easy

**Office 2016**

Patrice-Anne Rutledge

que®

800 East 96th Street

Indianapolis, Indiana 46240

# CONTENTS

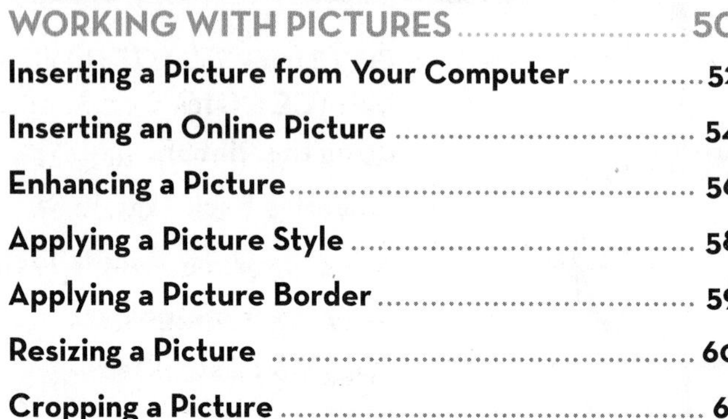

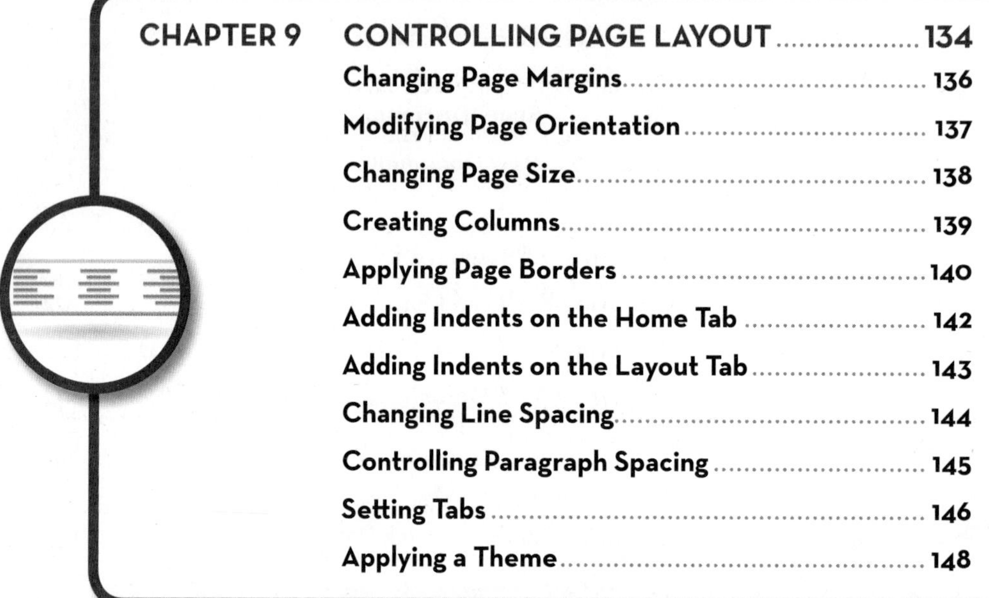

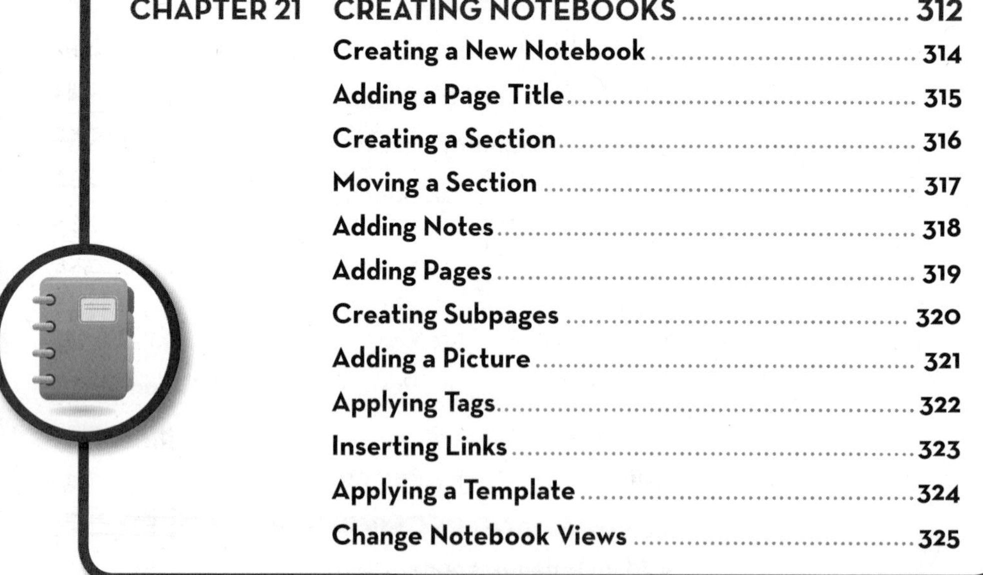



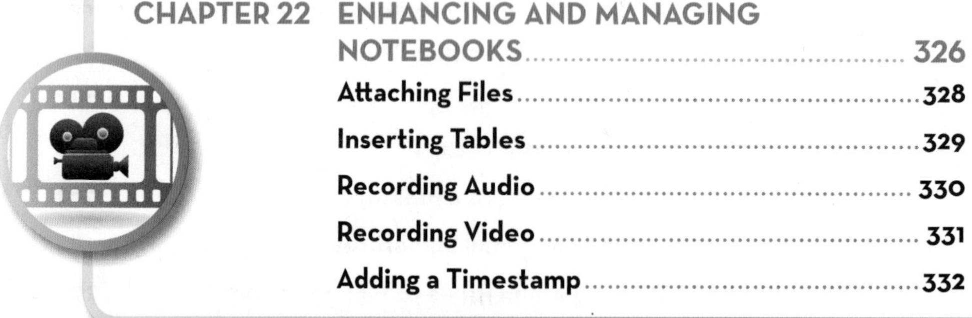

# EASY OFFICE 2016



ISBN-13: 978-0-7897-5505-6
ISBN-10: 0-7897-5505-X

Library of Congress Control Number: 2015945801

Printed in the United States of America

First Printing: October 2015

## TRADEMARKS

All terms mentioned in this book that are known to be trademarks or service marks have been appropriately capitalized. Que Publishing cannot attest to the accuracy of this information. Use of a term in this book should not be regarded as affecting the validity of any trademark or service mark.

## WARNING AND DISCLAIMER

Every effort has been made to make this book as complete and as accurate as possible, but no warranty or fitness is implied. The information provided is on an "as is" basis. The author and the publisher shall have neither liability nor responsibility to any person or entity with respect to any loss or damages arising from the information contained in this book.

## SPECIAL SALES

For information about buying this title in bulk quantities, or for special sales opportunities (which may include electronic versions; custom cover designs; and content particular to your business, training goals, marketing focus, or branding interests), please contact our corporate sales department at corpsales@pearsoned.com or (800) 382-3419.

For government sales inquiries, please contact governmentsales@pearsoned.com.

For questions about sales outside the U.S., please contact international@pearsoned.com.

**Editor-in-Chief**
Greg Wiegand

**Acquisitions Editor**
Michelle Newcomb

**Development Editor**
Charlotte Kughen

**Managing Editor**
Sandra Schroeder

**Senior Project Editor**
Tonya Simpson

**Copy Editor**
Barbara Hacha

**Indexer**
Erika Millen

**Proofreader**
The Wordsmithery LLC

**Technical Editor**
Vince Averello

**Editorial Assistant**
Cindy Teeters

**Cover Designer**
Mark Shirar

**Compositor**
Trina Wurst

# ABOUT THE AUTHOR

**Patrice-Anne Rutledge** is a business technology author and consultant who specializes in teaching others to maximize the power of new technologies. Patrice has used—and has trained others to use—Microsoft Office for many years. She is the author of numerous books about Office for Pearson Education, including *Easy Office 2013*, *Office 2013 All-In-One Absolute Beginner's Guide*, and *PowerPoint 2013 Absolute Beginner's Guide*. She can be reached through her website at www.patricerutledge.com.

# DEDICATION

*To my family, with thanks for their ongoing support and encouragement.*

# ACKNOWLEDGMENTS

Special thanks to Michelle Newcomb, Charlotte Kughen, Vince Averello, Barbara Hacha, and Tonya Simpson for their feedback, suggestions, and attention to detail.

# WE WANT TO HEAR FROM YOU!

As the reader of this book, *you* are our most important critic and commentator. We value your opinion and want to know what we're doing right, what we could do better, what areas you'd like to see us publish in, and any other words of wisdom you're willing to pass our way.

We welcome your comments. You can email or write to let us know what you did or didn't like about this book—as well as what we can do to make our books better.

*Please note that we cannot help you with technical problems related to the topic of this book.*

When you write, please be sure to include this book's title and author as well as your name and email address. We will carefully review your comments and share them with the author and editors who worked on the book.

Email: feedback@quepublishing.com

Mail: Que Publishing
ATTN: Reader Feedback
800 East 96th Street
Indianapolis, IN 46240 USA

# READER SERVICES

Visit our website and register this book at quepublishing.com/register for convenient access to any updates, downloads, or errata that might be available for this book.

# IT'S AS EASY AS 1-2-3

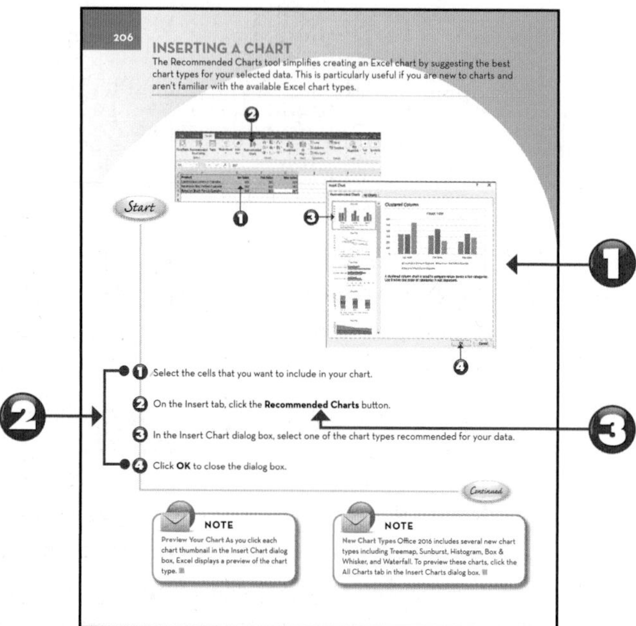

206

INSERTING A CHART

The Recommended Charts tool simplifies creating an Excel chart by suggesting the best chart types for your selected data. This is particularly useful if you are new to charts and aren't familiar with the available Excel chart types.



1. Select the cells that you want to include in your chart.
2. On the Insert tab, click the **Recommended Charts** button.
3. In the Insert Chart dialog box, select one of the chart types recommended for your data.
4. Click **OK** to close the dialog box.

Continued

**NOTE**

Preview Your Chart As you click each chart thumbnail in the Insert Chart dialog box, Excel displays a preview of the chart type.

**NOTE**

New Chart Types Office 2016 includes several new chart types including Treemap, Sunburst, Histogram, Box & Whisker, and Waterfall. To preview these charts, click the All Charts tab in the Insert Charts dialog box.

Each part of this book is made up of a series of short, instructional lessons, designed to help you understand basic information.

1. Each step is fully illustrated to show you how it looks onscreen.
2. Each task includes a series of quick, easy steps designed to guide you through the procedure.
3. Items that you select or click in menus, dialog boxes, tabs, and windows are shown in **bold**.

Tips, notes, and cautions give you a heads-up for any extra information you might need while working through the task.

**How to Drag:** Point to the starting place or object. Hold down the mouse button (right or left per instructions), move the mouse to the new location, and then release the button.

**Click:** Click the left mouse button once.

**Click and Type:** Click once where indicated and begin typing to enter your text or data.

**Selection:** Highlights the area onscreen discussed in the step or task.

**Double-click:** Click the left mouse button twice in rapid succession.

**Right-click:** Click the right mouse button once.

**Pointer arrow:** Highlights an item on the screen you need to point to or focus on in the step or task.

# INTRODUCTION TO *EASY OFFICE 2016*

Microsoft Office 2016 is the latest version of Microsoft's popular suite of business software applications. Using Office, you can quickly create documents such as letters, reports, and resumes; calculate and analyze data in spreadsheets; design and deliver presentations; send and receive email; store data in digital notebooks; and create publications such as newsletters and brochures.

The world is becoming increasing mobile, and so is Office 2016. This new version is integrated with OneDrive (Microsoft's online storage solution) as well as Office Online, which offers web-based versions of Word, Excel, PowerPoint, and OneNote. Office 2016 makes it easy to access, edit, and create Office files on the go, using a mobile device such as a tablet or smartphone.

*Easy Office 2016* is designed to get you up and running on Office as quickly as possible. This book covers six of the most popular Office applications—Word, Excel, PowerPoint, Outlook, OneNote, and Publisher—and provides visual, step-by-step instructions that help you master tasks with little effort. For now, turn to Chapter 1, "Getting Started with Microsoft Office 2016," to begin exploring this powerful application suite.

## WHO THIS BOOK IS FOR

This book is for you if...

- You want to become productive with the latest version of Office as quickly as possible and are short on time.
- You're new to Office and need to learn the basics in an easy-to-understand format.
- You're a visual learner and want to see what to do rather than read lengthy paragraphs describing what to do.

## HOW THIS BOOK IS ORGANIZED

*Easy Office 2016* is divided into seven parts.

Part I, "Microsoft Office 2016," introduces Office fundamentals, such as navigating applications, using the Ribbon and Backstage view, getting help, and saving and opening files. If you're an experienced computer user but are new to Office, these chapters provide a foundation for using the Office suite. If you've used Office in the past, they can serve as a quick review and introduce you to the new, exciting features of Office 2016.

In Part II, "Microsoft Word 2016," you continue on to one of the most popular Office applications: Microsoft Word. In this section, you learn how to create and format documents, modify page layout, and perform a collaborative review of your documents before you print, publish, or send.

Next, you can start exploring Excel, Office's spreadsheet application. Part III, "Microsoft Excel 2016," shows you how to create and format Excel workbooks and worksheets and introduces you to cell formulas and functions. Finally, you can analyze your worksheet data using visual tools such as charts, PivotTables, and sparklines (mini charts).

Part IV, "Microsoft PowerPoint 2016," shows you how to create eye-catching presentations using PowerPoint's powerful collection of ready-made tools, even if you're design challenged. You also learn how to edit and format presentations; incorporate audio, video, and animation; and prepare for delivery, either in person or on the Web.

Part V, "Microsoft Outlook 2016," helps you get up and running quickly with the Office email, calendaring, and scheduling tools.

Part VI focuses on OneNote, the Office digital notebook application that helps you organize masses of data. "Microsoft OneNote 2016" introduces you to OneNote basics, such as creating, enhancing, managing, and sharing notebooks.

Finally, you explore Publisher in Part VII, "Microsoft Publisher 2016." In this section, you discover how to create publications including newsletters, brochures, flyers, and more.

# GETTING STARTED WITH MICROSOFT OFFICE 2016

Although Microsoft Office 2016 is intuitive and easy to use, it's worth spending several minutes exploring its interface and navigation tools. The most common of these include the Ribbon, the Backstage view, the Quick Access toolbar, the mini toolbar, contextual tabs, and task panes.

If you're upgrading from Office 2007 or later, the basic Office interface should be reasonably familiar. There are enhancements to the Ribbon and the Backstage view, but these key features still work in much the same way. If you're upgrading from a previous Office version, however, take your time exploring the new ways to use and navigate Office.

The first thing you notice when you start most Office 2016 applications is the start screen that welcomes you. This color-coded screen is available for Word, Excel, PowerPoint, and Publisher. Outlook and OneNote, however, open directly to the Home tab, bypassing the start screen.

For now, let's start with a quick tour of Microsoft Office 2016.

# MICROSOFT OFFICE 2016 START SCREEN (WORD)

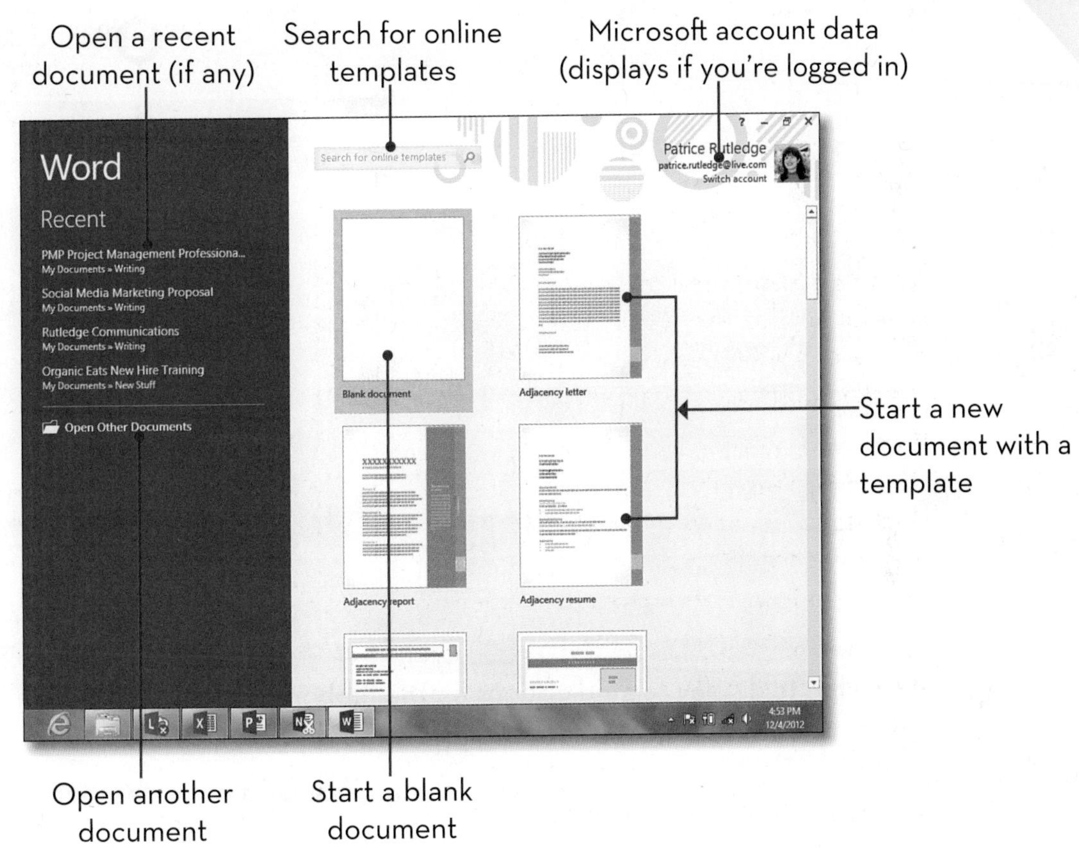

# USING THE RIBBON

The *Ribbon*, which replaces the menu structure found in Office 2003 and earlier, provides an easy way to access common commands and buttons using the least amount of space possible. To start, explore some common Ribbon features.

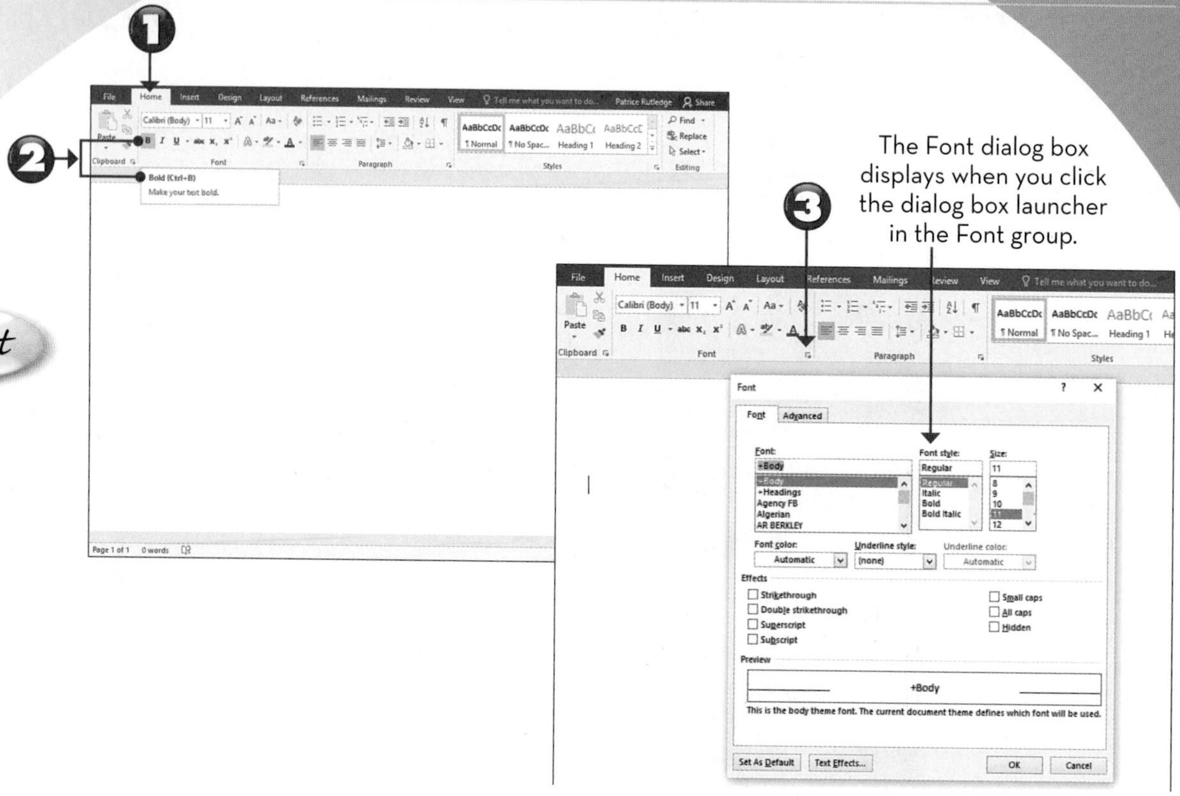

The Font dialog box displays when you click the dialog box launcher in the Font group.

Start

1. Click a tab to display related options on the Ribbon.
2. Pause your mouse over a Ribbon command to display a basic description.
3. Click a dialog box launcher to open a dialog box of related options.

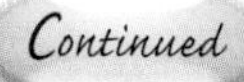

## NOTE

**The Ribbon** The Ribbon is divided into tabs, such as Home, Insert, Design, and so forth. Each Ribbon tab includes groups and buttons of related features. ■

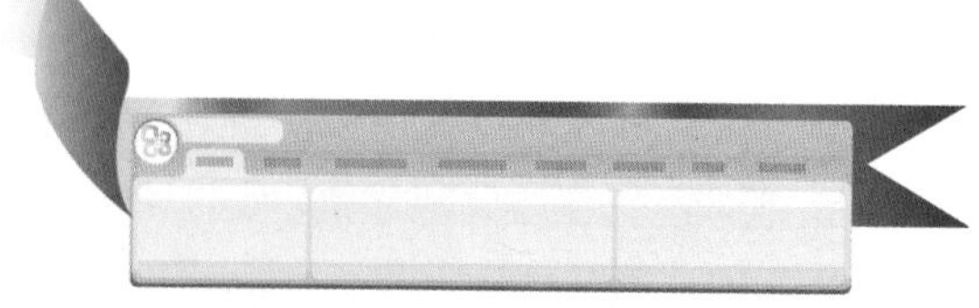

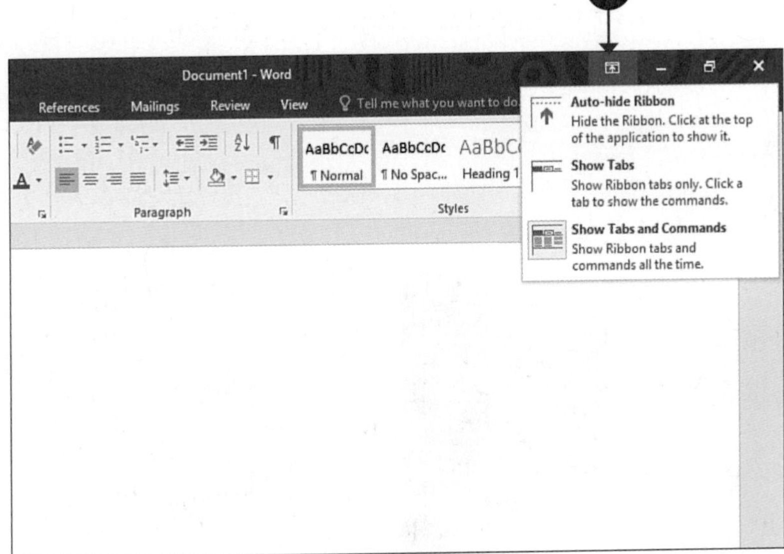


4 Click the **Ribbon Display Options** button to specify your Ribbon display preference: Auto-Hide Ribbon, Show Tabs, or Show Tabs and Commands.

End

## NOTE

**Ribbon Display Options** By default, Office displays both the Ribbon tab and its related commands and buttons. If you want to save screen space, you can choose to show tabs only or hide the Ribbon entirely. If you show tabs only, you can click a tab to display its commands temporarily. ■

# EXPLORING BACKSTAGE VIEW

*Backstage view* enables you to perform common Office file-related tasks in one place.

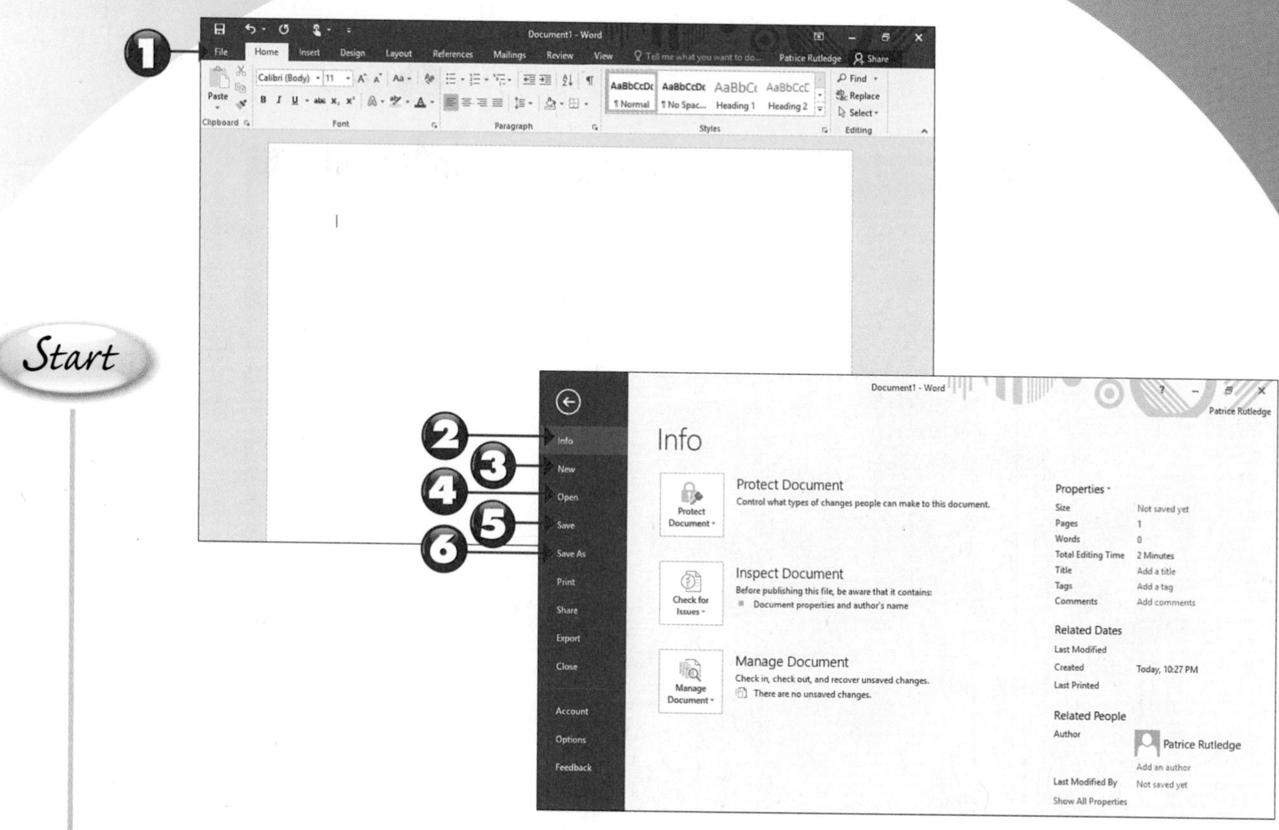


Start

1. Click the **File** tab.
2. View the Info window, which displays by default. This window enables you to control access to your document and view its properties.
3. Click **New** to create a new document, either a blank document or one from a template.
4. Click **Open** to open an existing document or view a list of recent documents.
5. Click **Save** to save your document to your computer or OneDrive, Microsoft's online file-sharing site.
6. Click **Save As** to save an existing document under a new name.

Continued

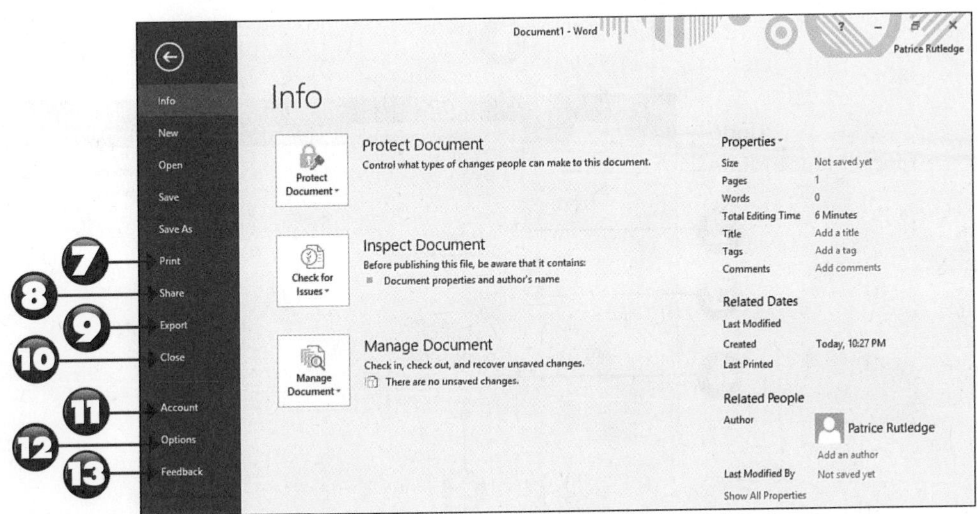


7 Click **Print** to print your document and specify print preferences.

8 Click **Share** to share your document via email, by instant message, or online.

9 Click **Export** to create a PDF/XPS document or change your document's file type.

10 Click **Close** to close your document.

11 Click **Account** to set up or modify your Microsoft account.

12 Click **Options** to access customization options.

13 Click **Feedback** to send feedback to Microsoft.

*End*

**NOTE**

**Backstage View Differences** The options available in Backstage view vary by application but are similar to the options shown in this section for Microsoft Word. ■

# USING THE QUICK ACCESS TOOLBAR

The *Quick Access Toolbar* is a small toolbar that displays in the upper-left corner of your screen and is available no matter which Ribbon tab you select.

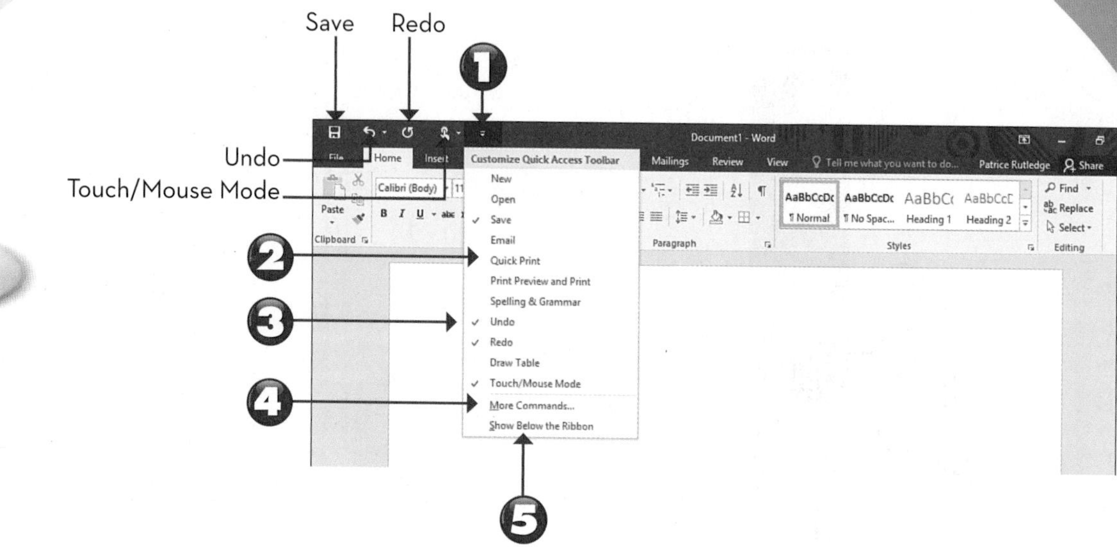


Start

1. Click the down arrow to display a menu of additional options.
2. Select a command to display it on the Quick Access Toolbar.
3. Deselect a selected command to remove it from the toolbar.
4. Open the Options dialog box for advanced customization options.
5. Move the toolbar below the Ribbon.

End

## NOTE

**Quick Access Toolbar Default Buttons** By default, the Quick Access Toolbar contains three buttons: Save, Undo, and Redo; but you can customize it to include almost any command. If you have a touch-enabled computer, the Touch/Mouse Mode button also displays by default. ■

## TIP

**Touch/Mouse Mode** If your computer is touchscreen enabled, click the Touch/Mouse Mode button to switch between these modes. Touch mode includes more space between commands for easier access. Mouse mode is optimized for use with a mouse. ■

## USING THE MINI TOOLBAR

The *mini toolbar* is a small contextual toolbar that displays only when you perform specific tasks. For example, when you select text, this toolbar displays with options related to text formatting.

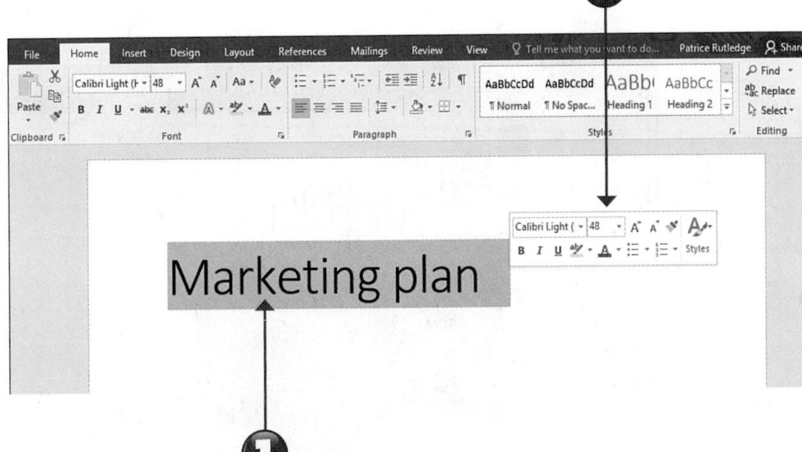


Start

1. Select any text.
2. View the mini toolbar.

End

**NOTE**

**Mini Toolbar Versus the Ribbon** Although you can perform the same tasks using the commands on the main Ribbon tab, using the mini toolbar makes these commands available in a more convenient location. ■

**TIP**

**Mini Toolbar Button Descriptions** Pause your mouse over a mini toolbar button to view its description. ■

10

# USING CONTEXTUAL TABS

Although the main tabs always display on the Ribbon, Office also includes several contextual Ribbon tabs that appear only when you perform specific tasks. For example, take a look at the Drawing Tools-Format tab, which displays only when you select a shape.

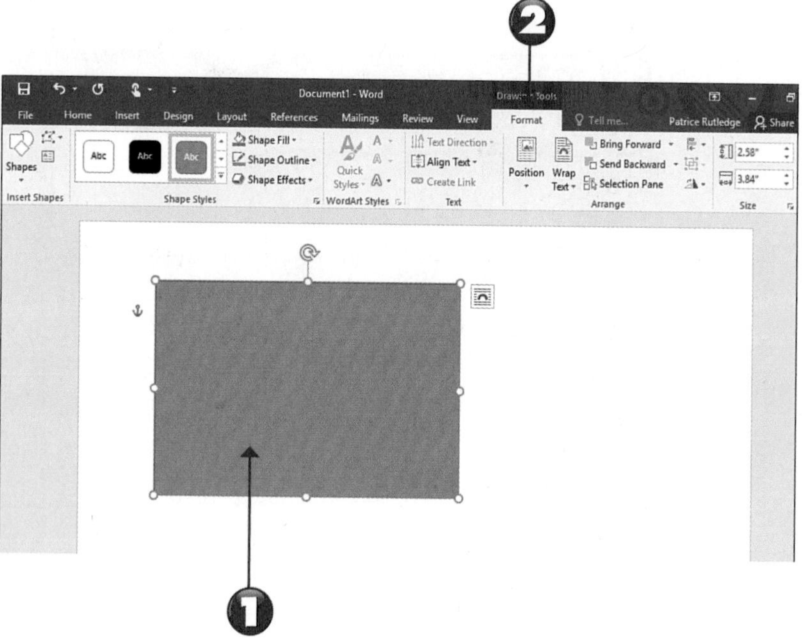


Start

1. Select a shape. (You can insert one by clicking the **Shapes** button on the Insert tab as described in Chapter 5, "Working with Shapes, SmartArt, and Screenshots.")
2. Click the **Drawing Tools-Format** tab to display options that are specific to working with shapes.

End

## NOTE

**Contextual Tab Examples** Some examples of contextual tabs include the following: the Picture Tools-Format tab displays when you select a picture; the Drawing Tools-Format tab displays when you select a shape; and the Chart Tools-Design and Chart Tools-Format tabs display when you select a chart. ■

## NOTE

**Where Did It Go?** A contextual tab remains visible as long as the related object is selected. When you click elsewhere, it disappears. ■

## USING TASK PANES

A *task pane* is a window that enables you to perform common tasks without covering your document (such as a dialog box does). For example, open the Format Shape pane.

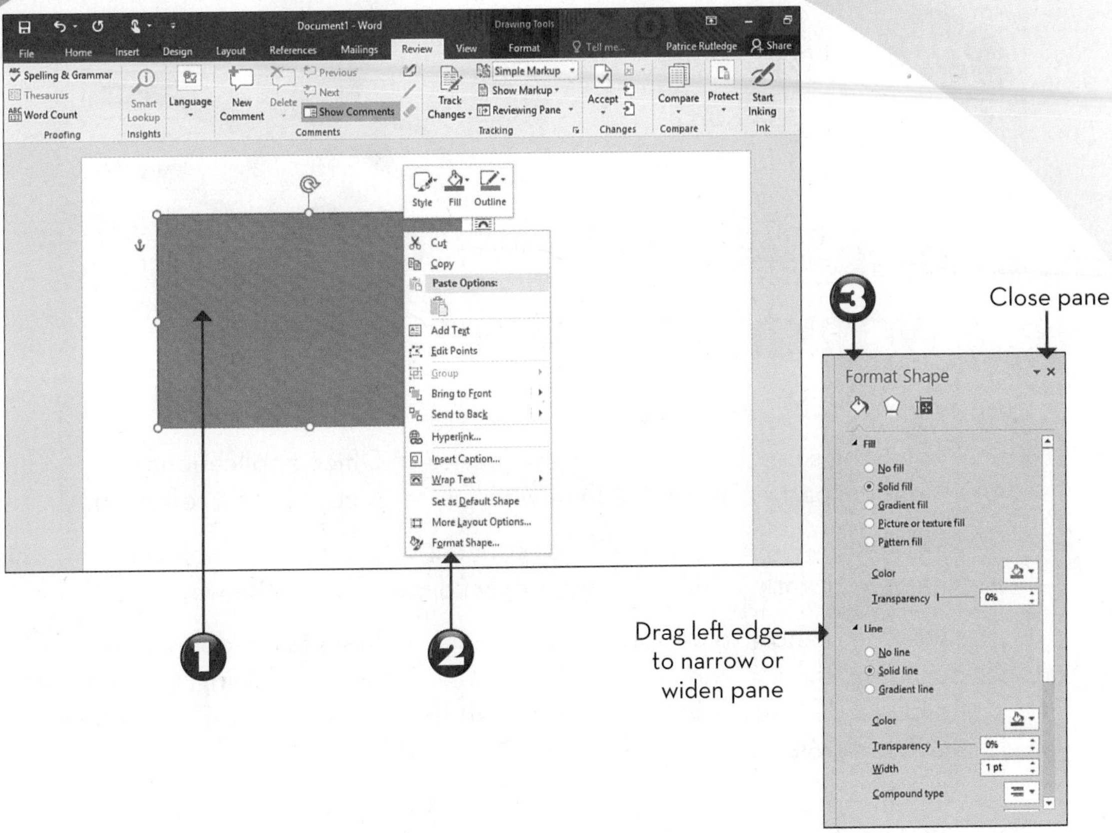

Start

Close pane

Drag left edge to narrow or widen pane

1. Right-click a shape. (You can insert one by clicking the **Shapes** button on the Insert tab, as described in Chapter 5.)
2. Select **Format Shape** from the menu that displays.
3. On the Format Shape pane, adjust the format settings to change the look of your shape.

End

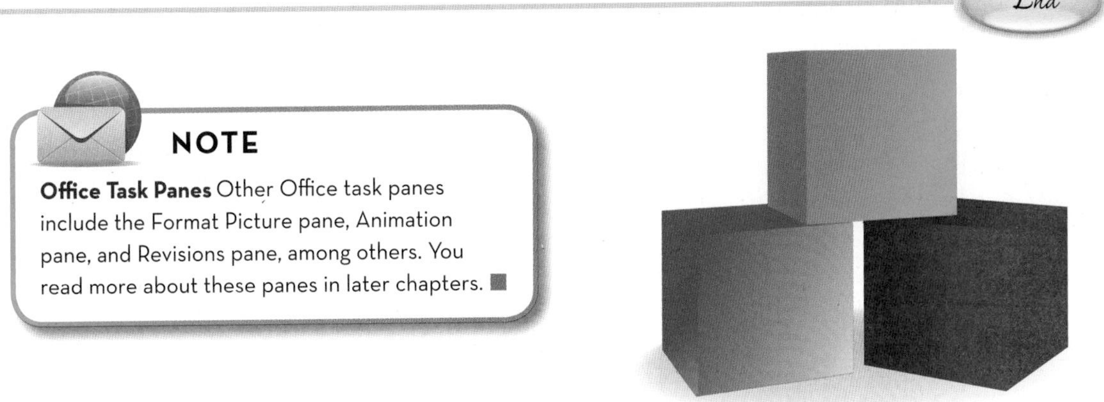

### NOTE

**Office Task Panes** Other Office task panes include the Format Picture pane, Animation pane, and Revisions pane, among others. You read more about these panes in later chapters.

# WORKING WITH OFFICE APPLICATIONS

Spending some time mastering the basics of Office applications pays off in the long run, particularly if you're new to Office or could use a refresher.

First, you should set up Office to connect with your Microsoft account, which helps you work in today's increasingly connected, mobile world.

Next, learn how to perform Office's most common tasks: opening, saving, printing, sharing, and closing files, as well as cutting, copying, and pasting using clipboard functionality. Although these should be familiar if you're upgrading, Office 2016 does include some changes and new features.

Finally, spend a few minutes customizing Office defaults to suit your own work style and preferences.

# EXPLORING OFFICE

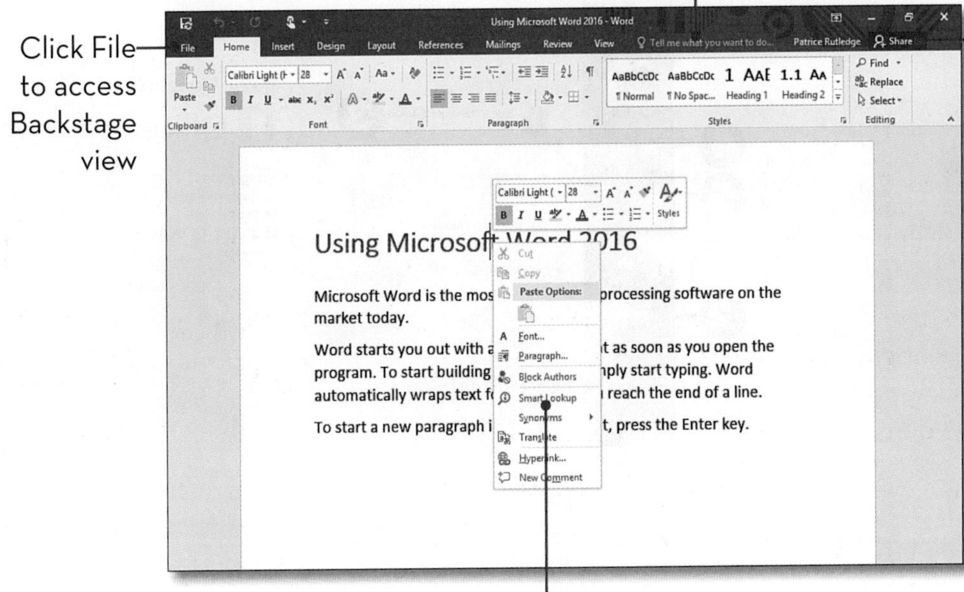

# SETTING UP YOUR ACCOUNT

The *Account window* is where you set up your Microsoft account and connected services, which are both important for taking full advantage of Office 2016. When you first start using this new version of Office, be sure to take a few minutes to handle this important task.

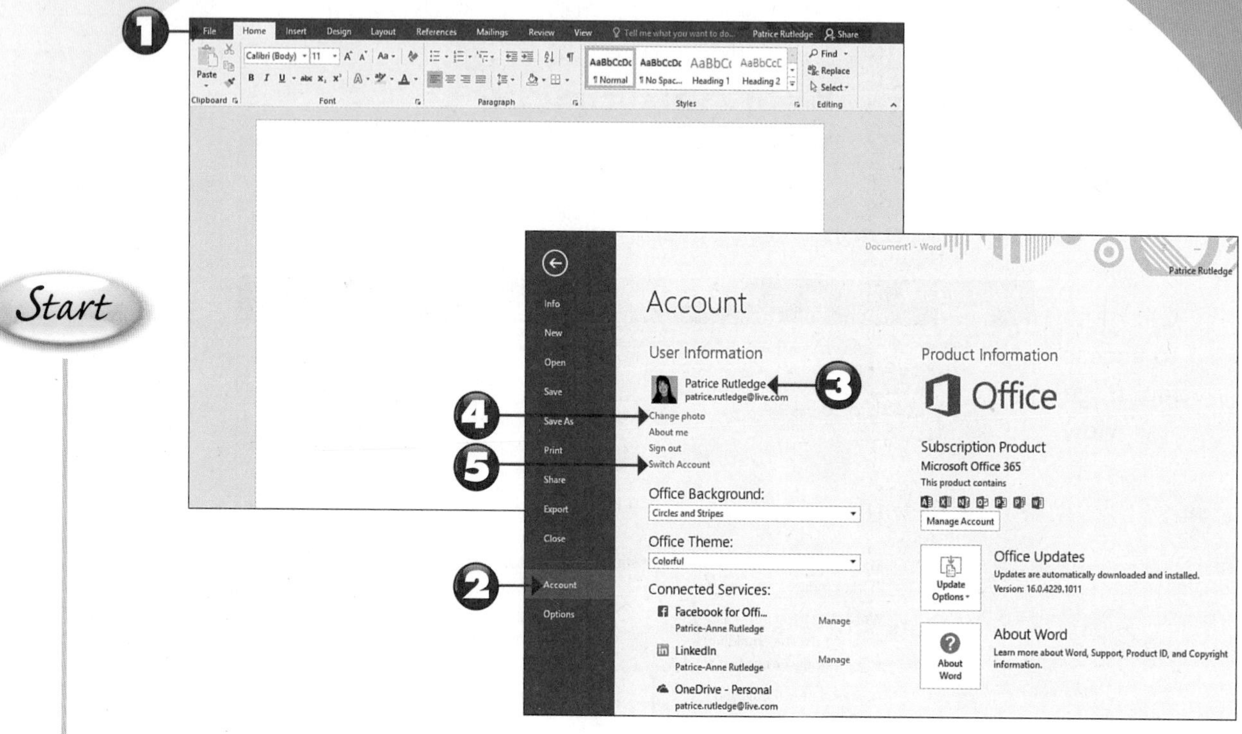

Start

1. Click the **File** tab.
2. Click **Account**.
3. Office displays information about the Microsoft account you used to install Office 2016.
4. Click **Change photo** to upload a new photo of yourself.
5. Click **Switch Account** to switch to another Microsoft account.

Continued

## NOTE

**Microsoft Account** Office 2016 connects you to the Web with your Microsoft account: an email and password you use to access all Microsoft services, such as OneDrive, Skype, and Outlook.com. To create a new Microsoft account, go to https://signup.live.com.

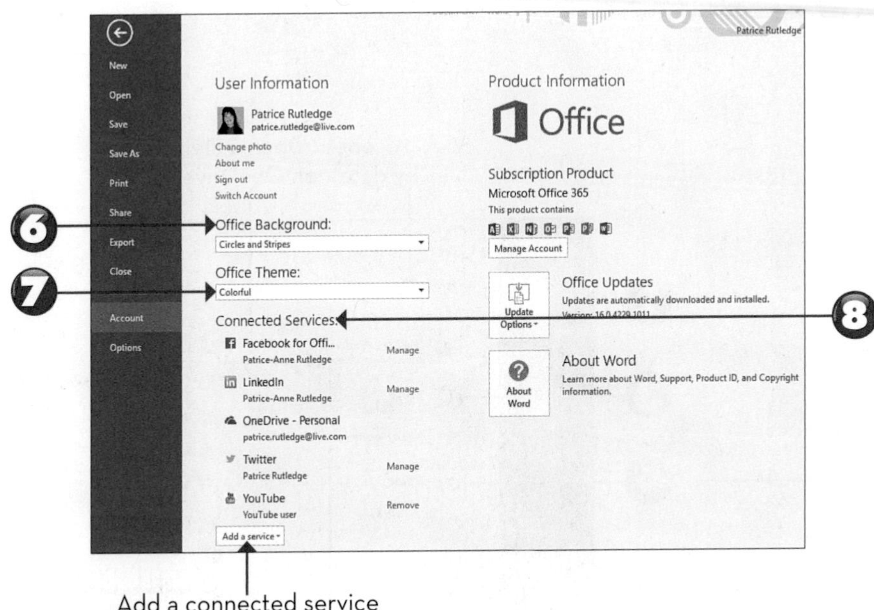


Add a connected service

6 Select an Office background. The default is Circles and Stripes, but you can select another option, including Clouds, Straws, or no background.

7 Select an Office theme: Colorful (the default), Dark Gray, or White.

8 Specify the connected services you want to use with Office.

*End*

## NOTE

**Office Theme** The Office theme controls the appearance of the Office interface, not the appearance of any documents you create. The default Office 2016 theme is Colorful, but you can change it back to the previous default theme (White) if you want.

## NOTE

**Connected Services** The Account window displays the services you've already connected with. (Office finds some services automatically based on your Microsoft account email address.) Click the **Add a service** button to add more services, including Flickr, YouTube, Office 365 SharePoint, OneDrive, Facebook, LinkedIn, and Twitter. See "Sharing a File with Other People" later in this chapter to learn how to share Office files on the social sites to which you connect.

# OPENING A FILE

You can easily find and open existing files in Microsoft Office. In this example, you open a file on your computer.

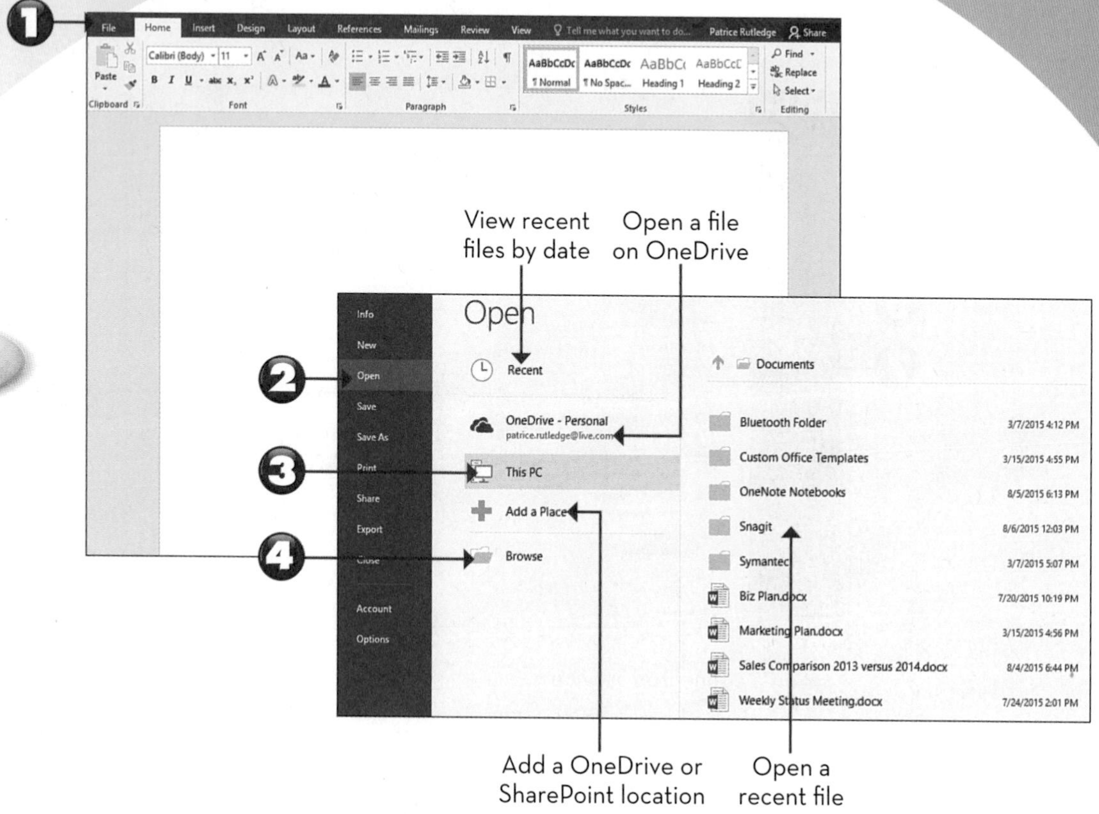

View recent files by date

Open a file on OneDrive

Start

Add a OneDrive or SharePoint location

Open a recent file

1. Click the **File** tab.
2. Click **Open**.
3. Click **This PC**.
4. Click the **Browse** button.

Continued

## NOTE

**Open a Recent Document** As a shortcut, click **Recent** in the Open window, and select a recent document to open.

## NOTE

**Open a File Stored on OneDrive** If the file you want is stored on OneDrive, click **OneDrive** in the Open window and browse to find your file.

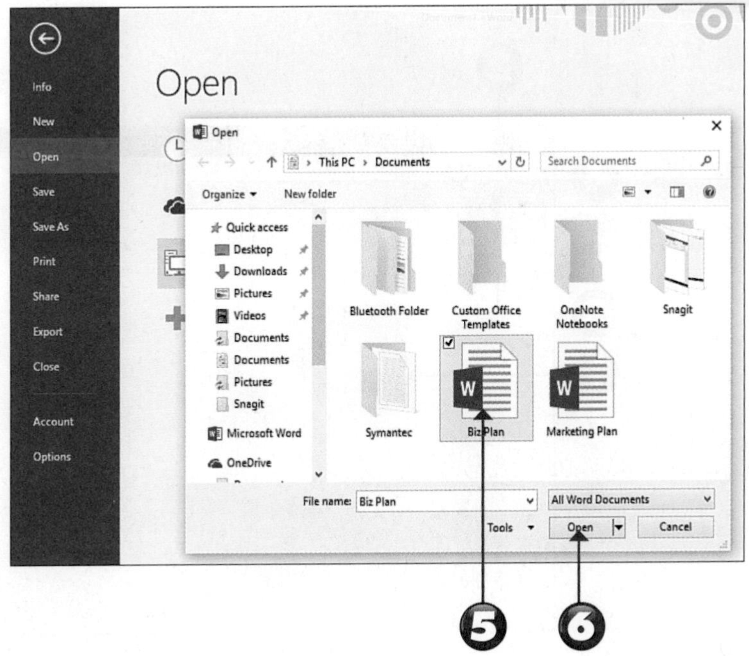


5 In the Open dialog box, navigate to the file you want to open.

6 Click the **Open** button.

End

**TIP**

**Rename a File** To rename a file in the Open dialog box, right-click it and select **Rename** from the menu. To delete a file, right-click it and select **Delete** from the menu.

**TIP**

**File-Opening Option** You can also open a file by double-clicking its name in File Explorer or by pressing Ctrl+O to display the Open dialog box directly.

# USING THE CLIPBOARD TO CUT, COPY, AND PASTE

Using the options in the Clipboard group on the Home tab, you can cut, copy, and paste objects. In Office, an *object* refers to any of the components you include in your documents, such as text, shapes, pictures, text boxes, placeholders, SmartArt, charts, WordArt, and so forth.

Start

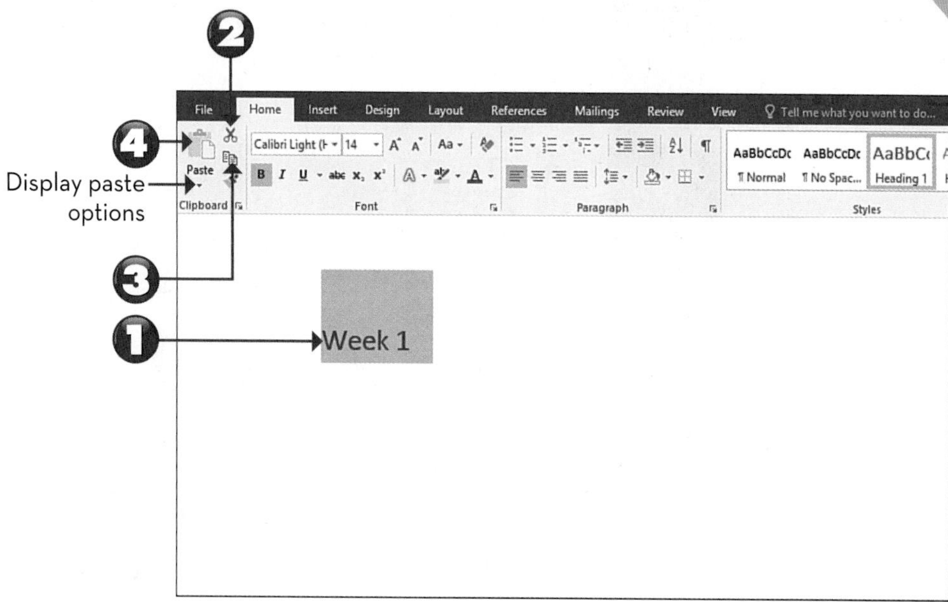


1. Select an object.
2. Click **Cut** (or press Ctrl+X) to cut the object or....
3. Click **Copy** (or press Ctrl+C) to copy the object.
4. Click **Paste** (or press Ctrl+V) to paste the object in a new location.

Continued

**NOTE**

**Paste Options Box** Optionally, click the down arrow below the Paste button to open the Paste Options dialog box. Pause your mouse over each option button to preview the pasted object. Options include Keep Source Formatting, Use Destination Theme, Picture (convert object to picture; not available with basic text), or Keep Text Only.

**TIP**

**Cut or Copy Multiple Objects** To cut or copy more than one object, hold down the Shift key while selecting objects, or drag a selection box around all the objects with the mouse. If the objects aren't contiguous, hold down the Ctrl key.

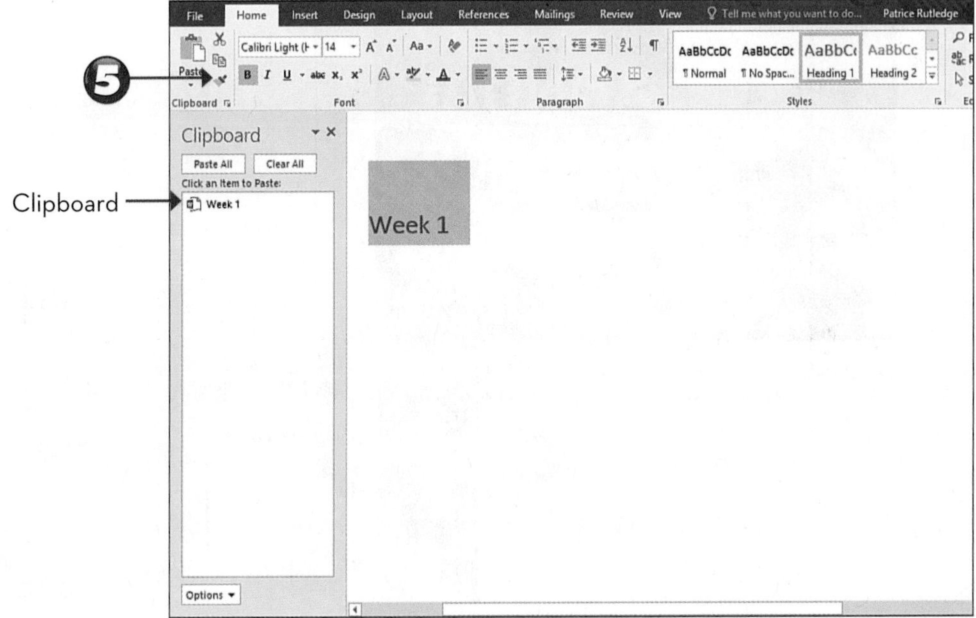


5 Click **Format Painter** to copy the attributes of one object and apply them to another object you select.

End

## TIP

**Format Painter** The Format Painter is a timesaving tool if you want to reuse formatting you've applied to an object. For example, if you select an object with 3D effects, click the **Format Painter** button, and then select another object so that new object gets the same 3D effects.

## NOTE

**The Clipboard** When you copy an object, it displays on the Clipboard. To view the Clipboard, click the down arrow to the right of the Clipboard group on the Home tab to open the Clipboard pane. You can also select which item to paste on this pane.

# SAVING A FILE TO YOUR COMPUTER

Saving files as you work is a good practice and a good way to avoid losing critical data. In this section, you find out how to save a file for the first time.

Start

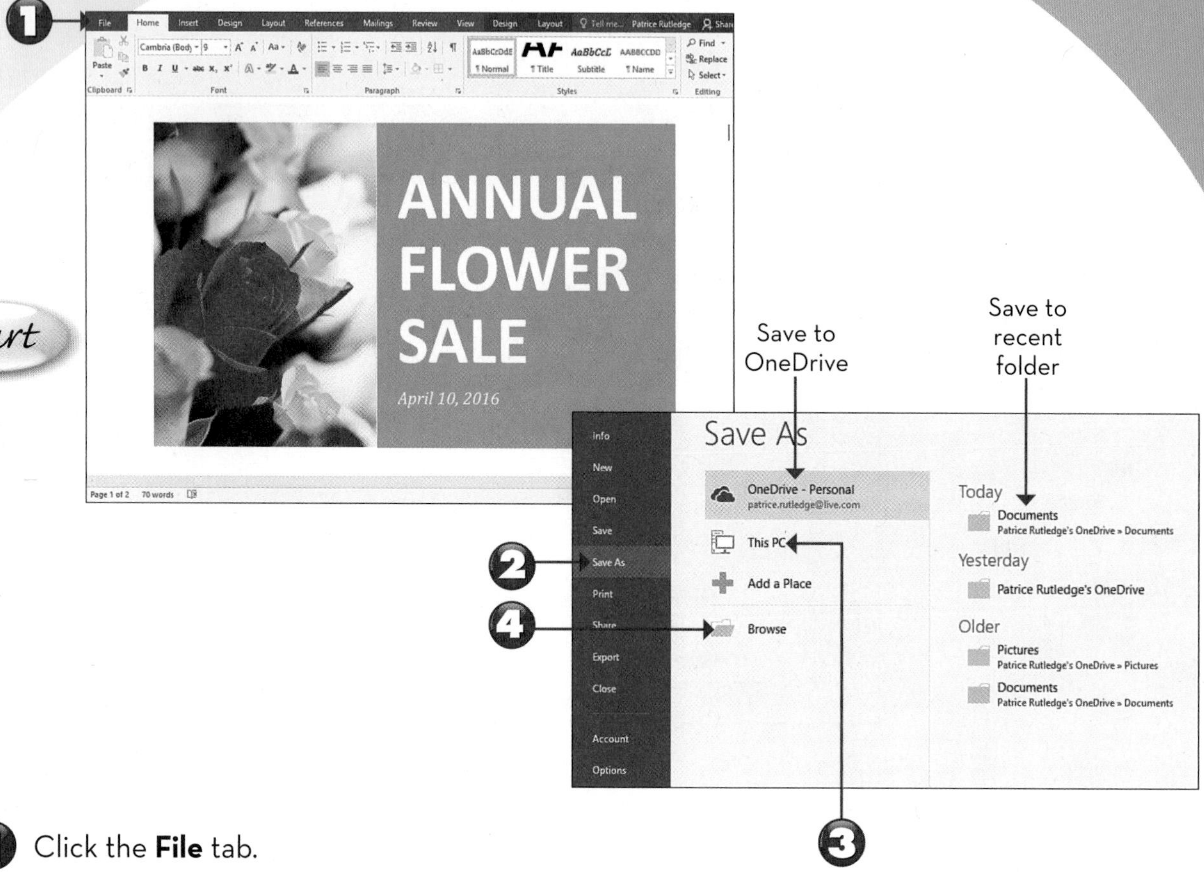

Save to OneDrive

Save to recent folder

1. Click the **File** tab.
2. Click **Save As**.
3. Click **This PC**.
4. Click the **Browse** button.

Continued

## TIP

**Saving Shortcuts** After you save for the first time, press Ctrl+S or click the **Save** button on the Quick Access toolbar to save new changes without opening the Save As dialog box. If you want to save an existing file to a new location or change its name, click the **File** tab and select **Save As**.

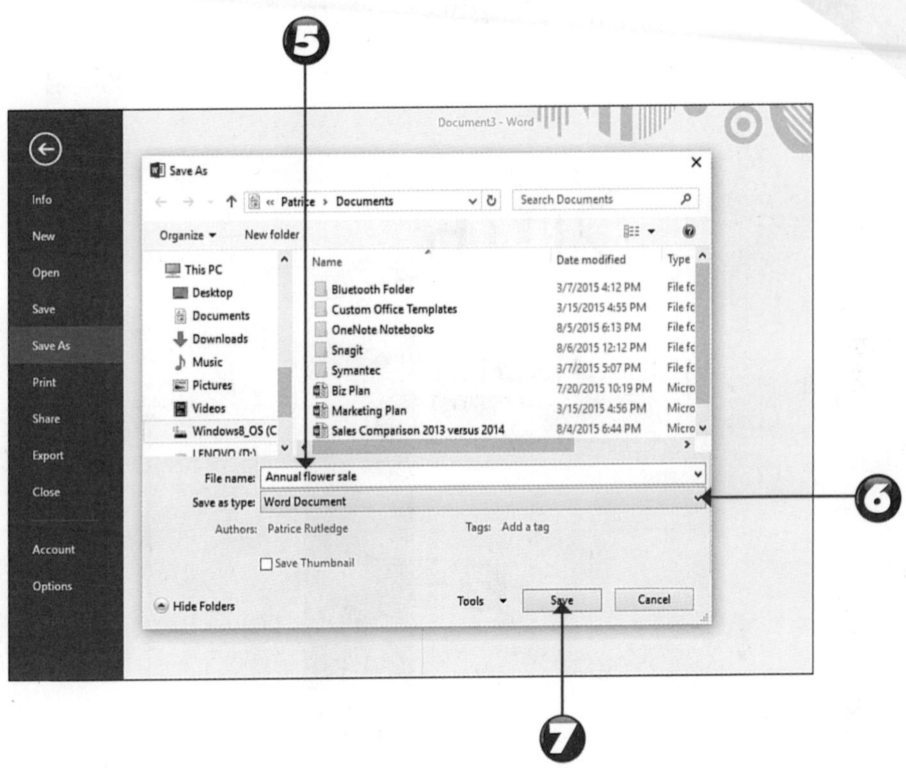


5 Type a filename.

6 Select a file format from the Save as Type drop-down list if you don't want to save in the default format.

7 Click **Save** to save the file.

End

## TIP

**Recent Folders** Optionally, you can save time by selecting one of the options on the right side of the screen, which displays your recent folders. If you often save to the same folder, pause your mouse over that folder name, and click the **Pin This Item to the List** icon to ensure that this folder is always at the top of the list for easy convenience.

## TIP

**Save to OneDrive** You can also save to OneDrive (Microsoft's online storage and file-sharing solution) from the Save As window. On the left side of the window, click **OneDrive**, click the **Browse** button, and select a folder.

# SAVING AS A PDF OR AN XPS DOCUMENT

Office enables you to save a file directly as a PDF or an XPS document without requiring an add-in.

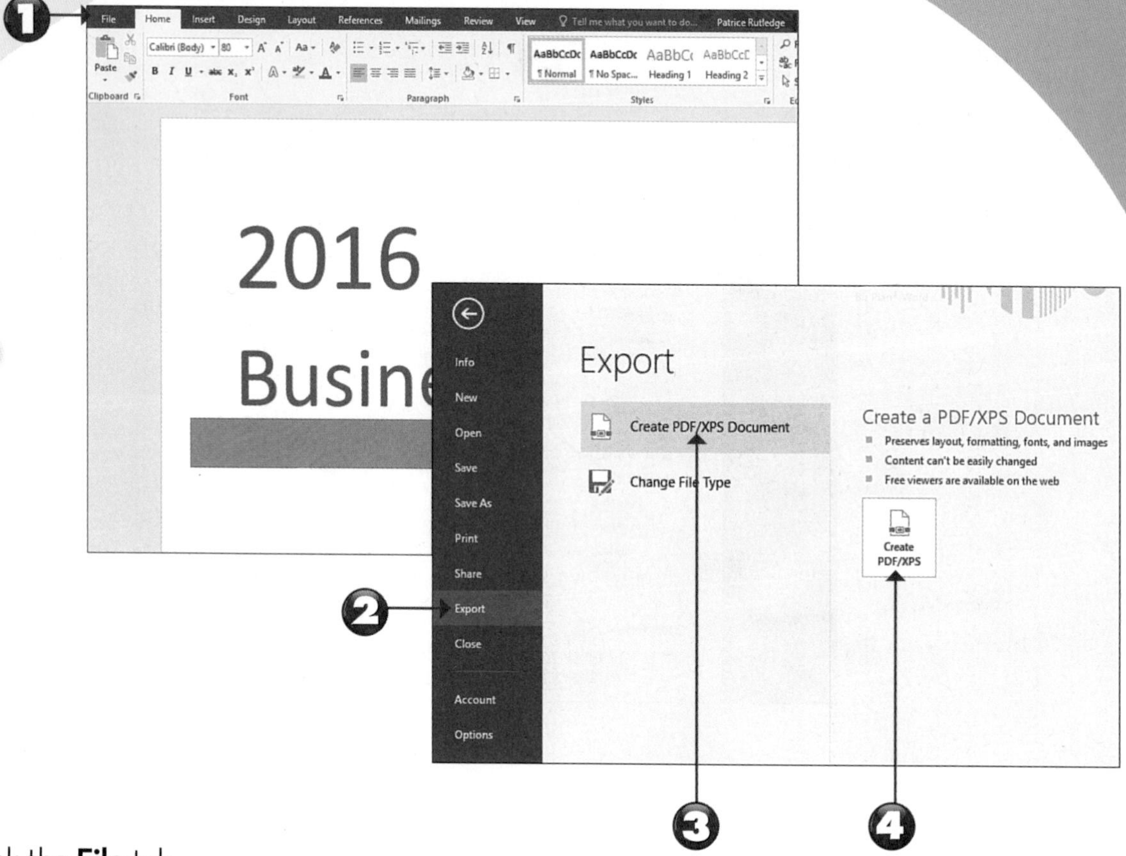

Start

1. Click the **File** tab.
2. Click **Export**.
3. Click **Create PDF/XPS Document**.
4. Click the **Create PDF/XPS** button.

Continued

## NOTE

**PDF Versus XPS** PDF (Portable Document Format) is a file format that makes your Office documents readable by anyone who has the free Adobe Reader software. XPS (XML Paper Specification) enables you to create documents readable with the XPS Viewer. PDF is by far the more common format.

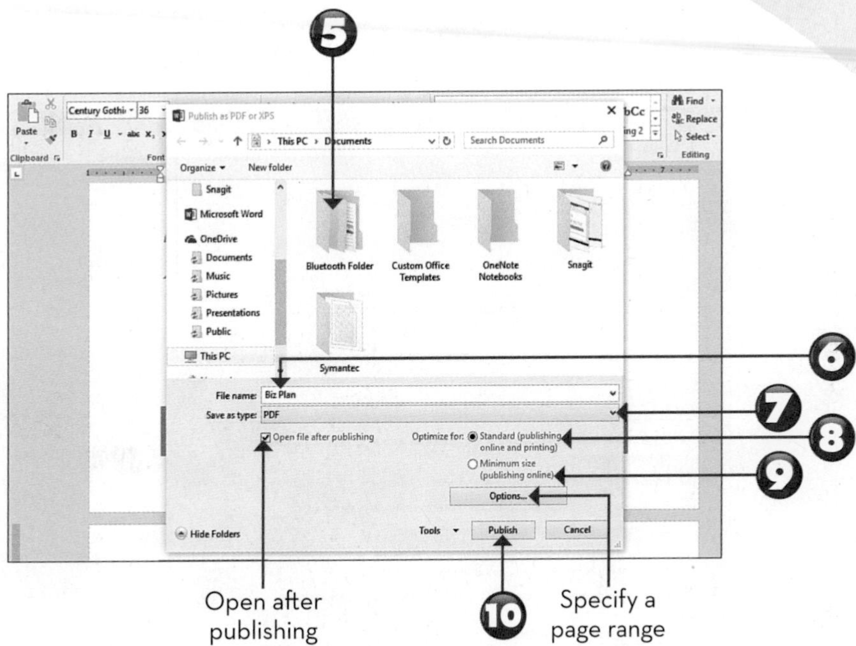


5. Select the folder in which to save your document.

6. Type a filename.

7. Select either PDF or XPS Document.

8. Select **Standard** to create a document that's suitable for both online viewing and printing.

9. Select **Minimum size** if you just want to view online.

10. Click the **Publish** button to create your document.

End

**TIP**

**Save First** Be sure to save your file in your Office application before you save as PDF or XPS documents.

# SHARING A FILE WITH OTHER PEOPLE

The Share pane makes it easy to share files with other people. This pane is available in Word, Excel, and PowerPoint.

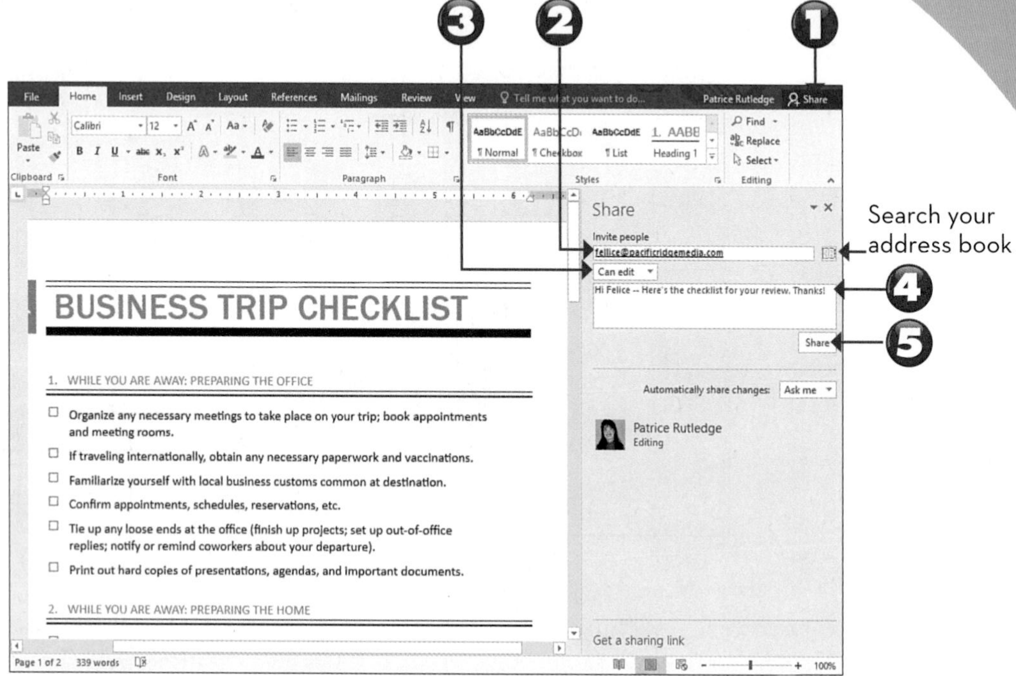


Start

1. Click the **Share** button.
2. Enter the email address of the person (or people) you want to share with.
3. Specify whether this person can edit the file or only view it.
4. Enter an optional message.
5. Click **Share** to send your sharing invitation.

Continued

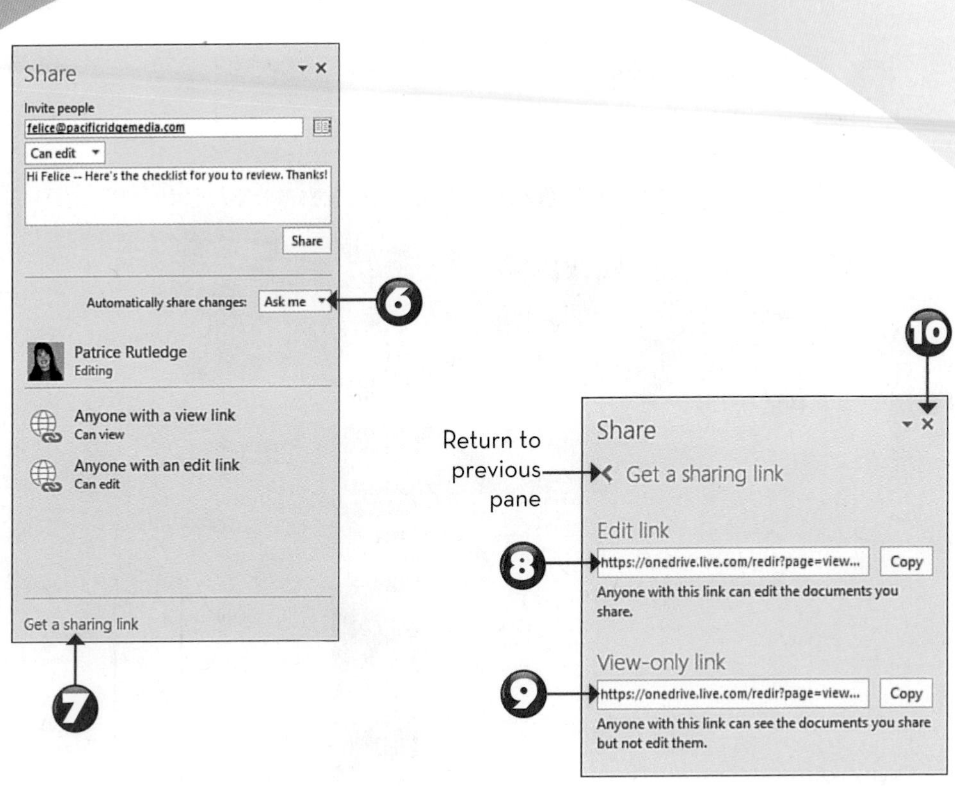


6. Specify whether you want Office to ask you before notifying people of document changes (the default), to always share changes, or to never share changes.

7. Click **Get a sharing link** if you want to share your document with a link.

8. Share an edit link if you want others to be able to change your document.

9. Share a view-only link if you want others to only be able to view your document.

10. Click the **Close** (**x**) button to close the Share pane.

End

## TIP

**Save to the Cloud First** You must save your file to OneDrive before you can share it with other people. If you haven't done so yet, the Share pane prompts you to save by displaying the Save to Cloud button.

## CAUTION

**Don't Overshare** Think carefully before sharing any file. Remember that someone you give a sharing link to could share this link with others.

# EXPLORING OTHER SHARING OPTIONS

You can find other sharing options in the Share window in Backstage view. In this example, you explore the Share window in PowerPoint.

Start

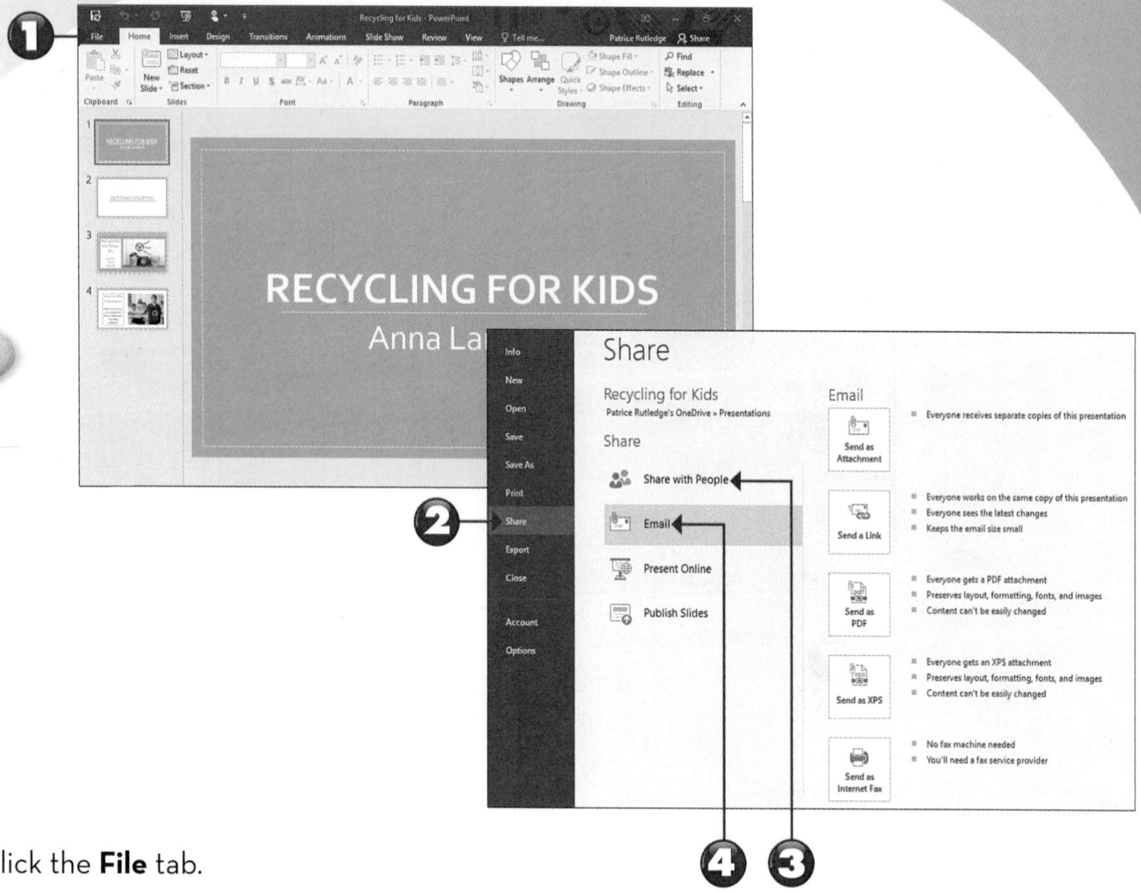

1. Click the **File** tab.
2. Click **Share**.
3. Click **Share with People** to open the Share pane and invite people to view or edit your file.
4. Click **Email** to share via email.

Continued

## NOTE

**Email Sharing Options** Office offers several ways to share via email. You can send as an attachment, send a link, send as a PDF, send as an XPS, or send as an Internet fax.

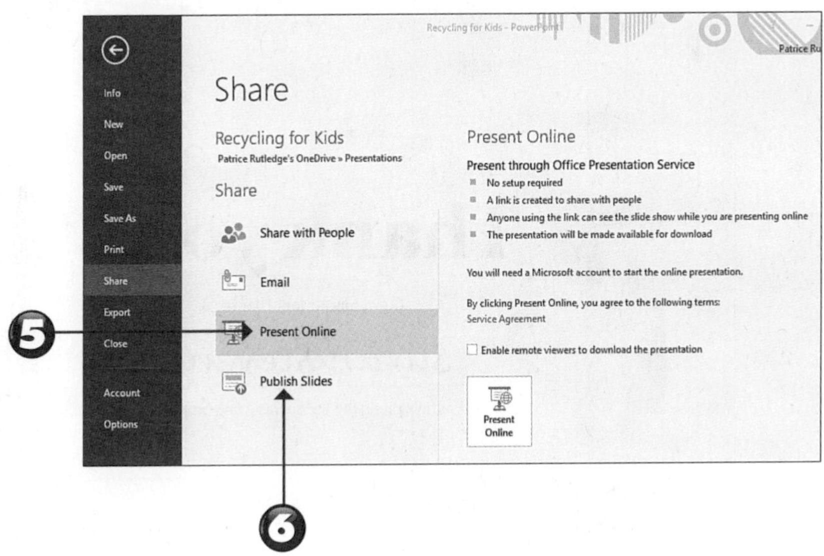


5 Click **Present Online** to start an online presentation.

6 Click **Publish Slides** to publish your slides to a slide library or to a SharePoint site.

End

## NOTE

**Share Window Differences** Depending on the application you use, the Share window might have additional options or fewer options. For example, Word enables you to post a document to your blog and PowerPoint lets you publish slides online. Excel has only two sharing options: Share with People and Email. In OneNote, you specify the people you want to share with on the Share window rather than the Share pane.

# PRINTING A FILE

The Print window simplifies printing Office files. Although the specific printing options available in this window vary by application, they all follow the same basic steps. In this example, you explore the Print window in Microsoft Word.

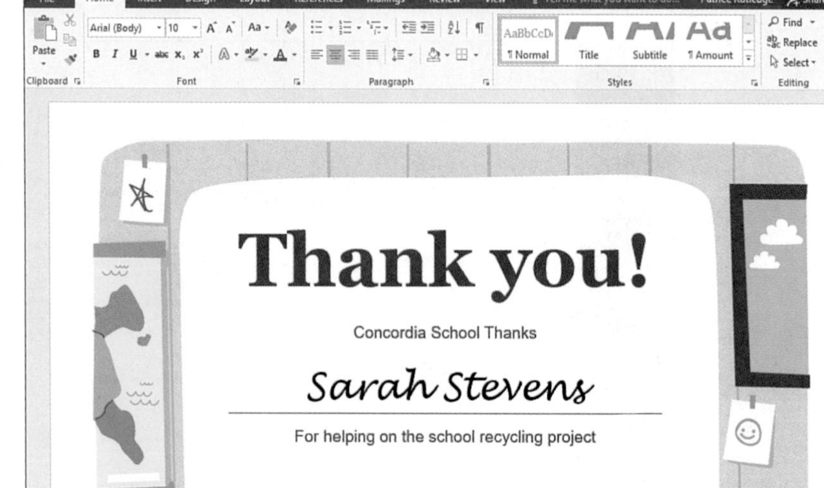


Start

1. Click the **File** tab.

Continued

**TIP**

**Printing Alternatives** Consider a greener alternative to distributing multiple printed copies. For example, you could save to a OneDrive folder to which your colleagues have access.

**NOTE**

**Print Window Differences** Although the print process works in much the same way, each Office application includes specific print options. For example, you might want to specify the exact page range to print, a portrait or landscape orientation, page size (such as letter or legal), and any collation options if you're printing multiple copies.

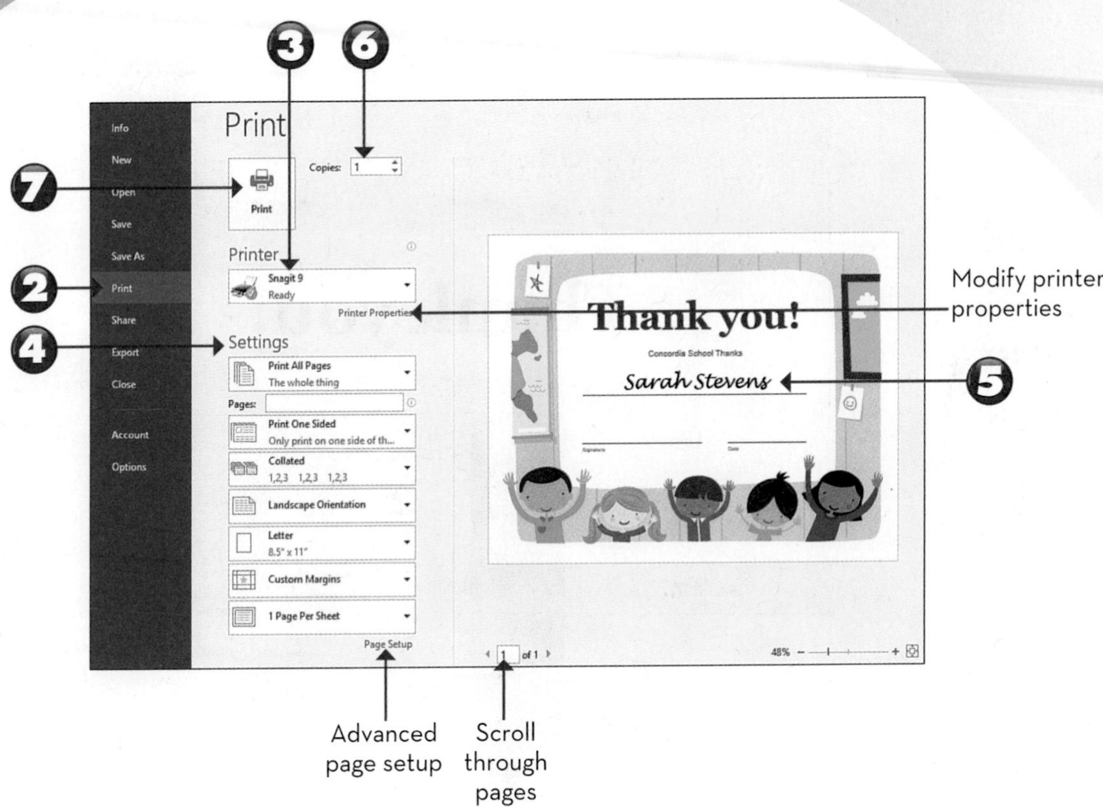


2. Click **Print**.

3. Select a printer.

4. Specify settings specific to your Office application.

5. Preview your document.

6. Select the number of copies to print.

7. Click the **Print** button.

End

# CLOSING A FILE

At times, you might want to close a file without exiting an application. This is particularly useful if you have many files open and want to save memory.

Start

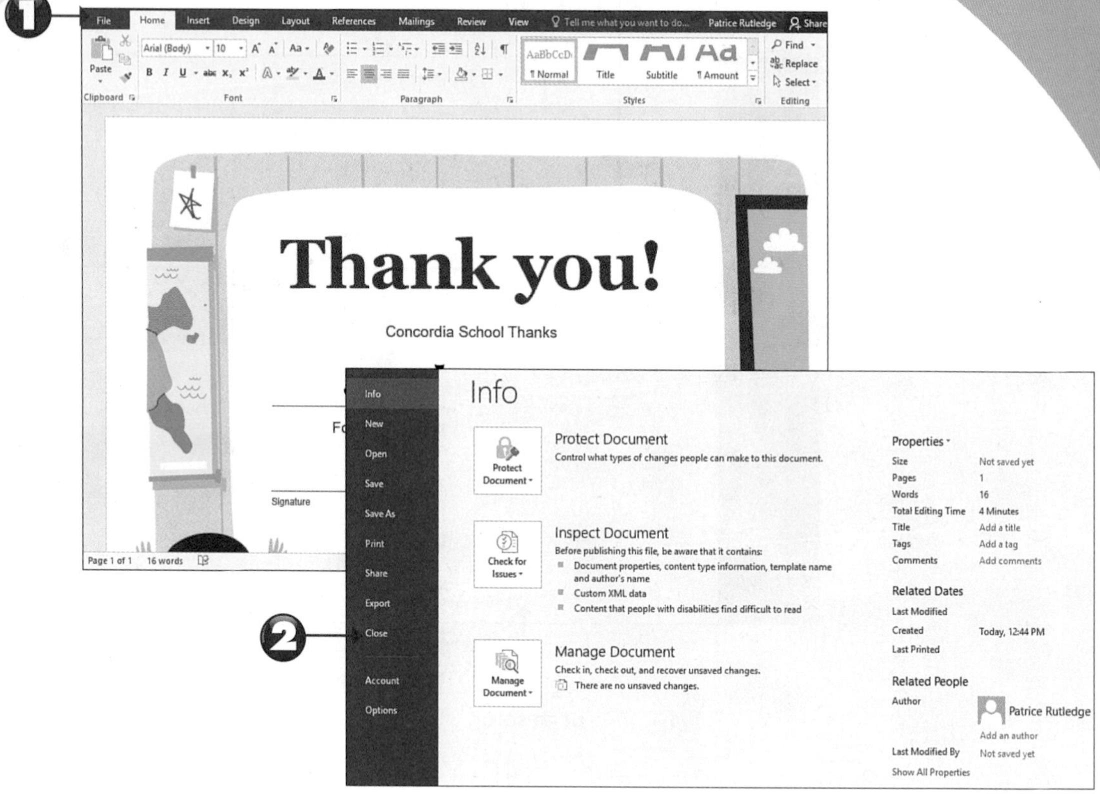

1. Click the **File** tab.
2. Click **Close**.

Continued

**NOTE**

**Previously Saved Files** If you've already saved your file, Office doesn't prompt you to do so, and you don't need to complete steps 4 through 6.

**NOTE**

**File Closing Options** You can also click the **Close** (**x**) button in the upper-right corner of the screen to close an open file. Note, however, that if this is the only file you have open, this action also closes the application. Optionally, pressing Ctrl+W closes the current file without closing the application.

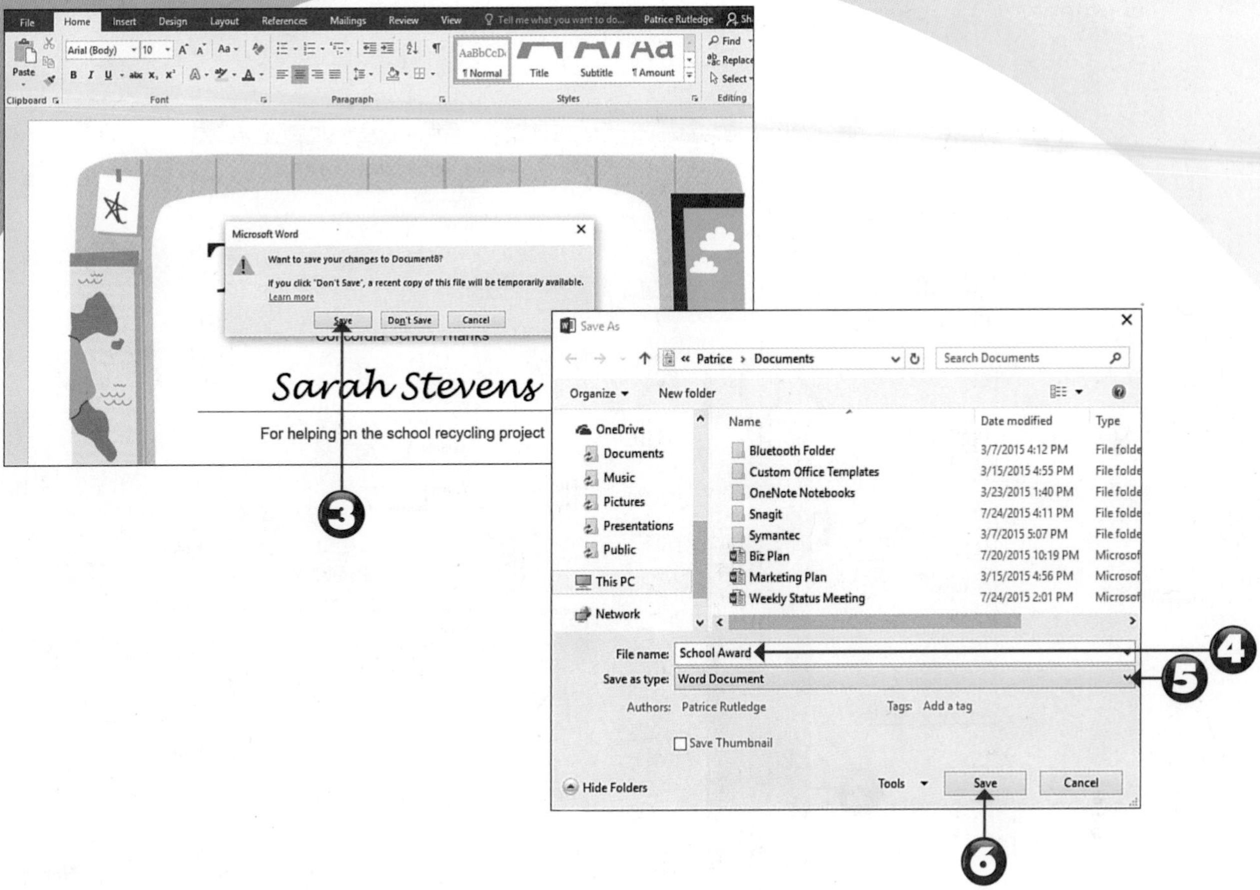

3. Click **Save** to open the Save As dialog box.

4. Type a filename.

5. Select a file format from the Save as Type drop-down list if you don't want to save in the default format.

6. Click **Save** to save and close the file.

End

# CUSTOMIZING OFFICE

The Options dialog box enables you to customize Office applications to suit your work style and needs.

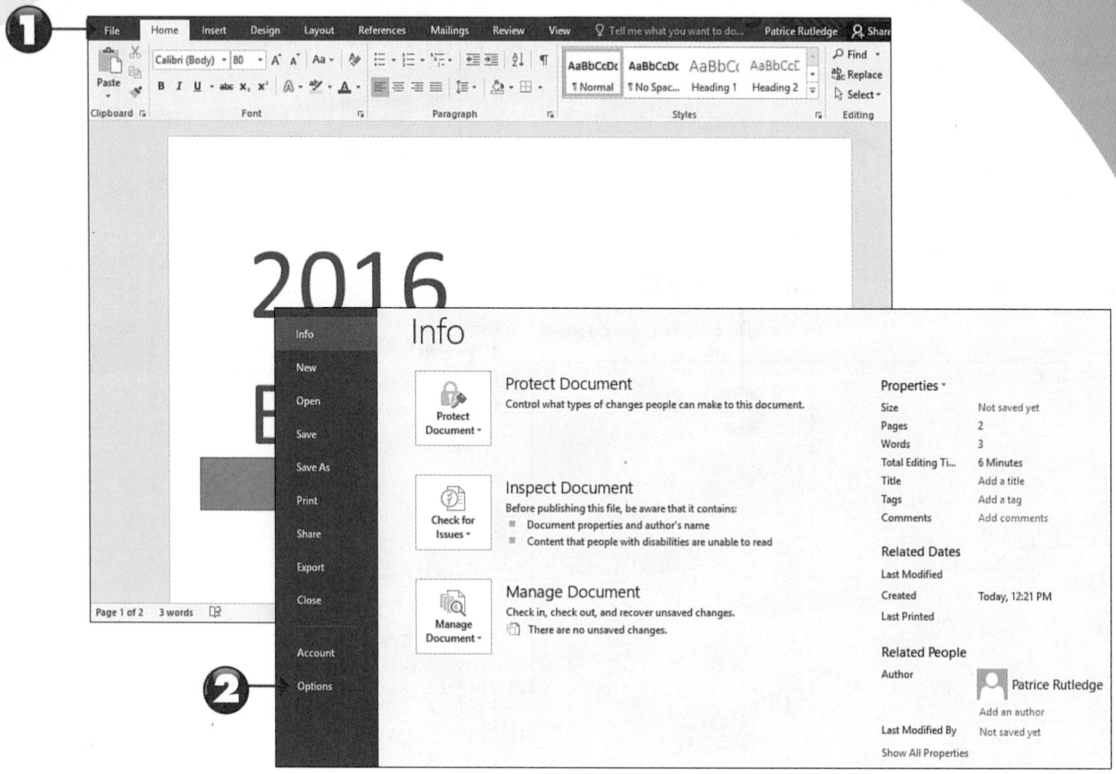

Start

1. Click the **File** tab.
2. Click **Options**.

Continued

## TIP

**Don't Overlook Customization** Although all the available options might seem overwhelming at first, it's worth it to spend a few minutes reviewing the tabs in the Options dialog box to verify which of the defaults you want to change, if any.

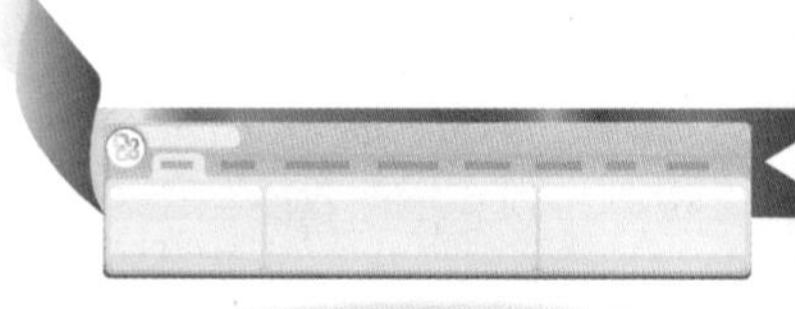

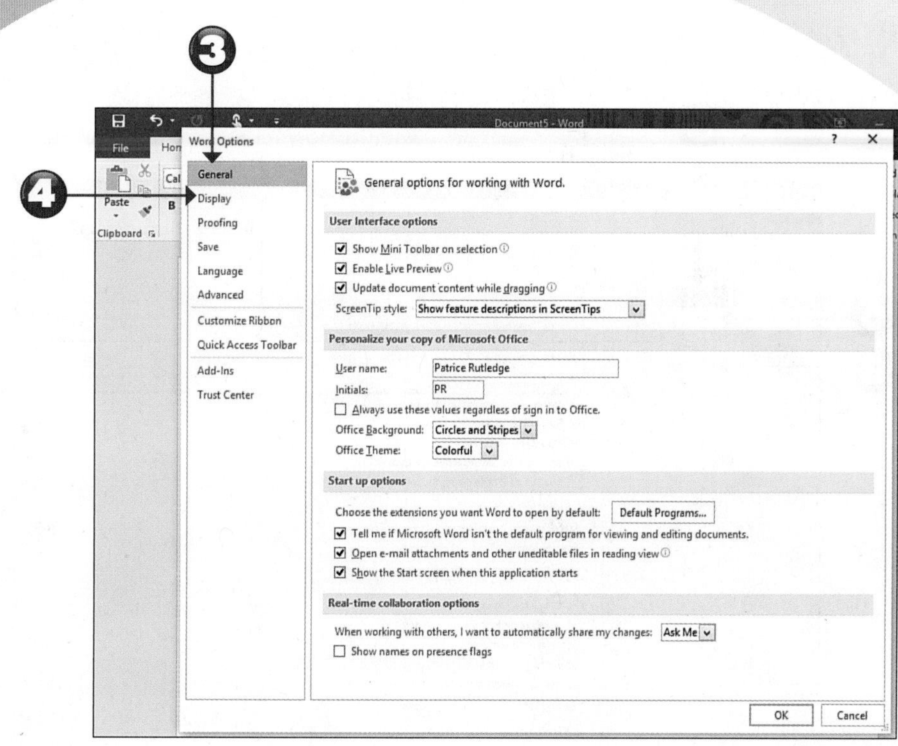


3. Click **General** to customize the user interface and start-up options. This tab is selected by default.

4. Click **Display** to change page display, formatting marks, and printing options.

*Continued*

**NOTE**

**Options Dialog Box Differences** Each Office application has a unique Options dialog box, even though most of the settings are common to all applications. This example shows the Word Options dialog box.

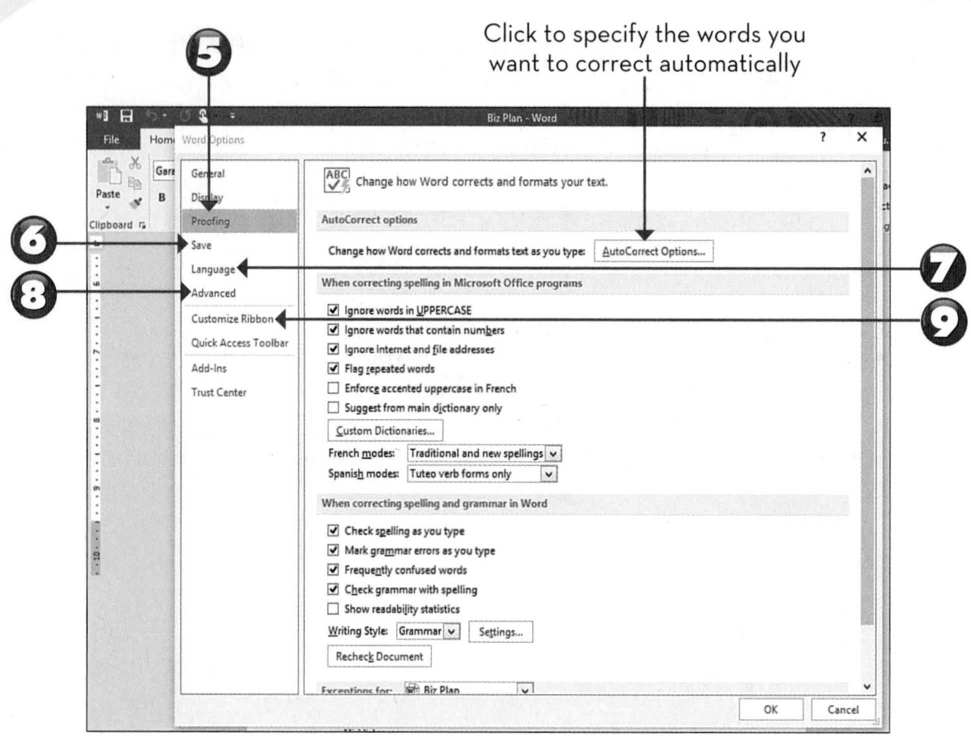


5 Click **Proofing** to customize AutoCorrect, spelling, and grammar.

6 Click **Save** to specify how and where you want to save documents.

7 Click **Language** to enable additional editing languages if you plan to create documents in more than one language.

8 Click **Advanced** to specify Clipboard, chart, display, and print options.

9 Click **Customize Ribbon** to add and remove buttons on the Ribbon.

Continued

## NOTE

**One Setting for All Apps** After you set an option in one Office application, that setting carries over to all the other applications as well.

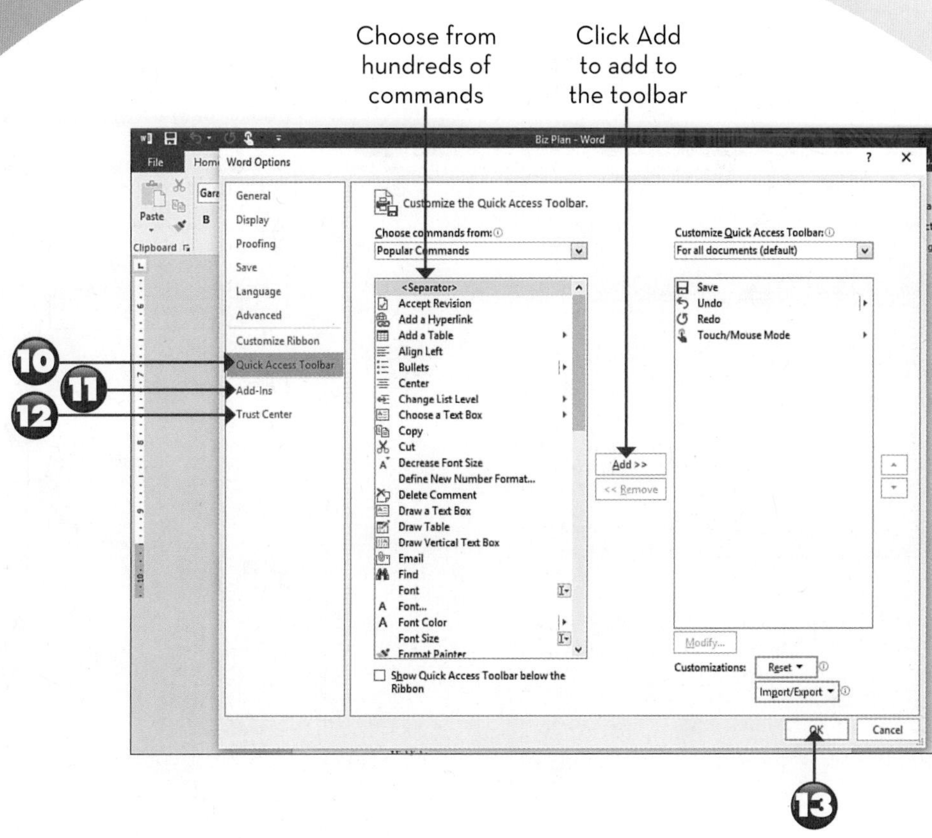


10 Click **Quick Access Toolbar** to add and remove buttons on the Quick Access toolbar.

11 Click **Add-Ins** to view and manage add-ins (for advanced users only).

12 Click **Trust Center** to view Microsoft privacy statements.

13 Click OK when you finish customizing.

*End*

## CAUTION

**Customize Carefully** Although it's a good idea to customize Office to your own needs, don't try customizing too much at once; instead, focus on a few customizations at a time and verify whether they work for you. That way, you can quickly undo any changes you made.

# USING THE TELL ME BOX

The Tell Me box is a new Office 2016 feature that makes it easier to get help on common tasks. In this example, you use Tell Me to discover how to insert a chart in Excel and open the Insert Chart dialog box.

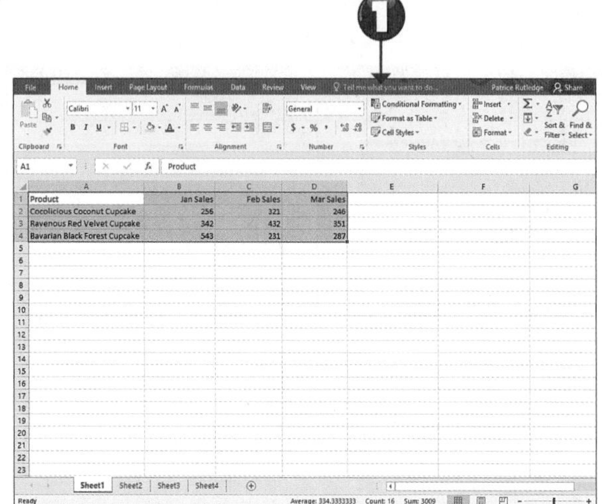


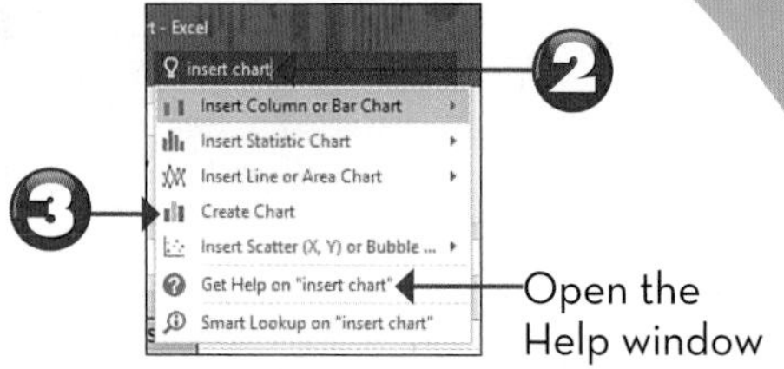


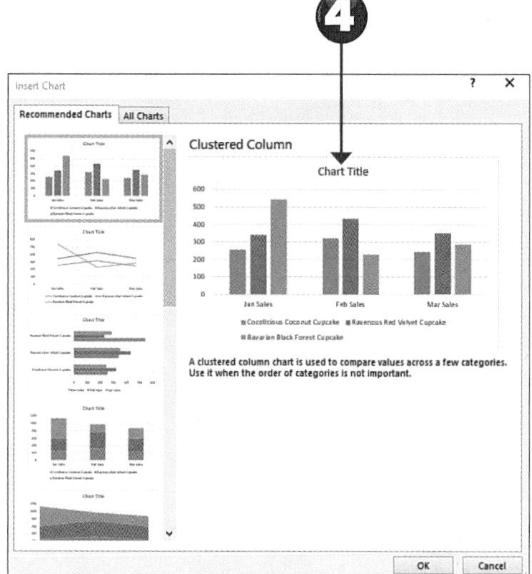


Start

1. Click the **Tell Me** box.
2. Start typing the task you want to do.
3. Click a command.
4. Office goes to that feature; for example, it might open a dialog box or highlight a button on the Ribbon.

End

**TIP**

**Other Help Options** From the Tell Me menu you can also open the Help window or the Insights pane, both discussed later in this chapter.

**NOTE**

**Where's the Tell Me Box?** The Tell Me box is available only in Word, Excel, PowerPoint, and Outlook. OneNote and Publisher use the Help window.

## GETTING HELP

OneNote and Publisher don't use the Tell Me box and rely on the standard Office Help window for providing user assistance. In this example, you search for help on inserting a screen clipping in OneNote.

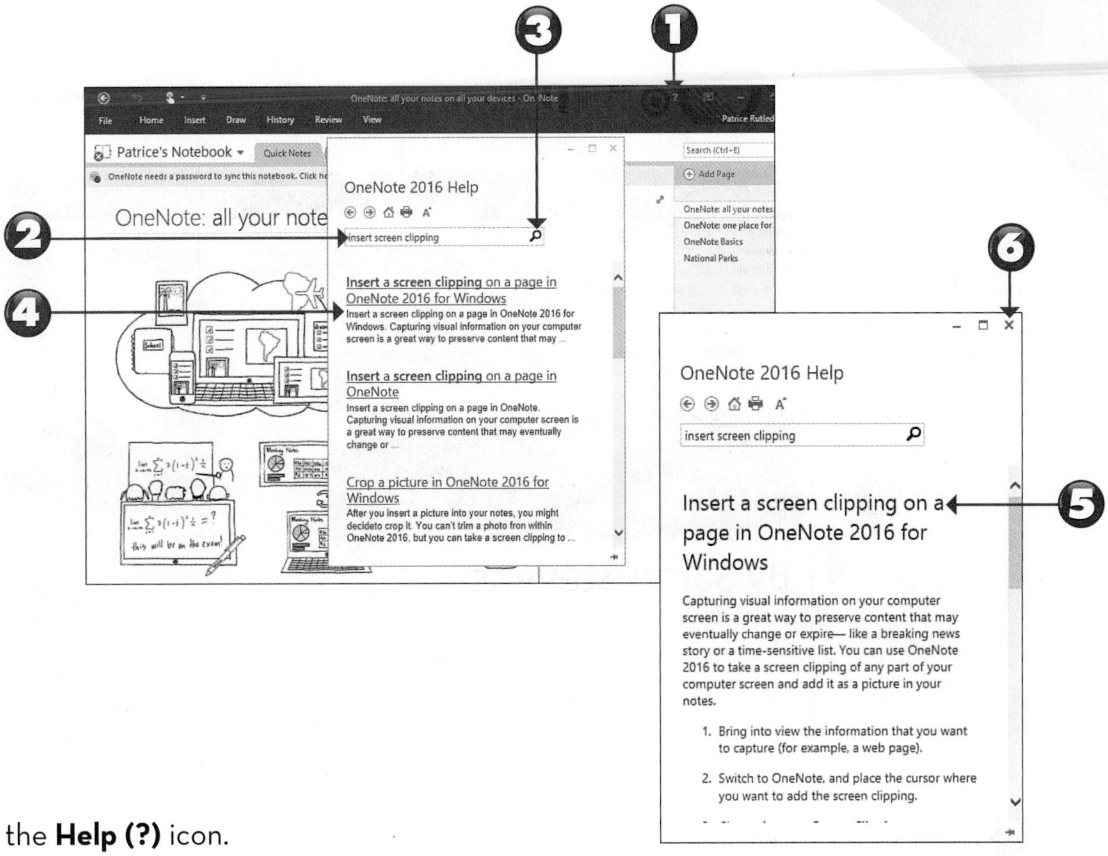

Start

1. Click the **Help (?)** icon.
2. Enter keywords to describe what you're looking for.
3. Press the **Search** button.
4. Click a help topic.
5. View detailed information about this topic.
6. Click the **Close** (**x**) button to close the Help window.

End

**TIP**

**Another Help Option** Another way to open the Help window is to press F1 on your keyboard.

# USING INSIGHTS TO SEARCH THE WEB

Insights is a new Office 2016 feature that enables you to search the Web for information about any topic you mention in Word, Excel, PowerPoint, and Outlook. In this example, you search for information on Lake Tahoe from Word.

Start

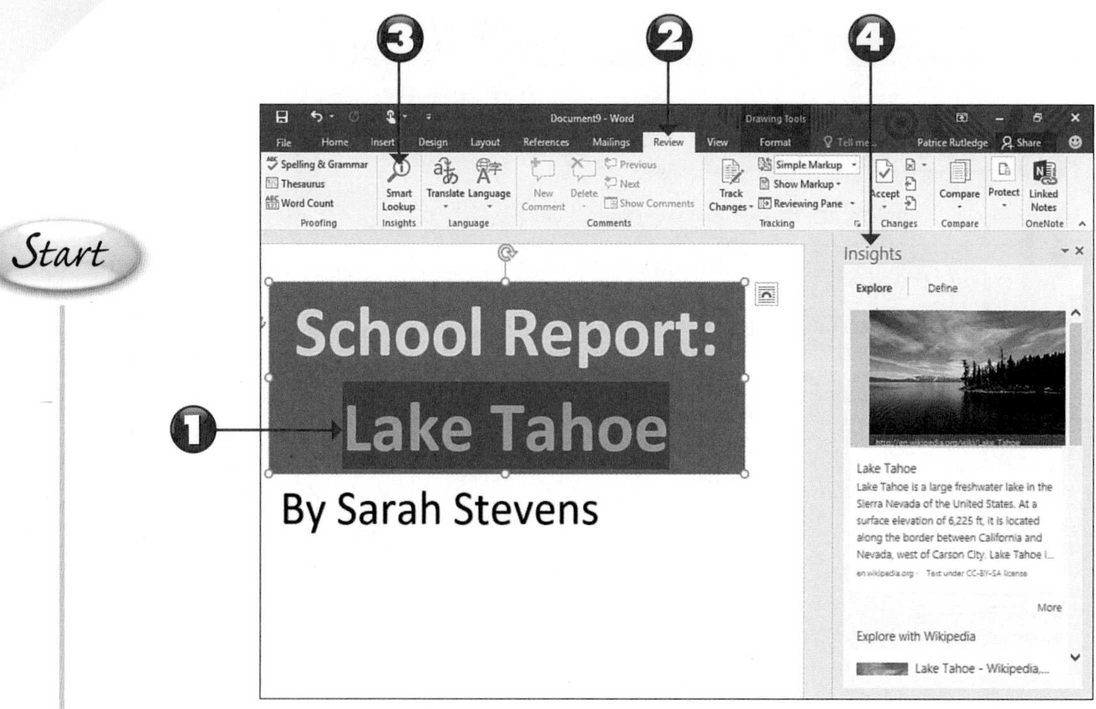


1. Select the text you want to research.
2. Click the **Review** tab.
3. Click the **Smart Lookup** button.
4. The Insights pane opens, displaying basic information about your topic.

Continued

## NOTE

**How Does Insights Work?** Powered by Bing, Insights provides information about selected text from multiple online sources such as Wikipedia, Bing Image Search, Bing Snapshot, the Oxford English Dictionary, and other sites across the Web. Because you can view this data on the Insights pane directly in your Office application, it's a great timesaver for anyone who needs to do research or check facts.

## TIP

**Insights Privacy Statement** The first time you use Insights, Office prompts you to review its related privacy statement and then click the **Got It** button.

5 Scroll down the pane to view additional information, such as results from Bing Image Search and the Web.

6 Click the **Define** tab to display a definition of your selected term from the Oxford English Dictionary.

7 Click the **Close** (**x**) button to close the Insights pane.

*End*

**TIP**

**Improve Insights Results** If the Insights pane doesn't display the information you're looking for, try selecting additional text. For example, selecting a phrase might yield more specific results than selecting only a single word. Also, Insights uses the content surrounding the words you select to help determine what you're looking for (smart lookup). Adding more content to your page can help Insights better understand what your document is about.

**TIP**

**Another Way to Access Insights** You can also open the Insights pane by right-clicking selected text and selecting **Smart Lookup** from the menu.

# WORKING WITH TEXT

Adding text in an Office application is easy; just start typing. If the default text formatting doesn't suit your needs, however, Office also offers numerous text formatting and customization options.

The Home tab in Word, PowerPoint, Publisher, and Excel is home to a solid collection of text-formatting tools, giving you the option to select a font style and size; change text color; or apply bold, italic, and underlining to your text. You can also align text, use WordArt to create sophisticated text objects, search for and replace text, and use the Font dialog box for more advanced formatting.

Finally, you can fix any spelling errors by performing a spell check—something you need to do on every Office document.

## FORMATTING TEXT ON THE HOME TAB (WORD)

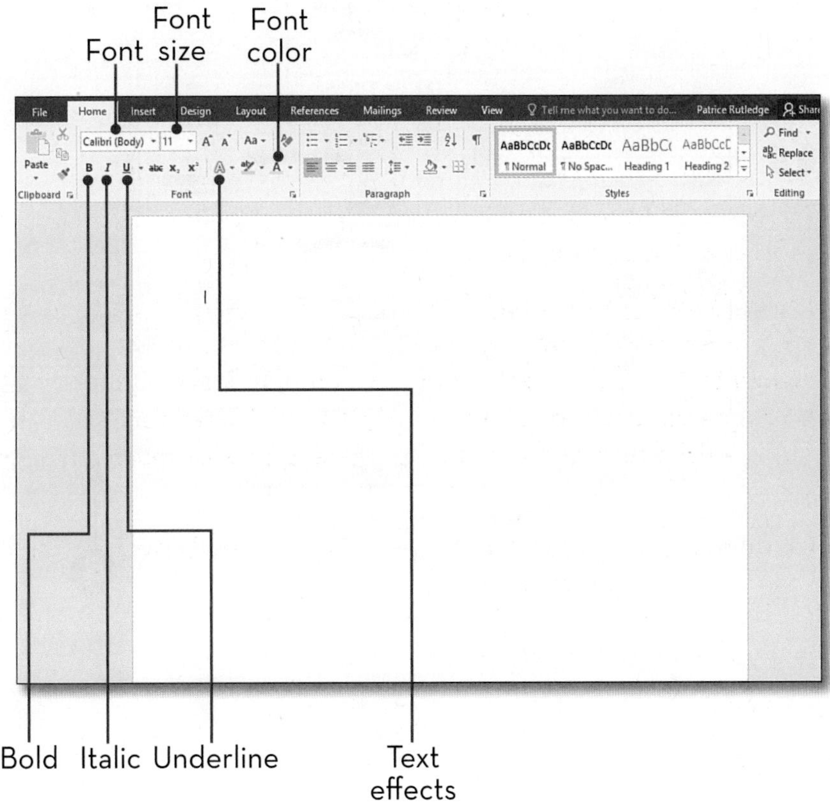

# USING THE FONT DIALOG BOX TO FORMAT TEXT

The Font dialog box offers some advanced formatting options not available on the Home tab.

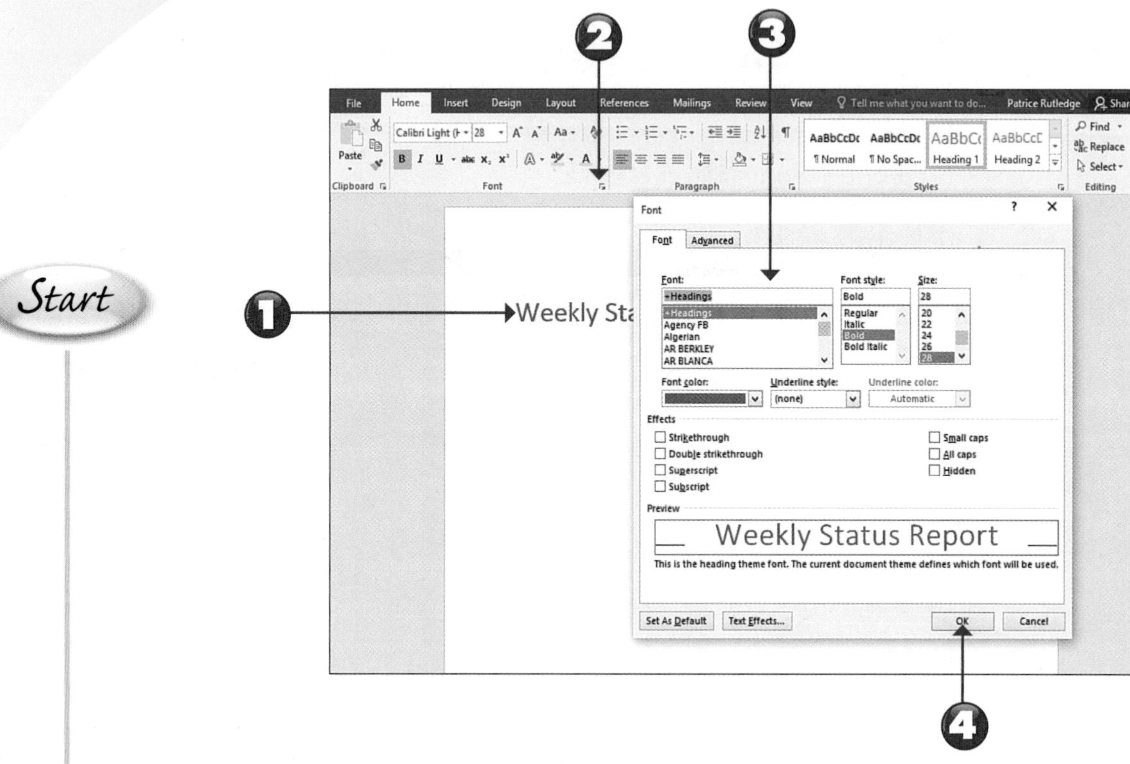


1. Select the text you want to format.
2. Click the dialog box launcher in the Font group.
3. In the Font dialog box, select a formatting option.
4. Click the **OK** button to close the dialog box and apply the font formatting.

End

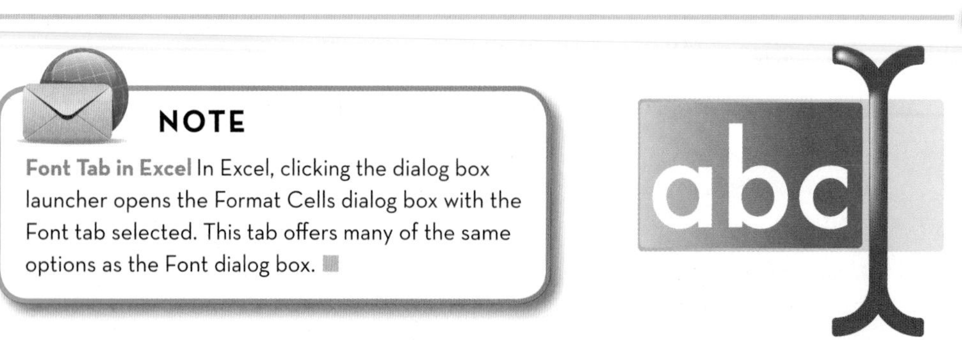

## NOTE

**Font Tab in Excel** In Excel, clicking the dialog box launcher opens the Format Cells dialog box with the Font tab selected. This tab offers many of the same options as the Font dialog box.

# ALIGNING TEXT

You can quickly align text using buttons on the Home tab.

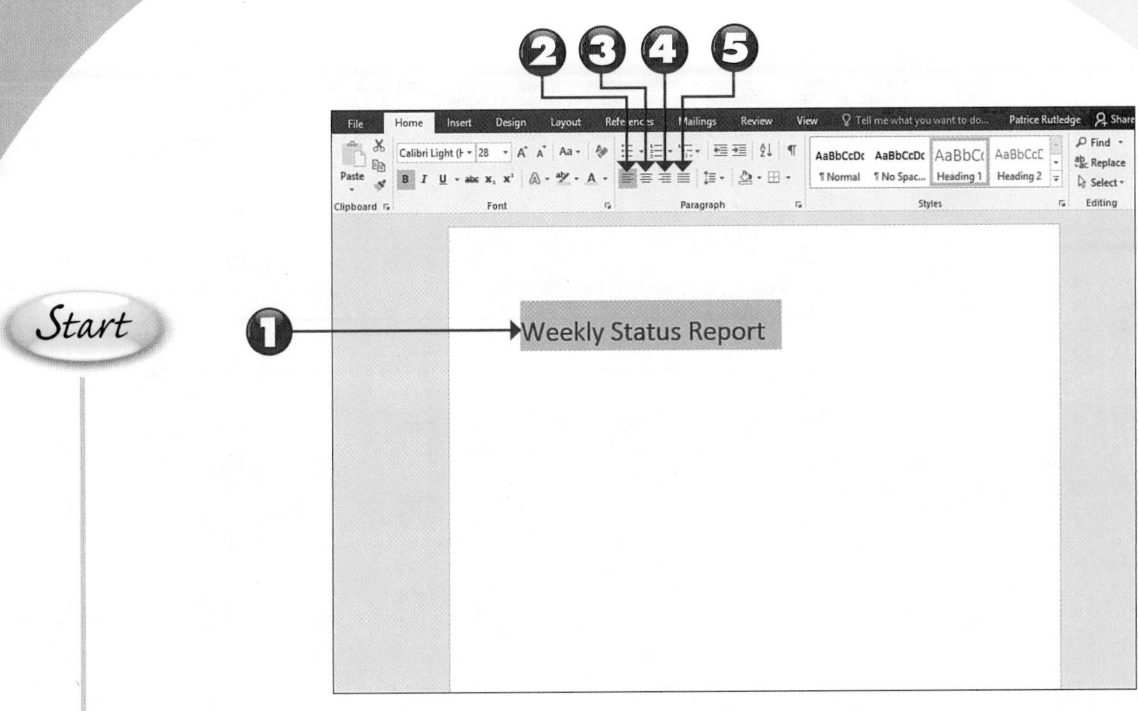


1. Select the text you want to align.
2. Click the **Align Left** button to align your text to the left (the default).
3. Click the **Center** button to center your text, such as a heading.
4. Click the **Align Right** button to align your text to the right.
5. Click the **Justify** button to justify your text.

End

**NOTE**

**Justified Text** When you justify text, it's stretched or compressed to align to both the left and the right.

# REPLACING TEXT

At times, you might need to change a word or phrase that's used throughout a document. The Find and Replace dialog box makes it easy to replace text, especially in long documents.

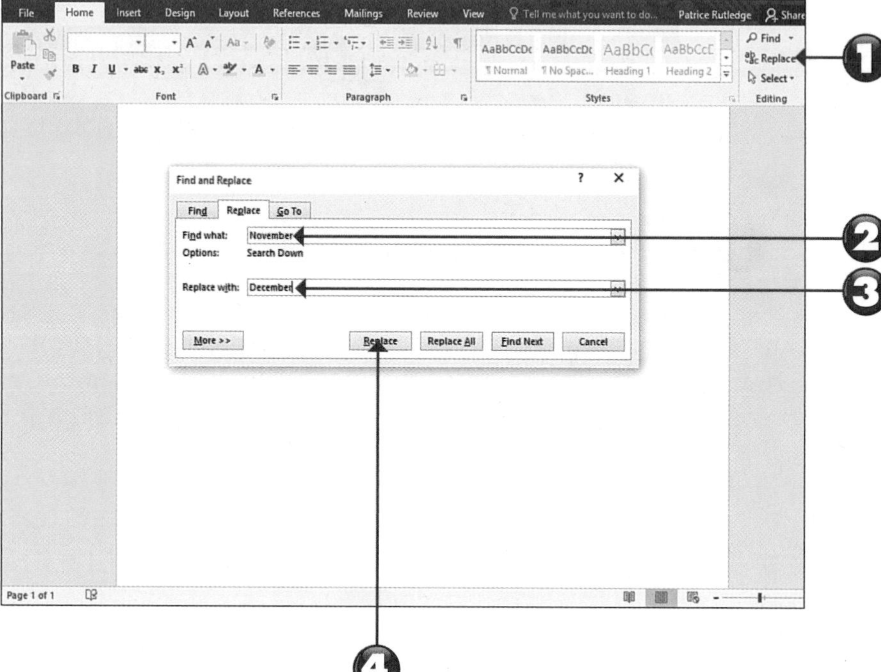


1. On the Home tab, click the **Replace** button.
2. In the Find and Replace dialog box, enter the text you're searching for in the **Find what** box.
3. Enter the replacement text in the **Replace with** box.
4. Click the **Replace** button to make the replacement.

Continued

## NOTE

**Replace All Instances** If you don't want to approve each instance of a replacement, you can click the **Replace All** button to handle this process all at once.

## NOTE

**Excel Navigation** In Excel, click the **Find & Select** button, and select **Replace** from the menu to open the Find and Replace dialog box.

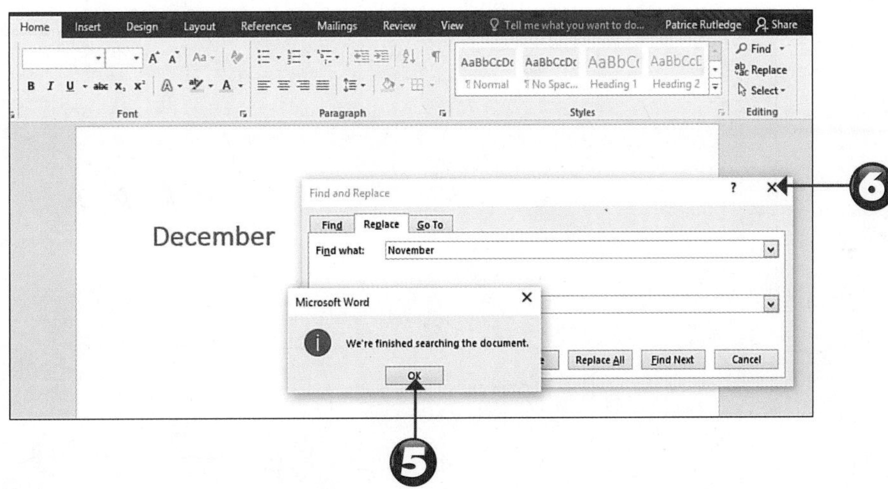


5 Office notifies you when the process is finished. Click **OK** to close the notification.

6 Click the **Close** button to close the Find and Replace dialog box.

*End*

## NOTE

**Find Text** Just want to find specific text rather than replace it? Enter the text in the Find What box, and click the **Find Next** button. You can also click the **Find** button on the Home tab to perform a search.

## NOTE

**More Options** Click the **More** button to display more find-and-replace options. For example, you might want to replace only text with matching case or search only for whole words.

# INSERTING WORDART

WordArt enables you to create special text effects such as shadowed, rotated, stretched, and multicolored text.

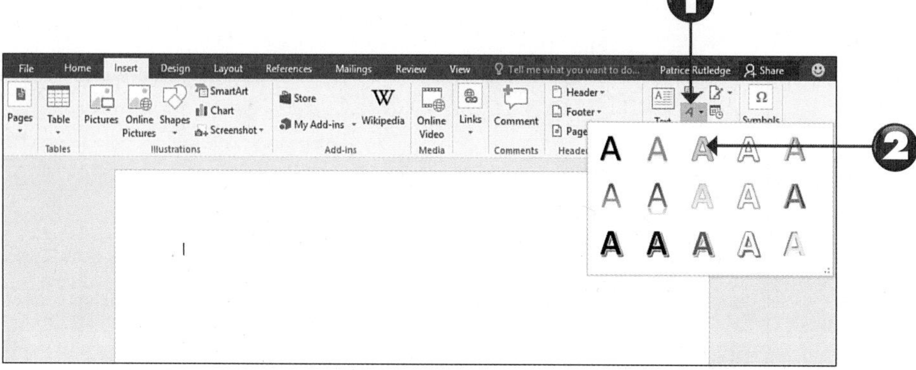


Start

1. On the Insert tab, click the **WordArt** button.
2. In the WordArt gallery, click the WordArt style you prefer.
3. Replace the placeholder text with text you want to format using WordArt.

End

## CAUTION

**Don't Overuse WordArt** Be careful not to overuse WordArt in your document or presentation, or it can become cluttered and confusing. Use WordArt only for emphasis.

## NOTE

**Excel WordArt Navigation** This example demonstrates adding WordArt in Microsoft Word. In Excel, click the **Text** button on the Insert tab, and select **WordArt** from the menu.

# FORMATTING WORDART

Office offers a wide selection of formatting options for WordArt. You can apply a Quick Style, gradients, textures, bevels, rotations, and more.

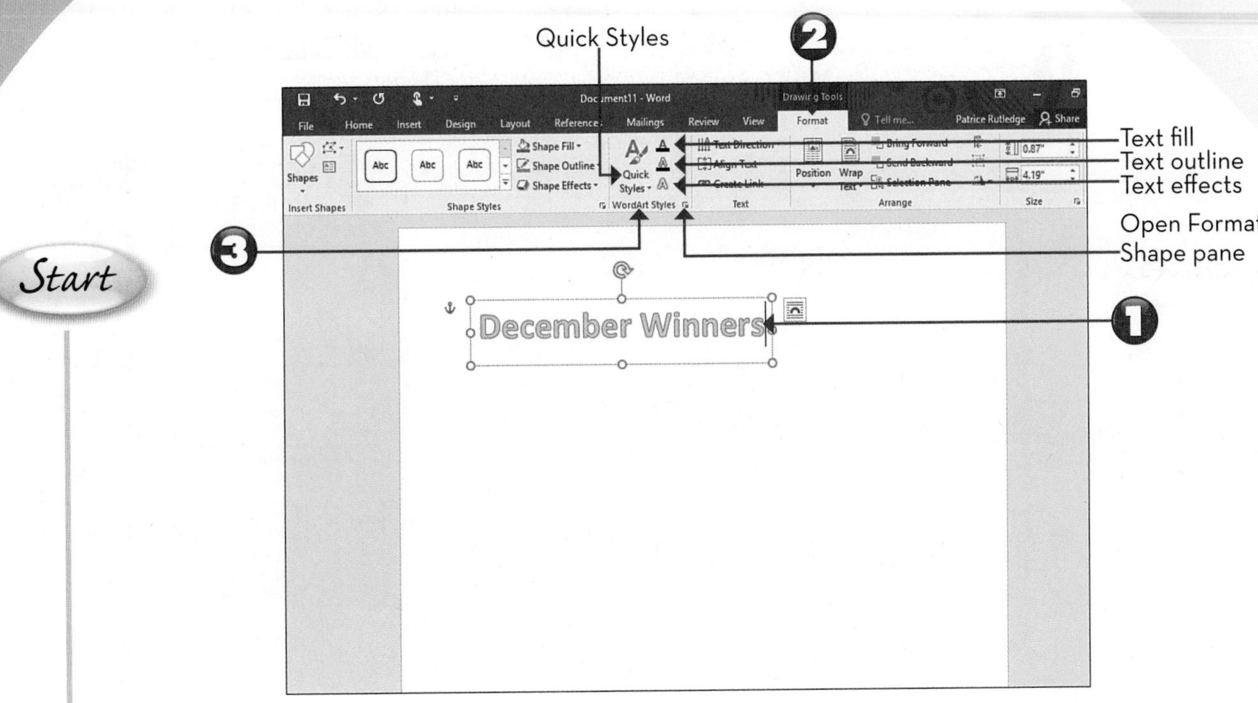


1. Select the WordArt object you want to format.
2. The Drawing Tools–Format tab displays.
3. Format your WordArt object using the options on this tab, in particular those in the WordArt Styles group.

End

## NOTE

**Text Fill and Text Outline** The Text Fill button and Text Outline button include a down arrow to their right that displays an extensive menu of options. Clicking the button directly applies the default. Clicking the **Text Effects** button, however, displays the menu; there is no default to apply.

# CHECKING SPELLING

Creating quality, error-free, and easy-to-read content is a natural objective when you use an Office application. Fortunately, Office offers a spelling checker to help eliminate spelling errors. You can also spell check your entire presentation at once.

Start

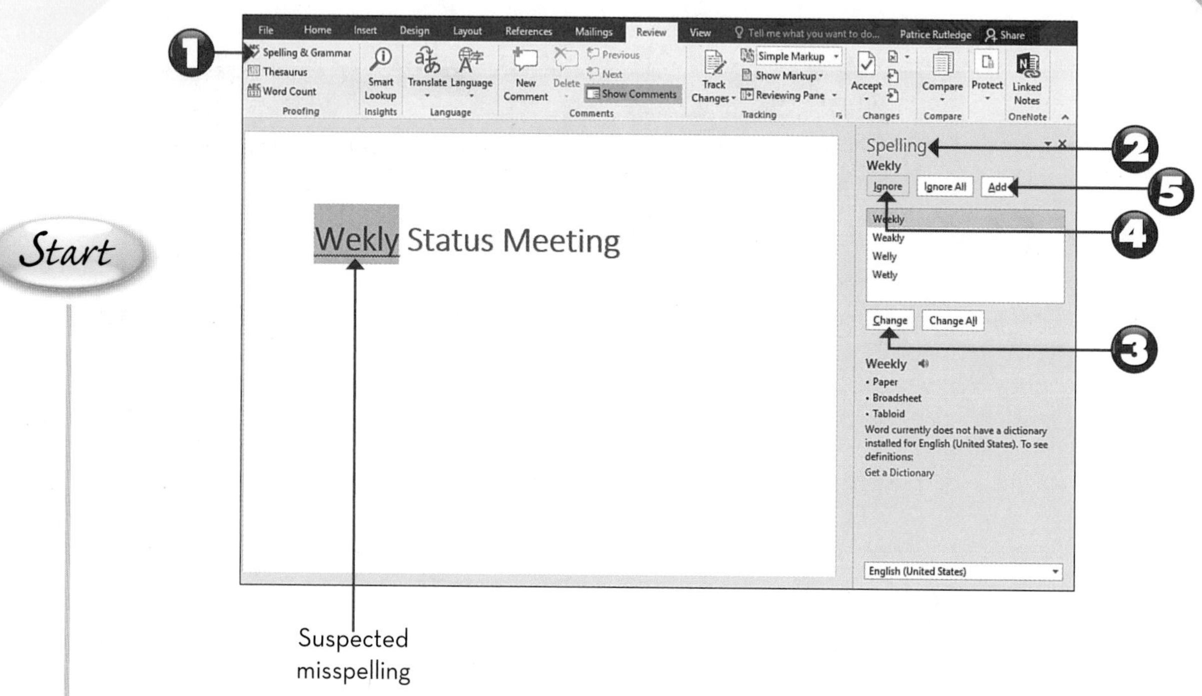


Suspected misspelling

1. On the Review tab, click the **Spelling & Grammar** button. (In Excel and PowerPoint, this is called the Spelling button.)
2. The Spelling pane opens, and the spell checker starts examining your document.
3. Select the correct spelling, and click the **Change** button.
4. Click the **Ignore** button if the suspected misspelling isn't an error.
5. Click the **Add** button to add the word as-is to the dictionary.

Continued

**NOTE**

**No Spelling Errors** If your document contains no errors, Office displays a dialog box informing you of this and doesn't open the Spelling pane.

**TIP**

**Change or Ignore All** To save time, you can click either the **Change All** button or **Ignore All** button to resolve all instances of the suspected error at once.

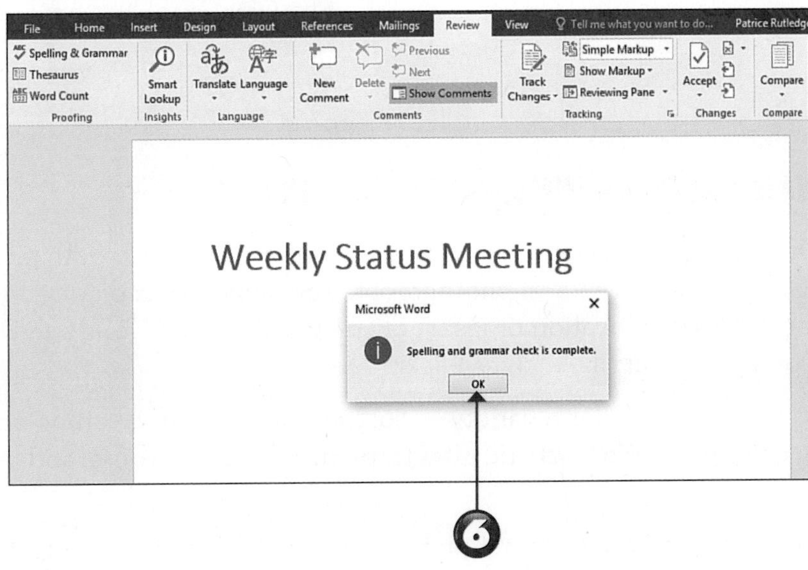


6

6 Office notifies you when the spelling checker is finished. Click **OK** to close the notification.

*End*

**CAUTION**

**Spelling Checker Limitations** Keep in mind that, although an automated tool can help you catch errors, it isn't foolproof and doesn't take the place of thorough proofreading by a person.

**NOTE**

**Spelling Options** By default, Office checks spelling as you type and displays a red squiggly line under all suspected misspellings. To modify the default spell-checking options, click the **File** tab, select **Options** in Backstage view, and click **Proofing**.

Chapter 4

# WORKING WITH PICTURES

Microsoft Office offers several ways to enliven your documents with pictures, including both illustrations and photographs. You can insert a picture from your computer or network location or insert online pictures from your OneDrive account or an external site such as Flickr.

In addition, Office provides a variety of customization and formatting options, including color correction, artistic effects, picture styles, borders, and much more.

You can insert, modify, and format pictures in Word, PowerPoint, Publisher, Outlook, and Excel. You also can insert pictures in OneNote, but you can't modify them because OneNote doesn't include the Picture Tools–Format tab.

## PICTURE TOOLS–FORMAT TAB

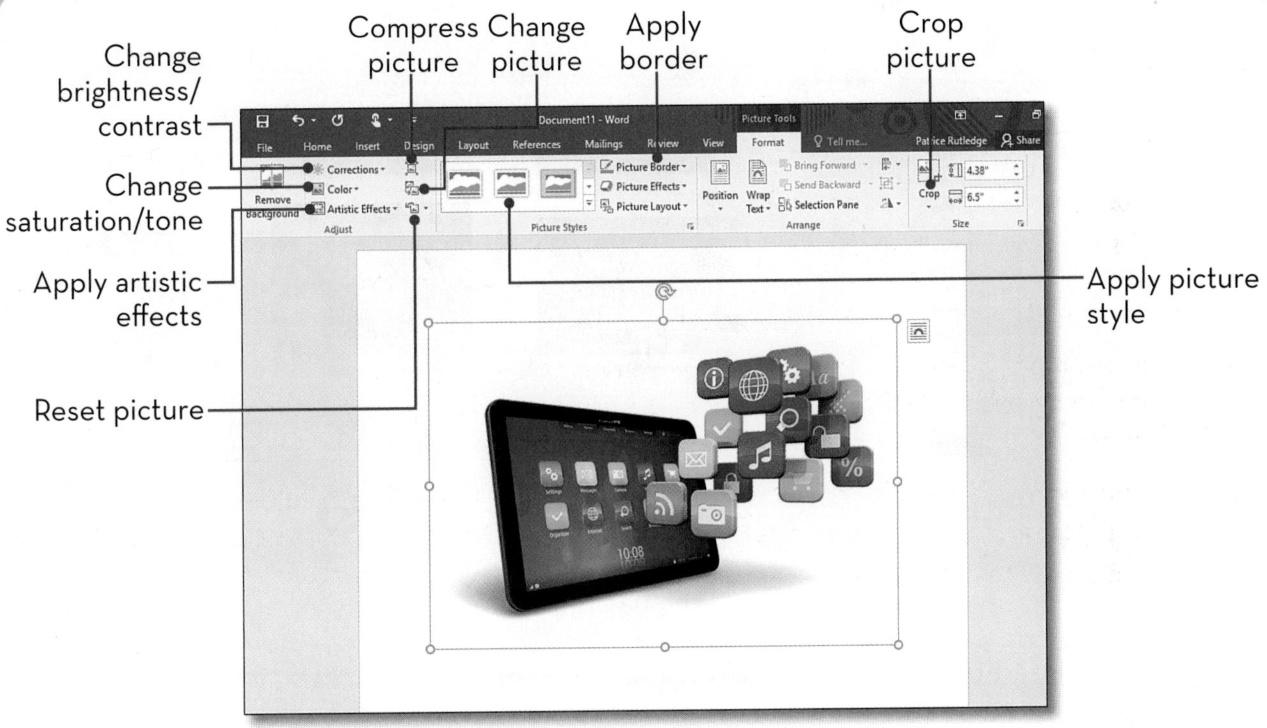

# INSERTING A PICTURE FROM YOUR COMPUTER

Office makes it easy to insert a picture from your computer or a network location.

Start

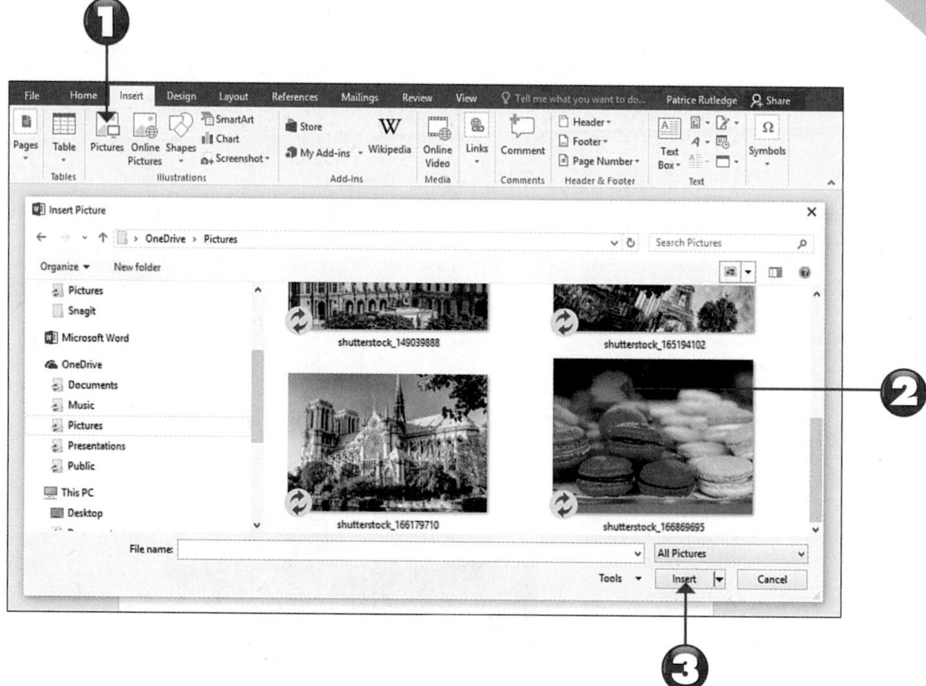

1. On the Insert tab, click the **Pictures** button.
2. In the Insert Picture dialog box, select the picture you want to insert.
3. Click the **Insert** button.

Continued

## TIP

**Where's the Pictures Button?** Depending on your screen size and resolution, you might have to click the **Illustrations** button on the Insert tab and then select **Pictures** from the menu.

**4** Office inserts the picture.

End

## NOTE

**Picture File Types** Office works with two basic types of pictures. *Bitmap* pictures are composed of pixels (tiny dots of color), such as photos from a digital camera. Common bitmap file formats include .bmp, .gif, .jpg, .png, and .tif. *Vector* pictures are composed of points, lines, and curves and are popular for pictures you need to modify and resize, such as logos. Common vector file formats include .eps and .wmf.

## TIP

**Select Multiple Pictures** To select multiple pictures, hold down the **Shift** key as you select. If the pictures aren't contiguous, hold down the **Ctrl** key.

# INSERTING AN ONLINE PICTURE

You can use Bing Image Search to find images that are licensed under Creative Commons.

Start

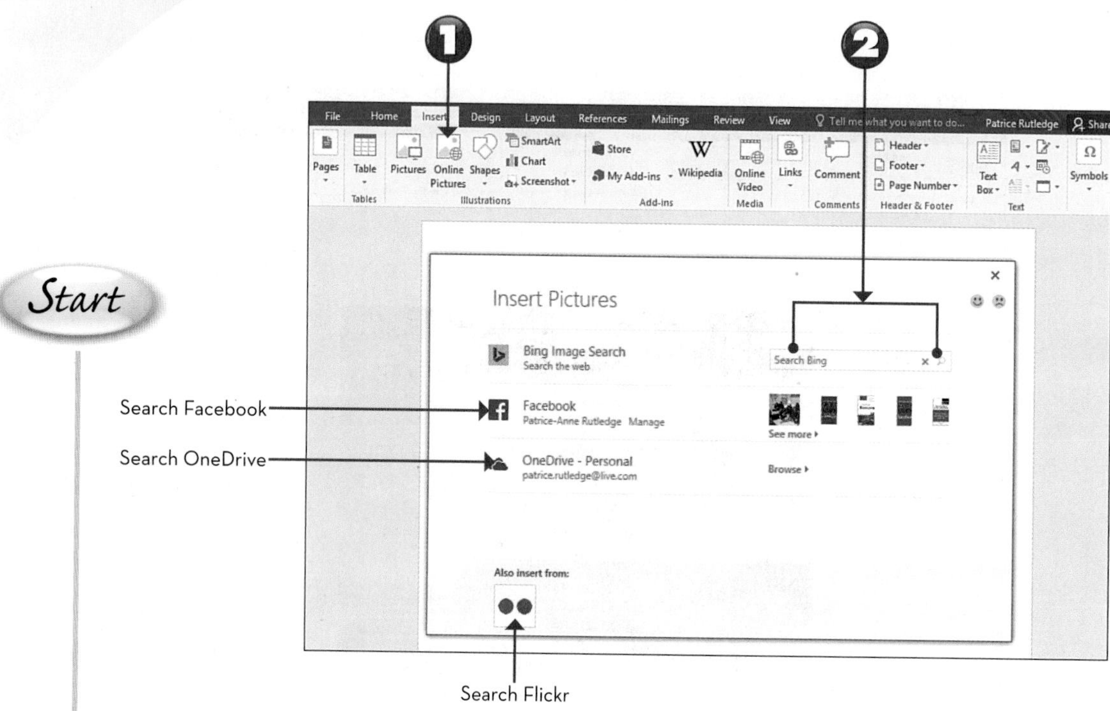


1. On the Insert tab, click the **Online Pictures** button.

2. In the Insert Pictures dialog box, enter a keyword or keywords in the Bing Image Search field, and then click the **Search** button.

Continued

**TIP**

**Where's the Online Pictures Button?** Depending on your screen size and resolution, you might have to click the **Illustrations** button on the Insert tab and then select **Online Pictures** from the menu.

**NOTE**

**Online Picture Options** From the Insert Pictures dialog box, you can also insert pictures from your OneDrive account, Facebook, and Flickr.

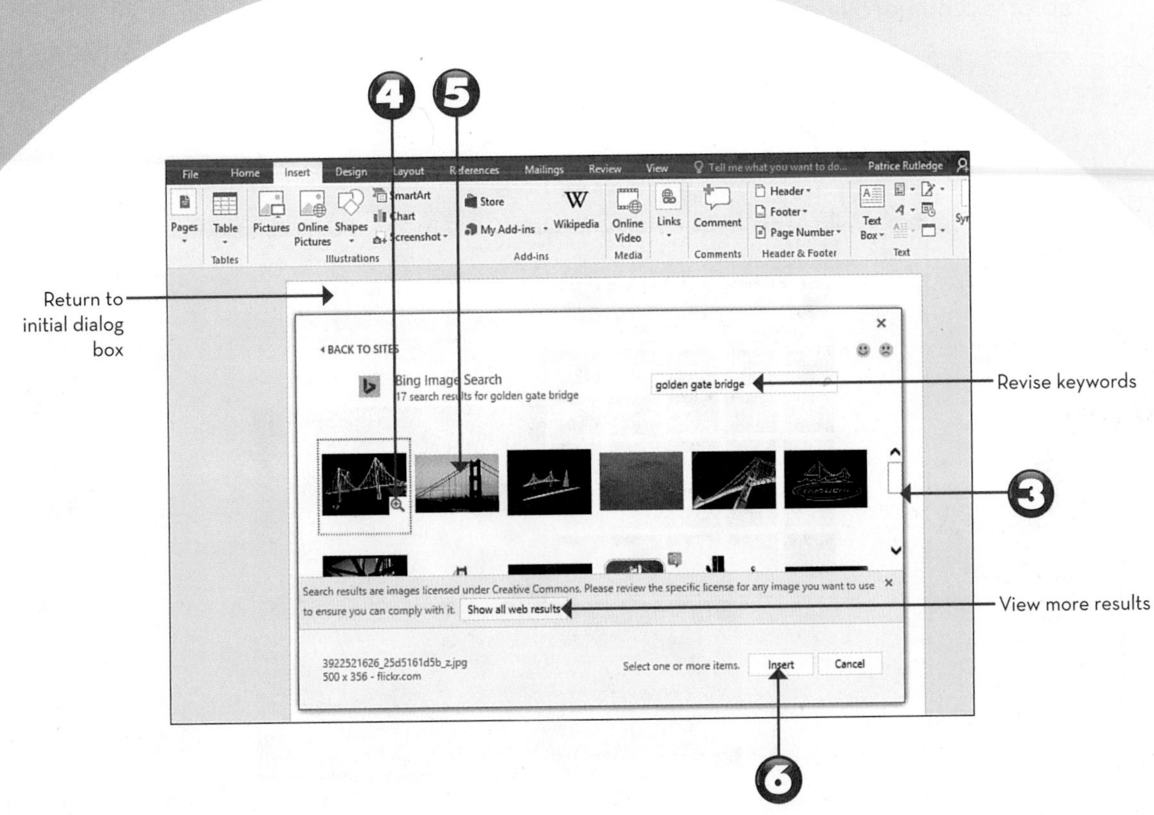


3 Scroll down the right side of the dialog box to view all results that match your keywords.

4 Click the **View Larger** button to enlarge a picture.

5 Select one or more pictures from the matching results.

6 Click the **Insert** button to insert the picture.

*End*

## TIP

**Select Multiple Pictures** To select multiple pictures, hold down the **Shift** key as you select. To select noncontiguous pictures, hold down the **Ctrl** key.

## CAUTION

**Creative Commons Limitations** A Creative Commons license gives you the right to use copyrighted work, such as a picture. Be sure to view the details of the license before using a picture, however. Some licenses prohibit derivative works or commercial use.

# ENHANCING A PICTURE

When you select a picture, the Picture Tools-Format tab displays. The Adjust group on this tab offers numerous picture enhancement options.

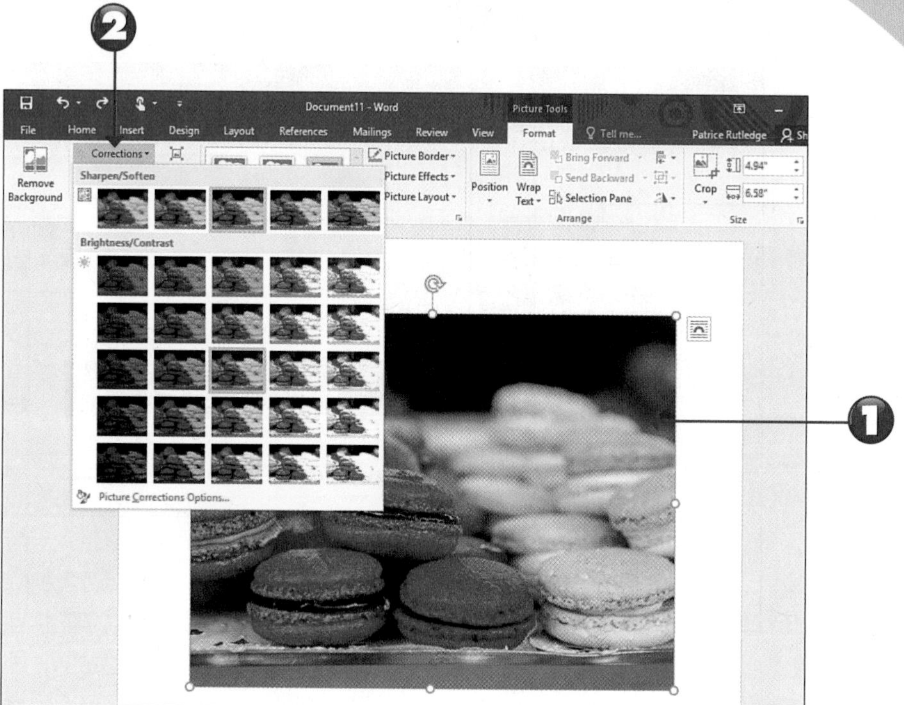


Start

1. Select the picture you want to enhance.
2. On the Picture Tools-Format tab, click the **Corrections** button to adjust sharpness, softness, brightness, or contrast.

Continued

## NOTE

**Other Picture Enhancements** The Adjust group on the Picture Tools-Format tab also enables you to remove picture backgrounds, compress a picture to reduce its size, change to a different picture, or reset a picture after changing it.

Click the **Color** button to modify color saturation and color tone or to recolor your picture.

Click **Artistic Effects** to apply artistic effects such as Pencil Sketch, Mosaic Bubbles, or Paint Brush.

End

## CAUTION

**Don't Overdo Enhancements** Although the tools in the Adjust group give you many creative options for modifying your pictures, be careful not to overdo it and make your picture unrecognizable.

# APPLYING A PICTURE STYLE

To enliven a picture, consider using a picture style. For example, you might apply a rotated white border or a soft-edge oval shape to your picture.

Start

1. Select the picture to which you want to apply a style.
2. On the Picture Tools–Format tab, click the down arrow in the lower-right corner of the Picture Styles box.
3. Select your preferred picture style from the gallery that displays.
4. Office applies the style to your selected picture.

End

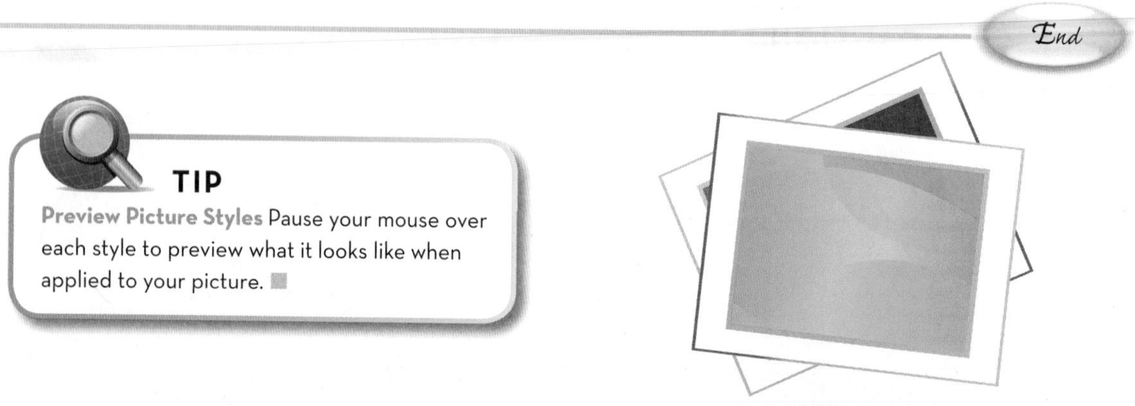

**TIP**

**Preview Picture Styles** Pause your mouse over each style to preview what it looks like when applied to your picture.

# APPLYING A PICTURE BORDER

Applying a simple border to your picture can give it a professional look and distinguish it from a background of a similar color.

Start

1 Select the picture to which you want to apply a border.

2 On the Picture Tools–Format tab, click the **Picture Border** button.

3 Select a border color.

4 Click the **Picture Border** button again, and select a border weight from the Weight menu option.

5 Office applies the selected border options.

End

## TIP

**Picture Border Options** From the Picture Border menu, you can also select **More Outline Colors** to customize a border color or **Dashes** to create a border with dashed lines.

# RESIZING A PICTURE

If your picture is either too large or too small, you can resize it easily by dragging a corner with your mouse.

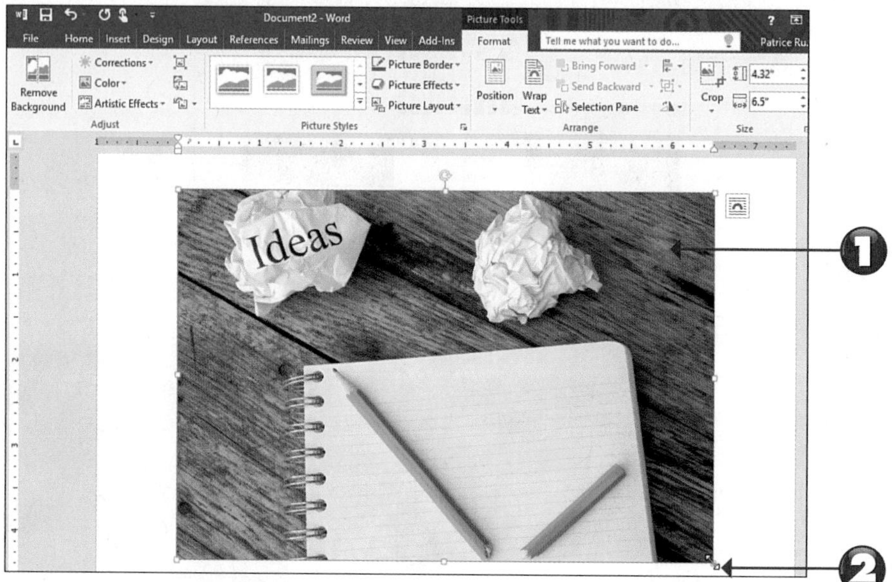

1. Select the picture you want to resize.
2. Position your mouse over a picture corner. The mouse pointer becomes a double arrow.
3. Drag the corner to make the picture larger or smaller.

End

## CAUTION

**Resize to Avoid Distortion** Be sure to drag a picture corner to size the picture proportionally. If you drag a picture from its side, you'll distort it.

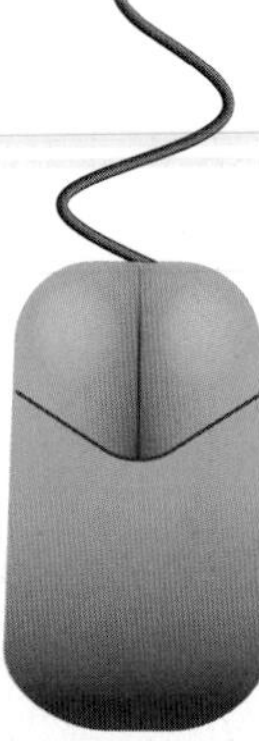

# CROPPING A PICTURE

If you don't want to include an entire picture, you can crop it to your exact specifications. For example, you might want to zero in on an object in the center of a picture or remove extra content at the top of a picture.

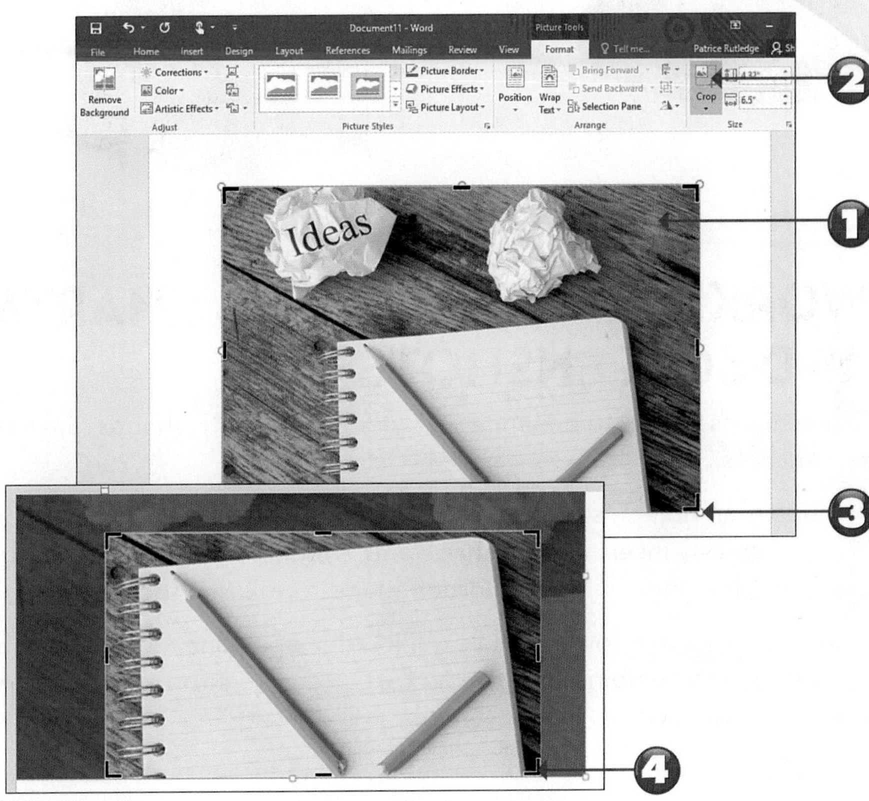

Start

1. Select the picture you want to crop.
2. On the Picture Tools –Format tab, click the **Crop** button.
3. Handles surround the picture, enabling you to specify the exact content you want to retain.
4. Drag the mouse to determine your cropping area.

End

**TIP**

**Crop to Fit a Shape** You can also crop a picture to fit in a specific shape by clicking the down arrow below the Crop button and selecting **Crop to Shape** on the menu.

# WORKING WITH SHAPES, SMARTART, AND SCREENSHOTS

Office makes it easy to enhance your documents with shapes, SmartArt, and screenshots.

A *shape* is an object, such as a line, arrow, rectangle, circle, square, or callout. You can quickly insert a basic shape and, optionally, customize it to meet your exact needs using Office's numerous shape-formatting tools.

*SmartArt* takes the power and flexibility of shapes one step further. SmartArt enables you to combine shapes and text to create informative lists, matrices, pyramids, and more.

Finally, Office gives you the option of inserting *screenshots* without the need for a screen-capture tool. For example, you might want to capture something from another Office application or from an external website.

You can insert and modify shapes, SmartArt, and screenshots in Word, PowerPoint, Outlook, and Excel. You can insert and modify shapes in Publisher.

# INSERT TAB

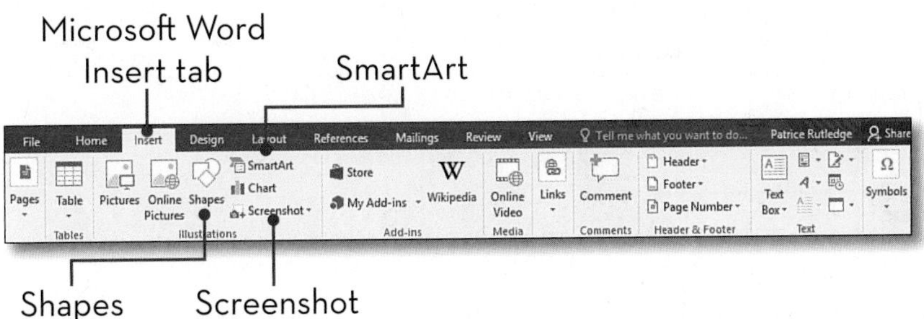
Microsoft Word
Insert tab
SmartArt
Shapes
Screenshot

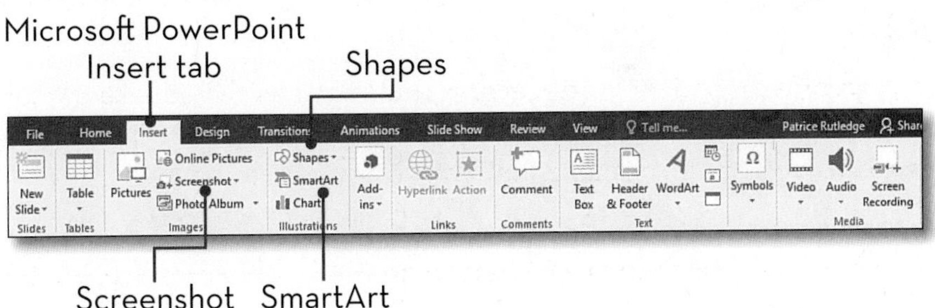
Microsoft PowerPoint
Insert tab
Shapes
Screenshot
SmartArt

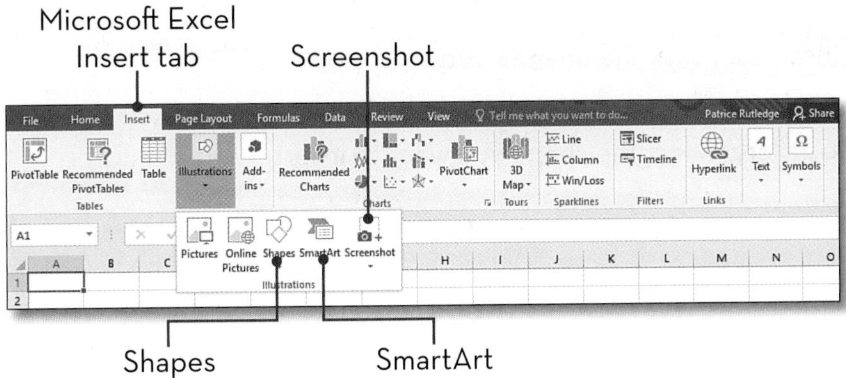
Microsoft Excel
Insert tab
Screenshot
Shapes
SmartArt

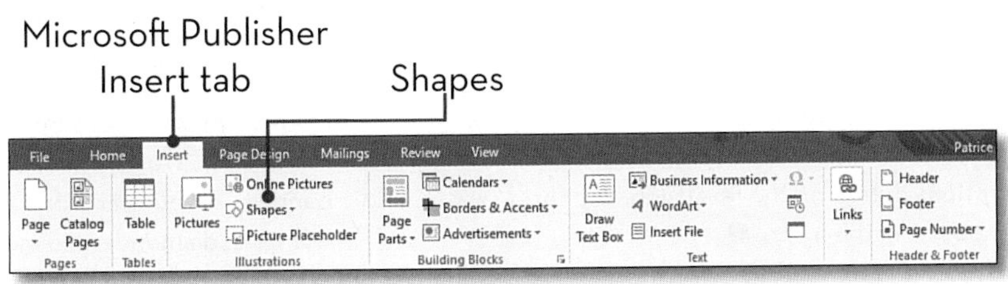
Microsoft Publisher
Insert tab
Shapes

# INSERTING A SHAPE

Office offers dozens of ready-made shapes for you to use.

Start

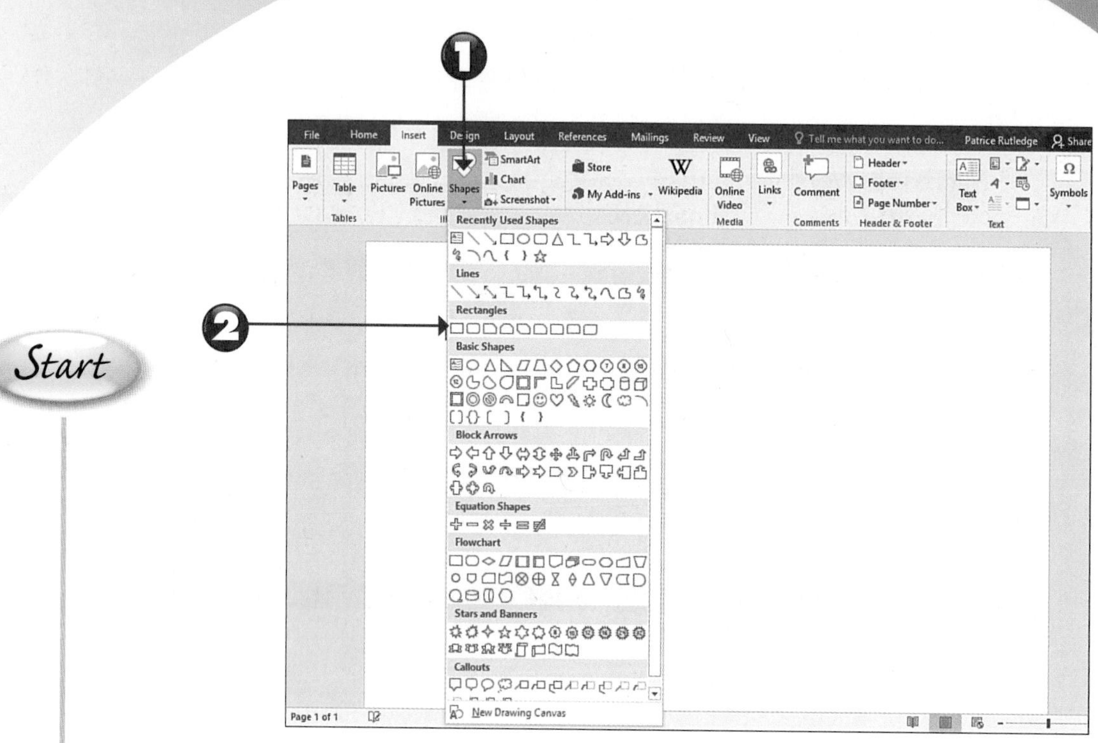


1. On the Insert tab, click the **Shapes** button.

2. From the gallery, select the shape you want to insert.

Continued

## TIP

**Where Is the Shapes Button?** Depending on your screen size and resolution, you might have to click the **Illustrations** button on the Insert tab, and then select **Shapes** from the menu. ■

## NOTE

**Shape Options** Shape options include lines, rectangles, arrows, equations, flowcharts, stars, banners, callouts, and basic shapes such as ovals, triangles, diamonds, and more. ■

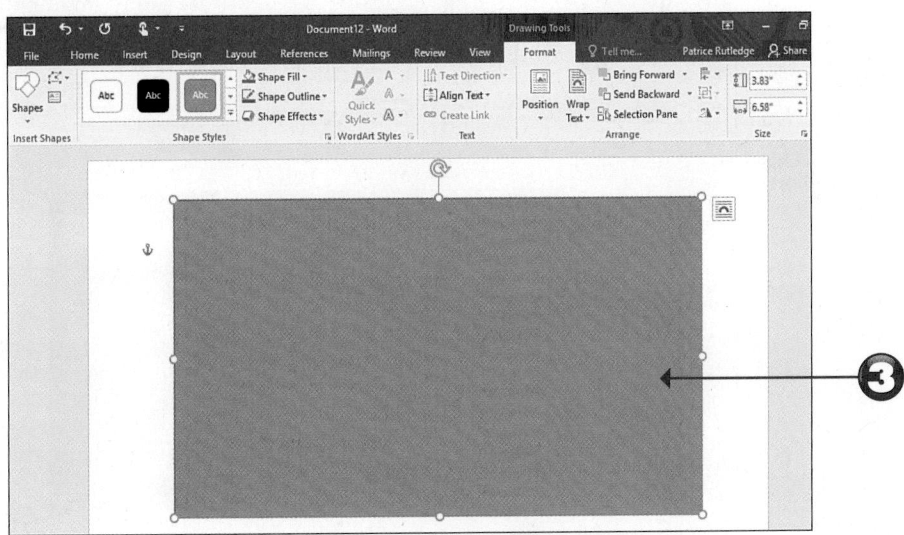


3 Click where you want the shape to appear, and then drag until the shape is the size you want.

End

**TIP**

**Squares and Circles** To create a square, insert a Rectangle shape and press the **Shift** key while you draw. To create a circle, insert an Oval shape and press the **Shift** key while you draw. ■

**NOTE**

**Draw a Straight Line** To draw a straight horizontal or vertical line, press the **Shift** key as you drag the mouse. ■

# FORMATTING A SHAPE

When you select a shape, the contextual Drawing Tools–Format tab appears. This tab offers numerous options for shape formatting and enhancement, which you explore in this section.

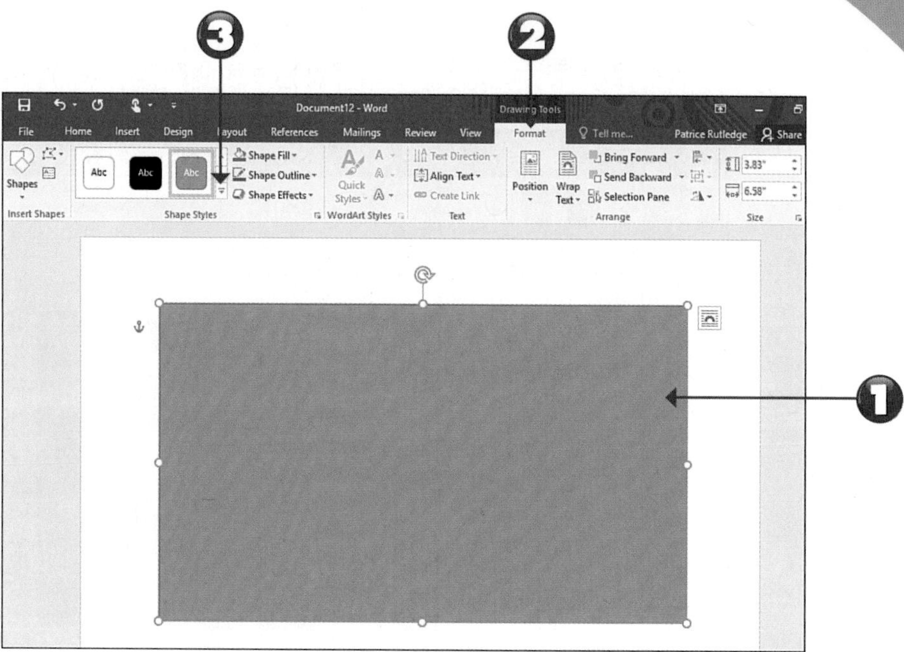


Start

1. Select the shape you want to format.
2. The Drawing Tools–Format tab displays.
3. Select a **Shape Style** to apply a gradient or shaded fill to your shape.

Continued

## NOTE

**Drawing Tools–Format Tab Differences** The Drawing Tools–Format tab in each Office application has slight differences. If your application doesn't match the figure in this book exactly, pause your mouse over the Ribbon tab buttons to find the right option. ■

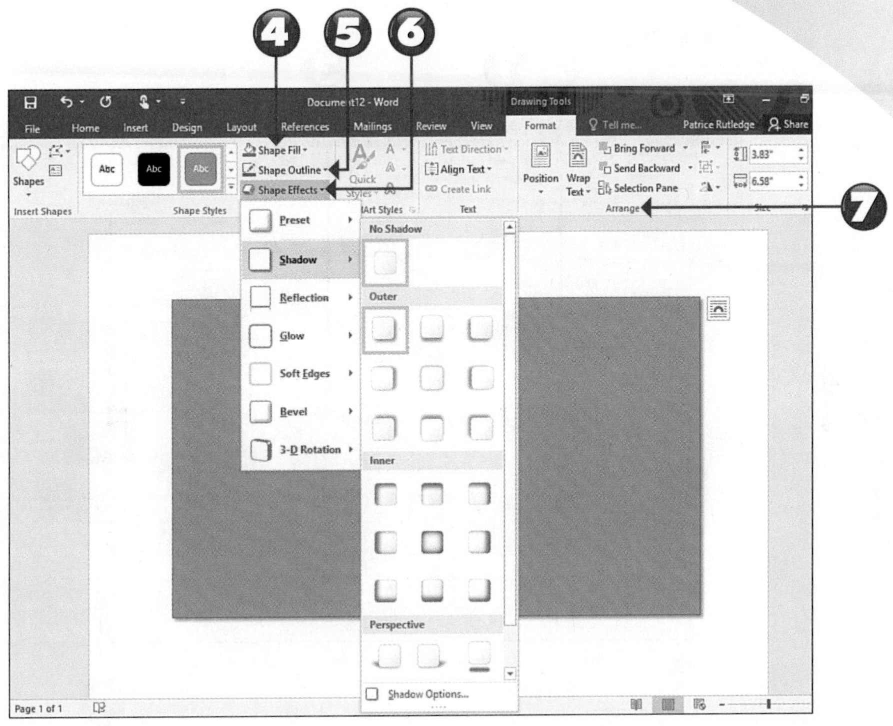

4 Click the **Shape Fill** button to change the shape's color or apply other gradient or texture effects.

5 Click the **Shape Outline** button to apply a shape border.

6 Click the **Shape Effects** button to apply a shadow, reflection, glow, or other special effect.

7 Select an option in the Arrange group to position, group, rotate, or align a shape.

End

## TIP

**Format Shape Pane** You can use the Format Shape pane to apply numerous formatting changes from one place. To open this pane, right-click a shape and choose **Format Shape** from the menu that displays.

# INSERTING A SMARTART GRAPHIC

SmartArt offers a unique opportunity to present content, such as an organization chart or a process, in a way that makes the most of Office's sophisticated design features.

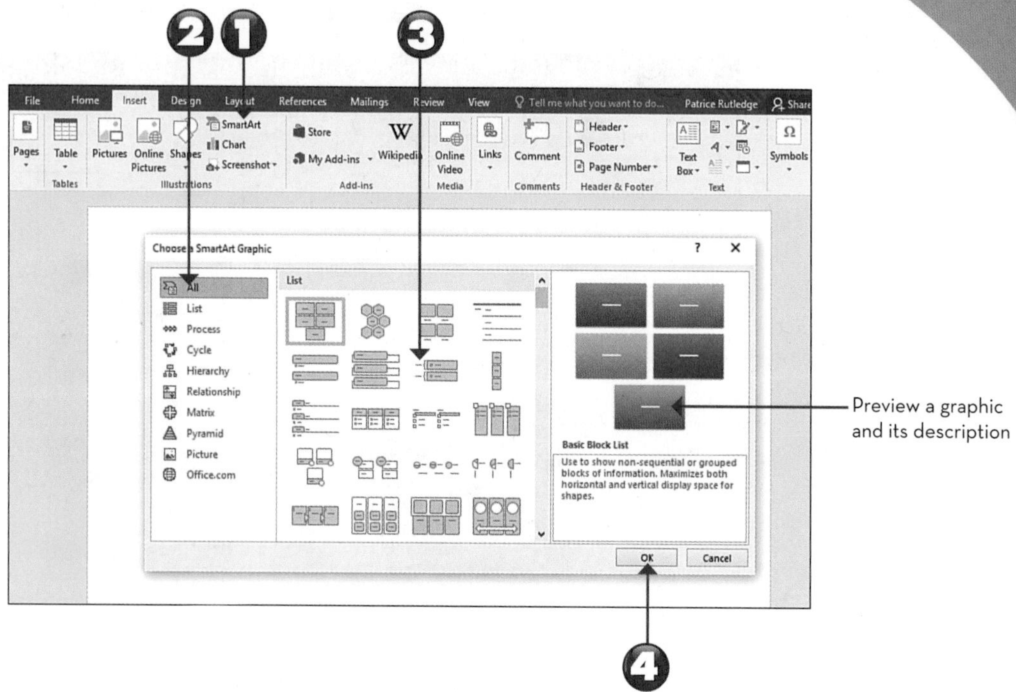


Start

1. On the Insert tab, click the **SmartArt** button.
2. In the Choose a SmartArt Graphic dialog box, select a SmartArt type.
3. Select a SmartArt graphic.
4. Click **OK** to insert the SmartArt graphic.

*Continued*

## NOTE

**SmartArt Types** You can create many types of SmartArt graphics, including the following: list, process, cycle, hierarchy, relationship, matrix, pyramid, and picture. The Choose a SmartArt Graphic dialog box includes samples and descriptions of each SmartArt type. ■

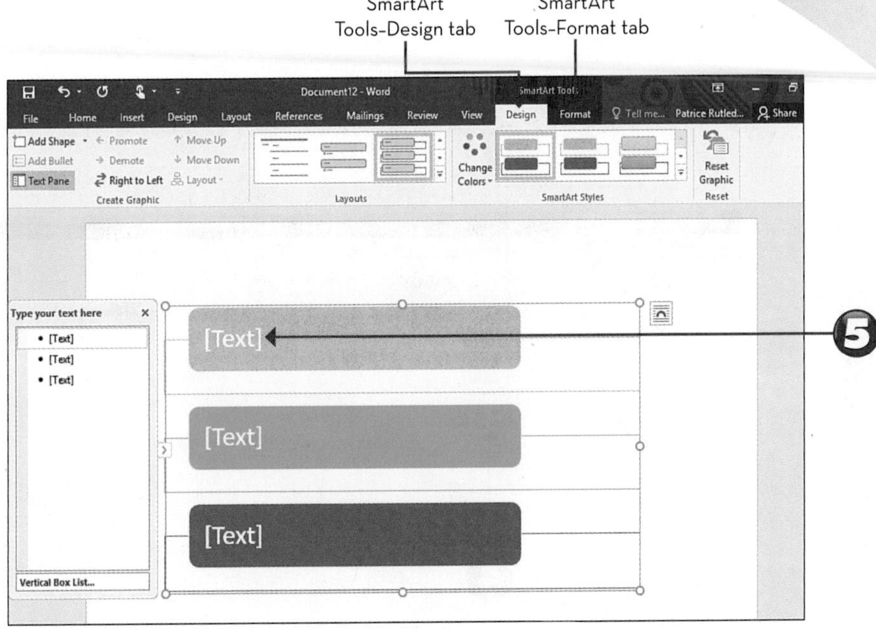


**5** Enter your text in the placeholders.

End

## TIP

**SmartArt Tools Tabs** When you select a SmartArt graphic, the SmartArt Tools-Design and SmartArt Tools-Format tabs become available. On these tabs, you can modify your SmartArt graphic, change its colors, apply a SmartArt style, and more. ■

## TIP

**PowerPoint Options** In PowerPoint, a good way to add a SmartArt graphic to your presentation is to use a slide layout that contains the content palette. You can add a new slide by clicking the **New Slide** button on the Home tab. ■

# INSERTING A SCREENSHOT

Rather than using an external application to take screenshots, Office offers its own screen-capture tool.

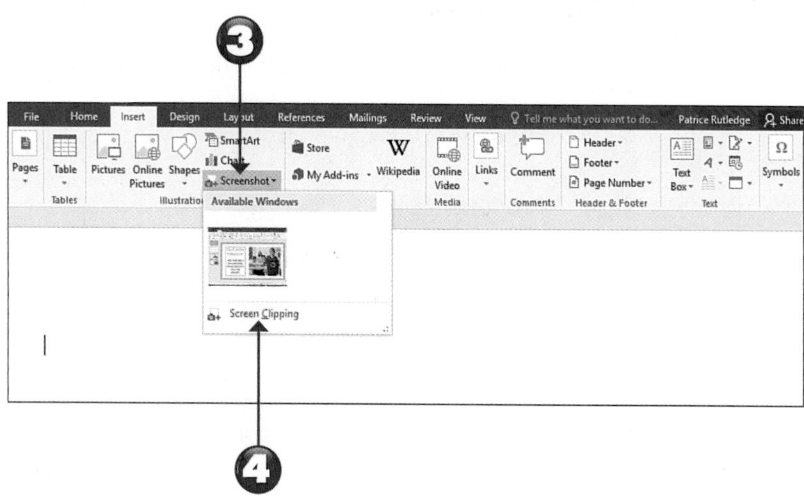


1. Open the application from which you want to take a screenshot.
2. Open the Office document where you want to place the screenshot.
3. On the Insert tab, click the **Screenshot** button.
4. Click **Screen Clipping**.

Continued

**TIP**

**Insert the Entire Window** If you want to insert a screenshot of the entire window, select that window from the list that displays. ■

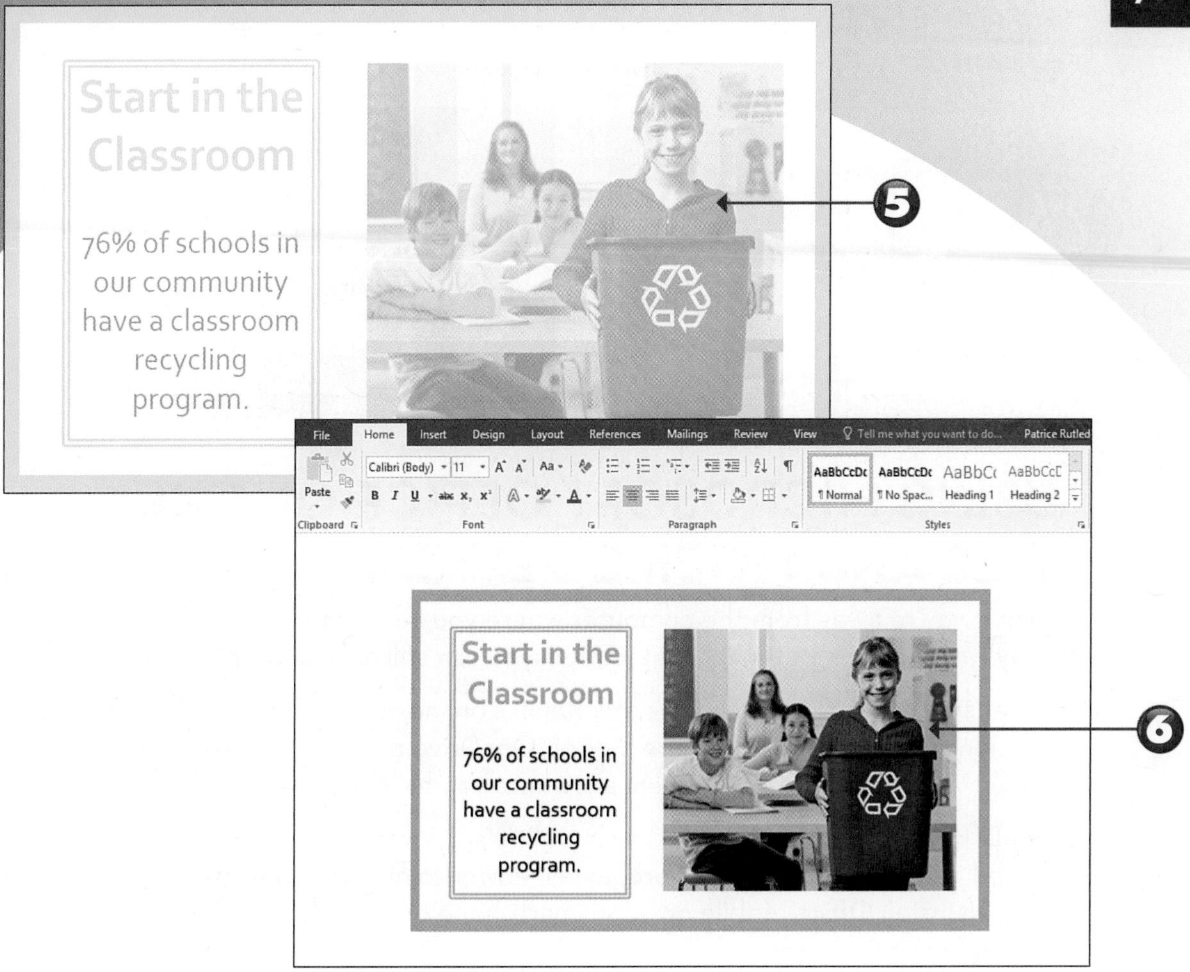

5 Select the area you want to include in your presentation using your mouse pointer (which now appears as a crosshair).

6 Release the mouse to insert the screenshot.

End

**NOTE**

**Screen Clippings** Selecting **Screen Clipping** minimizes your Office application and displays other open applications and the desktop with a white semitransparent layer. ■

# USING MICROSOFT OFFICE ON THE WEB AND MOBILE DEVICES

Even if you're away from the computer where you installed Office 2016—or away from any computer, for that matter—you can still access your Office files.

To get started, explore OneDrive, Microsoft's online storage and file-sharing solution. You can store and share files on OneDrive directly from your Office applications and then access them anywhere you have Internet access.

OneDrive also offers access to Office Online apps, which enable you to create and edit files remotely using Word, Excel, PowerPoint, and OneNote. Finally, you can install Office Mobile on your smartphone or tablet for another way to access Office on the go.

## EXPLORING ONEDRIVE

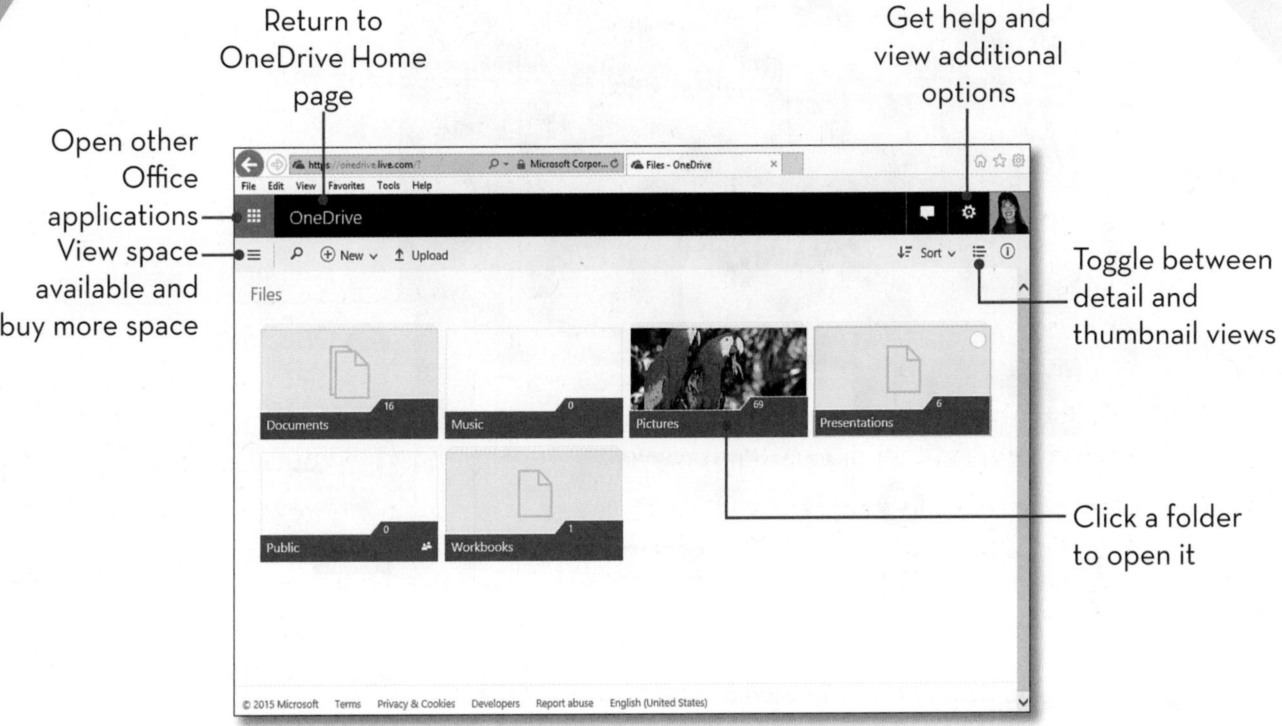

# GETTING STARTED WITH ONEDRIVE

OneDrive offers 15 gigabytes of free online storage that you can use to collaborate with colleagues anywhere in the world using a PC, Mac, or mobile device (such as a smartphone, iPad, or other tablet).

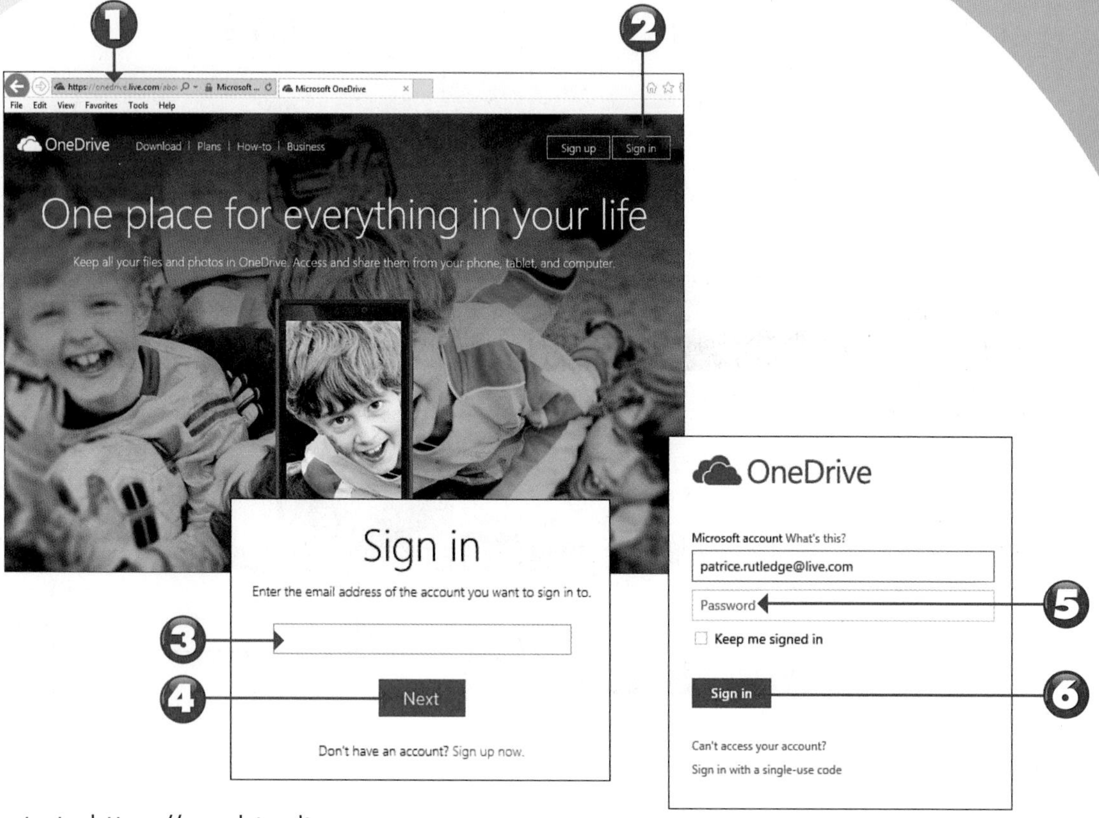


Start

1. Navigate to https://onedrive.live.com.
2. Click the **Sign In** button.
3. Enter the email address of your Microsoft account.
4. Click **Next**.
5. Enter your password.
6. Click **Sign In**.

End

**NOTE**

**OneDrive Basics** To access OneDrive you must have a free Microsoft account or an existing account with another Microsoft application, such as Windows 8, Office 365, Skype, Outlook.com, Xbox Live, or Hotmail. If you don't, you can sign up for an account by clicking the **Sign Up** button.

**NOTE**

**Additional Storage** If you want more than 15GB of storage, you can sign up for a monthly plan. Office 365 users (see https://products.office.com) receive 1TB of OneDrive storage.

# CREATING A NEW FOLDER

Just like on your computer, you store OneDrive files in folders. You can add files to OneDrive default folders or create your own.

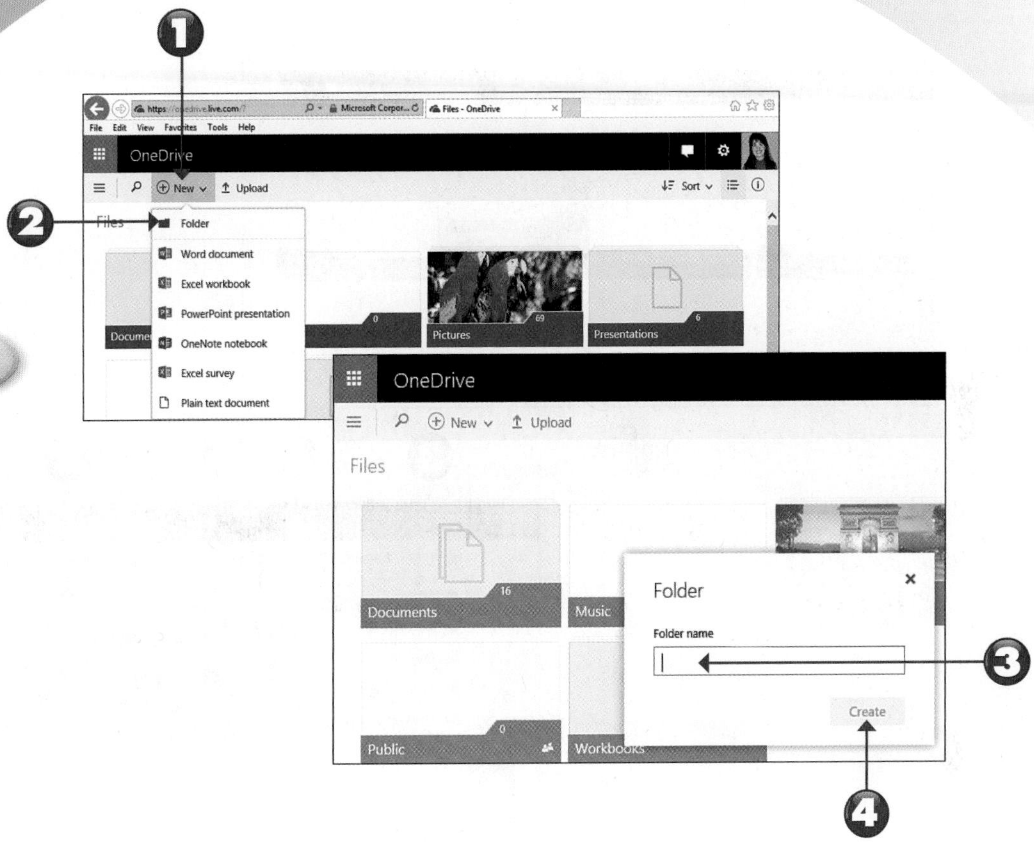

Start

1. Click **New**.
2. Click **Folder**.
3. Enter a folder name.
4. Click **Create**.

End

### TIP

**Folder Organization** Although you can organize folders by topic or by file type, you should also consider organizing them by the people you want to share with. That way, you don't risk sharing personal files with the wrong audience.

# MANAGING FOLDERS

OneDrive makes it easy to manage your folders, including the capability to share, delete, and move them.

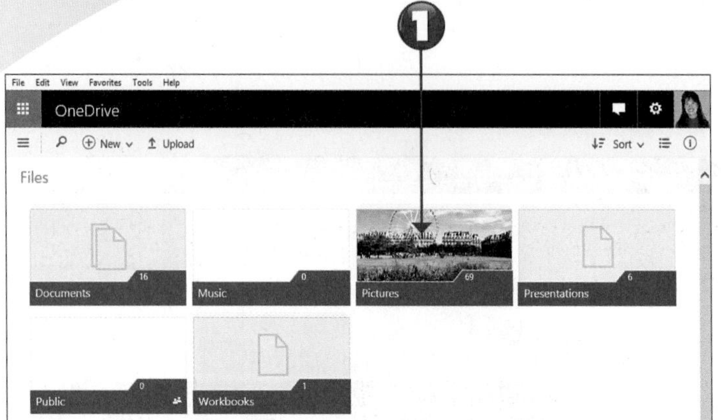


Start

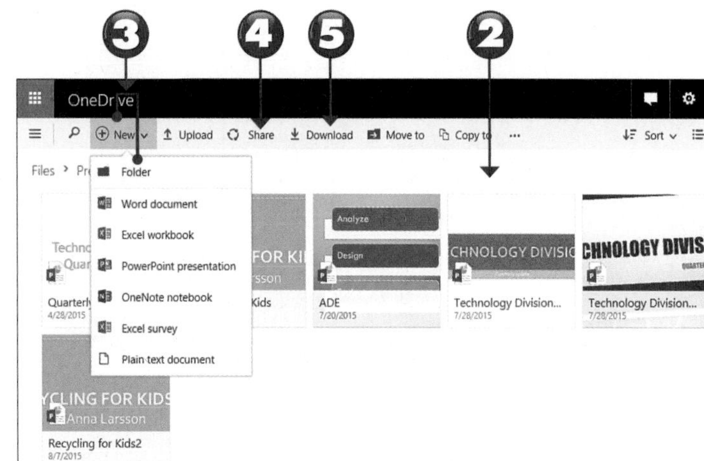


1. Click a folder to open it.
2. OneDrive displays the files it contains.
3. Click **New** and then **Folder** to create a new subfolder within this folder.
4. Click **Share** to share this folder with other users.
5. Click **Download** to download a zipped file with this folder's content to your computer.

Continued

**CAUTION**

**Folder-Sharing Considerations** Consider carefully who should have access to specific content before sharing it.

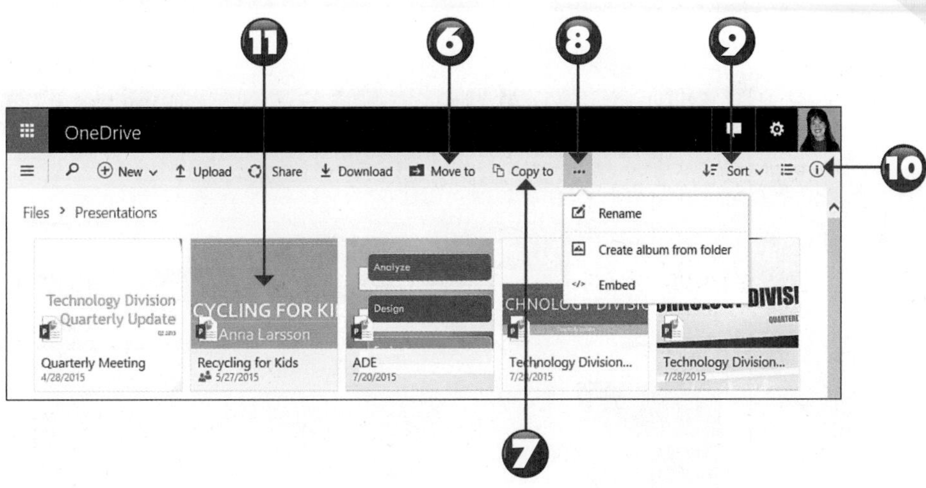


6 Click **Move to** to move this folder into another folder.

7 Click **Copy to** to copy this folder to another folder.

8 Click **...** to rename, embed, or create an album from this folder.

9 Click **Sort** to sort files in this folder by name, date, or size.

10 Click Properties to view more information about this folder.

11 Click a file in a folder to open it.

End

**TIP**

**Shortcut Menu** Another option is to right-click a folder to view a shortcut menu with many of these same options.

**NOTE**

**Folder Properties** Folder properties provide information about folder size, creation date, sharing status, and more.

# UPLOADING FILES TO ONEDRIVE

Although you can save your Office files to OneDrive directly from an Office application, you can also upload them manually.

Start

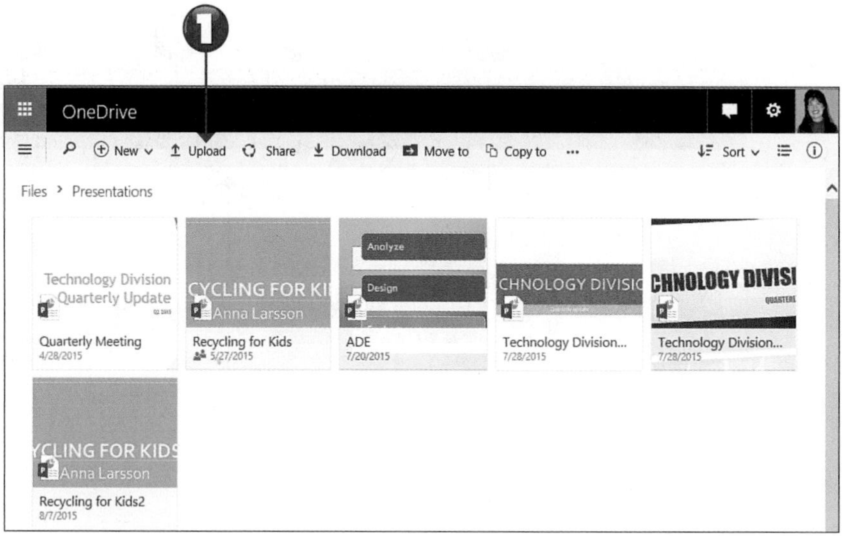


1. In the folder where you want to upload your file, click **Upload**.

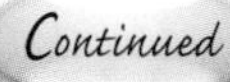

**TIP**

**Upload Many Types of Files** Uploading files to OneDrive isn't limited to files you create in Office. You can also store any other files on OneDrive, such as photos, PDFs, and so forth.

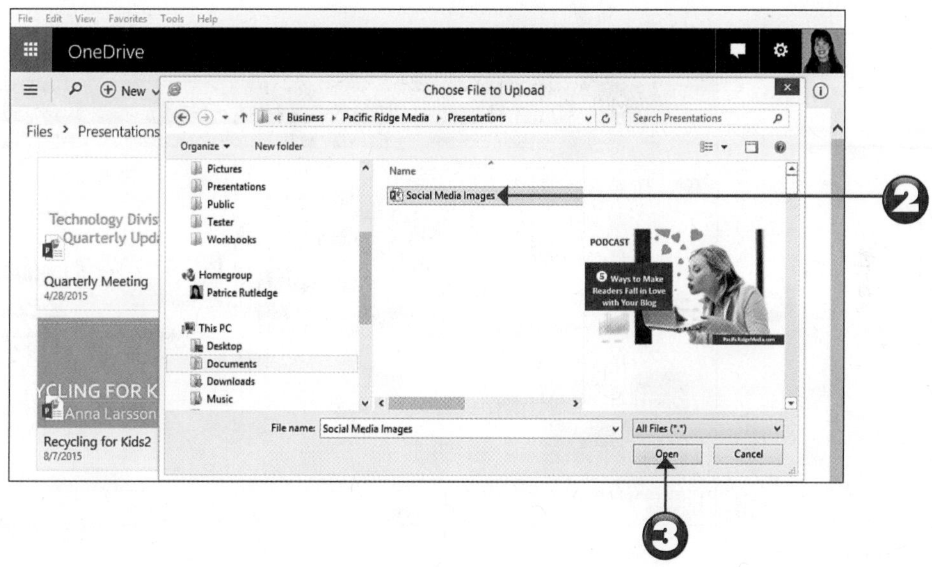


2. Select the file you want to upload.

3. Click the **Open** button to upload and return to OneDrive.

End

## TIP

**Upload Multiple Files** You can also select multiple files to upload by pressing the **Shift** key as you select files. To select noncontiguous files, press the **Ctrl** key. ■

# CREATING A NEW FILE IN ONEDRIVE

OneDrive isn't just for storing files; you can also create a new file directly in OneDrive. In this example, you create a new PowerPoint presentation.

Start

1. In the folder where you want to store your new file, click **New**. In this case, you want to create a presentation in the Presentations folder.

2. Select **PowerPoint Presentation** from the menu.

Continued

## NOTE

**Office Online** When you create an Office file from OneDrive, the associated online version of that application opens: Word Online, Excel Online, PowerPoint Online, or OneNote Online. These online applications are part of Office Online and were formerly called Office Web Apps. They contain most, but not all, of the features of their associated desktop applications.

## TIP

**Other Options** You can also create Excel surveys or plain text documents from this menu. When you create an Excel survey, people can open and respond to it by clicking the provided link, and you can view results in one place online.

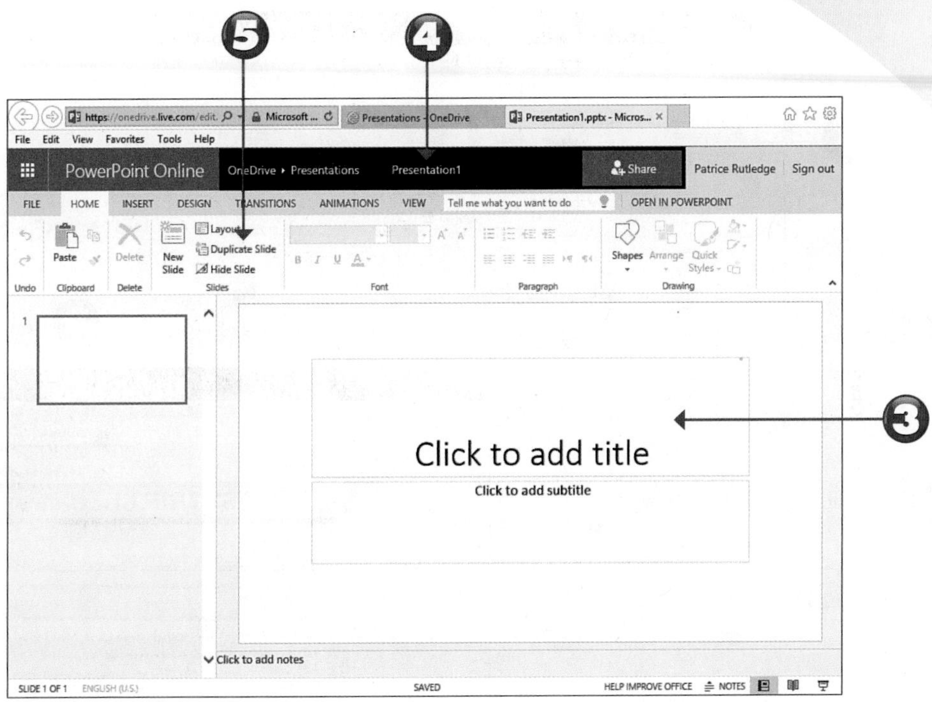


3. PowerPoint Online opens in Edit mode.
4. Enter a presentation name.
5. Create and design your presentation as you would in the desktop version of PowerPoint.

End

## NOTE

**Where's the Save Button?** PowerPoint Online doesn't have a Save button because it saves your changes automatically.

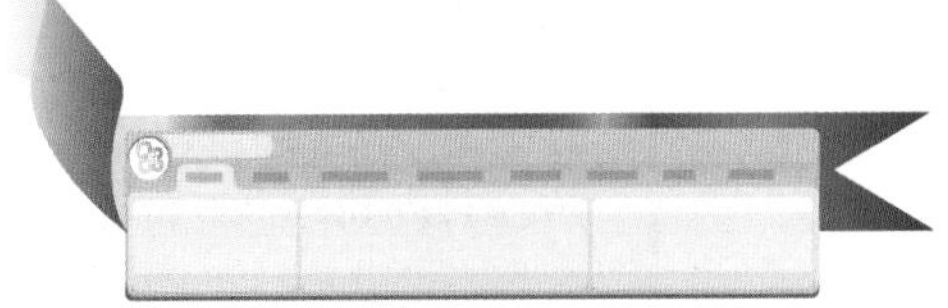

# EDITING A FILE IN ONEDRIVE

You can edit Word, Excel, PowerPoint, and OneNote files that you create or store in OneDrive using their associated online application. In this example, you edit a Word document in Word Online.

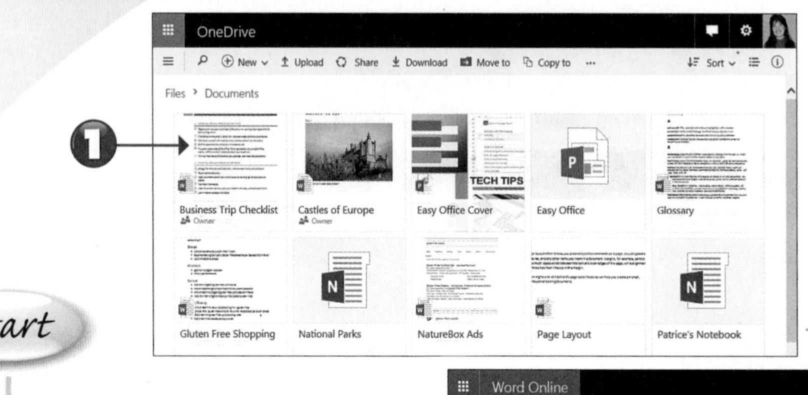


Start

1. Click the Word document you want to edit.
2. Click **Edit Document**.
3. Select **Edit in Word Online** from the menu.

Continued

## TIP

**Open in the Desktop App** You can also open this file directly in Word. For example, select **Edit in Word** from the menu to open in the desktop version of Word on your computer.

## TIP

**Print a Document** Editing isn't the only option on this screen. You can also click **Print** to print the document.

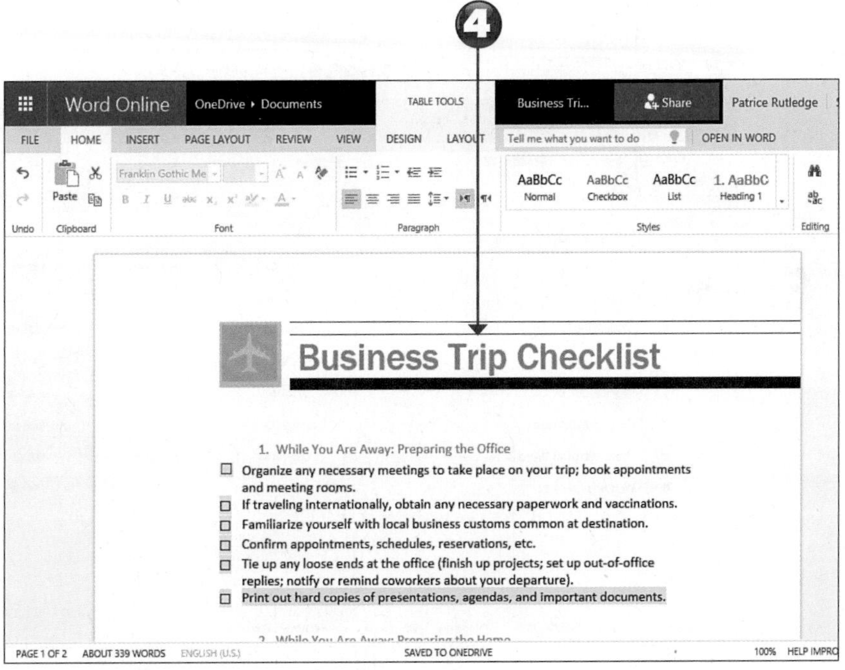


**4** Edit your document as you would in the desktop version of Word.

*End*

## NOTE

**Word Online Editing** The commands and buttons on these tabs function in much the same way as they do in the desktop version of Word. The main difference is that you can perform the commands online on a computer that doesn't have Word installed.

## TIP

**Share a File** If you want to share a file with others, click the **Share** button to send an email to people inviting them to view or edit on OneDrive. Optionally, you can also post a link to your document. Before sharing, however, remember to think carefully about who should have access to this file.

# MANAGING FILES IN ONEDRIVE

OneDrive offers numerous file-management options in addition to editing. You can also download, share, embed, rename, delete, and copy files.

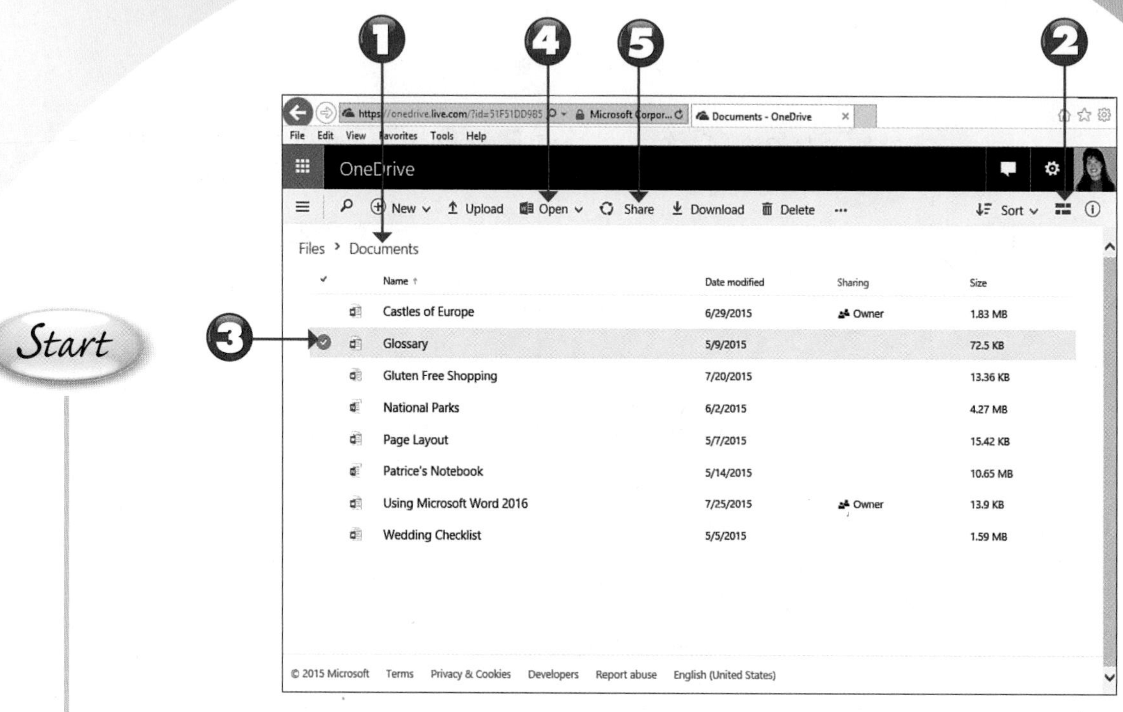

Start

1. Open the folder whose files you want to manage.
2. Click the **View** button to toggle to Detail view if it doesn't already display.
3. Select the check box next to the file you want to manage.
4. Click **Open** to open the file.
5. Click **Share** to share the file with others via email or a link.

Continued

## TIP

**Select Multiple Files** You can select multiple files if you want to perform the same action on them. For example, you might want to download multiple files at the same time. If you want to select all files in a folder, click the check box to the left of the Name field.

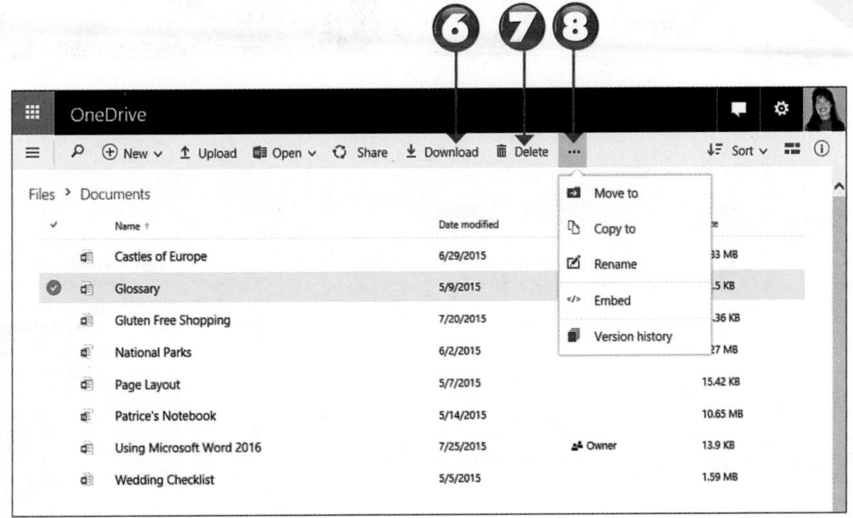


6. Click **Download** to download the file to your computer.

7. Click **Delete** to delete the selected file.

8. Click **...** to view a list of additional options: Move To, Copy To, Rename, Embed, or Version History.

*End*

### TIP

**Shortcut Menu** You can also right-click a file to view a shortcut menu with many of these same options.

### NOTE

**Version History** Version history enables you to view previous versions of a file. For example, if you're editing a presentation and then realize you deleted something by mistake, you can view and restore a previous version.

# DOWNLOADING ONEDRIVE

OneDrive isn't available only on the Web. You can also download a OneDrive app for Windows, Android, Mac OS X, iOS, Windows Phone, and Xbox for easy access on your computer, smartphone, or tablet.

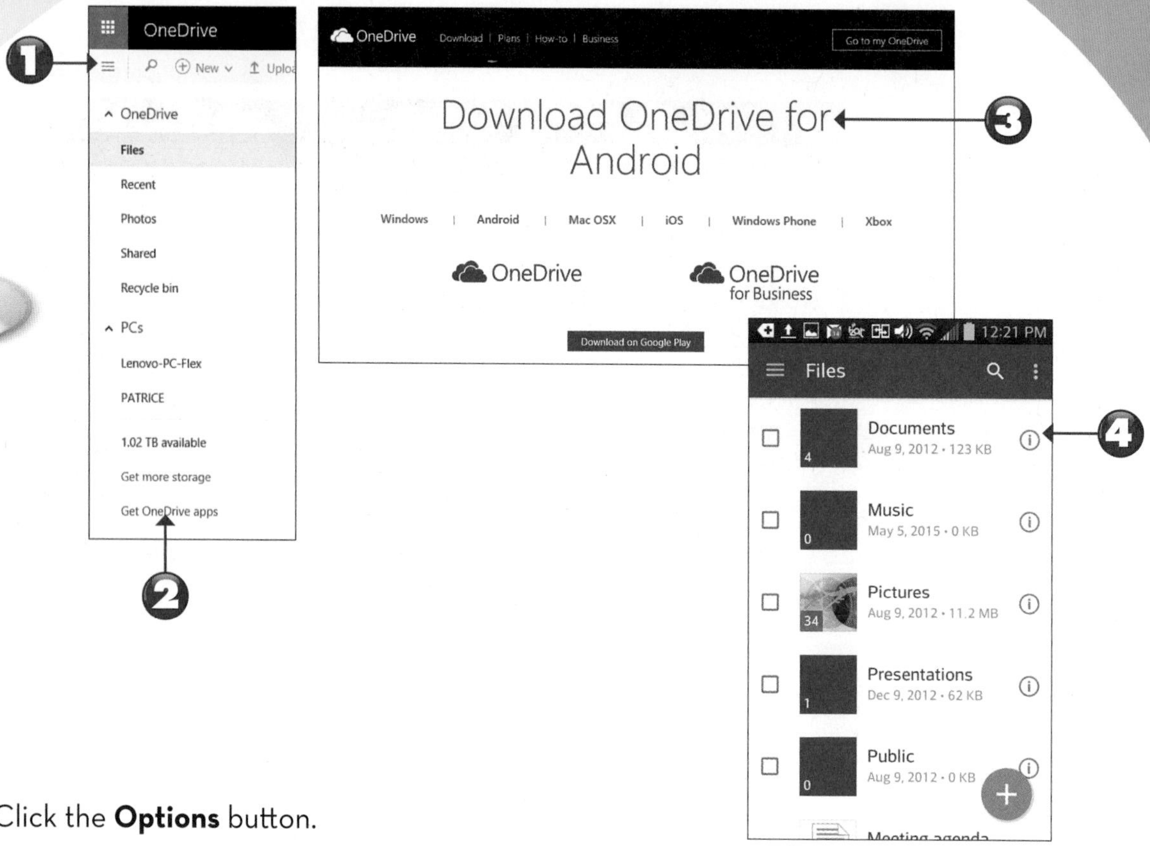

Start

1. Click the **Options** button.

2. Click **Get OneDrive apps**.

3. Select the OneDrive app you want to install, and follow the onscreen directions.

4. View OneDrive on your selected device. In this example, you view OneDrive on an Android smartphone.

End

## TIP

**Download from Your Mobile Device** You can also download the OneDrive app directly from your mobile device using the Google Play Store, the iTunes Store, or the Windows Phone Store.

## NOTE

**Windows 8.1 or Later** If you use Windows 8.1 or later, you don't need to download OneDrive to your computer; it comes preinstalled. You can access your OneDrive files in File Explorer just like any other files on your computer.

# GETTING STARTED WITH OFFICE ONLINE

OneDrive isn't the only way to access Office Online applications or your Office files online. You can also access them from the Office Online website.

Start

1. Navigate to https://office.live.com.
2. Click an application to open its online version: **Word Online**, **Excel Online**, **PowerPoint Online**, or **OneNote Online**.
3. Click **OneDrive** to open your OneDrive account.
4. Click **Outlook.com** to access this online email service.

End

## NOTE

**What's Outlook.com?** Outlook.com is Microsoft's free web-based email service (formerly known as Hotmail). By clicking **Outlook.com**, you can access email accounts using the outlook.com, hotmail.com, or live.com domain. You can also access people (contacts) and your calendar associated with this account. The desktop version of Outlook 2016 is covered in Part V of this book.

## TIP

**Universal Office Apps for Windows 10** If you use Windows 10, also consider the Universal Office apps for Windows 10, which are optimized for touch and mobile. You can download apps for Word, Excel, PowerPoint, Outlook, and OneNote from the Windows Store (http://windows.microsoft.com).

# INSTALLING OFFICE ON A MOBILE DEVICE

Microsoft offers free mobile versions of Word, Excel, PowerPoint, and Outlook for a variety of mobile devices including iPhone, iPad, Android phone, Android tablet, Windows phone, and Windows tablet. In this example, you install Office Mobile on an Android phone.

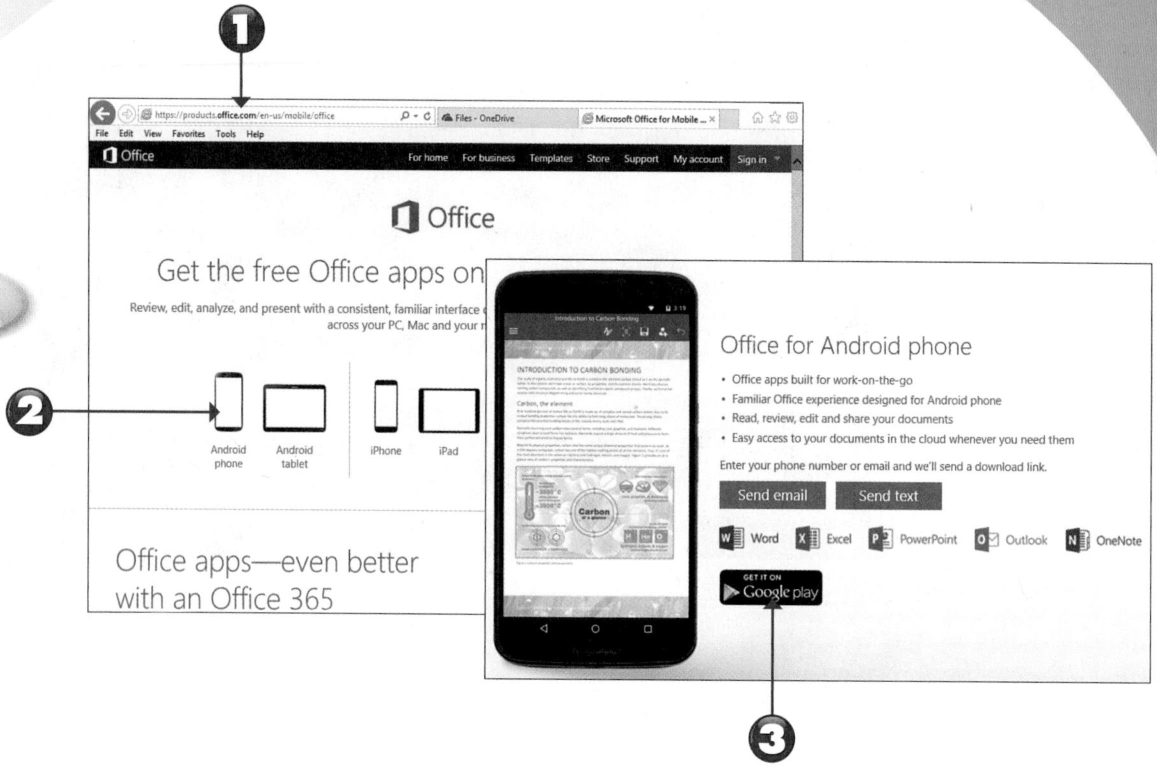

Start

1. Navigate to http://products.office.com/en-us/mobile/office.

2. Click **Android phone**.

3. Click **Get It on Google Play**.

Continued

## TIP

**Receive a Download Link** If you don't want to install via Google Play, you can click **Send email** to receive an email with a download link or **Send text** to receive a text message with a download link.

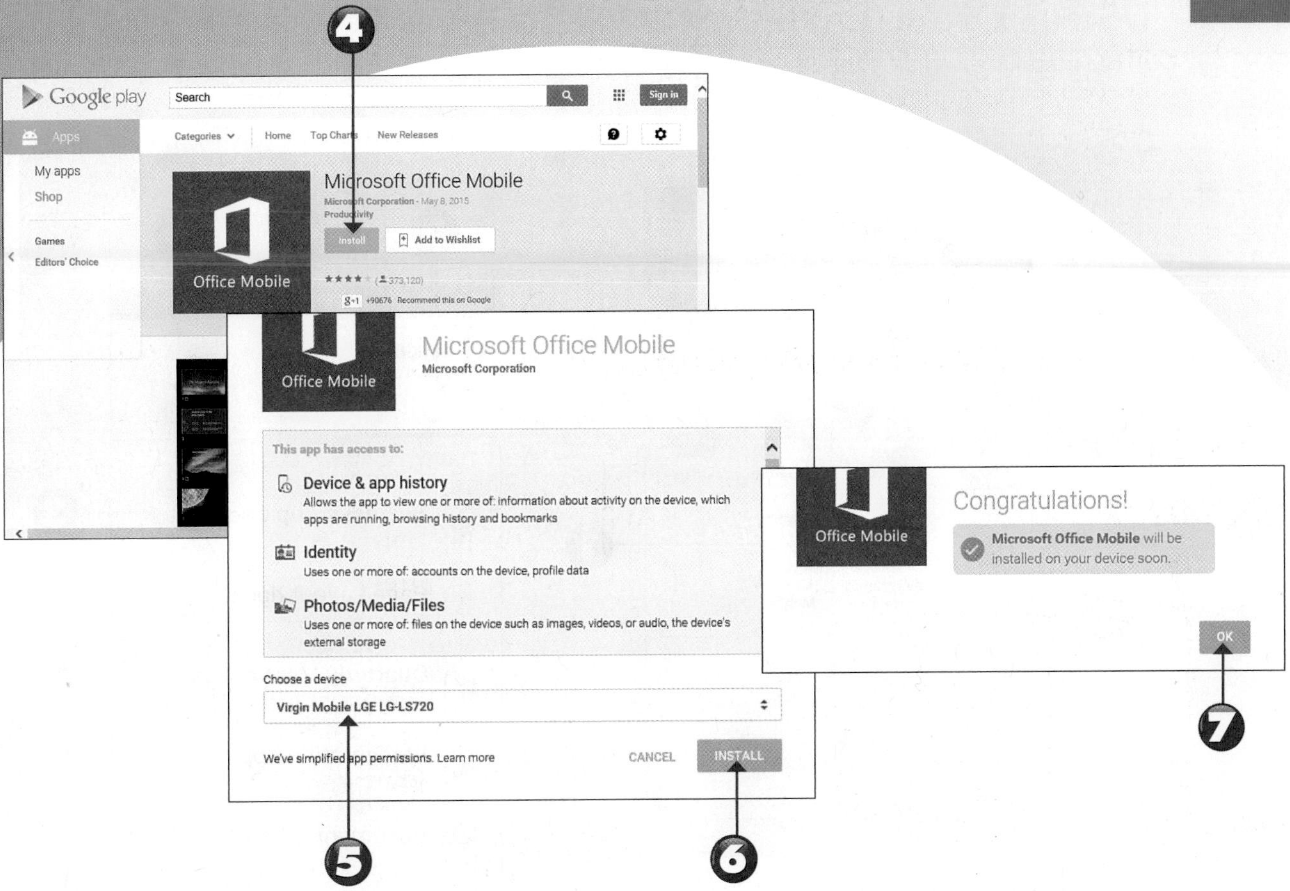

4. Click **Install**.
5. Select your mobile device.
6. Click **Install**.
7. Click **OK**.

End

**TIP**

**Download from Your Mobile Device** You can also download the Office Mobile app directly from your mobile device using the Google Play Store, the iTunes Store, or the Windows Phone Store.

# USING OFFICE ON A MOBILE DEVICE

After installing Office Mobile, you can access, edit, and create selected Office files on the go.

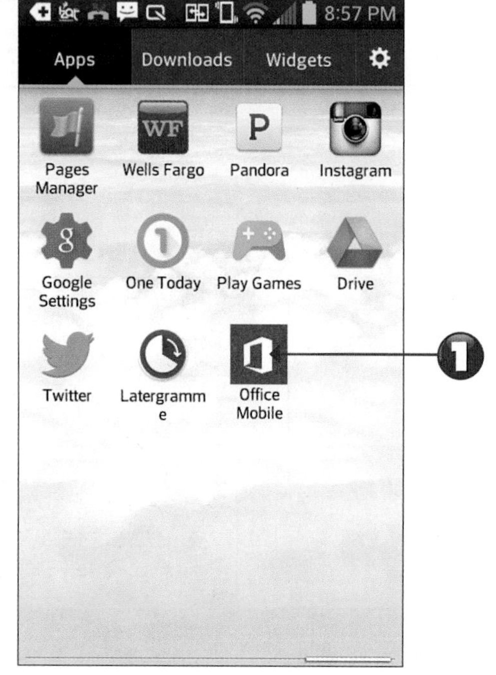


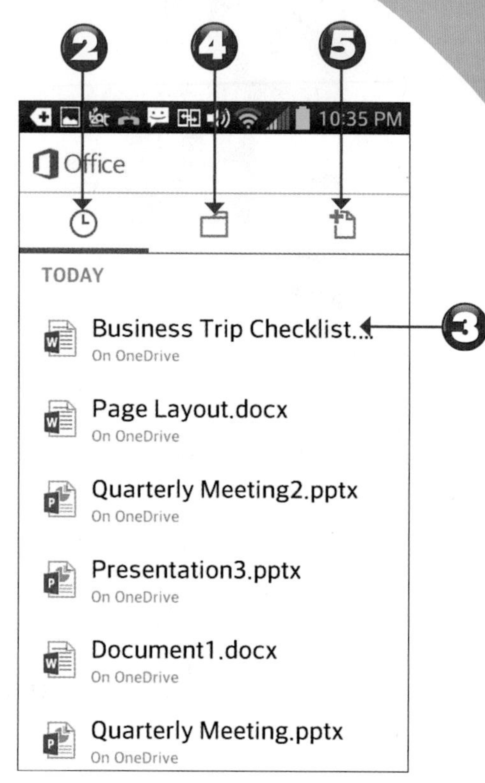


Start

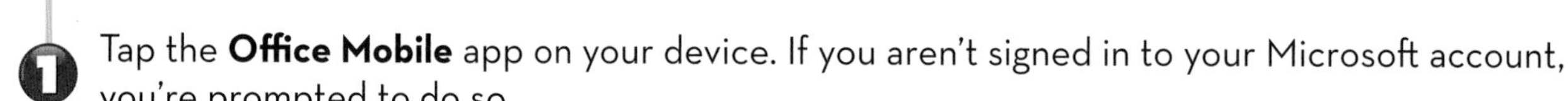

1. Tap the **Office Mobile** app on your device. If you aren't signed in to your Microsoft account, you're prompted to do so.
2. View your most recent Office files.
3. Tap a file to open it.
4. Tap to view your OneDrive folders.
5. Tap to create a new Office file. In this example, you create a Word file.

Continued

**NOTE**

**Where Are My Files?** You can view files stored on OneDrive using Office Mobile, not files stored on your physical computer.

**NOTE**

**Office Mobile Limitations** Because Office Mobile is designed to create files on the go, it doesn't offer the full features of the desktop version of Office 2016. Create a basic document on your mobile device, and then add more when you have access to Word Online or Word 2016.

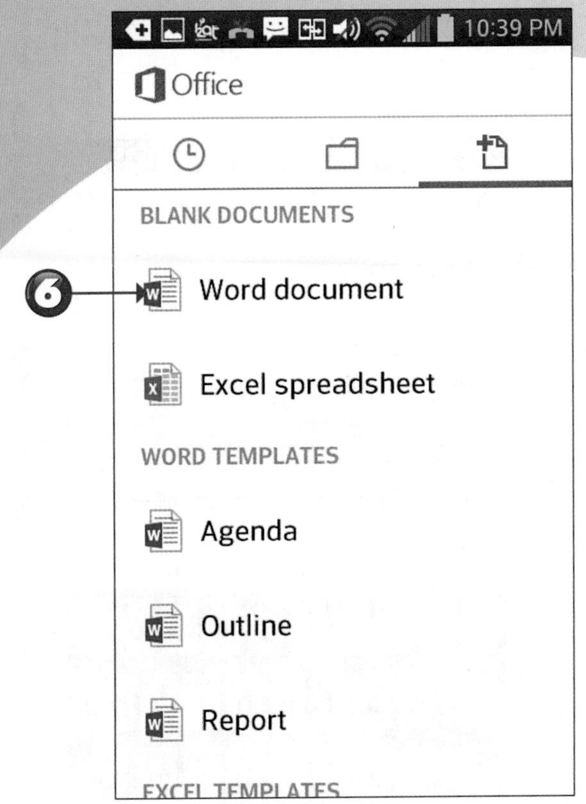

6 Tap **Word document**.

7 Type text on your document.

8 Tap when you finish your document.

Continued

## TIP

**Create an Excel Spreadsheet** You can also create a simple spreadsheet by tapping **Excel spreadsheet**. Office Mobile enables you to enter basic spreadsheet data and perform simple calculations.

## TIP

**Use a Template** Office Mobile helps the file-creation process with templates for Word and Excel, such as agenda, reports, budgets, and mileage trackers.

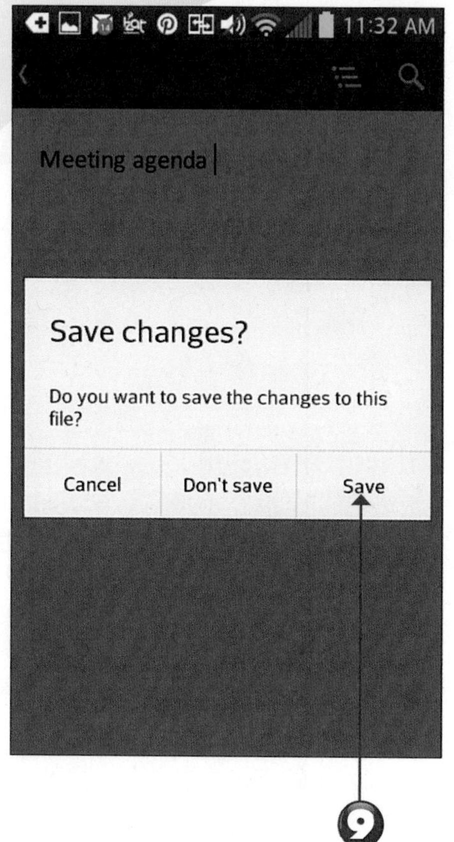


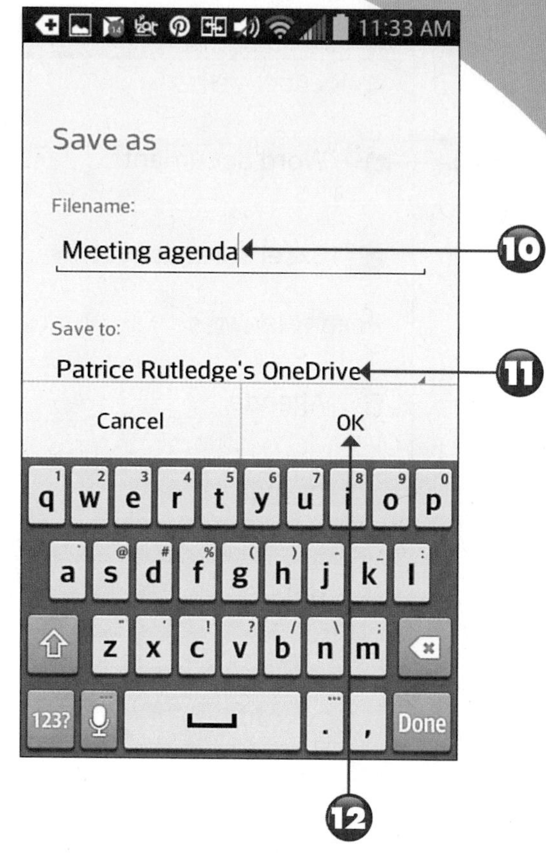


9 Tap **Save**.

10 Type a filename.

11 Specify where you want to save your file, such as OneDrive.

12 Tap **OK**.

*Continued*

**NOTE**

**Where Can I Save?** Office Mobile doesn't give you a choice of folders when saving to OneDrive. You can optionally move the files you create on your phone to another location at a later time.

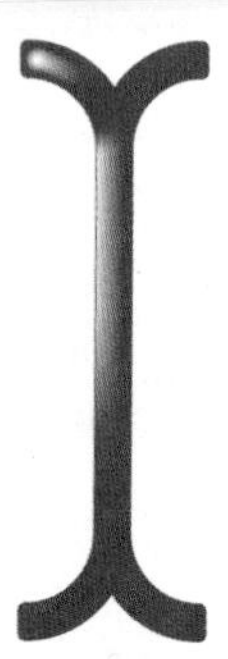

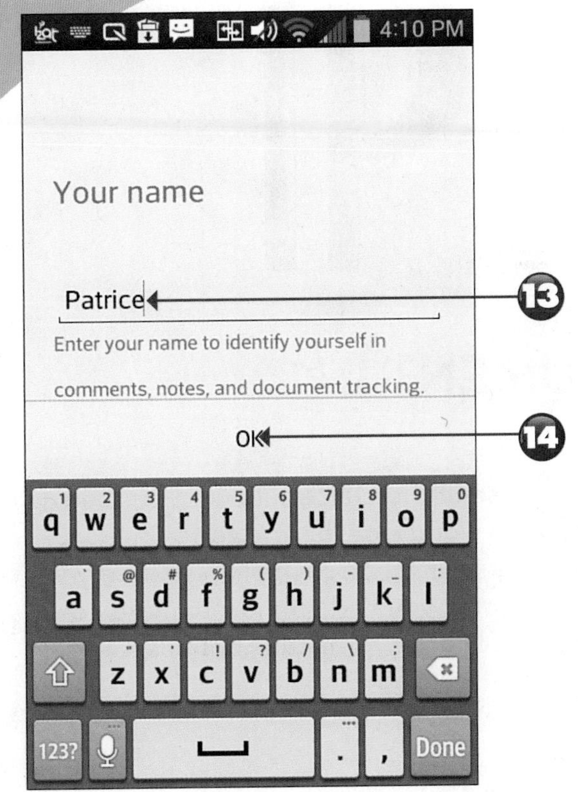


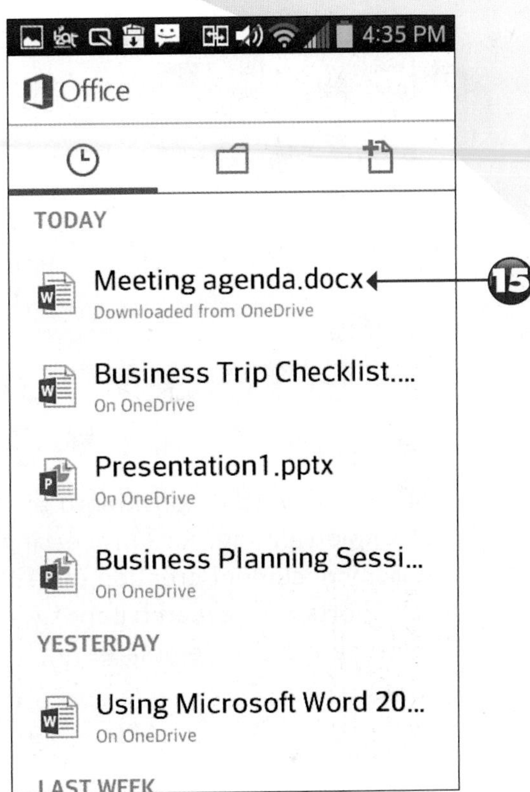


13 Enter your name to identify yourself in comments and notes.

14 Tap **OK**.

15 View your newly saved file on the Office Mobile home page.

End

## NOTE

**Next Steps** After saving your document, you can edit and view it again using Office Mobile or the location where you stored it, such as OneDrive.

# CREATING A DOCUMENT IN MICROSOFT WORD

Microsoft Word is considered the workhorse of the Office suite and the leading champion among word processing software worldwide. It's the go-to program for any document-creation tasks that come your way, from memos and letters to reports and research papers. In this chapter, you find out how to make new documents using templates and how to apply basic formatting options.

## NAVIGATING THE WORD PROGRAM SCREEN

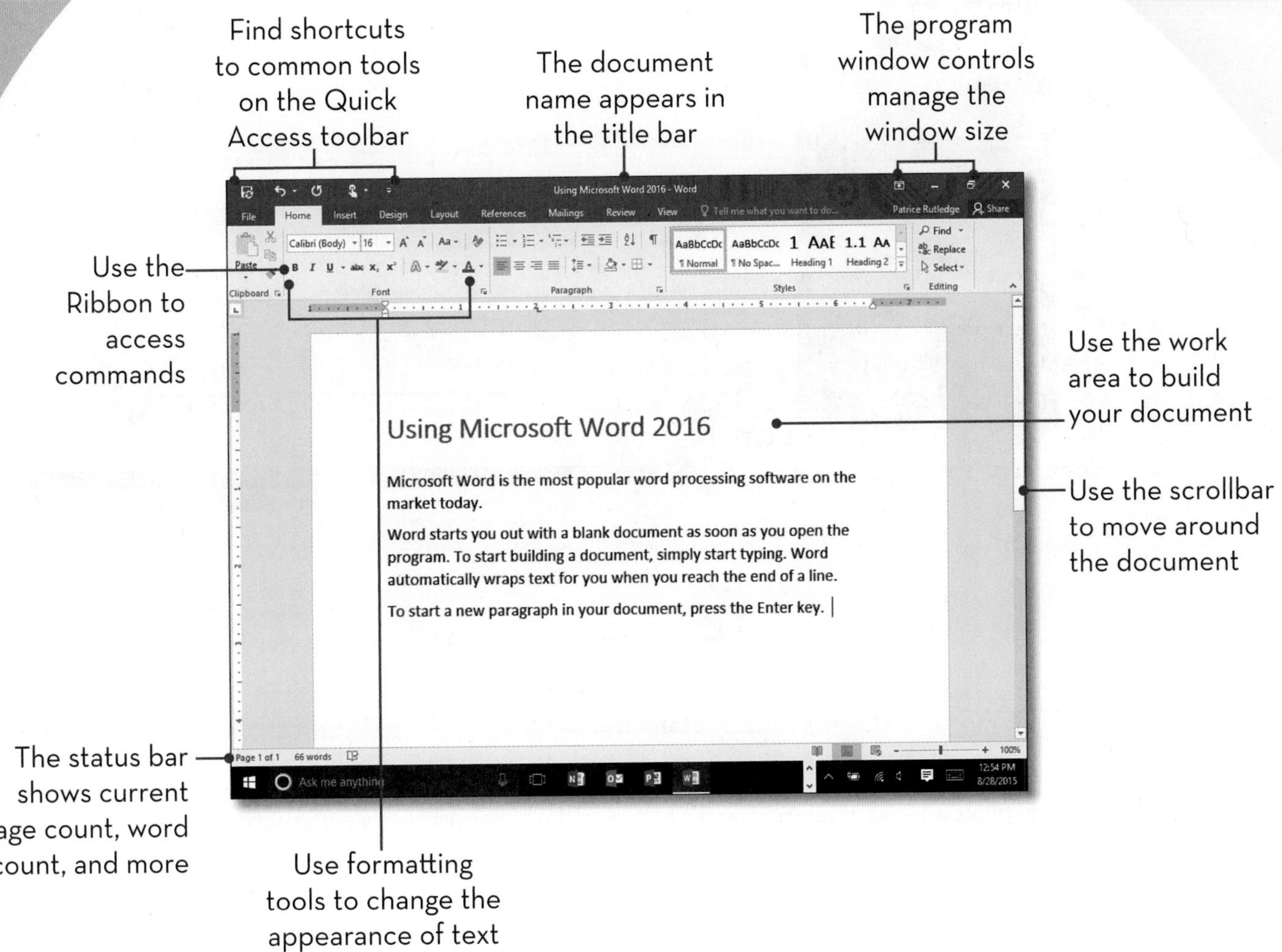

# STARTING A BLANK DOCUMENT

When you first open Microsoft Word, it lists several templates you can use to create a new document. The blank document, which is the default choice, is just as the name implies—an empty document waiting for you to add your own text and formatting.

Start

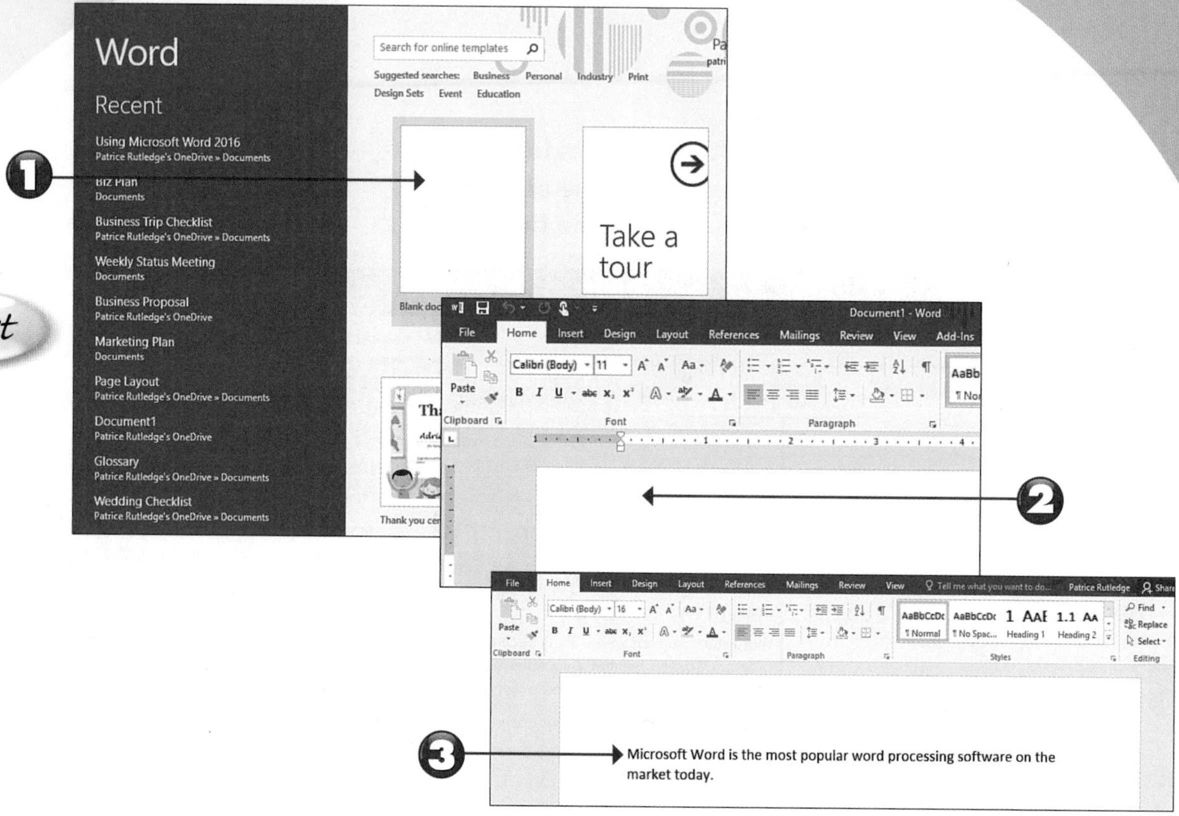

1. From the Word start screen, click **Blank document**.
2. Word displays a blank document with a cursor flashing and ready for you to start typing in text.
3. Type in your text, and Word automatically wraps the text for you when you reach the end of a line.

Continued

## NOTE

**Word 2016 Default File Format** The default file format for a Word 2016 document is .docx, such as quarterlyreport.docx. This has been the default format since Word 2007. Optionally, you can save your document using the .doc format that was the default with previous versions (Word 2003 and earlier).

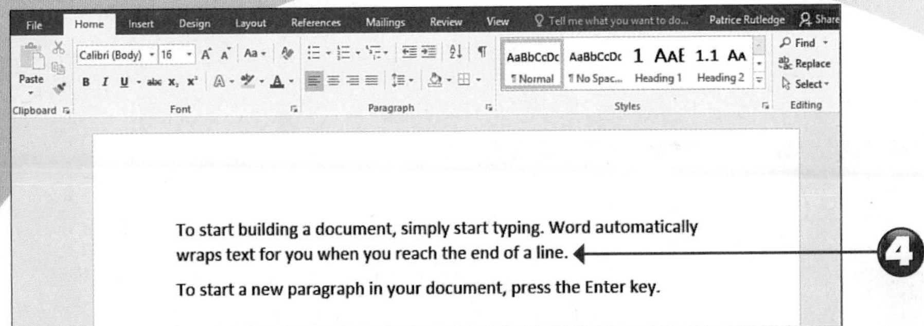


To start building a document, simply start typing. Word automatically wraps text for you when you reach the end of a line.

To start a new paragraph in your document, press the Enter ke

5

To start building a document, simply start typing. Word automatically wraps text for you when you reach the end of a line.

To start a new paragraph in your document, press the Enter key.

6

4. Press **Enter** when you want to start a new paragraph.
5. To remove a character while typing, press the **Backspace** key.
6. To edit a word in the middle of a sentence, click where you want to edit, and press **Backspace** to remove characters to the left of the cursor, or press **Delete** to remove characters to the right.

*End*

## TIP

**Save It!** To save your work, click the **Save** button on the Quick Access toolbar. You can also click the **File** tab and choose **Save**. Word prompts you to choose a location for the document, such as storing it online, on your computer, or at another location.

# STARTING A NEW DOCUMENT

You can start a new document file anytime you need one, even when other files are open. You can choose to base the new document on the default blank document or on a specific template.

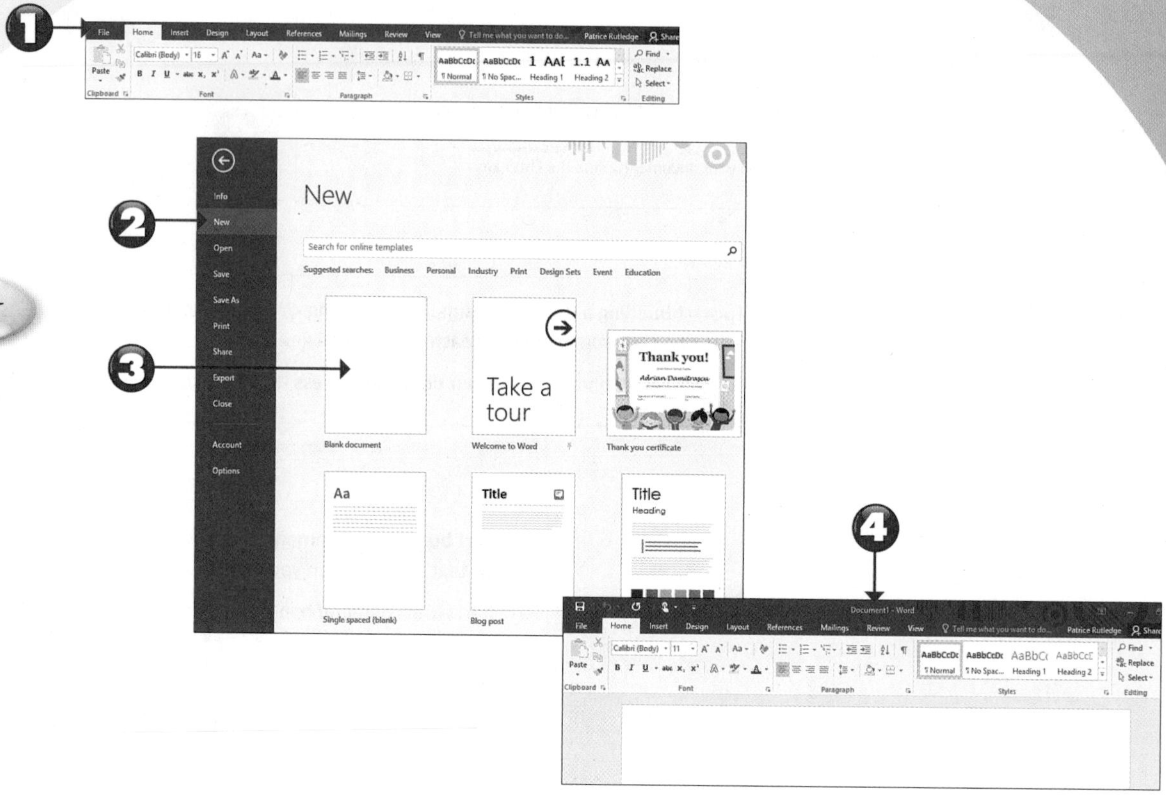

Start

1. Click **File**.

2. Click **New**.

3. Click **Blank document**, or choose from among the available templates.

4. Word opens the document onscreen with a default name in the title bar.

End

**TIP**

**Open It!** To open a document stored on your computer, click the **File** tab and click **Open**. Choose where the file is located, such as on your computer; then choose a folder. (If you used the file recently, it appears listed among the Recent Documents category for quick access.) The Open dialog box appears, and you can navigate to the file and click **Open**.

# SELECTING TEXT

As you build your document, you can select text to perform various tasks, such as applying formatting, moving and copying text, or deleting text. You can select a single character, word, sentence, paragraph, or the entire document. You can use a mouse-clicking method to select text, or you can click and drag across the words you want to select.

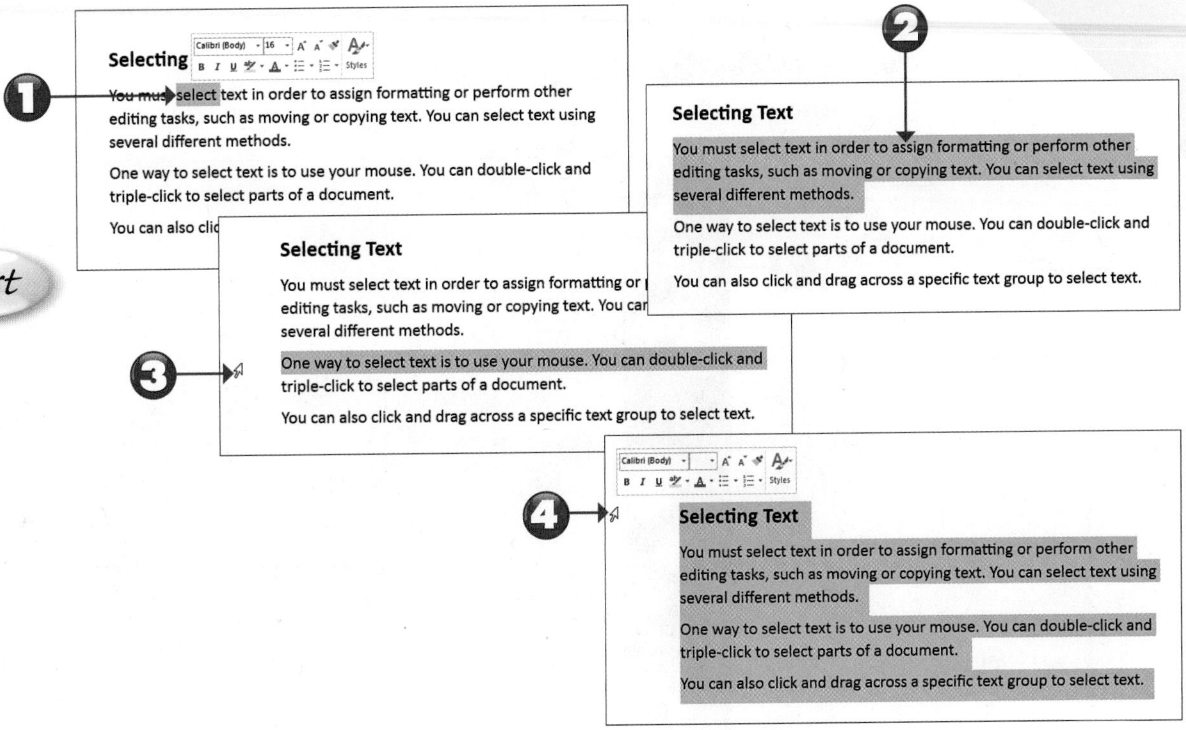

Start

1. Double-click a word to select it. Word displays the mini toolbar with optional commands you can activate, if needed.
2. Triple-click to select a paragraph.
3. Click in the left margin to select the adjacent line of text.
4. Triple-click in the upper-left corner of the document area (not in the header area) to select the entire document.

End

## NOTE

**Click and Drag** You can also click and drag across the text you want to select. Click in front of the first character, and then hold the mouse button down while dragging across the rest of the text you want to include in the selection.

## NOTE

**Mini Toolbars** Word displays a mini toolbar next to selected text to offer you quick access to commonly used features. You can click to make a selection from the toolbar, or just ignore it and keep working—it eventually disappears.

# CREATING A DOCUMENT FROM A TEMPLATE

Templates are the underlying structure for a document, a fill-in-the blanks skeleton to help you build files. You can find ready-made templates in Word to help you create letters, memos, labels, and more. Templates offer preset formatting and styles—all you need to do is add your own text. Even the blank document, for example, is a template, but an empty one.

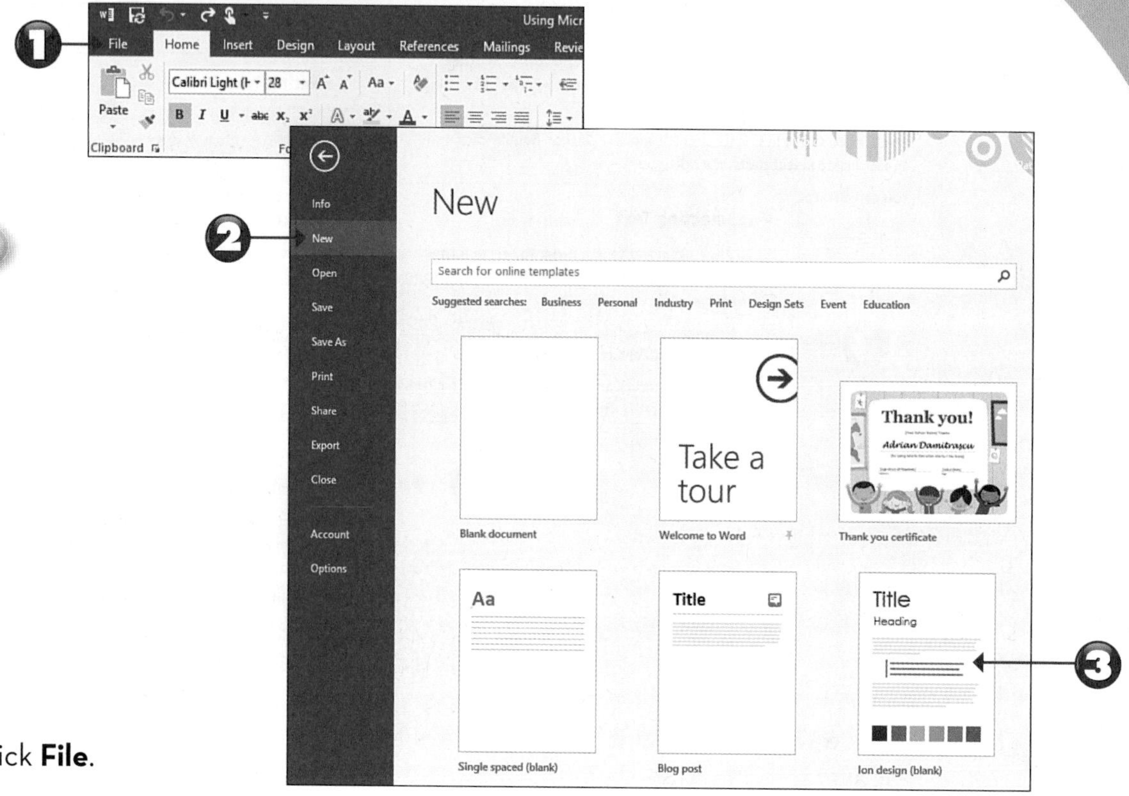

Start

1. Click **File**.
2. Click **New**.
3. Click a template.

Continued

## NOTE

**Search Online!** To use Microsoft's vast library of ready-made templates, first verify whether you're connected to the Internet. From the New screen, type a template category into the Search box, and press **Enter** or click **Search**. Word displays any matching results for you to choose from.

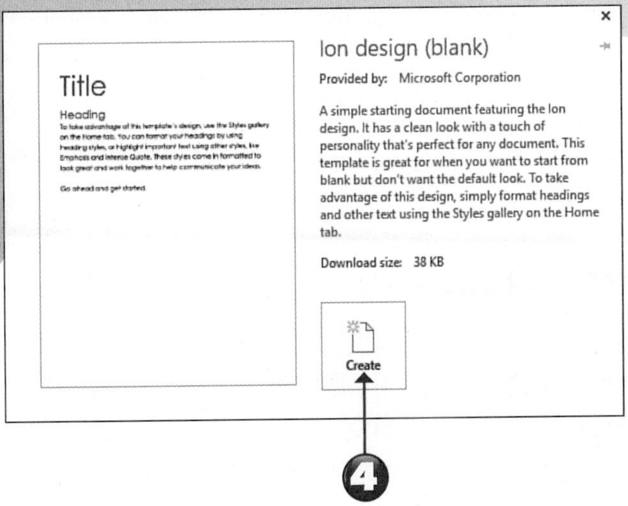

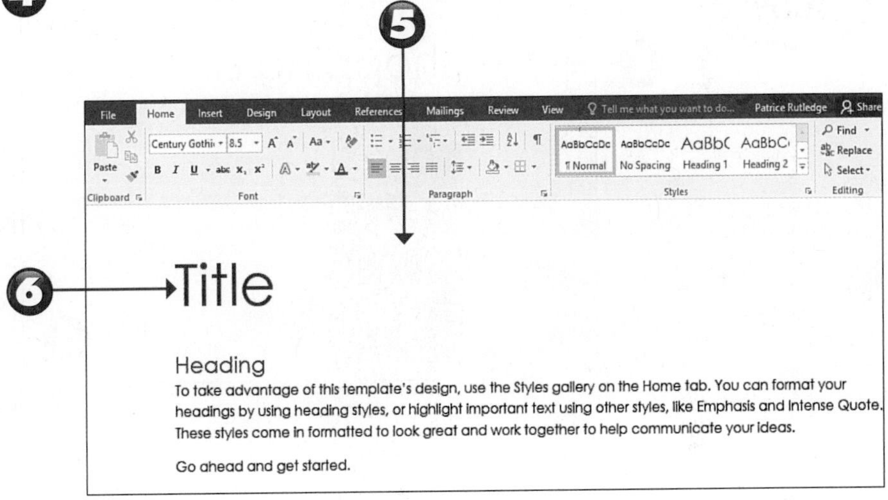

Ion design (blank)

Provided by: Microsoft Corporation

A simple starting document featuring the Ion design. It has a clean look with a touch of personality that's perfect for any document. This template is great for when you want to start from blank but don't want the default look. To take advantage of this design, simply format headings and other text using the Styles gallery on the Home tab.

Download size: 38 KB

Create

Title

Heading

To take advantage of this template's design, use the Styles gallery on the Home tab. You can format your headings by using heading styles, or highlight important text using other styles, like Emphasis and Intense Quote. These styles come in formatted to look great and work together to help communicate your ideas.

Go ahead and get started.

4 Click **Create**.

5 Word opens the template.

6 Click the placeholder text you want to replace, and type in your own text.

End

**TIP**

**Make Your Own Template** You can turn any document into a template to reuse. Click the **File** tab and click **Save As**. Choose a location for the file; then in the Save As dialog box, choose **Word Template** from the **Save as Type** drop-down list.

# CREATING BULLETED LISTS

You can use Word's bulleting features to present polished lists or draw attention to important text. A bulleted list inserts bullets or circles in front of each listed item, which you can customize to create the right effect.

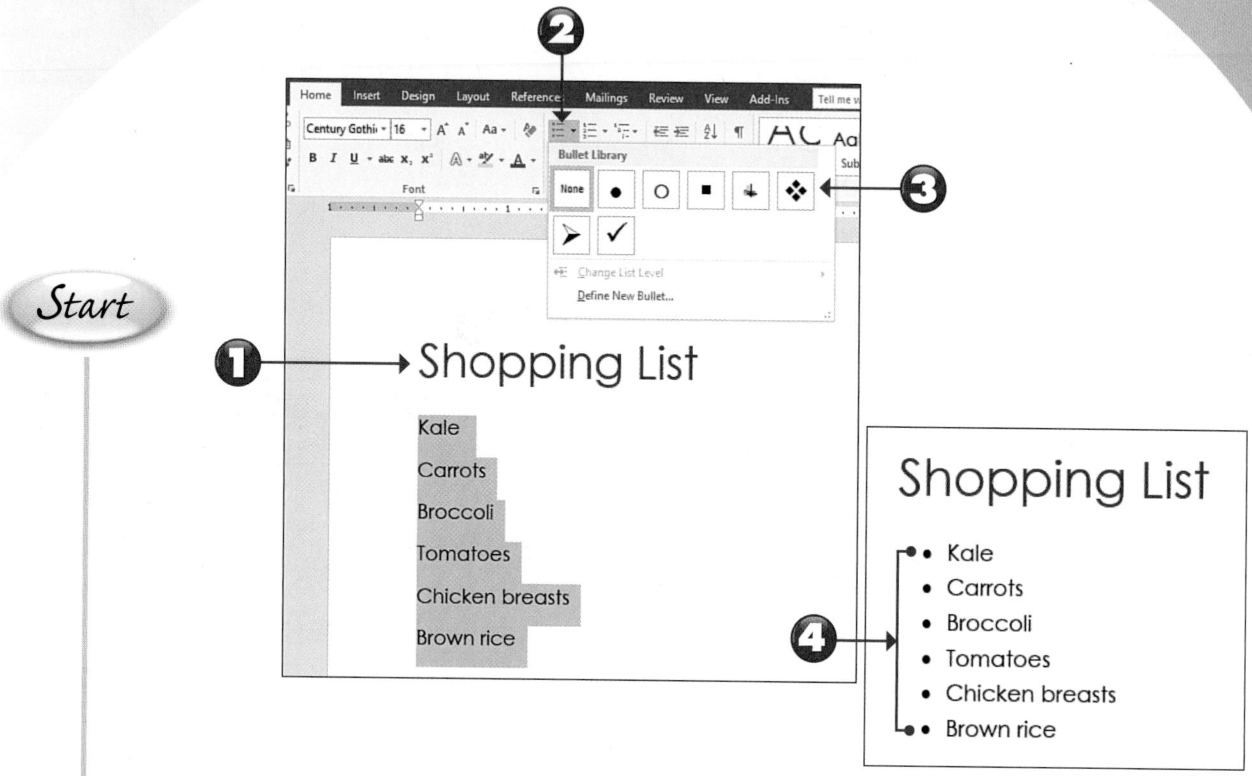

Start

Shopping List

Kale
Carrots
Broccoli
Tomatoes
Chicken breasts
Brown rice

Shopping List

- Kale
- Carrots
- Broccoli
- Tomatoes
- Chicken breasts
- Brown rice

1. Select the text to which you want to add bullets.
2. On the Home tab, click the **Bullets** drop-down arrow.
3. Click the bullet style you want to apply.
4. Word adds bullets to the selected text.

End

## NOTE

**Add to the List** You can continue growing your bulleted or numbered list by adding a line immediately following the last bulleted or numbered item. Click at the end of the line, and press **Enter**. Word assumes you want to keep adding to the list and automatically inserts the next bullet or number for you. When you press **Enter** at the end of the last list item, press the **Backspace** key to reset the document to Normal text.

# CREATING NUMBERED LISTS

Numbered lists are similar to bulleted lists except each item is preceded by numbers or letters.

Start

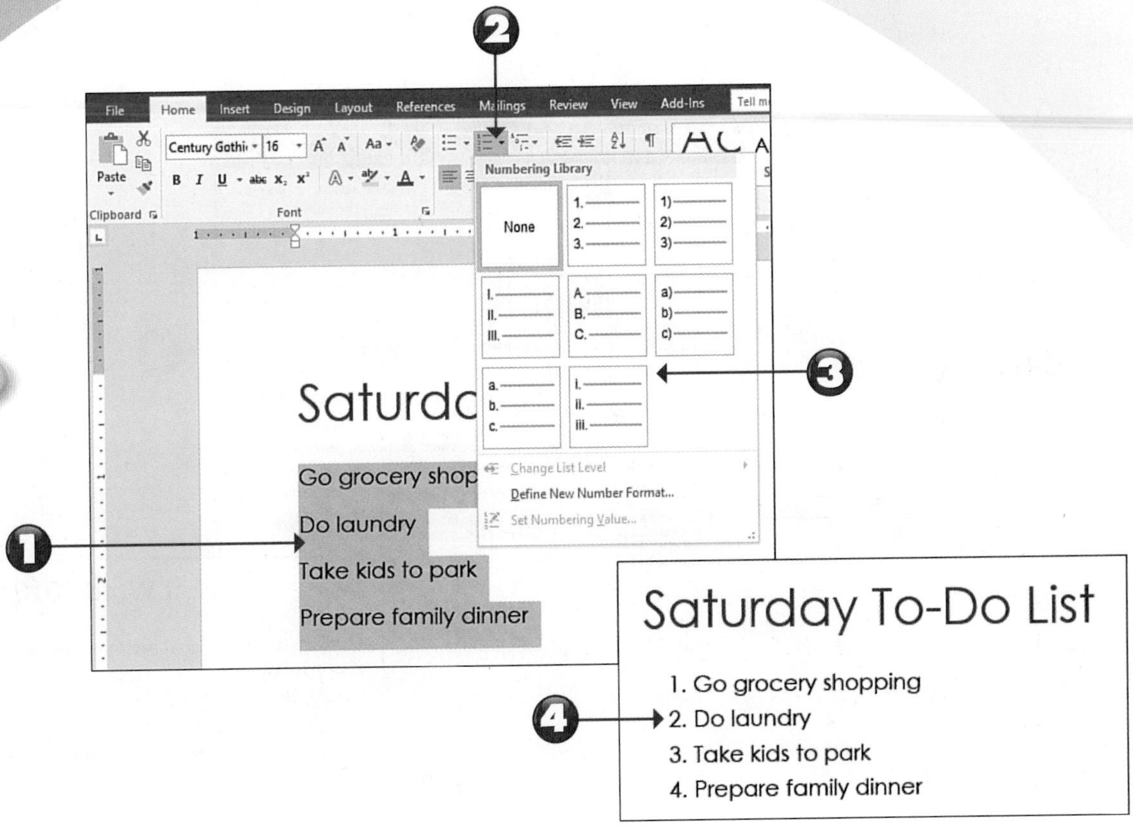

1. Select the text to which you want to add numbers.
2. On the Home tab, click the **Numbering** drop-down arrow.
3. Click the number style you want to apply.
4. Word adds numbers to the selected text.

End

**TIP**

**Customize It** Word offers you a variety of bullet and number styles in the library, but you can also create your own custom bullet or number style. From the Bullets drop-down menu, select **Define New Bullet**. From the Numbering drop-down menu, select **Define New Number Format**. This opens a dialog box in which you can choose another style source.

**TIP**

**Use the Default Setting** Apply the default bullet or number by clicking the **Bullets** button or **Numbering** button directly.

# CHANGING TEXT COLOR

You can apply color to your Word text through font color formatting. You can choose from a palette of colors that are theme related or from Word's standard colors. Always keep legibility in mind when choosing font colors.

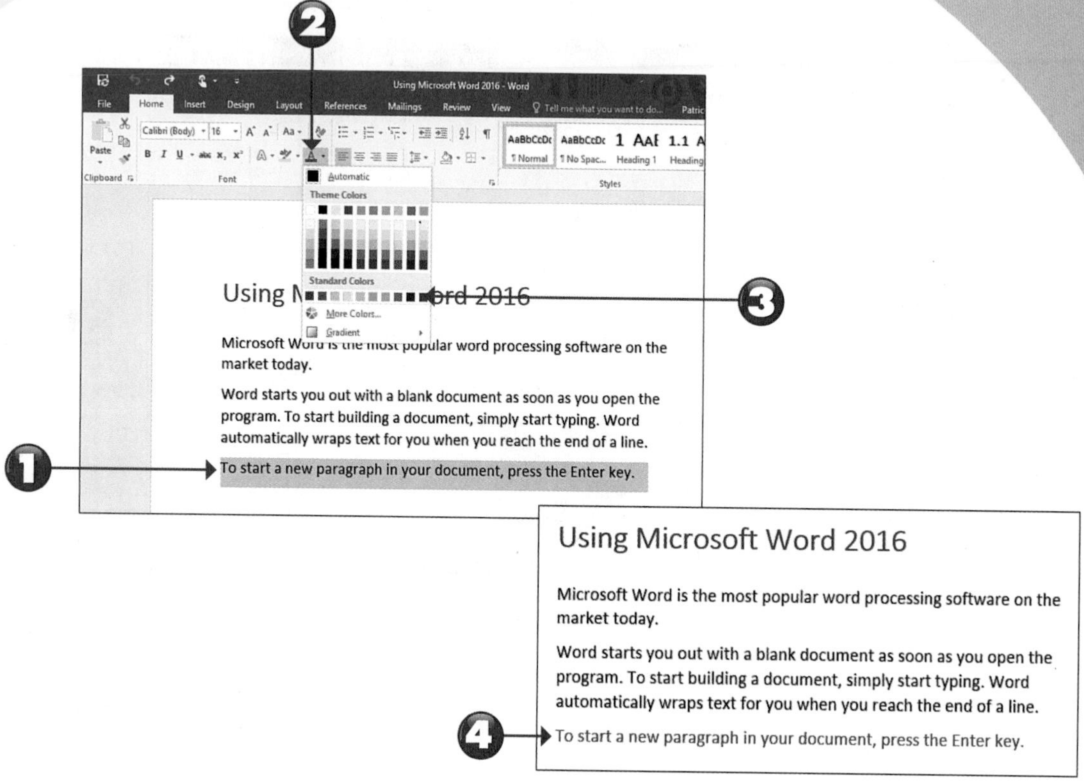

Start

1. Select the text you want to format.
2. On the Home tab, click the **Font Color** drop-down arrow.
3. Click a color.
4. Word applies the formatting to the selected text.

End

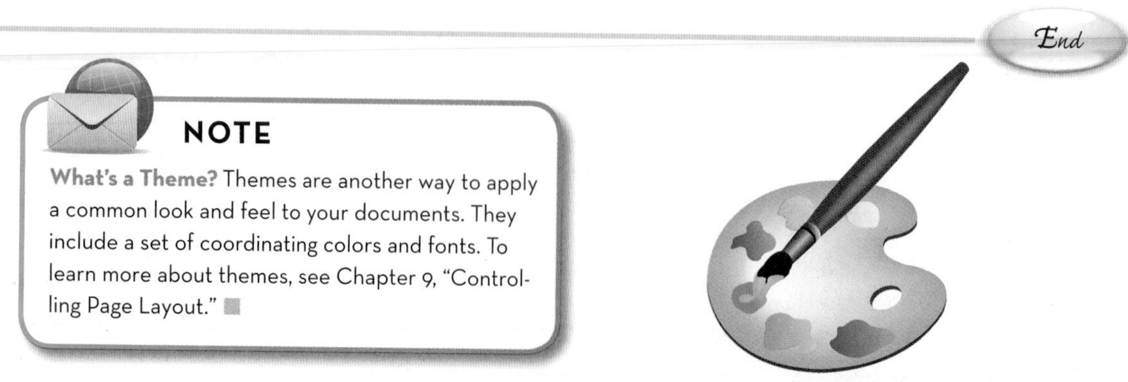

## NOTE

**What's a Theme?** Themes are another way to apply a common look and feel to your documents. They include a set of coordinating colors and fonts. To learn more about themes, see Chapter 9, "Controlling Page Layout."

# APPLYING STYLES

You can use Word's Quick Styles to quickly and easily apply preset formatting to your document text. You can use the Quick Styles gallery—a pop-up menu on the Ribbon's Home tab—to preview a style before you apply it.

Start

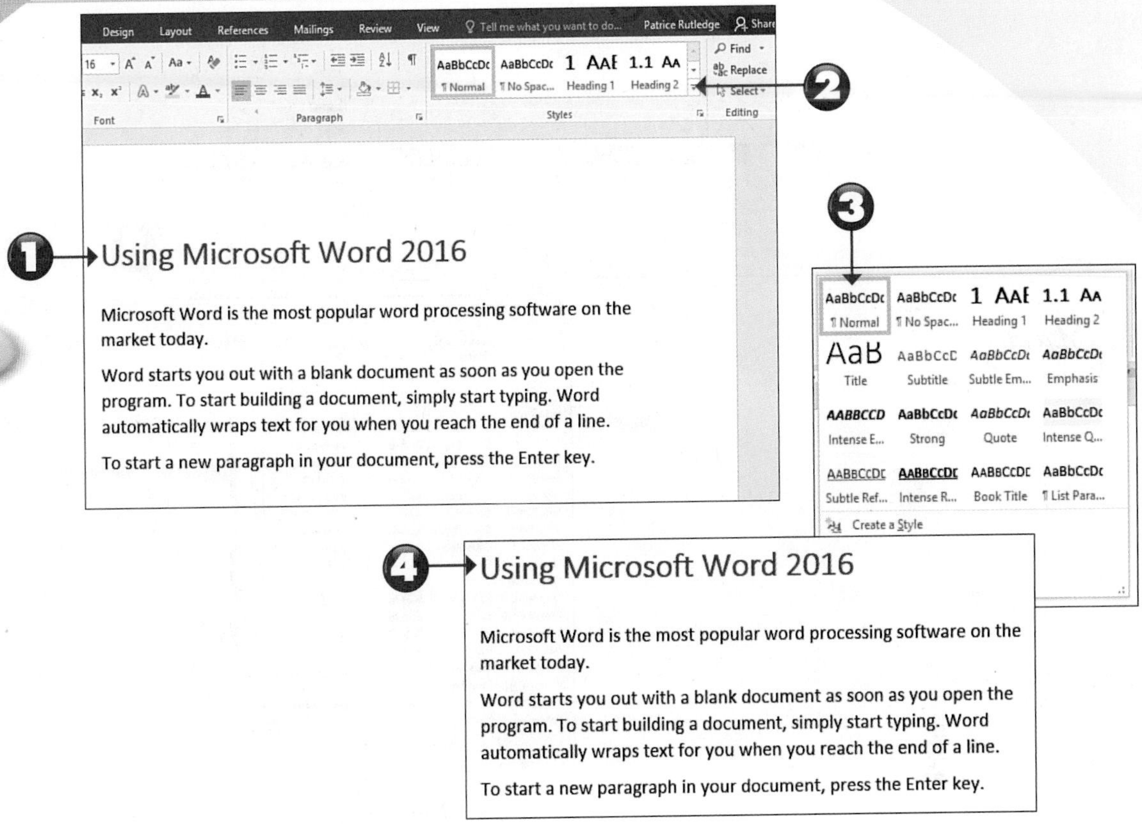

1. Select the text to which you want to apply a style.
2. On the Home tab, click the **More** button in the Styles group to view the full Quick Styles gallery.
3. Click a style from the gallery.
4. Word immediately applies it to the text.

End

TIP

**Clear a Style** To remove a style from your text, click the **Clear All Formatting** button in the **Font** group on the **Home** tab. This command removes all the formatting applied to the selected text.

TIP

**Make a Style** Format the text the way you want; then click the **More** button and choose **Create a Style**. This opens the Create New Style from Formatting dialog box where you can name the style.

# ADDING QUICK PARTS

Word's Quick Parts offers you dozens of premade content elements, called *building blocks*, you can insert into your documents. Building blocks include text boxes, tables, page numbers, and more. Reusable Quick Parts elements make it easy to build your documents.

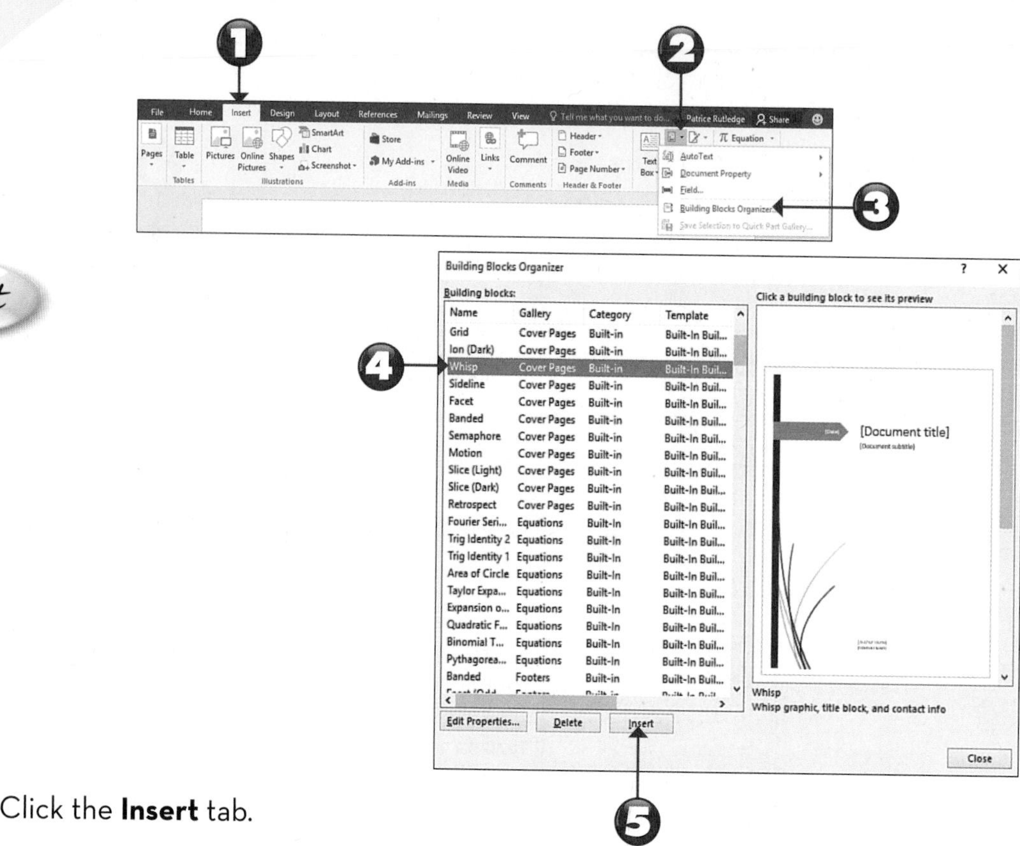


Start

1. Click the **Insert** tab.
2. Click **Quick Parts**.
3. To view all the building blocks available, click **Building Blocks Organizer** to open a full list of reusable elements.
4. Click a building block element to see a preview.
5. Click **Insert** to add it to your document.

End

## NOTE

**Types of Quick Parts** Word's Quick Parts library includes elements such as cover pages, bibliographies, tables of content, headers and footers, text boxes, and watermarks, to list a few. You can add other types of items as needed and choose your own classifications to describe the items. ■

# CREATING CUSTOM QUICK PARTS

If you don't see what you need in the Quick Parts library, you can add your own custom quick parts to the mix.

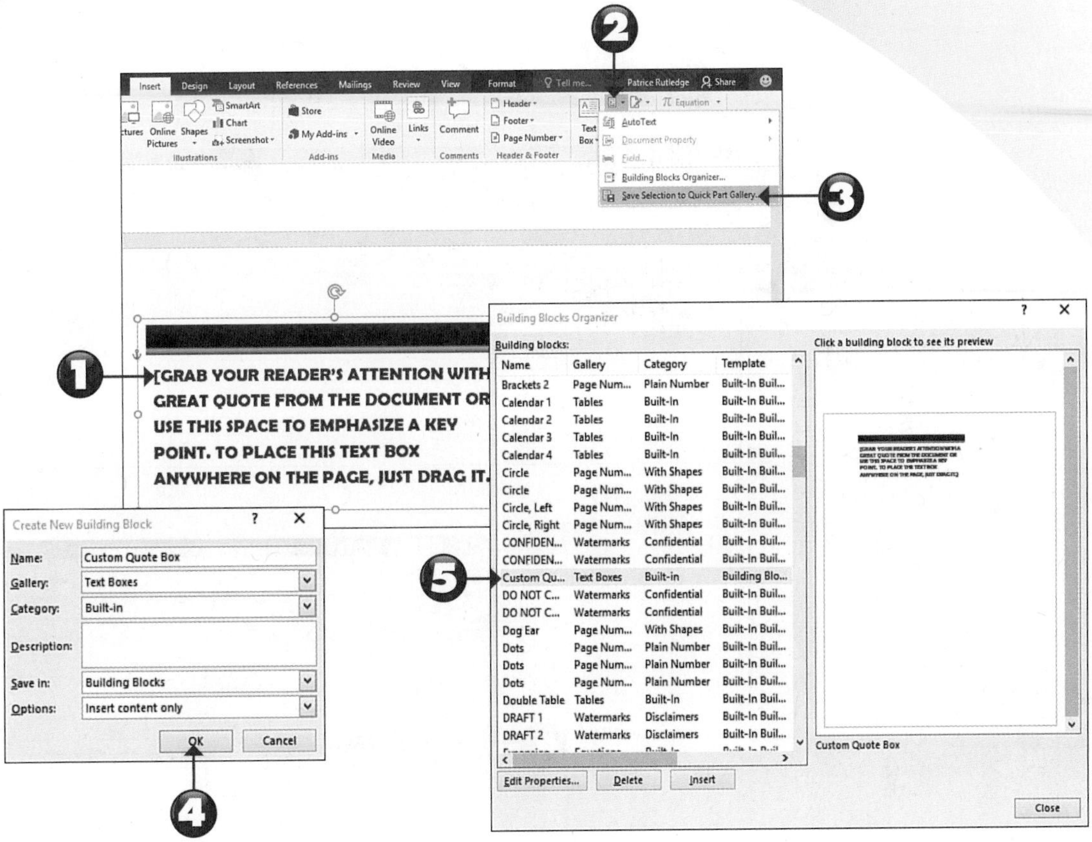

Start

1. To turn text into a building block, first select the text in the document.

2. Click **Quick Parts**.

3. Click **Save Selection to Quick Part Gallery**.

4. Fill out any details you want to save along with the text element, and click **OK**.

5. Word displays the text in the gallery the next time you click Quick Parts.

End

## TIP

**Remove It** To remove an item from the Quick Part Gallery, open the Building Blocks Organizer and select the element you want to remove. Next, click the **Delete** button. After you confirm deletion, Word removes it from the Building Blocks Organizer list and out of the gallery that appears when you click the **Quick Parts** menu.

# CREATING A TABLE

You can use tables in Word to present information in an organized fashion. Tables are composed of intersecting columns and rows that form *cells*, which hold data.

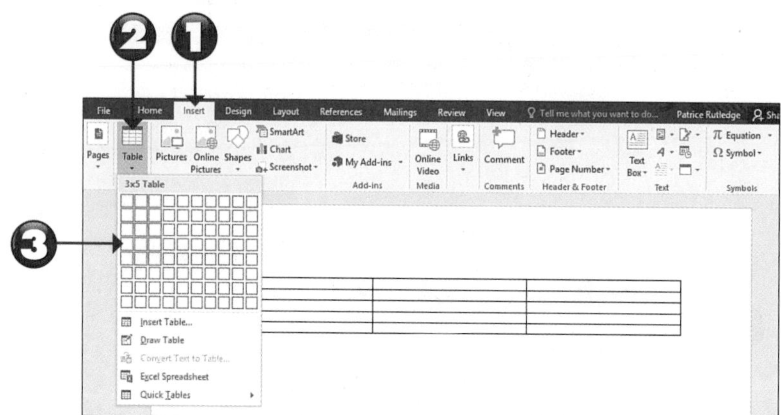


Start

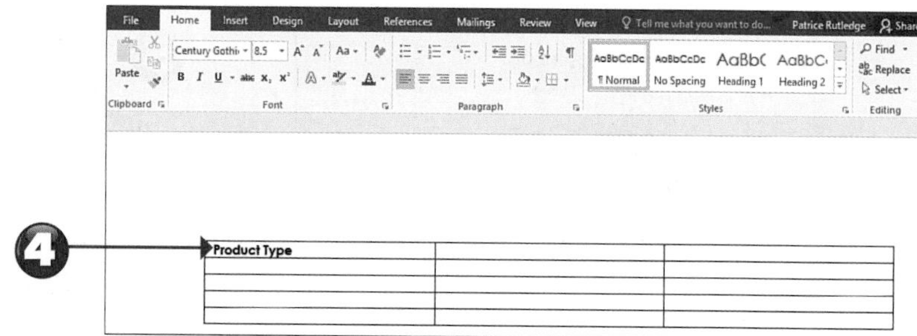


1. Click the **Insert** tab.

2. Click **Table**.

3. Click and drag across the number of columns and rows you want to create.

4. Word inserts the table, and you can start typing text into each cell.

End

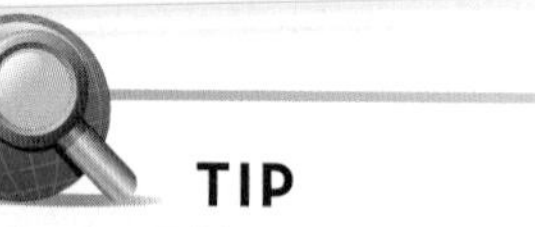

**TIP**

**Navigating Tables** You can press the **Tab** key to move from cell to cell in a table. You can press **Shift+Tab** to move back to the previous cell.

**TIP**

**Selecting Rows and Columns** You can select cells, rows, and columns to perform edits to the table data, such as applying formatting. To select a cell, click the top-left edge of the cell. To select a table row, click the far-left edge of the row. To select a column, click the top edge of the column. To select the entire table, click the top-left corner of the table.

# CREATING A QUICK TABLE

Word installs with several preset tables you can instantly insert, called Quick Tables. You can use Quick Tables to insert calendars, tabular lists, and other common table designs.

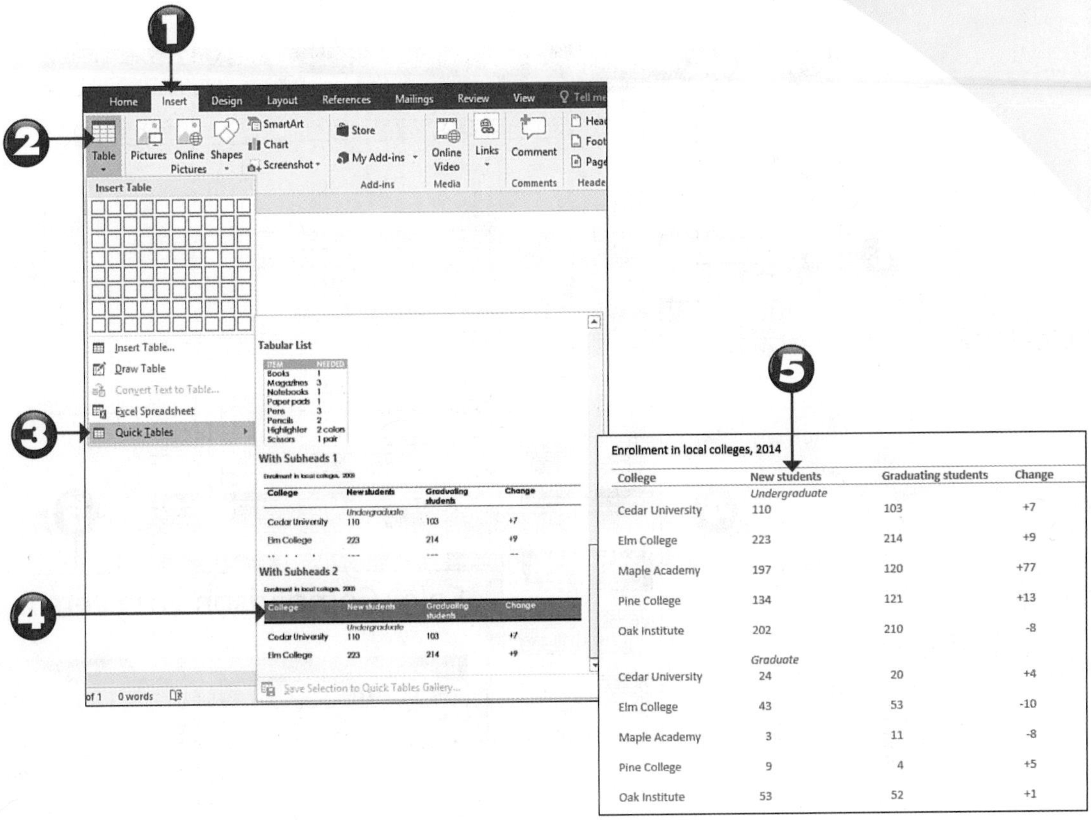

Start

**Enrollment in local colleges, 2014**

| College | New students | Graduating students | Change |
|---|---|---|---|
| | *Undergraduate* | | |
| Cedar University | 110 | 103 | +7 |
| Elm College | 223 | 214 | +9 |
| Maple Academy | 197 | 120 | +77 |
| Pine College | 134 | 121 | +13 |
| Oak Institute | 202 | 210 | -8 |
| | *Graduate* | | |
| Cedar University | 24 | 20 | +4 |
| Elm College | 43 | 53 | -10 |
| Maple Academy | 3 | 11 | -8 |
| Pine College | 9 | 4 | +5 |
| Oak Institute | 53 | 52 | +1 |

1. Click the **Insert** tab.
2. Click **Table**.
3. Click **Quick Tables**.
4. Scroll through the selection, and click a built-in table.
5. Word inserts the table, and you can start replacing any placeholder text with your own text.

End

## TIP

**Edit Quick Tables** Like other templates and Quick Parts you add in Word, you can customize a Quick table and add your own text and other data. Just select any preset text and replace it with your own. You can also change the formatting, as needed.

## NOTE

**New Tabs** When working with tables, two new tabs appear on the Ribbon: the Table Tools–Design tab and the Table Tools–Layout tab. They both offer special table tools and features.

# APPLYING A TABLE STYLE

You can apply a preset table style to quickly add formatting to a table, such as cell borders and shading, or colors.

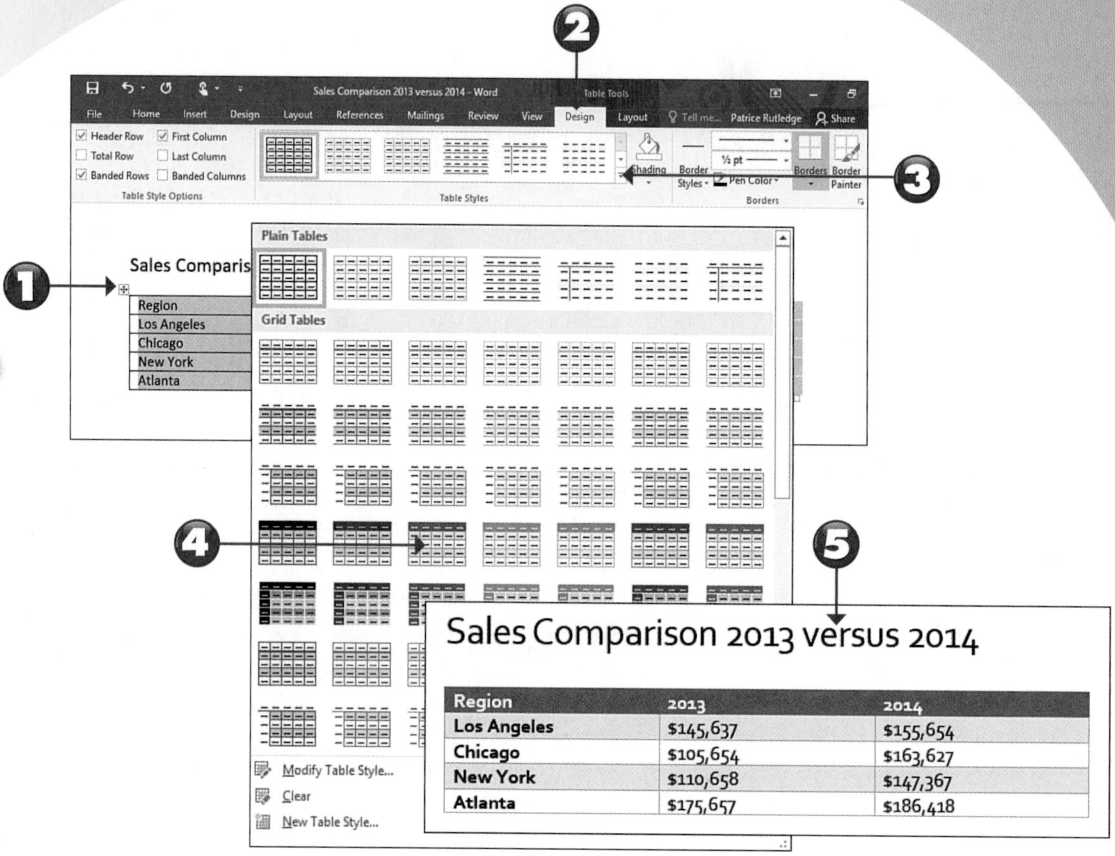

Sales Comparison 2013 versus 2014

| Region | 2013 | 2014 |
|---|---|---|
| Los Angeles | $145,637 | $155,654 |
| Chicago | $105,654 | $163,627 |
| New York | $110,658 | $147,367 |
| Atlanta | $175,657 | $186,418 |

Start

1. Click the upper-left corner of the table to select the entire table.
2. Click the **Design** tab.
3. Click the **More** button in the Table Styles group.
4. Click a style in the Quick Tables Gallery.
5. Word applies the new style to the table.

End

## TIP

**Customize and Save It** You can customize any preset table style to suit your own design needs; just make the necessary changes to the formatting. You can also save the new table formatting as a new table style to reuse later. Select the customized table, and display the Quick Tables Gallery; click **New Table Style**. The Create New Style from Formatting dialog box opens; give the style a name and click **OK**.

## TIP

**Format Tables** You can format table text just as you can any other text in Word. You can change fonts and sizes, apply color to text, add background shading to the cells, change the gridline colors, and more.

# INSERTING ROWS AND COLUMNS

You can add rows and columns in your table as you work. Naturally, your table expands to include new rows or columns.

Start

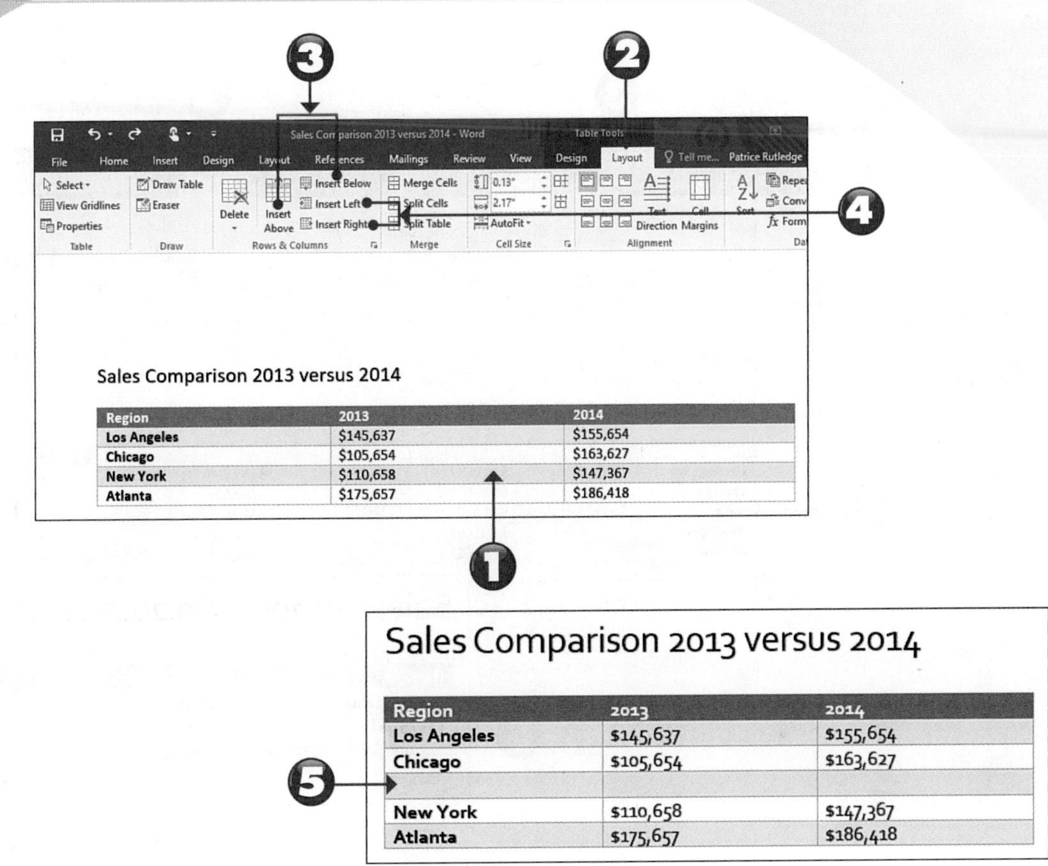


1. Click where you want to insert a new row or column in the table.

2. Click the **Layout** tab.

3. Click **Insert Above** to add a row above the current location, or click **Insert Below** to add a row below.

4. Click **Insert Left** to add a column to the left of the current location in the table, or click **Insert Right** to add a column to the right.

5. In this example, a new row is added to the table.

**TIP**

**Right-Click Shortcut** You can also right-click on a table cell where you want to add a column or row and choose **Insert**; then specify where you want the new row or column inserted.

# DELETING ROWS AND COLUMNS

You can delete rows and columns you no longer need. When you delete columns and rows, the rest of the table structure shifts to fill in the space. Any data within the rows or columns is also deleted.

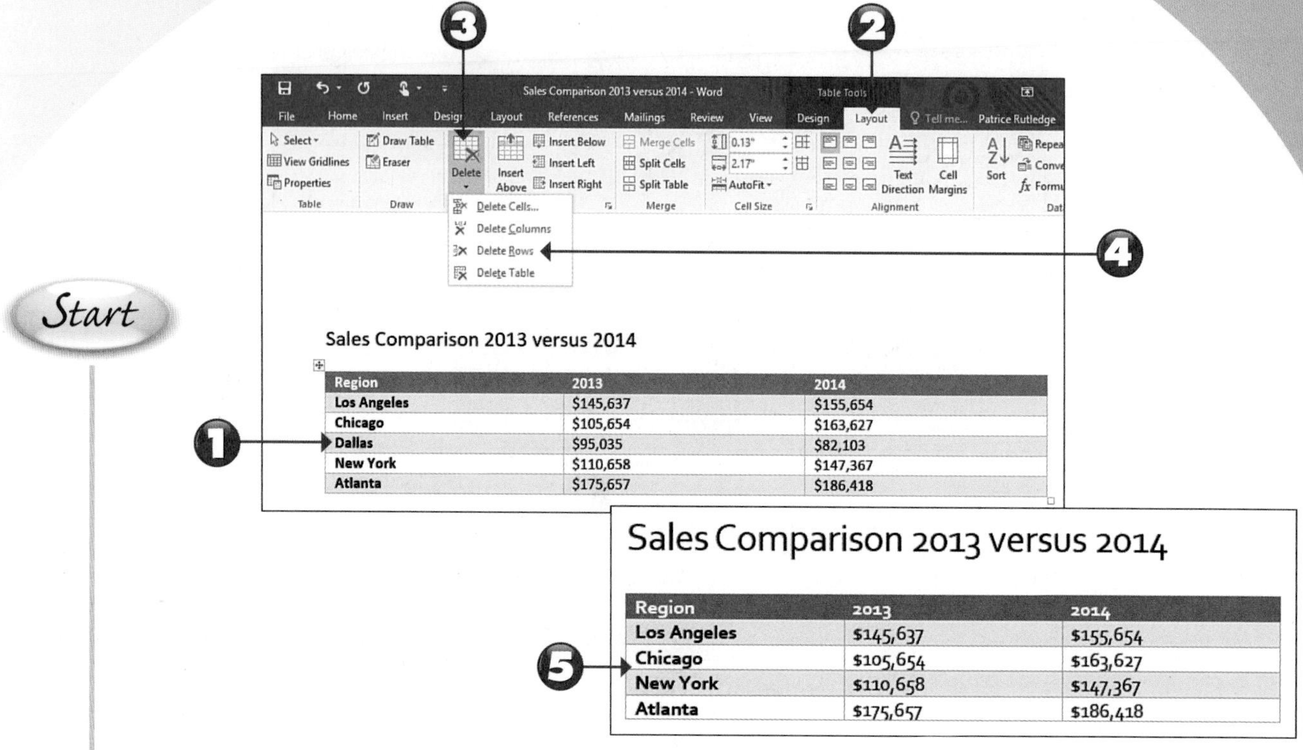

Start

Sales Comparison 2013 versus 2014

| Region | 2013 | 2014 |
|---|---|---|
| Los Angeles | $145,637 | $155,654 |
| Chicago | $105,654 | $163,627 |
| Dallas | $95,035 | $82,103 |
| New York | $110,658 | $147,367 |
| Atlanta | $175,657 | $186,418 |

Sales Comparison 2013 versus 2014

| Region | 2013 | 2014 |
|---|---|---|
| Los Angeles | $145,637 | $155,654 |
| Chicago | $105,654 | $163,627 |
| New York | $110,658 | $147,367 |
| Atlanta | $175,657 | $186,418 |

1. Select the column or row you want to delete, or click in a corresponding cell.
2. Click the **Layout** tab.
3. Click **Delete**.
4. Click **Delete Columns** or **Delete Rows**.
5. Word removes the column or row; in this example, a row is deleted.

End

**TIP**

**Oops!** If you accidentally delete the wrong row or column, click the **Undo** button on the Quick Access toolbar to quickly fix the mistake, or press **Ctrl+Z** on your keyboard.

**TIP**

**Remove Cells** You can also choose to delete cells in a table rather than entire rows or columns; click the **Delete** button on the **Layout** tab and then click **Delete Cells**. Deleting cells removes the cell and its content, and Word prompts you to choose how you want to fill in the gap, by moving surrounding cells either up or left.

# DELETING A TABLE

You can easily delete a table you no longer need in a document. Just remember that deleting a table removes all the content as well.

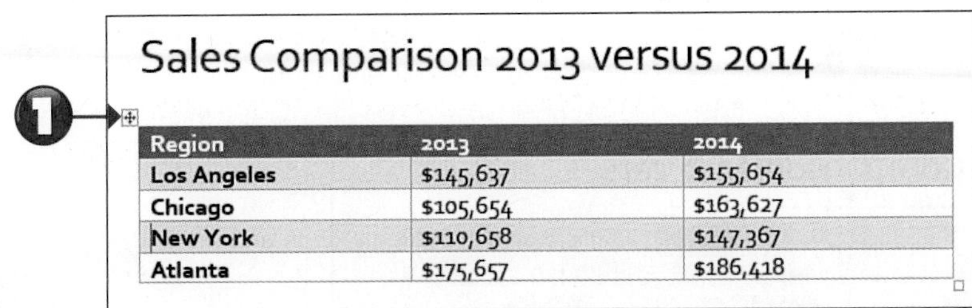

Sales Comparison 2013 versus 2014

| Region | 2013 | 2014 |
|---|---|---|
| Los Angeles | $145,637 | $155,654 |
| Chicago | $105,654 | $163,627 |
| New York | $110,658 | $147,367 |
| Atlanta | $175,657 | $186,418 |

Start

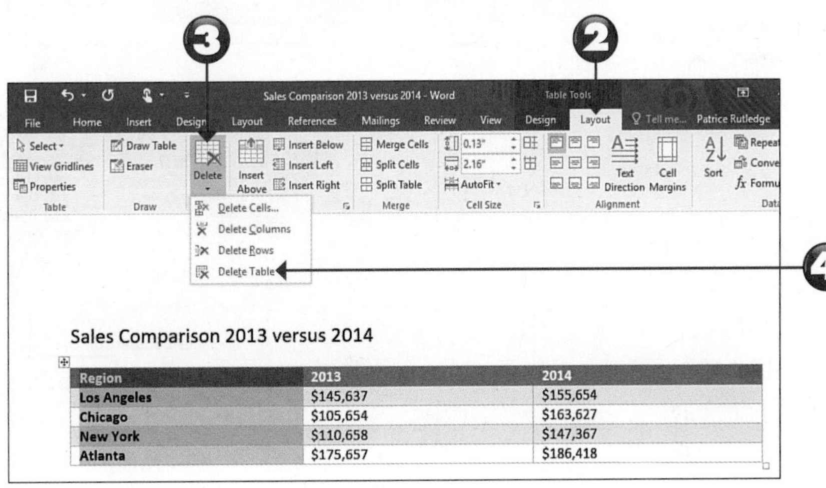


1. Click the table corner to select the table you want to delete.
2. Click the **Layout** tab.
3. Click **Delete**.
4. Click **Delete Table**.

End

**TIP**

**Not the Delete Key!** You might assume that pressing the Delete key will remove a table from your document, but it does not. Pressing Delete removes the table's contents only. You must use the **Delete Table** command to completely remove a table.

**TIP**

**Deletion Shortcut** You can also right-click over a selected table and click **Delete Table** from the pop-up menu that appears.

# MERGING TABLE CELLS

You can merge two or more cells in a table to create one larger cell. You might use this technique to create a title cell that spans several columns, for example, or a large cell to contain a special note. You can merge cells across rows or down a column.

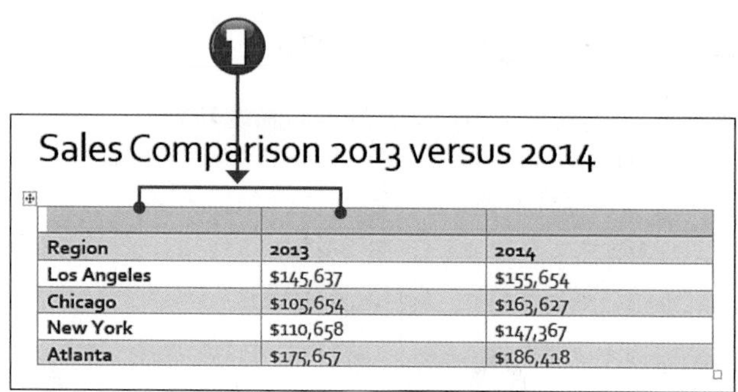
Sales Comparison 2013 versus 2014

| | | |
|---|---|---|
| Region | 2013 | 2014 |
| Los Angeles | $145,637 | $155,654 |
| Chicago | $105,654 | $163,627 |
| New York | $110,658 | $147,367 |
| Atlanta | $175,657 | $186,418 |

Start

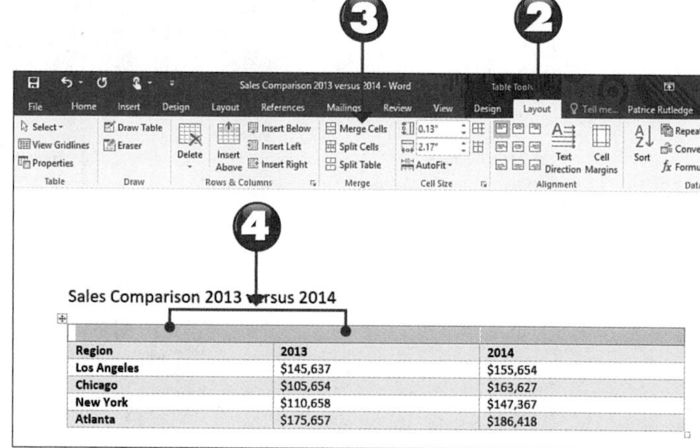

Sales Comparison 2013 versus 2014

| | | |
|---|---|---|
| Region | 2013 | 2014 |
| Los Angeles | $145,637 | $155,654 |
| Chicago | $105,654 | $163,627 |
| New York | $110,658 | $147,367 |
| Atlanta | $175,657 | $186,418 |

1. Select the cells you want to merge.
2. Click the **Layout** tab.
3. Click **Merge Cells**.
4. Word merges the cells.

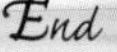

**TIP**

**Resize It** You can easily resize your table, rows, and columns by dragging a border. For example, to resize a row, drag the top or bottom of the row's border. To resize a column, drag the left or right column border.

# SPLITTING TABLE CELLS

Just as you can merge cells to create one large cell, you can also split a large table cell into two or more cells. When you split a cell, Word prompts you to choose how to split the cell, either into row or column format. Any text contained within the cells is merged into one cell, unless you specify differently.

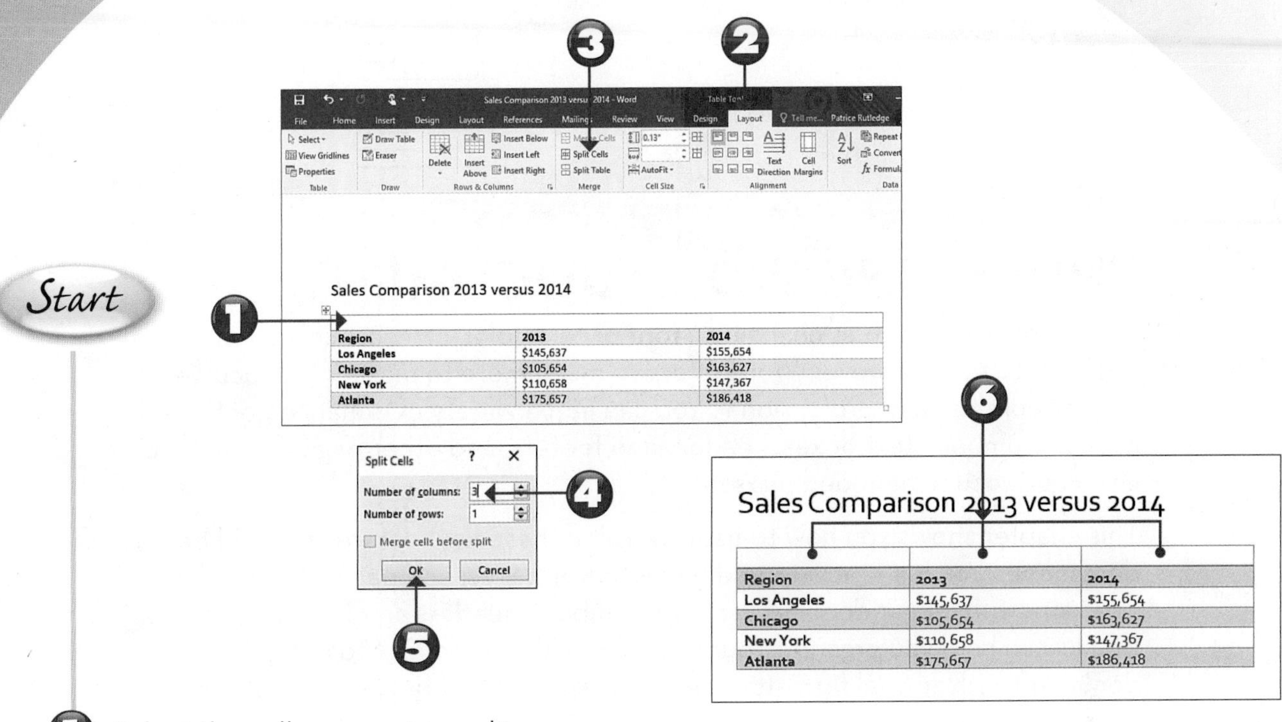

Start

1. Select the cell you want to split.
2. Click the **Layout** tab.
3. Click **Split Cells**.
4. Specify whether you want to split the cell by column or rows and indicate the number of each.
5. Click **OK**.
6. Word splits the cells as directed.

End

## TIP

**Split Tables** You can also split a table into two tables using the Split Table command located directly below the Split Cells command on the Layout tab.

## NOTE

**Add Tables** You can add tables from other sources to appear in your Word document. For example, you might copy and paste an Excel worksheet into a report you are preparing in Word. You can also build an Excel table from scratch directly in Word and use some of Excel's formula tools. To do so, click the **Insert** tab, click **Table**, and click **Excel Spreadsheet**.

# ENHANCING WORD DOCUMENTS

Basic formatting, such as changing a font or text color, can certainly spruce up a document's text. However, Word offers so much more to make your document appear polished and professional. You can add a variety of enhancements, such as page numbers, text boxes, headers and footers, and other page elements to give your document added pizzazz.

This chapter shows you how to use several of these key features to build better documents. You learn how to add pages, cover pages, and page numbers. When you work with longer documents, page numbers, headers and footers, and page breaks can help you organize your pages. You also learn how to enhance your document with special formatting features, such as text boxes, symbols, and drop caps.

# ADDING HEADERS AND FOOTERS IN WORD

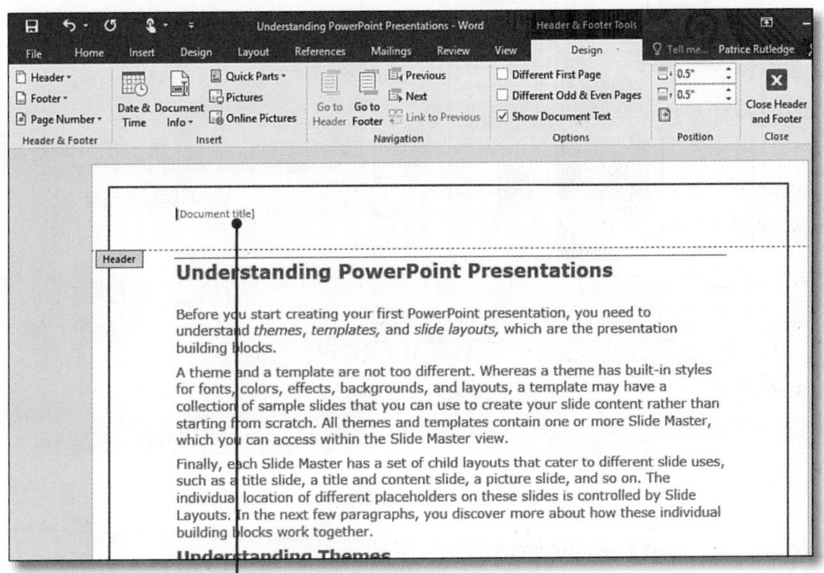


You can add headers and footers to your documents to add repeating page text, such as page numbers, author name, or document title

# INSERTING A COVER PAGE

You can add a cover page to your document to display a title, author information, or other text of your choosing. Cover pages are templates with preset designs and placeholder text. Simply replace the template text with your own.

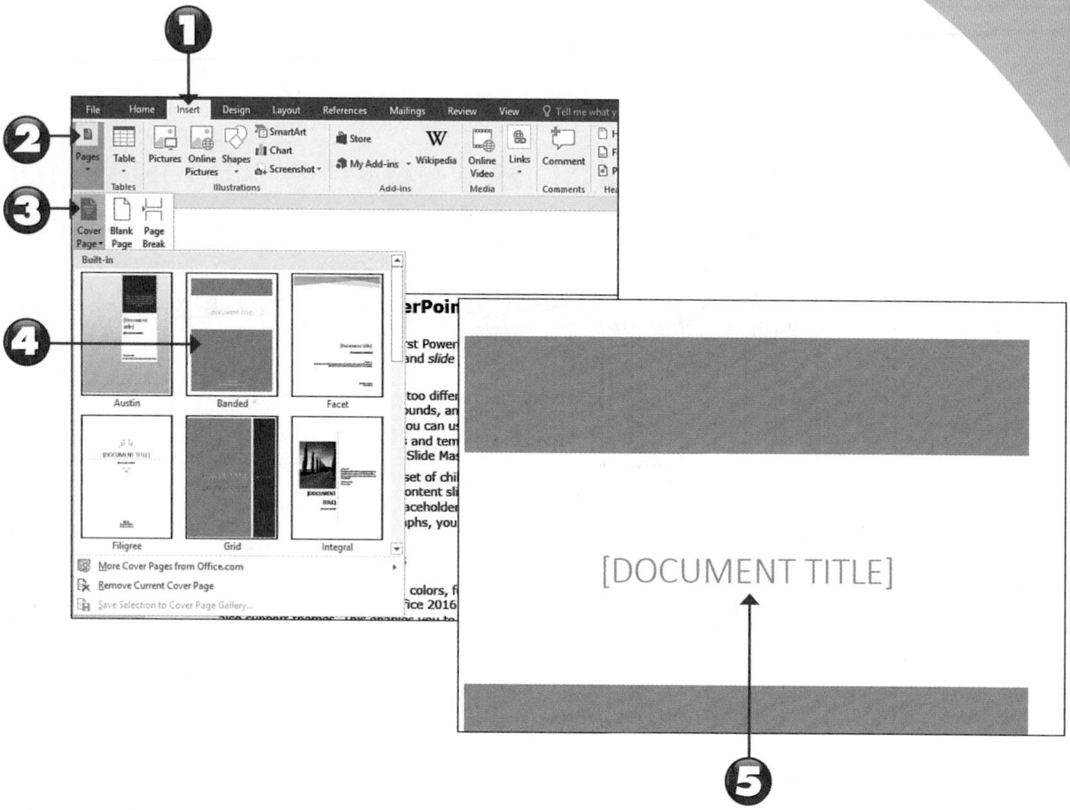

Start

1. Click the **Insert** tab on the Ribbon.
2. Click **Pages**.
3. Click **Cover Page**.
4. Scroll through and click a cover page template.
5. Word adds the page; you can now fill it in as needed.

End

## NOTE

**Screen Resolution Differences** The layout of the Insert tab varies based on your screen resolution. For example, the Cover Page button displays directly on the Insert tab rather than on a menu below the Pages button with some resolutions. If your screen doesn't match the figures in this chapter, look for the button you want elsewhere in the Ribbon tab group.

## TIP

**Remove It** To remove a cover page you no longer want, click the page, click the **Insert** tab, click **Pages**, click **Cover Page**, and then click **Remove Current Cover Page**.

# INSERTING A BLANK PAGE

Although Word creates a new page for you as you type when you reach the end of the current page, you might also need to insert a blank page from time to time. For example, you might need a new page in the middle of two existing pages to insert a chart or graphic. Inserting blank pages where you need them is easy.

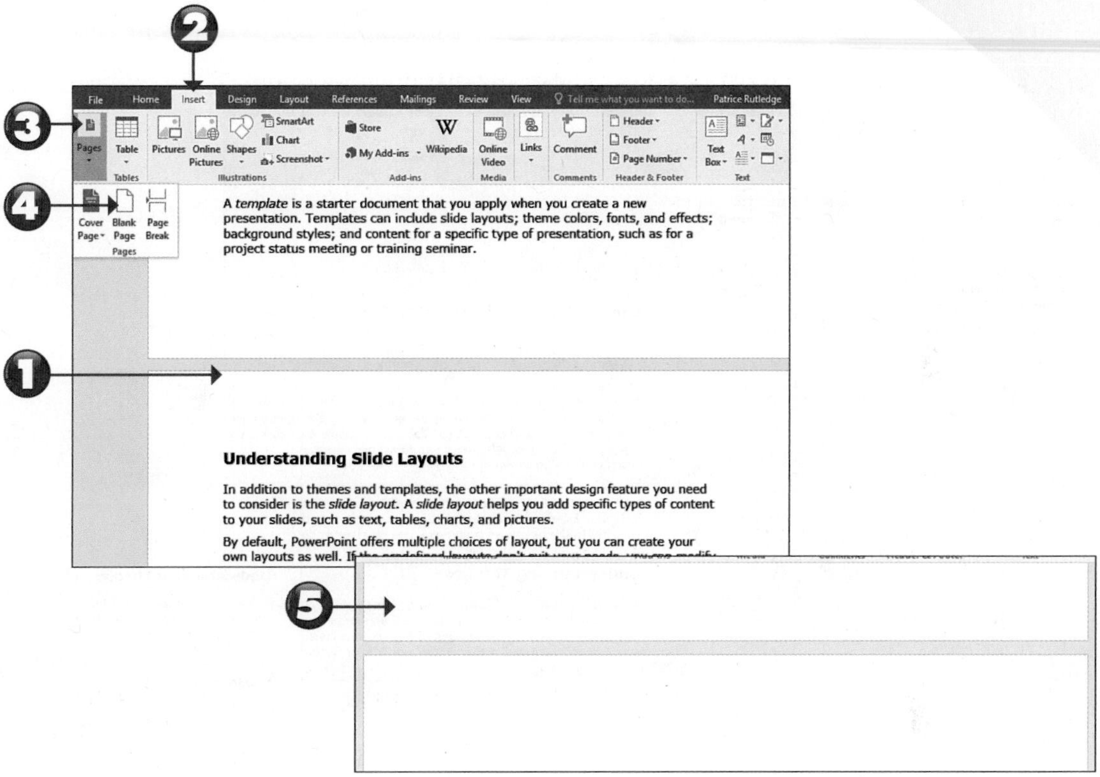

Start

1. Click anywhere on the page that you want to appear after the newly inserted page.
2. Click the **Insert** tab.
3. Click **Pages**.
4. Click **Blank Page**.
5. Word adds the page.

End

**NOTE**

**Delete It!** To remove a blank page, click the bottom of the page that precedes it, and press **Delete** until the blank page is removed.

**TIP**

**Type a Title** Did you know you can type text, such as a title, anywhere on a page? For example, if you just added a blank page to start a new section, you can double-click the center of the page and start typing there.

# INSERTING A PAGE BREAK

You can insert a page break anytime you need to manually start a new page. For example, you might want a longer paragraph at the end of a page to remain as a single block of text rather than be broken onto two pages. You can also insert a page break to start a new chapter or topic.

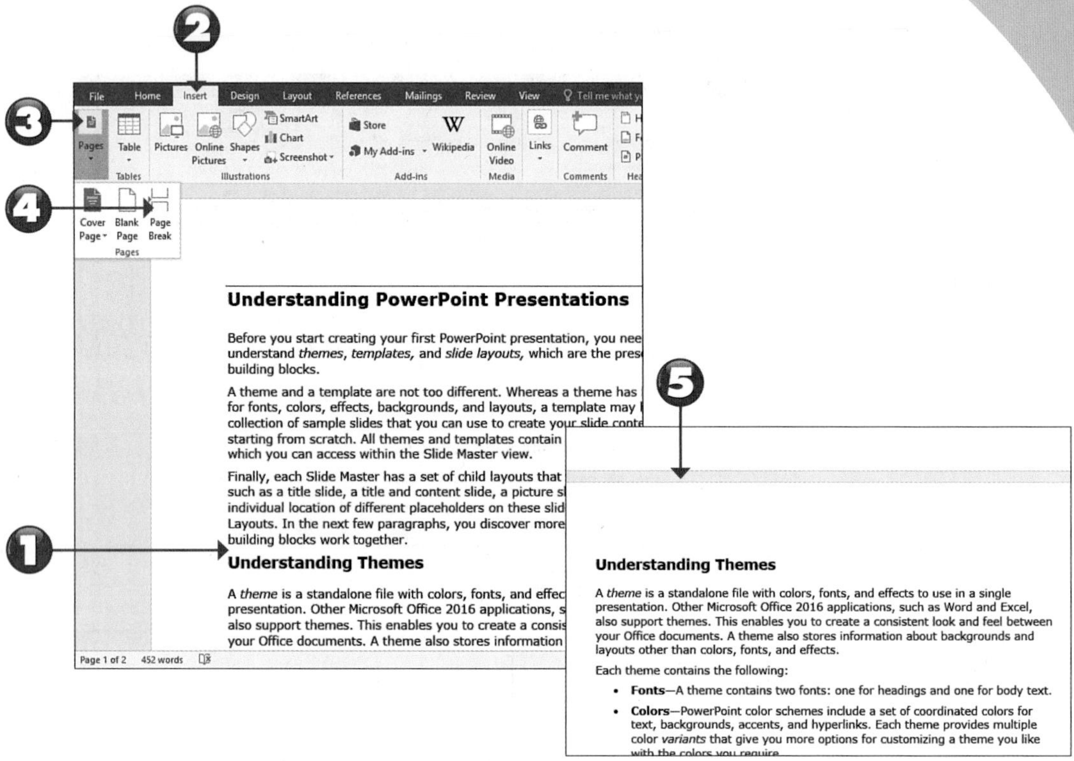

Start

1. Click where you want the page break to appear.
2. Click **Insert**.
3. Click **Pages**.
4. Click **Page Break**.
5. Word inserts a page break.

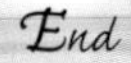

## TIP

**Shortcut!** You can also insert a page quickly using the keyboard shortcut Ctrl+Enter. This command immediately starts a new page where the cursor currently sits.

## NOTE

**More Breaks** You can use several kinds of breaks in Word in addition to page breaks. You can insert column breaks to control how text flows from one column to the next or insert section breaks to help manage long documents. To find more break options, click the **Layout** tab, and click the **Breaks** drop-down menu.

# INSERTING PAGE NUMBERS

You can insert page numbers to appear in the header and footer areas of your documents. Page numbers are particularly helpful with longer documents, especially when you print them out and need to organize the pages.

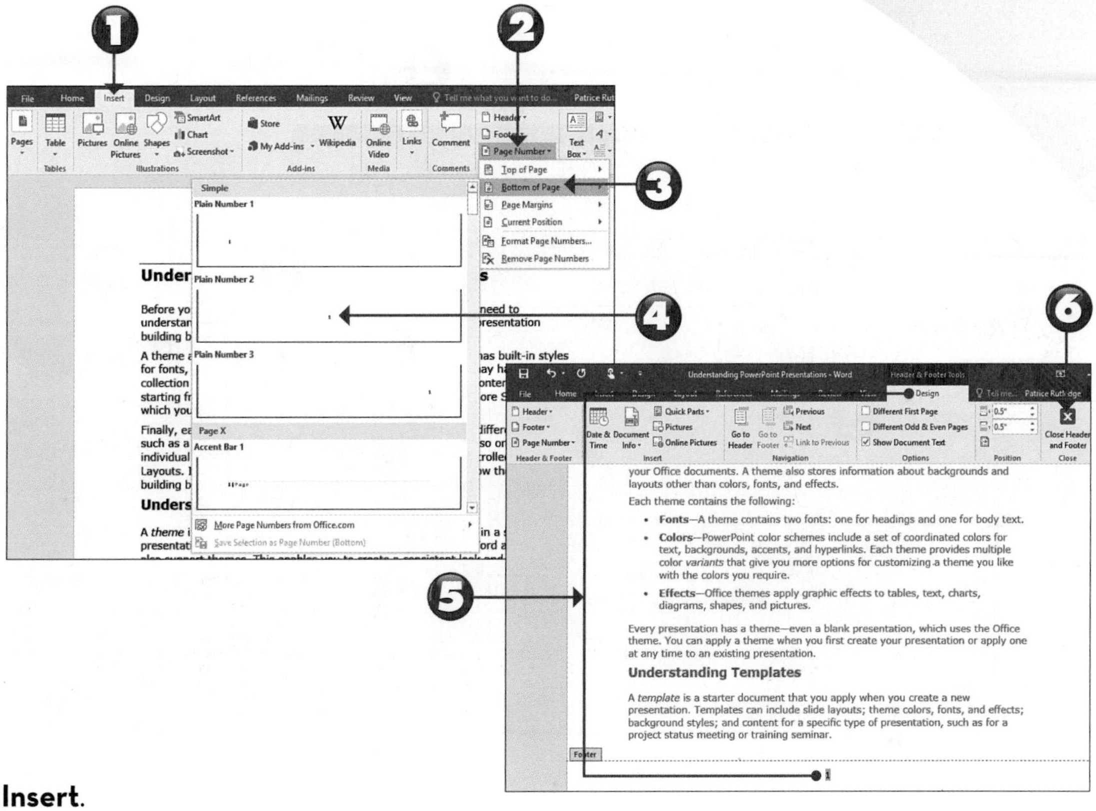

Start

1. Click **Insert**.
2. Click **Page Number**.
3. Click a page location for the numbers.
4. Click a style.
5. Word applies the numbers to your document pages and opens the Header & Footer Tools on the Ribbon.
6. Click **Close Header and Footer** to exit.

End

## NOTE

**Format Them!** You can easily change the formatting for page numbers. To change font, size, or color, for example, select the page number in the header or footer area and apply any formatting from the Home tab, such as making the numbers bold or red. To change the number style, click the **Page Number** drop-down menu on the Header & Footer Tools-Design tab, and then click **Format Page Number**. This opens a dialog box where you can specify other styles, such as Roman numerals. Learn more about headers and footers in the next task.

# ADDING HEADERS AND FOOTERS

You can use headers and footers in your documents to add special information to every page, such as a title and date at the top of each page, or a company name and address at the bottom. Header and footer information appears outside the regular text margins at the top (headers) or bottom (footers) of the document.

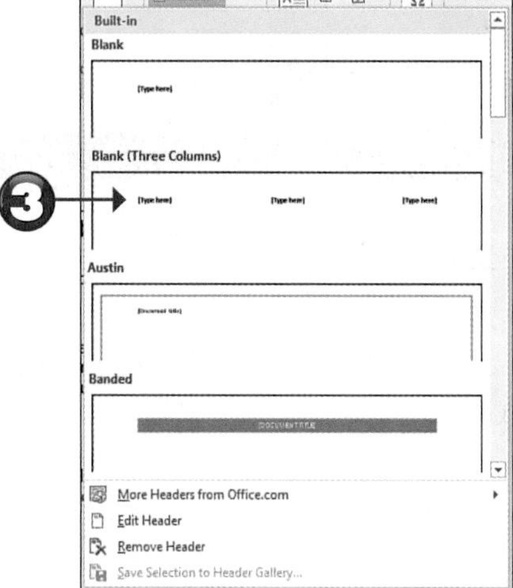

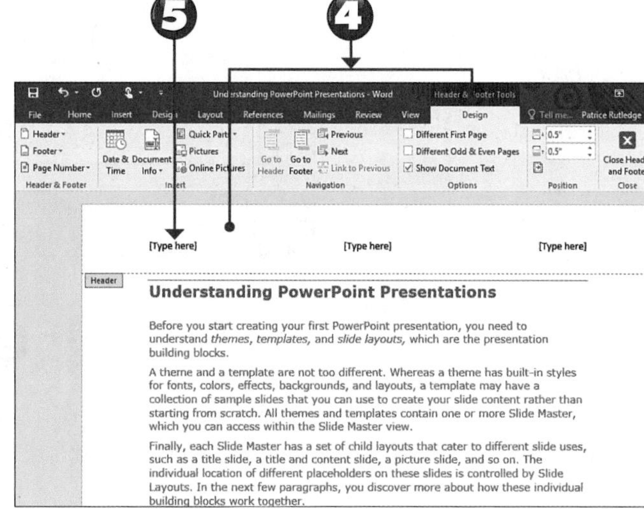

1. Click **Insert**.
2. Click **Header** or **Footer**.
3. Scroll through and click a header or footer style.
4. Word applies it to the document and displays the Design tab for Header & Footer Tools. In this example, a header is added.
5. Replace any placeholder header or footer text.

## NOTE

**Working with Fields** Header and footer elements are built out of *fields*, which hold pieces of information that update, such as page numbers or dates. You can add and subtract specific fields from a header or footer to customize it. For example, you can insert a date and time field that updates every time you open the document.

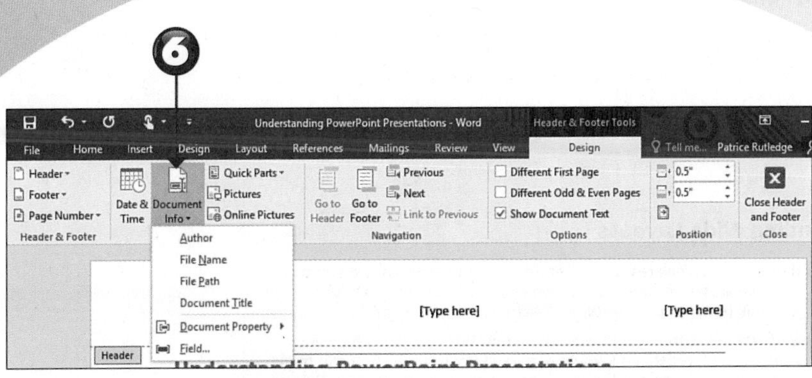


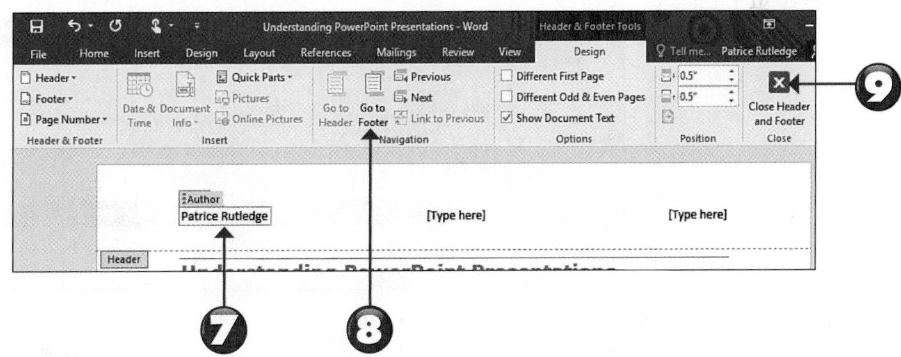


6 To insert a specific field, such as the document title or author name, click **Document Info** on the Header & Footer Tools–Design tab, and select a field.

7 Word inserts the specified field; in this example, an author name field is added to the header.

8 To navigate between headers and footers, click the **Go to Header** or **Go to Footer** button.

9 To exit the header and footer area of a document, click the **Close Header and Footer** button.

*End*

**TIP**

**Header and Footer Shortcuts** When you work with headers and footers, a dotted line separates the header or footer area from the rest of the document page. If you double-click outside the header or footer area, or press **Esc**, Word automatically closes the Header/Footer view for you. To reopen the view again, double-click inside the header or footer area at the top or bottom of the page.

# EDITING HEADERS AND FOOTERS

You can edit your headers and footers to make changes to the text or fields. You can add new fields, remove others, and adjust the formatting to suit your preferences. You can also delete headers and footers you no longer want.

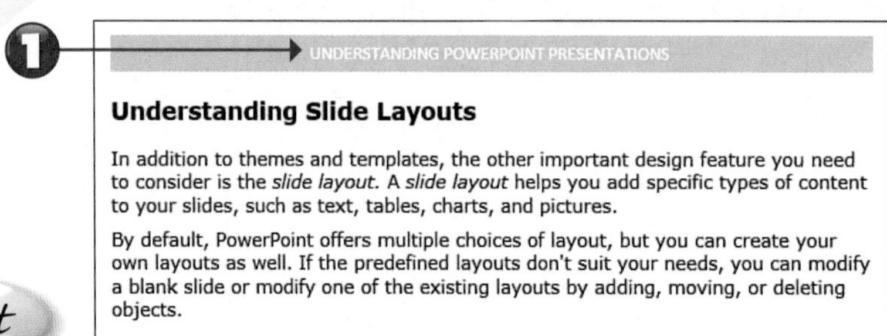

UNDERSTANDING POWERPOINT PRESENTATIONS

**Understanding Slide Layouts**

In addition to themes and templates, the other important design feature you need to consider is the *slide layout.* A *slide layout* helps you add specific types of content to your slides, such as text, tables, charts, and pictures.

By default, PowerPoint offers multiple choices of layout, but you can create your own layouts as well. If the predefined layouts don't suit your needs, you can modify a blank slide or modify one of the existing layouts by adding, moving, or deleting objects.

Start

1. Double-click in the header or footer area you want to edit.
2. Select and make any changes to the header or footer elements as needed, such as formatting, typing in different text, or adding more fields.
3. Use the **Options** tools to change how headers, footers, and documents appear while working in Header and Footer mode.
4. Use the **Position** tools to change the position and alignment of header and footer elements.

Continued

**TIP**

**Navigating Tools** You can use the tools in the Navigation group on the Design tab to navigate back and forth between header and footer areas in your document. For example, click the **Go to Footer** button to quickly view and make changes to the footer area.

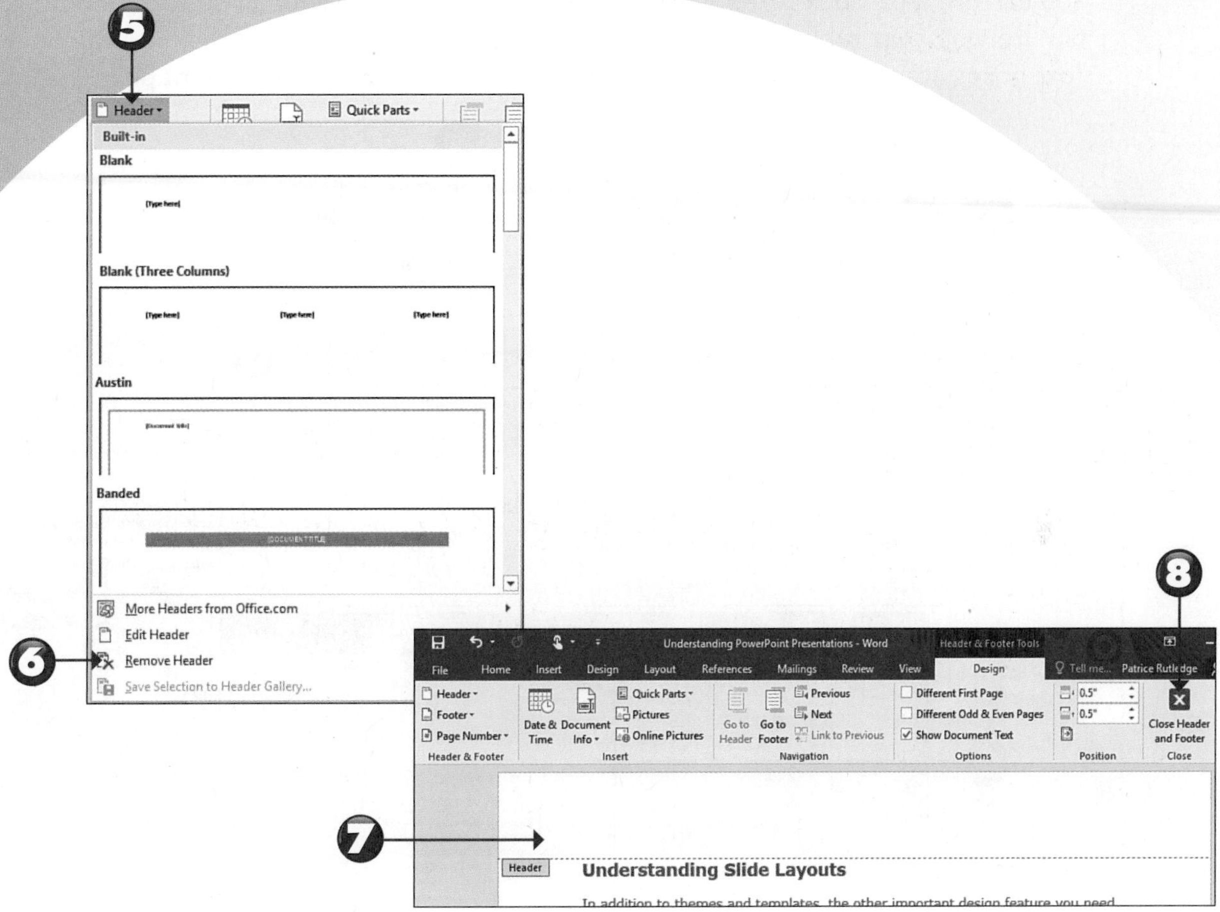

5 To remove a header or footer, click the **Header** or **Footer** button on the Header & Footer Tools–Design tab.

6 Click **Remove Header** or **Remove Footer**.

7 Word removes the header or footer.

8 To exit the header and footer area, click the **Close Header and Footer** button.

End

**TIP**

**Customize Headers and Footers** Headers and footers display on every page unless you specify otherwise. To control this, click the **Layout** tab, and then click the **More** button in the lower-right corner of the Page Setup group. On the Layout tab of the Page Setup dialog box you find options for placing different odd and even or first-page headers and footers.

# INSERTING A TEXT BOX

You can use a text box to add text to a picture, such as a caption or title, or to hold a picture, quote, or other element you want to appear separate from the main document text. Text boxes act as containers that you can move around on the document page.

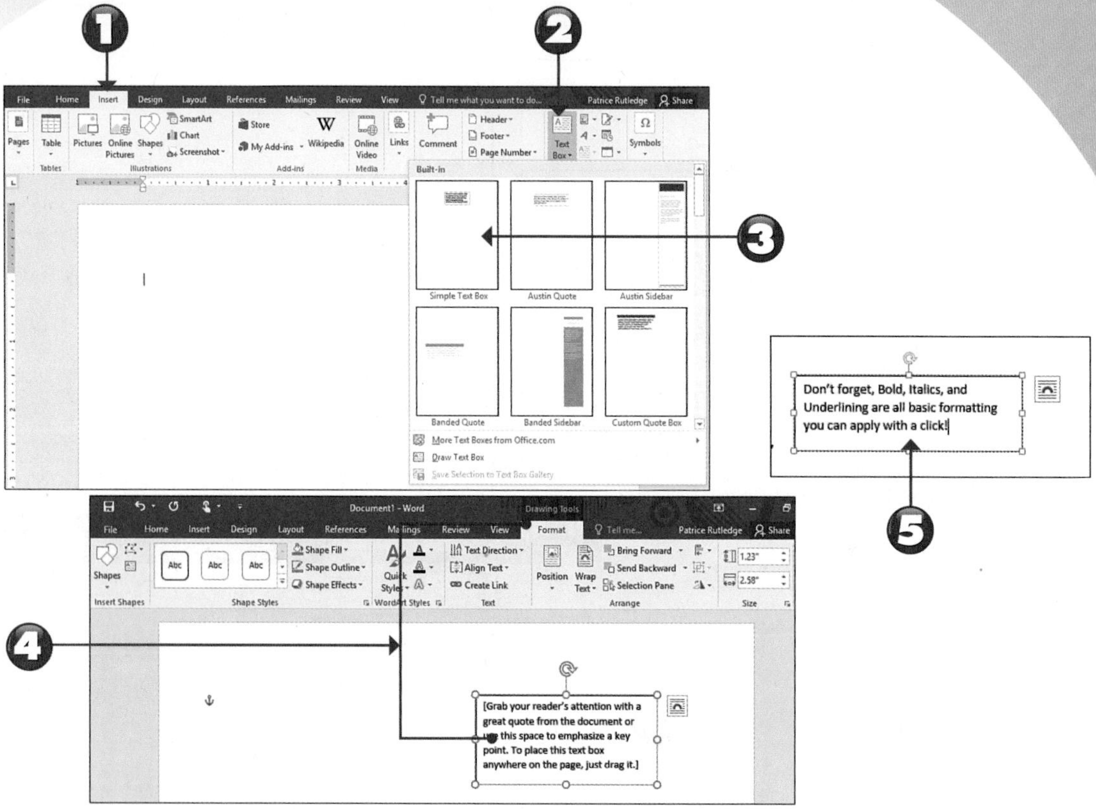

1. Click **Insert**.

2. Click **Text Box**.

3. Click a text box style.

4. Word inserts a placeholder box and displays the Format tab on the Ribbon.

5. Type the text you want to appear in the box.

## TIP

**Text Box Variety** Text boxes come in a variety of preset styles you can choose from, or you can insert a simple text box and add your own formatting later. To check online for more text box styles, click the **More Text Boxes from Office.com** command in the Text Box drop-down gallery.

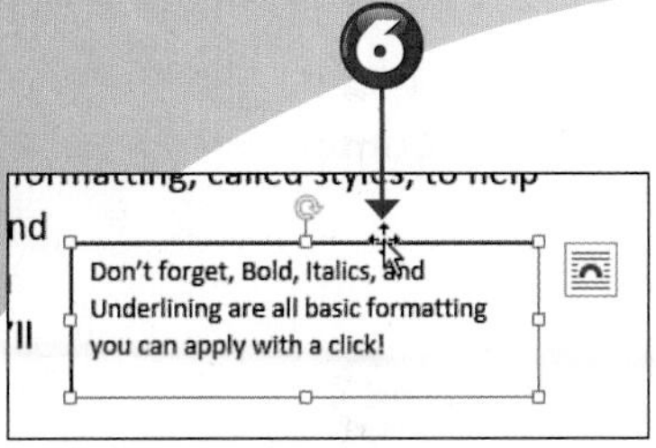

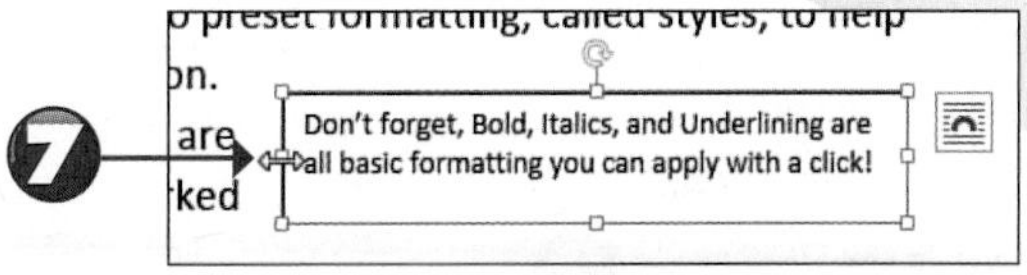

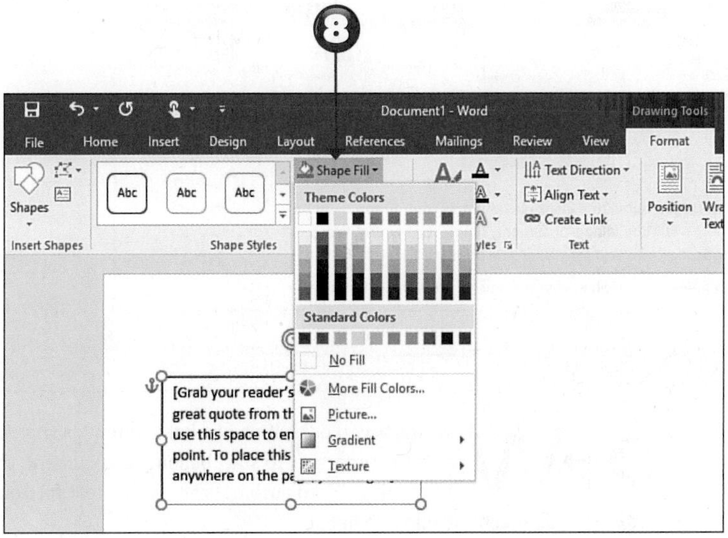

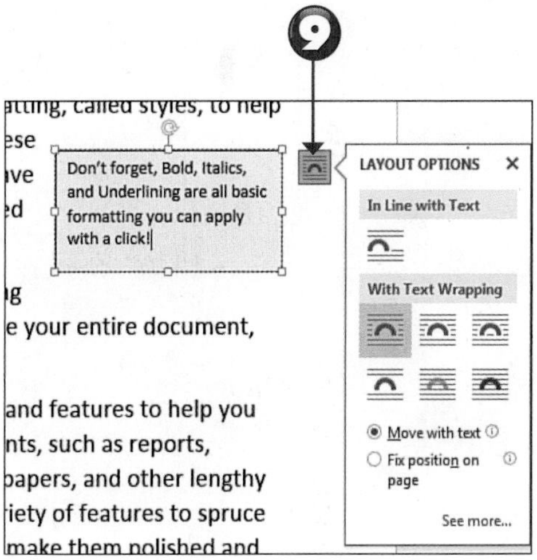

6 To move a text box, position the mouse pointer over an edge of the box and then drag it to a new location onscreen.

7 To resize the box, click and drag a selection handle.

8 To add shading to a text box background, click the **Shape Fill** button and choose a shading color.

9 To control additional layout options, click the **Layout Options** button and choose a text wrap selection.

End

## TIP

**Easy Formatting** You can format text within a text box using the same controls you use to format the rest of your document text. In addition, you can use the Drawing Tools–Format tab to make changes to the text box shape, color, background, and alignment.

# INSERTING A DROP CAP

A drop cap typically appears at the start of a paragraph, usually much larger in size than the rest of the text. Drop caps are commonly used in book publishing to mark the opening paragraph of a new chapter. You can use drop caps to add visual emphasis to your text.

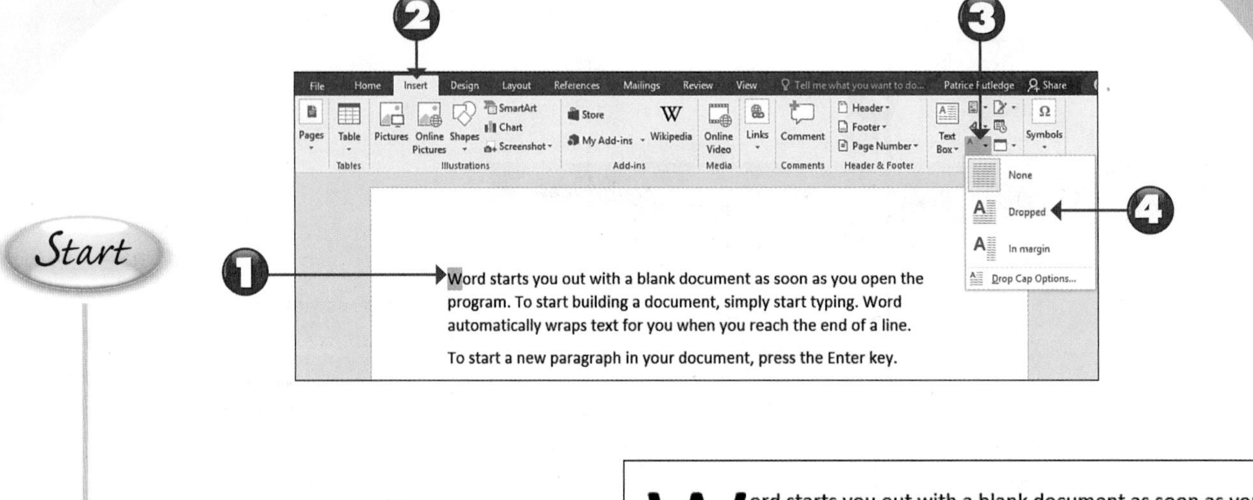


1. Select the text character you want to turn into a drop cap.
2. Click the **Insert** tab.
3. Click the **Add a Drop Cap** button.
4. Click **Dropped**.
5. The drop cap is added and you can format it to suit your needs.

End

**TIP**

**Remove It** To delete a drop cap, select it, click the **Add a Drop Cap** button, and choose **None** from the drop-down menu.

# INSERTING A DATE

You can insert a date or time field into a document that automatically updates every time you open the file. You can also keep the date static (that is, unchanging) if you like.

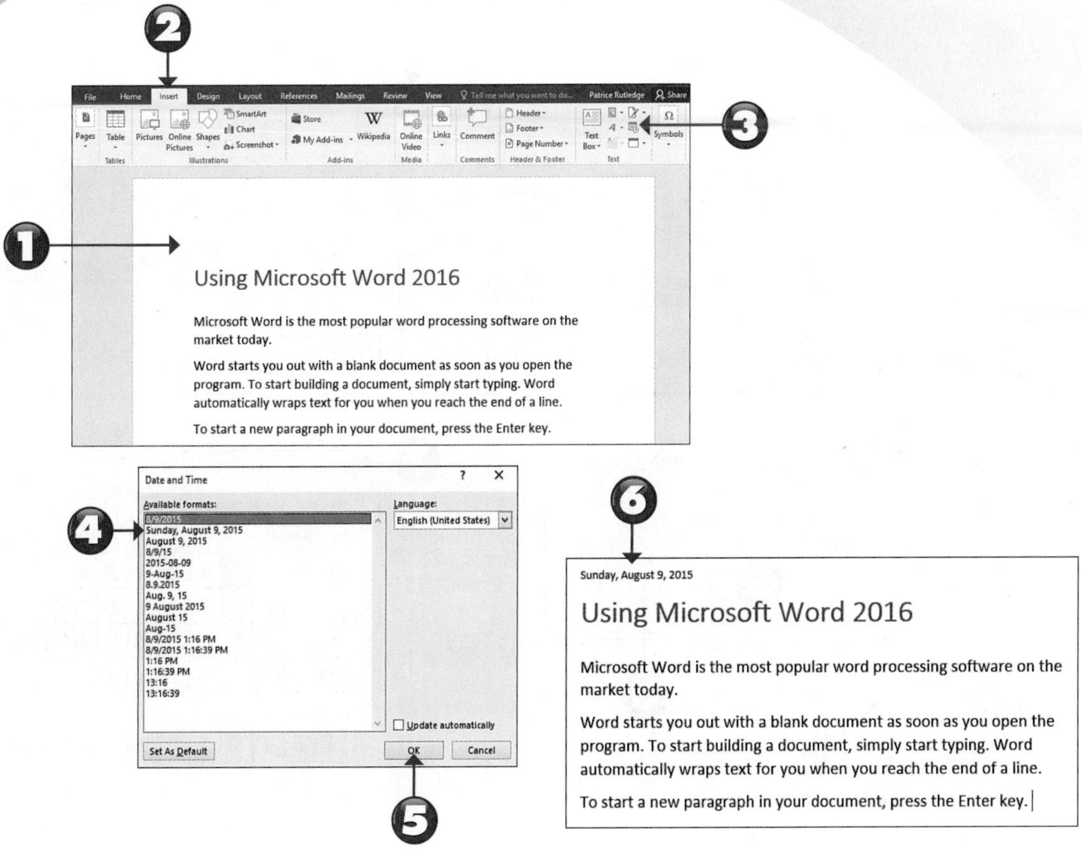

Start

1. Click where you want to insert a date.
2. Click the **Insert** tab.
3. Click the **Insert Date and Time** button.
4. Word opens the Date and Time dialog box; click a format for the date or time.
5. Click **OK**.
6. The current date and time are added.

End

**TIP**

**Automatic Update** If you want the date or time to update automatically, make sure you click the **Update Automatically** check box in the Date and Time dialog box.

# INSERTING A SYMBOL

You might need to insert special symbols or characters from time to time, such as a copyright symbol or a registered trademark. Special symbols also include mathematical signs, special quotes, foreign language symbols, and more.

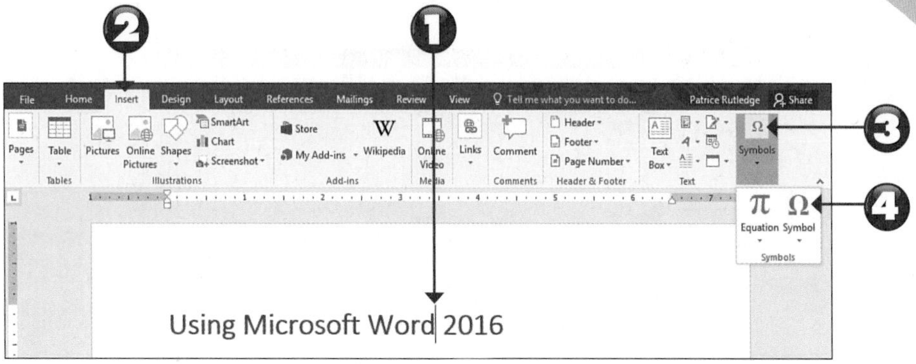

Start

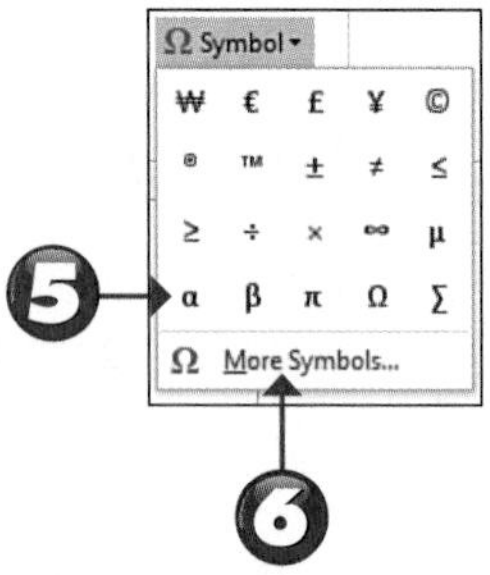

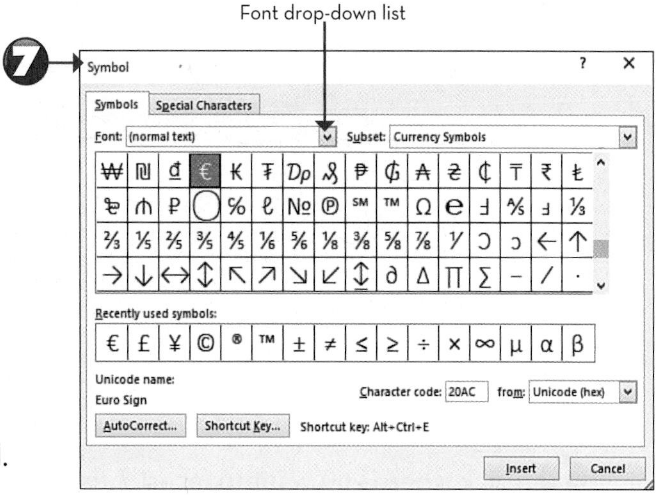

Font drop-down list

1. Click where you want to insert a symbol.
2. Click the **Insert** tab.
3. Click **Symbols**.
4. Click **Symbol**.
5. Click a symbol from the list.
6. To view more symbols, click **More Symbols**.
7. Word opens the Symbol dialog box; click the **Symbols** tab to view symbols.

Continued

## TIP

**More Symbols** If you don't see the symbol or special character you're looking for, you can switch to another font or symbol subset in the Symbol dialog box using the drop-down arrows.

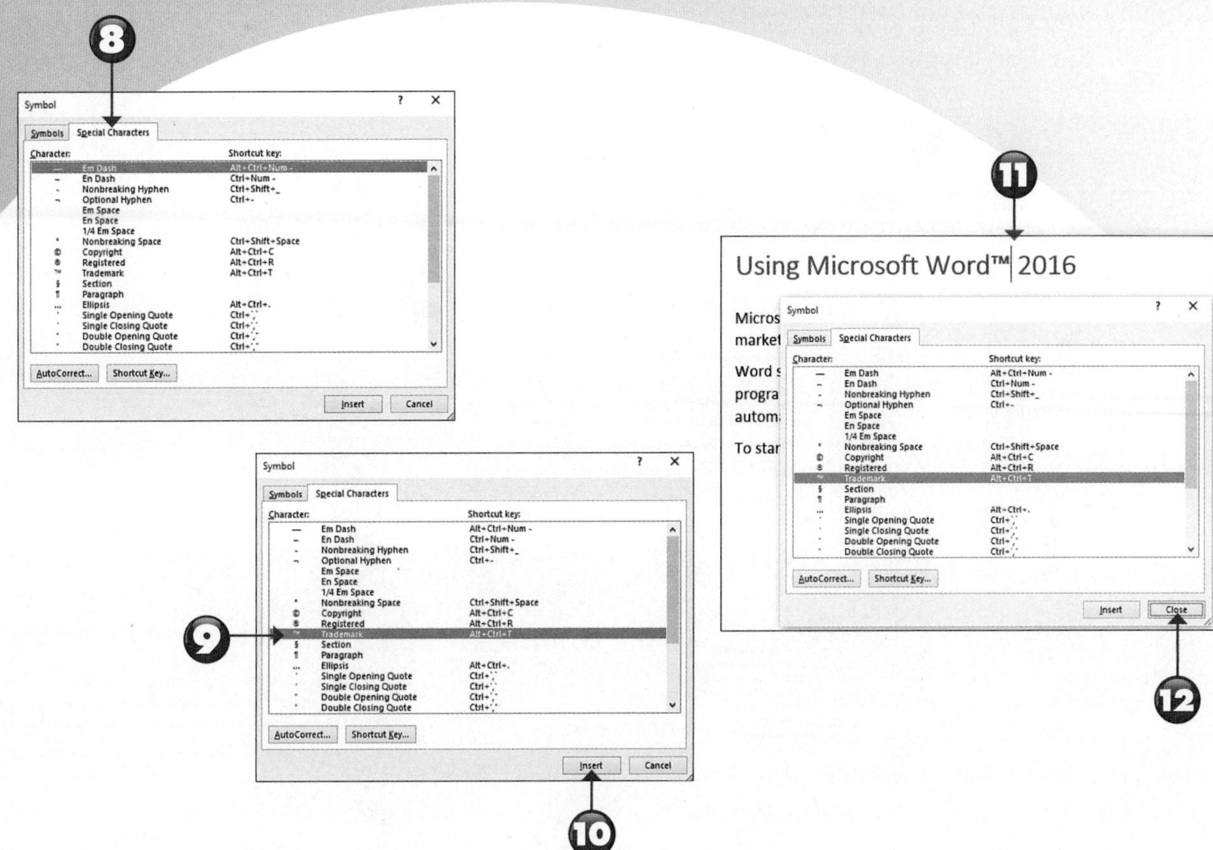


8. Click the **Special Characters** tab to view special characters.

9. Click the symbol or character you want to add.

10. Click **Insert**.

11. The symbol appears in the document.

12. Click **Close** to exit the dialog box.

*End*

### TIP

**Symbol Shortcuts** Some symbols have their own shortcut keys you can press to quickly add the symbol to any spot in a document. For example, pressing **Alt+Ctrl+C** inserts the copyright (©) symbol, and pressing **Alt+Ctrl+R** inserts the registered symbol (®). Look for keyboard shortcut keys for common symbols on the Special Characters tab in the Symbol dialog box.

# INSERTING A HYPERLINK

You can insert a hyperlink into a document that, when clicked, jumps you to another location in your existing document, another document, or a web page on the Internet.

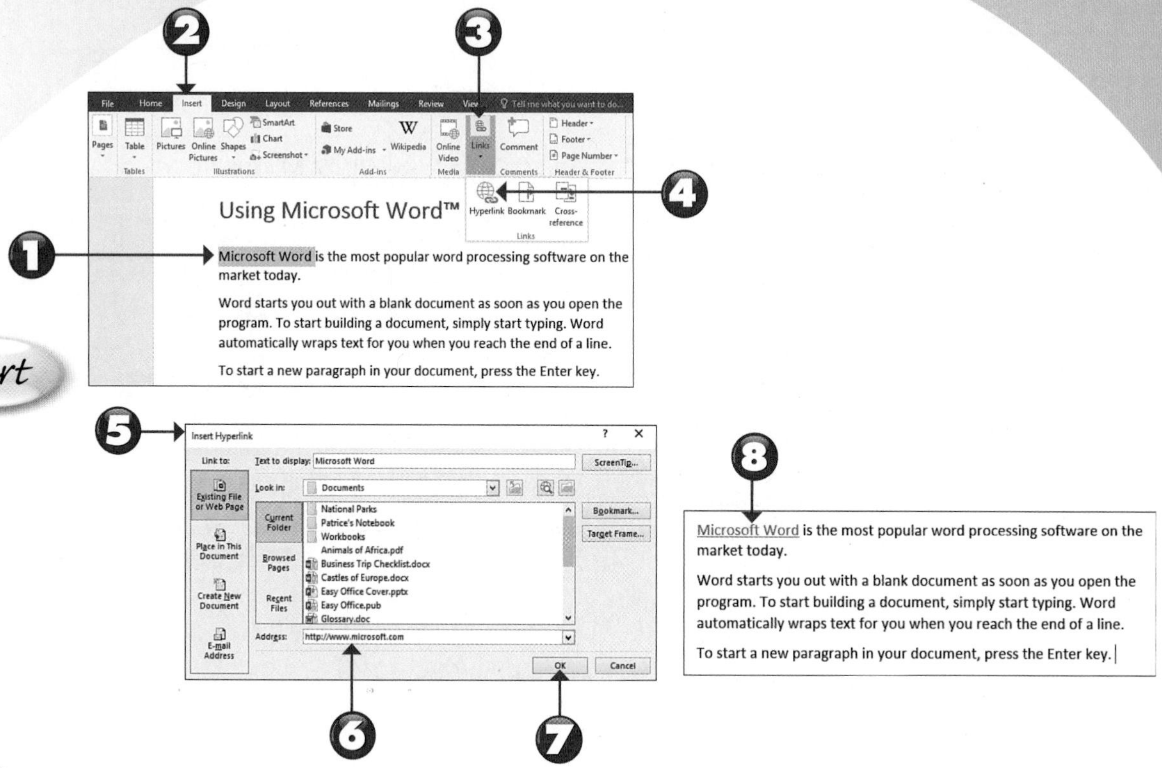

Start

1. Select the text or graphic you want to turn into a hyperlink.
2. Click the **Insert** tab.
3. Click **Links**.
4. Click **Hyperlink**.
5. The Insert Hyperlink dialog box opens; click which type of link you want to create.
6. Navigate to the item you want to link to; depending on the type of link you create, different options are available for selection.
7. Click **OK**.
8. Word formats the selected text as a hyperlink.

End

## NOTE

**Add a ScreenTip** You can add text that displays whenever you hover the mouse pointer over the link. In the Insert Hyperlink dialog box, click the **ScreenTip** button, and type in your text.

# INSERTING A BOOKMARK

You can insert a hyperlink into a document that, when clicked, jumps you to another location in your existing document, another document, or a web page on the Internet.

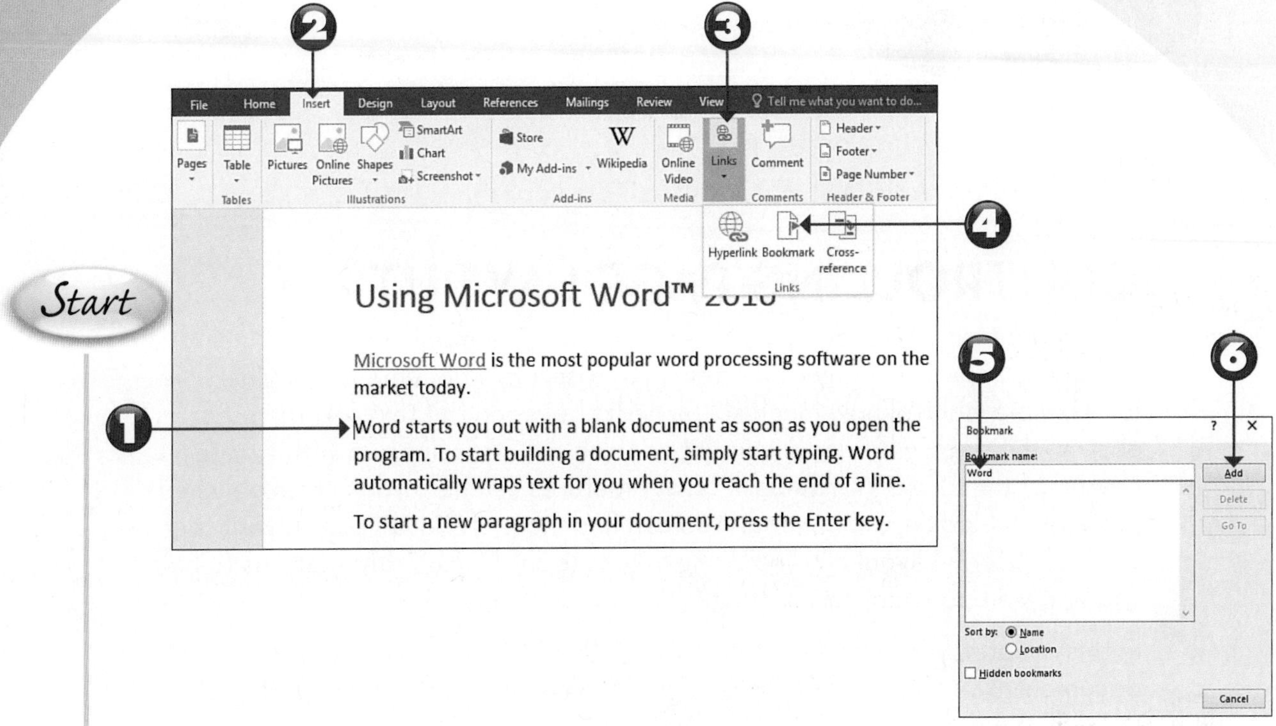

1. Select the text or graphic you want to turn into a hyperlink.
2. Click the **Insert** tab.
3. Click **Links**.
4. Click **Bookmark**.
5. The Bookmark dialog box opens; type a name for the new bookmark.
6. Click **Add** and Word saves the bookmark.

## NOTE

**Navigate to a Bookmark** To navigate to a bookmark in your document, click the **Home** tab on the Ribbon, click **Find**, and click **Go To**. Word opens the Find dialog box. In the **Go To** tab, click **Bookmark**, and then select your bookmark from the drop-down list.

# CONTROLLING PAGE LAYOUT

*Page layout* refers to how you place and position elements on a page, including text and graphics, and any other items you insert in a document. Margins, for example, control how much space exists between the text and the outer edge of the page, whereas alignment controls how text lines up with a margin. Learning how to use Word's page layout features can help you create polished, professional-looking documents. You can find most of Word's page layout tools on the Ribbon's Layout tab, including access to the Page Setup features to help you ready a document for printing.

In this chapter, you find out how to change the default margins to suit your document. You also see how to change the page orientation from portrait, which is the default setting, to landscape. This chapter shows you how to change the page size and add special borders, create columns on a page, and apply a theme.

## CONTROLLING PAGE LAYOUT IN WORD

Find preset themes you can apply on the Design tab

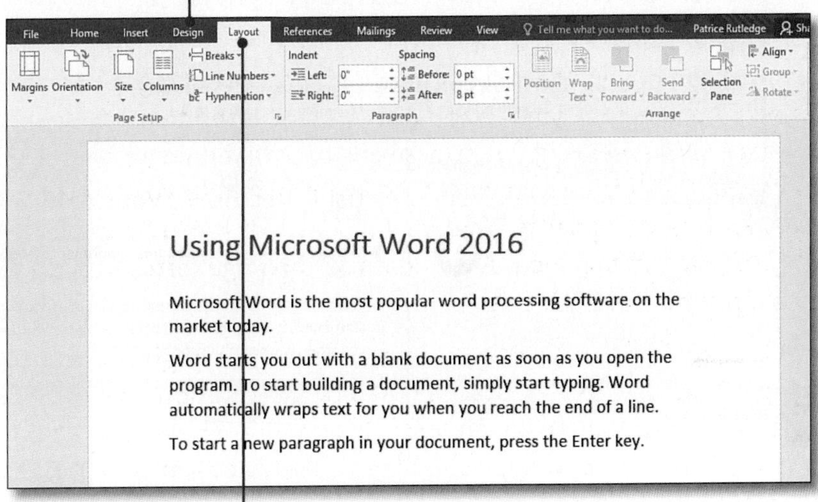


The Layout tab offers a variety of tools for controlling the layout of elements on a document page

# CHANGING PAGE MARGINS

Page margins control how text is positioned on a page as it relates to the edges of the page. By default, Word sets margins to 1" on all sides of the page: top, bottom, left, and right. You can change any or all margins as needed, or choose from several presets.

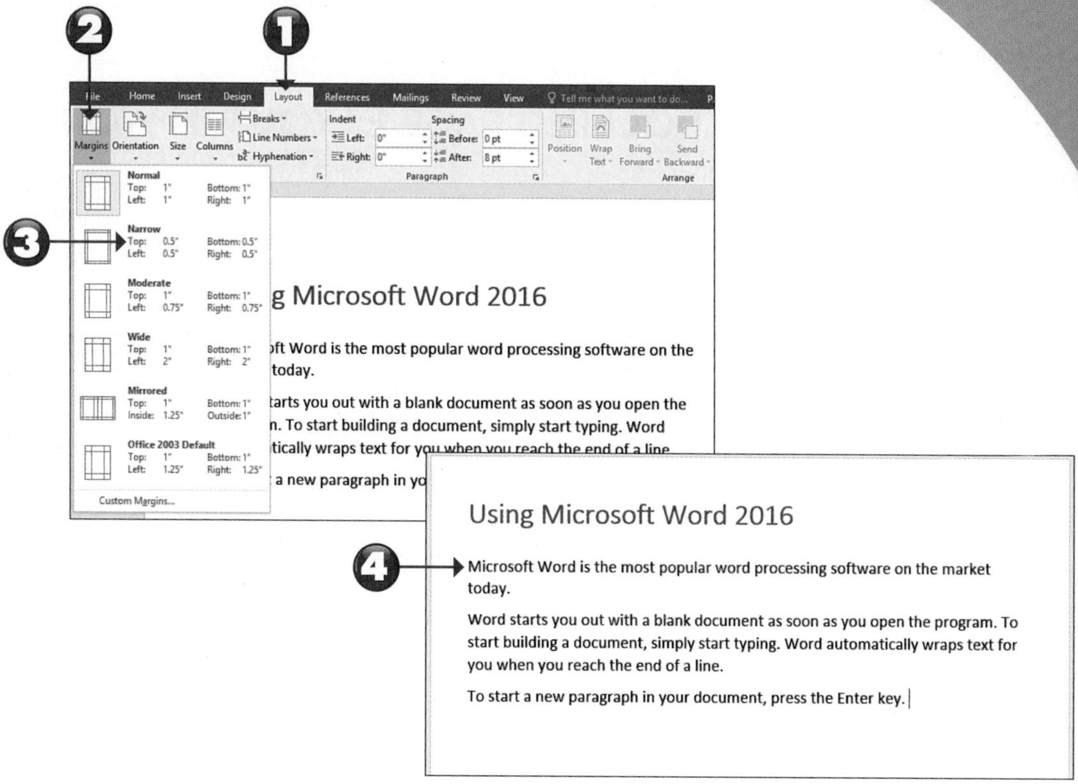

Start

1. Click the **Layout** tab on the Ribbon.
2. Click **Margins**.
3. Click the margins settings you want to apply.
4. Word applies the new margins to the document pages.

End

## TIP

**Display the Ruler** Need help gauging margins? Display Word's ruler. Click the **View** tab on the Ribbon, and then click the **Ruler** check box in the Show group of tools. This turns on both the horizontal and vertical rulers. You can drag the margin markers on the rulers to reset the margins around the document. You can uncheck the **Ruler** check box to turn the ruler display off again. ■

## TIP

**Custom Margins** To set your own custom margins, open the Page Setup dialog box. From the Margins drop-down menu on the Ribbon, click **Custom Margins**. Click the **Margins** tab where you can set all four margins per your requirements. Click **OK** to exit the dialog box and apply the changes. ■

# MODIFYING PAGE ORIENTATION

By default, Word applies a portrait page orientation, which means the page is taller than it is wide (8.5" x 11"). If your document needs to be wider than it is tall (11" x 8.5"), you can switch it to landscape orientation.

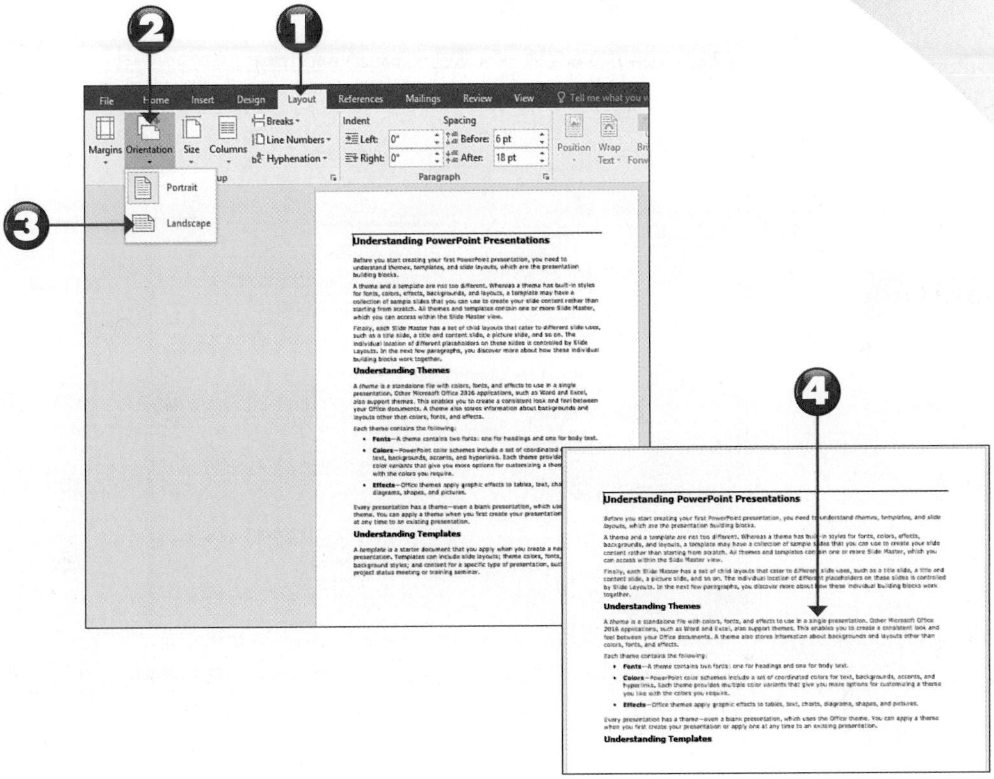

Start

1. Click the **Layout** tab.
2. Click the **Orientation** button.
3. Click an orientation.
4. Word applies the new orientation to the page.

End

## TIP

**Page Setup** You can also find the page orientation options in the Page Setup dialog box. To access the dialog box, click the **Page Setup** icon in the corner of the Page Setup tools on the Layout tab. The orientation controls are on the Margins tab in the dialog box. ■

## NOTE

**Recheck Your Page Elements!** When you switch page orientation, Word resets any existing text to fit the new document width and depth. This might require you to recheck the placement of page elements, such as lines and paragraphs of text or artwork. ■

# CHANGING PAGE SIZE

Depending on your printer's capabilities, you can create and print all kinds of document sizes in Word. For example, you can type up an address and return address in Word to print on an envelope, or you can print legal size pages, and so on.

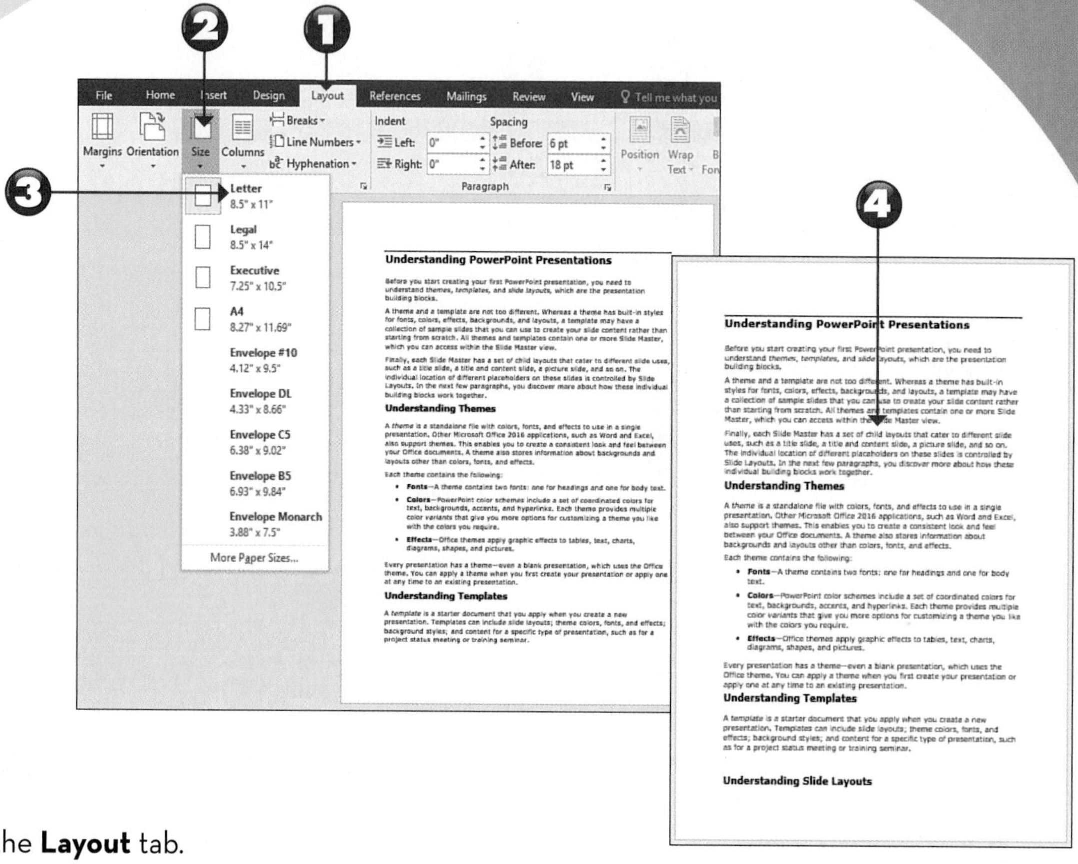

Start

1. Click the **Layout** tab.
2. Click the **Size** button.
3. Click a paper size.
4. Word applies the new size to the page.

End

## TIP

**Dialog Box Option** You can also change paper sizes through the Page Setup dialog box. At the bottom of the Size drop-down menu, click **More Paper Sizes**. The Page Setup dialog box opens to the Paper tab options, including options for selecting a paper source for your printer. ■

# CREATING COLUMNS

You can turn a page of text into columns, much like those found in a newspaper or magazine. With the column feature, text flows from column to column on a page.

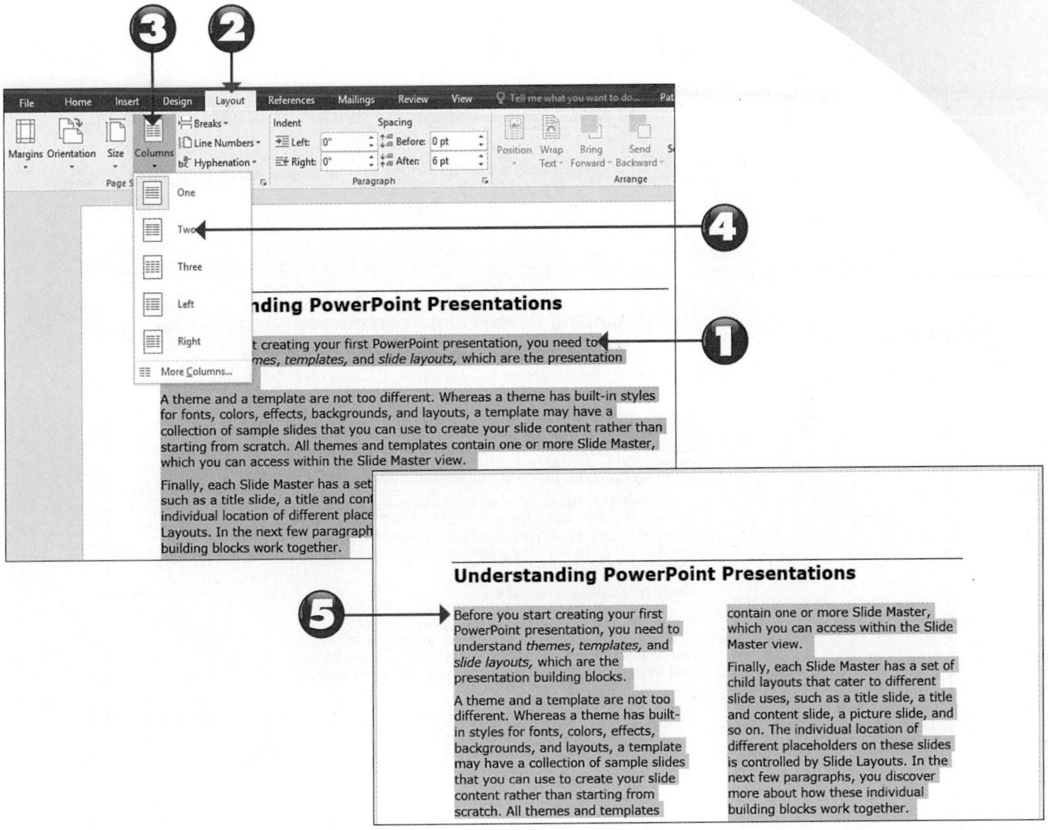

Start

1. Select the text you want to turn into columns.
2. Click the **Layout** tab.
3. Click the **Columns** button.
4. Click the number of columns you want to create.
5. Word applies the column format to the text.

End

## NOTE

**Customized Columns** You can use the Columns dialog box to create customized column widths and spacing, and even insert a dividing line to run between columns. To open the dialog box, click the **More Columns** command at the bottom of the Columns menu on the Layout tab. ■

# APPLYING PAGE BORDERS

You can add a border to a document using the Borders and Shading tools. You can specify a border type, such as a box or shadow effect, and choose from a variety of line styles, such as solid, dots, or dashes. In addition, you can specify a color and thickness for the border.

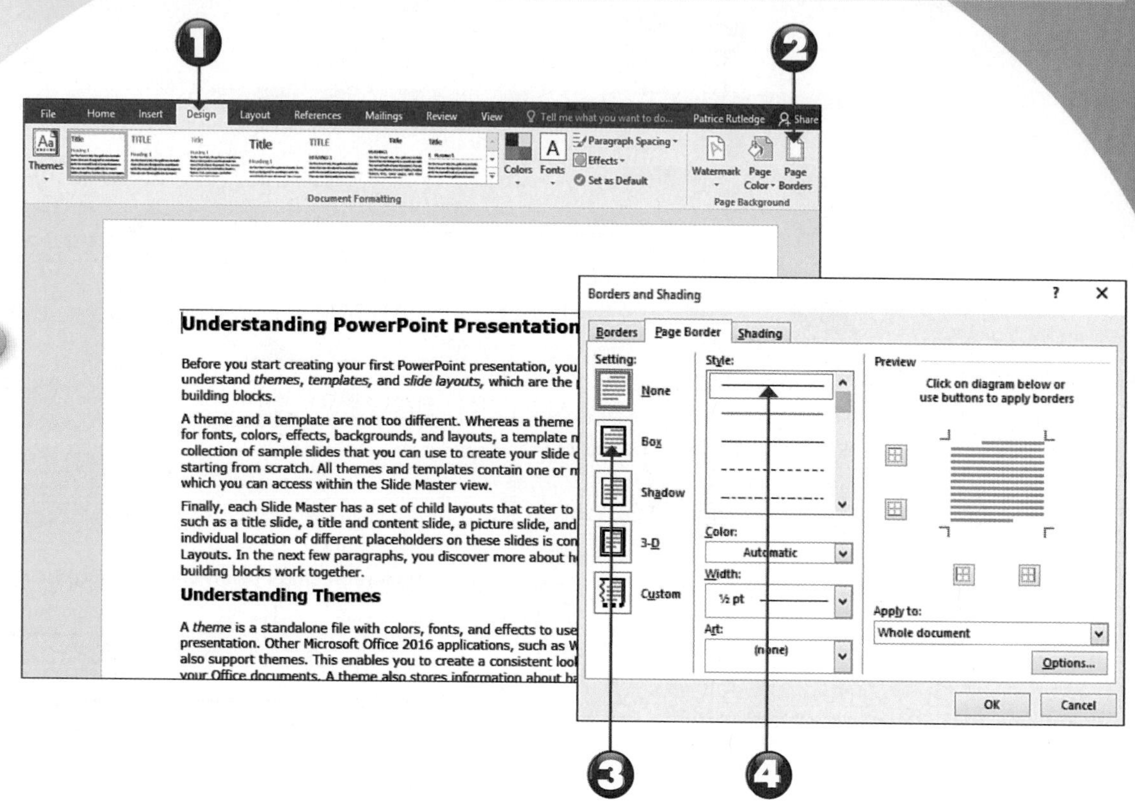


Start

1. Click the **Design** tab.
2. Click the **Page Borders** button.
3. Choose a border setting.
4. Click a style.

Continued

**TIP**

**Custom Borders** You can also create a custom page border that has only one or two sides. Using the edging buttons in the Preview area of the Borders and Shading dialog box, you can turn borders on or off for the top, bottom, right, and left edges of the document. ■

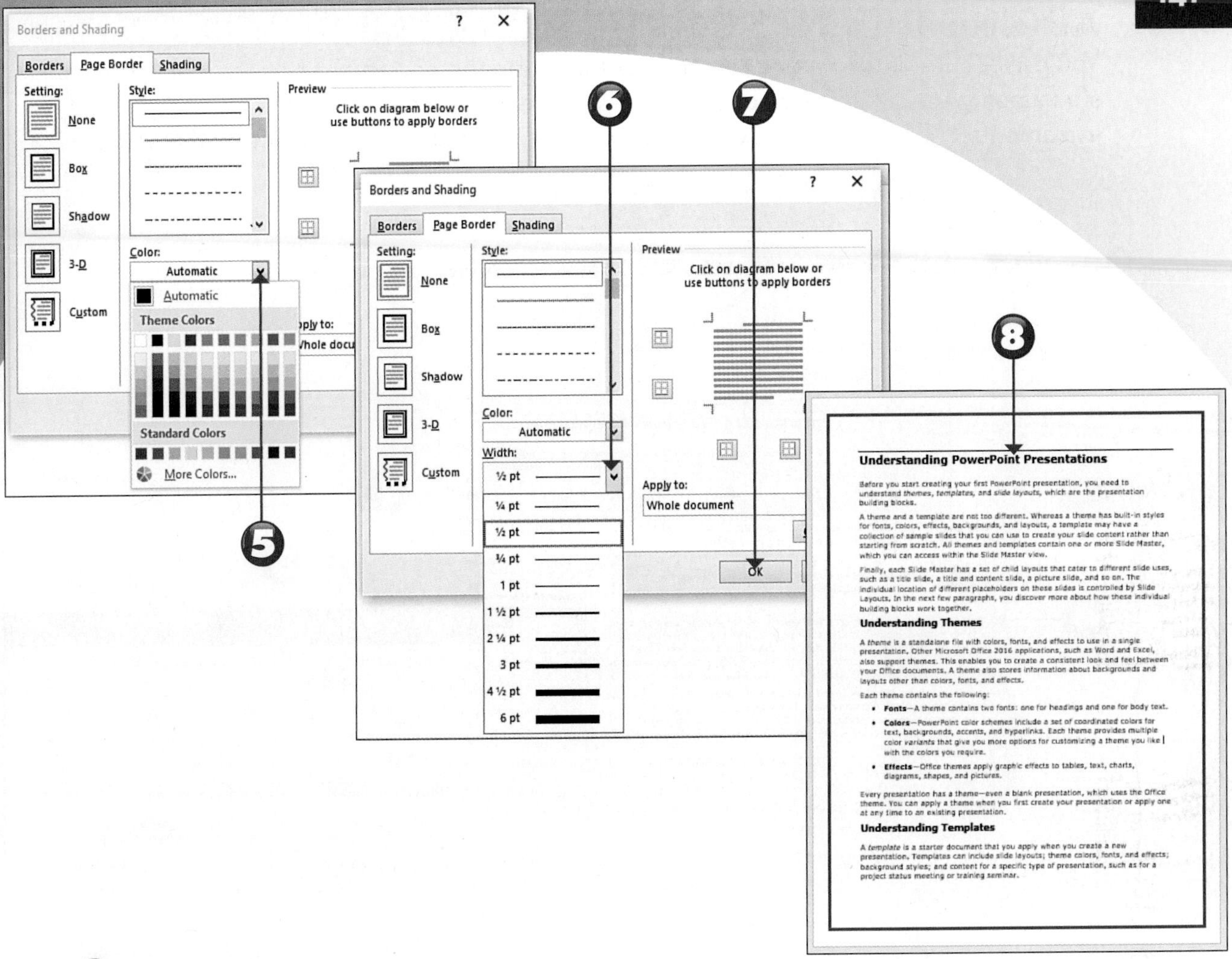

**5** Click the **Color** drop-down arrow to choose a color.

**6** Click the **Width** drop-down arrow to choose a line thickness.

**7** Click **OK**.

**8** Word applies the border to your page.

*End*

### TIP

**More Options** If you click the **Options** button in the Borders and Shading dialog box, you can open the Border and Shading Options dialog box and specify margin settings for your page border. By default, Word sets the page border at 1/2 points all around, but you can customize the setting to suit your own document. ■

# ADDING INDENTS ON THE HOME TAB

You can use indents to move text horizontally from the page margin to set it apart from surrounding text. The Increase Indent and Decrease Indent commands create left indents in increments.

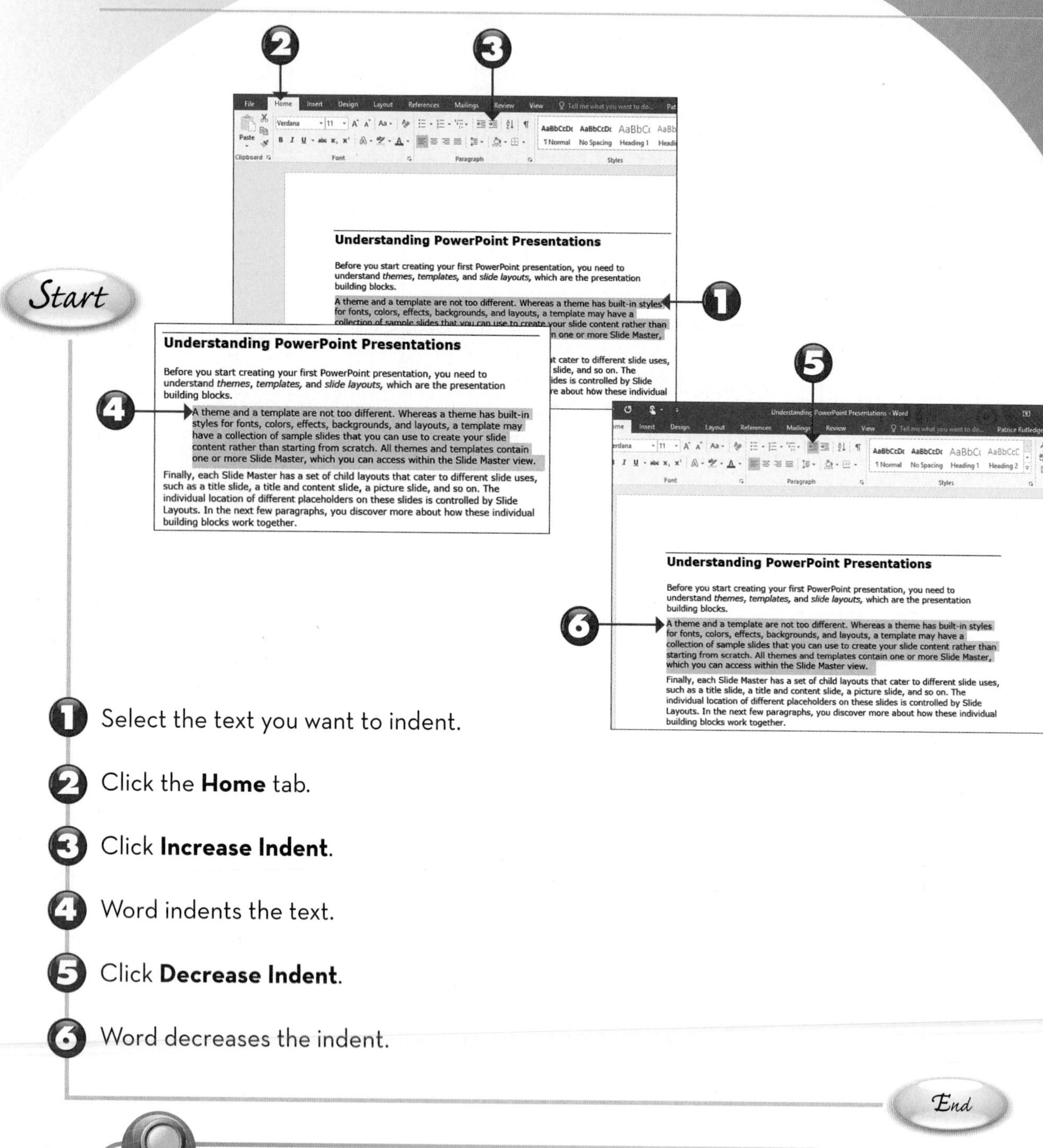


1. Select the text you want to indent.
2. Click the **Home** tab.
3. Click **Increase Indent**.
4. Word indents the text.
5. Click **Decrease Indent**.
6. Word decreases the indent.

End

### TIP

**Ruler Trick** You can also control indents using Word's ruler. Click the **View** tab, and click the **Ruler** check box to turn on the rulers. The top horizontal ruler has indent and margin markers you can drag on the ruler to set new indents and margins for a page. ■

# ADDING INDENTS ON THE LAYOUT TAB

You can set more precise indents using the Layout tab, including tools for indenting from the right side of a page.

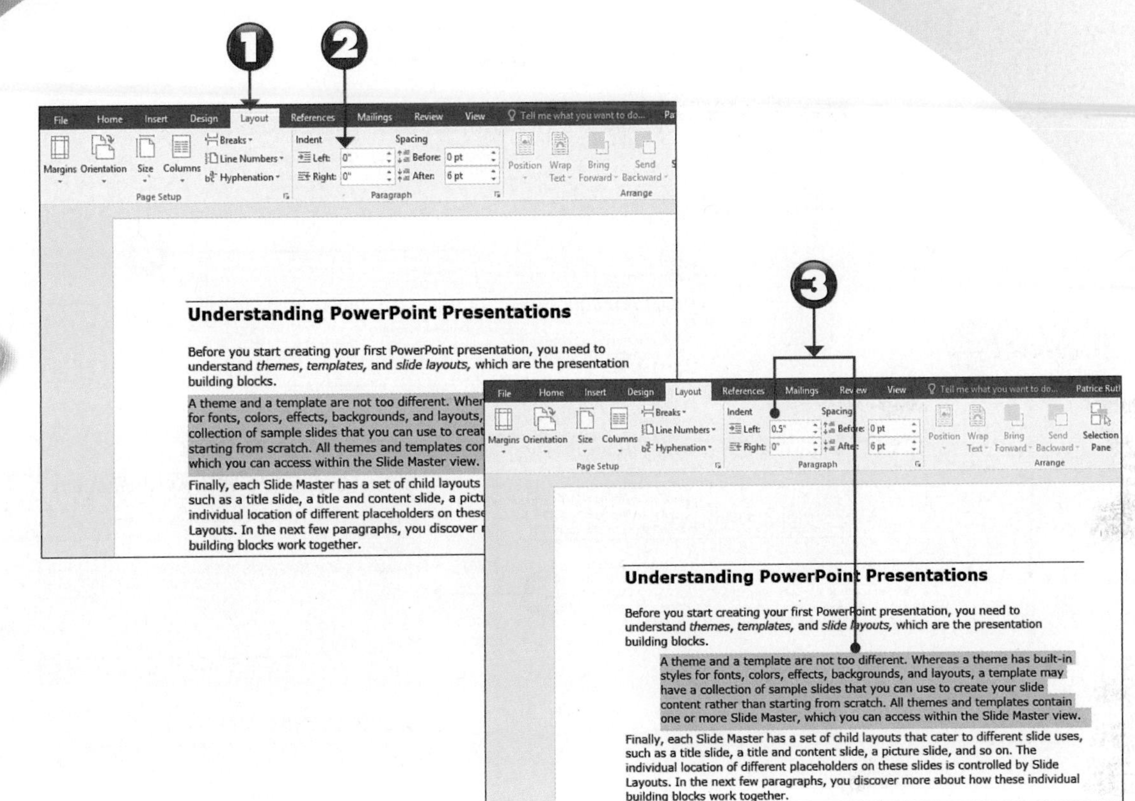

Start

1. Click the **Layout** tab.

2. Click the spinner arrows for the **Left** or **Right** indents to specify an indentation amount.

3. Word applies the indent to the selected text.

End

## NOTE

**Types of Indents** You can set several types of indents in Word, including left and right indents. You can also set a *first line* indent, which indents just the first line of text in a paragraph, or a *hanging indent*, which indents everything in the paragraph except the first line. You can find draggable markers for these indents on the horizontal ruler; click the **View** tab and click **Ruler** to display the ruler. You can also find special indents through the Paragraph dialog box; click the **Paragraph Settings** icon in the Paragraph group of tools on the Home tab. ■

# CHANGING LINE SPACING

Line spacing refers to the amount of space between lines of text and paragraphs. You can choose from several preset line spacing amounts. By default, multiple line spacing is assigned unless you specify something else.

Start

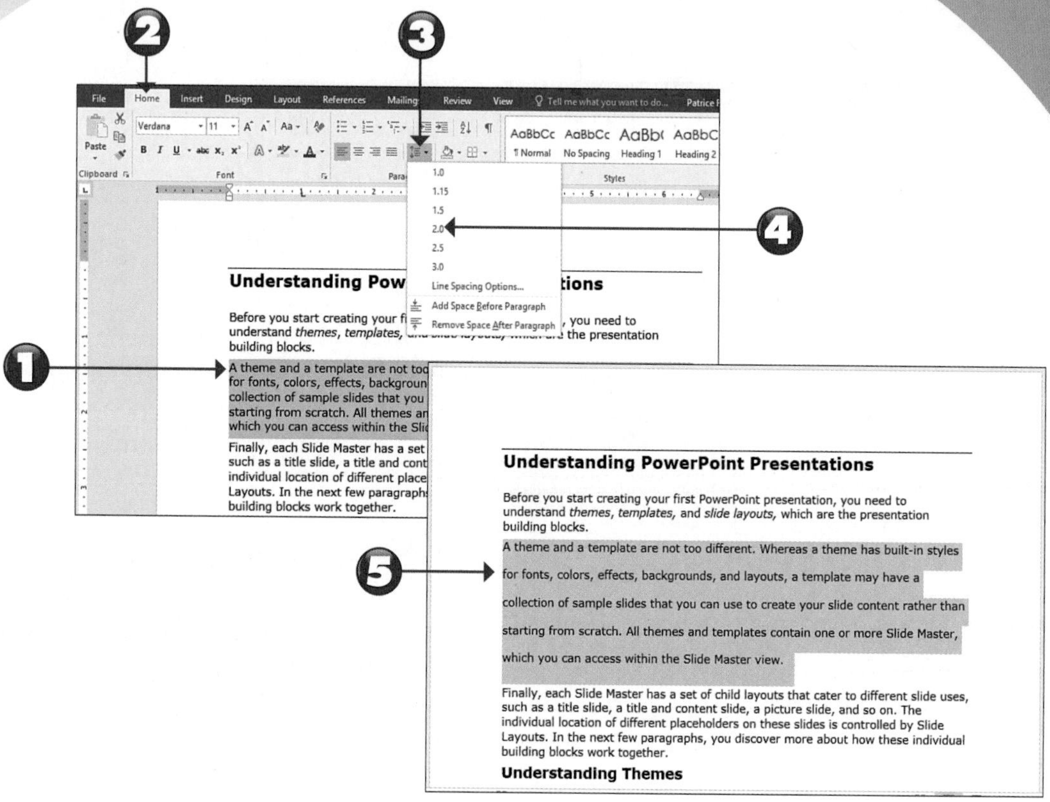

1. Select the text you want to modify.

2. Click the **Home** tab.

3. Click line and paragraph spacing.

4. Click the spacing you want to apply.

5. Word applies the spacing to the text.

End

## TIP

**Character Spacing** You can also control spacing between characters of text. Sometimes called *tracking*, character spacing can help you place typed characters closer together or farther apart. You can find character spacing controls in the Font dialog box. From the Home tab, click the **Font** icon in the corner of the Font group of tools. This opens the Font dialog box. Click the **Advanced** tab to find character spacing controls. ■

# CONTROLLING PARAGRAPH SPACING

Word adds extra space below every paragraph by default. You can control the spacing to suit your own document needs. You can specify how much space to include before and after paragraphs.

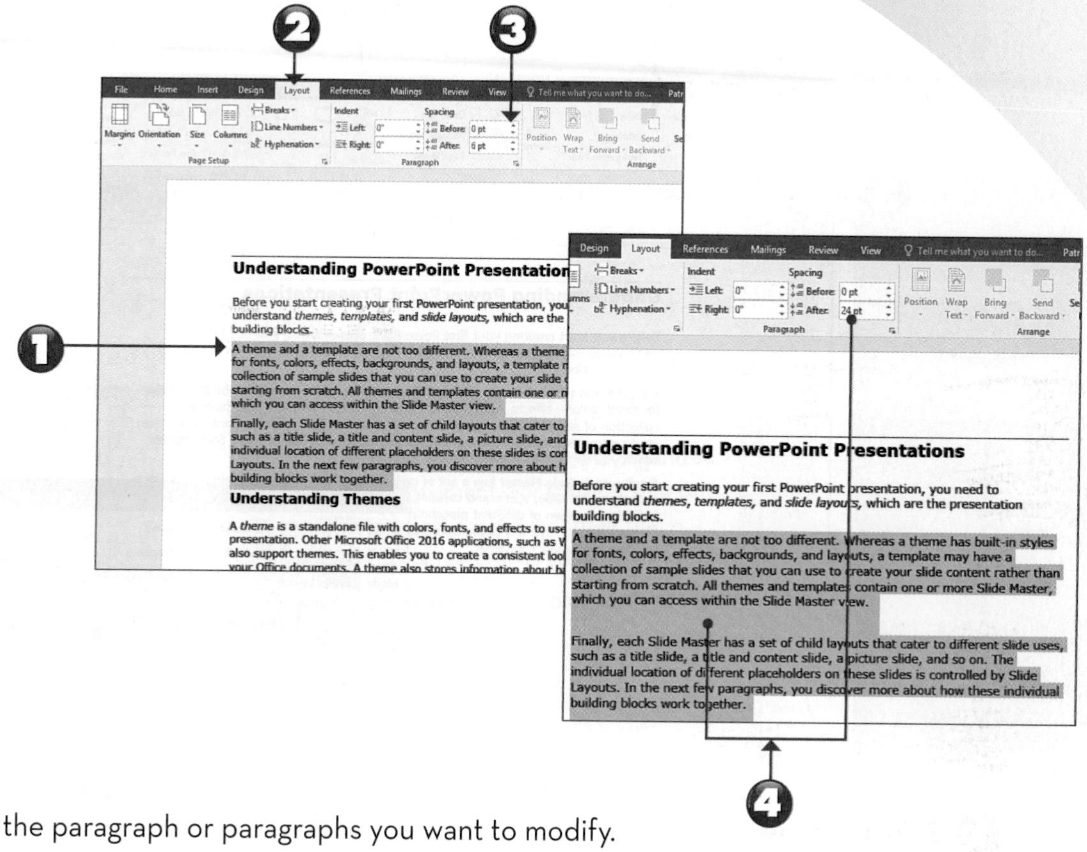

1. Select the paragraph or paragraphs you want to modify.
2. Click the **Layout** tab.
3. Click the **Spacing** spinner arrows to select the measurement you want to assign; click **Before** to add space before a paragraph, or click **After** to add space after a paragraph.
4. Word applies the spacing to the text.

## NOTE

**More Spacing** Word automatically adds extra spacing between lines using a default setting called Multiple Line Spacing. The measurement for this setting is 1.08; however, you might prefer single line (1.0) spacing instead. You can click the **Home** tab and click **Line and Paragraph Spacing** to change the line spacing. ■

## SETT

You can
Word's t
pressing

Start

1. Click t
2. Click t
3. Click t
differe
4. Click t

Tabs
click
Parag
stops



# APPLYING A THEME

Another way to add formatting to an entire document is to apply a theme. Themes include a set of coordinating colors, fonts, and effects you can apply to make sure your documents present a professional appearance. You can choose from a variety of preset themes or browse for more themes online.

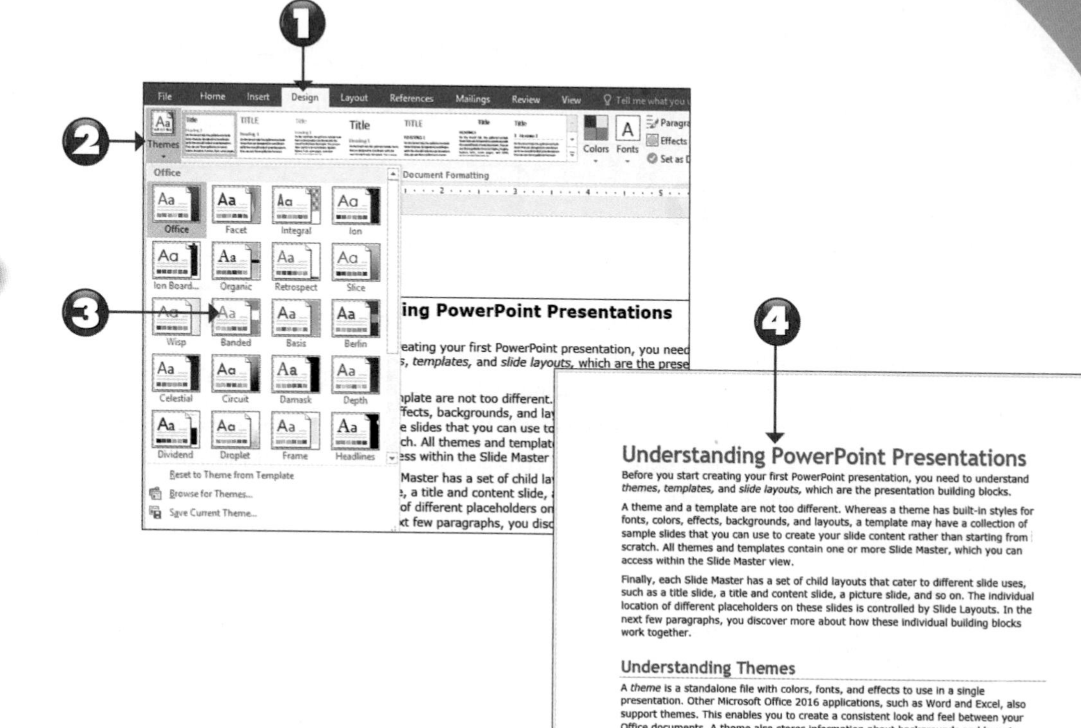


Start

1. Click the **Design** tab.
2. Click **Themes**.
3. Click the theme you want to apply.
4. Word applies the new theme to the document.

Continued

## TIP

**More Themes** You can browse your computer or network for more themes. Click the **Themes** button, and click **Browse for Themes**. ■

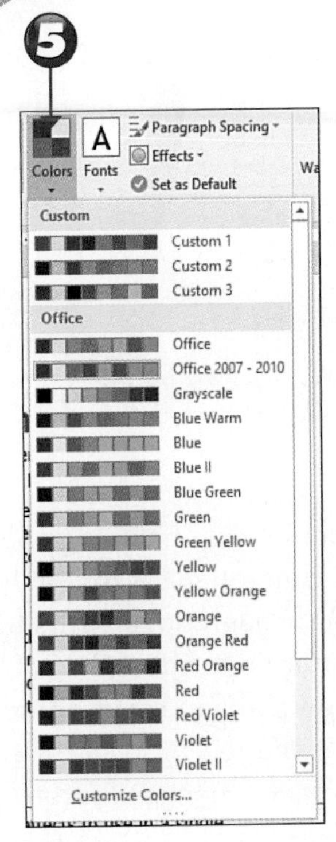


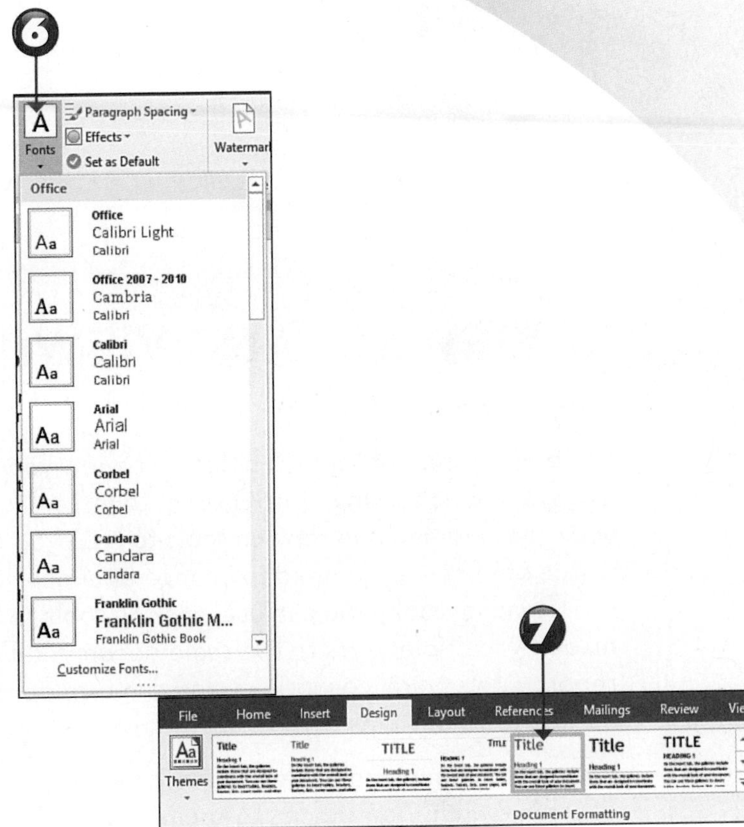


**5** Click the **Colors** drop-down arrow to change the color scheme associated with the theme.

**6** Click the **Fonts** drop-down arrow to change the fonts associated with the theme.

**7** To change the document formatting, make a selection from the palette, or click the **More** button to view all the choices and choose a style.

*End*

## NOTE

**What's in a Theme?** When you assign a theme, Word looks for and replaces the formats of each of the styles to the document elements. A theme includes fonts for any headings and body text assigned, including color, type style, and spacing. Themes also include 3D effects, shadows, and lighting effects. ■

## TIP

**Default Theme** Any blank documents you start in Word already have a default theme assigned—the Office theme. To return to this default, select **Office** from the Themes palette that appears when you click the Themes button. ■

# REVIEWING AND VIEWING WORD DOCUMENTS

Word offers a lot of tools to help you review your documents, including spelling and grammar checking, AutoCorrect to instantly fix common mistakes while you type, and find and replace tools to help you look through documents for words or phrases you need to change or check. In addition to these basic proofreading tools, you can use tracking tools to help you keep review changes made by multiple users to the same document. For example, if you share a report with several co-workers, you can turn on the Track Changes feature and easily see who makes what changes and compare them all.

Word also offers numerous ways to view your documents using View modes. You can switch View modes to see how your document looks when printed or in a web browser, or you can use the Read mode to read through your document just like a book. You can also zoom in or out of your document to get a better look at text or page elements and layout.

## REVIEWING TOOLS IN WORD

Use the Reviewing Pane to check revisions to a shared document.

The Review tab houses all kinds of tools and features for editing a document with other reviewers.

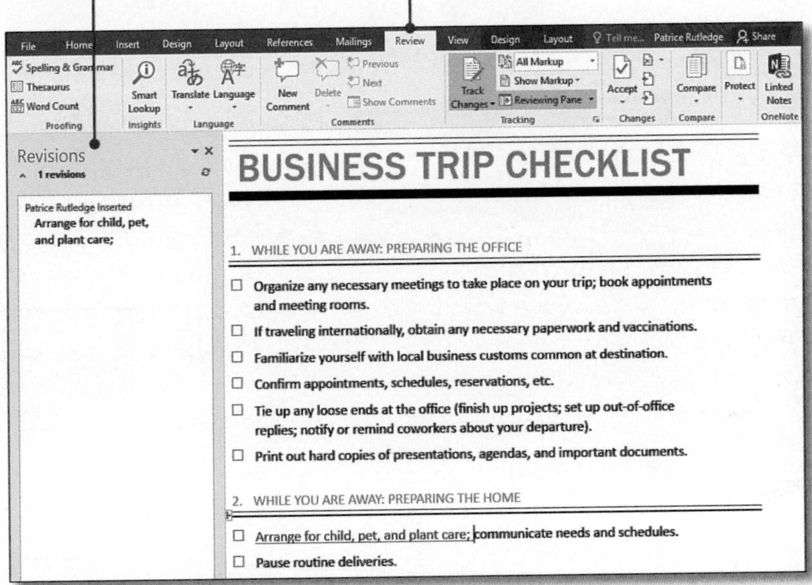

# TRACKING CHANGES WITH DOCUMENT REVIEWERS

If you share your documents with other Word users in an editorial environment, you can turn on Word's Track Changes feature and keep track of who makes what changes to the text.

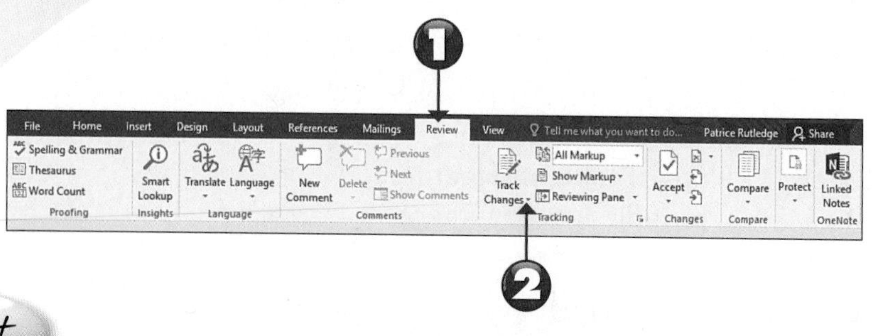


Start

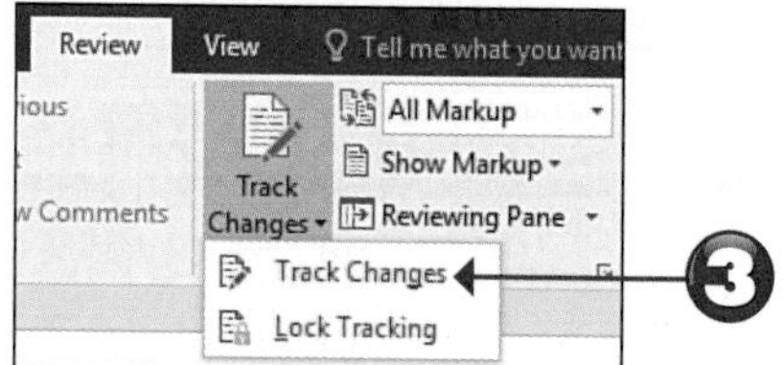

1. Click the **Review** tab.
2. Click the **Track Changes** arrow.
3. Click **Track Changes** to turn on the feature.
4. The button turns dark gray when Track Changes is on.

Continued

**TIP**

**Lock It** To lock the tracking feature on, select the **Lock Tracking** option from the drop-down menu. The Lock Tracking dialog box opens, and you must assign a password. Type a password, confirm the password, and then click **OK**.

**TIP**

**Review Changes** When everyone finishes editing a document, you can review the changes. See the task "Accepting or Rejecting Changes," later in this chapter, to learn how.

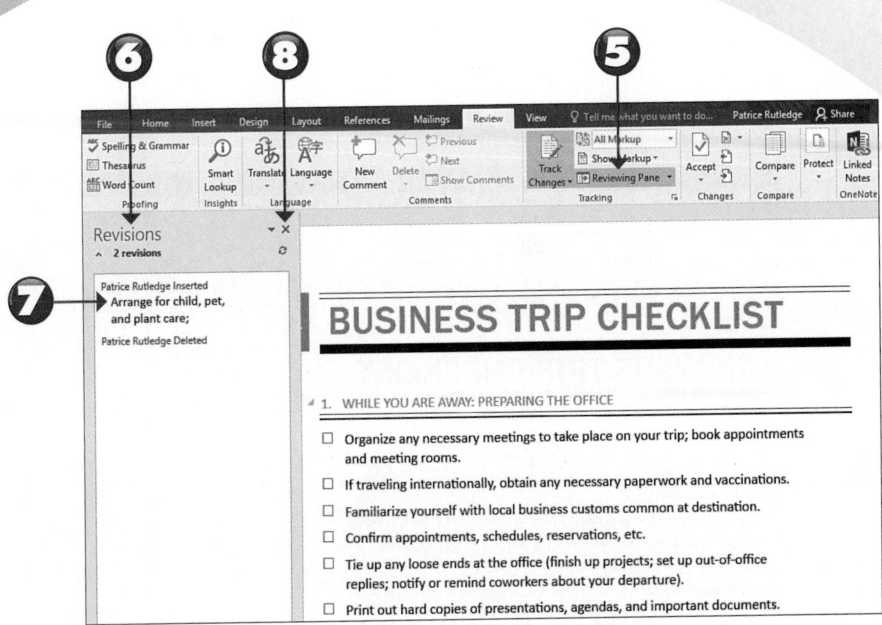


5. Click **Reviewing Pane**.

6. Any revisions made to the document appear in this pane, along with the name of the person who made the changes.

7. Click an item in the list to quickly move to its location in the document.

8. To close the pane, click the **Close** button (x).

*End*

## NOTE

**Reviewing Pane** Be aware that although the button on the Review tab says Reviewing Pane, the actual pane says Revisions in its title.

## TIP

**Change the Pane** You can click the down arrow next to the Reviewing Pane button on the Review tab and choose whether you want to display the pane on the left side or at the bottom of the document.

# ADDING COMMENTS

Comments enable you to share feedback and commentary on documents with other people. They appear in the markup area in the right margin of a document or on the Reviewing Pane.

Start

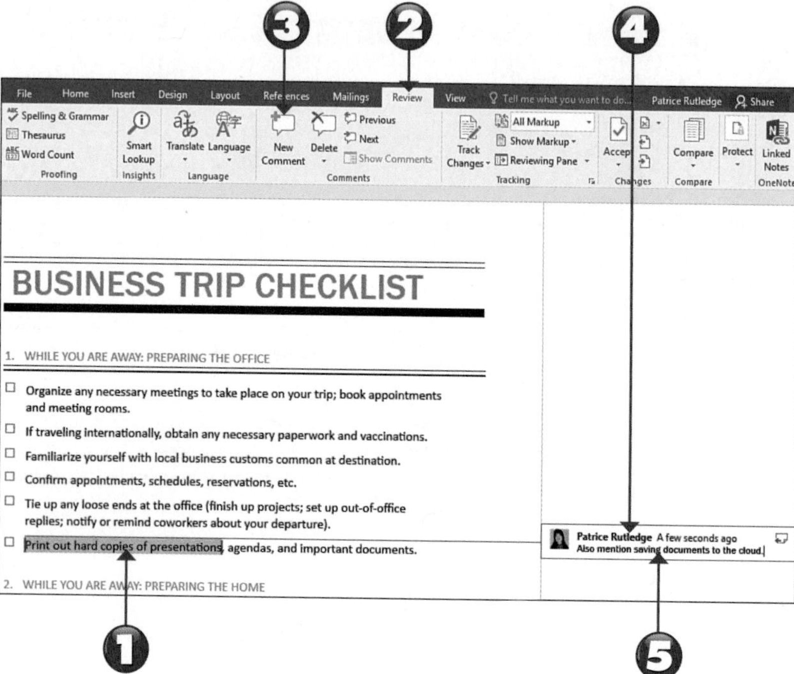


1. Click where you want to insert a comment, or select the text relating to the comment.
2. Click the **Review** tab.
3. Click **New Comment**.
4. Word displays a comment box in the markup area in the right margin.
5. Type your comment text.

Continued

**TIP**

**View Comments on the Reviewing Pane** Optionally, you can also view comments on the Revisions pane. To open this pane, click the **Reviewing Pane** button on the Review tab.

**TIP**

**Edit It** To edit or add to a comment, click it and type your changes. You can edit in a comment balloon or on the Reviewing Pane.

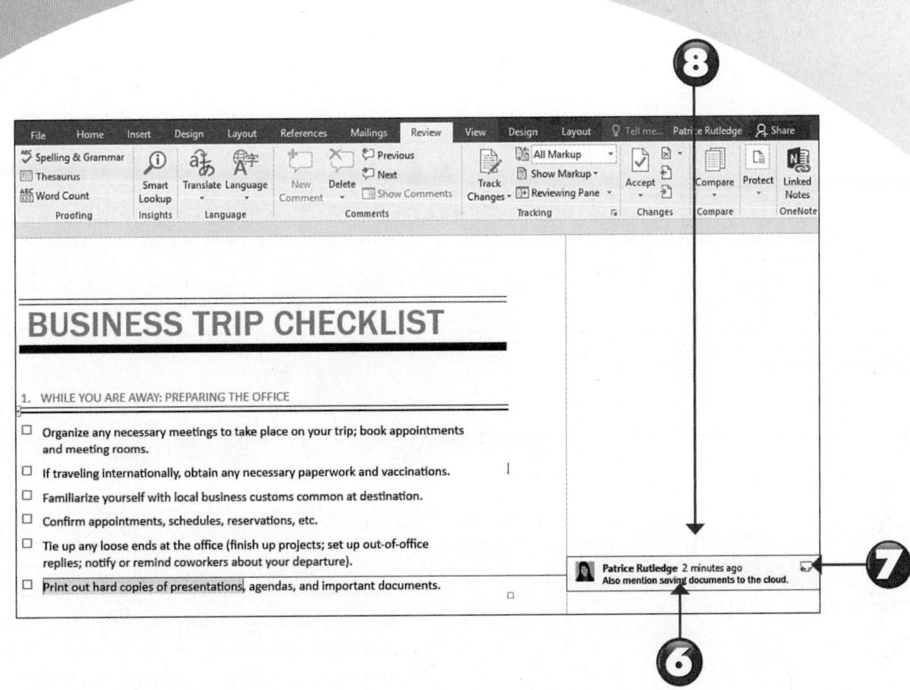


6 When you finish entering a comment, Word displays it as a balloon icon in the right margin.

7 Click to add a reply to a comment.

8 Click in the document (not in the markup area) to close it.

End

**TIP**

**Remove It** To delete a comment, click it and click the **Delete Comment** button on the Review tab. To delete all comments, click the down arrow and select **Delete All Comments in Document**.

# VIEWING DOCUMENT MARKUP

If you are reviewing a document and keeping track of changes you and other users make, you can change the way in which you view those changes—called *markup*. You can choose to view all the changes, just the simple changes, no markup at all, or the original document.

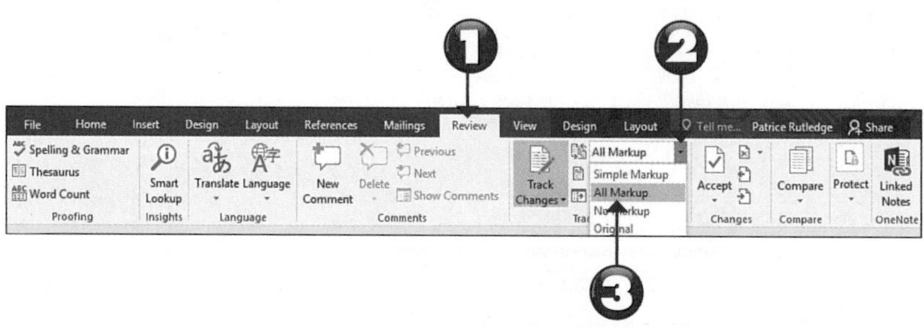


Start

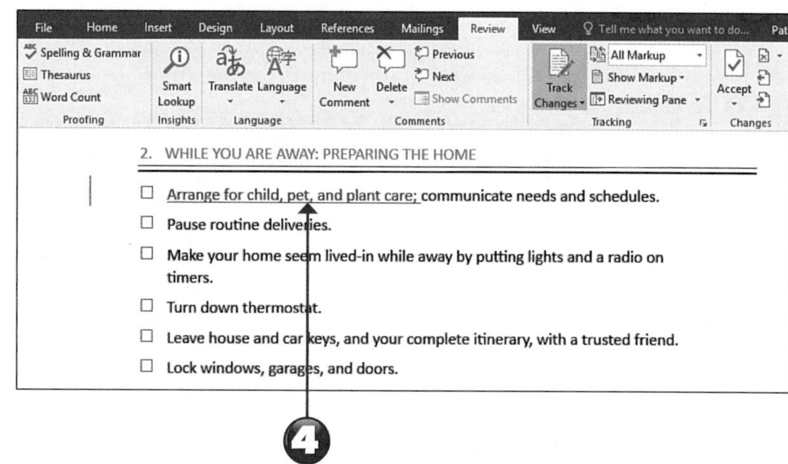


1. Click the **Review** tab.
2. Click the **Markup** drop-down arrow.
3. Click a markup setting.
4. Word applies the new view; in this example, all the document markup displays.

End

## TIP

**Choose Your Markup** You can use the **Show Markup** drop-down menu on the Review tab to specify exactly which types of markup changes to view in a document, including comments, insertions and deletions, and formatting changes. ■

## TIP

**Use the Reviewing Pane** It helps to have the Reviewing pane open as you check changes; you can quickly see details about who made the change or added comments. Click the **Reviewing Pane** button on the Review tab to display the pane. ■

# ACCEPTING OR REJECTING CHANGES

After using Word's Track Changes feature to record everyone's changes to a document, you can go through and decide which edits to keep or disregard.

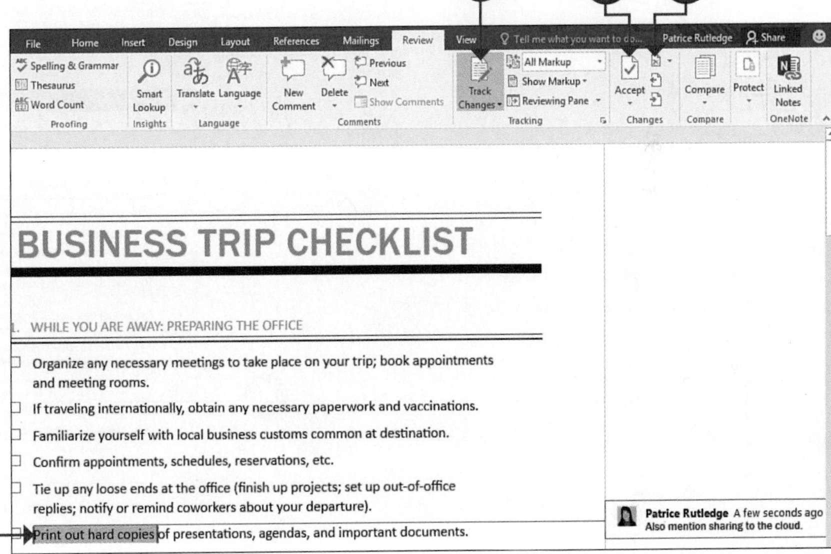


1. With the edited document displayed, click the **Review** tab.
2. Click **Next Change**.
3. Word highlights the first edit.
4. Click **Accept** to okay the change and move to the next edit.
5. Click **Reject and Move to Next** to forgo the change and move to the next edit.
6. When you complete the review, you can turn off the tracking feature; click **Track Changes**.

End

**TIP**

**More Options** Click the **Accept** button's drop-down arrow to view a menu of more options, such as accepting all the changes in the document.

**TIP**

**Comparing Documents** If reviewers have made changes to two of the same file, click the **Review** tab and click **Compare**. Then click **Compare** to compare the two documents, or click **Combine** to combine the two documents into one.

# EXPLORING DOCUMENT VIEWS

Word offers several view modes you can use to view your document. The default view, Print Layout, shows you how your document will look when printed. You can switch to Web Layout view to see how your document looks in a web browser, or Read Mode to view your document much like a book, with side-by-side pages.

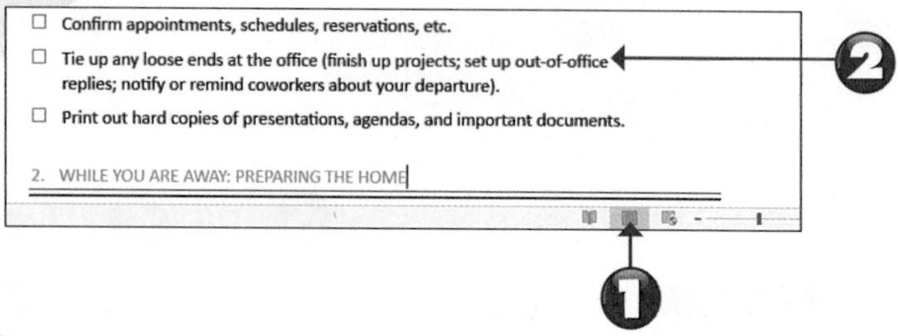

*Start*

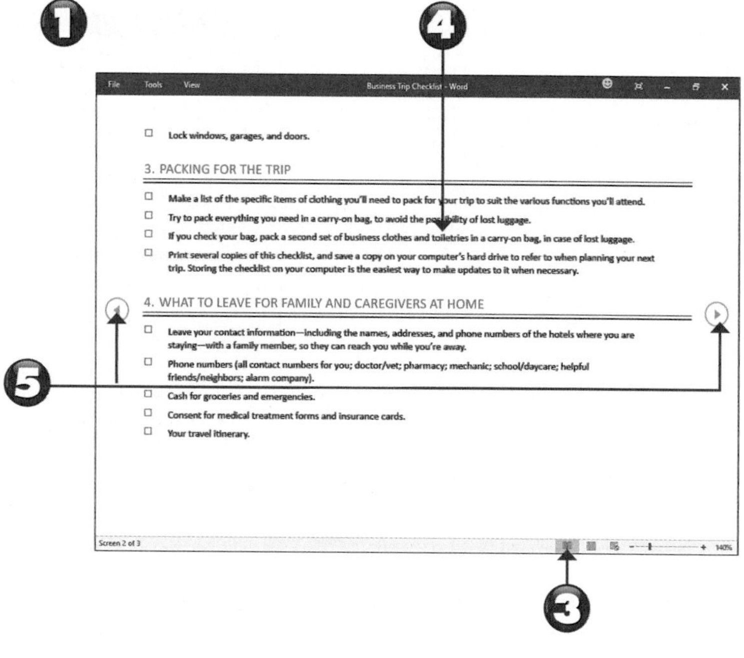

1. Click the **Print Layout** button.
2. Word displays the document in Print Layout view mode (the default view).
3. Click the **Read Mode** button.
4. Word displays the document in Read mode.
5. Click the navigation arrows to move back and forth between pages.

*Continued*

## TIP

**Viewing Other Elements** You can find other ways to view your document, including viewing elements such as the ruler or gridlines, through the View tab.

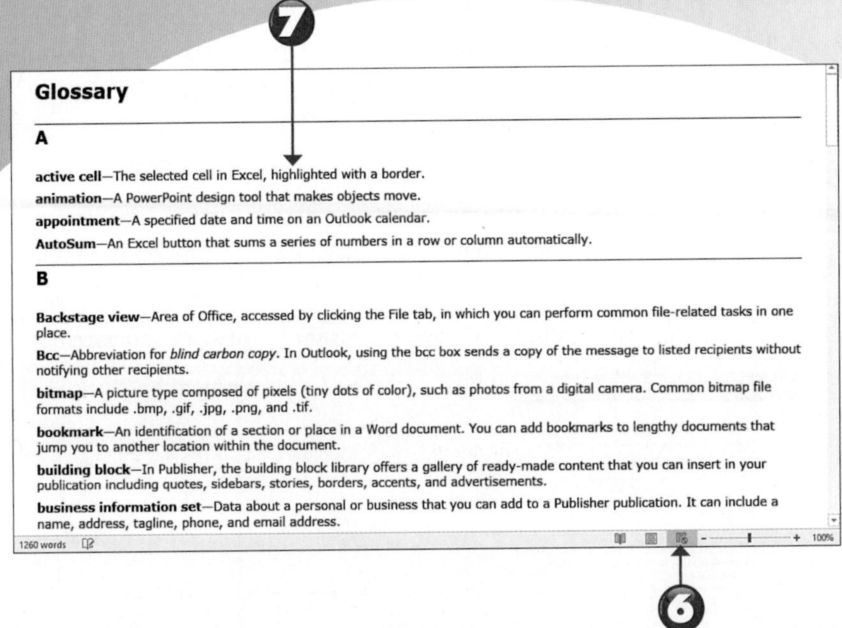


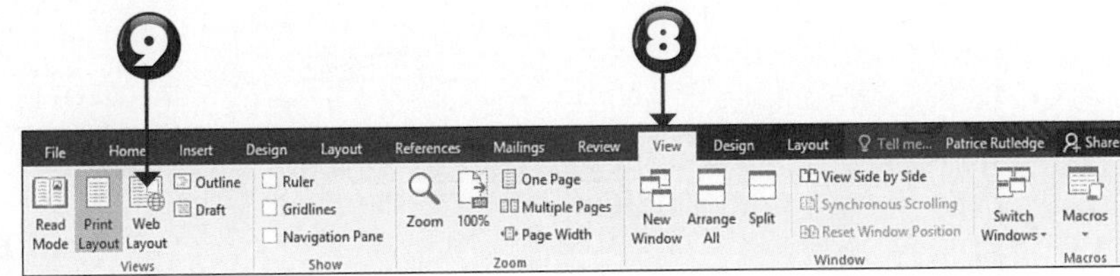


6. Click the **Web Layout** button.

7. Word displays the document in Web Layout view mode.

8. You can also change view modes through the Ribbon's View tab; click the **View** tab.

9. Click a view mode.

End

**TIP**

**More Views** You can also view your document in Draft mode, which hides any graphics elements, so you can focus on just the text. If your document is composed of headings and document levels, you can use Outline mode to see your document in an outline format. Both options are available as buttons on the View tab. See Word's Help feature to learn more about using Draft and Outline modes.

# ZOOMING IN AND OUT OF DOCUMENTS

You can use the Zoom controls to zoom in and out of a document. Zooming in increases the magnification level, enabling you to enlarge the document for a closer look. Zooming out decreases the magnification level, enabling you to see more of the page.

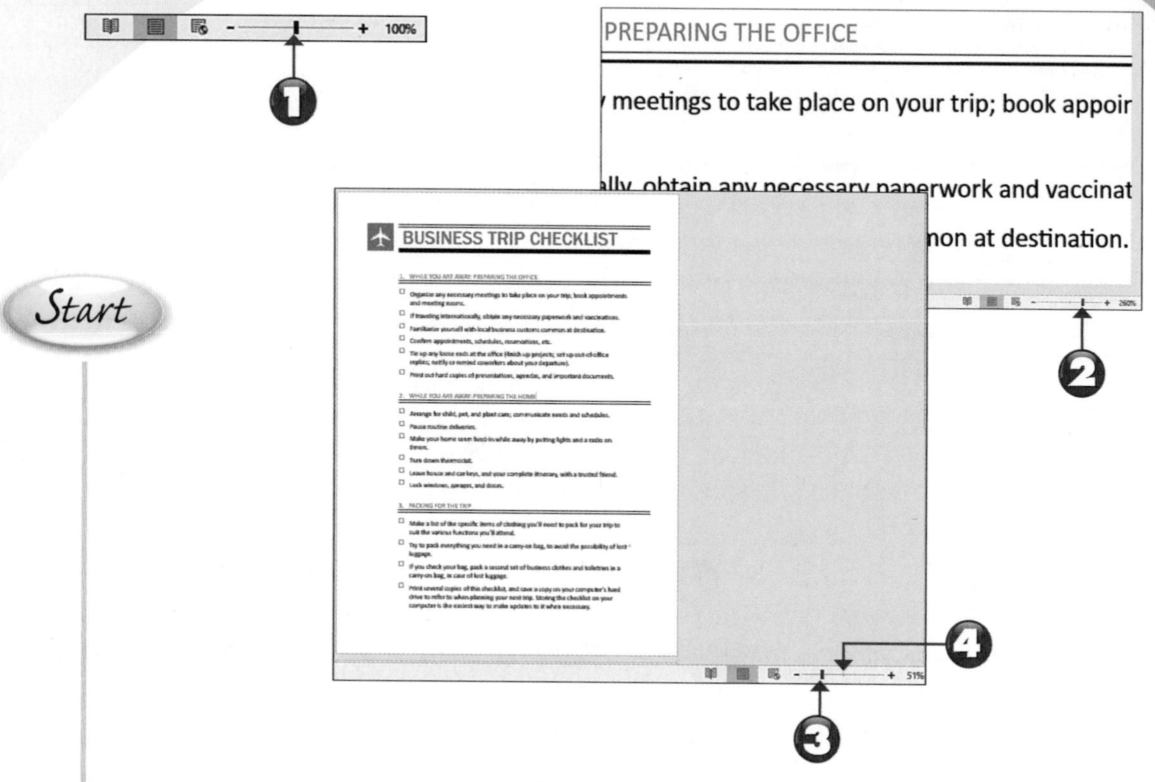


1. To quickly zoom in or out, drag the **Zoom** slider on the Zoom bar.
2. Drag the **Zoom** slider right to zoom in.
3. Drag the **Zoom** slider left to zoom out.
4. Drag the slider to the middle to return to 100%.

*Continued*

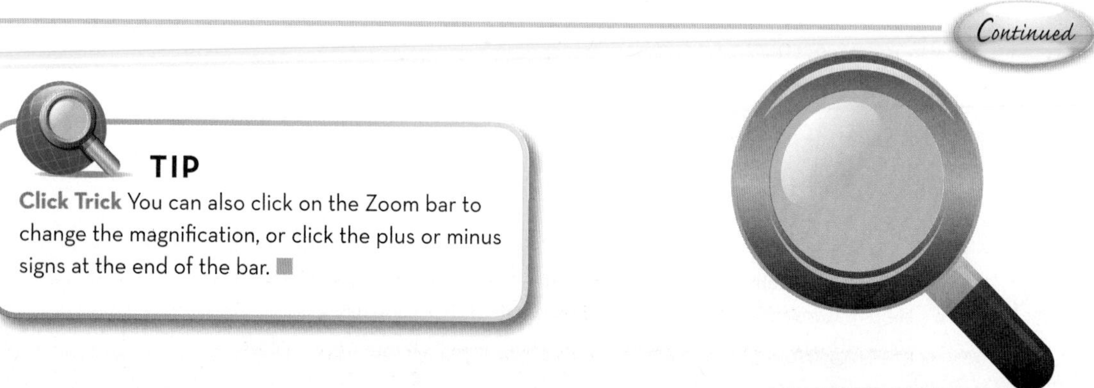

**TIP**

**Click Trick** You can also click on the Zoom bar to change the magnification, or click the plus or minus signs at the end of the bar.

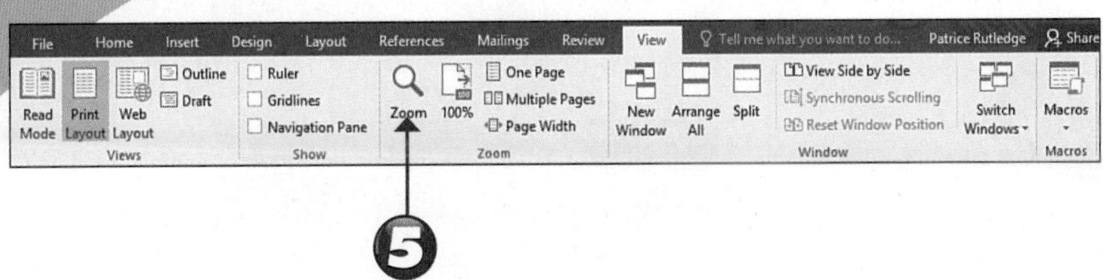


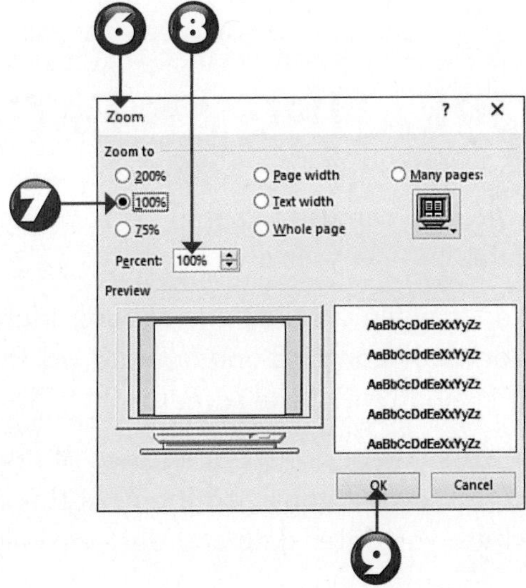


5. To set a specific zoom percentage, click the **Zoom** button on the View tab.
6. Word opens the Zoom dialog box.
7. Choose a zoom setting.
8. Type a percentage number here to set a specific zoom amount.
9. Click **OK** and Word applies the zoom.

*End*

**NOTE**

**More Zoom Tools** The View tab includes buttons for zooming quickly to 100% or choosing to display multiple pages, full page width, or a single page.

# CREATING AN EXCEL WORKBOOK

Excel is the full-featured spreadsheet program that's part of Microsoft Office 2016. You can use Excel to perform calculations, create charts, and analyze data.

An Excel file is called a *workbook*, identified with the extension .xlsx. Each workbook contains one or more *worksheets*, each identified with a unique tab at the bottom of the screen.

A worksheet consists of a series of rows and columns; up to 256 columns and 16,384 rows, if you need them. At the intersection of a column and row is a cell, where you enter data and perform calculations.

# GETTING STARTED WITH EXCEL

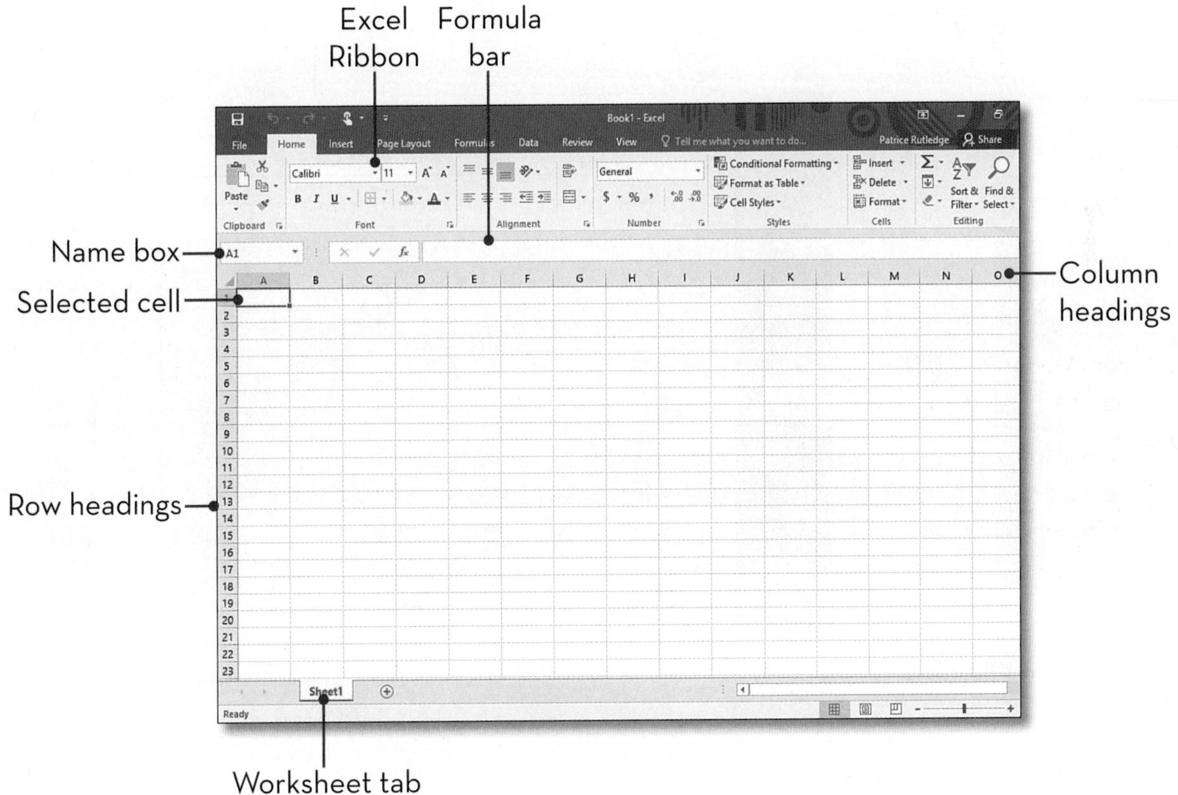

# CREATING A WORKBOOK FROM A TEMPLATE

Creating an Excel workbook from a template helps you save time because you can use a ready-made spreadsheet customized to your needs.

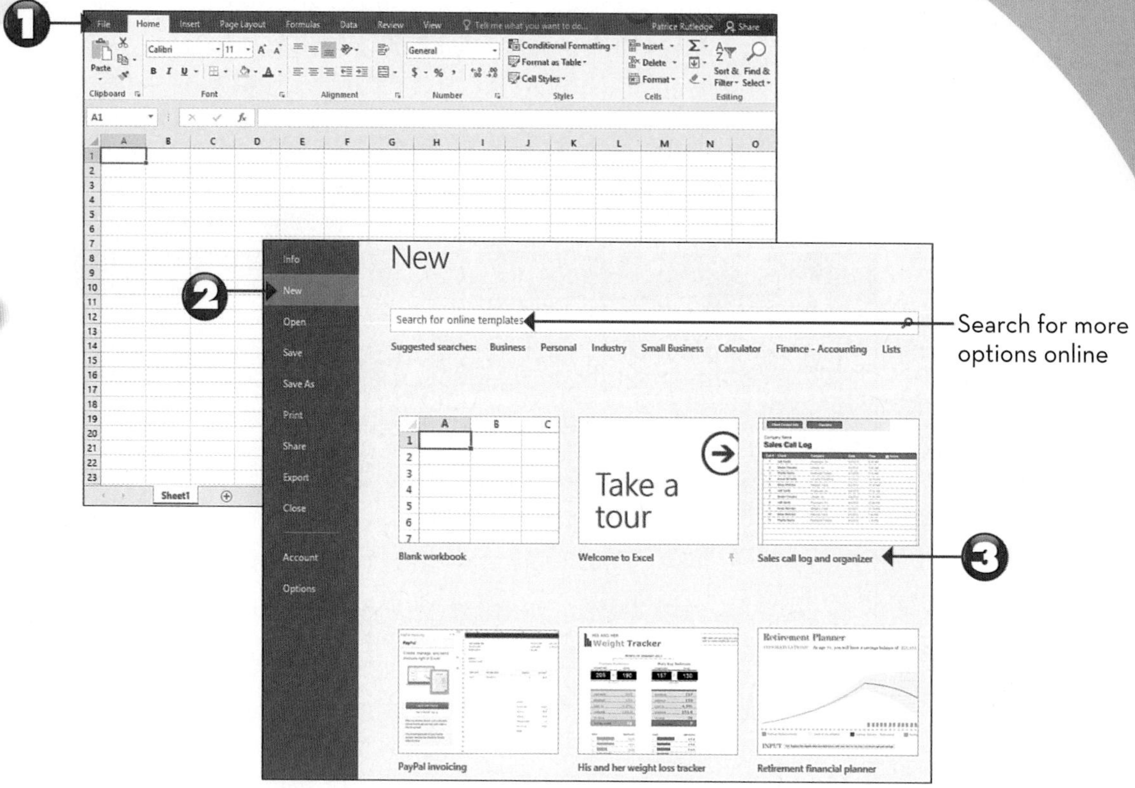

Start

Search for more options online

1. Click the **File** tab.
2. Click **New**.
3. In the New window, select one of the thumbnail templates.

Continued

## TIP

**Search for More Templates Online** Microsoft offers a vast collection of templates on its website. If one of the default templates doesn't suit your needs, enter a description of the type of template you want in the **Search for online templates** box, and click the **Start Searching** button (small magnifying glass).

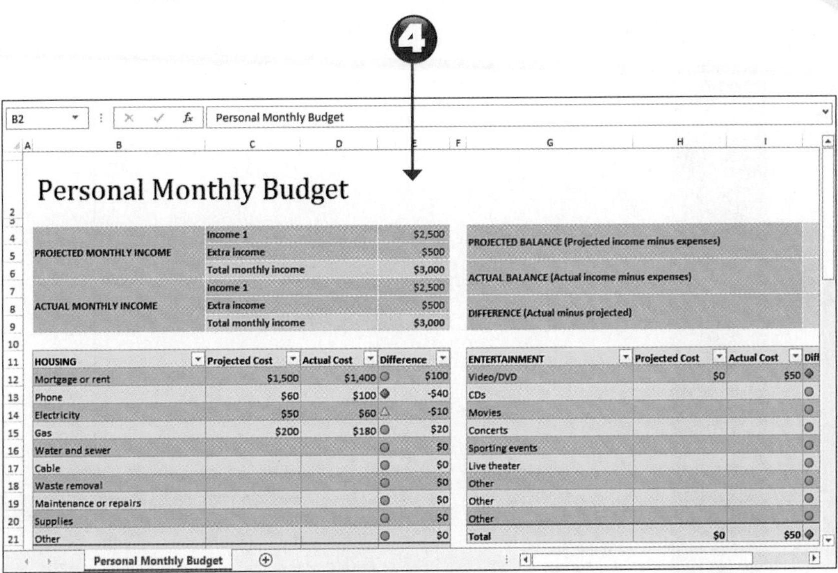


**4** Excel opens a new workbook based on the template you select.

End

## TIP

**Save Your Workbook** Remember to save your new workbook by clicking the **Save** button on the Quick Access toolbar.

## NOTE

**Template Examples** Some sample Excel templates include billing statements, expense reports, sales reports, personal budgets, time cards, and more. It's very likely that a template exists for the exact type of workbook you want to create.

# CREATING A BLANK WORKBOOK

If you need just a basic spreadsheet, you can create a blank workbook.

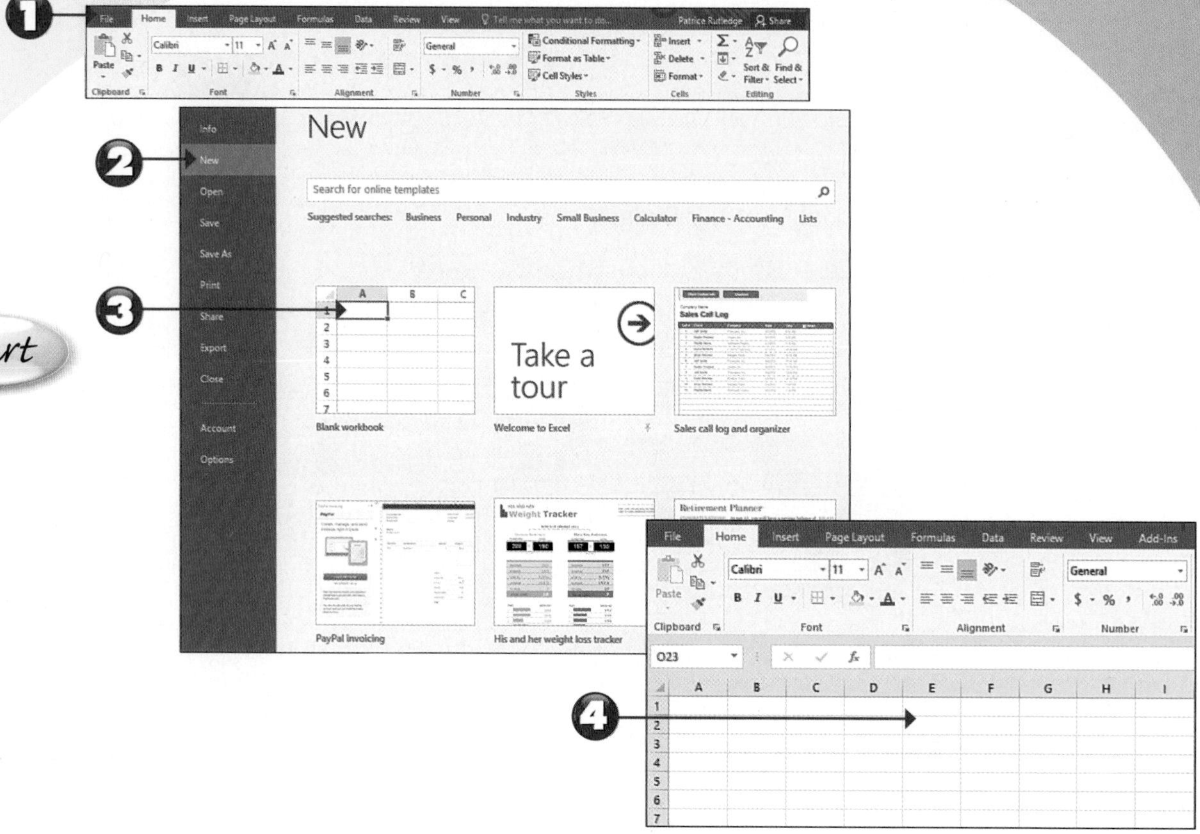

Start

1. Click the **File** tab.
2. Click **New**.
3. Click **Blank workbook**.
4. Excel opens a new workbook without data or formatting.

End

## TIP

**Plan Your Workbook Content** Before getting started adding data to your workbook, take a minute to think about its content and organization. What columns and rows do you need? Is one worksheet sufficient or do you need multiple worksheets? What formatting and coloring do you want to apply?

# NAVIGATING THE WORKSHEET SCREEN

You can use your mouse or keyboard to quickly navigate in an Excel worksheet.

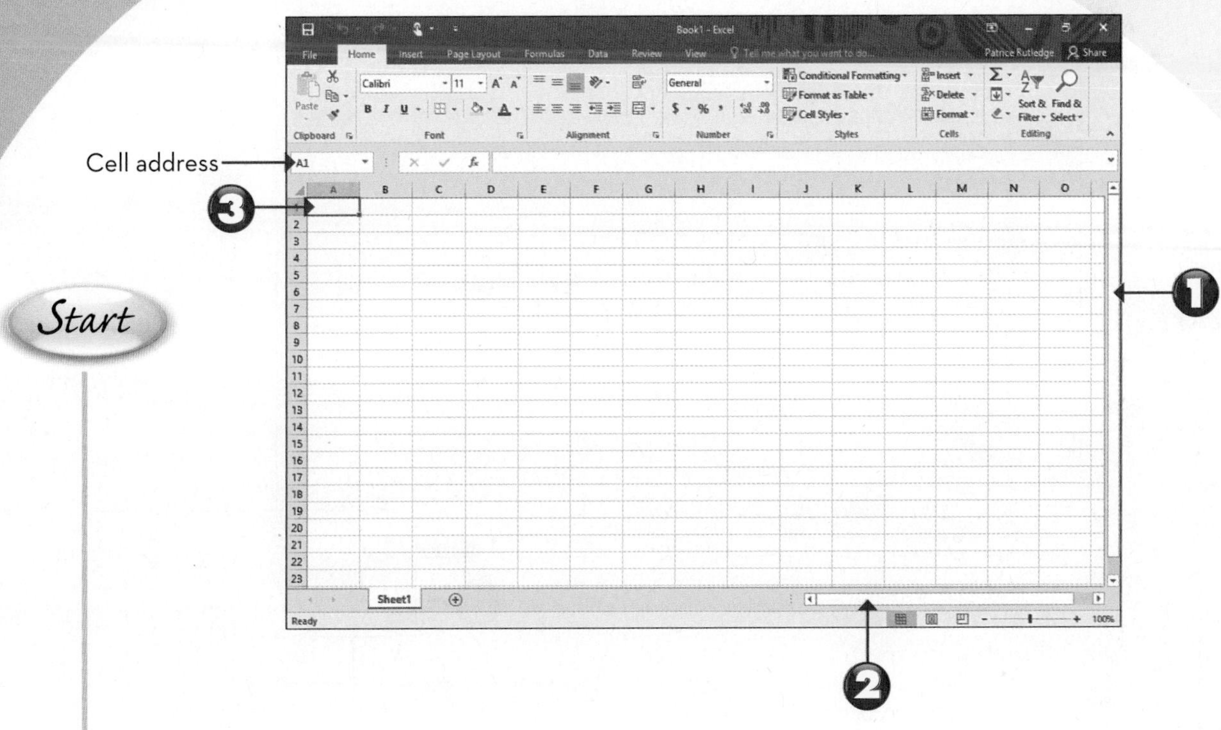


1. Select and drag the vertical scrollbar with your mouse until the row you are looking for is visible.

2. Select and drag the horizontal scrollbar until the column you are looking for is visible.

3. Click the wanted cell. It becomes the current cell.

End

## NOTE

**Cell Address** The name box in the upper-left corner of the screen displays the *cell address* of the selected cell. A cell address is composed of the column letter and row number, such as cell A1 or cell D8.

## TIP

**Other Ways to Navigate a Worksheet** You can also navigate your worksheet using the arrow keys on your keyboard to move one cell at a time up, down, left, or right. Using the Page Up and Page Down keys is another navigation option. If you have a touchscreen device, you can also navigate a worksheet by touch.

# ENTERING DATA

You can enter a variety of data on an Excel worksheet such as numbers, text, dates, or times.

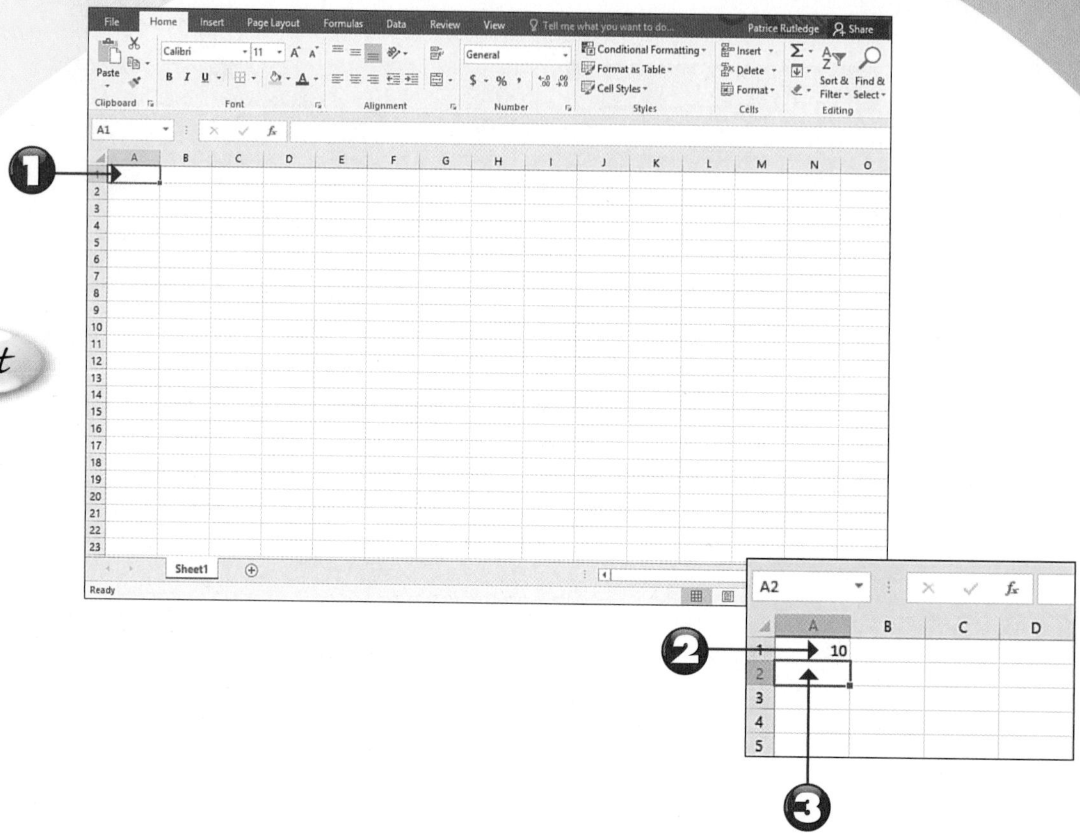

Start

1. Click the cell where you want to enter data. A border appears around the selected cell.

2. Enter your data. A blinking insertion point appears.

3. Press **Enter** to accept the value. Excel enters the data into the cell, and the selection moves to the next cell down.

End

**TIP**

**Data Entry Option** Optionally, you can press an arrow key instead of the Enter key. This not only accepts the data you entered but also moves to the next cell in the direction of the arrow key at the same time.

**TIP**

**Entering Sequential Data** If you want to enter sequential data, make your first few entries, select them with your mouse, and then drag the lower-right corner of your selection to have Excel continue entering data. For example, you could enter a series of numbers, days of the week, or months and have Excel finish your work for you.

# INSERTING A NEW ROW

Occasionally, you might need to insert a row into the middle of data that you have already entered. Inserting a row moves existing data down one row.

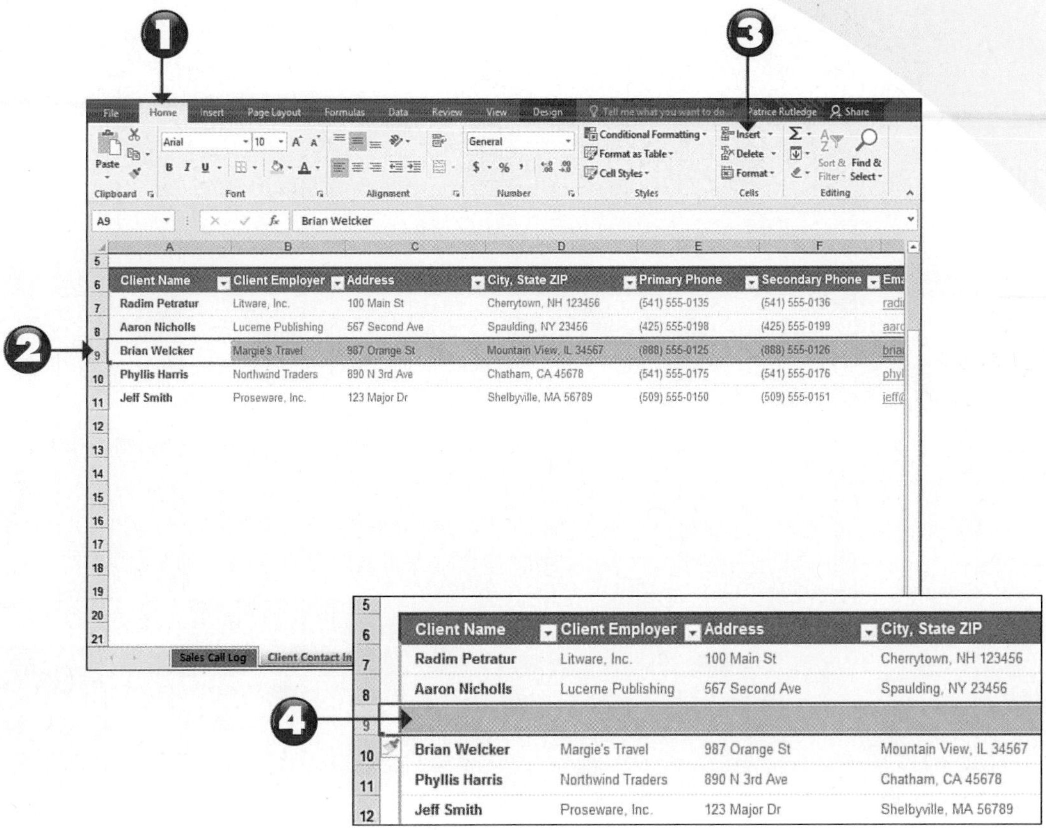

Start

1. Click the **Home** tab.
2. Click the row heading number where you want to insert the new row. Excel selects the entire row.
3. Click the **Insert** button.
4. Excel moves the existing row down and inserts a new blank row.

End

**TIP**

**Enter Multiple Rows** To enter more than one row, select the number of rows you want to enter with your mouse, and click the **Insert** button. For example, if you select rows 7 through 9, Excel moves the existing rows down and inserts three blank rows, numbered 7 through 9.

# INSERTING A NEW COLUMN

You can also insert a new column on a worksheet with existing data. Inserting a column moves the existing data to the right of the new column.

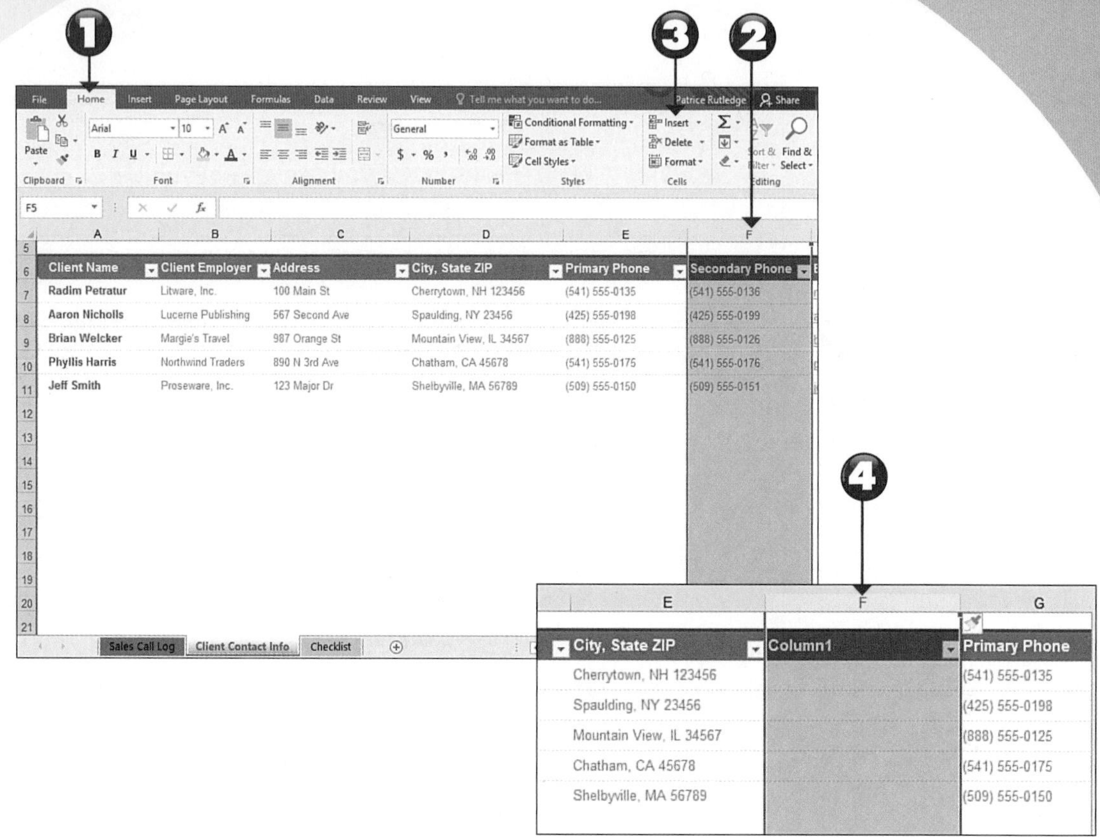


*Start*

1. Click the **Home** tab.
2. Click the column heading letter where you want to insert the new column. Excel selects the entire column.
3. Click the **Insert** button.
4. Excel moves the existing column to the right and inserts a new column.

*End*

**TIP**

**Enter Multiple Columns** To enter more than one column, select the number of columns you want to enter with your mouse, and click the **Insert** button. For example, if you select columns A through C, Excel moves the existing columns to the right and inserts three blank columns, labeled A through C.

# DELETING ROWS AND COLUMNS

You can delete Excel rows and columns easily and quickly. Remember that deleting a row or column removes all content from the selected row or column, not just the content of a single cell.

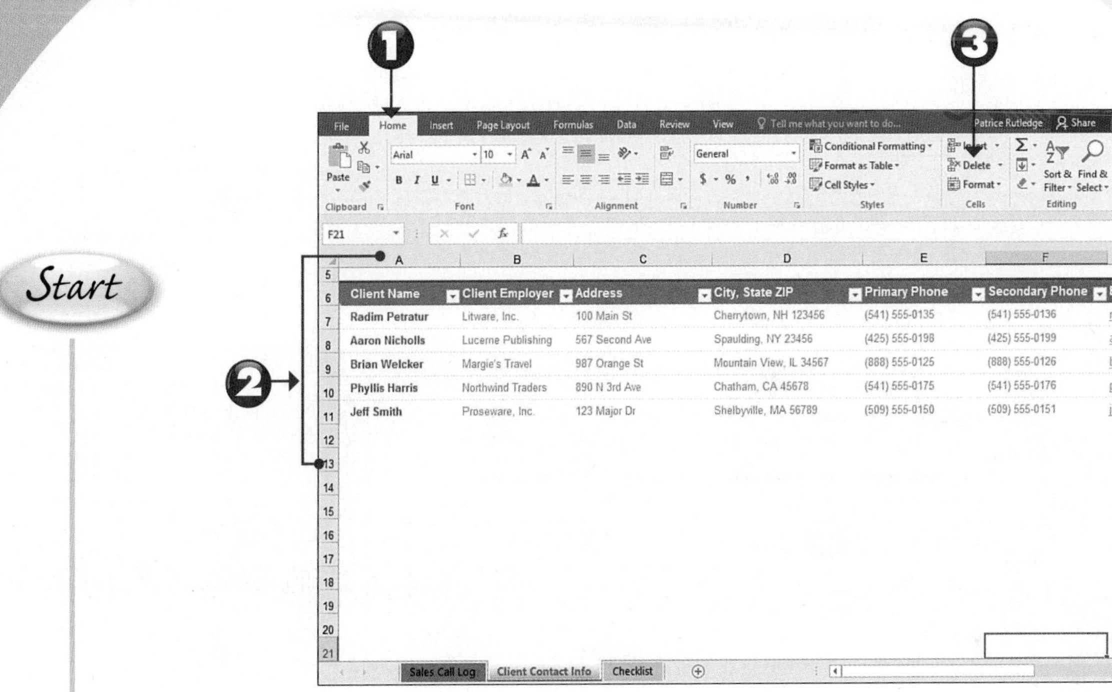


1. Click the **Home** tab.
2. Click the column heading letter or row heading number of the column or row you want to delete.
3. Click the **Delete** button. Excel deletes the selected content.

End

**TIP**

**Delete Multiple Columns or Rows** To delete more than one column or row, select the content you want to delete with your mouse and click the **Delete** button. For example, if you select the row heading numbers for rows 7 through 9, Excel deletes those rows.

# INSERTING A NEW WORKSHEET

By default, a new Excel workbook contains a single worksheet named Sheet1. If you like, you can add more worksheets to your workbook. For example, you might want a worksheet for every month of the year, for specific products or projects, and so forth.

Start

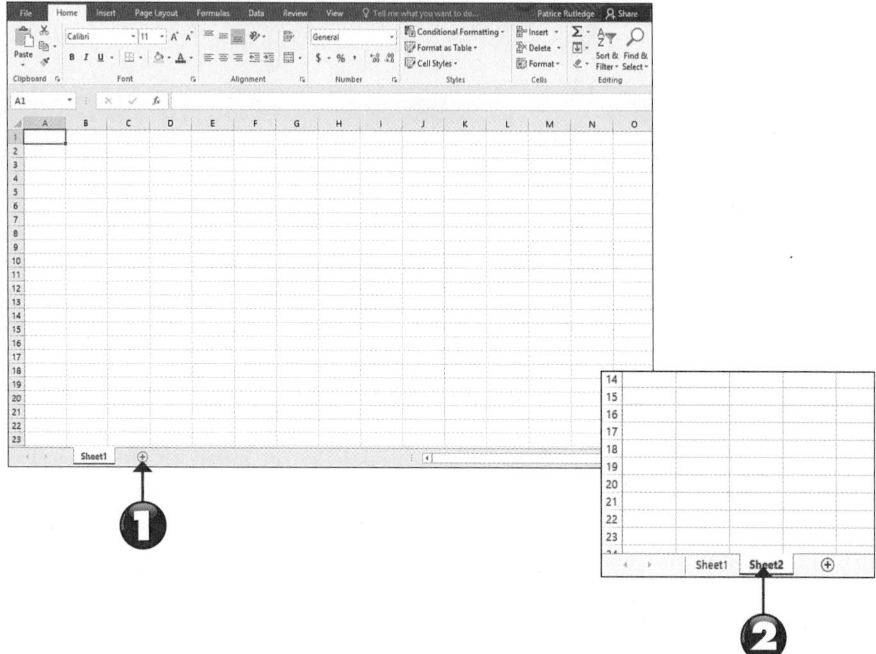


1. Click the plus sign (+) to the right of the Sheet1 tab.

2. Excel inserts a new sheet, named Sheet2.

End

**TIP**

**Optional Way to Insert New Worksheets** You can also insert a new worksheet by clicking the down arrow to the right of the **Insert** button on the **Home** tab and selecting **Insert Sheet** from the menu.

# RENAMING WORKSHEET TABS

Excel names your worksheets consecutively as Sheet1, Sheet2, Sheet3, and so forth. You can easily customize these tab names to something more meaningful, however.

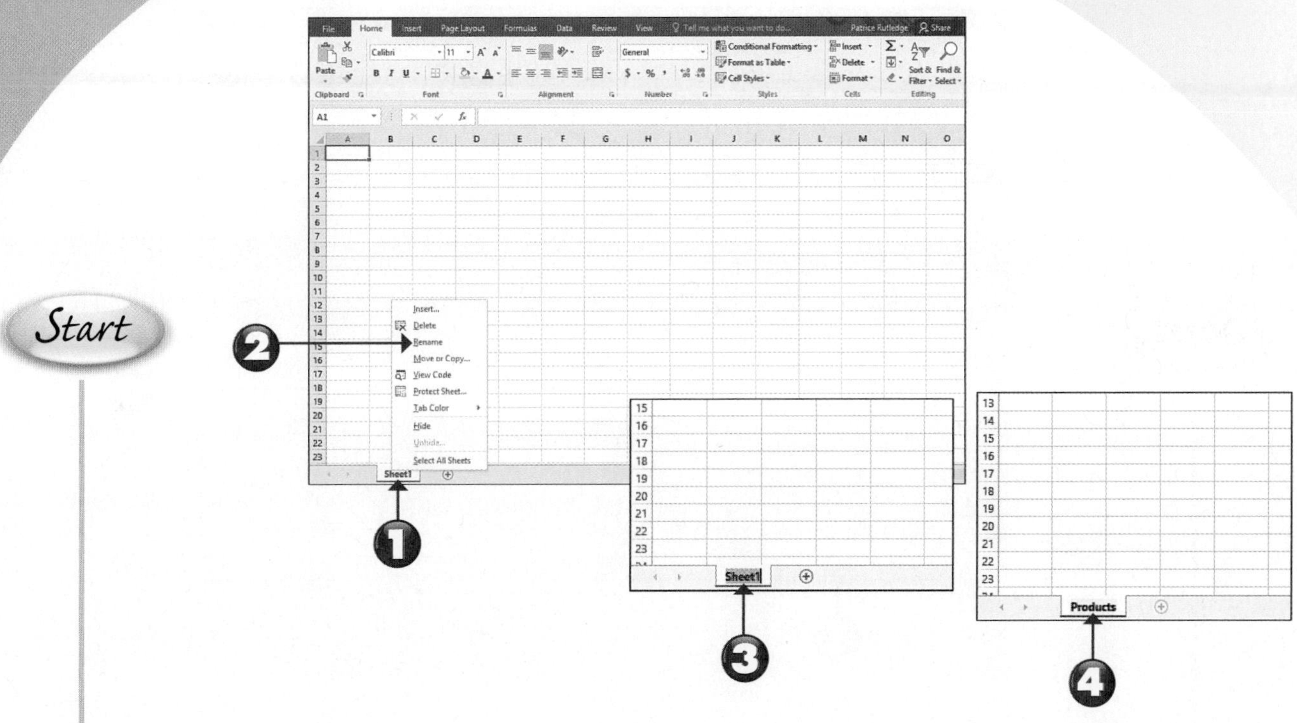


1. Right-click the tab you want to rename.

2. Select **Rename** from the menu.

3. Excel highlights the tab name.

4. Type a new name for the tab, and press **Enter** to confirm your entry.

End

**TIP**

**Color a Worksheet Tab** If your workbook has numerous worksheets, you can identify them with colors and labels. To apply a color to a selected worksheet tab, click it, select **Tab Color** from the menu, and select your preferred color.

# DELETING A WORKSHEET

If you no longer need a worksheet, or create one by mistake, you can delete it.

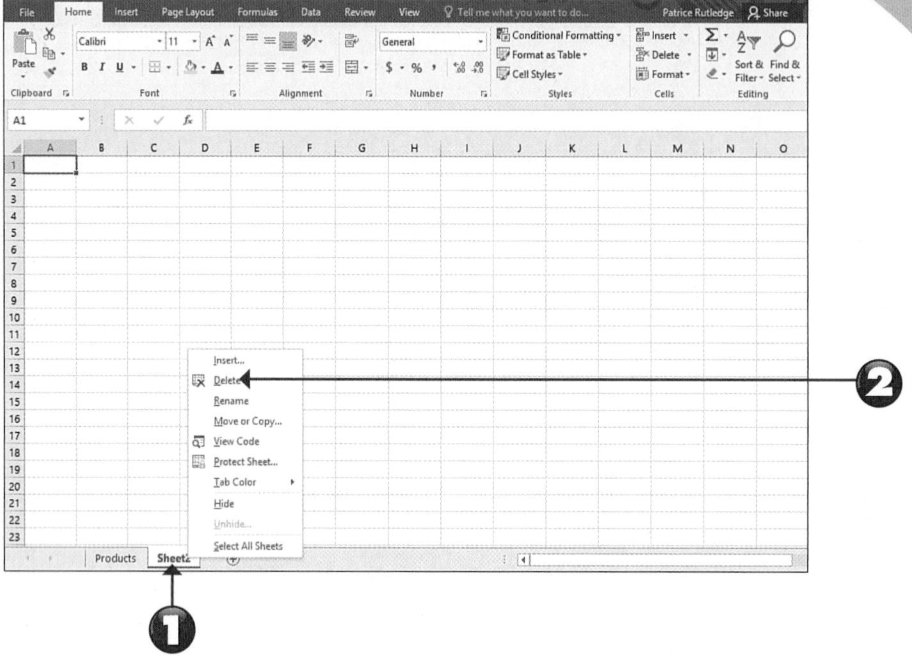


Start

1. Right-click the worksheet you want to delete.

2. Select **Delete** from the menu.

End

## TIP

**Delete Multiple Worksheet** If you want to delete more than one worksheet, hold down the **Ctrl** key, and select the worksheets you no longer want. Then, right-click and select **Delete** from the menu.

## CAUTION

**Excel Workbooks Require at Least One Worksheet** Because Excel requires at least one worksheet, you can't delete all the worksheets in your workbook. If you no longer need any of the worksheets in a workbook, you should delete the entire workbook instead.

# HIDING A WORKSHEET

If you aren't ready to delete a worksheet, but don't want it to display in your workbook, you can hide it.

Start

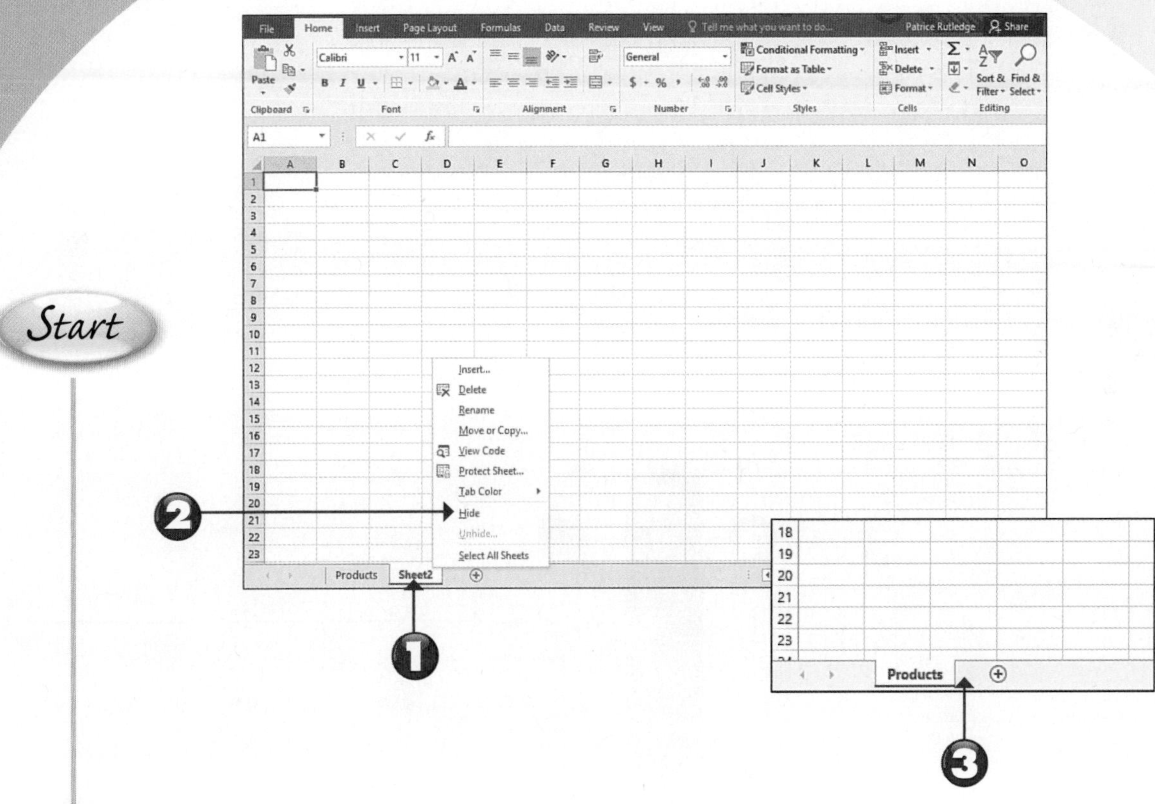


1. Right-click the tab you want to hide.
2. Select **Hide** from the menu.
3. Excel hides the tab on the worksheet.

End

## TIP

**Unhide a Worksheet** If you want to display a worksheet again, you can unhide it. To do so, click the **Format** button on the **Home** tab, and select **Hide & Unhide**, **Unhide Sheet** from the menu. In the Unhide dialog box, you can select the sheet you want to restore.

# PROTECTING A WORKBOOK WITH A PASSWORD

If your workbook contains confidential information that you want to share only with a select audience, you can protect it with a password. This way, only people who have the password can open the workbook and view its contents.

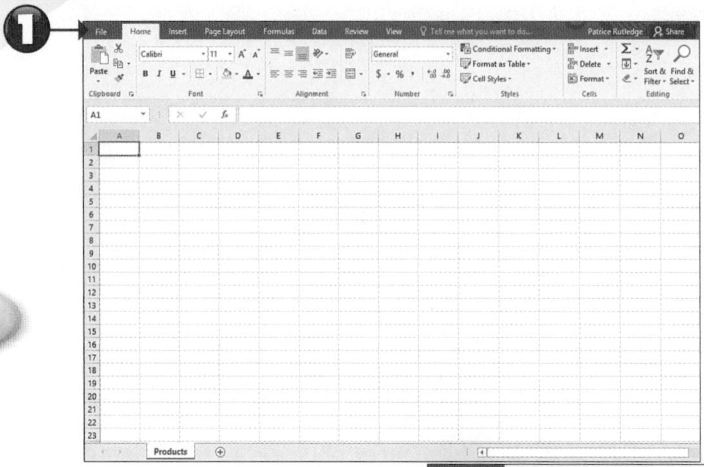

Start

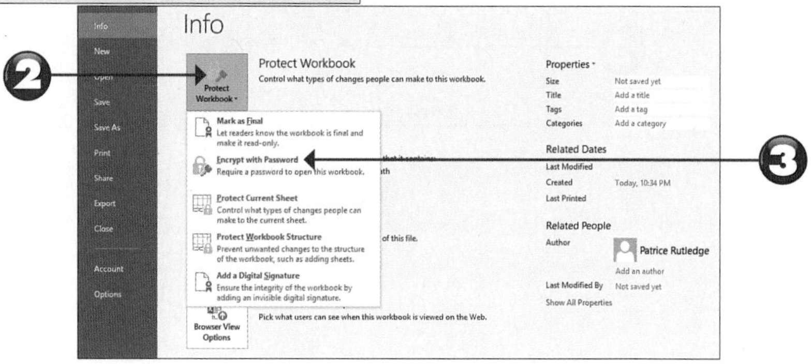

1. Click the **File** tab.
2. Click the **Protect Workbook** button.
3. Select **Encrypt with Password** from the menu.

Continued

## TIP

**Make Your Workbook Read-Only** An alternative to protecting your workbook with a password is to make it read-only if you're more concerned about potential changes than data confidentiality. To make a workbook read-only, select **Mark as Final** from the Protect Workbook menu.

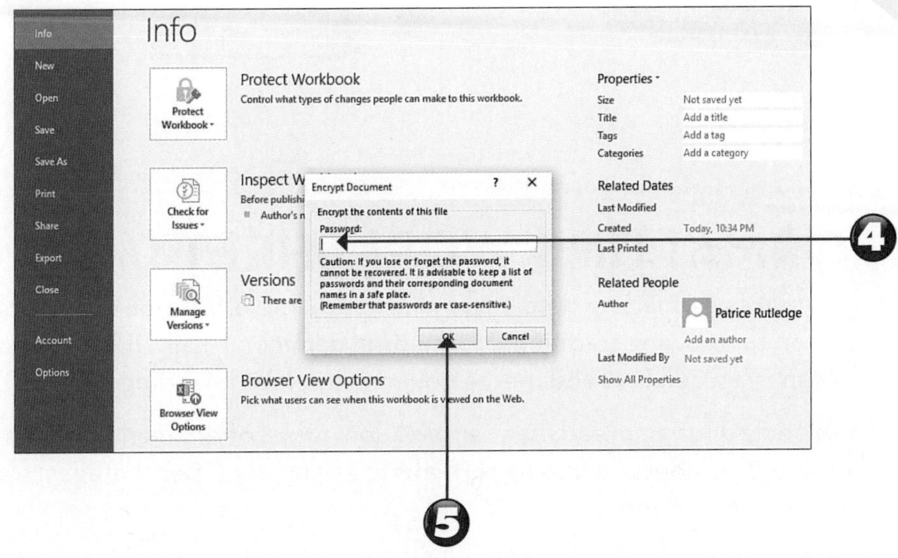


4 In the Encrypt Document dialog box, enter a case-sensitive password for your workbook.

5 Click **OK**.

End

**TIP**

**Protect Worksheet Data** Another alternative to protecting an entire workbook is to protect specific worksheet data. Doing this enables people to open your workbook but not perform functions you specify, such as format, insert, or delete rows and columns. To protect a worksheet, right-click it and select **Protect Sheet** from the menu.

# FORMATTING WORKSHEET DATA

Excel makes formatting data easy with many simple, yet powerful, tools. In addition to applying traditional formatting common to all Office applications, you can wrap cell text and merge columns to create headings in Excel.

As expected for a spreadsheet application, Excel offers many options for formatting numbers, including formatting as currency, percentages, fractions, dates, times, and more.

If your worksheet contains a lot of data, Excel makes it easy for you to find a specific cell or even replace cell content automatically. Freezing row numbers and column letters also makes it easier to find what you're looking for.

Formatting your worksheet data using colored cell styles or as a table are other options that enhance your table's design and functionality.

# FORMATTING BASICS

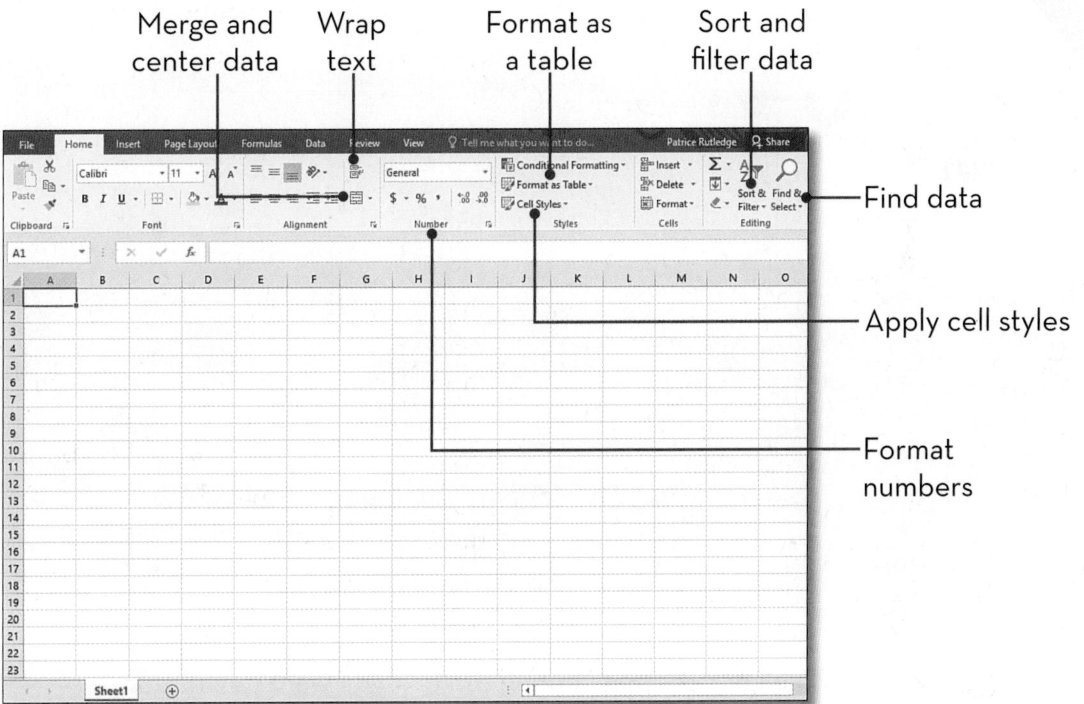

# WRAPPING TEXT

Wrapping text in cells is useful when the text is too long to fit in one cell, and you don't want it to overlap to the next cell.

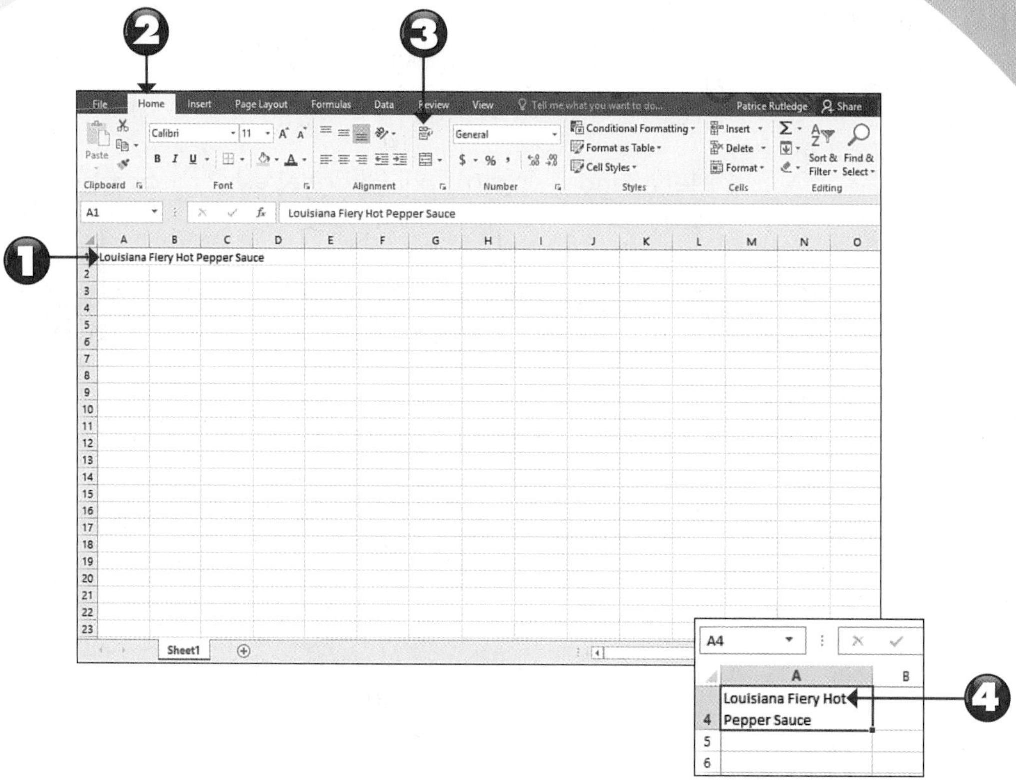

Start

1. Select the cell or cells that contain the text you want to wrap.
2. Click the **Home** tab.
3. Click the **Wrap Text** button.
4. Excel wraps your text in the selected cells.

End

## TIP

**Wrap Text Automatically** To wrap worksheet text automatically, select the cells you want to format, click the **Format** button on the Home tab, and select **Format Cells** from the menu. On the Alignment tab of the Format Cells dialog box, select the **Wrap Text** check box.

# MERGING AND CENTERING TEXT

The Merge & Center button makes it easy to create attractive headings that display across multiple columns. For example, if your worksheet contains data in columns A through H, you could merge and center a heading across these columns.

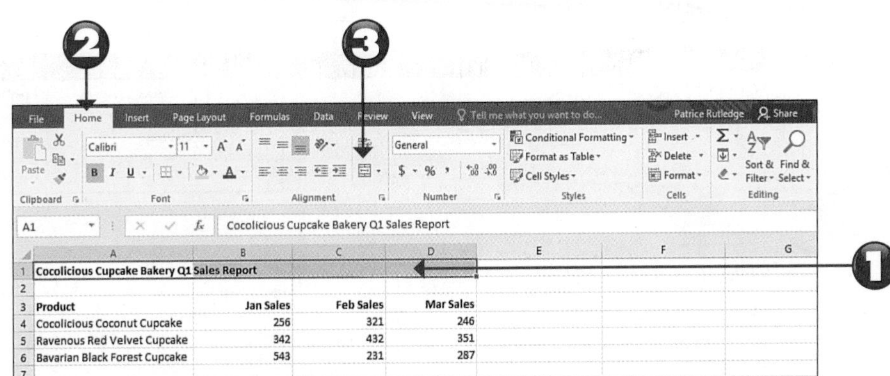


Start

4

| | A | B | C | D |
|---|---|---|---|---|
| 1 | Cocolicious Cupcake Bakery Q1 Sales Report | | | |
| 2 | | | | |
| 3 | **Product** | **Jan Sales** | **Feb Sales** | **Mar Sales** |
| 4 | Cocolicious Coconut Cupcake | 256 | 321 | 246 |
| 5 | Ravenous Red Velvet Cupcake | 342 | 432 | 351 |
| 6 | Bavarian Black Forest Cupcake | 543 | 231 | 287 |
| 7 | | | | |

1. Select the cells to be included in the heading.
2. Click the **Home** tab.
3. Click the **Merge & Center** button.
4. Excel merges and centers the selected cells.

End

**NOTE**

**Identify Merged Cells** Notice the gridlines have disappeared and the cells appear to be joined together.

# FORMATTING NUMBERS

By default, values display as general numbers. You can also display values as currency, percentages, fractions, dates, or in many other formats.

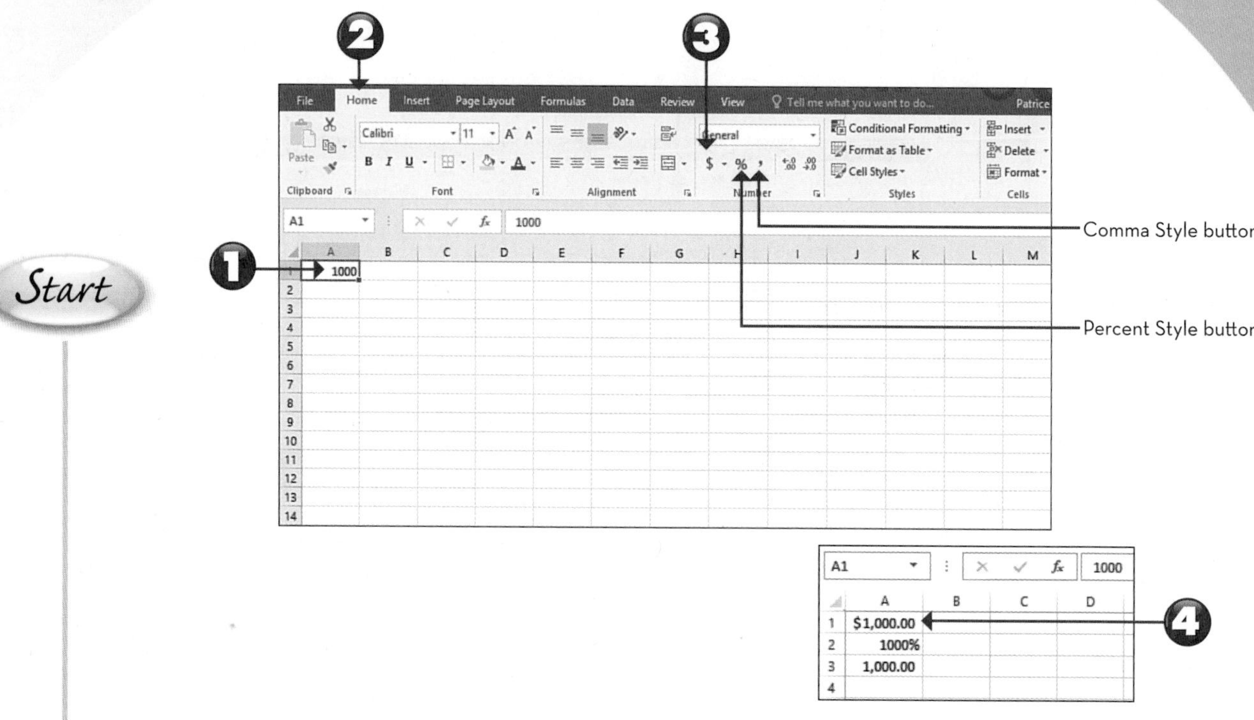


1. Select the cell or cells you want to format.
2. Click the **Home** tab.
3. Click the **Accounting Number Format** button to format the selected cells as your default currency.
4. Excel formats your selected cells.

End

## TIP

**More Number Formatting** For additional number formatting options, right-click the cells you want to format and select **Format Cells** from the menu. The Numbers tab on the Format Cells dialog box includes formatting options not available on the Ribbon Home tab.

## CAUTION

**What Happened to My Number?** Don't be alarmed if some of the cells display a series of number signs (######) or in scientific format (1E+08) instead of your values. This is because the column width is too small. You learn how to change column width later in this chapter.

# APPLYING CELL STYLES

Cell styles enable you to apply colored formatting instantly to your worksheets. These styles can make your data easier to read.

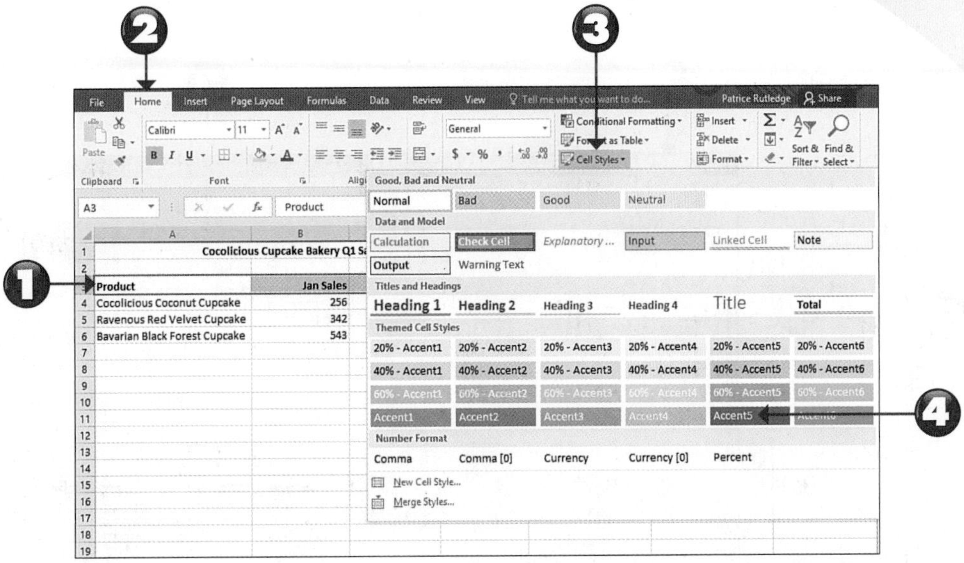

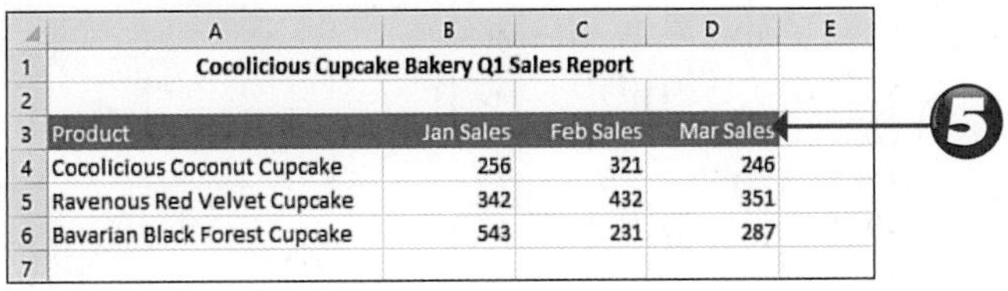

| | A | B | C | D | E |
|---|---|---|---|---|---|
| 1 | Cocolicious Cupcake Bakery Q1 Sales Report | | | | |
| 2 | | | | | |
| 3 | Product | Jan Sales | Feb Sales | Mar Sales | |
| 4 | Cocolicious Coconut Cupcake | 256 | 321 | 246 | |
| 5 | Ravenous Red Velvet Cupcake | 342 | 432 | 351 | |
| 6 | Bavarian Black Forest Cupcake | 543 | 231 | 287 | |
| 7 | | | | | |

1. Select the cells you want to format with a cell style.
2. Click the **Home** tab.
3. Click the **Cell Styles** button.
4. Click a cell style in the gallery.
5. Excel applies the cell style.

## TIP

**Cell Styles for Headings** One of the most common uses of cell styles is to format titles and headings. Select your heading cells, and then use a cell style to distinguish heading cells from regular data.

## TIP

**Themed Cell Styles** The Cell Styles gallery also includes themed cell styles in a variety of colors and shadings. You can use these as an alternative to a standard heading or as a way to call attention to other important data.

# FORMATTING AS A TABLE

Formatting worksheet data as a table is another way to distinguish cell data with color. You can also filter and summarize table data using the tools on the Table Tools–Design tab.

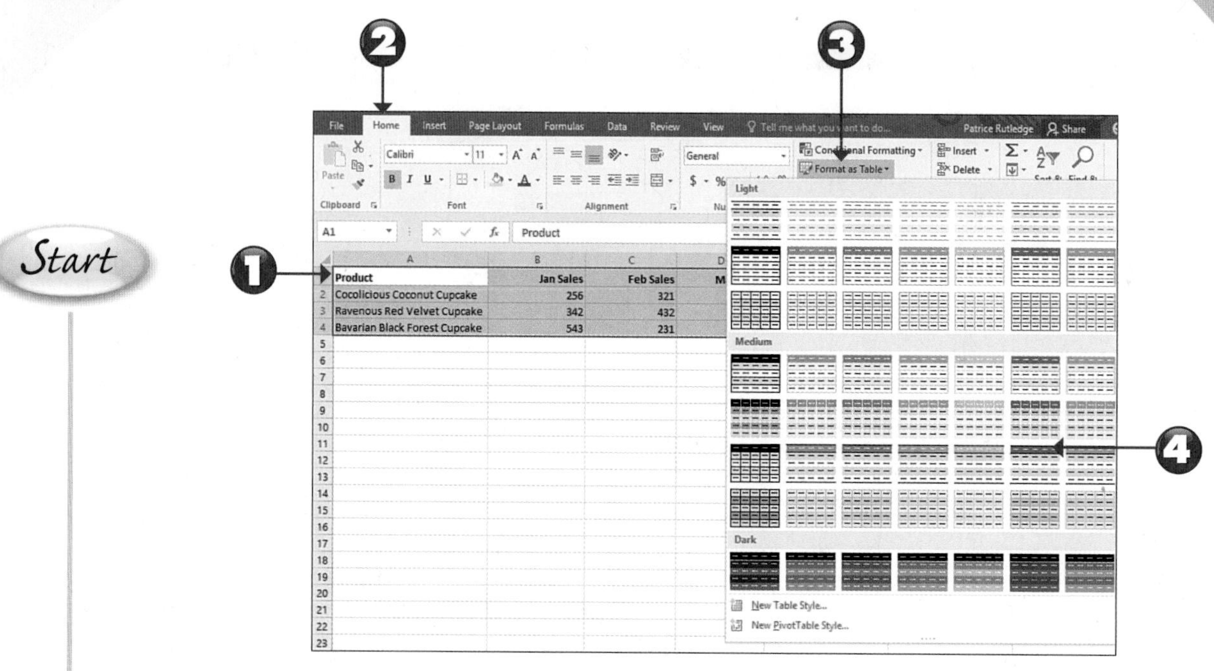


1. Select the cells you want to format as a table.
2. Click the **Home** tab.
3. Click the **Format as Table** button.
4. Select a table design from the gallery.

Continued

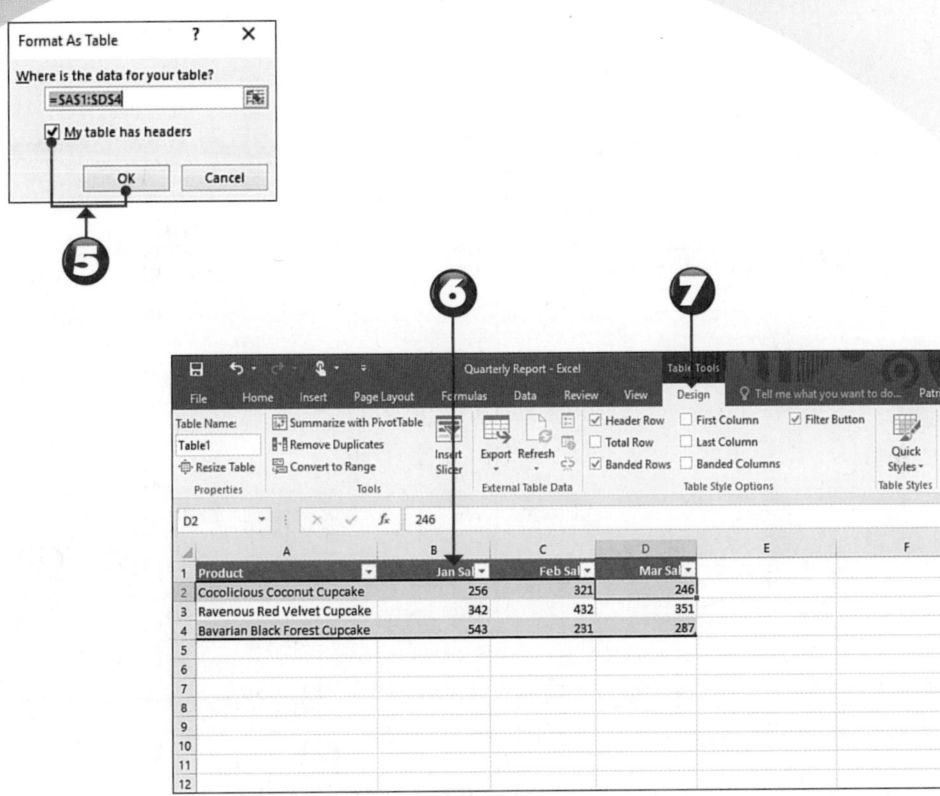


5. In the Format as Table dialog box, select the **My table has headers** check box if you want to distinguish table headers, and then click **OK**.

6. Excel applies the table design you selected.

7. The Table Tools–Design tab displays, offering additional table formatting options.

End

## NOTE

**Filter Tables** When you format cells as a table, Excel also enables you to filter your data. See "Filtering Data" later in this chapter for more information.

## TIP

**Add Table Totals** To add a total row to your table, click the **Total Row** check box on the Table Tools–Design tab.

# ADJUSTING COLUMN WIDTH

The default width of an Excel column is 8.43 characters, but you can adjust each column from 0 to 255 characters wide.

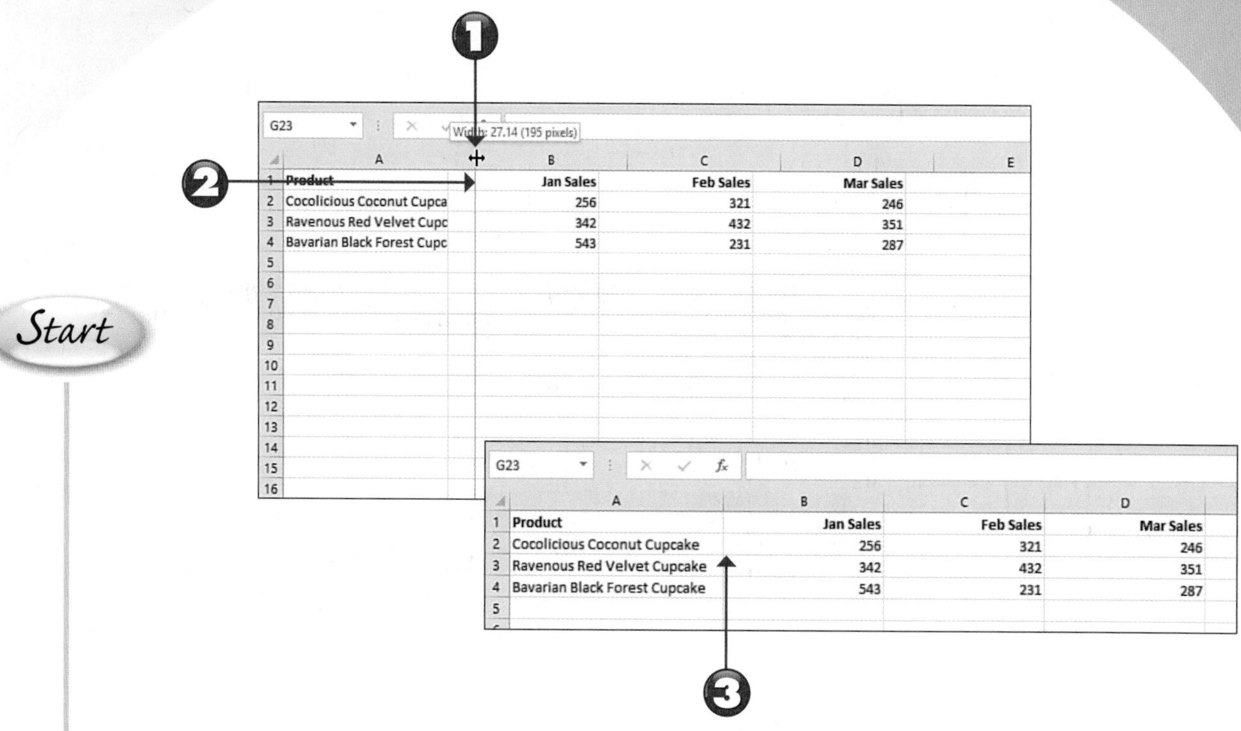


1. Position the mouse pointer to the right of the column you want to adjust. The mouse pointer becomes a crosshair.
2. Press and hold the mouse button, and drag the column line to the right to increase the column width or to the left to decrease it.
3. Release the mouse button. The column width will be changed.

End

**TIP**

**Adjust Columns Automatically** To automatically adjust column width to exactly fit the contents of the cell, double-click the mouse after the pointer becomes a crosshair.

## ADJUSTING ROW HEIGHT

The default height of an Excel row is 15 points, but you can adjust each row from 0 to 409 points.

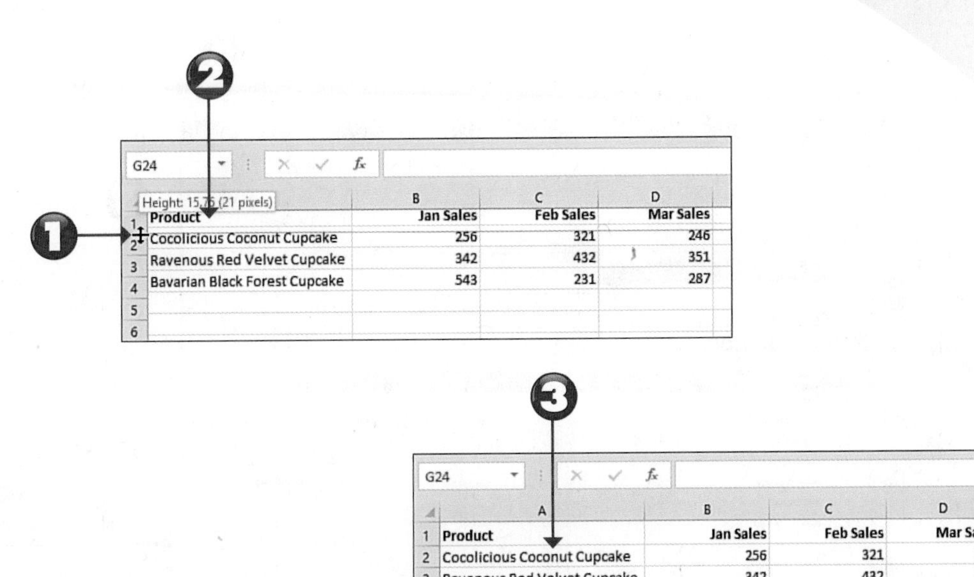


Start

1. Position the mouse pointer below the row you want to adjust. The mouse pointer becomes a crosshair.
2. Press and hold the mouse button and drag the row line down to increase the row height or up to decrease it.
3. Release the mouse button. The row height will be changed.

End

**TIP**

**Adjust Rows Automatically** To automatically adjust row height to exactly fit the contents of the cell, double-click the mouse after the pointer becomes a crosshair.

# FINDING DATA

If your worksheet contains a lot of data, it can be hard to find the right cell at times. Fortunately, Excel makes it easy to search your worksheet data.

Start

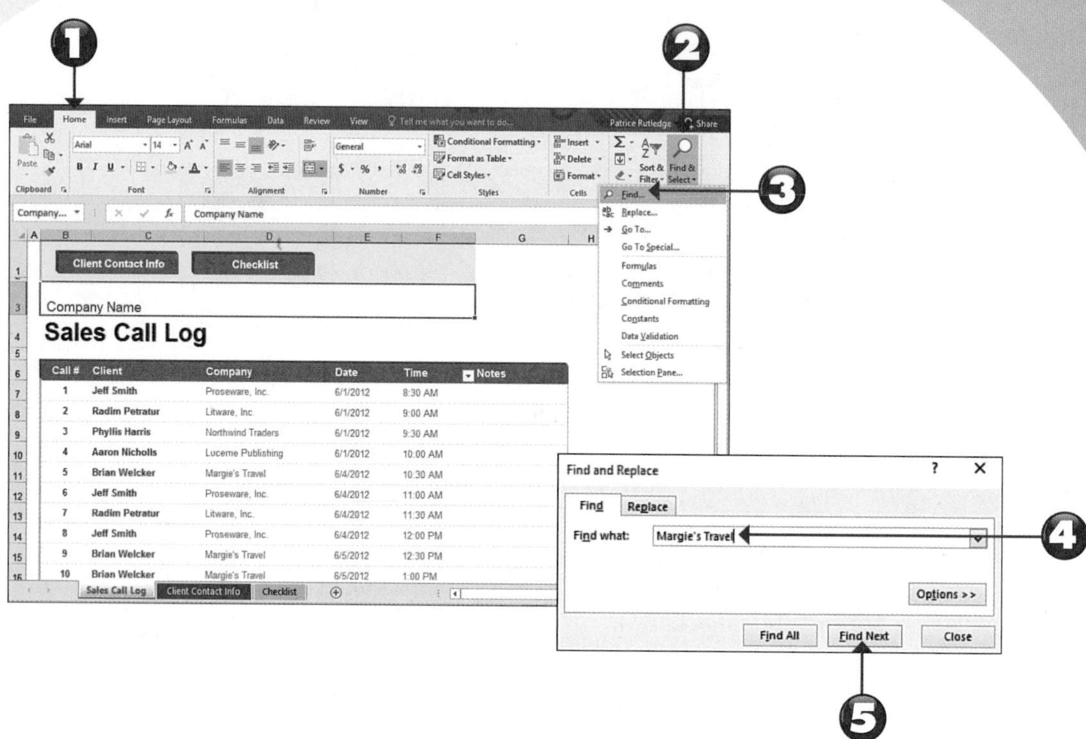


1. Click the **Home** tab.
2. Click the **Find & Select** button.
3. Select **Find** from the menu.
4. In the Find and Replace dialog box, enter the data you're searching for.
5. Click the **Find Next** button to find the next instance of this data.

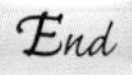

**TIP**

**Replace Data** In addition to finding data, you can also find and replace it. To do so, click the **Replace** tab in the Find and Replace dialog box.

# FREEZING PANES

You can freeze columns, rows, or both so that your row and column headings remain in view as you scroll instead of scrolling off the screen with the rest of the worksheet. This is particularly helpful with larger worksheets.

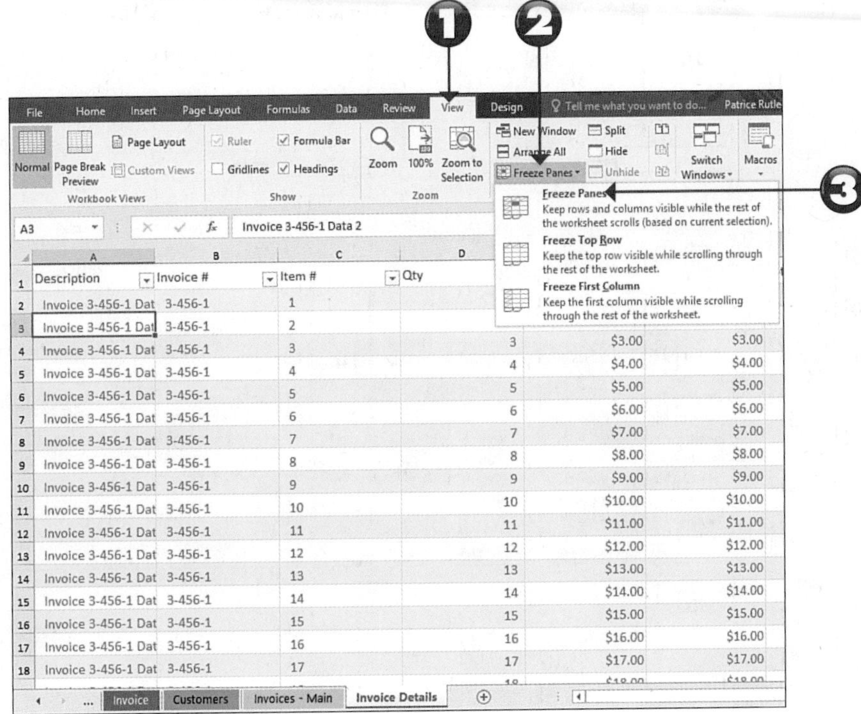


Start

1. Click the **View** tab.
2. Click the **Freeze Panes** button.
3. Select **Freeze Panes** from the menu to freeze both columns and rows.

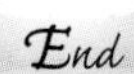

## TIP

**Unfreeze Panes** To unfreeze panes, click the **Freeze** button and select **Unfreeze Panes** from the menu.

## TIP

**Customize Freezing** From the Freeze Panes menu, you can optionally choose to freeze only the top row or only the first column.

# SORTING DATA

If your worksheet data isn't in the right order, you can sort it.

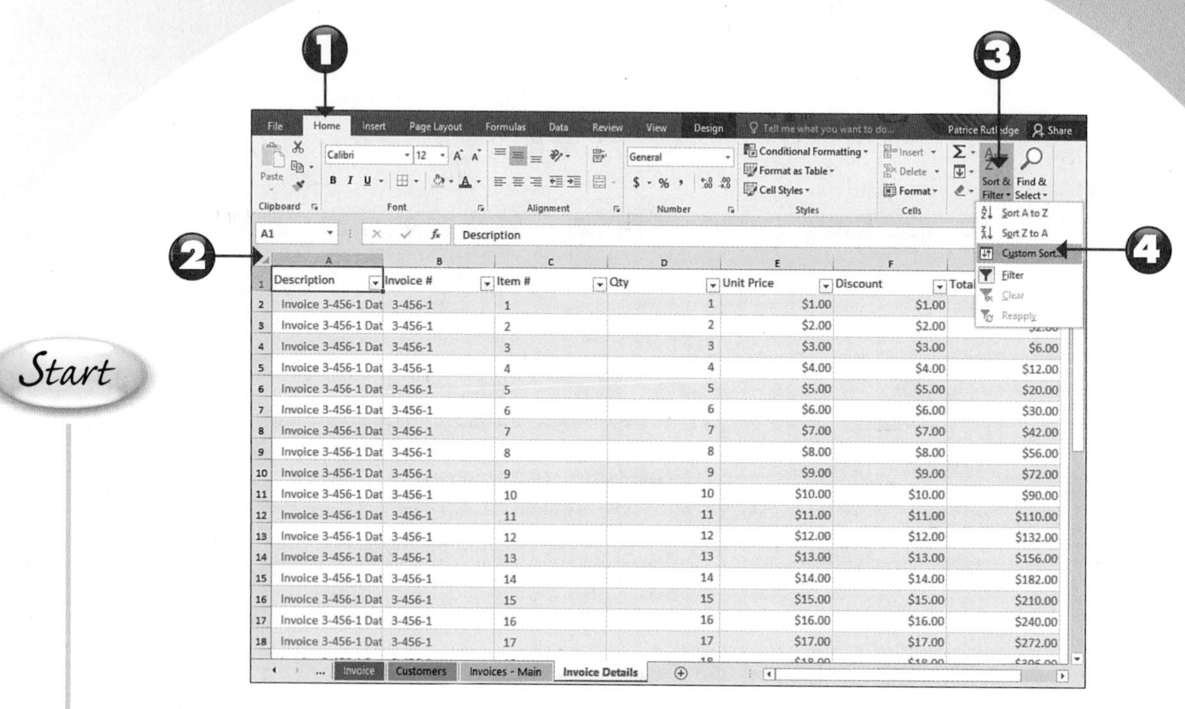

1. Click the **Home** tab.
2. Click the **Select All** button to select all your worksheet data.
3. Click the **Sort & Filter** button.
4. Select **Custom Sort** from the menu.

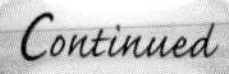


## NOTE

**Column Headers** Column headers are useful for identifying your worksheet data. For example, you can use headers to identify the months of the year, product names, regions, and so forth.

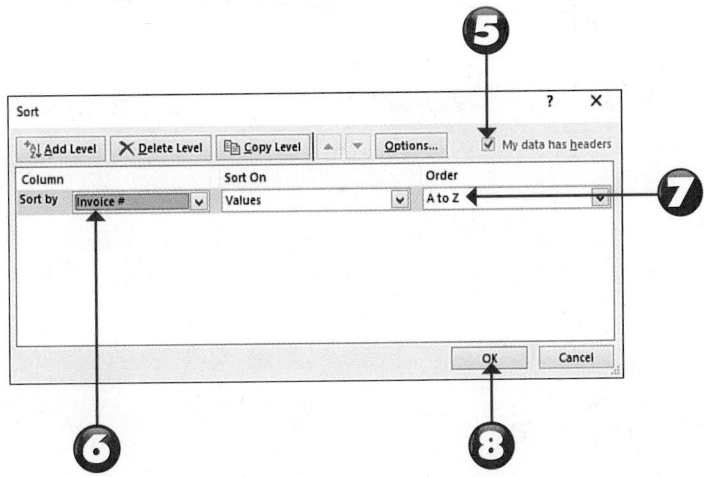


5. Select the **My data has headers** check box if your worksheet includes column headers.
6. Specify the column you want to sort by.
7. Specify your preferred sort order, such as A to Z or Z to A.
8. Click **OK**.

End

**TIP**

**Sort on Multiple Columns** To sort on more than one column, click the **Add Level** button in the Sort dialog box, and add an additional column.

# FILTERING DATA

Filtering data is another way to control what displays on your Excel worksheet. By applying a filter, you can hide data temporarily, making it easy to focus on the data you need to see.

Start

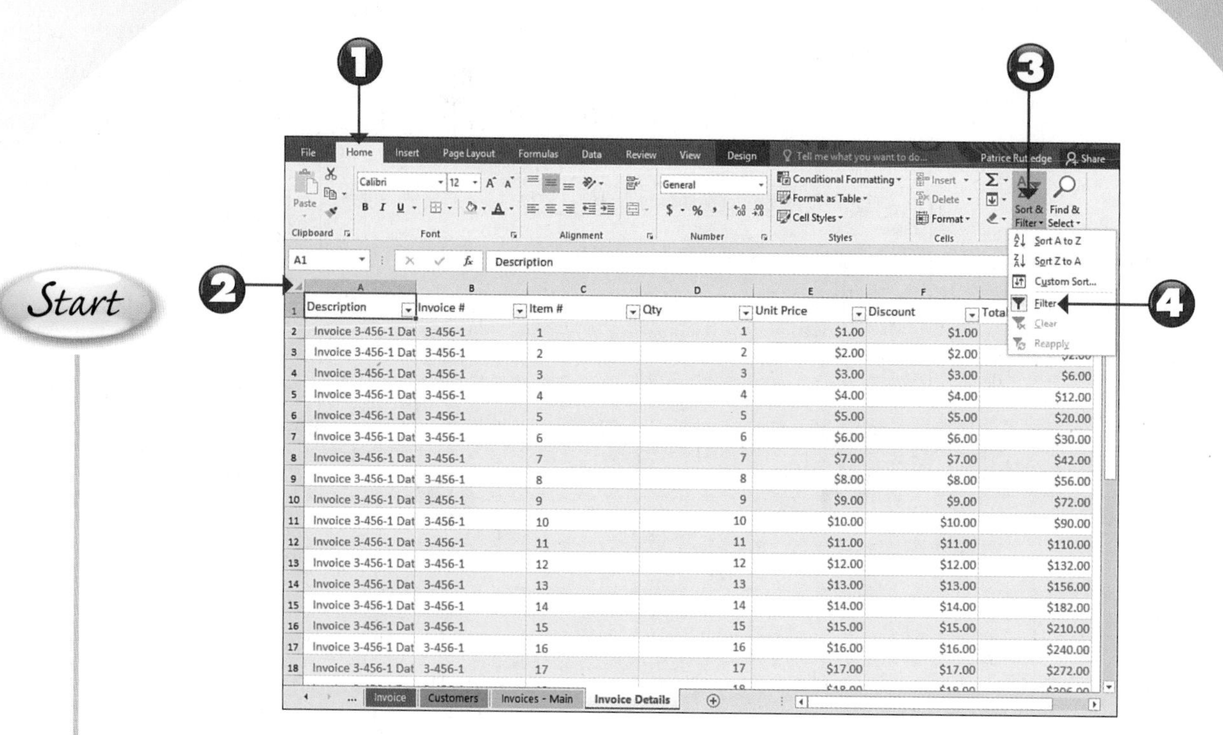

1. Click the **Home** tab.

2. Click the **Select All** button to select all your worksheet data.

3. Click the **Sort & Filter** button.

4. Select **Filter** from the menu.

Continued

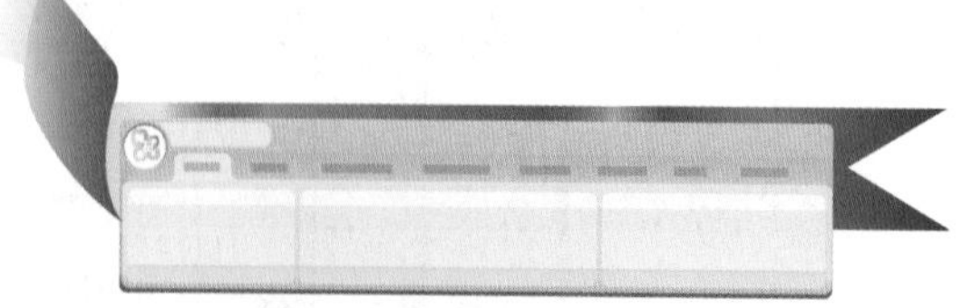

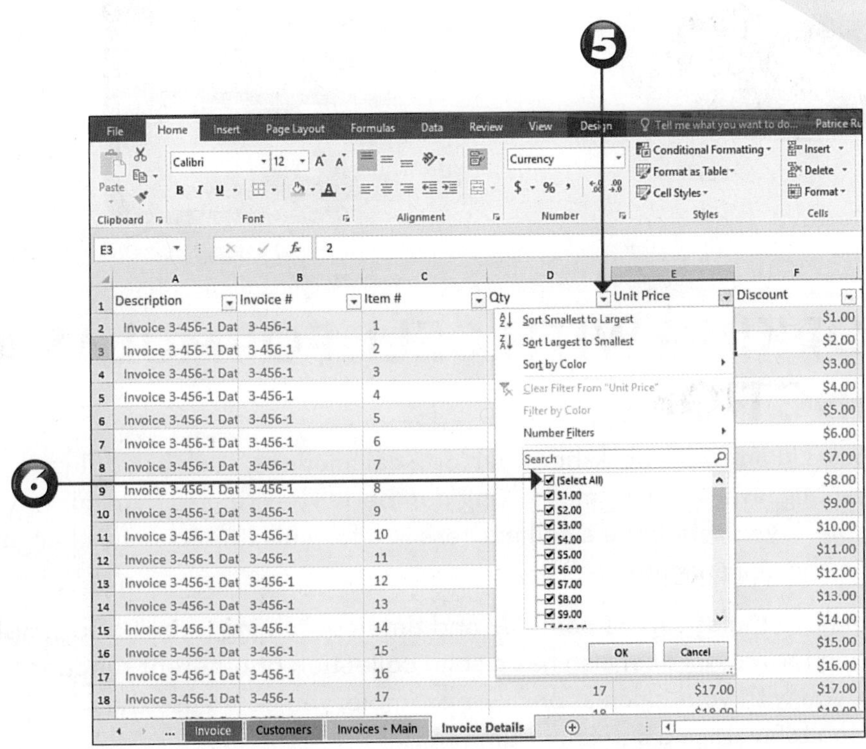

5 Excel displays a down arrow to the right of each column. Click the arrow to the right of the column you want to filter.

6 Click to remove the check next to any data you don't want to display.

*End*

**TIP**

**Remove a Filter** To remove a filter you applied, click the **Sort & Filter** button, and select **Filter** from the menu.

**TIP**

**Sort with a Filter** Applying a filter also makes it easier to sort columns. From the **Filter** menu, you can sort from smallest to largest or from largest to smallest.

# WORKING WITH CELL FORMULAS AND FUNCTIONS

Formulas in an Excel worksheet perform calculations, such as adding, subtracting, averaging, or multiplying numbers. They're also dynamic—for example, if you reference a cell address in a formula, the formula changes if the data in the cell changes.

At times, formulas can be complex and time-consuming to build. To simplify creating formulas, Excel also has a solid collection of different functions to assist you with your calculations. For example, you could use the AVERAGE function to average a series of numbers.

# CELL FORMULA BASICS

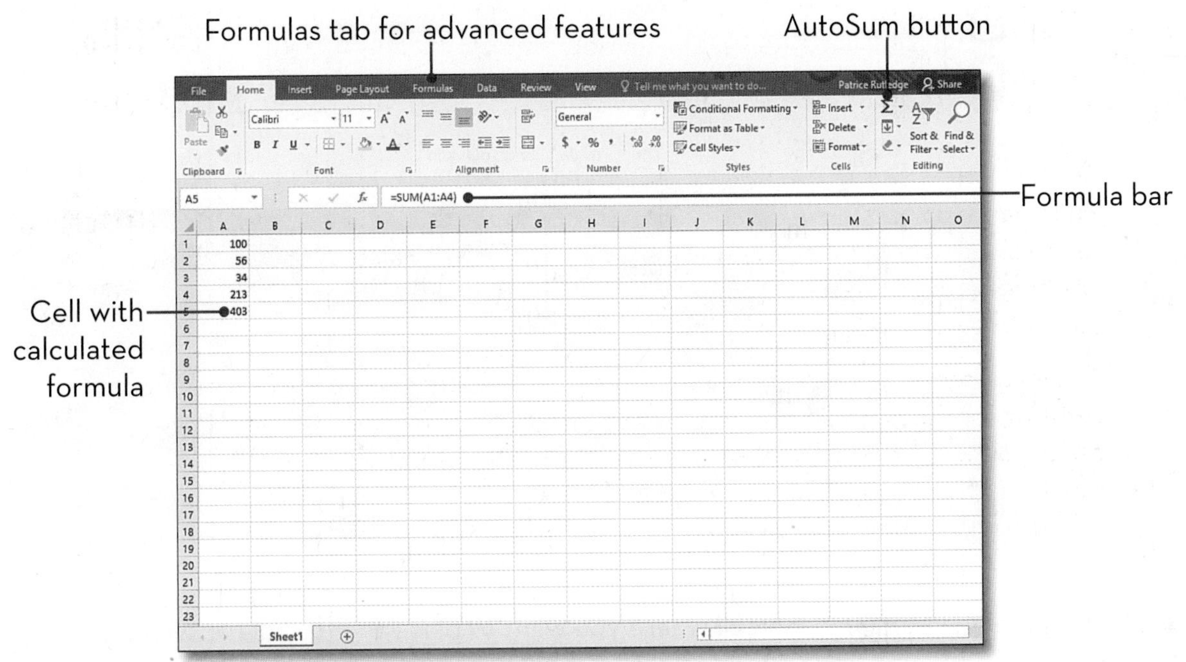

# CREATING A SIMPLE FORMULA

You can use a simple formula to add, subtract, multiply, or divide two numbers. An example of a simple formula is =A1+A2, which adds the contents of cells A1 and A2.

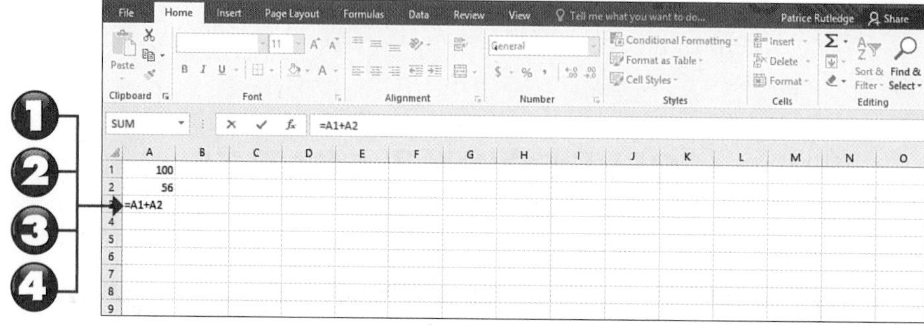

Start

The formula also displays in the Formula bar

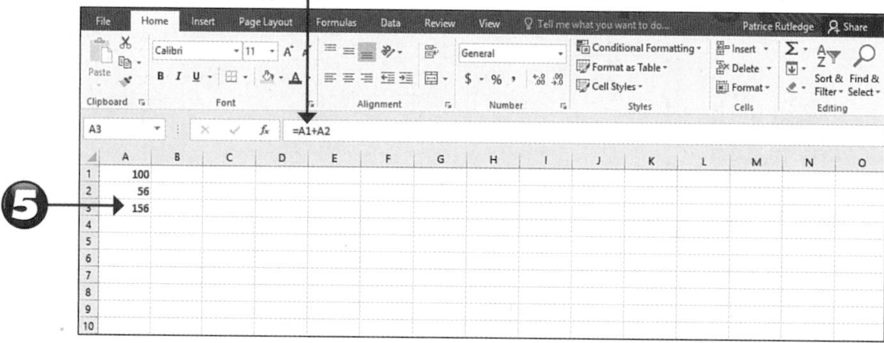

1. Type an equal sign (**=**) in the cell where you want to place the formula answer.
2. Type the cell address (such as **A1**) of the first cell to include in the formula. This is called the cell reference.
3. Type an operator to indicate the action to perform: plus (**+**), minus (**–**), multiply (*****), or divide (**/**).
4. Type the reference to the second cell of the formula.
5. Press **Enter**. The result of the calculation displays in the cell.

End

## NOTE

**Start a Formula** All formulas must begin with the equal (=) sign, regardless of whether the formula consists of adding, subtracting, multiplying, or dividing. ■

## NOTE

**Formula Case Sensitivity** Excel formulas are not case sensitive. For example, A5 is the same as a5. ■

## TIP

**Numbers in Formulas** You can also include an actual number in a formula instead of two cell references. For example, you could create a formula such as =A6-10, which subtracts 10 from the amount in cell A6. ■

# COPYING FORMULAS USING FILL

Similar to filling a pattern of days or months, Excel can also fill cells with the pattern of a formula. For example, you might want to copy a formula if you have multiple rows or columns that require the same calculation.

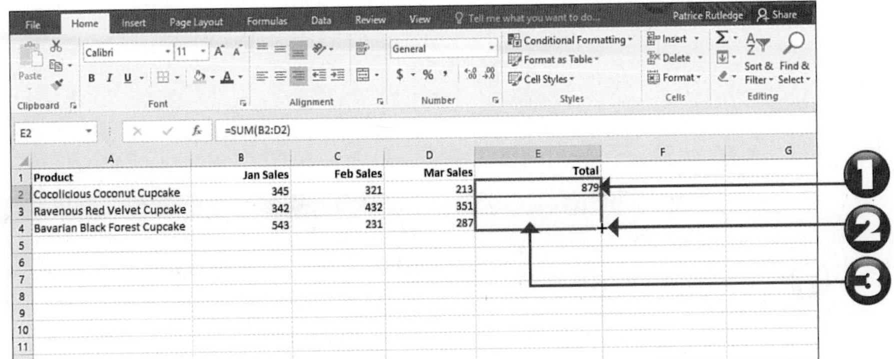


Start

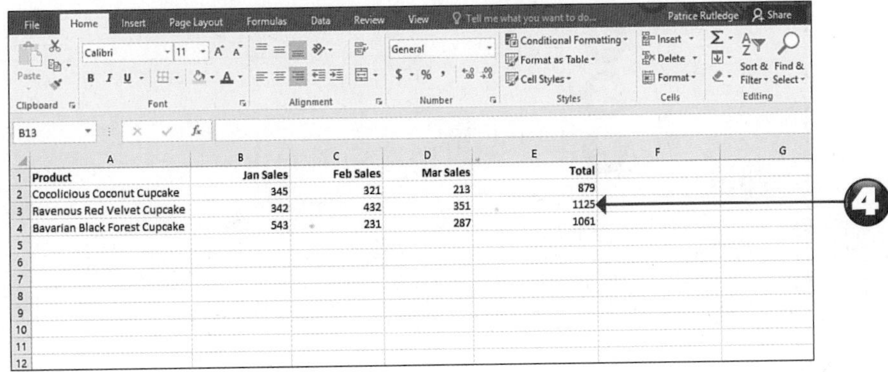


1. Select the cell that has the formula you want to copy.
2. Position the mouse pointer on the lower-right corner of the beginning cell. The mouse pointer becomes a crosshair.
3. Press and hold the mouse button, and drag to select the next cells to be filled in.
4. Release the mouse button. Excel copies the formula to all the selected cells.

End

## TIP

**Copy Formulas with Copy and Paste** Another time-saving method for duplicating formulas is to use the Copy and Paste buttons on the Home tab. ■

## NOTE

**How Excel Copies Formulas** When Excel copies a formula, the references change as the formula is copied. If the original formula was =A10–A19 and you copied it to the next cell to the right, the formula would read =B10–B19. Then, if you copied it to the next cell to the right, it would be =C10–C19, and so on. ■

# CREATING A COMPOUND FORMULA

If you need more than one operator for a calculation, you can use a compound formula. Examples of a compound formula include =B7+B8+B12 or =B11–B19–A23.

Start

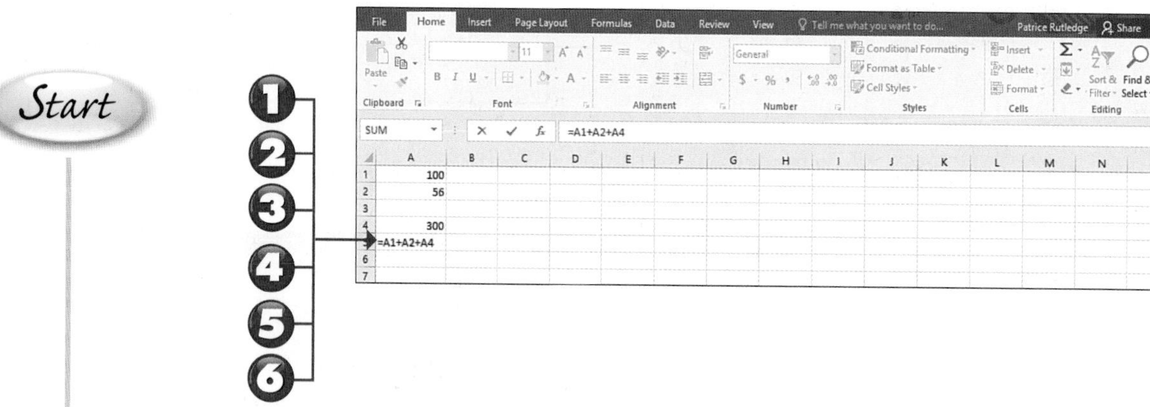


1. Type an equal sign (=) in the cell where you want to place the formula answer.
2. Type the reference to the first cell of the formula.
3. Type the operator.
4. Type the reference to the second cell of the formula.
5. Type the next operator.
6. Type the reference to the third cell of the formula.

Continued

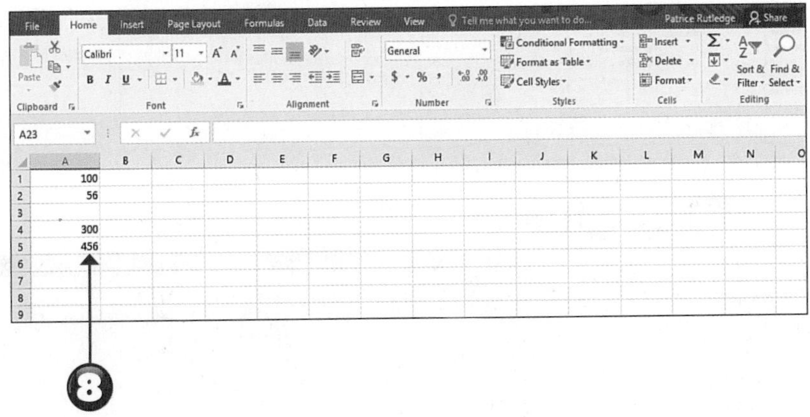


7 Repeat steps 5 and 6 until the formula is complete, adding parentheses wherever necessary.

8 Press **Enter** to accept the formula. The result of the calculation displays in the cell.

End

TIP

**Update Formulas Automatically** Try changing one of the values you originally typed in the worksheet and watch the answer to the formula change. ■

NOTE

**Calculation Precedence** In a formula, Excel performs multiplication and division before addition and subtraction unless you use parentheses to indicate calculation precedence. For example, Excel calculates the formula =A4+B4*C4 in a different order than =(A4+B4)*C4. In the first formula, Excel multiples B4 by C4 and then adds A4. In the second formula, Excel adds A4 and B4 and then multiples it by C4. ■

# CREATING AN ABSOLUTE REFERENCE IN A FORMULA

Sometimes when you copy a formula, you don't want one of the cell references to change. That's when you need to create an absolute reference. You use the dollar sign ($) to indicate an absolute reference.

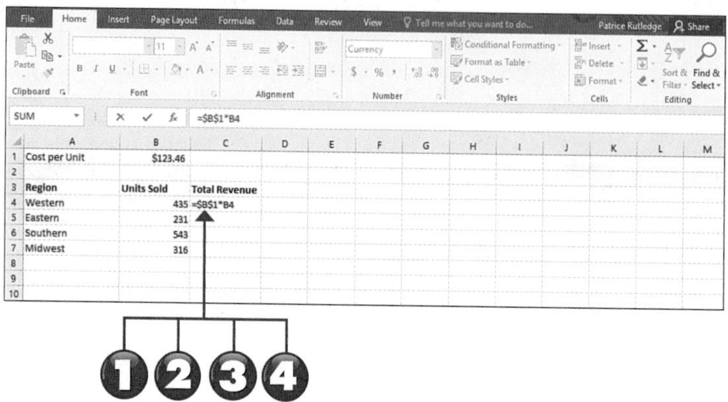


Start

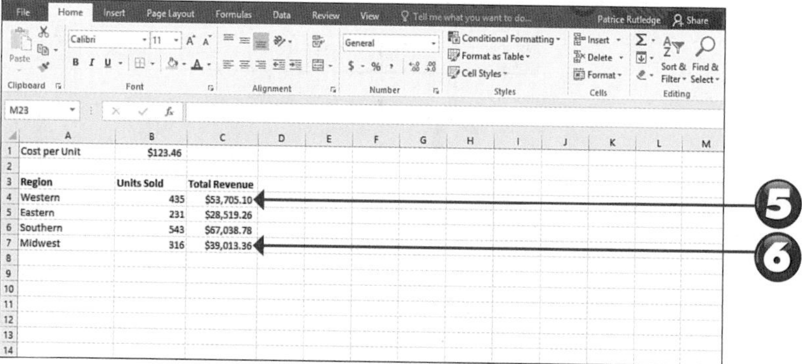


1. Type the equal (=) sign in the cell where you want to place the formula answer.
2. Type the reference to the first cell of the formula. If this reference is to be an absolute reference, add dollar signs (**$**) in front of both the column reference and the row reference.
3. Type the operator.
4. Type the reference to the second cell of the formula. If this reference is to be an absolute reference, add dollar signs (**$**) in front of both the column reference and the row reference.
5. Press **Enter**. The result of the calculation displays in the cell.
6. Copy the formula to the adjacent cells using either the Fill or Copy and Paste methods.

End

**NOTE**

**Absolute References** It's called an *absolute reference* because when you copy it, it absolutely stays that cell reference and never changes. An example of a formula with an absolute reference might be =B21*$B$23. The reference to cell B23 will not change when copied. ■

**NOTE**

**Compound Formulas** Although this example uses a simple formula, compound formulas can also have absolute references. ■

# USING THE SUM FUNCTION

The SUM function totals a range of values. The syntax for this function is =SUM(*range of values to total*). An example might be =SUM(B4:B7).

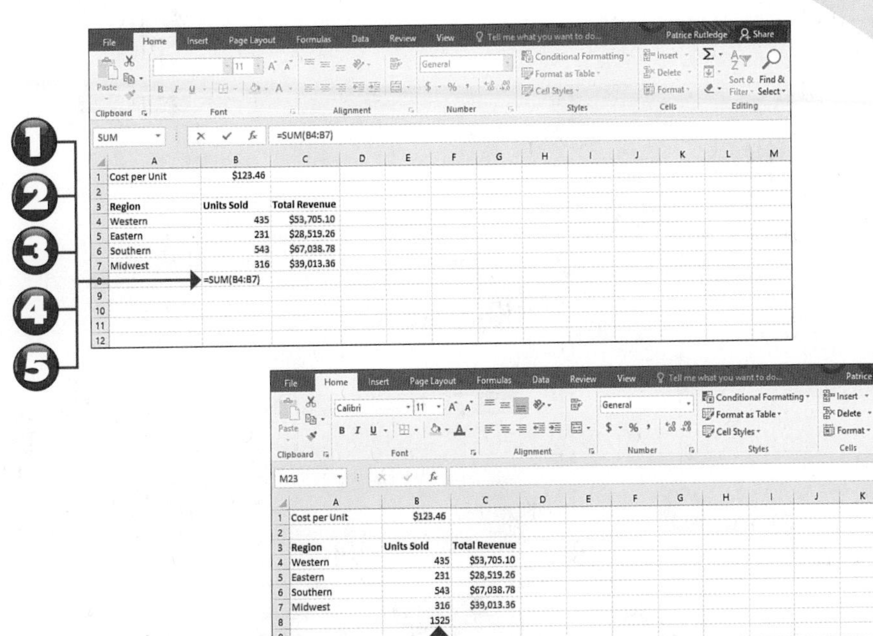


1. Type the equal (=) sign in the cell where you want to place the sum of values.
2. Type the function name **SUM**.
3. Type the open parentheses symbol.
4. Type the range to be totaled, such as **B4:B7**.
5. Type the close parentheses symbol.
6. Press **Enter**. The result of the calculation displays in the cell.

End

## NOTE

**Nonsequential Sums** There are two ways to reference a range of values. If the cells to be included are sequential, they are separated by a colon (:). If the range is nonsequential, the cells are separated by a comma (,). For example, the range (B8:D8) would include cells B8, C8, and D8; the range (B8:D8, F4) would include cells B8, C8, D8, and F4. ■

# USING THE AUTOSUM BUTTON

Excel's AutoSum button simplifies creating a basic addition formula. You can calculate a string of numbers in either a row or a column using this easy feature.

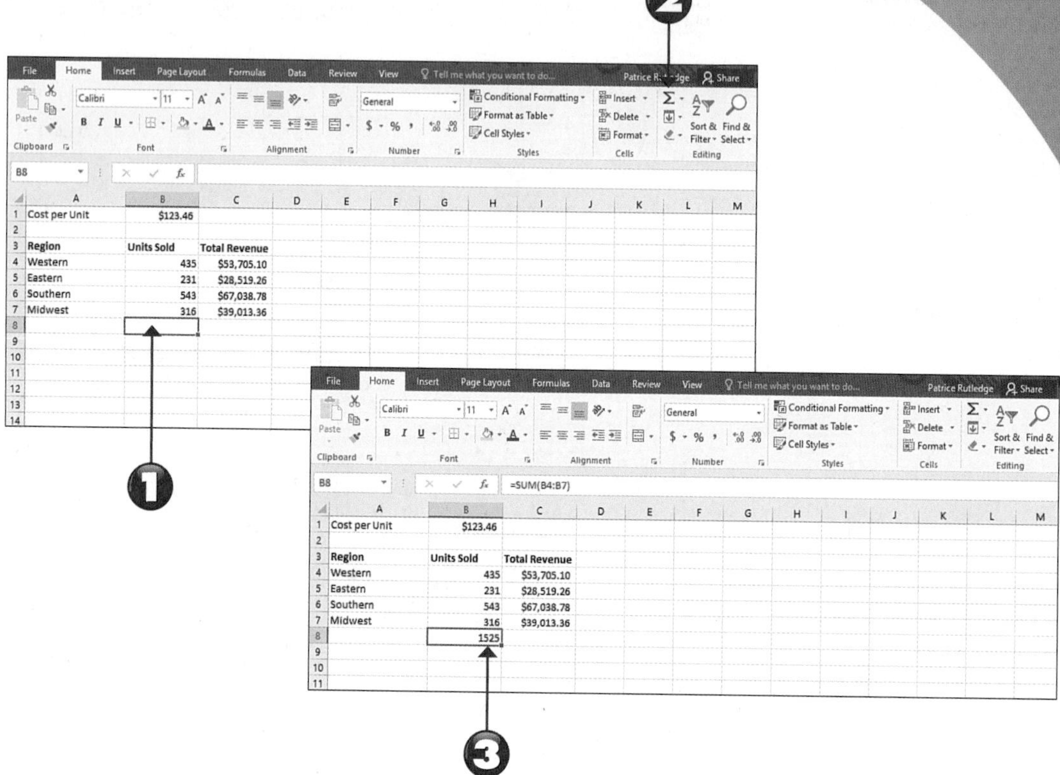

Start

1. Select the cell below or to the right of the values to be totaled.

2. On the Home tab, click the **AutoSum** button.

3. Press **Enter**. The result of the calculation displays in the selected cell.

End

## CAUTION

**AutoSum Looks for Sequential Numbers** AutoSum adds only sequential numbers. If you have empty cells in a column or row, AutoSum adds only the cells following the empty cell. For example, if cells A1 through A10 have numbers, cell A11 is blank, and cells A12 through A14 have numbers; using AutoSum in cell A15 adds only cells A12 through A14. ■

## NOTE

**Sum Directions** Excel sums the values directly above the selected cell first. If no values are above it, Excel looks for values in the cells to the left. ■

# USING THE AVERAGE FUNCTION

The AVERAGE function finds an average value of a range of cells. The syntax for this function is =AVERAGE(*range of values to average*). An example might be =AVERAGE(B7:D7).

Start

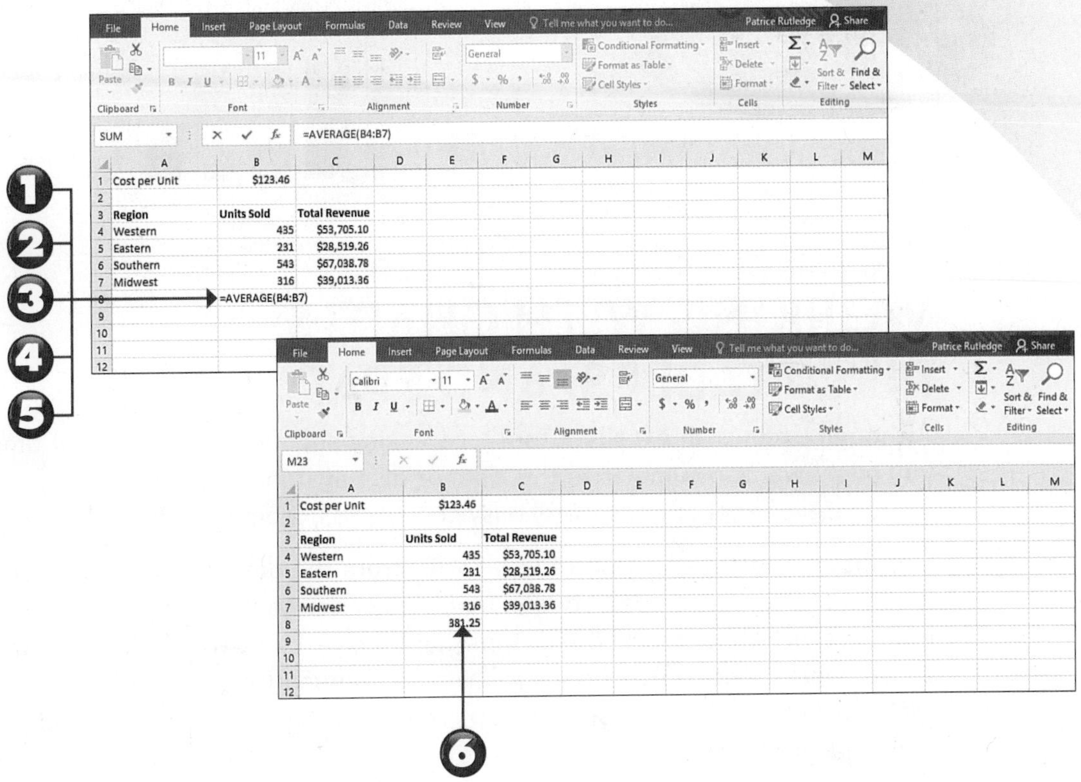

1. Type the equal (=) sign in the cell where you want to place the average.
2. Type the function name **AVERAGE**.
3. Type the open parentheses symbol.
4. Type or highlight the range to be averaged.
5. Type the close parentheses symbol.
6. Press **Enter**. Excel averages the values in the selected range.

End

## NOTE

**Consider Other Functions** Similar functions include the =MAX, =MIN, and =COUNT functions. The =MAX function finds the largest value in a range of cells. The =MIN function finds the smallest value in a range of cells. The =COUNT function counts the nonblank cells in a range of cells. Examples might include =MAX(C7:C15) or =COUNT(C7:C15).

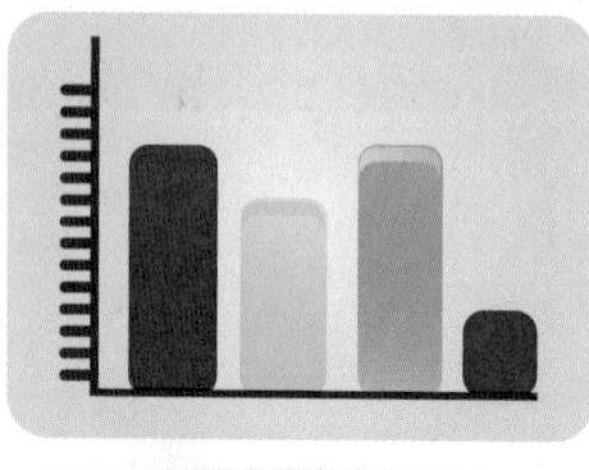

# WORKING WITH CHARTS, PIVOTTABLES, AND SPARKLINES

Although Excel is an excellent tool for tracking and calculating data, at times you might want to summarize this data or display it in a more visual way. Fortunately, Excel offers several easy options to accomplish this.

Creating a *chart* is an effective way to illustrate the data in your worksheet. It can make relationships between numbers easier to see because it turns numbers into shapes, and the shapes can then be compared to one another. If your worksheet contains data you want to summarize, consider creating a *PivotTable* report. A final option is to create a mini chart called a *sparkline* in a cell adjacent to your data.

# CHART AND PIVOTTABLE TOOLS

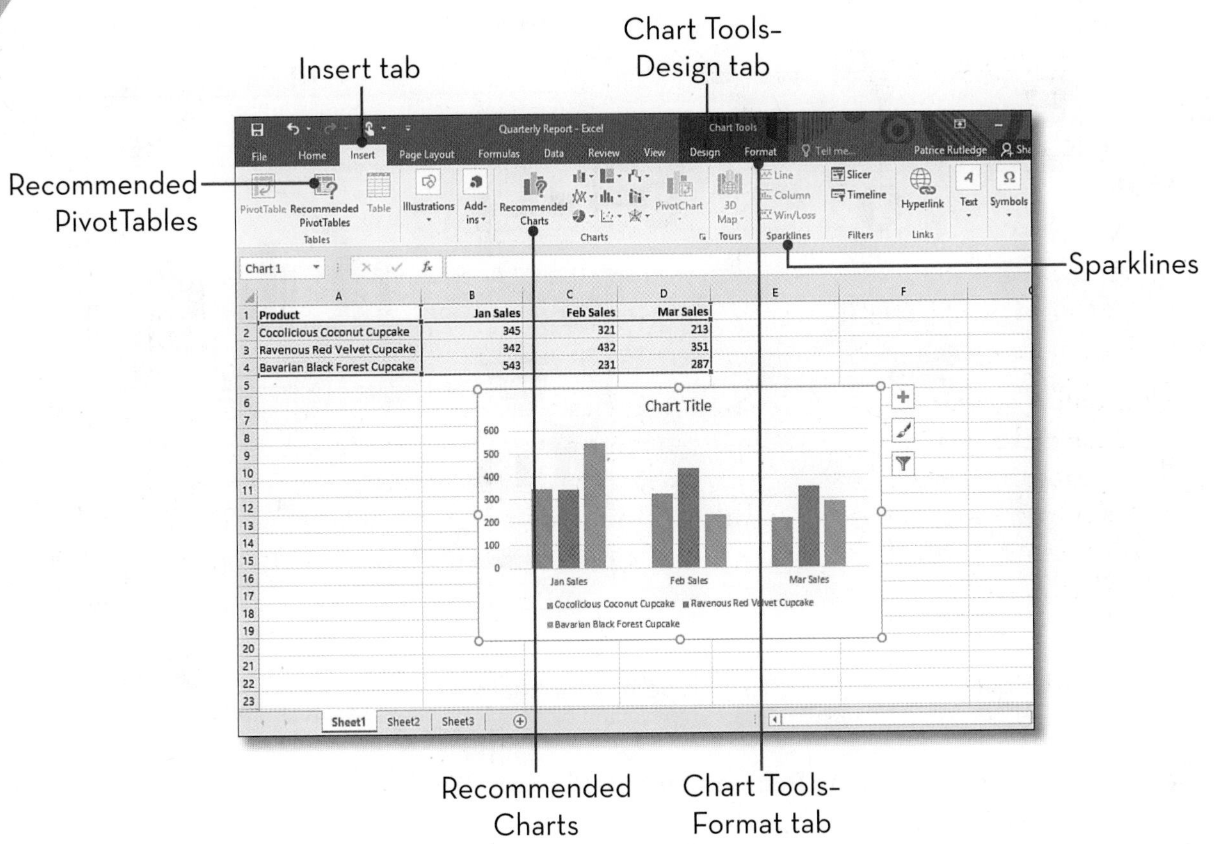

# INSERTING A CHART

The Recommended Charts tool simplifies creating an Excel chart by suggesting the best chart types for your selected data. This is particularly useful if you are new to charts and aren't familiar with the available Excel chart types.

Start

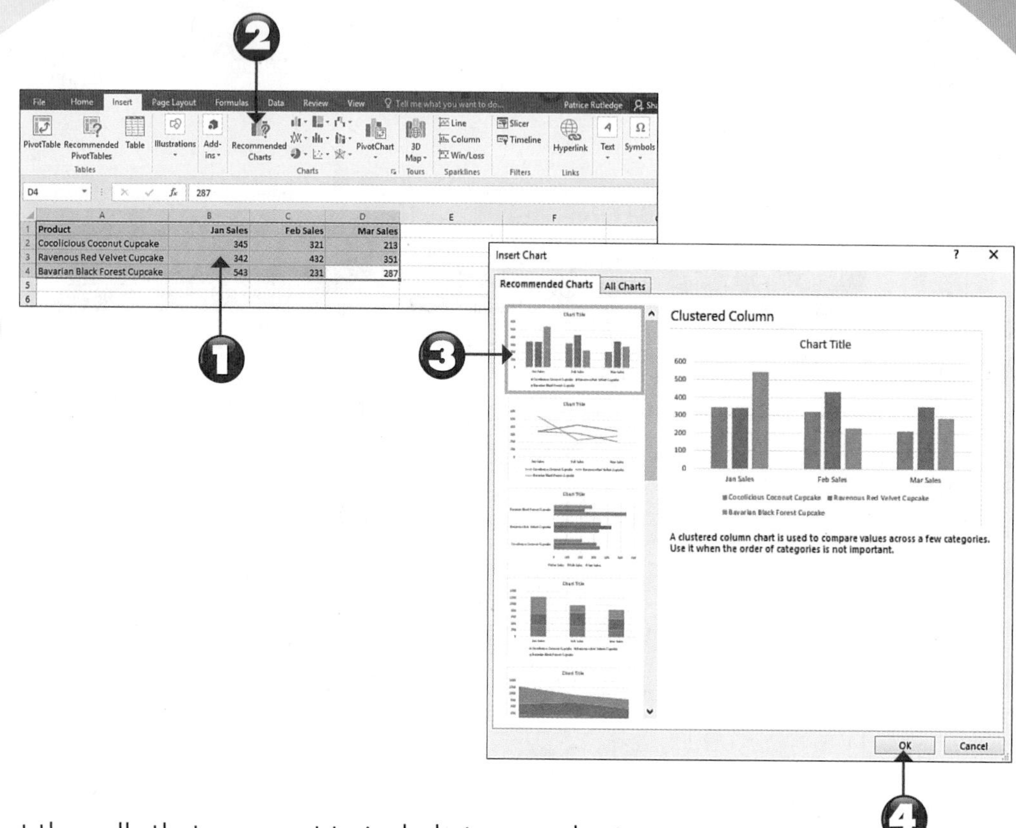


1. Select the cells that you want to include in your chart.
2. On the Insert tab, click the **Recommended Charts** button.
3. In the Insert Chart dialog box, select one of the chart types recommended for your data.
4. Click **OK** to close the dialog box.

Continued

**NOTE**

**Preview Your Chart** As you click each chart thumbnail in the Insert Chart dialog box, Excel displays a preview of the chart type. ■

**NOTE**

**New Chart Types** Office 2016 includes several new chart types including Treemap, Sunburst, Histogram, Box & Whisker, and Waterfall. To preview these charts, click the All Charts tab in the Insert Charts dialog box. ■

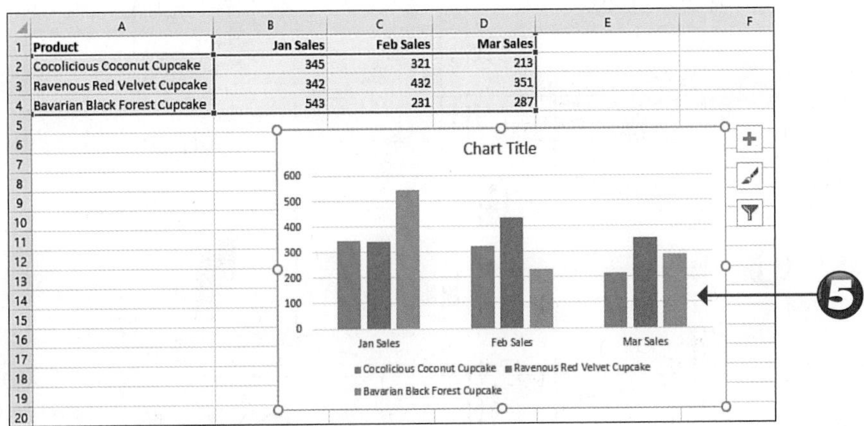


**5** Excel displays the chart on your worksheet.

*End*

## NOTE

**Excel Chart Types** Excel offers numerous chart types that display worksheet data in a graphical format. The most common chart types include column charts (compare values across categories), pie charts (show portions of a whole), line charts (display values across a line), and bar charts (compare values across categories that show duration). You can view all available chart types by clicking the **All Charts** tab in the Insert Chart dialog box.

# APPLYING A CHART STYLE

One easy way to modify the appearance of a chart is to apply a new chart style.

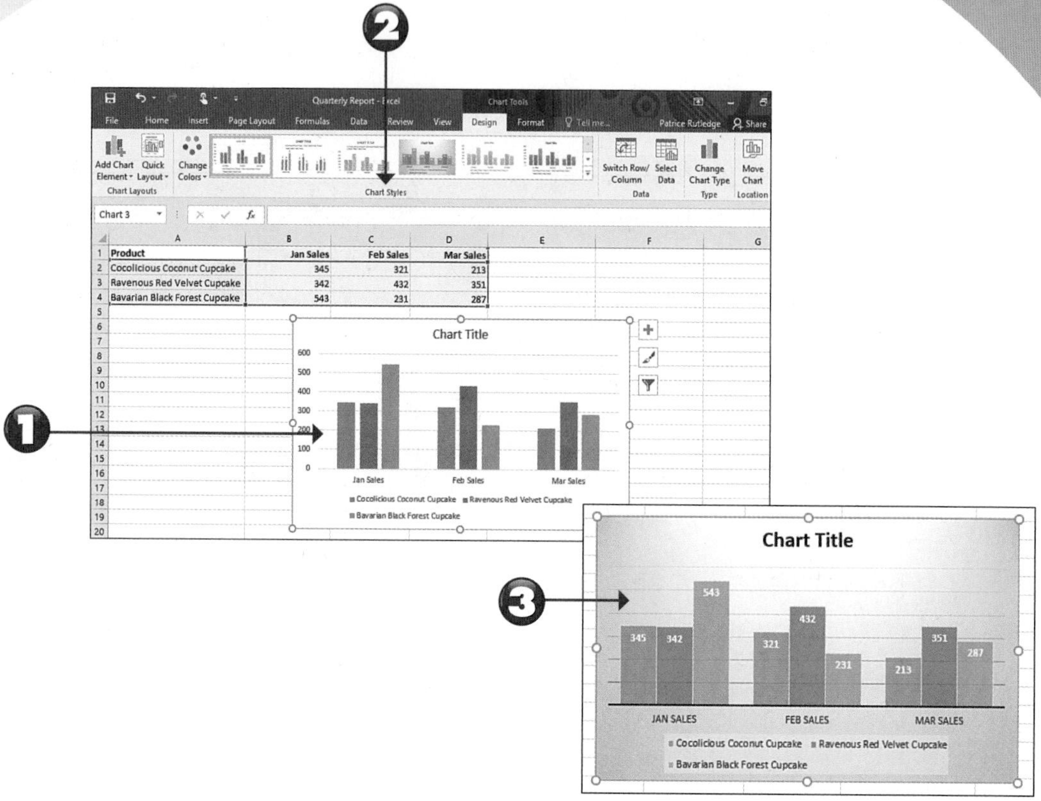

Start

1. Select the chart whose style you want to change.
2. On the Chart Tools-Design tab, select a new style in the Chart Styles group.
3. Excel applies the new chart style.

End

## NOTE

**Chart Styles** The chart styles available for a chart are associated with that workbook's theme and its colors. You can apply a new theme by clicking the **Themes** button on the Page Layout tab.

## TIP

**Preview Chart Styles** Pause the mouse over each option in the Chart Styles group to preview its effect on your chart.

# MODIFYING A CHART

Although Excel automates chart creation, you most likely still want to make a few changes. In this section, you learn several ways to modify an existing chart using the Chart Tools–Design tab.

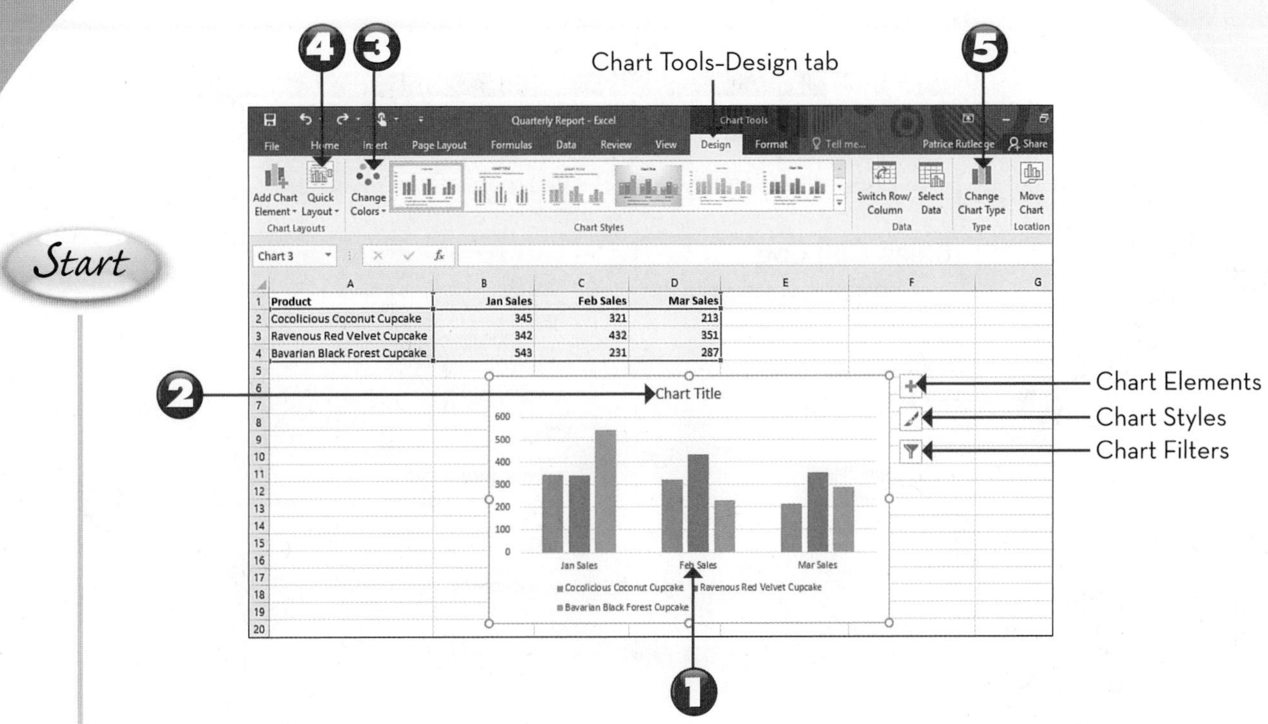


1. Select the chart you want to modify.

2. Click the **Chart Title** to remove the default text, and enter your own title.

3. Click the **Change Colors** button to apply a new color scheme.

4. Click the **Quick Layout** button to apply a new chart layout that works with your existing chart type.

5. Click the **Change Chart Type** button to select a different chart type, such as changing from a column chart to a bar chart.

End

**CAUTION**

**Modify with Caution** Although Excel offers a multitude of chart options, ensure that your chart is still readable after making changes.

# CREATING A PIVOTTABLE

If your worksheet contains extensive data, you can summarize it using a PivotTable report. For example, suppose you have a worksheet that lists every sale by product and customer over the past four quarters. You could use a PivotTable to summarize sales by product, customer, or quarter.

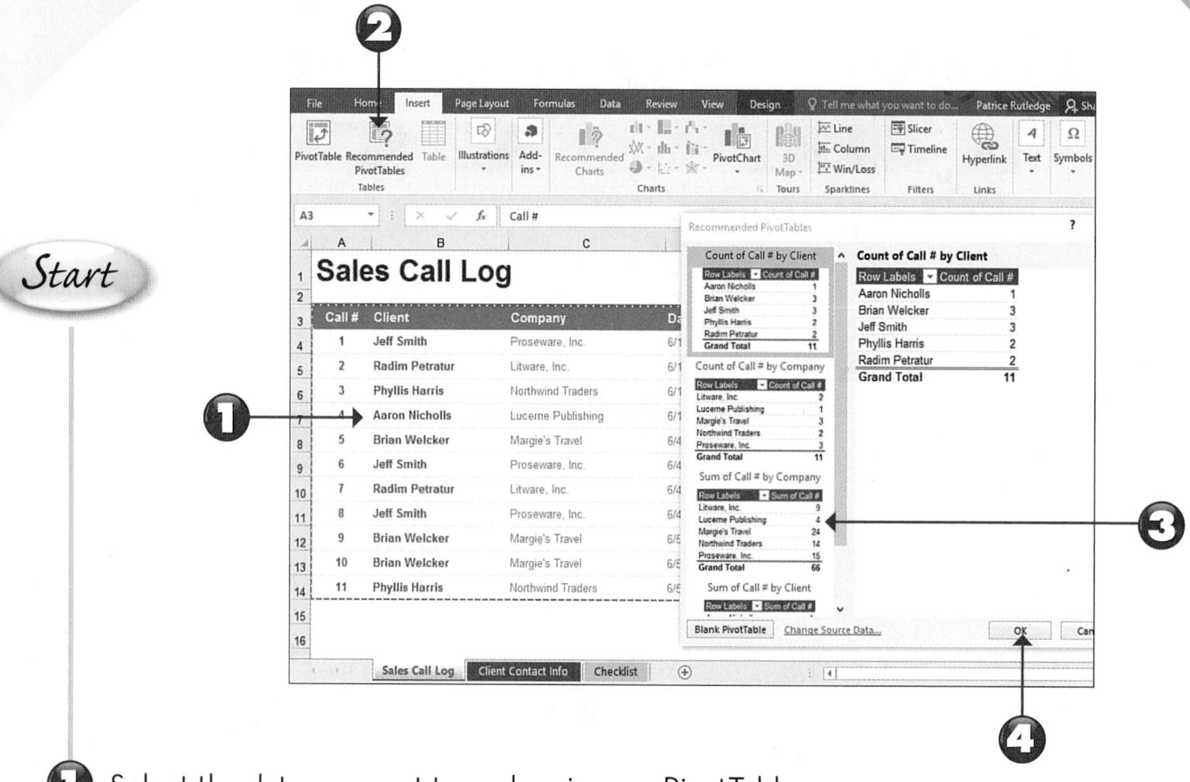


1. Select the data you want to analyze in your PivotTable.
2. On the Insert tab, click the **Recommended PivotTables** button.
3. In the Recommended PivotTables dialog box, select the report you want to create.
4. Click **OK** to close the dialog box.

Continued

**TIP**

**PivotTable Headings** If you don't like the headings in your PivotTable report, you can edit them.

**CAUTION**

**Not All Data Is Right for a PivotTable** Excel displays a warning message if your selected data won't work well as a PivotTable.

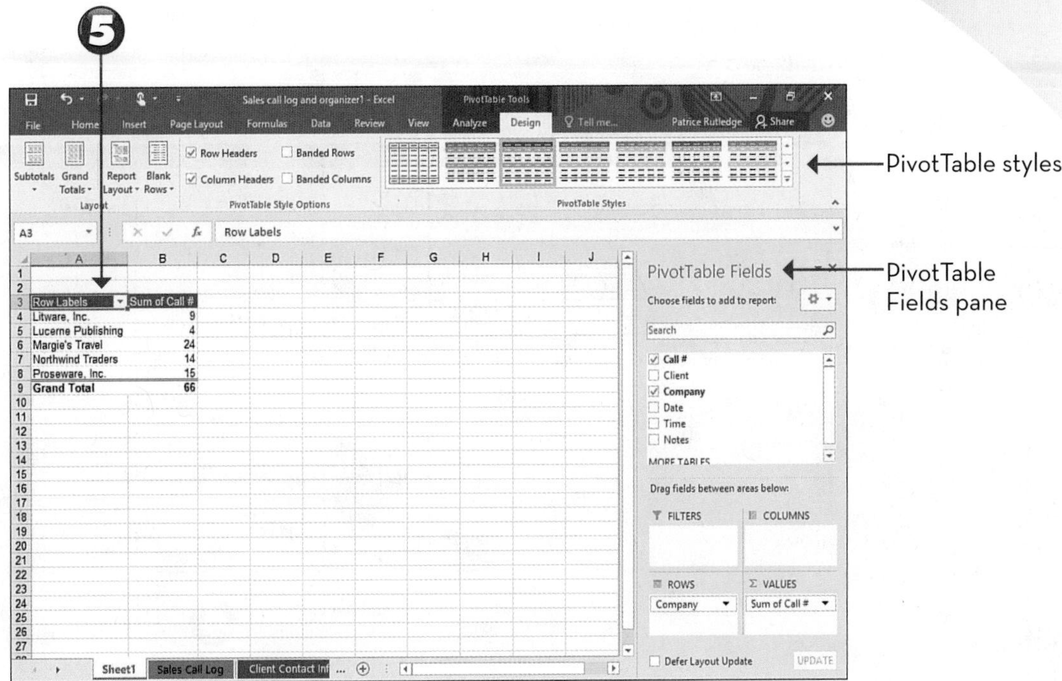


5 Excel displays the PivotTable report in a new worksheet in your workbook.

End

## NOTE

**PivotTable Fields Pane** You can modify your PivotTable on the PivotTable Fields pane, which displays when you select a PivotTable. For example, you can add and remove the fields analyzed.

## TIP

**PivotTable Styles** To apply a style to your PivotTable, select it and choose one of the PivotTable styles on the PivotTable Tools–Design tab.

# ADDING A SPARKLINE

Creating a sparkline—a mini chart that displays in a single cell—is another option for representing your worksheet data visually. In particular, a sparkline is a great tool for showing data trends.

Start

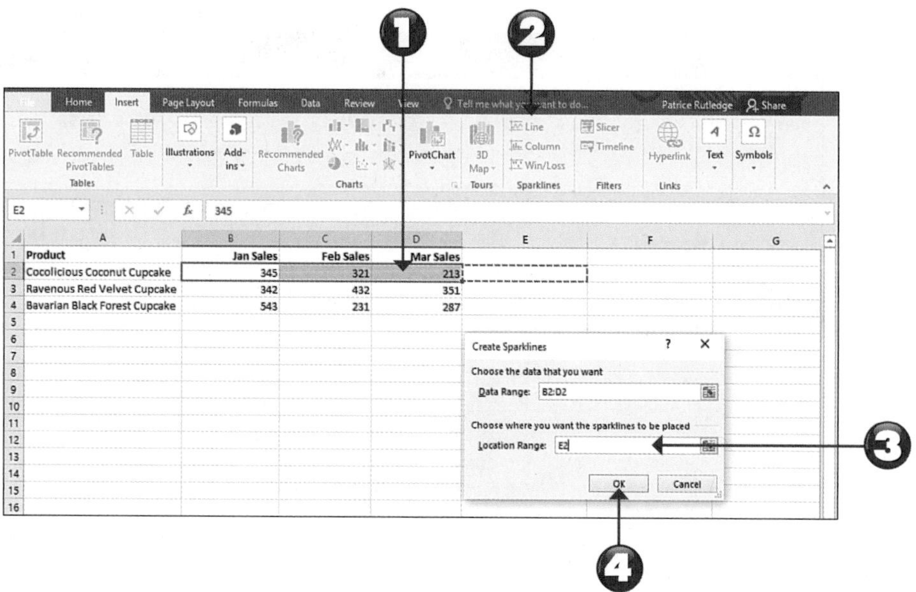

1. Select the data that you want to represent using a sparkline.
2. On the Insert tab, select the button for the type of sparkline you want to create: **Line**, **Column**, or **Win/Loss**.
3. In the Create Sparklines dialog box, enter the sparkline destination cell in the **Location Range** field.
4. Click the **OK** button.

Continued

## CAUTION

**Select the Right Data for a Sparkline** Be sure to select data that's suitable for a sparkline or Excel could give you an error message. A single row or column of numbers works best.

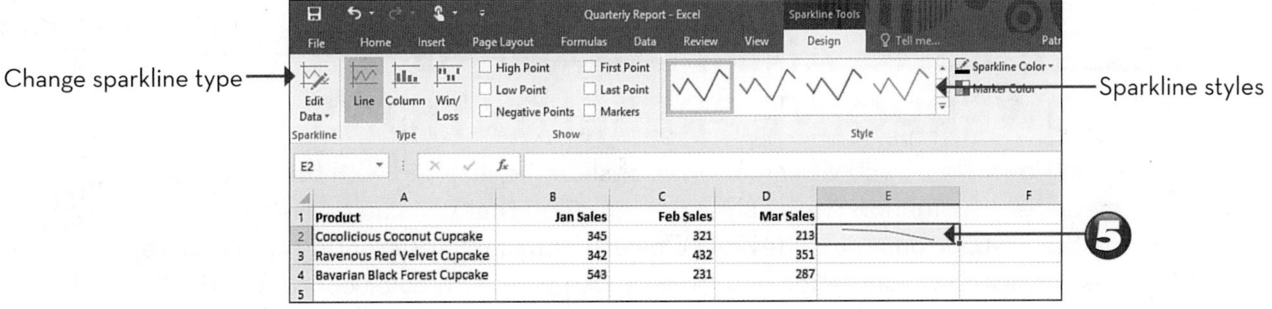


5 Excel displays the sparkline in the selected cell.

End

## NOTE

**Sparkline Types** Excel offers three kinds of sparklines: line, column, and win/loss. If you've created an Excel chart, you should be familiar with line and column sparklines. A win/loss sparkline is useful if your data contains negative numbers and you want to graphically represent losses in relation to gains (wins).

## TIP

**Sparkline Tools–Design Tab** When you select a sparkline, the Sparkline Tools–Design tab displays. On this tab you can apply sparkline styles, modify your sparkline content, or change its colors.

# CREATING AND MANAGING POWERPOINT PRESENTATIONS

With PowerPoint, you design a series of slides—enhanced with text, images, media, and animation—to create a presentation that you can deliver in person, on the Web, or on mobile devices. PowerPoint simplifies creating an effective, well-designed presentation with easy-to-use tools and color-coordinated themes.

Remember, however, that no matter how easy it is to create a basic series of slides, a great presentation requires strategic content, quality images, and a powerful delivery to truly motivate, inspire, and educate your audience.

# GETTING STARTED WITH POWERPOINT

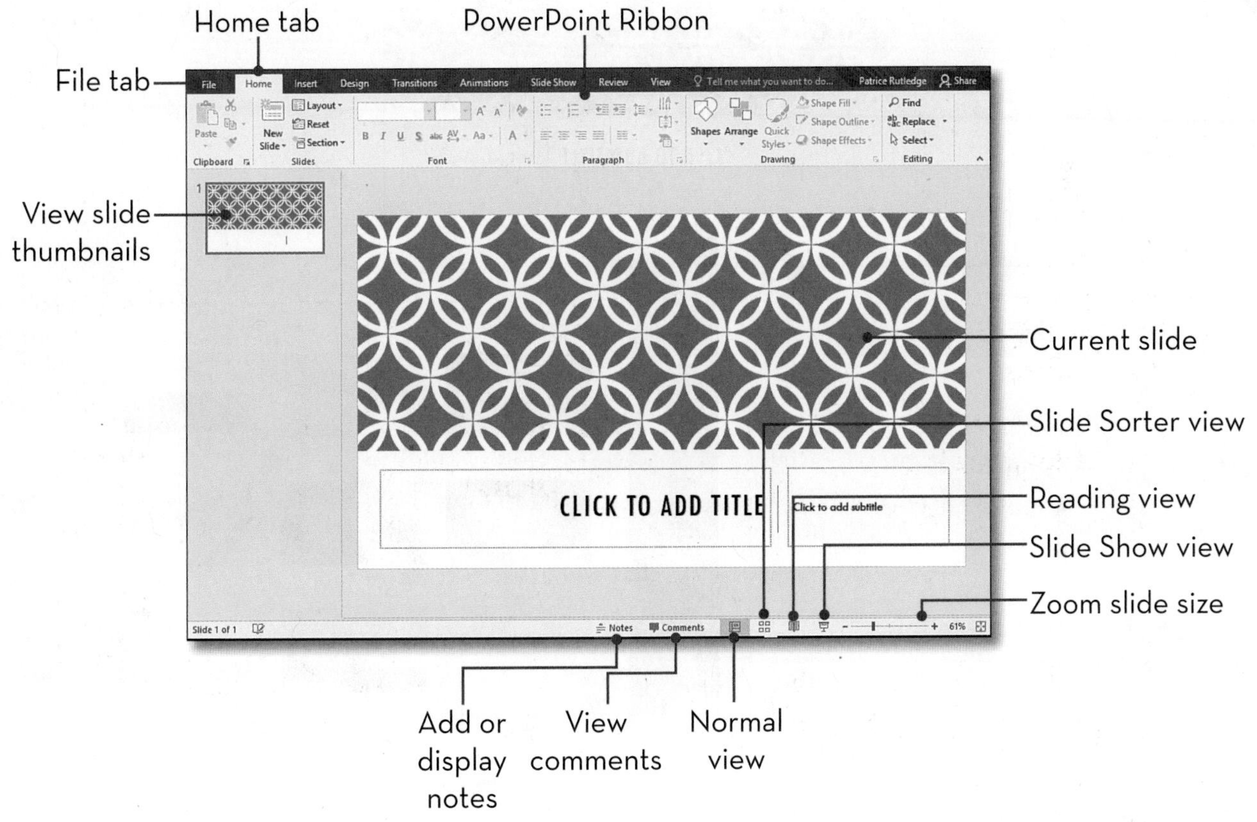

# CREATING A NEW POWERPOINT PRESENTATION

PowerPoint's professionally designed themes make it easy to create a quality presentation—even for the design challenged.

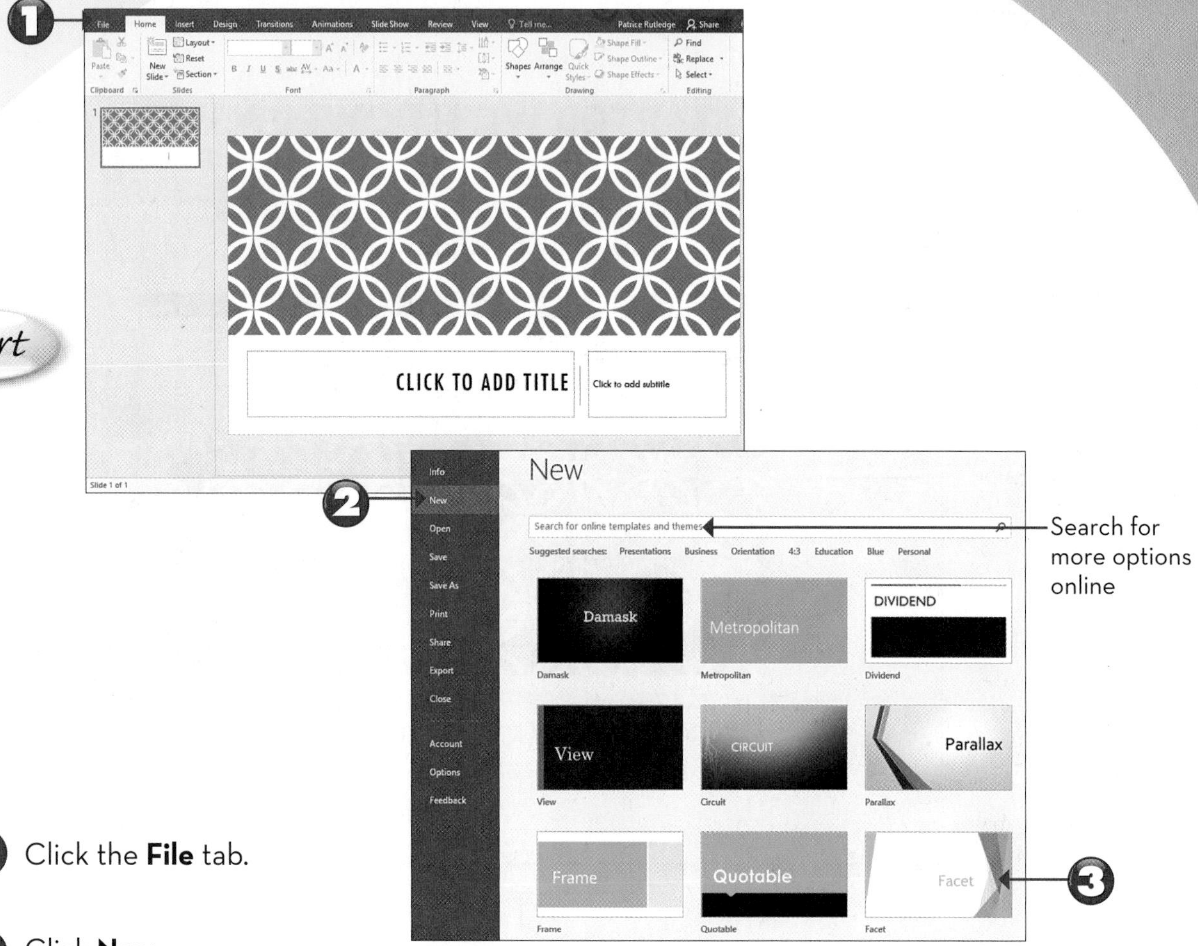

Search for more options online

Start

1. Click the **File** tab.
2. Click **New**.
3. Click the theme you want to apply to your presentation.

Continued

## NOTE

**PowerPoint Themes** A theme is a standalone file with coordinated colors, fonts, and effects to use in a single presentation. Other Microsoft Office 2016 applications—such as Word, Excel, and Publisher—also support themes, which enable you to create a consistent look and feel among Office documents.

## TIP

**Search for Other Themes** You can search for other themes and templates online in the **Search for Online Templates and Themes** box at the top of the New window.

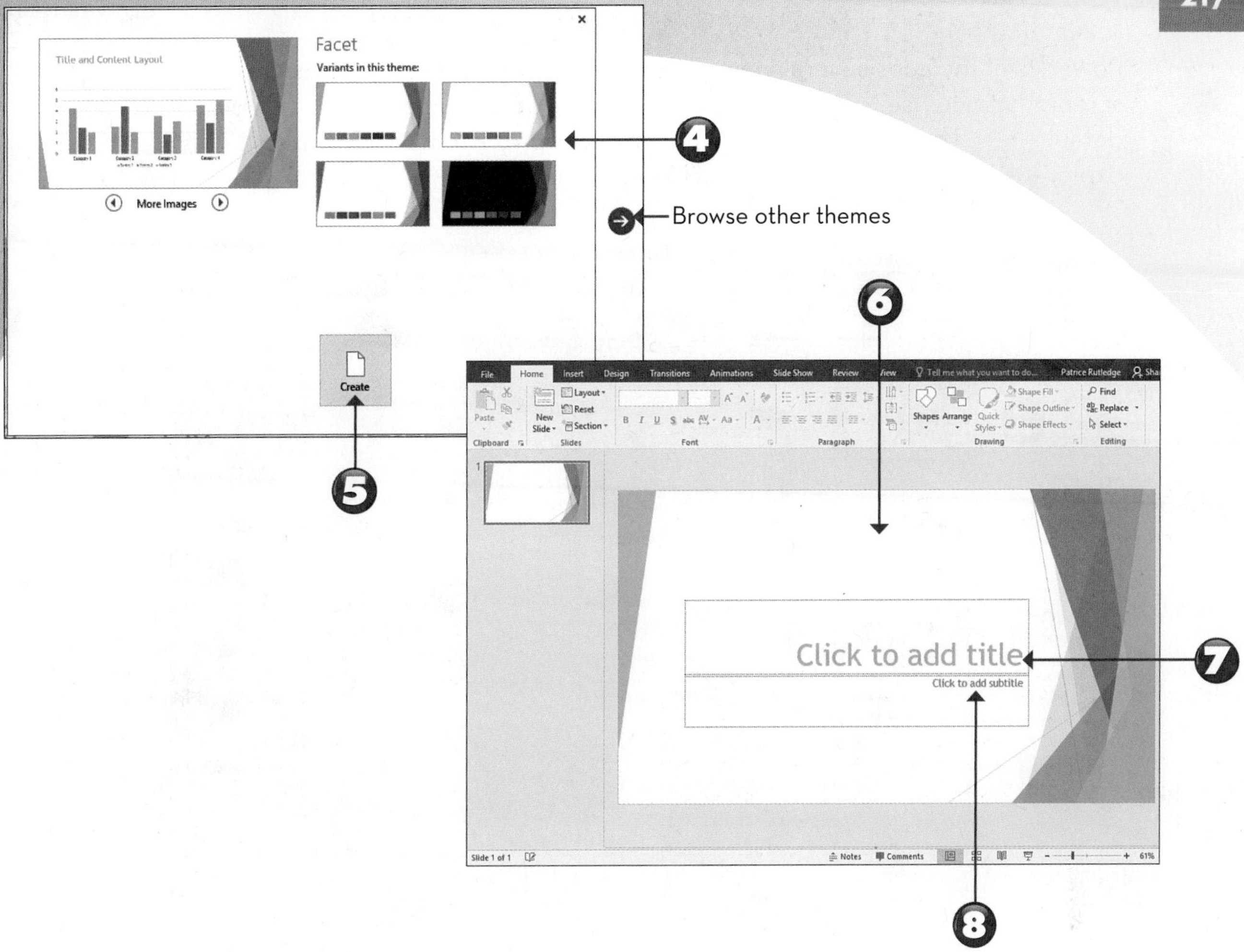

Browse other themes

4. Select the variant you prefer. Every PowerPoint theme has four variants.

5. Click the **Create** button.

6. PowerPoint opens a new presentation with a single slide in the Title Slide layout.

7. Click to add a title in the placeholder.

8. Click to add a subtitle in the placeholder.

End

**TIP**

**Change Your Theme** Don't like the theme you selected? Browse through other options by clicking the left or right arrows in the theme selection dialog box.

# EXPLORING NORMAL VIEW

PowerPoint includes several *views*, which are arrangements of slides and tools on the screen that you use to work with and view your presentation. Normal view is PowerPoint's default view. This is where you do most of your presentation design, so it's a good idea to explore this view and get to know its key elements.

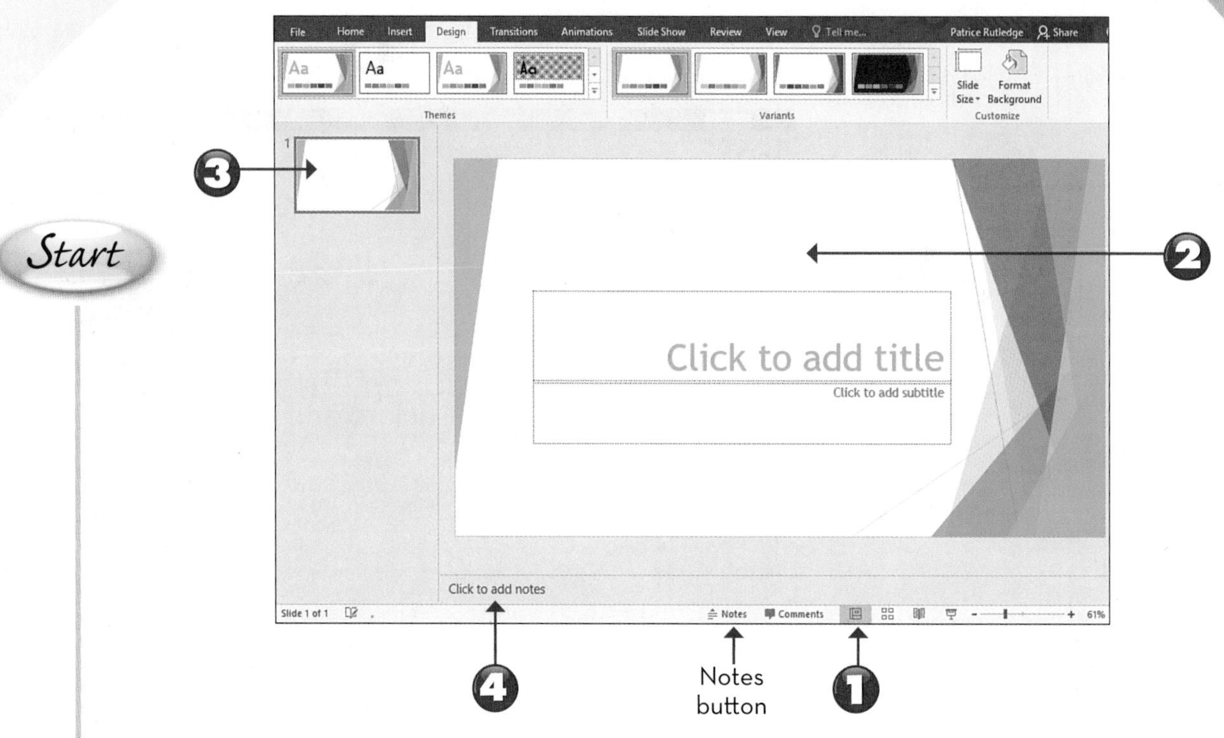


1. Click the **Normal** icon.
2. Click in the Slide pane to add text, graphics, tables, charts, and other objects to your presentation.
3. View images of your slides on the Thumbnails pane. You can rearrange and organize slides here or click a specific slide to display it in the Slide pane.
4. Click in the Notes pane to type speaker's notes or notes to yourself about your presentation.

End

**TIP**

**Another Way to Access Normal View** You can also access Normal view by clicking the **Normal View** button on the View tab.

**NOTE**

**Where's the Notes Pane?** If the Notes pane doesn't display, click the **Notes** button at the bottom of the screen.

# ADDING SLIDES TO YOUR PRESENTATION

You can add new slides to any open PowerPoint presentation. When you add a new slide, PowerPoint prompts you to select a predesigned slide layout.

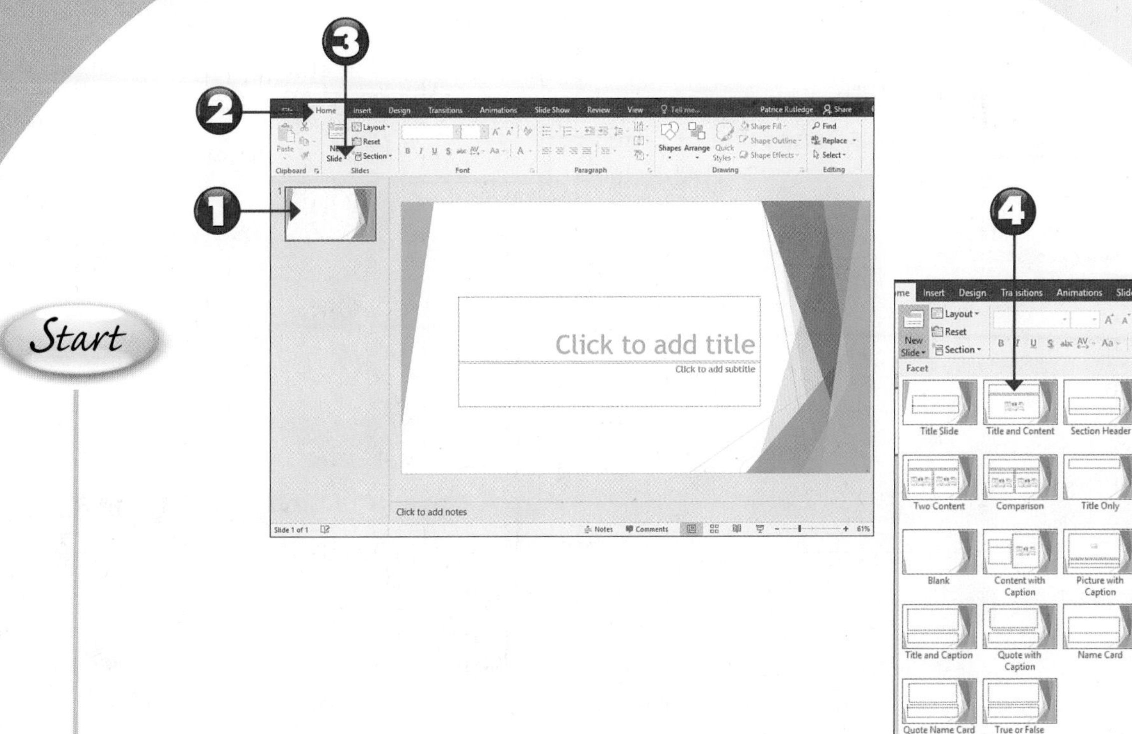


1. Select the slide that precedes the slide you want to add.
2. Click the **Home** tab.
3. Click the lower portion of the **New Slide** button.
4. Select a slide layout from the gallery that displays.

Continued

## NOTE

**Slide Layouts** A slide layout helps you add specific types of content to your slides, such as text, tables, charts, and pictures. Slide layouts include placeholders that enable you to position content in the correct location.

## TIP

**New Slide Shortcut** Clicking the top portion of the New Slide button adds a slide in the layout of the active slide automatically without opening the gallery. Pressing **Ctrl+M** also performs this same task.

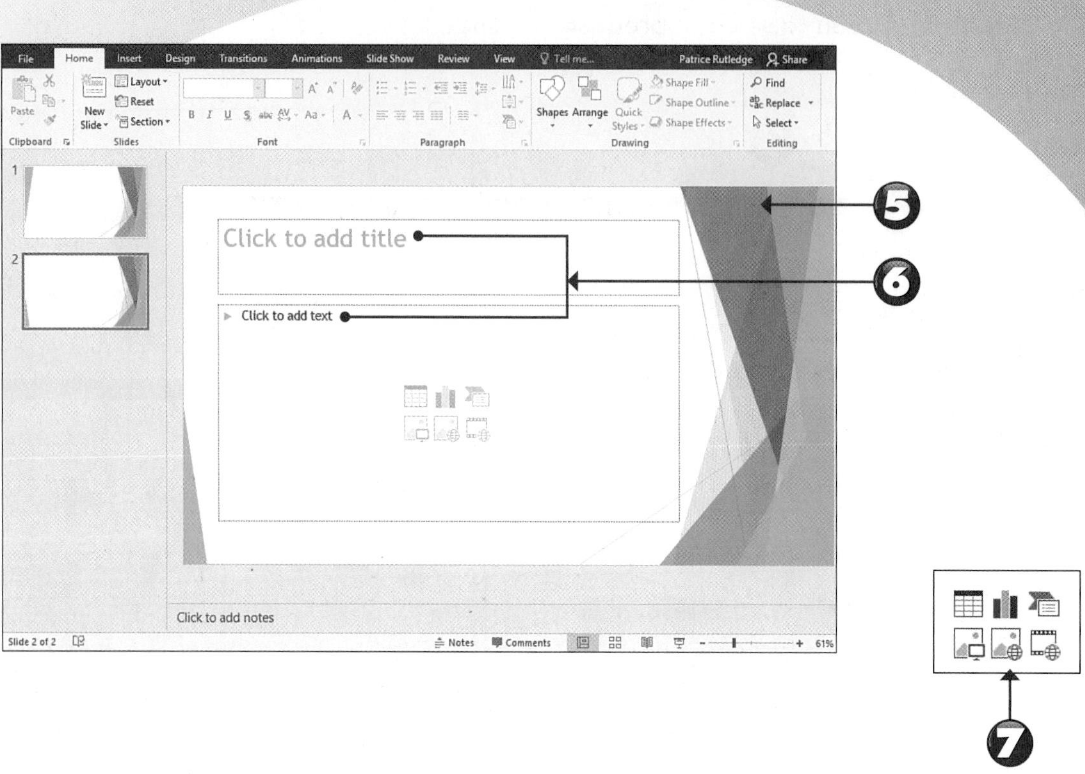


5 PowerPoint creates a new presentation with an initial slide in the layout you selected.

6 Add slide content in the placeholders.

7 If you selected a layout that includes the content palette, click the button on the palette that matches the type of content you want to insert. PowerPoint opens a dialog box that helps you insert that content type.

*End*

## NOTE

**Content Palette** The content palette enables you to add a table, chart, SmartArt graphic, picture, online picture, or video to your slide. Pause your mouse over each button on the content palette to view a description of the type of content that button inserts.

## TIP

**Switch to a New Layout** Didn't choose the right layout? Click the **Layout** button on the Home tab to apply a new layout to an existing slide.

# ADDING A SLIDE WITH A BULLET LIST

Although there is no slide layout specifically for bullet lists, you can create a list easily with the Title and Content layout.

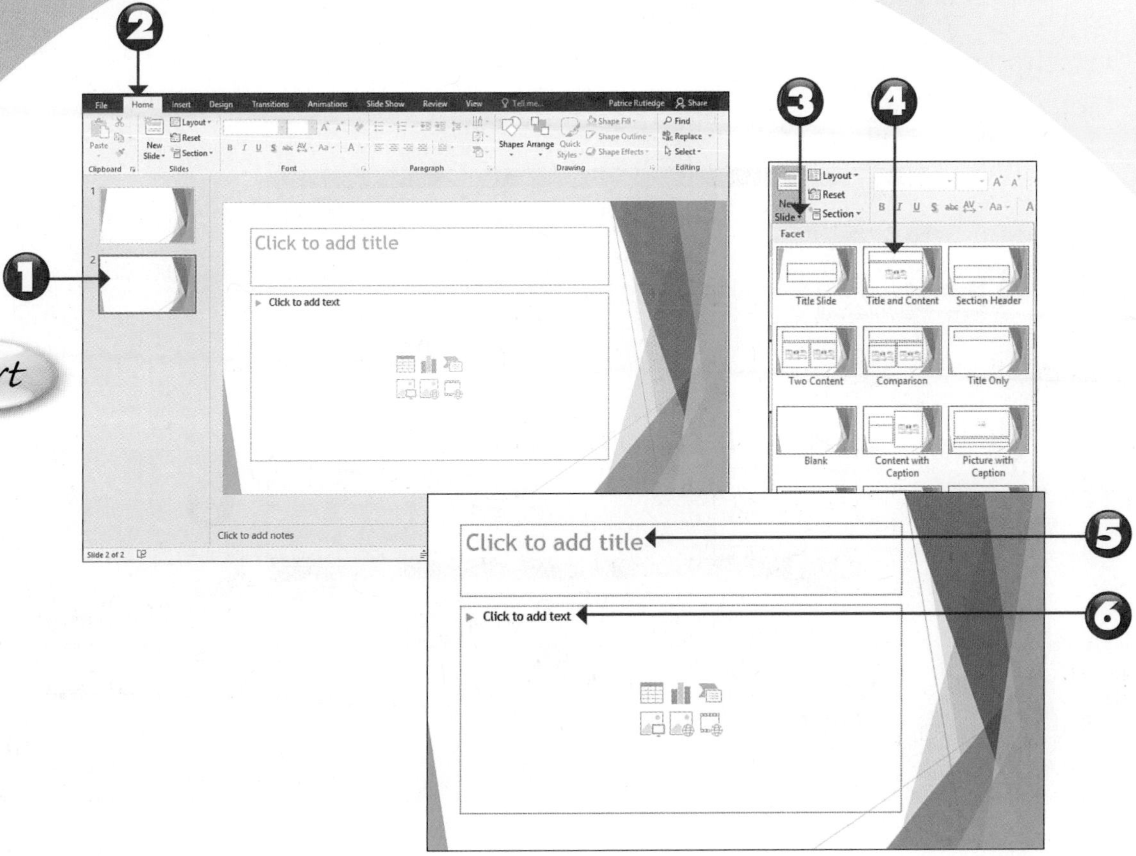

Start

1. In the Thumbnail pane, select the slide that precedes the slide you want to add.
2. Click the **Home** tab.
3. Click the lower portion of the **New Slide** button.
4. Click the **Title and Content** slide layout.
5. Click the title placeholder and type your slide title.
6. Click the starter bullet and start typing your bullet list, pressing the Enter key to move to a new line.

End

**TIP**

**Other Slide Layout Options** You can also create a bullet list by choosing any of the other slide layouts that include the content palette, including the following: Title and Content, Two Content, Comparison, and Content with Caption.

# ADDING SECTIONS TO YOUR PRESENTATION

Sections are particularly useful for large presentations where it's easy to get lost in a sea of slides. You can use sections to define presentation topics or distinguish between presenters, for example.

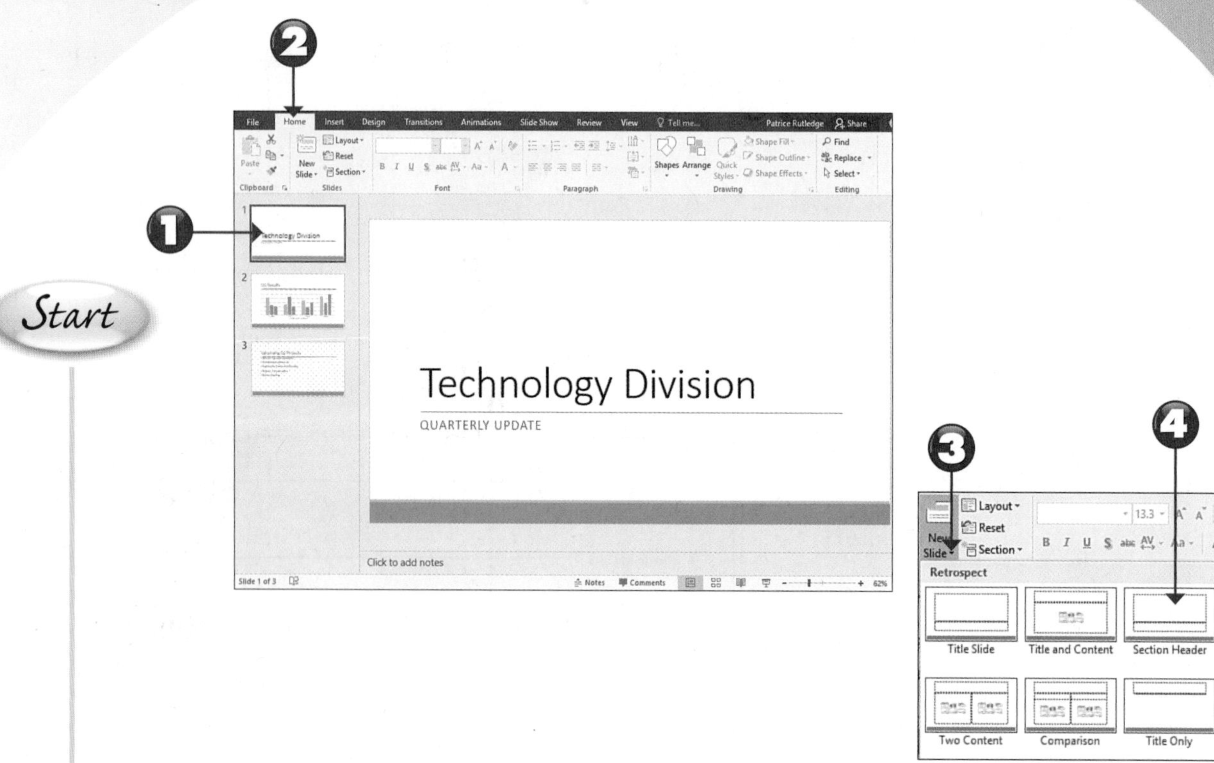


1. Select the slide that precedes the Section Header slide you want to add.
2. Click the **Home** tab.
3. Click the lower portion of the **New Slide** button.
4. Select the **Section Header** slide layout.

Continued

## TIP

**Move Sections** PowerPoint makes it easy to rearrange your presentation sections. Right-click the section you want to move and select either **Move Up** or **Move Down** from the menu.

## TIP

**Collapse and Expand Sections** If you have a lot of slides and sections, you might want to collapse them for easier viewing. To do so, right-click the section you want to collapse and select **Collapse All** from the menu. To expand again, select **Expand All** from the menu.

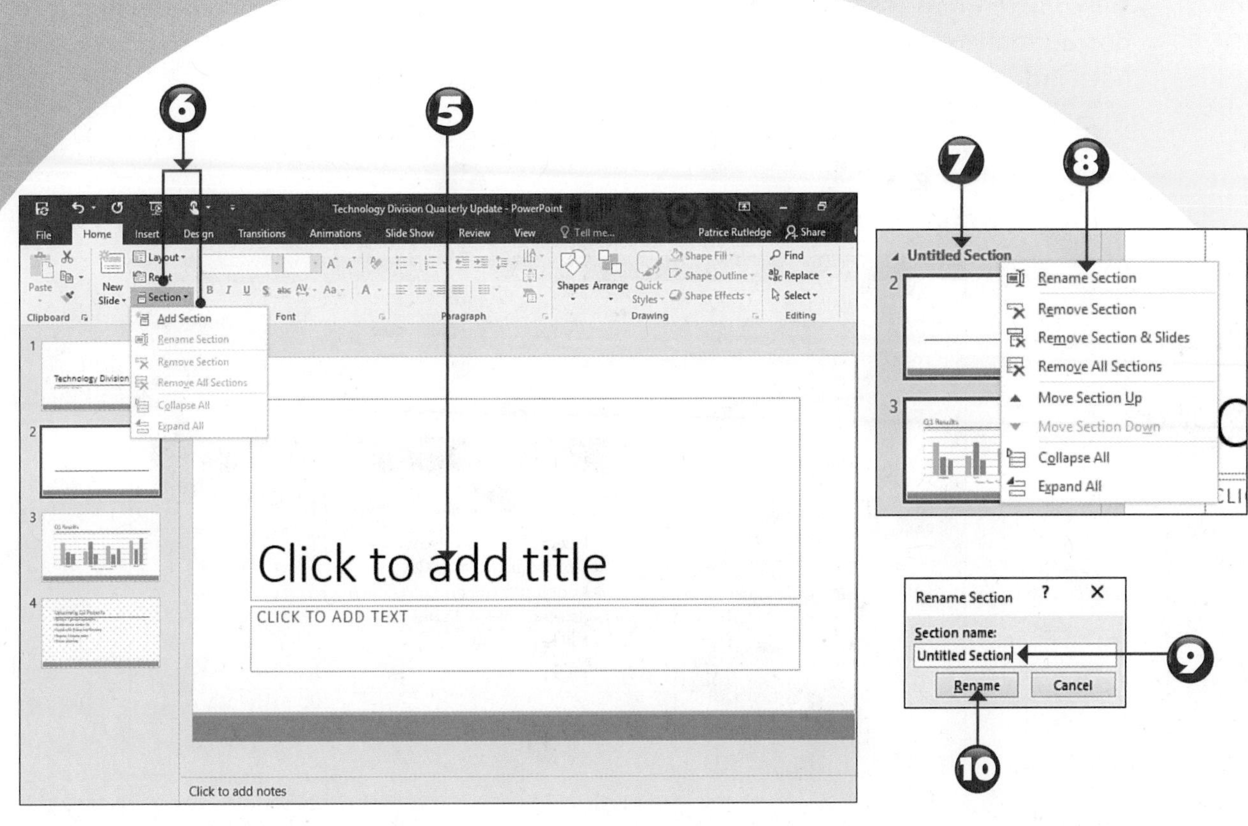


5. On the new slide, type a section title in the placeholder.
6. Click the **Section** button, and select **Add Section** from the menu.
7. On the left side of the screen, right-click **Untitled Section**.
8. Select **Rename Section** from the menu.
9. Enter a **Section name** in the Rename Section dialog box.
10. Click the **Rename** button.

End

## TIP

**Remove a Section** On the left pane, right-click the section you want to remove, and select **Remove Section** from the menu. PowerPoint deletes the section marker but not the slides in that section. If you want to remove all the slides in a section and not just the section marker, select **Remove Section and Slides** from the menu. To remove all sections, select **Remove All Sections** from the menu.

# CREATING A PRESENTATION OUTLINE

A solid, well-organized outline helps you achieve the goals of your presentation. In Outline view, PowerPoint organizes outline content in levels. For example, a slide is the first level on your outline. If your slide contains a bullet list, those bullets are the second level. If you have indented bullets, they are the third level of your outline.

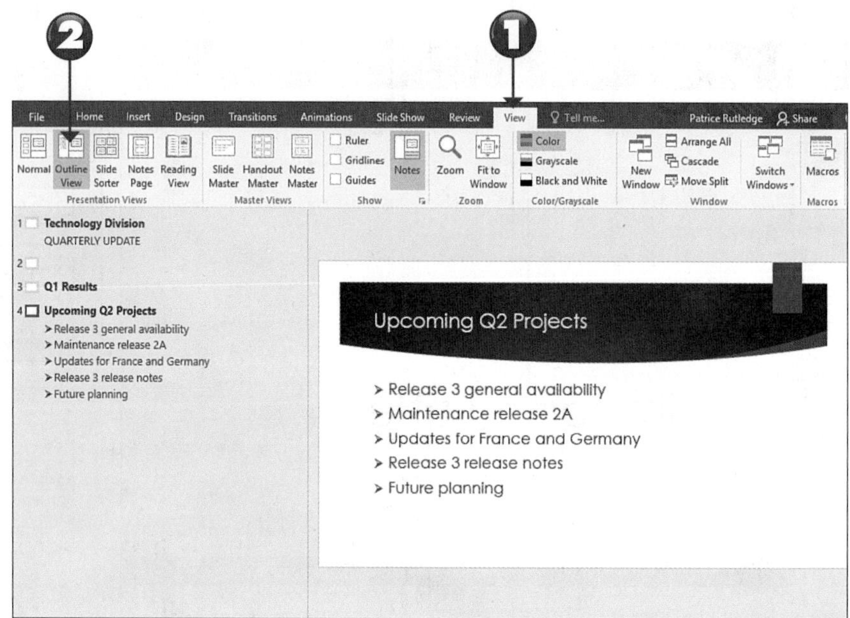


1. Click the **View** tab.
2. Click the **Outline View** button.

Continued

**CAUTION**

**When Not to Use Outline View** Outline view works best for slides that contain a lot of text, such as bulleted lists. Pictures, tables, charts, and other objects don't display in an outline. If your slides emphasize other types of content, such as graphics and charts, you'll find it more convenient to rearrange content directly on your slides.

**TIP**

**Delete Content** Select any outline content you want to delete, and press the **Delete** key on your keyboard. For example, you could delete a single bullet point or one or more slides.

**TIP**

**Collapse and Expand Your Outline** Collapsing hides all slide body text, which can make it easier to organize a long presentation. Right-click the Slide view, and then select **Collapse** and **Collapse All** from the menu. To expand again, select **Expand** and then **Expand All**.

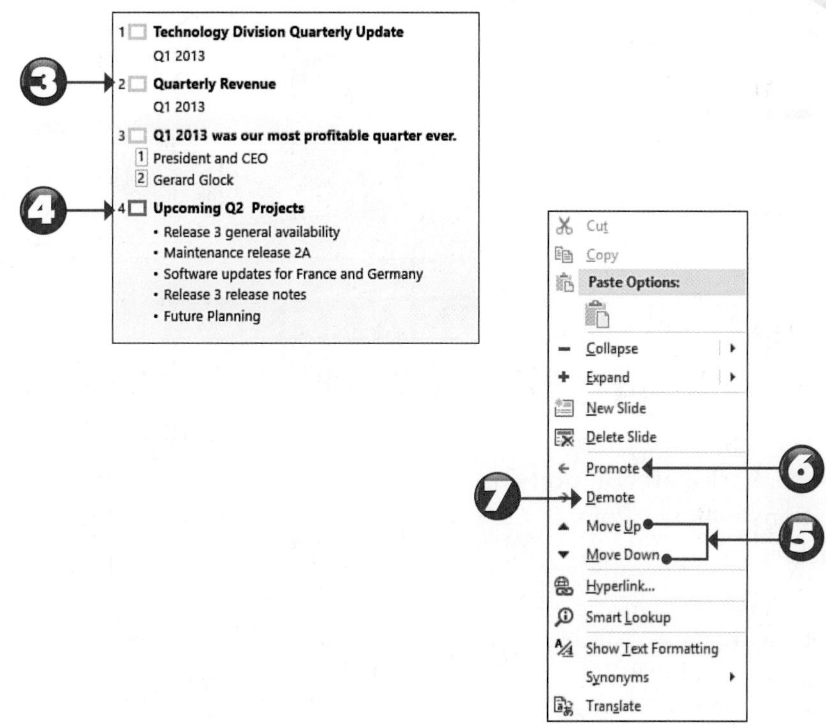


3. View an outline of your presentation. Each slide is numbered and followed by a slide icon and the title text.

4. Type new content, and press the **Enter** key on your keyboard to move to the next point.

5. Right-click a slide or slide content, and select **Move Up** or **Move Down** to move your selection.

6. Right-click slide content, and select **Promote** to change the selected text's outline level to the previous higher level.

7. Right-click slide content, and select **Demote** to change the selected text's outline level to the next lower level. Demoting a slide title moves the text of the selected slide to the previous slide.

End

**TIP**

**Import an Outline** If you create an outline in another application, such as Microsoft Word, you can import it into PowerPoint. Click the lower portion of the **New Slide** button, and select **Slides from Outline**.

# EDITING AND FORMATTING PRESENTATIONS

After you create a presentation, you'll most likely want to modify its appearance. Fortunately, modifying and organizing slides, content, and presentations in PowerPoint is easy using automated tools, the Slide Sorter, and slide masters.

When you finish with your presentation, you can print it for a final review or create handouts from your slides.

# POWERPOINT DESIGN OPTIONS

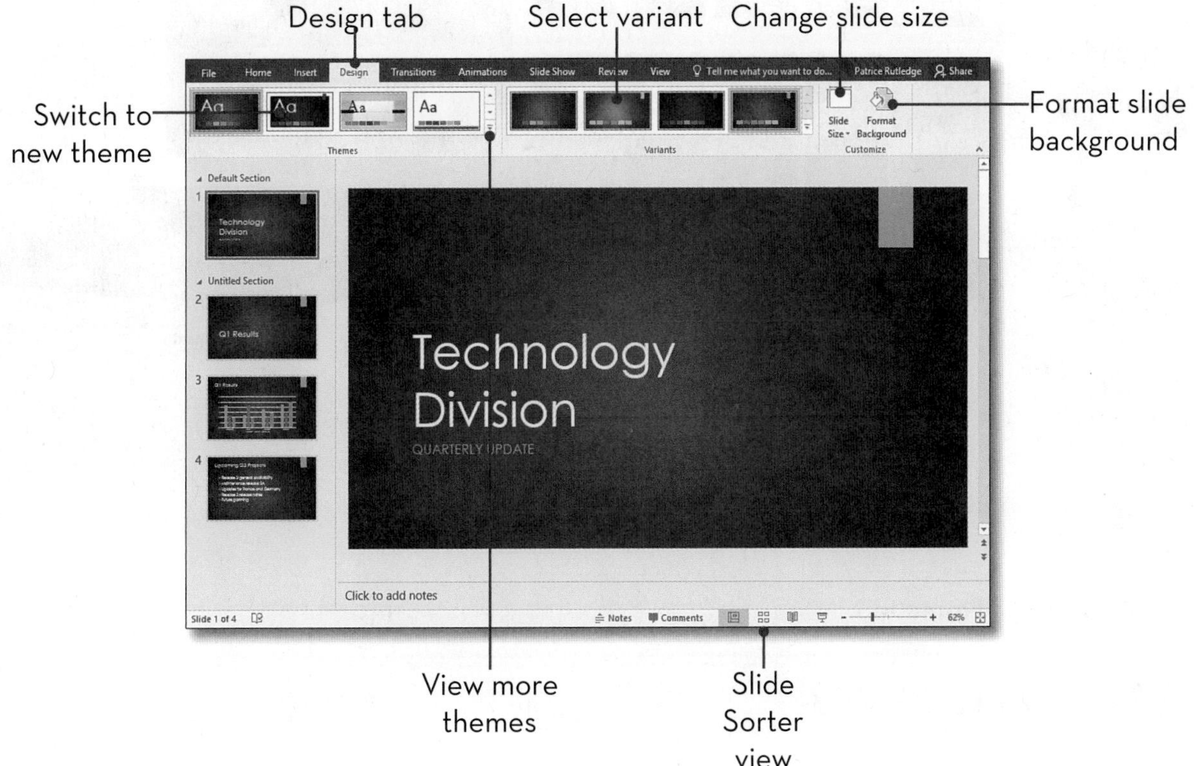

# APPLYING A NEW SLIDE LAYOUT

If you don't like the slide layout you applied to a slide—or you selected the wrong layout—you can apply a new layout easily.

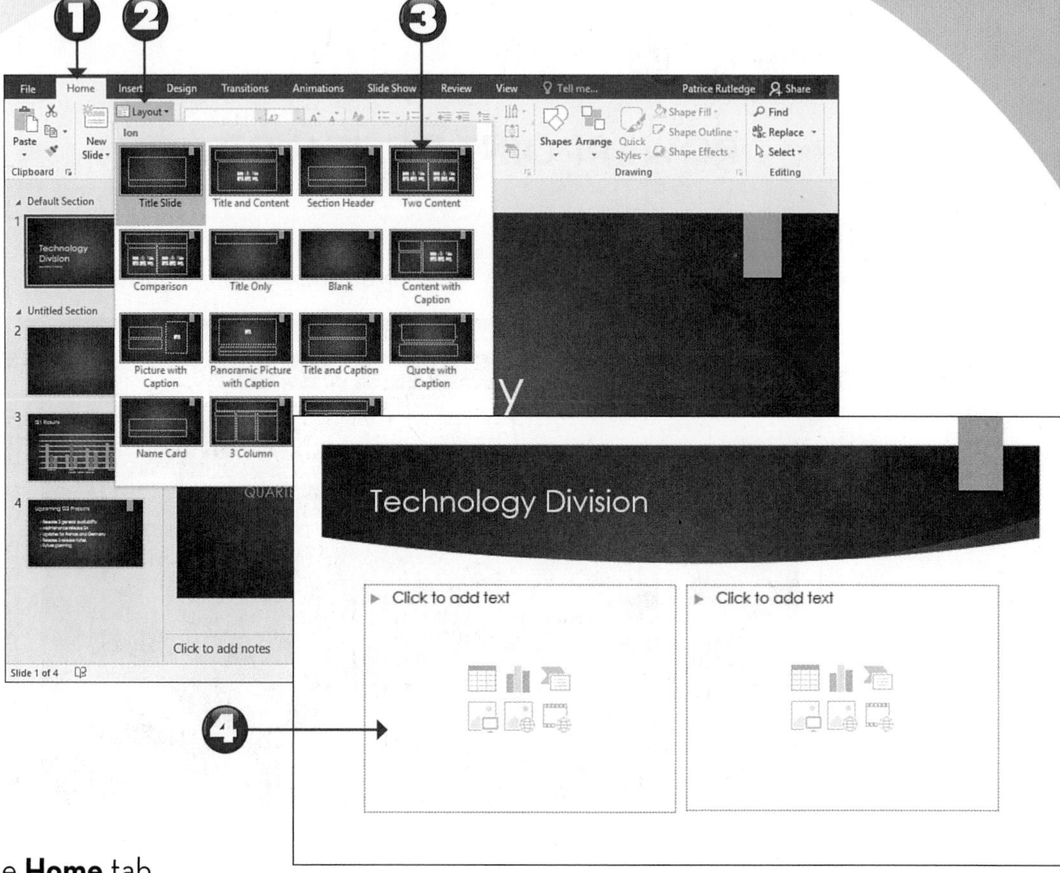

1. Click the **Home** tab.
2. Click the **Layout** button.
3. Select a slide layout from the gallery.
4. PowerPoint applies the new layout to your slide.

End

## TIP

**Slide Size** In addition to changing the slide layout, you can change the slide size. In PowerPoint 2016, the default slide size is widescreen (16:9) to match the dimensions of most computers and projectors. If you prefer, you can change your slide size to 4:3 by clicking the **Slide Size** button on the Design tab.

# APPLYING A NEW THEME

When you create a presentation, PowerPoint automatically applies a theme: a coordinated set of colors, fonts, and effects. However, you can easily change the existing theme in a matter of seconds.

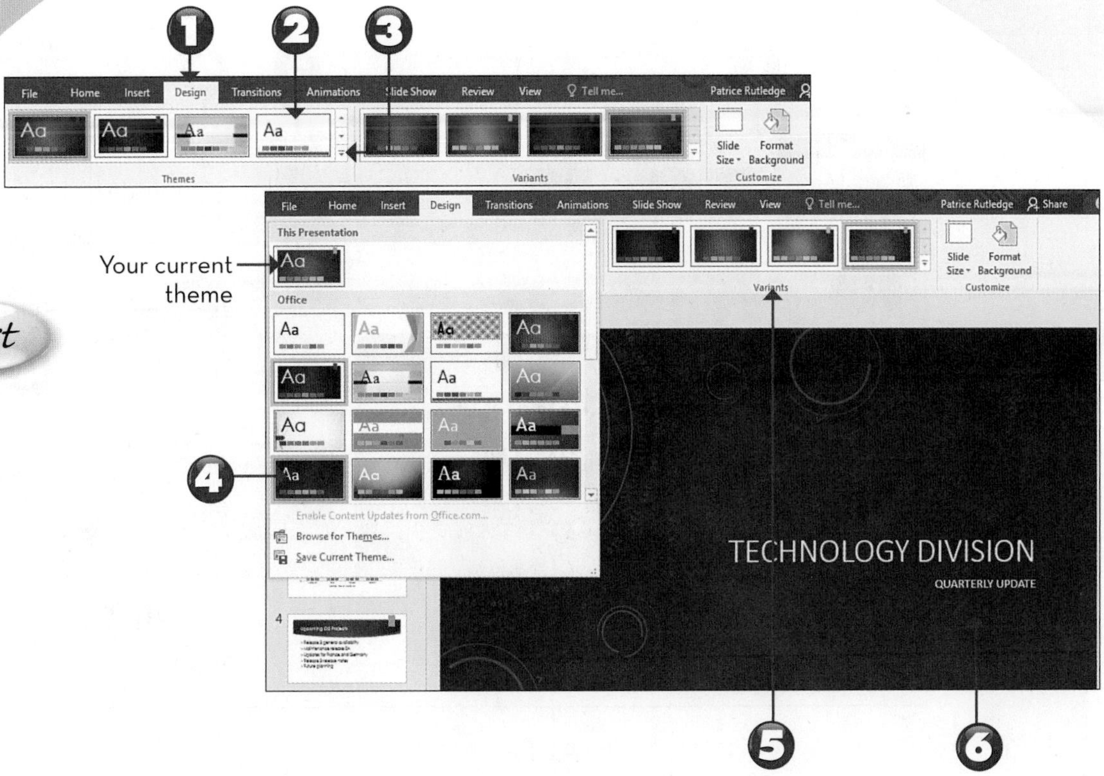

1. Click the **Design** tab.
2. Click one of the themes in the **Themes** group.
3. If none of the themes in the Themes group suit your needs, click the down arrow on the right side of the Themes box to display a gallery of additional themes.
4. Select the theme you want to use.
5. Select a variant to apply to your theme.
6. PowerPoint applies this new theme and its color variant to your presentation.

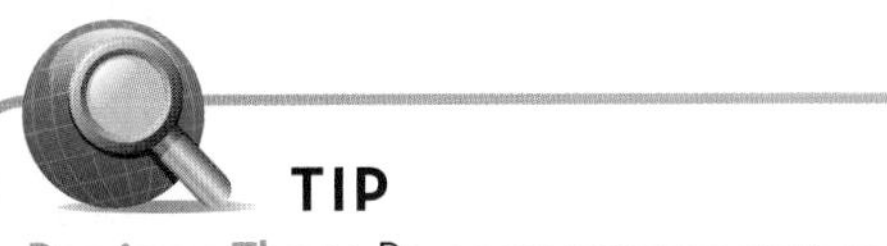

**TIP**

**Preview a Theme** Pause your mouse over each theme to preview it in your presentation.

# FORMATTING A SLIDE'S BACKGROUND

You can further customize your theme by applying, removing, and modifying its background. In addition to specific color backgrounds, you can also add special effects such as shading, patterns, textures, and pictures.

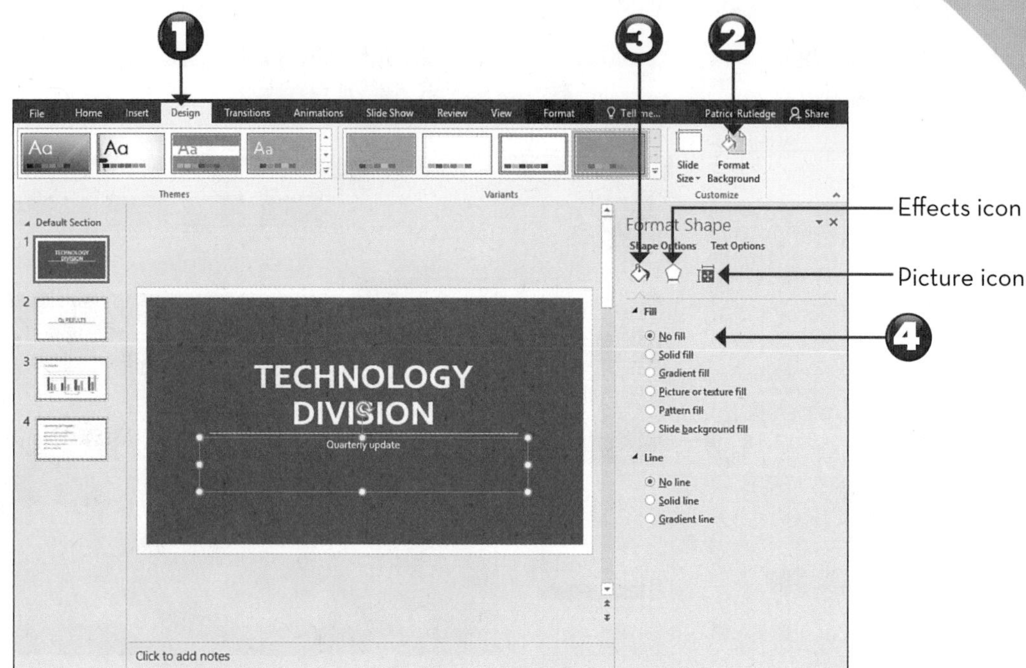


1. Click the **Design** tab.
2. Click the **Format Background** button.
3. Click the **Fill** icon to make changes to your background fill color, such as applying a solid, gradient, picture, texture, or pattern fill.
4. Specify the kind of fill you want to apply—such as a solid, gradient, or pattern—and select from the options that display at the bottom of the pane.

Continued

**TIP**

**Make the Right Changes** The Format Background pane includes numerous options for customizing your background's fill, effects, and pictures. Before making changes, be sure to review all the available options and make changes that truly enhance your presentation.

**NOTE**

**Format Effects and Pictures** You can also click the **Effects** icon or **Picture** icon to make additional background changes. Be aware that these formatting options are available for some, but not all, backgrounds.

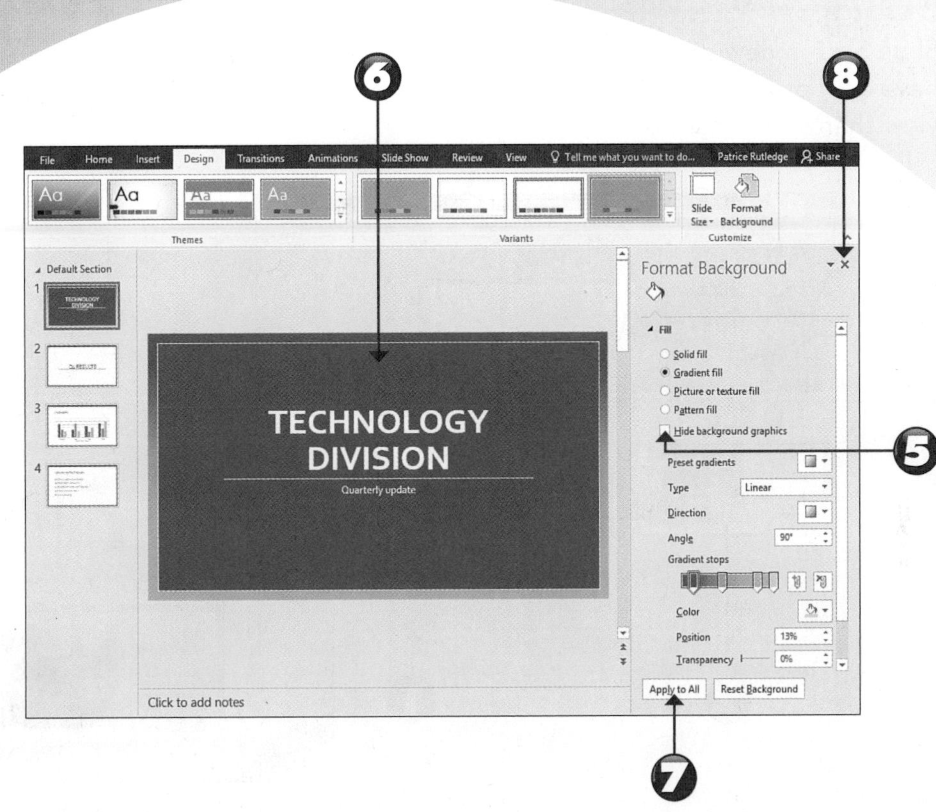


5. Select the **Hide background graphics** check box to hide the graphics included with your presentation theme. PowerPoint removes these objects but retains the original colors.

6. PowerPoint previews your changes in the Slide pane.

7. Click **Apply to All** if you want to apply this format to all slides in your presentation.

8. Click the **Close** button to close the Format Background pane.

End

### TIP

**Starting Over** If you don't like the formatting options you applied, click the **Reset Background** button to start again.

# ORGANIZING YOUR PRESENTATION WITH SLIDE SORTER VIEW

Slide Sorter view displays smaller versions of your slides in several rows and columns. If you have a lot of reorganization to do, it's usually easier to accomplish this task in Slide Sorter view than in Normal view.

Start

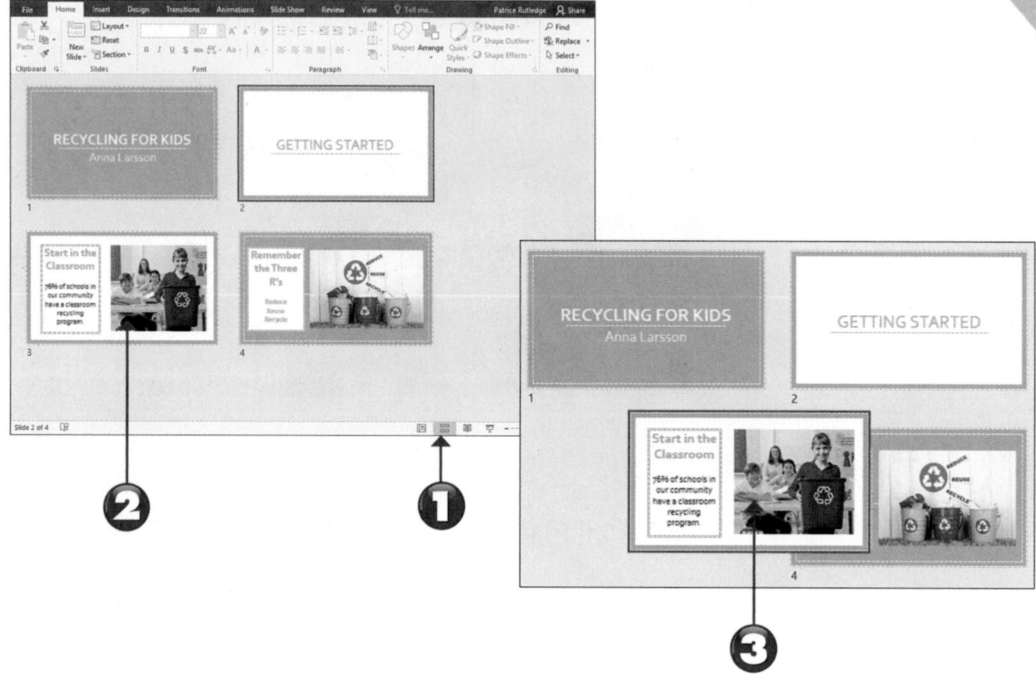


1. Click the **Slide Sorter** button on the lower-right corner of the PowerPoint window.
2. Select a slide you want to move. PowerPoint displays a red border around it.
3. Drag the slide to its new location.

Continued

**TIP**

**View Slide Detail** To view a particular slide in more detail, double-click it to open it in Normal view.

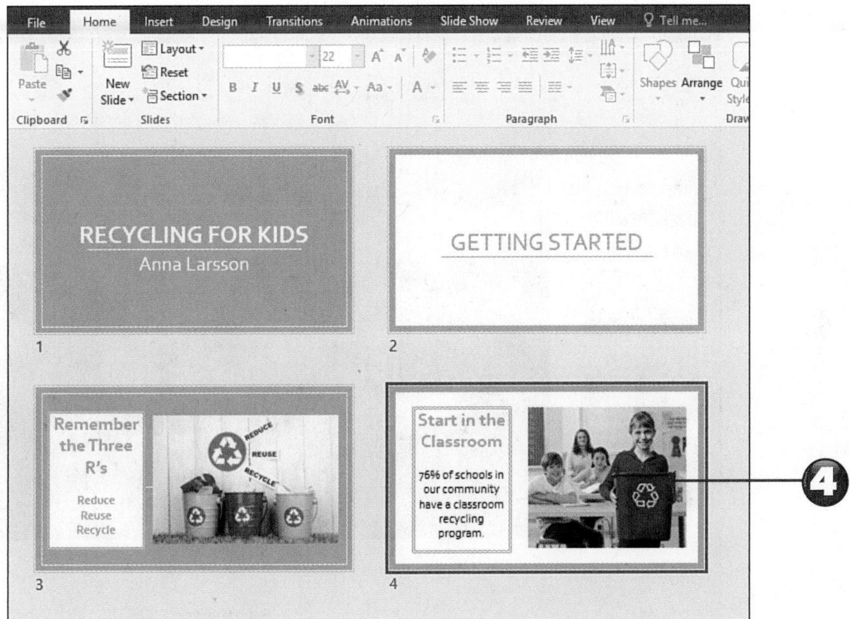


**4** PowerPoint displays the slide in its new location.

*End*

**TIP**

**Deleting Slides** To delete a slide, select it and press the **Delete** key on your keyboard.

**TIP**

**Delete Multiple Slides** To select multiple slides to delete, press **Ctrl**, select the slides, and then press the **Delete** key.

# COPYING AND MOVING SLIDES FROM ONE PRESENTATION TO ANOTHER

Using Slide Sorter view, you can copy or move slides from one presentation to another.

Start

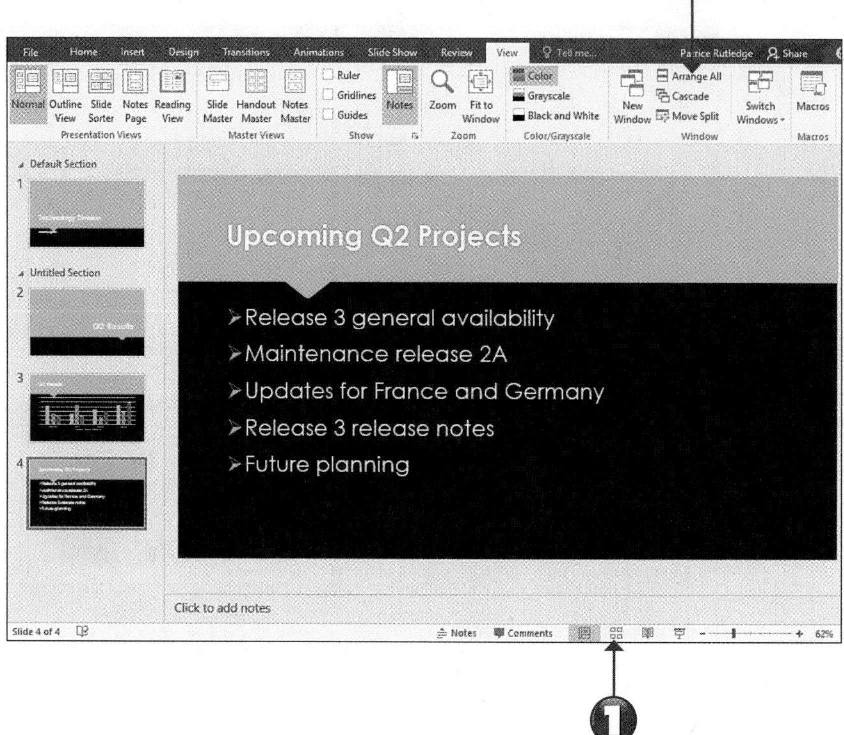

1. Open both the source and destination presentations in Slide Sorter view.

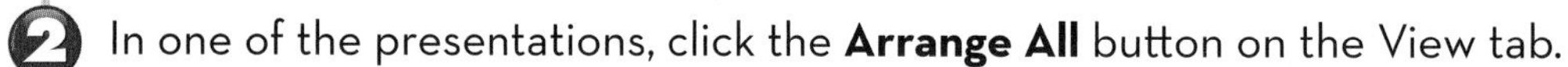

2. In one of the presentations, click the **Arrange All** button on the View tab.

Continued

## NOTE

**Presentation Themes** If each presentation uses a different theme, moving a slide changes its formatting to that of the new presentation, and the Paste Options button displays. To retain the formatting of the source presentation, click the down arrow to the right of the Paste Options button and choose **Keep Source Formatting**. Remember, however, that the best presentations use a consistent theme throughout.

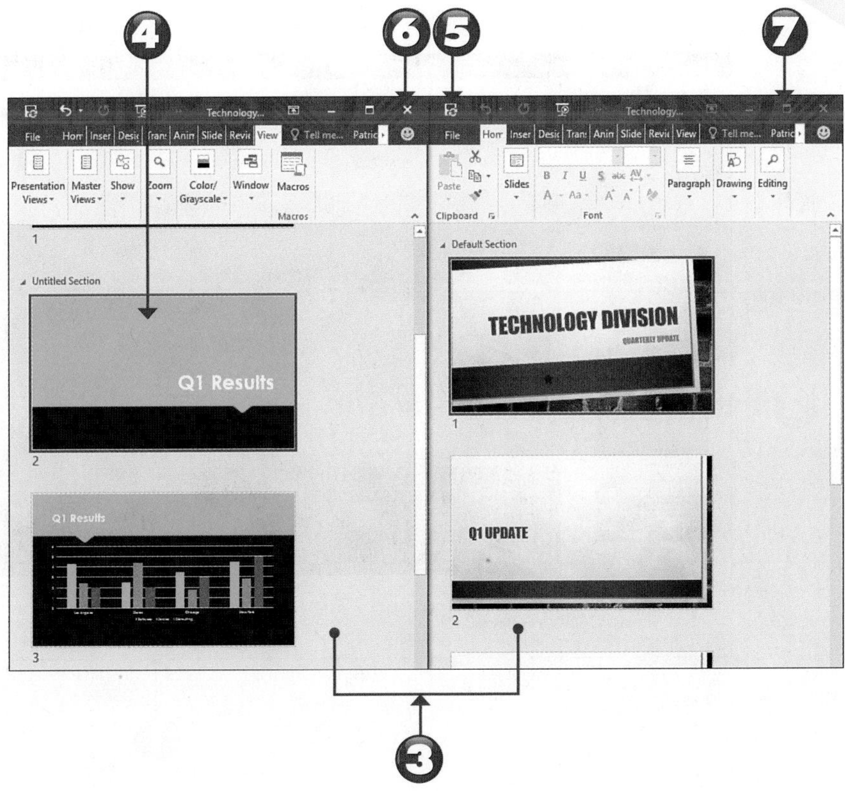


3. PowerPoint displays both presentations in different window panes in Slide Sorter view.

4. Drag and drop slides between presentations to copy them.

5. Click the **Save** button for any presentation you changed.

6. Click the **Close** button in the upper-right corner of the presentation you no longer want to view.

7. Click the **Maximize** button in the upper-right corner of the presentation you want to keep active.

End

## TIP

**Move a Slide** To move a slide, select it, press **Ctrl+X** on your keyboard, position the mouse in the new destination location, and press **Ctrl+V**. The slide is removed from the source presentation and inserted into the destination presentation.

# DELETING A SLIDE

If you no longer need a slide or make a mistake and want to start again, you can delete it.

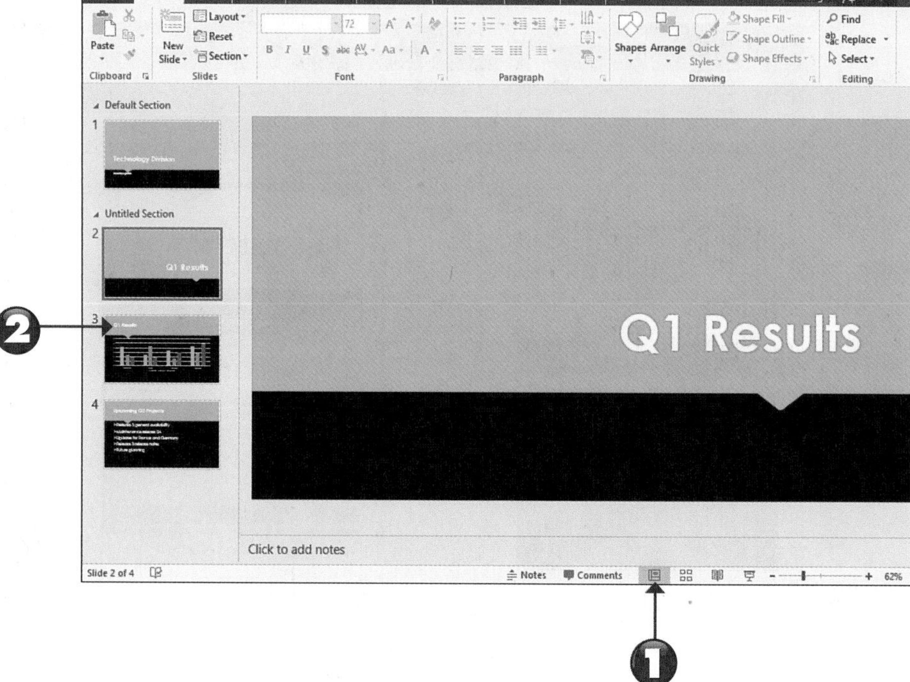


Start

1. Click the **Normal** button in the lower-right corner of the window if you aren't already using Normal view.
2. Select the slide you want to delete, and press the **Delete** key on your keyboard.

End

## TIP

**Delete Multiple Slides** To delete multiple consecutive slides, press the **Shift** key on your keyboard, select the first and last slides in the range, and press the **Delete** key. To delete multiple nonconsecutive slides, hold the **Ctrl** key, select the slides, and press the **Delete** key.

## NOTE

**Other Deletion Options** You can also delete slides in Slide Sorter view or Outline view. You can access these views on the View tab.

# USING SLIDE MASTERS

*Slide masters* help you achieve uniformity by storing data about a presentation's theme and slide layouts, such as colors, fonts, effects, background, placeholders, and positioning—and applying it consistently throughout your presentation.

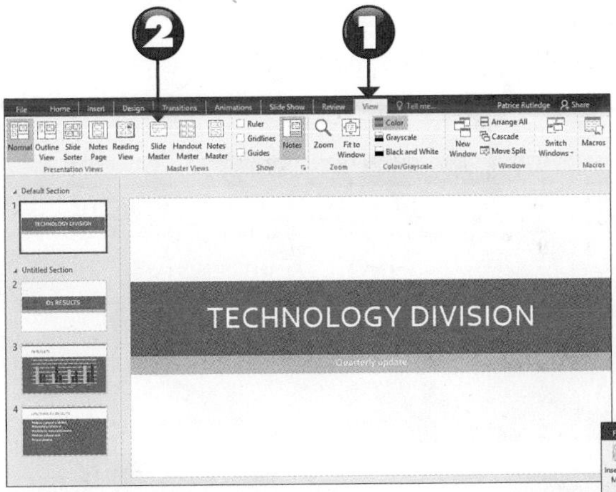

Start

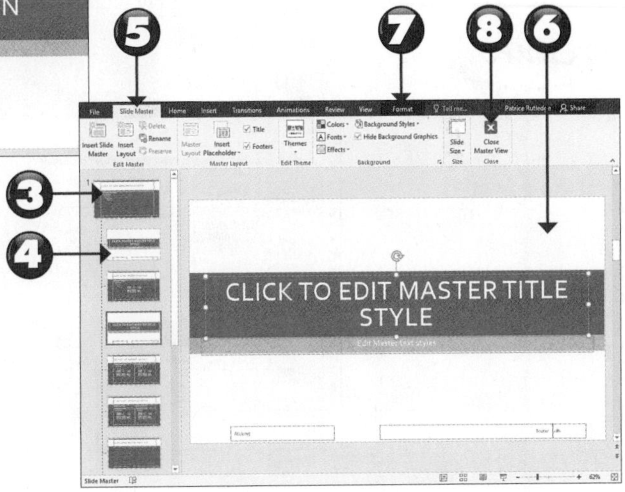

1. Click the **View** tab.
2. Click the **Slide Master** button.
3. If you want to change the entire presentation's design, click the slide master thumbnail.
4. If you want to edit the master for a specific slide layout, click the thumbnail for that layout.
5. PowerPoint displays the Slide Master contextual tab by default, where you can change the theme, colors, fonts, effects, and background styles.
6. Click the slide master editing screen.
7. Click the **Format** tab to makes changes to shapes and WordArt.
8. Click the **Close Master View** button on the Slide Master tab to save your changes and return to your presentation.

End

## NOTE

**Slide Masters** Each presentation contains at least one slide master. Editing a slide master is optional and suited to experienced users. One popular reason to edit a slide master is to add your company logo to all slides.

# INSERTING A HYPERLINK TO THE WEB

Inserting hyperlinks to external websites is a common use of PowerPoint's hyperlink feature. Inserting a hyperlink makes it easy to open a specific website or page during a presentation without having to manually enter its URL. You can add a hyperlink to text or to an object such as an image or shape.

Start

1. On the Slide pane in Normal view, select the text or object you want to link.
2. Click the **Insert** tab.
3. Click the **Hyperlink** button.
4. Type the URL into the **Address** field.
5. Click the **OK** button.

End

## TIP

**Insert Hyperlink Shortcut** Pressing **Ctrl+K** is another way to open the Insert Hyperlink dialog box.

## CAUTION

**URL Tips** Be sure to type the URL exactly as it appears, including uppercase and lowercase letters and all special characters (such as the tilde [~]). If you can, go to the site, copy the URL from the Address field in your browser, and paste it into this field.

# INSERTING A HYPERLINK TO ANOTHER SLIDE IN YOUR PRESENTATION

In addition to linking to websites, you can also link to other slides in your presentation. Creating links to other slides helps you customize your slideshow so that you can move quickly to the slides you need.

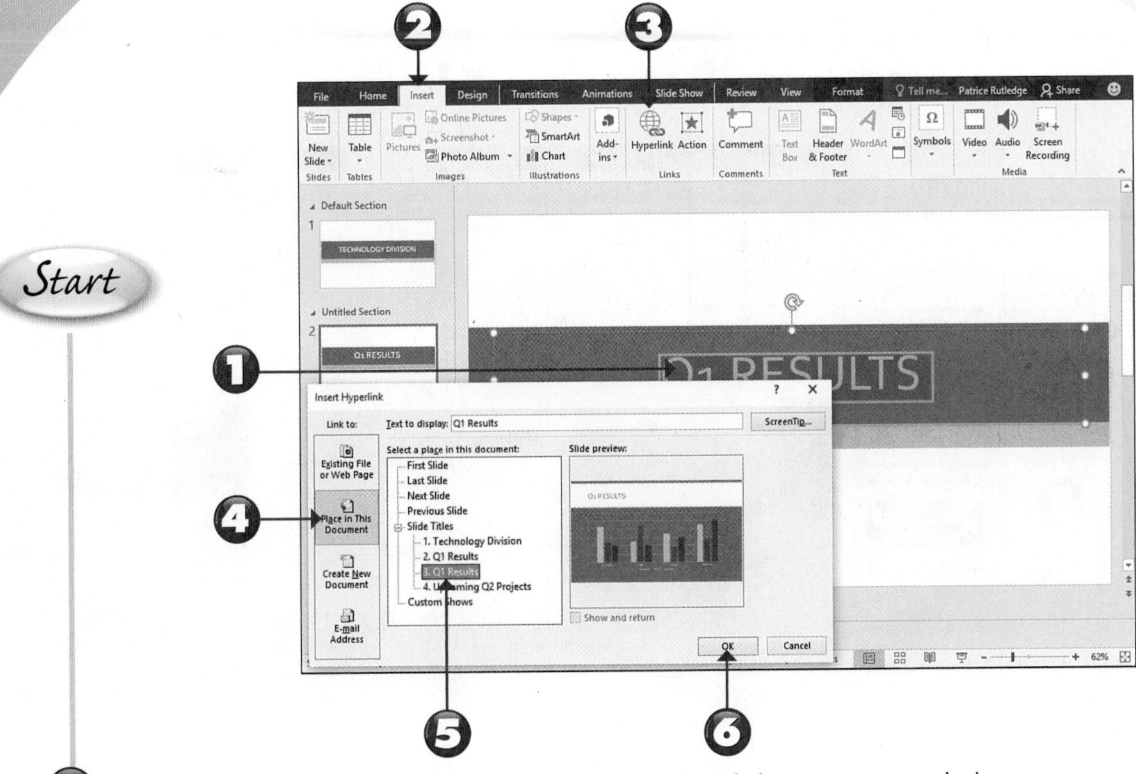


1. In Normal view, select the text or object on the slide you want to link.
2. Click the **Insert** tab.
3. Click the **Hyperlink** button.
4. Click the **Place in This Document** button.
5. Select the slide to which you want to link.
6. Click the **OK** button.

End

### TIP

**Removing Hyperlinks** After inserting a hyperlink, you might decide that you don't want it or that you need to link a different object instead. To remove a hyperlink, right-click it and select **Remove Hyperlink**.

### TIP

**Testing Hyperlinks** Before you present to an audience, test all your hyperlinks to make sure that you set them up correctly. The last thing you want during your presentation is a surprise when you click a hyperlink.

# ADDING HEADERS AND FOOTERS

If you plan to print your presentation—or create a PDF to distribute to participants—you can add headers and footers to your slides, notes, and handouts.

Start

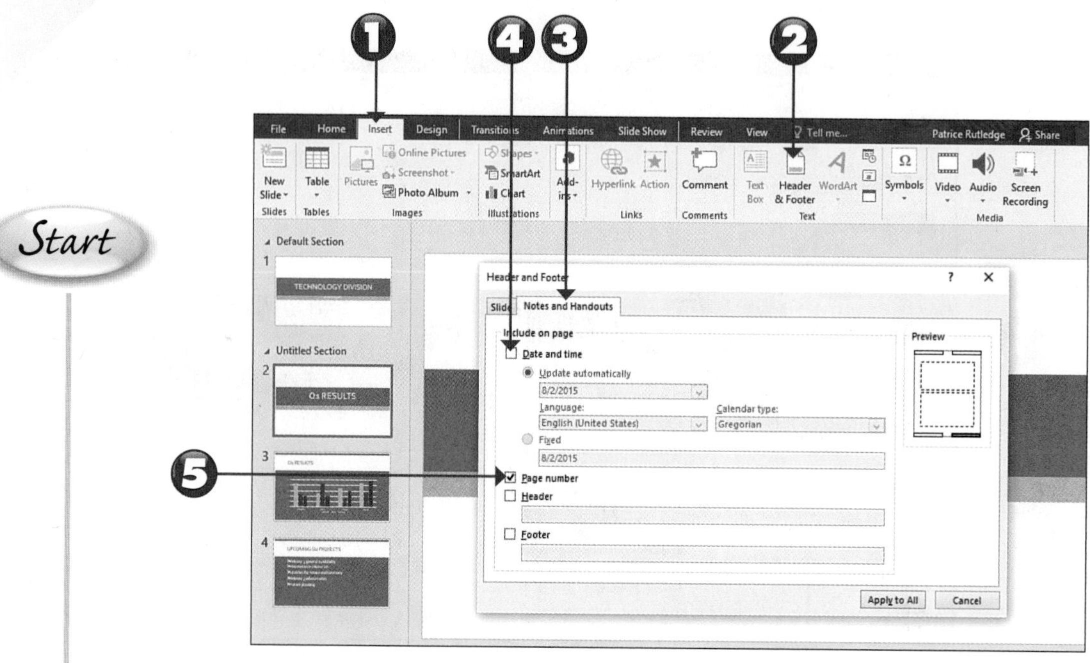


1. Click the **Insert** tab.

2. Click the **Header & Footer** button.

3. Click the **Notes and Handouts** tab on the Header and Footer dialog box.

4. Click the **Date and time** check box to print the date and/or time on each page, and select a formatting option from the drop-down list.

5. Click the **Page number** check box to print a page number on the lower-right corner of each page.

Continued

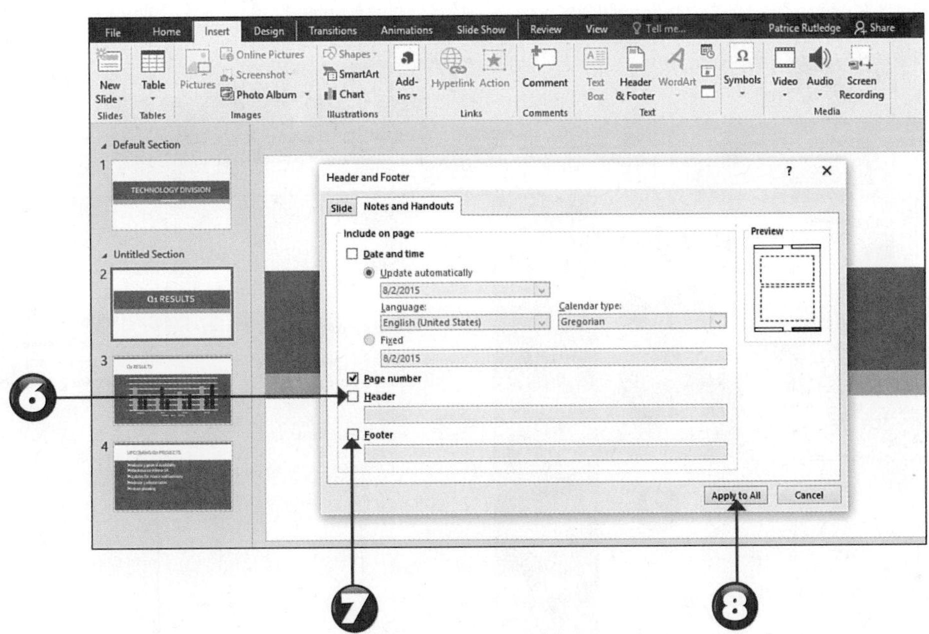


6 Click the **Header** check box to print a header on the upper-left corner of the page.

7 Click the **Footer** check box to print a footer on the lower-left corner of the page.

8 Click the **Apply to All** button to close the dialog box.

End

**TIP**

**Preview Headers and Footers** You can preview your changes on the right side of the Header and Footer dialog box.

# CREATING HANDOUTS IN MICROSOFT WORD

You can export the slides and notes from your PowerPoint presentation to Microsoft Word, where you can use Word's formatting to create more sophisticated handouts.

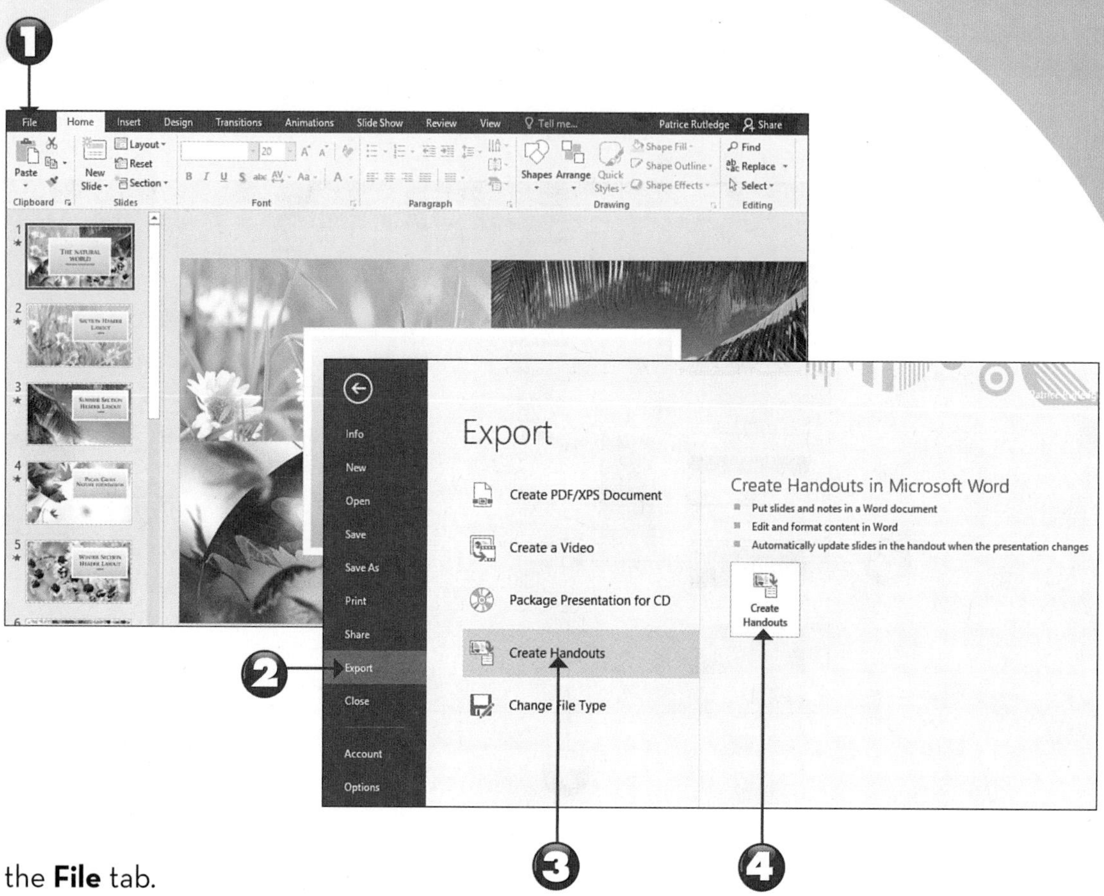

Start

1. Click the **File** tab.
2. Click **Export**.
3. Click **Create Handouts**.
4. Click the **Create Handouts** button.

Continued

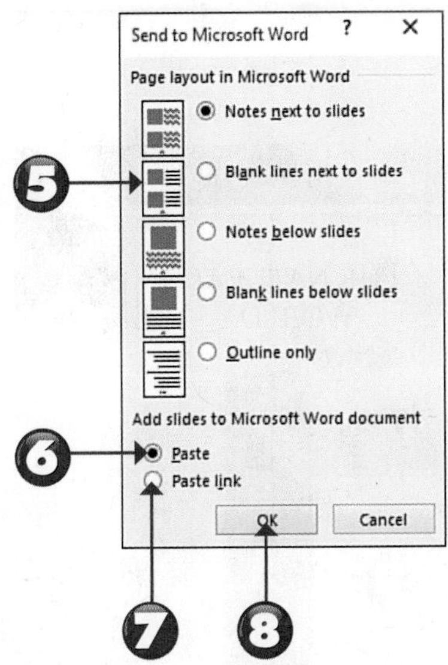


5 Select a page layout option for your handouts.

6 Select the **Paste** option button if you want to paste the slides into your Word document.

7 Select the **Paste link** option button if you want to update your Word document whenever you make changes in PowerPoint.

8 Click the **OK** button to open a Microsoft Word document in the layout you specified.

End

**NOTE**

**Preview Handout Layouts** The Send to Microsoft Word dialog box displays preview images of each page layout.

# PRINTING YOUR PRESENTATION

PowerPoint enables you to print more than just slides. You can also print notes to remind yourself of what you want to say while presenting, handouts to give to your audience, and outlines to help you proof your content. PowerPoint also includes numerous customization options for printing auxiliary materials.

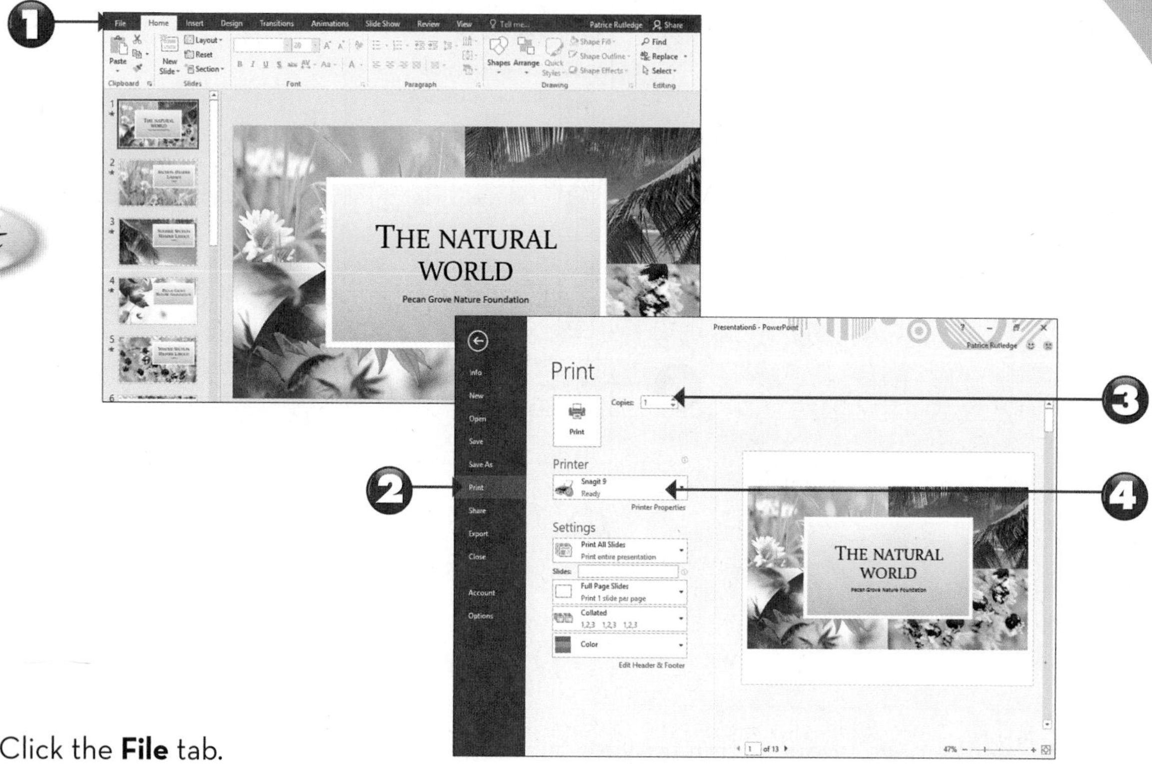

Start

1. Click the **File** tab.
2. Click **Print**.
3. Select the number of **Copies** you want to print.
4. Select your **Printer** from the drop-down list.

Continued

**TIP**

**Green Printing Alternatives** Consider a greener alternative to printing your presentation by saving it as a PDF and distributing it to your audience on the Web or on a company file-sharing site. Learn more at "Saving as a PDF or an XPS Document" on page 22. That way, you need to print only for personal review, not wide distribution.

**TIP**

**Scroll and Zoom** Below the slide, you can click the left and right arrows to scroll through the presentation. You can also use the zoom control to reduce or enlarge the size of the slides.

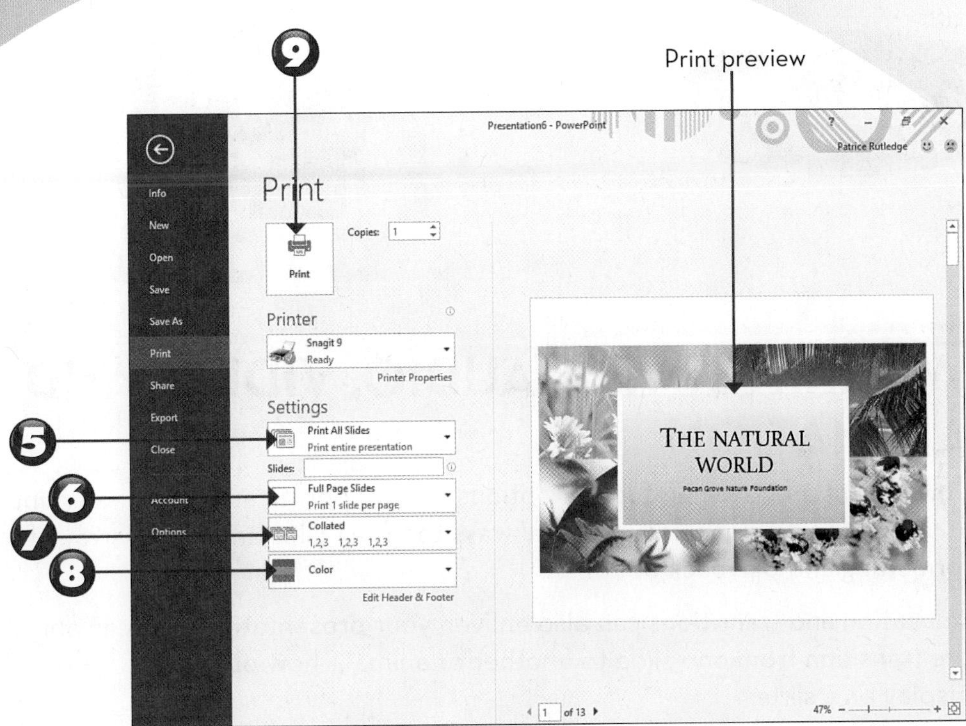


5 Select the slides you want to print. Your options include Print All Slides, Print Selection, Print Current Slide, or Custom Range.

6 Select the print layout you want to use. Options include Full Page Slides, Notes Pages, Outline, or nine Handout layouts.

7 Specify whether you want to collate your printouts (print in consecutive order). This option is valid only if you choose to print more than one copy of your presentation.

8 Specify color options for your printed presentation. You can print in color, grayscale, or pure black and white.

9 Click the **Print** button to print your formatted presentation to the printer you selected.

End

## NOTE

**Print Preview** Preview the way your presentation will display when printed on the right side of the Print window. Any changes you make to your presentation settings are reflected in this view, so you can verify before printing whether the choices you make work for you.

# WORKING WITH AUDIO, VIDEO, AND ANIMATION

PowerPoint offers a multitude of options to incorporate audio and video into your presentation, including several ways to insert clips and a vast array of formatting and playback options.

Animation and transitions can also enliven your presentation. You can animate the transition from one slide to another or animate how objects and text display on a slide.

Incorporating audio, video, transitions, and animation can give any presentation some pizzazz. Just remember that a little goes a long way, and focus on effects that truly enhance your presentation.

# ANIMATIONS TAB AND PANE

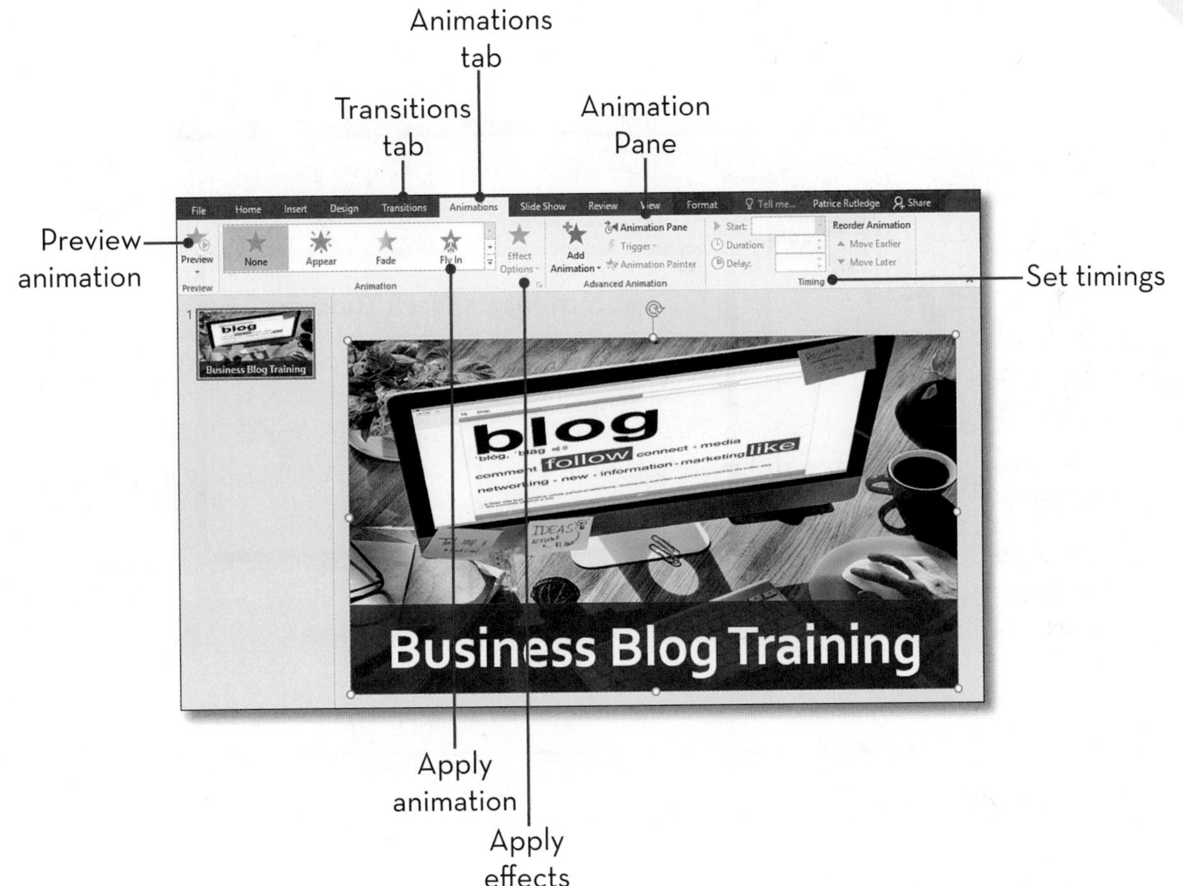

# INSERTING ONLINE VIDEO

Inserting online video is an easy way to add a visual element to your presentation. PowerPoint enables you to insert video clips from an external website, such as YouTube or Facebook. You can also insert a video from one of your OneDrive folders, or insert a video embed code.

Start

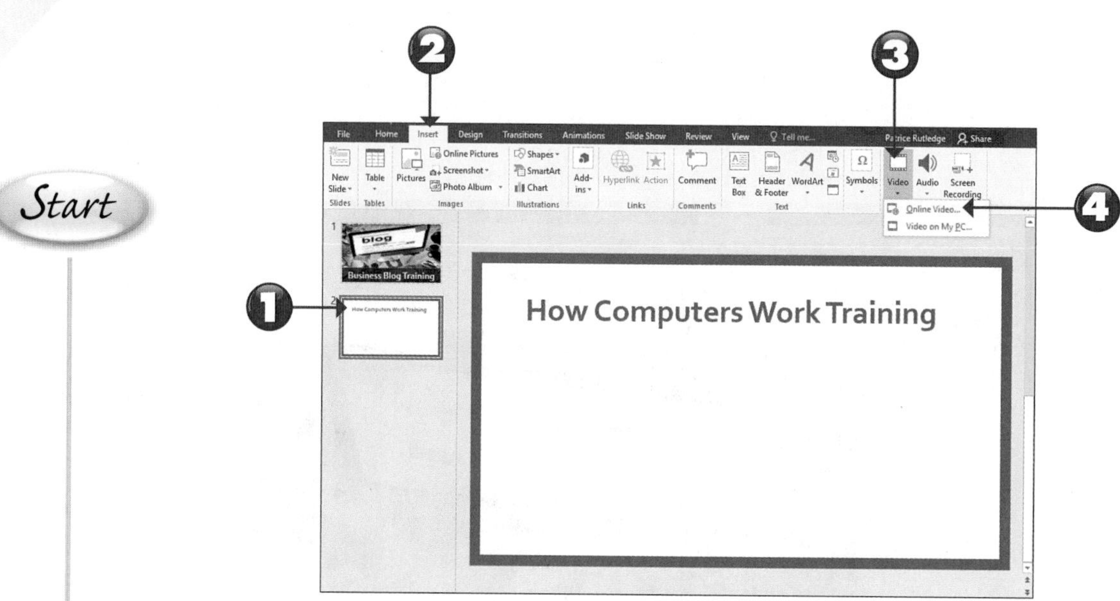


1. Select the slide where you want to insert your video clip.
2. Click the **Insert** tab.
3. Click the **Video** button.
4. Select **Online Video** from the menu.

Continued

**TIP**

**Insert Video from the Content Palette** Another way to insert online video is to use a slide layout that includes the content palette. Learn more in "Adding Slides to Your Presentation" on page 219. ■

**TIP**

**Video Embed Codes** A video embed code enables you to share web videos in other locations, including PowerPoint presentations. When you find a video on the Web that you want to use, clicking a Share link or button for that video usually leads to the video's embed code. ■

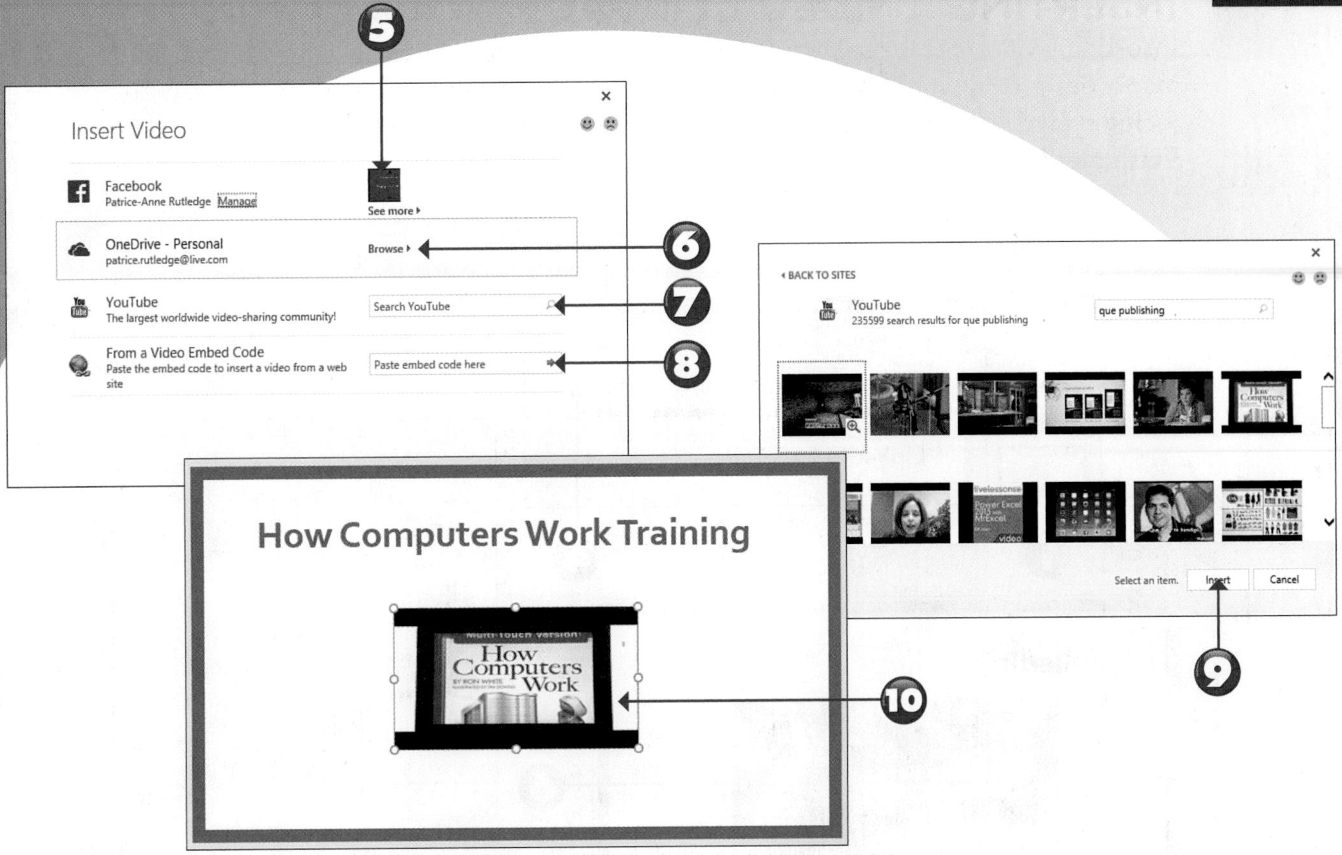

5 To search for a video you posted to Facebook, click the **Facebook** button. If you aren't already logged in to Facebook, you're prompted to do so.

6 To insert a video from OneDrive, click **Browse**.

7 To search for a video on YouTube, enter your search term, and click the **Search** button.

8 If you have an embed code from another website, paste it in the text box.

9 Follow the onscreen instructions to insert the video on your slide. For example, if you want to insert a YouTube video, select it and click the **Insert** button.

10 PowerPoint displays a thumbnail of the video on your slide.

End

**TIP**

**Resize a Video Clip** You can resize and reposition a video by dragging the handles that surround it when it's selected. ■

**TIP**

**Delete a Video Clip** To delete a video clip from a slide, select it and press the **Delete** key. ■

# INSERTING A VIDEO CLIP FROM YOUR COMPUTER

Inserting a video clip from your computer or a network location is another easy way to incorporate video into your presentation. PowerPoint supports many video formats, including the following: .ASF, .AVI, .MPEG, .WMV, .MOV, .MK3D, .MKV, .MP4, and Adobe Flash media.

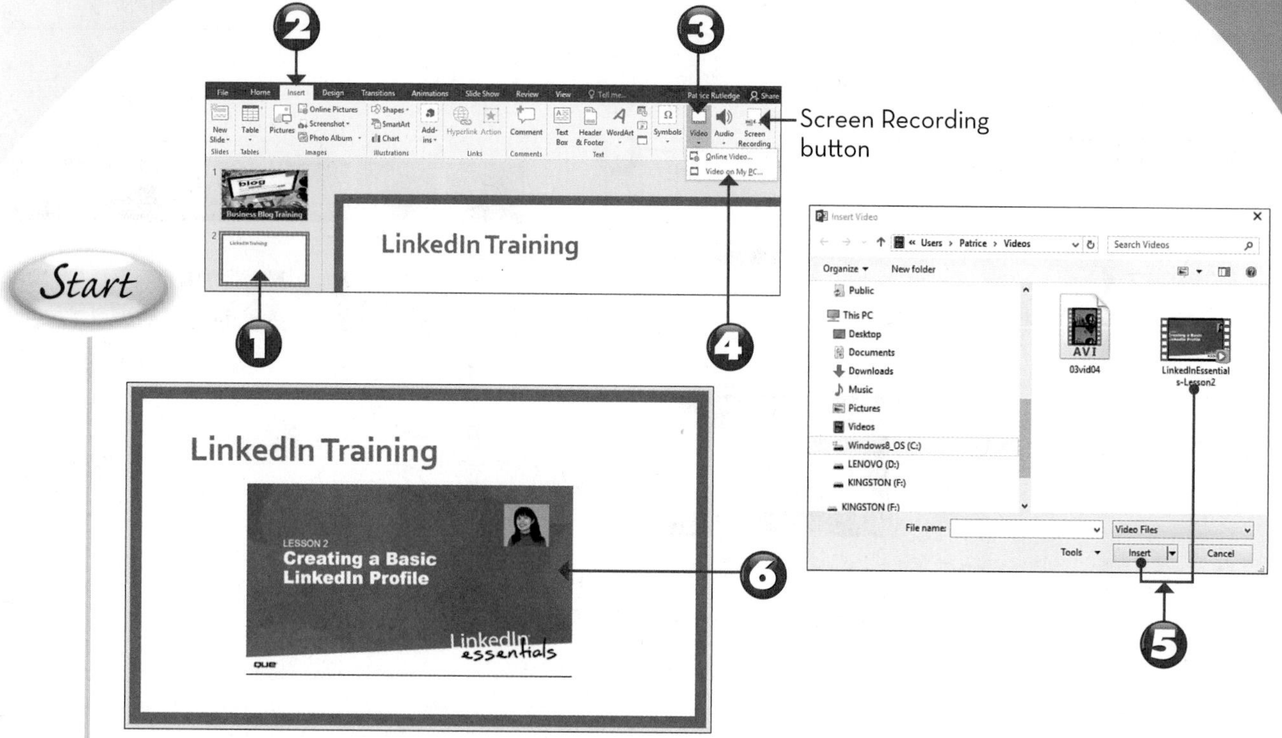

Screen Recording button

Start

1. Select the slide where you want to insert your video clip.
2. Click the **Insert** tab.
3. Click the **Video** button.
4. Select **Video on My PC** from the menu.
5. Navigate to the video you want, and click the **Insert** button.
6. PowerPoint inserts the video into your slide.

End

### TIP

**Video Player Controls** Select the video to display the player controls below it.

### TIP

**Screen Recordings** Another option is to create your own screen recordings directly from PowerPoint. Click the **Screen Recording** button on the Insert tab to start a recording.

# FORMATTING VIDEO CLIPS

The Format tab displays when you select a video clip on a PowerPoint slide. Now explore some of the most popular formatting features available on this tab.

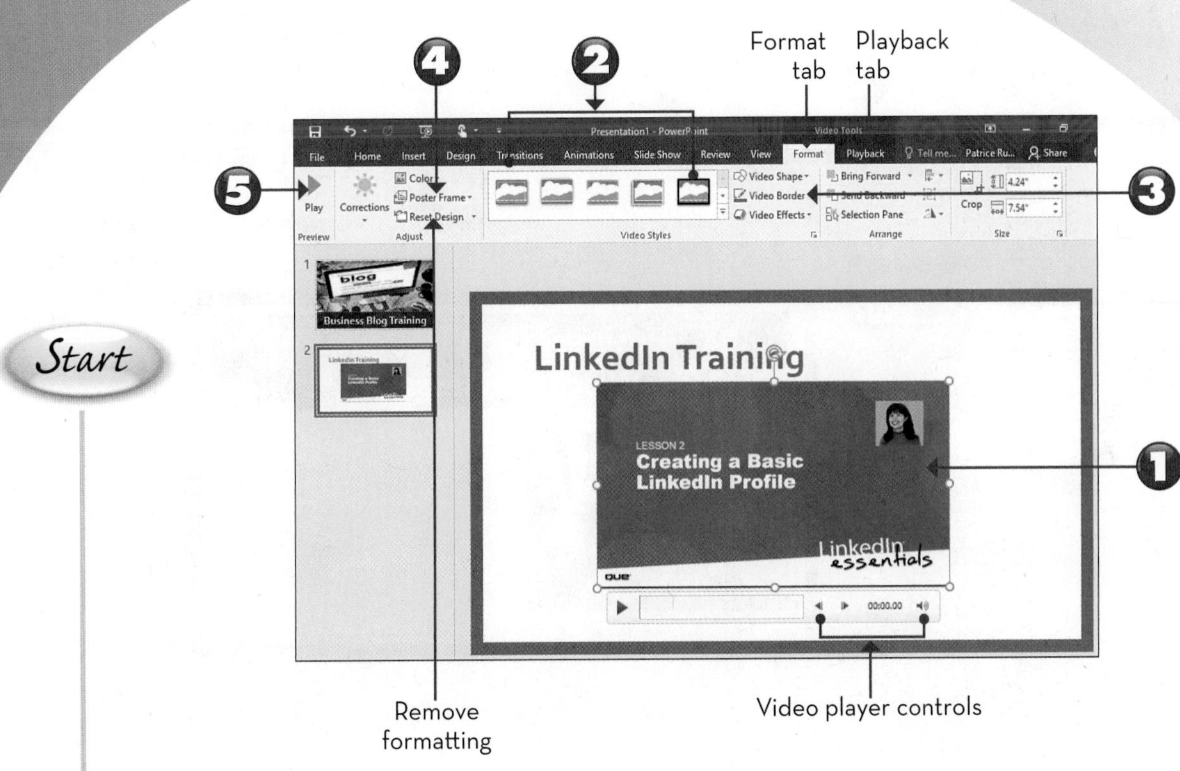


1. Select the video clip you want to format.
2. Select a **Video Style** to change the look of your video.
3. Click the **Video Border** button to apply a border to your video.
4. Click the **Poster Frame** button to specify your video's initial preview image. For example, you can display a static image from the video, a company logo, or even the photo of a speaker in the video.
5. Click the **Play** button to preview your video.

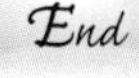

## NOTE

**Understanding Video Styles** A *video style* changes the appearance of a video on your slide but doesn't change the video itself. For example, you can use a video style to apply frames and shadows to your videos, rotate them, or even display them inside an oval. ■

## TIP

**Playback Options** Click the **Playback** tab for other video options, such as when you want to start playing your video: automatically or by clicking your mouse. ■

# INSERTING AN AUDIO CLIP FROM YOUR COMPUTER

You can insert an audio clip stored on your computer or a network location. PowerPoint supports the following audio file formats: .ADTS, .AIFF, .AU, .FLAC, .MIDI, .MKA, .MP3, .MP4, .WAV, and .WMA.

Start

1. Select the slide where you want to insert your audio clip.
2. Click the **Insert** tab.
3. Click the **Audio** button.
4. Select **Audio on My PC** from the menu.

Continued

**TIP**

**Record Your Own Audio** You can also record your own audio clip in PowerPoint. Click the **Insert** tab, click the **Audio** button, and select **Record Audio** from the menu. ■

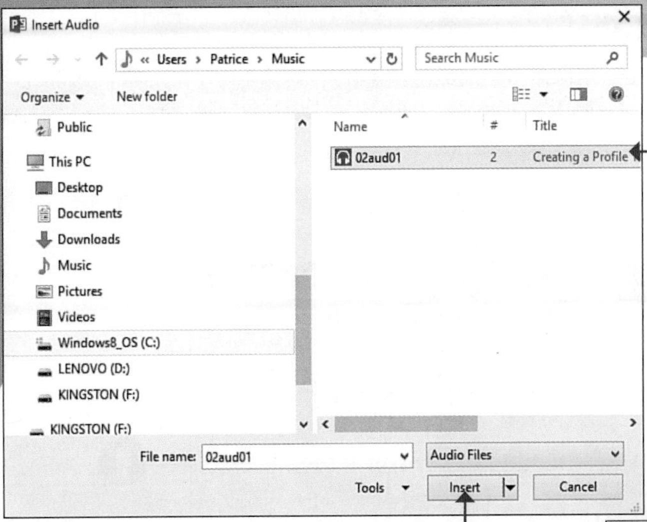

5 Navigate to the audio clip you want to insert.

6 Click the **Insert** button.

7 PowerPoint inserts the audio into your slide in the form of an Audio Clip icon.

8 Select the audio clip to display the player control bar below it.

End

TIP

**Reposition an Audio Clip** You can reposition and resize your audio clip if you want. For example, you might want to drag this icon into the lower-right corner of your slide to keep the audience's focus on the slide content. ■

TIP

**Delete an Audio Clip** To delete an audio clip from a slide, select it and press the **Delete** key. ■

# SETTING SLIDE TRANSITIONS

Setting slide transitions is one of the most common animation effects. You can apply a slide transition to the entire presentation or just to the current slide.

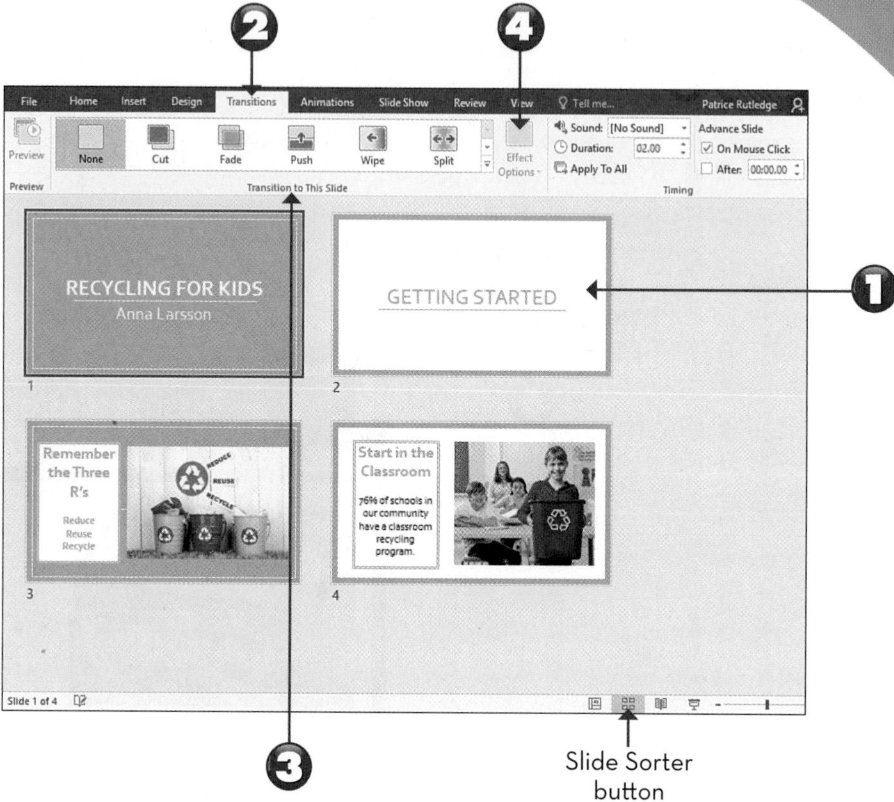

1. In Slide Sorter view, select the slides that you want to apply the transition to. To select all slides, press **Ctrl+A**.
2. Click the **Transitions** tab.
3. Select a transition in the **Transition to This Slide** group. For more options, click the down arrow.
4. Click the **Effect Options** button to select a directional effect, such as from the top or from the bottom right.

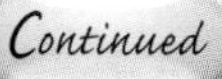

## NOTE

**Transition Options** PowerPoint offers a variety of transition options ranging from subtle to dynamic, including the capability to fade, wipe, reveal, or introduce a slide with a honeycomb effect. Most transitions enable you to choose a direction as well. For example, you can wipe up, down, left, or right. ■

## CAUTION

**Don't Overdo Transitions** As with so many PowerPoint features, use restraint with slide transitions. For the most professional results, choose one transition to use for every slide in a presentation. ■

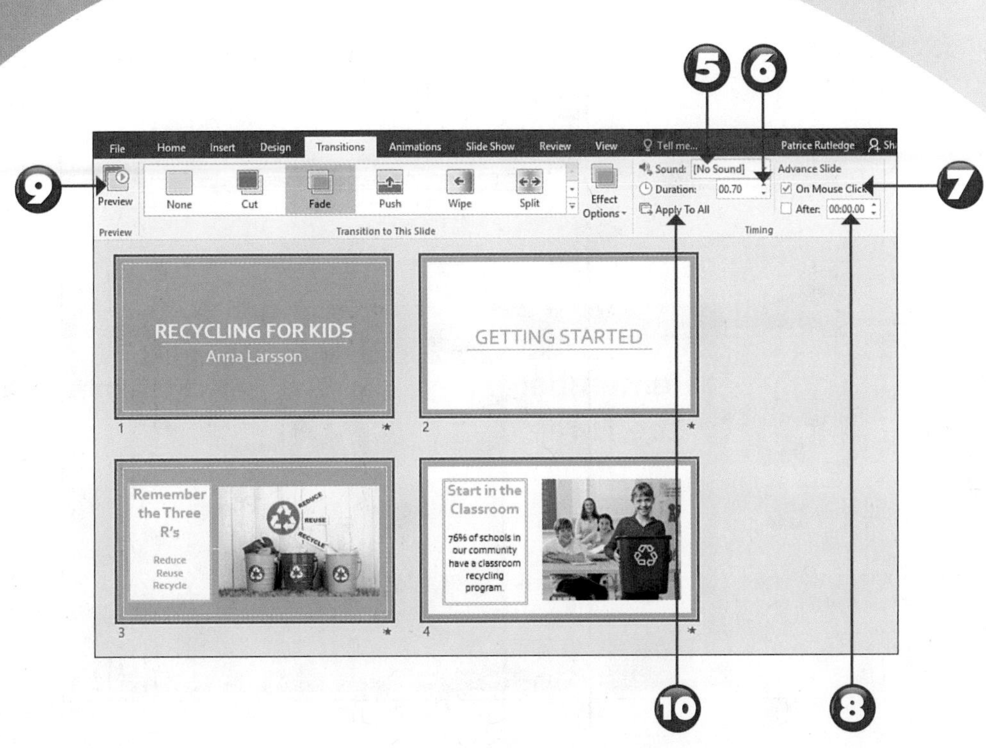


5. To add a sound effect to your transition, select a sound from the Sound drop-down list. If you want to use a sound stored on your computer, choose **Other Sound**.

6. Select the amount of time (in seconds) you want the transition to take to introduce each slide in the Duration field.

7. By default, PowerPoint starts transitions on a mouse click.

8. If you would rather transition to the next slide after a specified amount of time, select the **After** check box and enter a time.

9. Click the **Preview** button on the left side of the Transitions tab.

10. Click the **Apply to All** button to apply the transitions to all slides in your presentation.

End

## NOTE

**Advance Slides** If you select the **On Mouse Click** check box, PowerPoint also advances to the next slide when you press a key such as the spacebar, Enter, or Page Up. ■

# ANIMATING SLIDE OBJECTS

You can apply basic animation to objects such as shapes, text placeholders, text boxes, SmartArt graphics, pictures, and charts. For example, you can fly in text or make a shape spin.

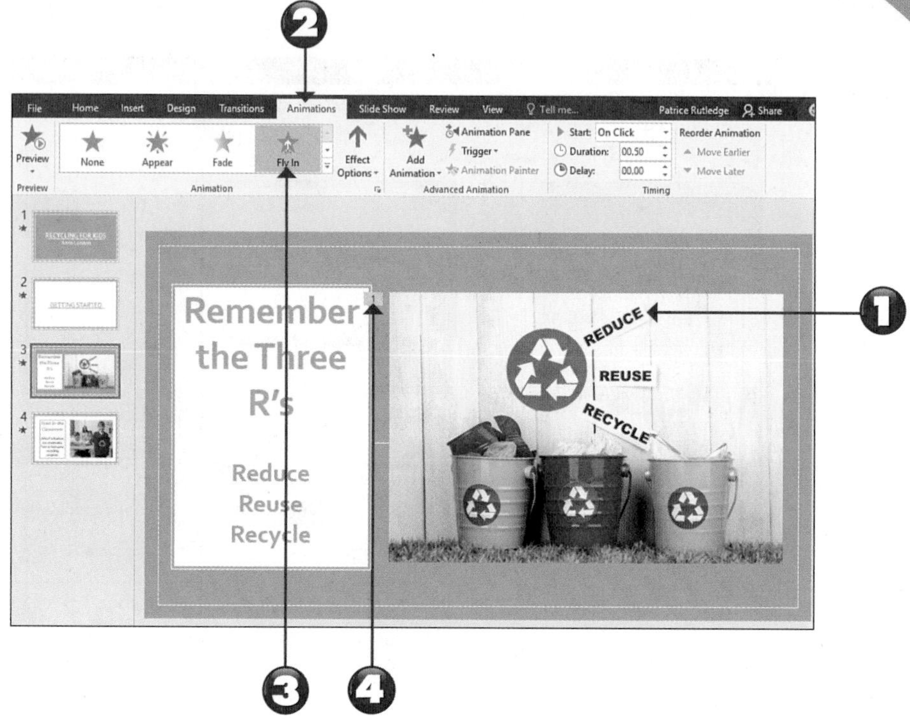


Start

1. Select the object or objects you want to animate.
2. Click the **Animations** tab.
3. Select the animation you want to apply from the Animation group. Click the down arrow to view additional options.
4. PowerPoint applies the animation to the selected object and numbers it.

Continued

## NOTE

**PowerPoint Animation Types** PowerPoint offers four categories of animations: entrance animations that determine how the text or object enters the slide, emphasis animations that add emphasis to the text or object, exit animations that determine how the text or object exits the slide, and motion path animations that set a path that the selected text or object follows. ■

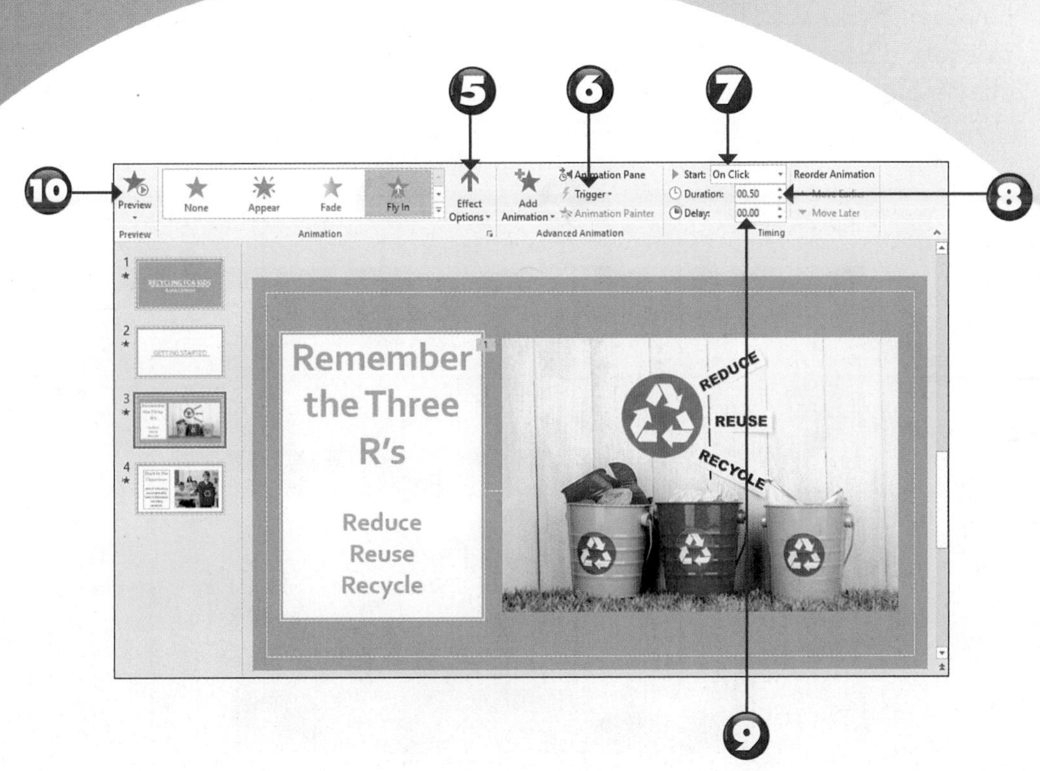


5 Click the **Effect Options** button to choose the direction to apply the animation, such as From Left or From Top-Right.

6 Click the **Trigger** button to specify what triggers this animation to start: the click of a specific object on the slide or a bookmark.

7 In the **Start** field, specify when to start the animation: with a mouse click, with the previous animation, or after the previous animation.

8 Select a **Duration**, in seconds, to determine how long the animation should last.

9 Select a **Delay**, in seconds, between each animation. If you don't want a delay, select **00.00** in this field.

10 Click the **Preview** button to preview your animation choices.

End

**NOTE**

**Animating Multiple Objects** If you select more than one object, PowerPoint applies the animation to both objects at the same time. If you want the animations to occur in sequence, you must apply each animation separately. ■

# CUSTOMIZING ANIMATIONS ON THE ANIMATION PANE

The tools available on the Animations tab should suit most of your animation needs; however, if you want to customize your animations even more, you can do so on the Animation pane. For example, you use this task pane to set animation effects for text, charts, SmartArt graphics, and media clips. Now explore this powerful tool.

Start

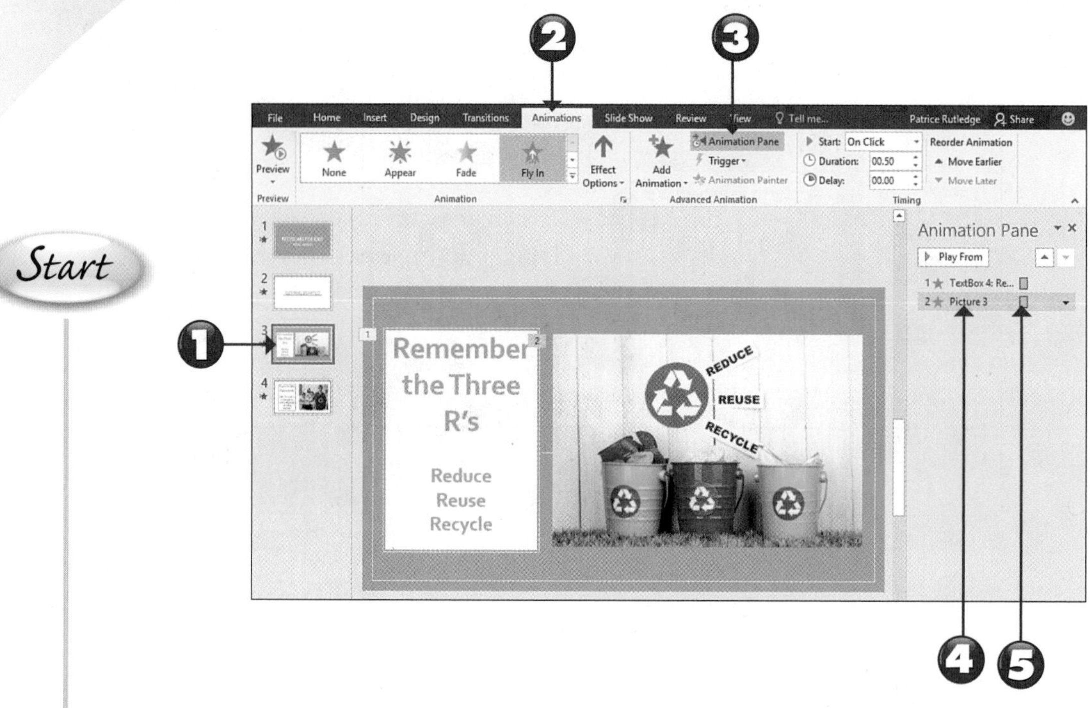


1. Select a slide to which you applied animation.
2. Click the **Animations** tab.
3. Click the **Animation Pane** button.
4. Each animation you applied displays in the Animation Pane in the order in which you applied it.
5. The light green bar that follows an animation indicates its duration.

Continued

NOTE

**Multiple Animations** If you have multiple animations in this list, the list is numbered, and the numbers also display on your slide to show where the animations are located. These numbers don't display in print or during a slide show, however. ■

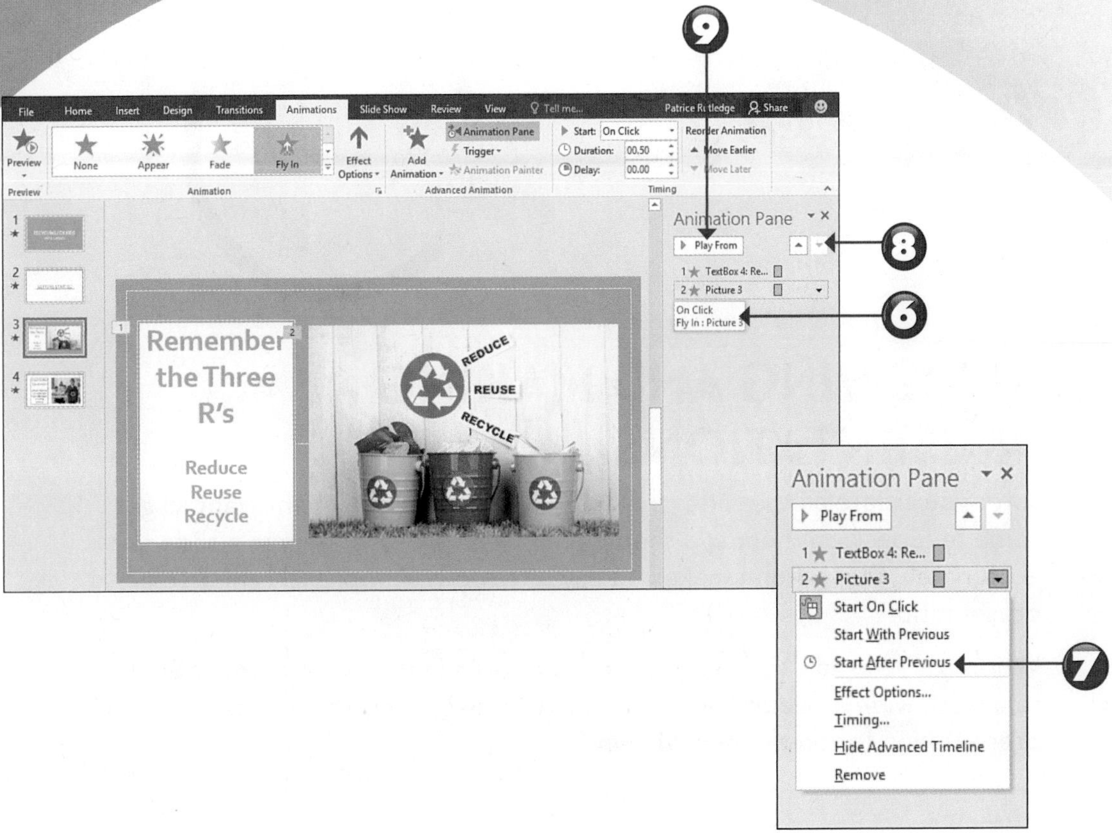

6. Pause the mouse over the animation in the list to display more information, such as the start option and effect type.

7. Select an animation in the list, and click the down arrow to its right to open a menu of additional options. For example, you can change the way an animation starts or its timing.

8. Reorder a selected animation by clicking the up arrow button or the down arrow button.

9. Click the **Play From** button to preview the animations in your current view.

*End*

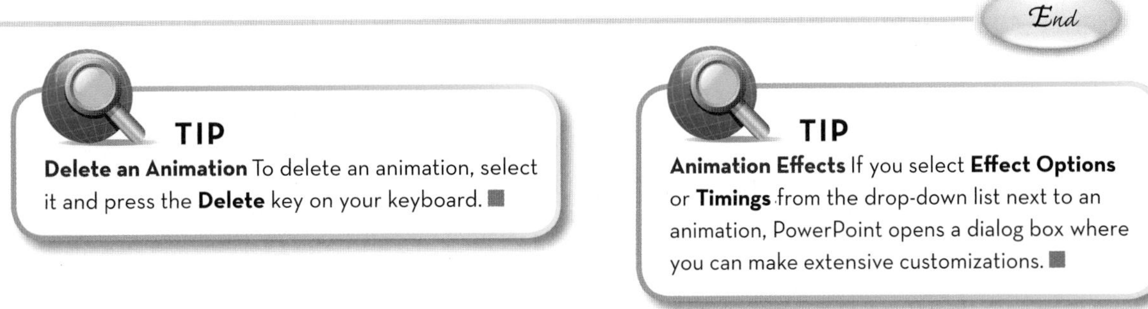

**TIP**

**Delete an Animation** To delete an animation, select it and press the **Delete** key on your keyboard. ■

**TIP**

**Animation Effects** If you select **Effect Options** or **Timings** from the drop-down list next to an animation, PowerPoint opens a dialog box where you can make extensive customizations. ■

# REVIEWING AND MAKING PRESENTATIONS

After you create all the slides in your presentation, you might want to get some feedback on them and then plan how to present them in a slide show. Fortunately, PowerPoint makes it easy to review, set up, and rehearse a presentation.

When you're ready, you can present to people in the same room as you or to a worldwide audience on the Web. You can also create a video from your presentation for on-demand viewing.

# SLIDE SHOW TAB

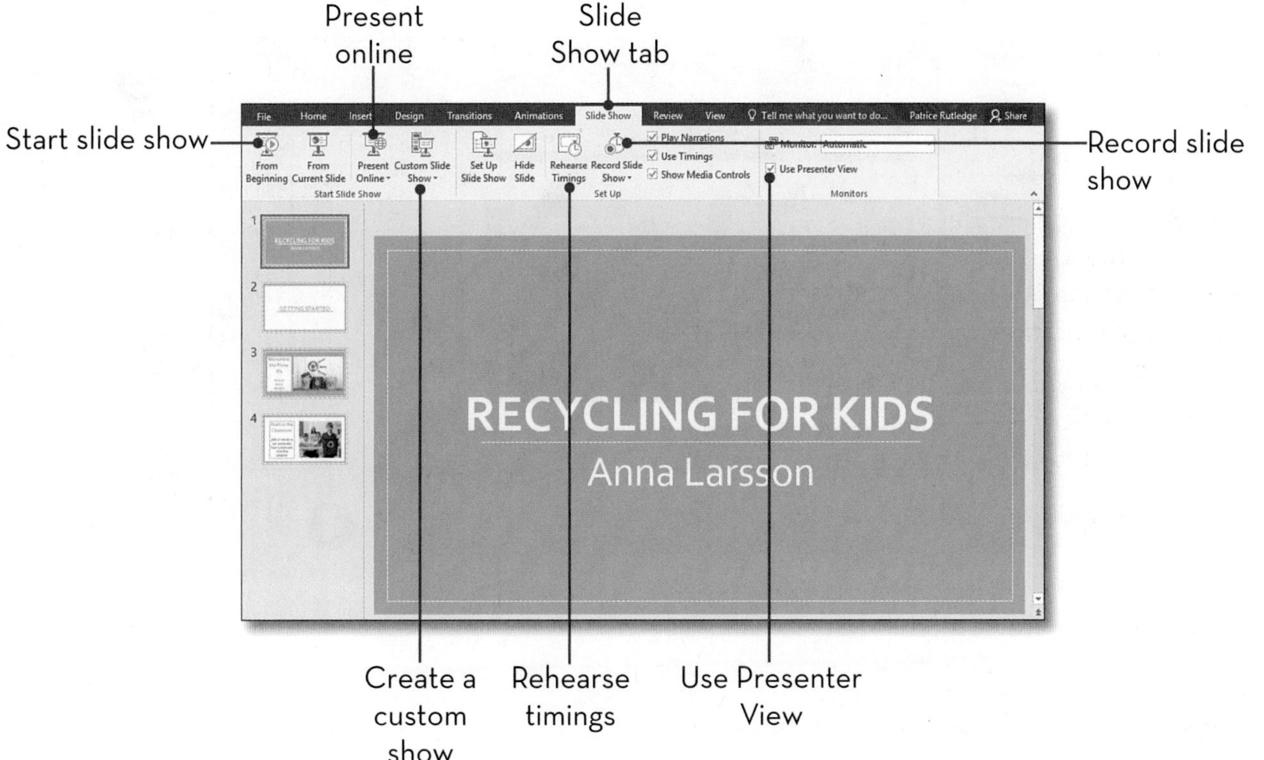

# ADDING COMMENTS

Providing and incorporating feedback on PowerPoint presentations is an important part of the presentation design process in many organizations. One of the best ways to communicate your suggested changes to a presentation's author is to add a comment.

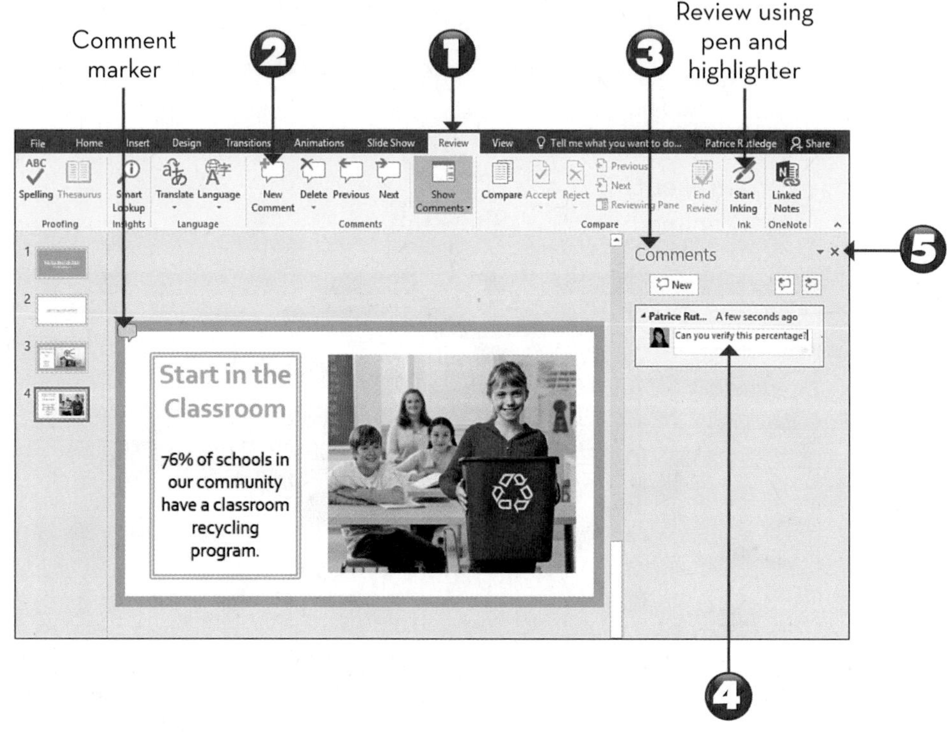

1. Click the **Review** tab.

2. Click the **New Comment** button.

3. The Comments pane opens.

4. Enter your comments in the box.

5. Click the **Close** button to close the Comments pane.

End

**NOTE**

**Add Comments in Normal View** You must use Normal view or Online view to add comments; Slide Sorter view doesn't support this feature.

**TIP**

**Comment on a Slide Element** You can also select a slide element to which you want to add a comment, such as a text box, chart, or graphic.

# MANAGING COMMENTS

After people comment on your presentation, you can review, edit, delete, and reply to their commentary.

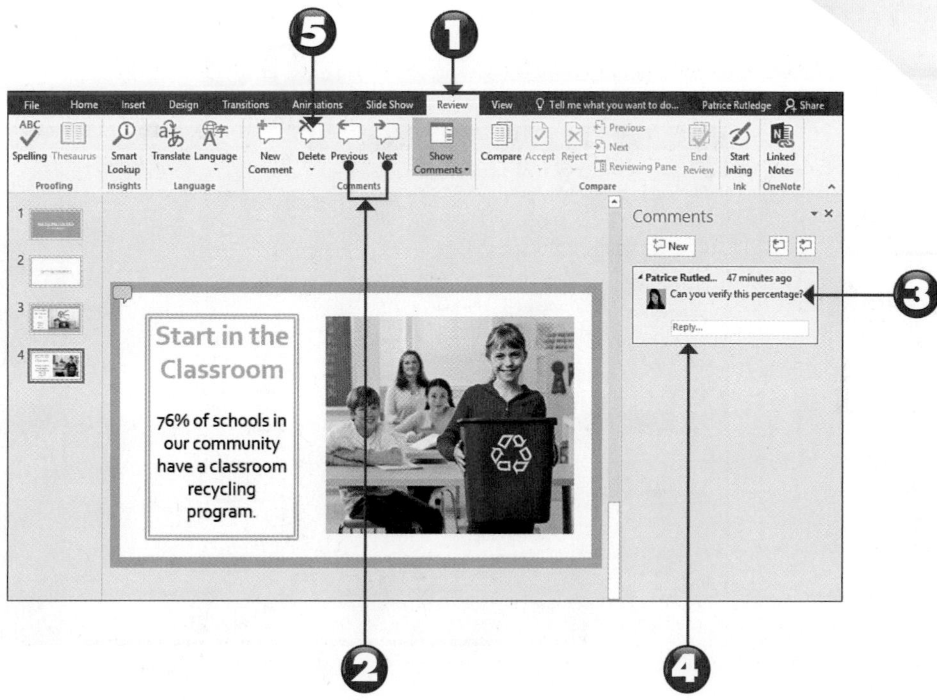


1. Click the **Review** tab.
2. Click the **Next** and **Previous** buttons to move from comment to comment.
3. Click in a comment box to edit the comment.
4. Click in the **Reply** box to reply to a comment.
5. Click the **Delete** button to delete a comment.

End

## TIP

**Delete All Comments** To delete all the comments in your entire presentation, click the down arrow below the Delete button and choose **Delete All Comments and Ink in This Presentation**. Ink refers to any ink annotations you created and saved during a slide show using the onscreen pen.

## NOTE

**Displaying Comments** If you can't see your comments, click the lower portion of the **Show Comments** button, and verify that Comments Pane and Show Markup are selected.

# COMPARING PRESENTATIONS

Although it's best if all reviewers comment on and edit the same version of a presentation, such as one stored in a central location, there are times when they will edit a separate version of your presentation. Fortunately, PowerPoint's Compare feature simplifies the process of analyzing and consolidating comments.

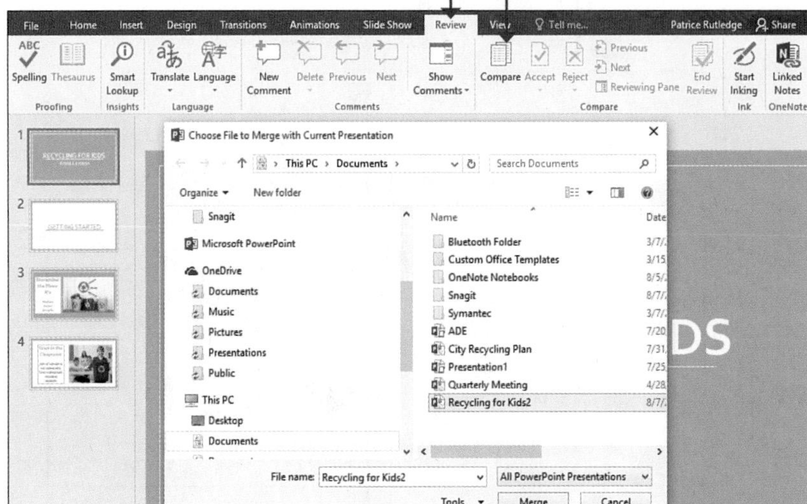

1. Click the **Review** tab.
2. Click the **Compare** button.
3. Navigate to the presentation you want to compare, and click the **Merge** button.

Continued

**TIP**

**Close the Revisions Pane** To close the Revisions task pane, click the **Close** button (x) in the upper-right corner. Alternatively, on the Review tab, click the **Reviewing Pane** button, which serves as a toggle for this pane.

**TIP**

**Accept All Changes** To accept all presentation changes, click the down arrow below the Accept button, and select **Accept All Changes to the Presentation** from the menu.

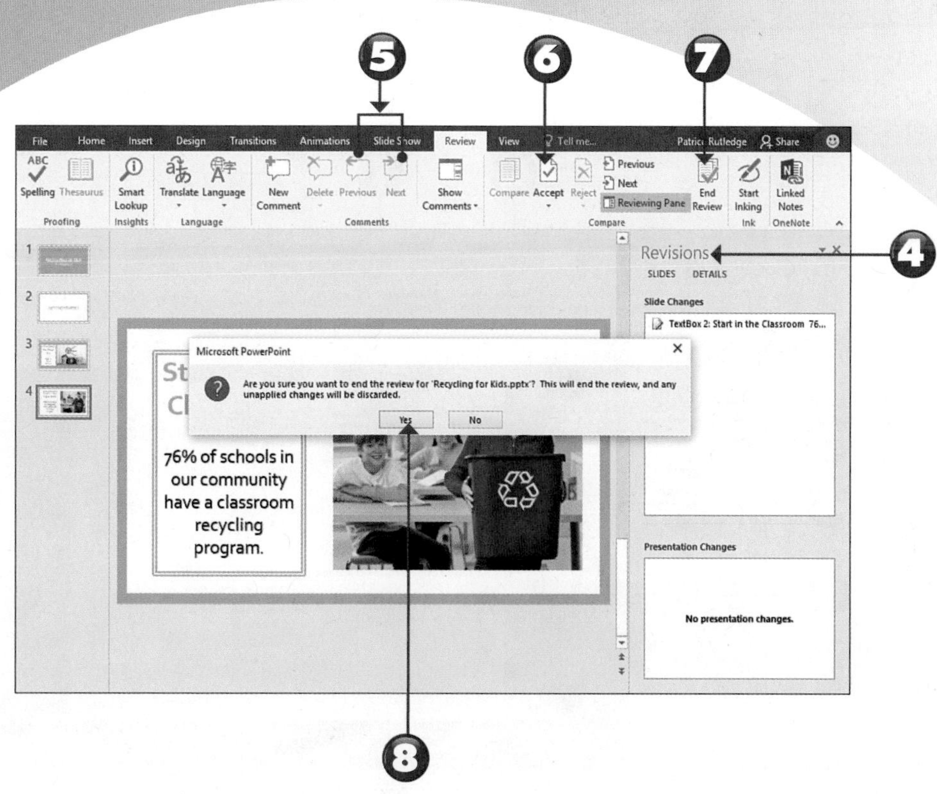


4. PowerPoint merges the two presentations and opens the Revisions task pane where you can view changes.
5. Use the **Next** and **Previous** buttons to scroll through changes.
6. Click the **Accept** button to accept a change.
7. When you finish comparing presentations, click the **End Review** button.
8. Click **Yes** to confirm that you want to end the review.

*End*

**TIP**

**Rejecting Changes** After you accept a change, the Reject button on the Review tab is available. If you want to reject the active change, click the upper part of the Reject button. For more options, click the down arrow below the Reject button.

**CAUTION**

**Ending Your Review** When you end your review, all your accepted changes are applied to your original presentation; changes you didn't accept are discarded. You can't undo this action.

# SETTING UP A SLIDE SHOW

Before delivering your slide show, you should set up all the show options you want to use.

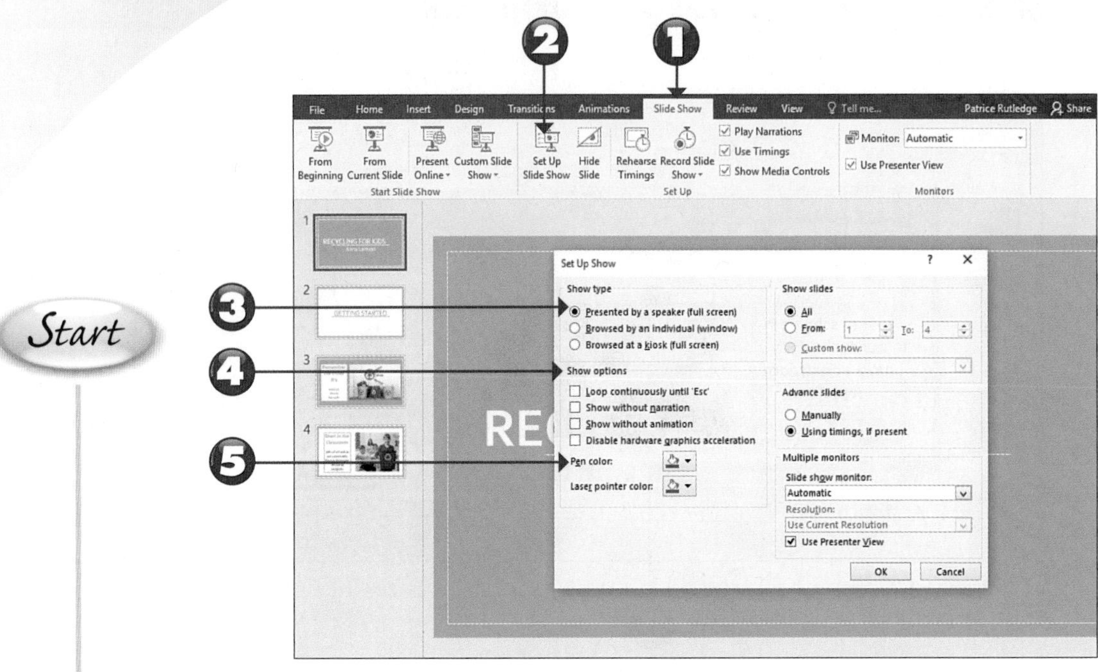


Start

1. Click the **Slide Show** tab.
2. Click the **Set Up Slide Show** button.
3. Select a Show Type. The default is Presented by a Speaker, which is the most common option.
4. Specify any Show Options you want to set.
5. Select a Pen Color if you plan to use a pen to draw onscreen during your presentation.

Continued

## TIP

**Slide Show Setup** Before you deliver a PowerPoint presentation, think through its entire visual flow. This is the time to rehearse in your mind what you want to present and how you want to present it, and plan for the technical aspects of your presentation.

## NOTE

**Show Options** By default, PowerPoint show options aren't active. Select one of these options only if you know you need this feature. For example, you might want to loop continuously or turn off narrations at a trade show.

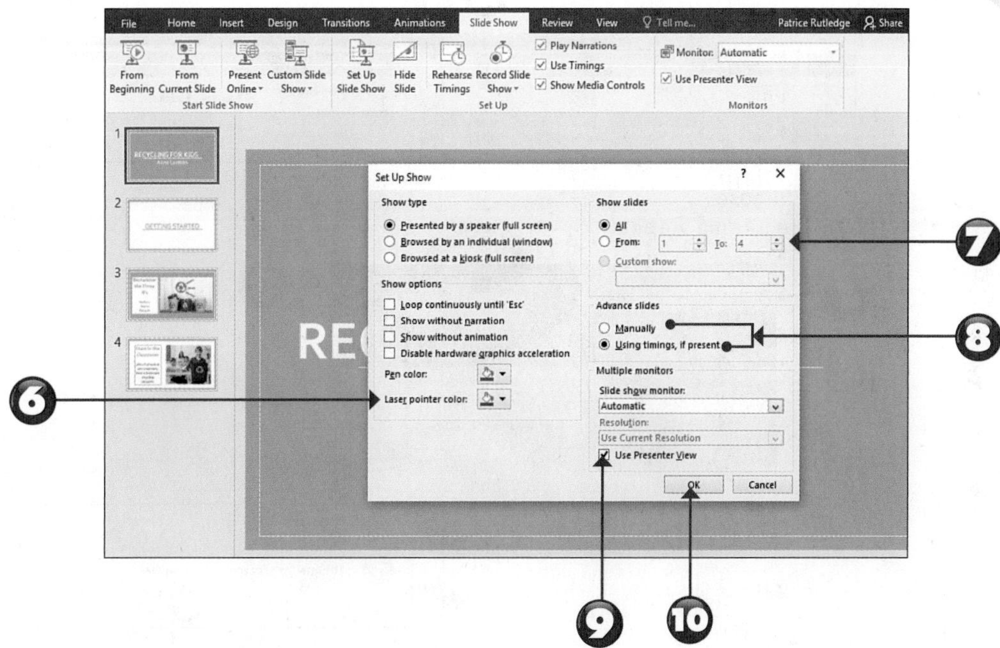


6. Select a Laser Pointer Color if you plan to use a laser pointer during your presentation.

7. Choose the slides you want to include in your presentation.

8. Specify how you want to advance slides: Manually or Using Timings, if Present.

9. Select the **Use Presenter View** check box if you want to use this view.

10. Click the **OK** button.

End

**TIP**

**Advancing Slides** To advance a slide manually, you must press a key or click the mouse. Choosing **Manually** in this field overrides any timings you previously set. See “Rehearsing Timings,” later in this chapter.

**NOTE**

**Presenter View** Presenter View enables you to display speaker’s notes, upcoming slides, the elapsed time of your presentation, and other useful information. See “Exploring Presenter View,” later in this chapter.

# REHEARSING TIMINGS

When you rehearse timings, PowerPoint keeps track of how long you spend on each slide. After you rehearse, you can use these timings to automate slide transitions or simply to help you adjust your presentation to fit in to an allotted amount of time.

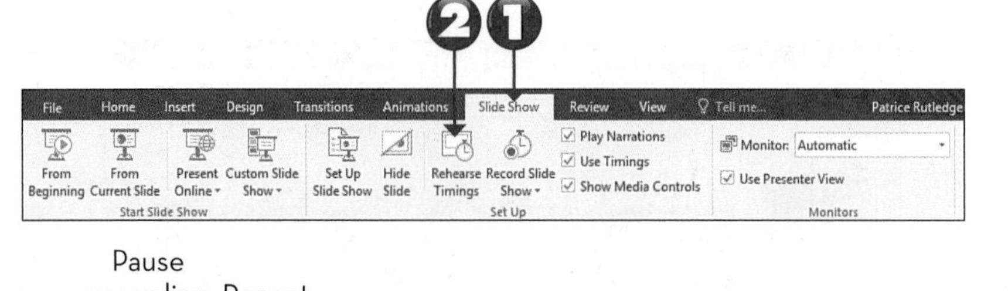


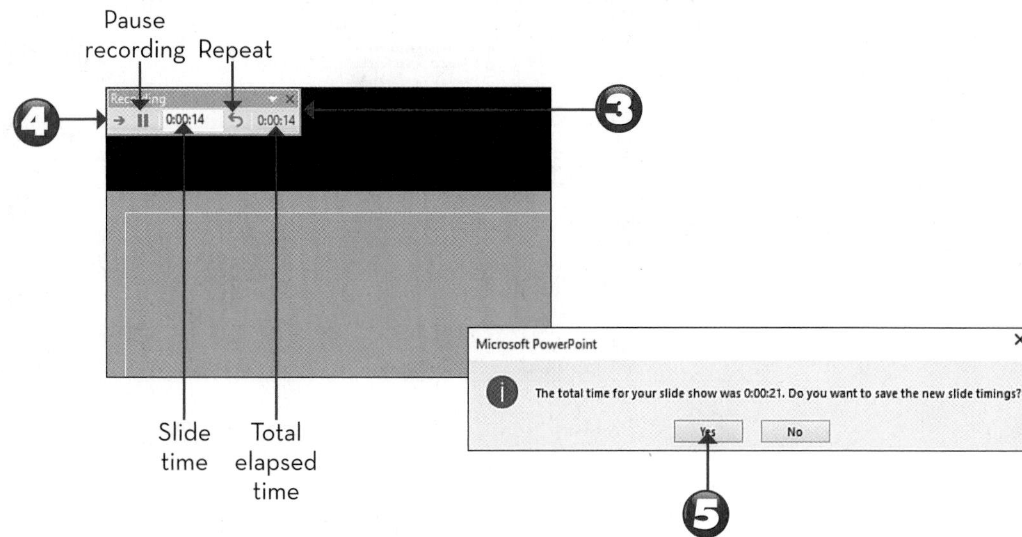


Start

1. Click the **Slide Show** tab.
2. Click the **Rehearse Timings** button.
3. The presentation displays in Slide Show view, opening the Recording toolbar in the upper-left corner.
4. Talk through your presentation, clicking the **Next** button to advance to the next slide.
5. After you rehearse the last slide, click **Yes** to save your timings.

End

**TIP**

**Using Timings** If you want to use slide timings during a slide show, verify that the **Use Timings** check box is selected on the Slide Show tab.

**TIP**

**Deleting Timings** To delete slide timings, click the down arrow below the **Record Slide Show** button on the Slide Show tab, and select **Clear** from the menu.

# RECORDING VOICE NARRATIONS

You can record your own voiceover to accompany a web-based presentation or an automated presentation, such as one you run continuously at a trade show booth.

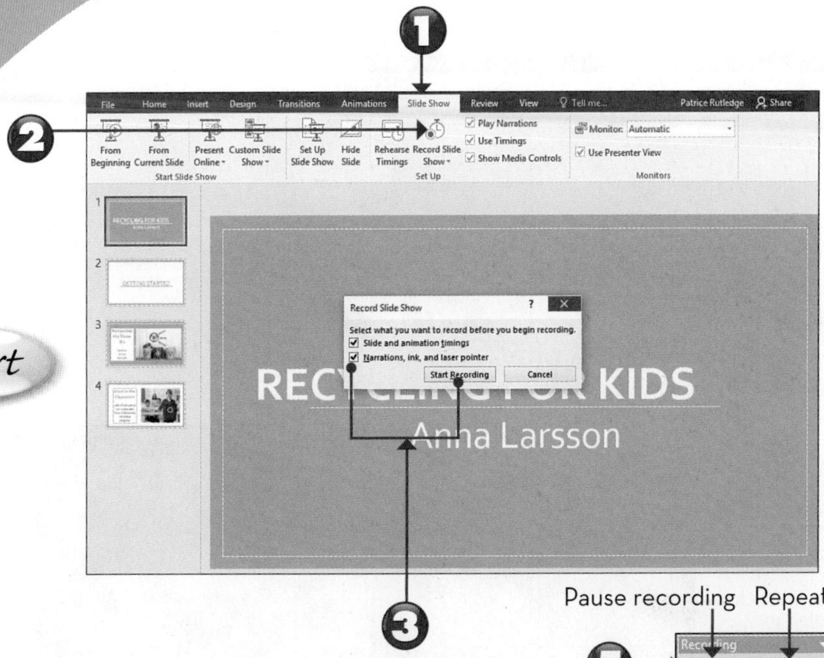

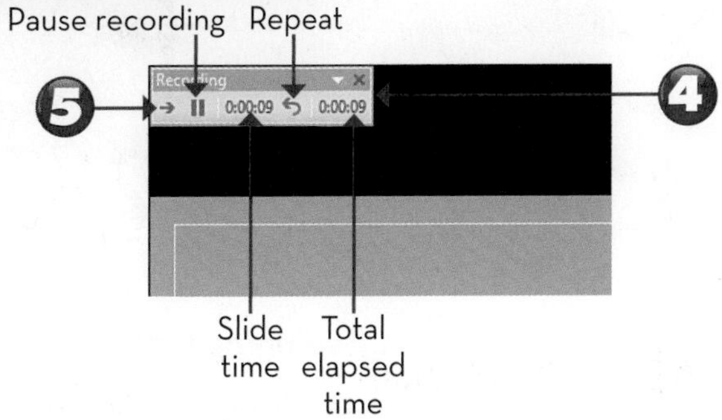

Start

Pause recording Repeat

Slide time

Total elapsed time

1. Click the **Slide Show** tab.
2. Click the **Record Slide Show** button.
3. Specify what you want to record, and then click the **Start Recording** button.
4. The presentation displays in Slide Show view, opening the Recording toolbar in the upper-left corner.
5. Record your presentation, clicking the **Next** button or spacebar to move to the next slide.

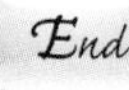

## NOTE

**Preparing to Record** You must have a microphone and a sound card to record a narration. And remember—the better the quality of the equipment you use, the more professional your narration will sound.

## TIP

**Playing and Deleting Narrations** To play voice narrations during a slide show, verify that the **Play Narrations** check box is selected on the Slide Show tab. To delete slide narrations, click the down arrow below the **Record Slide Show** button, and select **Clear**. From here, you can choose whether to clear timings or narrations on the current slide or all slides.

# PRESENTING YOUR SHOW

After you set up your PowerPoint slide show, it's time to present it. When you present a show, PowerPoint uses the settings you entered in the Set Up Show dialog box and on the Slide Show tab.

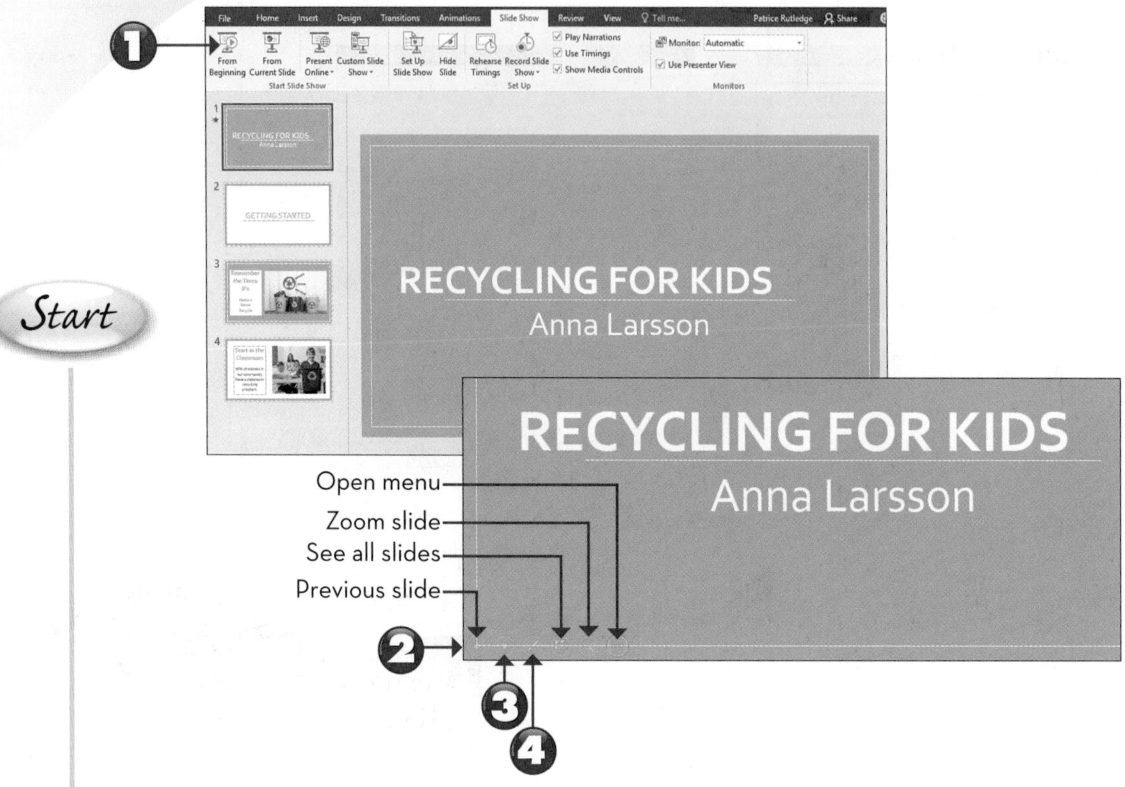


Start

1. Click the **From Beginning** button on the Slide Show tab to start your show. Alternatively, press **F5**.
2. Pause your mouse over the lower-left corner of your presentation to view PowerPoint's hidden navigation buttons.
3. Click the **Next** button to move to the next slide. Alternatively, press the **Page Down** key.
4. To use a pen or laser pointer, click the **Pen** navigation button, and select your preferred tool.

Continued

**TIP**

**Practice Before Presenting** Before presenting your show live, you should preview it to test content, flow, and narration. By simulating live conditions as much as possible in your practice sessions, you can increase your odds of delivering a perfect presentation.

**TIP**

**Check Your Spelling** Another thing to check before presenting is the spelling of any slide text by clicking the **Spelling** button on the Review tab. This is particularly important if you've made any last-minute changes.

5 Right-click to display a shortcut menu with options to show Presenter View, end your show, zoom, and more.

6 Select **End Show** from the menu to end your show. Alternatively, press the **Esc** key.

*End*

**TIP**

**Keyboard Commands** Navigating your slide show with keyboard shortcut commands is another option. Right-click anywhere on the screen, and choose **Help** from the shortcut menu to display a list of shortcuts.

**TIP**

**Arrow Pointer** By default, PowerPoint displays an arrow pointer when you move your mouse and hides it after three seconds of inactivity. If you want to always or never display the arrow, right-click the slide, and choose **Pointer Options**, **Arrow Options** from the menu.

# PRESENTING ONLINE

PowerPoint enables you to share your presentation in high fidelity with people on the Web, even if they don't have PowerPoint installed on their computers.

Start

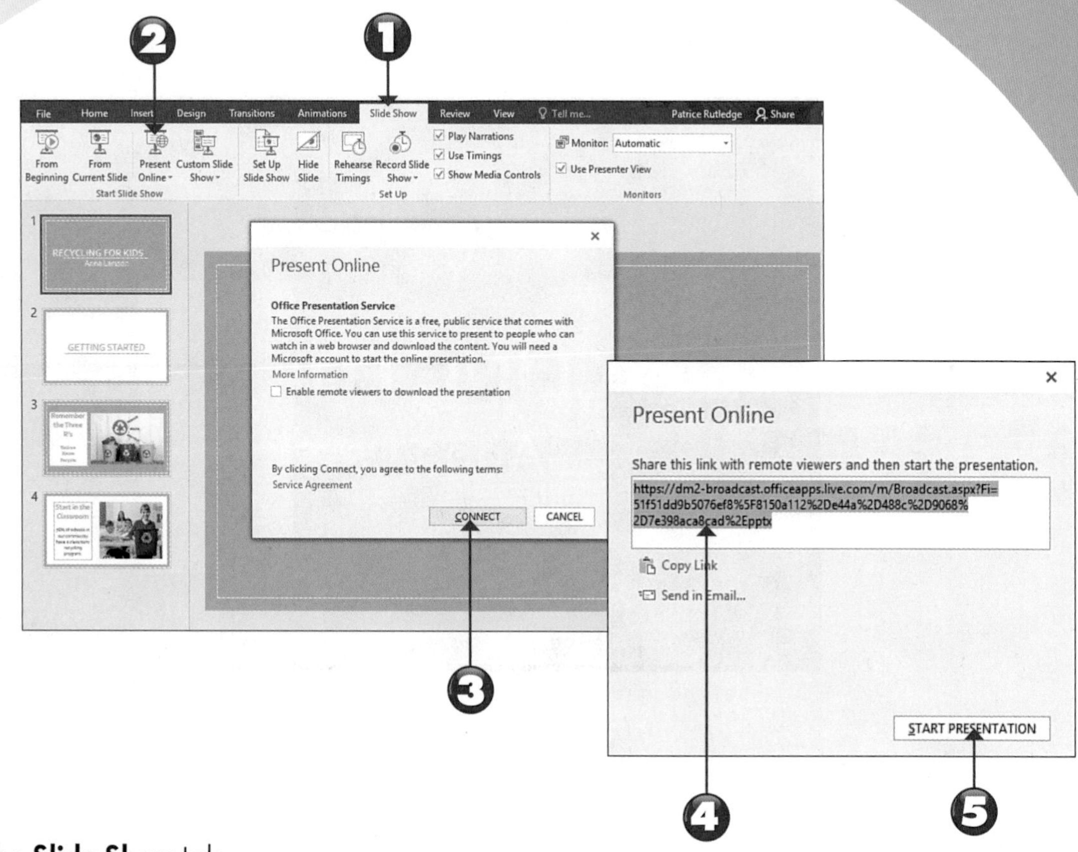


1. Click the **Slide Show** tab.
2. Click the **Present Online** button.
3. Click the **Connect** button.
4. The Present Online dialog box displays a link you can share with remote viewers.
5. When you're ready to present, click the **Start Presentation** button.

Continued

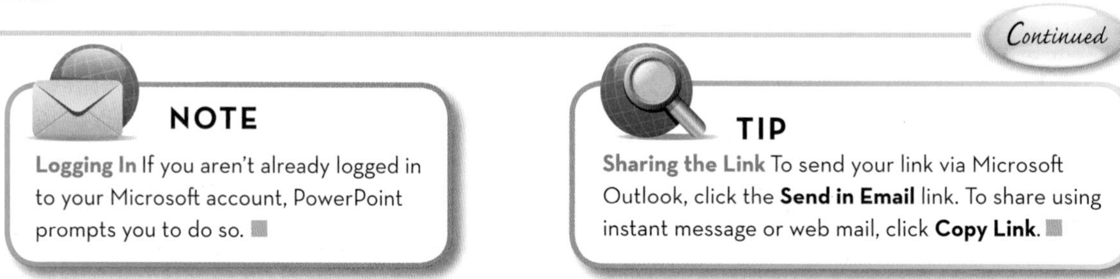

**NOTE**

**Logging In** If you aren't already logged in to your Microsoft account, PowerPoint prompts you to do so.

**TIP**

**Sharing the Link** To send your link via Microsoft Outlook, click the **Send in Email** link. To share using instant message or web mail, click **Copy Link**.

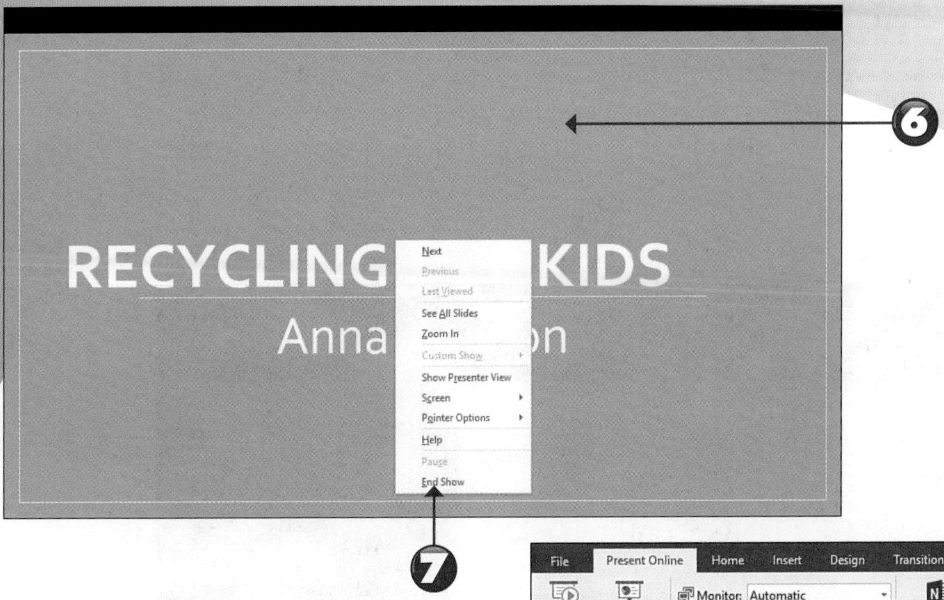

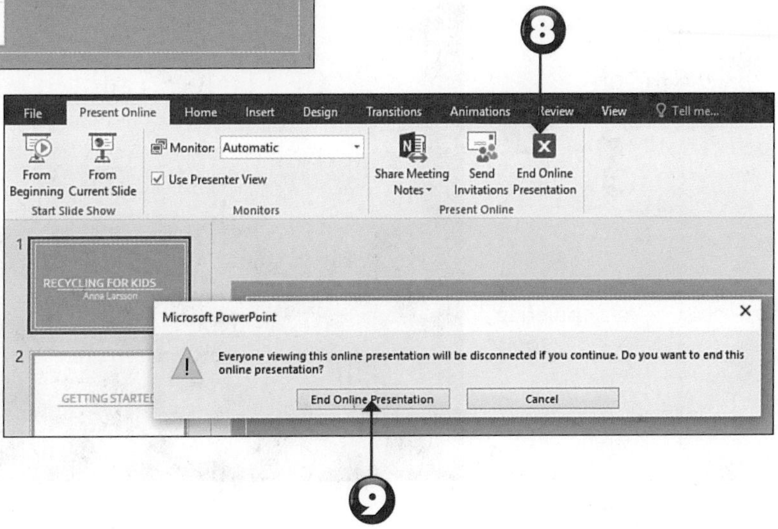

6 PowerPoint starts your slide show on the Web, where your viewers can see it.

7 When you finish your presentation, right-click and select **End Show**.

8 Click **End Online Presentation** on the Present Online tab to disconnect all your remote viewers.

9 Click **End Online Presentation** in the confirmation dialog box to confirm.

*End*

TIP

**Present Online Tab** Before broadcasting, review the options on the Present Online tab, where you can choose whether to start your show from the beginning or from the current slide, use Presenter View, share meeting notes, or send invitations.

TIP

**Starting Manually** To start Presenter View manually, right-click and select **Show Presenter View**. Learn more in the "Exploring Presenter View" section later in this chapter.

# EXPLORING PRESENTER VIEW

Presenter View enables you to display a full-screen presentation that your audience can see and another view for you (the presenter) that includes slide previews, speaker notes, a timer, and more. Now explore some of the useful tools that Presenter View offers.

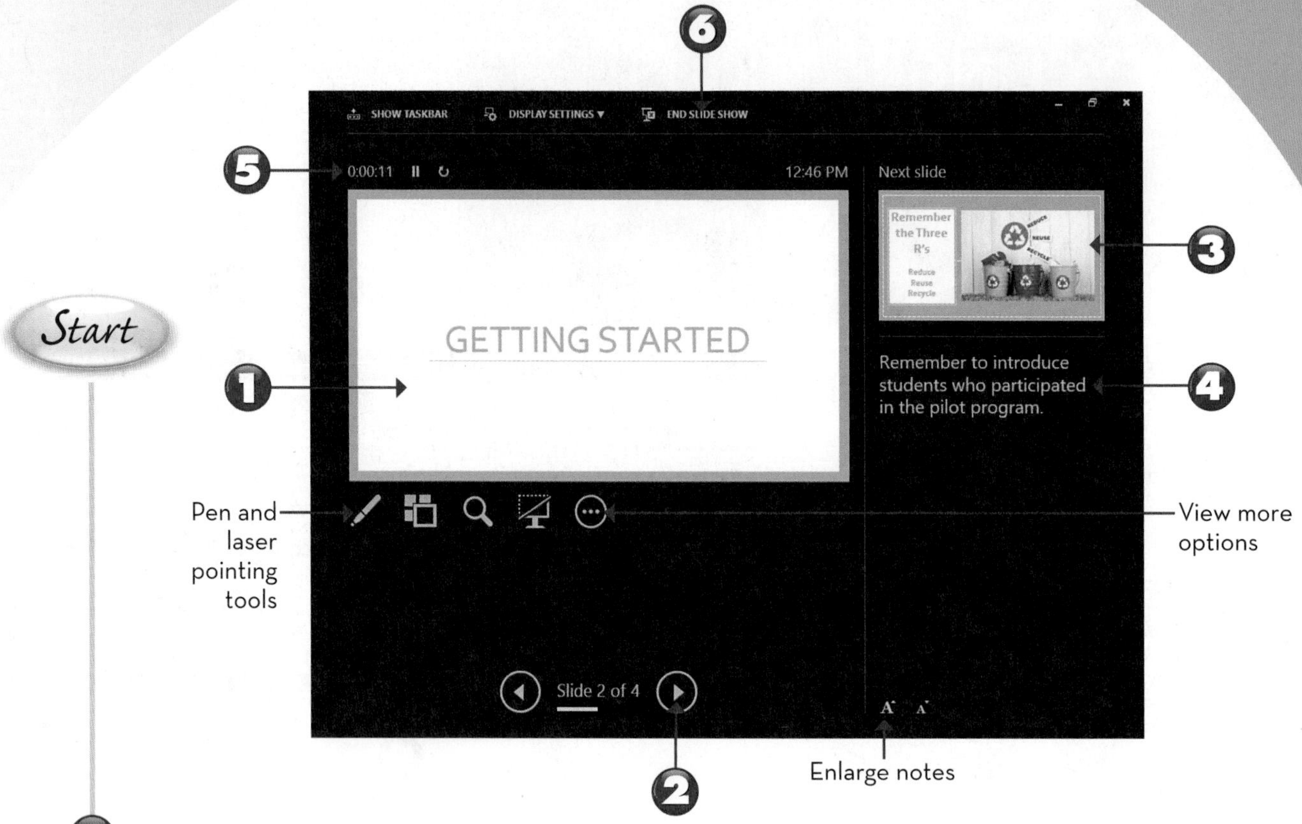

SHOW TASKBAR DISPLAY SETTINGS ▾ END SLIDE SHOW

0:00:11 12:46 PM Next slide

GETTING STARTED

Remember the Three R's Reduce Reuse Recycle

Remember to introduce students who participated in the pilot program.

Pen and laser pointing tools

View more options

Slide 2 of 4

Enlarge notes

Start

1. View your current slide in the main window.
2. Advance to the next slide.
3. Preview your next slide.
4. Display your notes, if any.
5. View how long you've been presenting.
6. End your slide show.

## NOTE

**Presenter View** To use Presenter View, select the **Use Presenter View** check box on the Slide Show tab. You can also right-click an in-progress presentation and select **Show Presenter View** from the menu.

# CREATING VIDEOS FROM POWERPOINT PRESENTATIONS

PowerPoint enables you to create full-fidelity video from your PowerPoint presentation in either a Windows Media Video (.wmv) or MPEG-4 Video (.mp4) format. You can distribute your video on the Web or mobile device, or through more traditional methods, such as on a DVD or through email.

Start

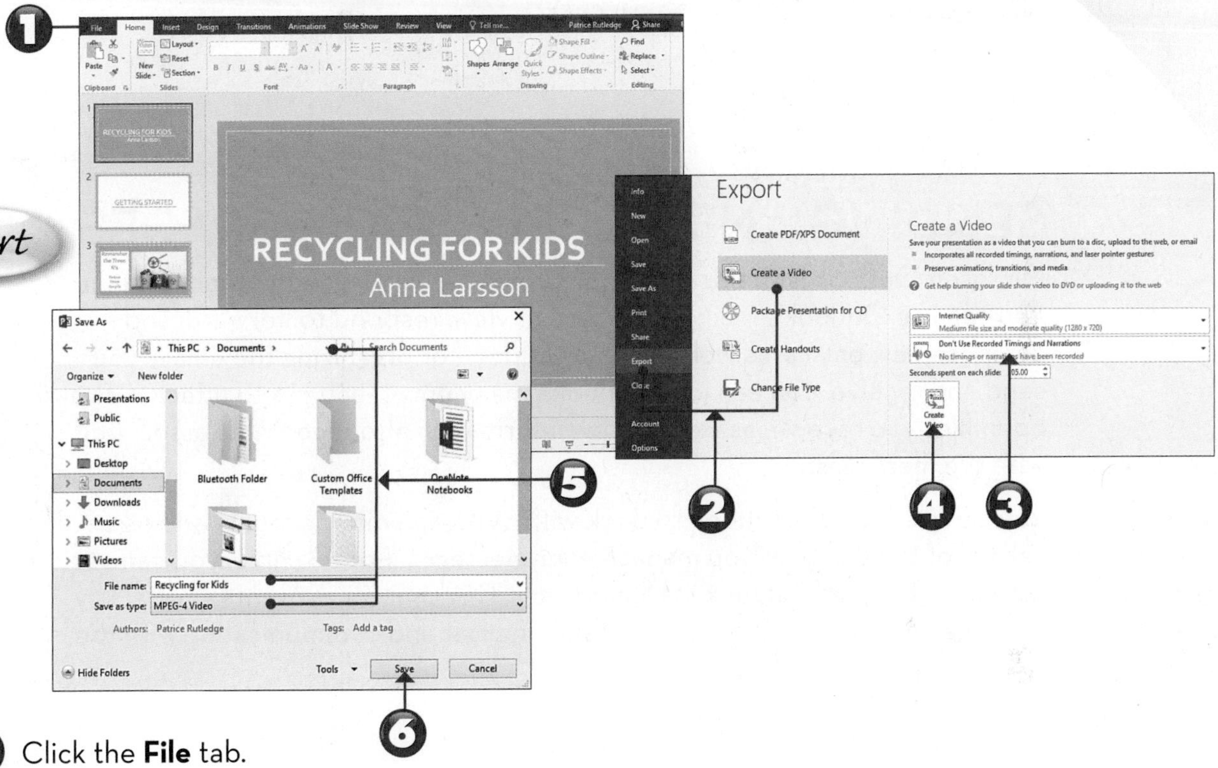

1. Click the **File** tab.
2. Select **Export** and then **Create a Video**.
3. Select your preferred video options.
4. Click the **Create Video** button.
5. Specify a filename, location, and video type.
6. Click the **Save** button.

End

**TIP**

**Video Options** Not sure which options to choose? PowerPoint offers explanations below each option that help you decide which is best for your presentation.

# SENDING AND RECEIVING MESSAGES

Microsoft Outlook is the perfect tool for communicating with others via email. You can use Outlook's Mail component to view, respond to, forward, and compose new emails, as well as create folders for organizing the emails you send and receive. You can use Outlook's many email features to attach files and open files you receive, as well as view information about contacts associated with the messages.

You can also set up Outlook to work with multiple email accounts and use a variety of tools to help you manage your messages. For example, you can set up a filter to weed out junk mail and spam. This chapter presents several key emailing features to get you up and running fast and communicating with the world at large.

# NAVIGATING THE OUTLOOK PROGRAM SCREEN

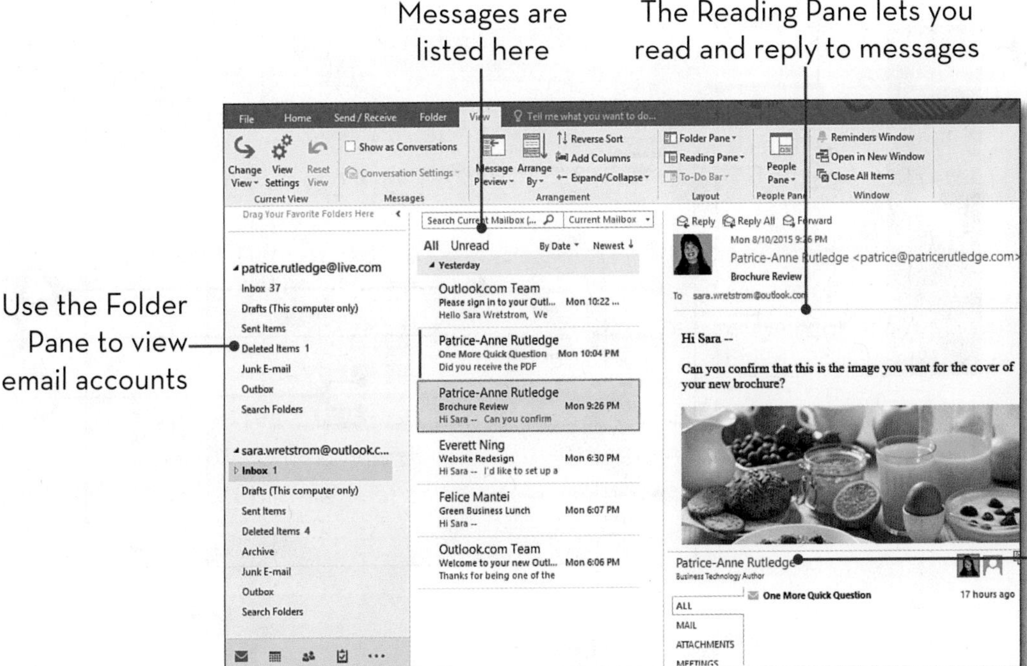

# ADD AN EMAIL ACCOUNT

You can set up Outlook to work with multiple email accounts from different services, such as Outlook.com, Hotmail, Gmail, or Yahoo!. This enables you to check all your email from various services in one convenient spot.

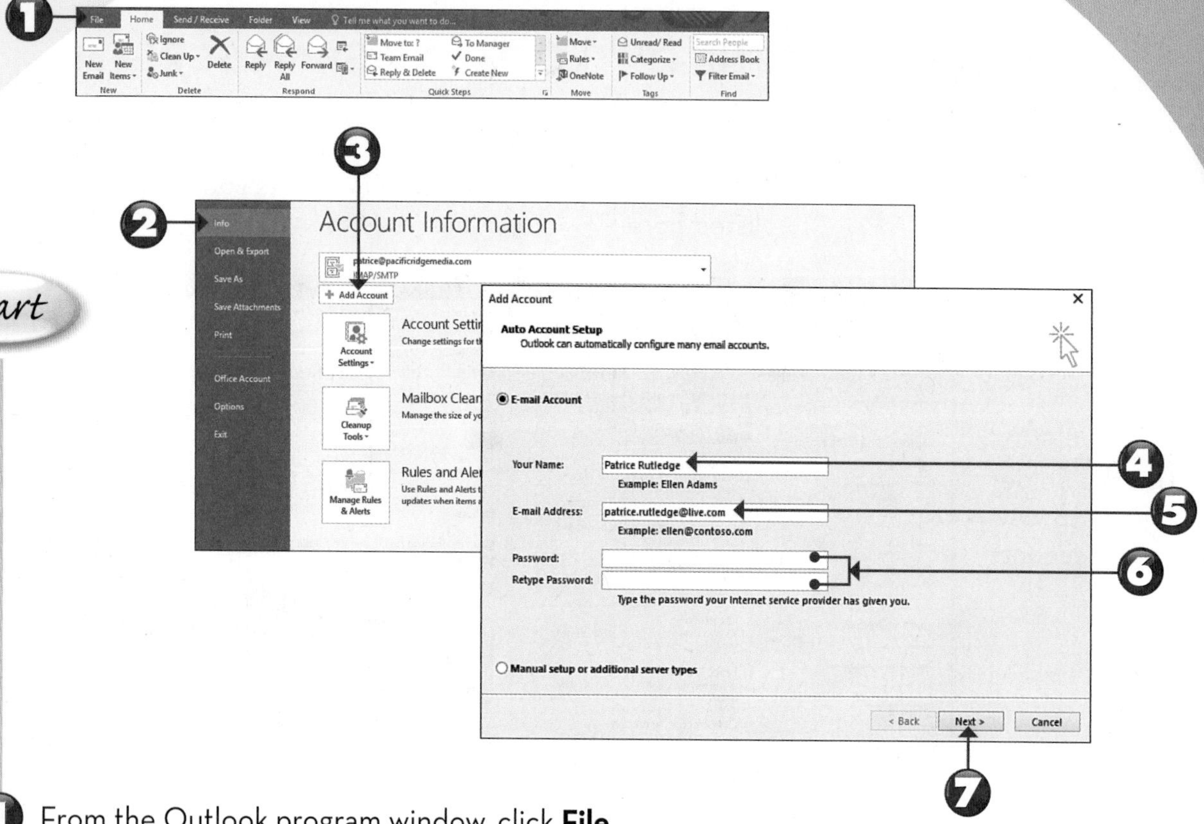

*Start*

1. From the Outlook program window, click **File**.
2. The Info page appears by default; if it doesn't, click **Info**.
3. Click **Add Account**.
4. Type your name.
5. Type your email address.
6. Type your password and then retype it.
7. Click **Next**.

*Continued*

## NOTE

**New to Outlook?** If you're new to Outlook, Microsoft displays a wizard that walks you through setting up your first email account. You can then use the steps in this section to add any additional accounts.

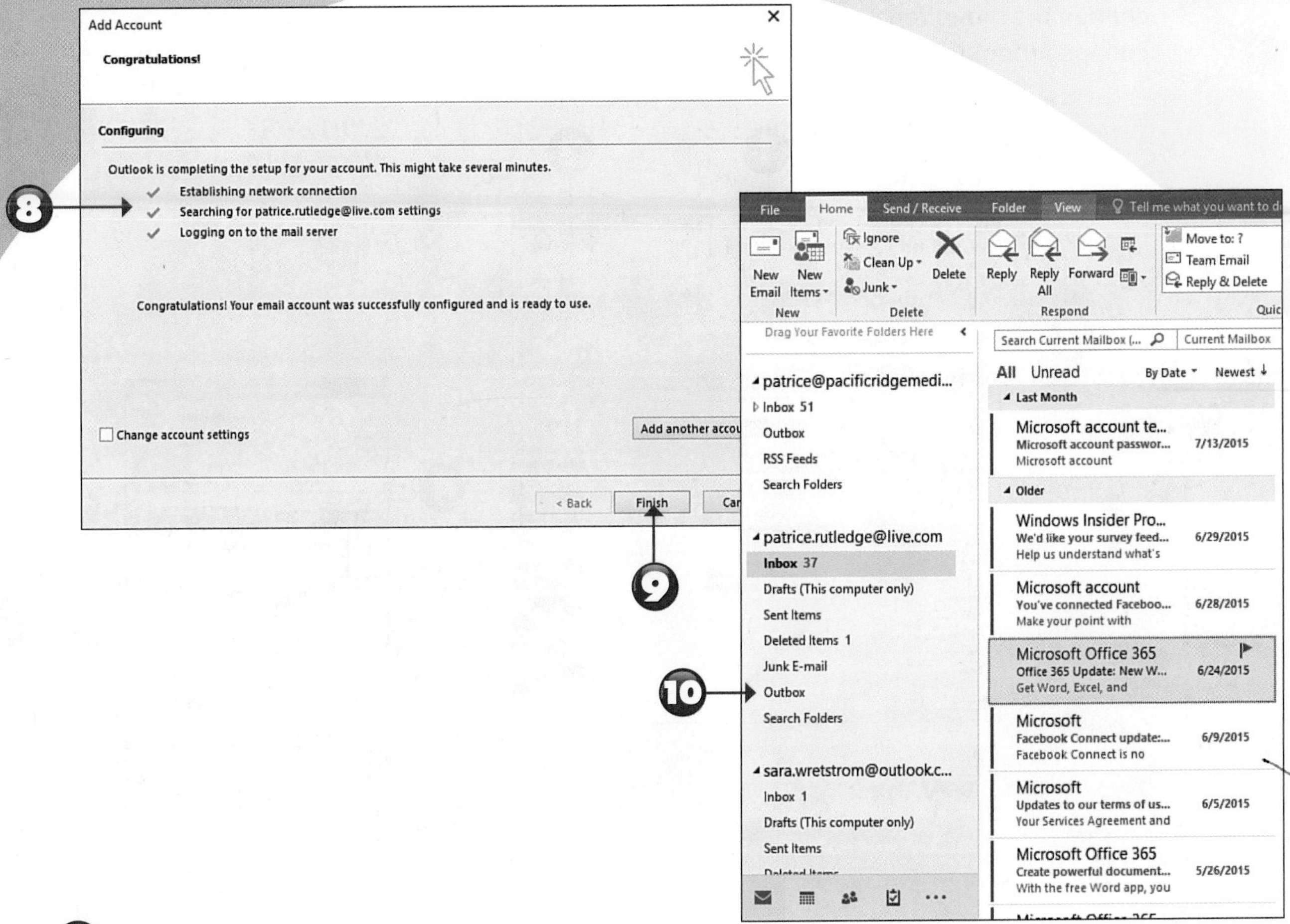

8 Outlook configures your account.

9 Click **Finish**.

10 Outlook displays your account.

End

## NOTE

**Manual Configuration** Outlook attempts to automatically configure new email accounts you add; however, some email service providers might require additional setup steps. If you have trouble, contact your provider for help and then try the **Manual setup or additional server types** option in the Add Account dialog box to set up the account manually.

## TIP

**Remove It!** To remove an email account you no longer use, click **File**, **Info**, and then click the **Account Settings** button; choose **Account Settings**. This opens the Account Settings dialog box where you can change, repair, or remove accounts. Click the account you want to remove from the list, and click the **Remove** button.

# EXPLORING THE OUTLOOK LAYOUT

Outlook's program window is divided into panes that you can expand and collapse to change the view. You can use the View tab to change how panes display, or expand and collapse them using their icons.

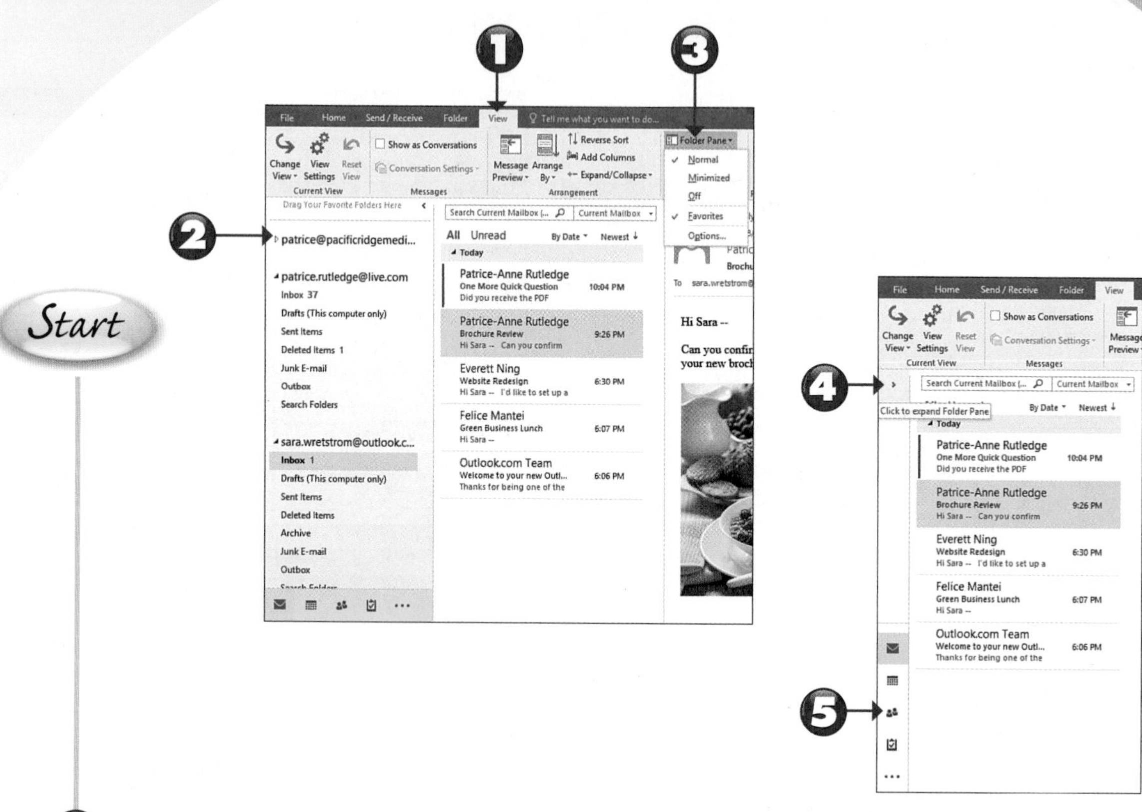

Start

1. Click the **View** tab.

2. The Folder Pane lists email accounts; click an arrow to expand or collapse an account.

3. Click the **Folder Pane** drop-down arrow on the View tab to change the pane's display or turn it off entirely.

4. If the pane is minimized, click to expand the Folder Pane again.

5. Other Outlook components are listed; click an icon to activate the component, such as your calendar, contacts, or tasks.

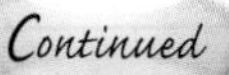
Continued

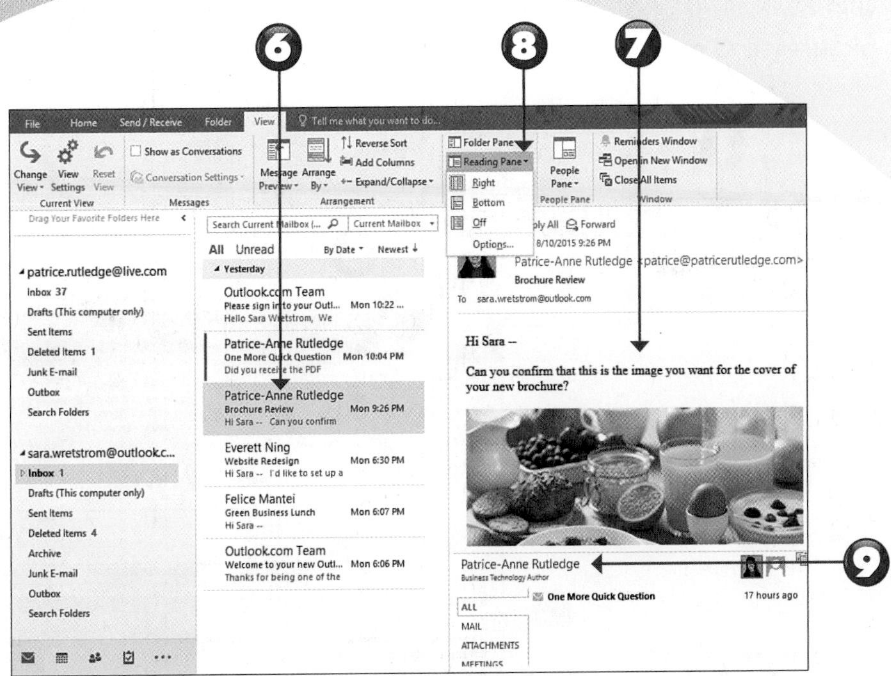


6 Messages are listed here; click the message you want to view.

7 You can read the selected message in the Reading Pane.

8 Click the **Reading Pane** drop-down arrow on the View tab to change the pane's display or turn it off entirely.

9 Read information about a particular contact in the People Pane.

End

## TIP

**Message Preview** In addition to controlling the Reading Pane, you can control how many lines from a message appear in the message list pane. By default, Outlook displays one line, but you can choose to view more or no message lines at all; click the **Message Preview** button on the View tab, and make a selection.

## TIP

**People Pane** Click the **People Pane** button on the View tab to control this pane. Your options include Normal, Minimized, and Off.

# SENDING AN EMAIL MESSAGE

When composing a message in Outlook, you can use a message window. The message window includes tabs of options for formatting message text, attaching files, adding pictures, and more.

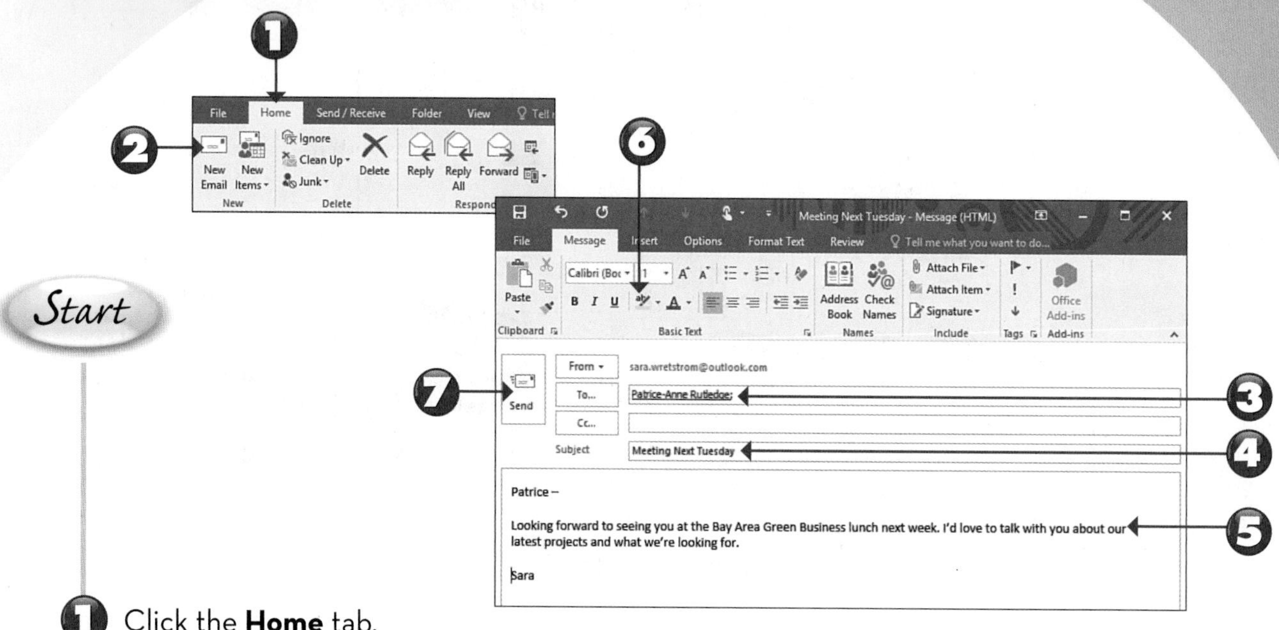


Start

1. Click the **Home** tab.
2. Click **New Email**.
3. Type the recipient's email address, or if it's already stored in your Address book, click the **To** button and choose the address.
4. Click in the **Subject** box and type a message title.
5. Click here and type your message text.
6. To change the formatting, such as a different font or size, choose from the Message tab's options, or click the **Format Text** tab for more formatting commands.
7. Click **Send** to send the message.

End

## TIP

**Send and Receive** To send any messages waiting in your outbox, click the **Send/Receive** tab, and click **Send/Receive All Folders**. You can also click the **Send/Receive All Folders** button on the Quick Access toolbar. This action also checks for new email messages.

## NOTE

**Cc and Bcc** You can copy someone else on a message, which means you send the message to a second party in addition to the primary addressee. Cc stands for courtesy copy or carbon copy, a leftover term from earlier days of correspondence. Click in the **Cc** field, and type another email address. You can also do a blind courtesy/carbon copy, or Bcc; this sends the message to another person without the primary addressee knowing. Click the **Cc** button to find the Bcc option.

# RECEIVING AND READING YOUR EMAIL

Each email account you have set up in Outlook is listed in the Folder Pane where you can choose which Inbox you want to view. You can read any message in your Inbox using the Reading Pane, or you can open the message in its own window.

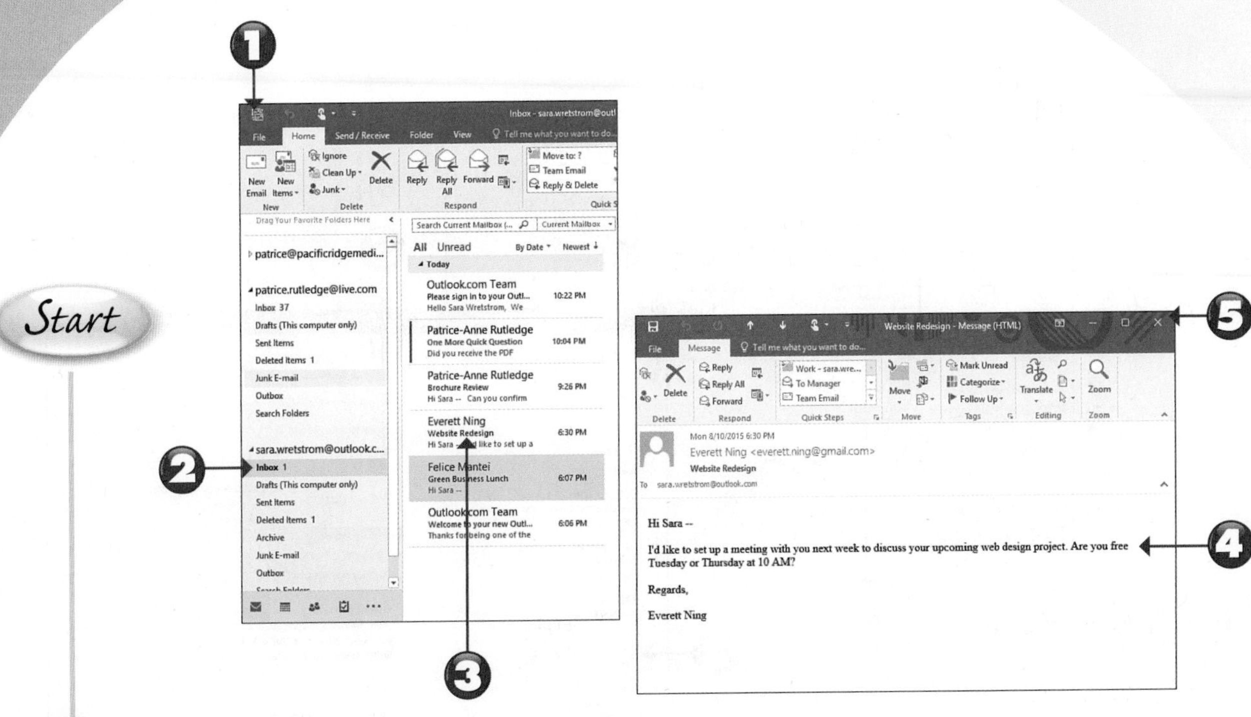


1. On the Quick Access toolbar, click **Send/Receive All Folders.**
2. From the Folder Pane, click the account Inbox you want to view.
3. Double-click the message you want to read.
4. Outlook opens the message in its own window.
5. Click the **Close** button (x) to close the window.

End

**TIP**

**The Reading Pane** You can also use the Reading Pane to read a selected message. If the pane is not visible, click the **View** tab, click **Reading Pane**, and then click **Right** or **Bottom** to turn on the pane.

**TIP**

**Reply and Forward Messages** You can reply to and forward messages you read in the Reading Pane. Click the **Reply**, **Reply All**, or **Forward** buttons at the top of the message and enter your new message. If you need more room to compose the reply or forward message, click the **Pop Out** button to open the message in its own window.

# REPLYING TO A MESSAGE

You can reply to a message from the Reading Pane or open the message window. The message window offers access to more commands and features for helping you format the message, proofread it, or insert pictures. When you reply to a message from the Reading Pane, an abbreviated group of commonly used formatting tools appears on the Message tab.

Start

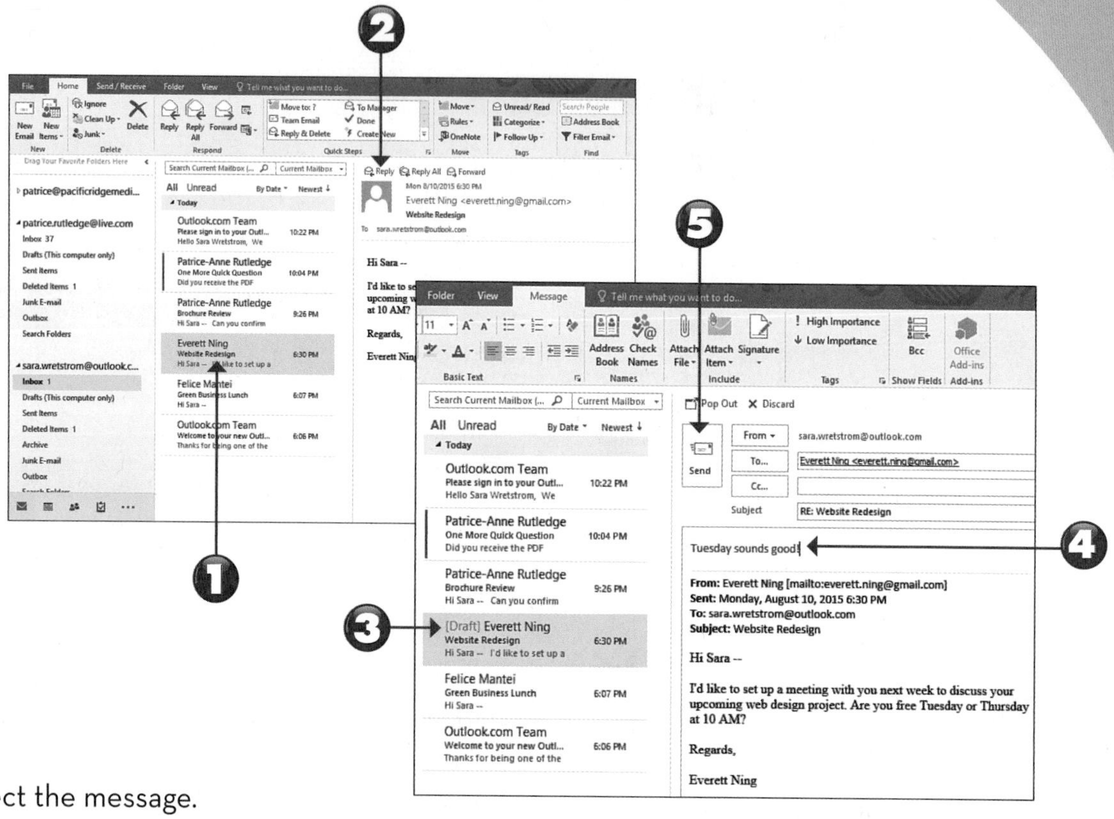

1. Select the message.
2. From the Reading Pane, click **Reply**.
3. Outlook adds draft status to the message here; you can use the Compose Tools Message tab on the Ribbon to add formatting to a message or apply other commands and features.
4. Type your reply.
5. Click **Send**.

**TIP**

**Reply to All** If the original message was sent to multiple people and you want to include them in your response, click **Reply All** instead of Reply.

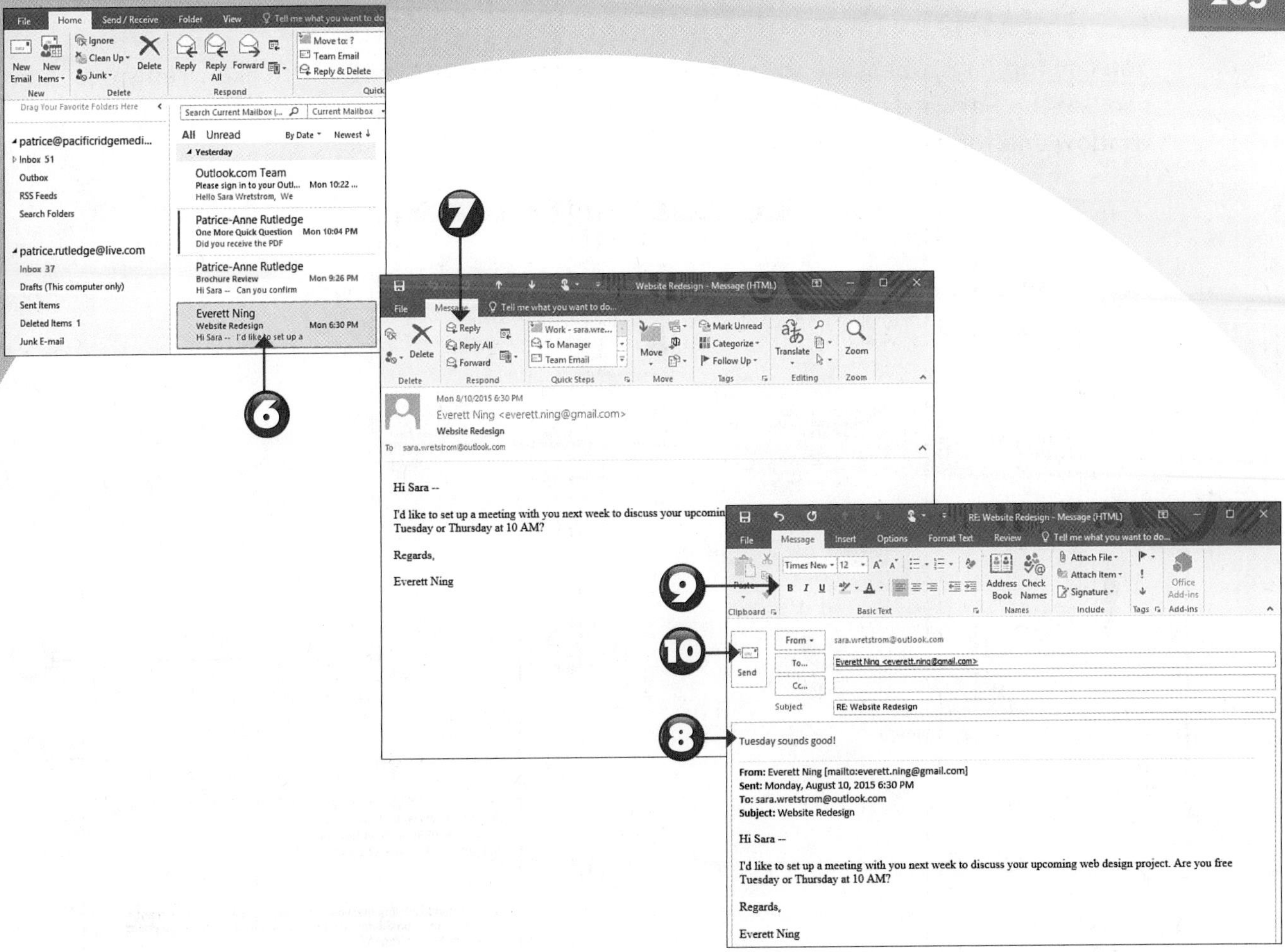

6 To reply to a message in its own window, double-click the message.

7 Click **Reply**.

8 Type your reply.

9 You can use the Ribbon tabs to assign formatting or activate other features.

10 Click **Send**.

*End*

**TIP**

**Proofread It!** Need to check your message for errors? You can check your text for spelling and grammar issues, look up words and synonyms, change the language, and more using the tools on the message window's Review tab.

# FORWARDING A MESSAGE

You can forward a message to send it along to another recipient. Much like a reply, you can use the Forward option in the Reading Pane, or you can open the message in its own window and forward it from there.

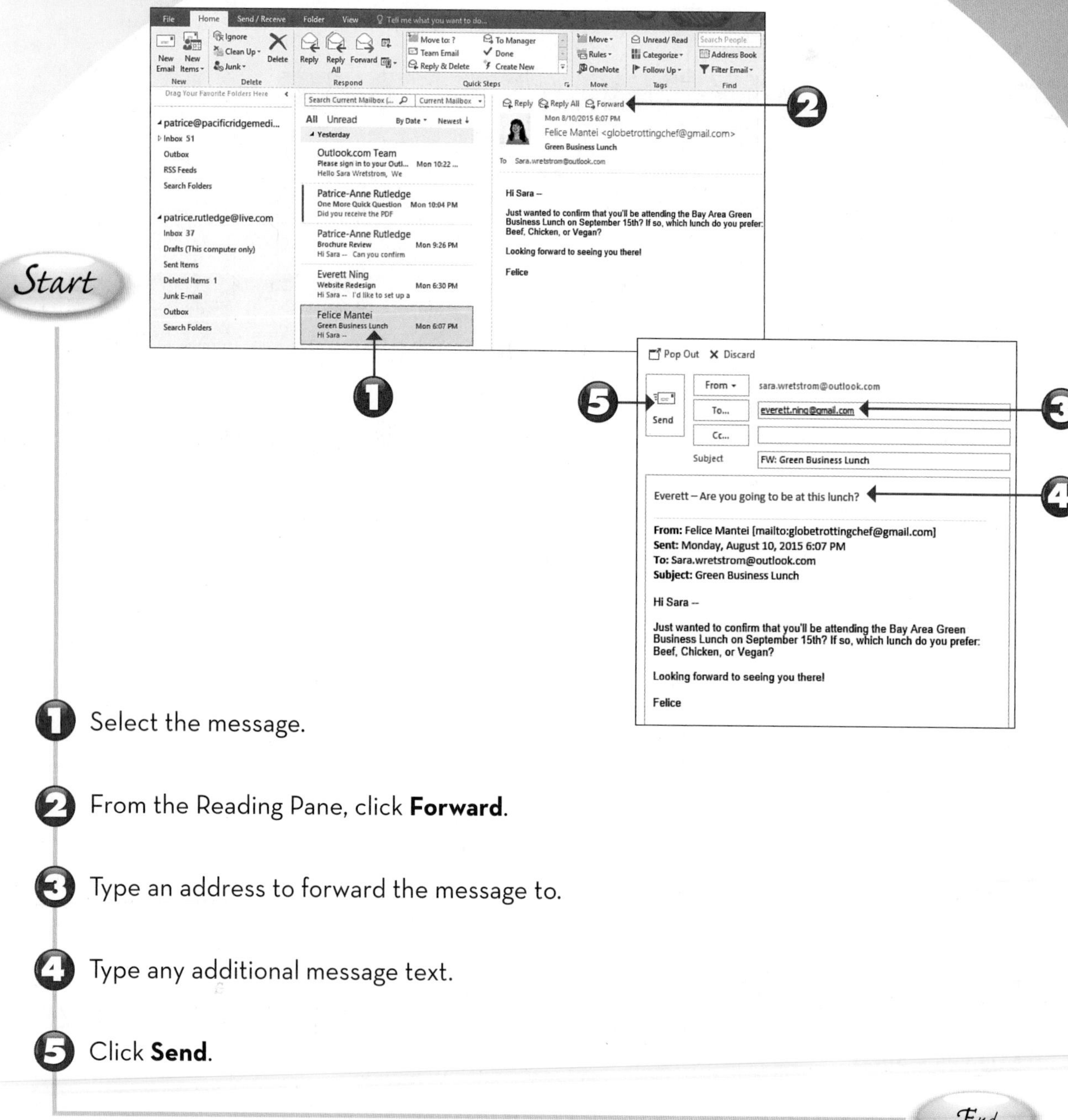


1. Select the message.
2. From the Reading Pane, click **Forward**.
3. Type an address to forward the message to.
4. Type any additional message text.
5. Click **Send**.

End

## TIP

**Think Before Forwarding** Always use caution when forwarding messages. The original sender might not want her email address included in the message text and header information. You might need to delete personal information before forwarding the message.

# ATTACHING FILES TO A MESSAGE

You can send files stored on your computer to other email recipients. For example, if you need to send a document file to a colleague, you can attach it to your message.

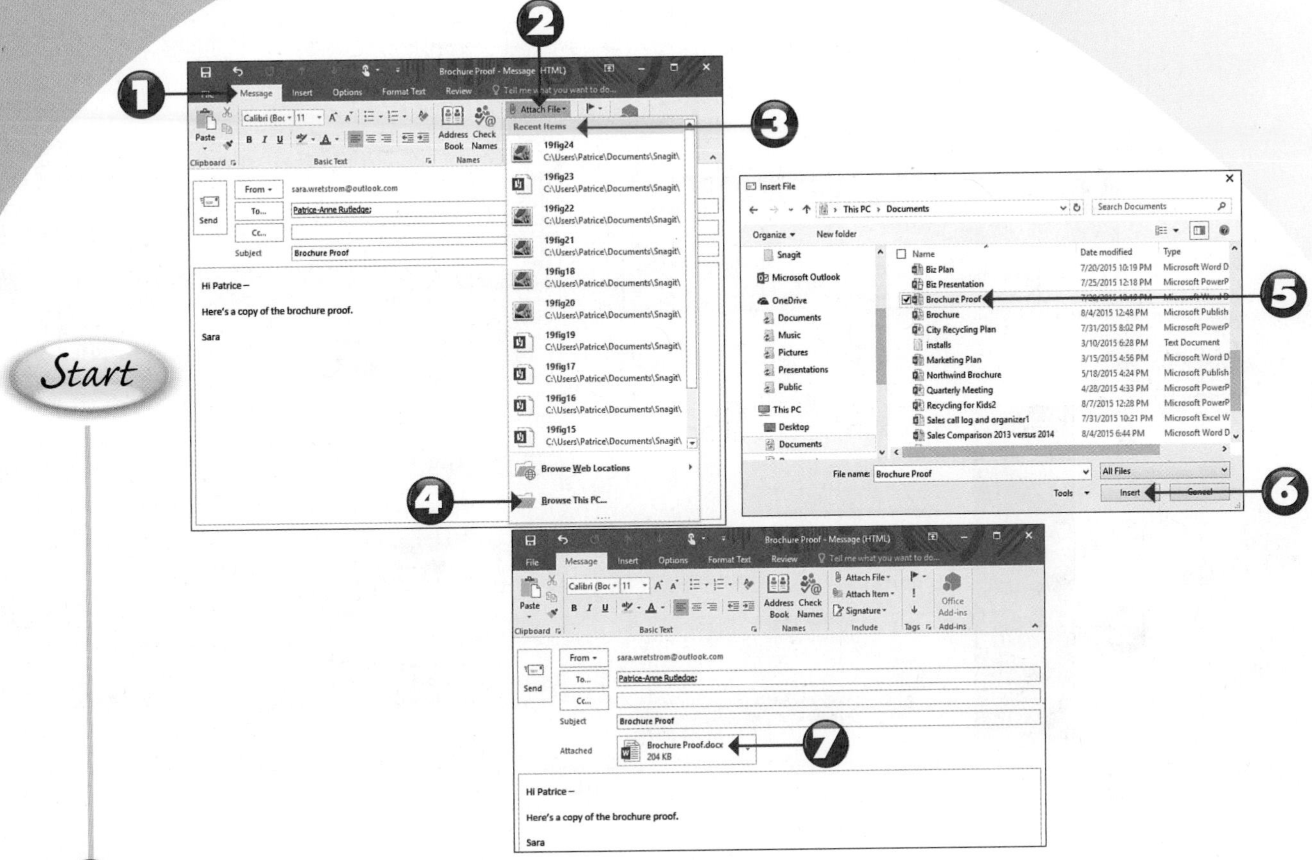

1. On the message window's Ribbon, click the **Message** tab.
2. Click **Attach File**.
3. The Recent Items list displays your most recent files; click a file to attach it.
4. If the file you want isn't in the list, click **Browse This PC** or **Browse Web Locations**. In this example, you browse your PC.
5. The Insert File dialog box opens; navigate to the file you want to attach and select the filename.
6. Click **Insert**.
7. Outlook attaches the file.

**TIP**

**Attach Items** You can use the **Attach Item** command on the **Message** tab to attach other Outlook items to the email, such as a business card, a calendar, another email, or a task.

# CREATING AN EMAIL SIGNATURE

A *signature* is a string of text that appears at the bottom of every email message you send. Signatures can include contact information, a personal quote or motto, or other special information.

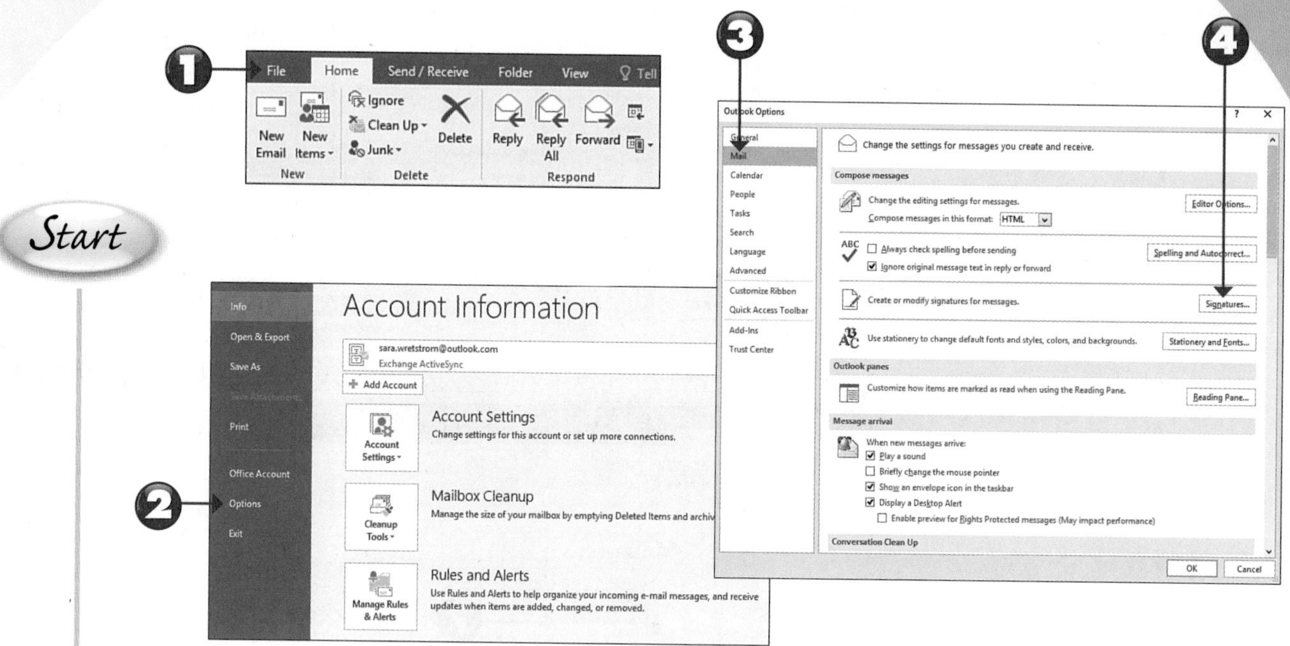

Start

1. Click **File**.
2. Click **Options**.
3. The Outlook Options dialog box opens; click **Mail**.
4. Click **Signatures**.

Continued

## TIP

**Delete a Signature** You can manage your signatures through the Signatures and Stationery dialog box. Click the signature you want to remove, and click the **Delete** button. You can also use the dialog box to specify when to add signatures to your messages.

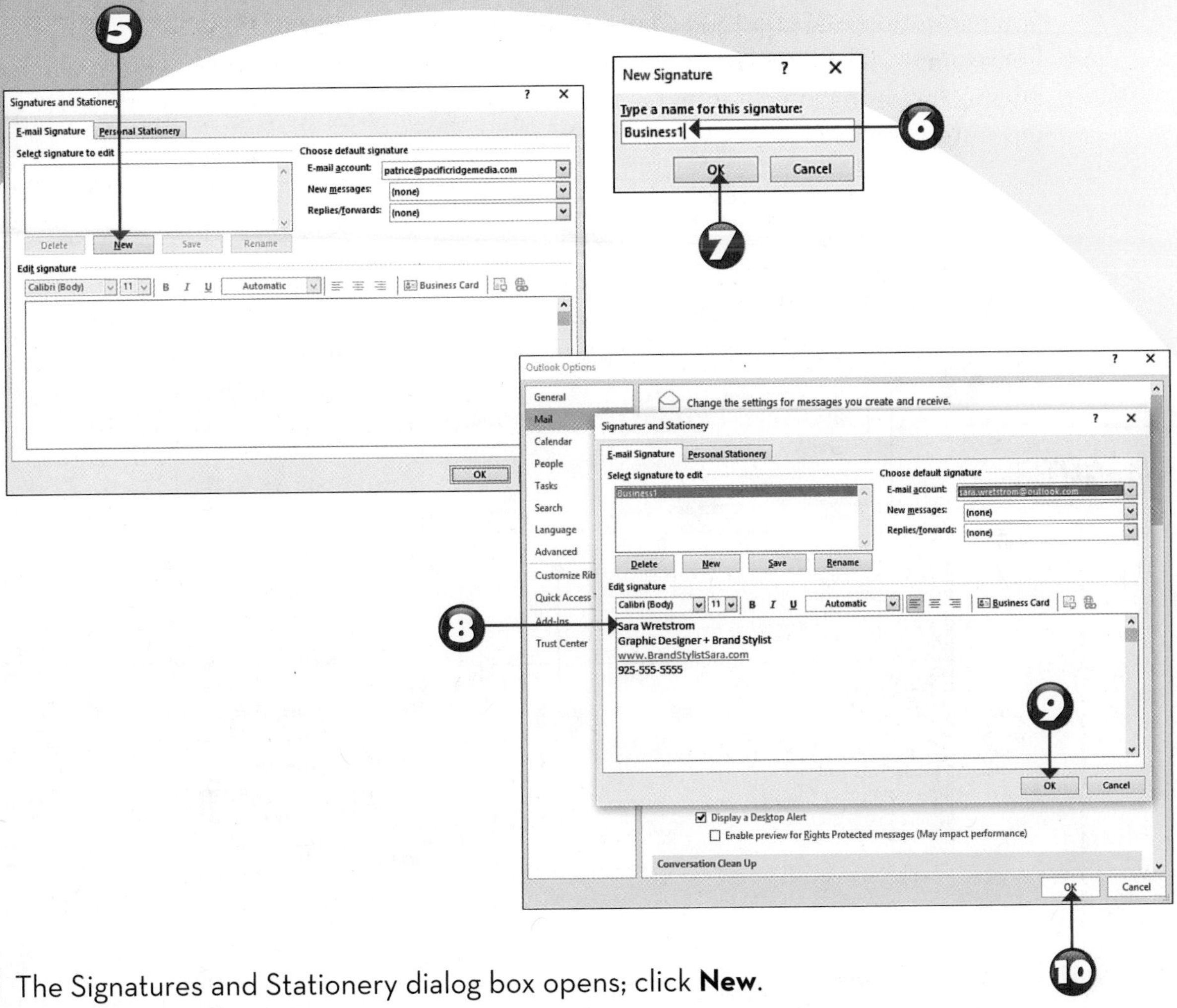

5 The Signatures and Stationery dialog box opens; click **New**.

6 Type a name for the signature.

7 Click **OK**.

8 Type your signature text and format it.

9 Click **OK**.

10 Click **OK**.

*End*

**TIP**

**Choose One!** If you create more than one signature, you can choose which one to add to a message. From the message window, click the **Signature** drop-down arrow and click the signature you want to apply.

# CREATING EMAIL RULES TO MANAGE SPAM

You can set up rules that tell Outlook what to do with different messages you receive. For example, if you receive a spam email, you can identify it as spam with a rule and keep it from appearing in your Inbox again. You can also create rules to filter other types of unwanted emails.

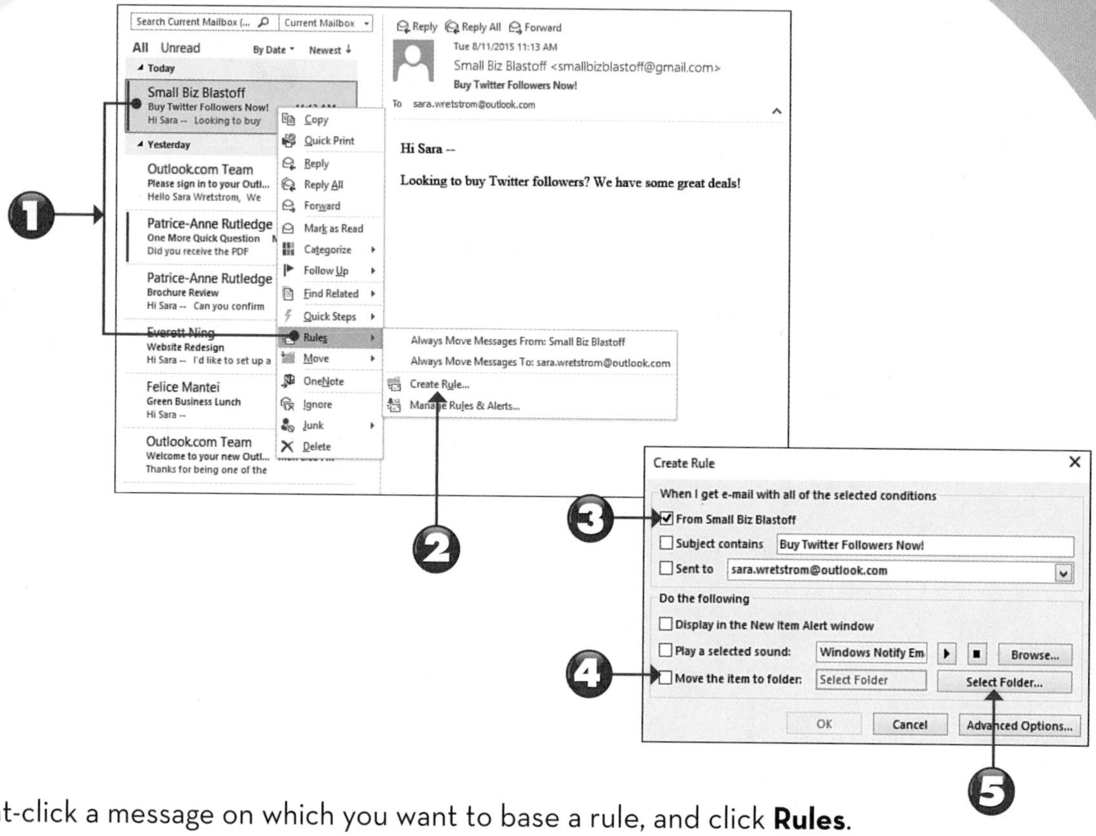

Start

1. Right-click a message on which you want to base a rule, and click **Rules**.
2. Click **Create Rule**.
3. The Create Rules dialog box opens; click any conditions you want to apply, including the **From** check box.
4. Click **Move the item to folder**.
5. Click the **Select Folder** button.

Continued

## NOTE

**Block a Sender** You can use Outlook's Block Sender feature to block future email from a specified address; right-click the message, click **Junk**, **Block Sender**. To view your list of blocked senders, right-click any message, click **Junk**, **Junk E-mail Options**, and then click the **Blocked Senders** tab.

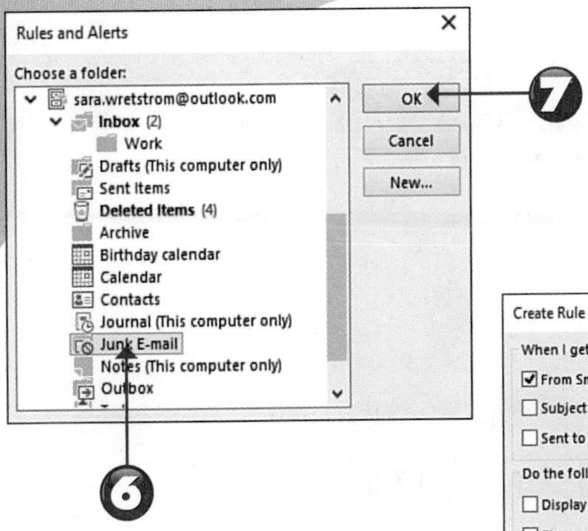

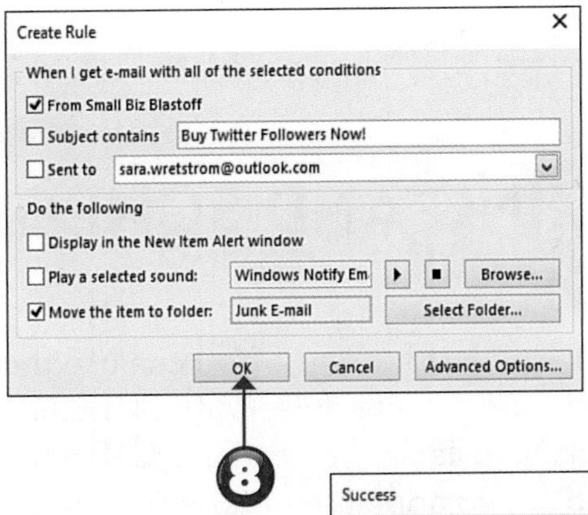

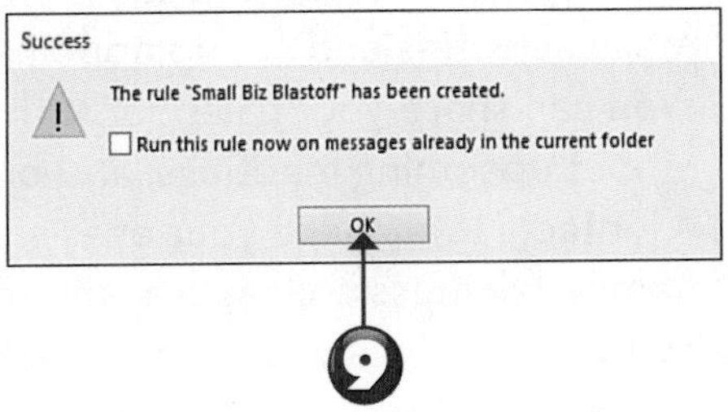

6. Click a folder where you want future messages from this address placed.

7. Click **OK**.

8. Click **OK**.

9. Outlook asks if you want to run the rule now; click the check box if you do, or just click **OK**.

*End*

**TIP**

**Move Messages** You can organize your messages into folders and move messages around as needed. For example, you might want to create folders for work-related projects, email newsletters, shopping notifications, bank updates, and so forth. To create a new folder in the Folder Pane, right-click the **Inbox**, click **New Folder**, and then give it a distinct name. To move a message to the folder, right-click the message, click **Move**, and then click **Other Folder**. The Move Items dialog box opens; specify which one and click **OK**.

# ORGANIZING AND SCHEDULING IN OUTLOOK

Microsoft Outlook isn't just for email. You can use the program to stay organized, on track, and on schedule. Outlook's other components include Calendar, Contacts, and Tasks. You can use Calendar to keep track of your daily activities and set up appointments, meetings, and other calendar items. You can share your calendar with others, set up alarms to remind yourself about upcoming meetings, and publish your calendar online. You can use Contacts to manage your ever-growing list of contacts, including friends and family, business colleagues, and more. You can use Tasks to help you organize important things you need to tackle, whether it's an office project or just a shopping list to take with you and check off on the way home from work.

# NAVIGATING THE OUTLOOK CALENDAR

You can use the Date Navigator to view a specific date on the calendar

The Calendar shows your schedule in daily, weekly, or monthly views

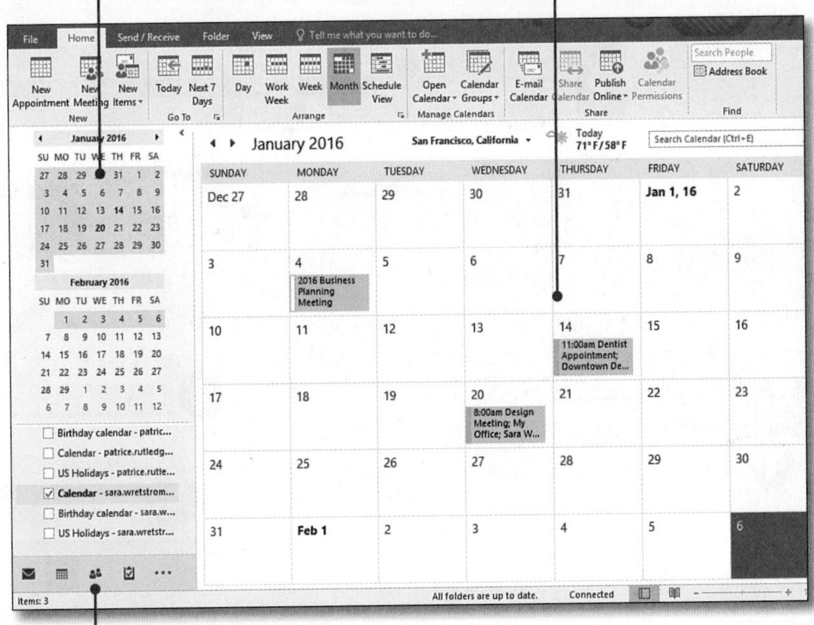


You can click a component icon to switch between Mail, Contacts, Calendar, Tasks, and Notes

# VIEWING YOUR CONTACTS

You can use Outlook's Contacts component, also called People, as a digital address book to manage all the people in your life, such as friends, work colleagues, clients, and such. You can keep relevant information, including phone numbers, email addresses, web pages, and more, just a glance away using the new People Cards.

Start

1. Click the **Contacts** icon.
2. Click the **Home** tab.
3. To change the way contacts display, click a view from the Current View gallery.
4. Click a contact to select it.
5. In this example, contacts appear as People Cards.

End

## TIP

**View the Gallery** Click the **More** icon in the bottom-right corner of the Current View gallery to see additional view options.

## TIP

**Conduct a Search** Outlook lists your contacts alphabetically using an alphabetized index that appears vertically on the page. You can click a letter on the index to view all the contacts associated with that letter. You can also search for a specific person; just type a name into the **Search Contacts** box.

# ADDING A NEW CONTACT

You can easily add new contacts to your contacts list and choose exactly which types of information to include. The new contact form offers the most fields for filling in contact information.

Start

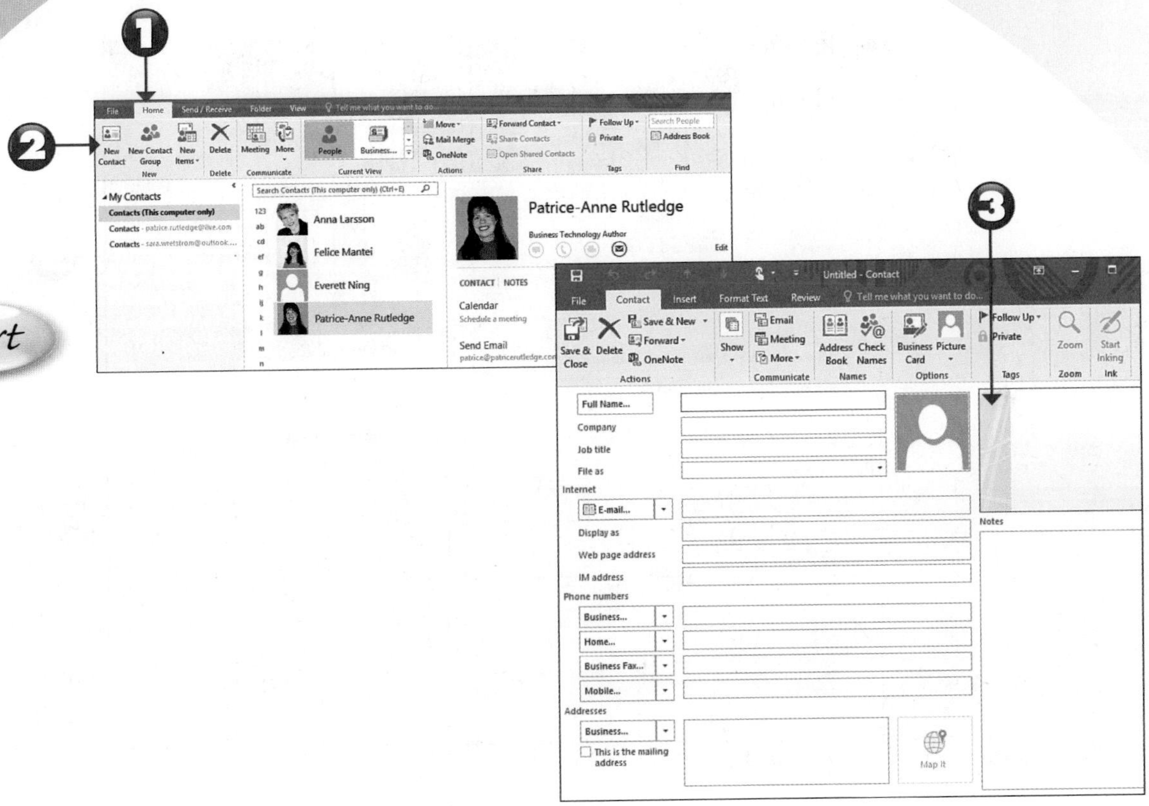

1. Click the **Home** tab.
2. Click **New Contact**.
3. An untitled contact form opens.

Continued

## TIP

**Delete It!** If you change your mind about adding a contact, click the **Delete** button on the Contact tab to exit the form and discard any data you entered. To remove a contact already in your contacts list, select it and click the **Delete** button on the Home tab.

4. Fill in the contact information you want to include.

5. Optionally, click to add a contact picture.

6. When finished, click **Save & Close**, and Outlook adds the new contact to your list.

*End*

## TIP

**Add Contact Notes** In the Notes field, you can add any notes about a contact, such as where you met this person or other important information.

## TIP

**Edit Contacts** You can make changes to contact information by clicking the **Edit** link in People view and choosing fields to edit. If you prefer to make your edits on the original form used to create the contact, double-click a contact name in any other view.

# EMAILING A CONTACT

Using Outlook's People Cards, you can quickly email a contact or schedule a meeting. Both options tap in to Outlook's other components: Mail and Calendar. This task shows you how to email a contact.

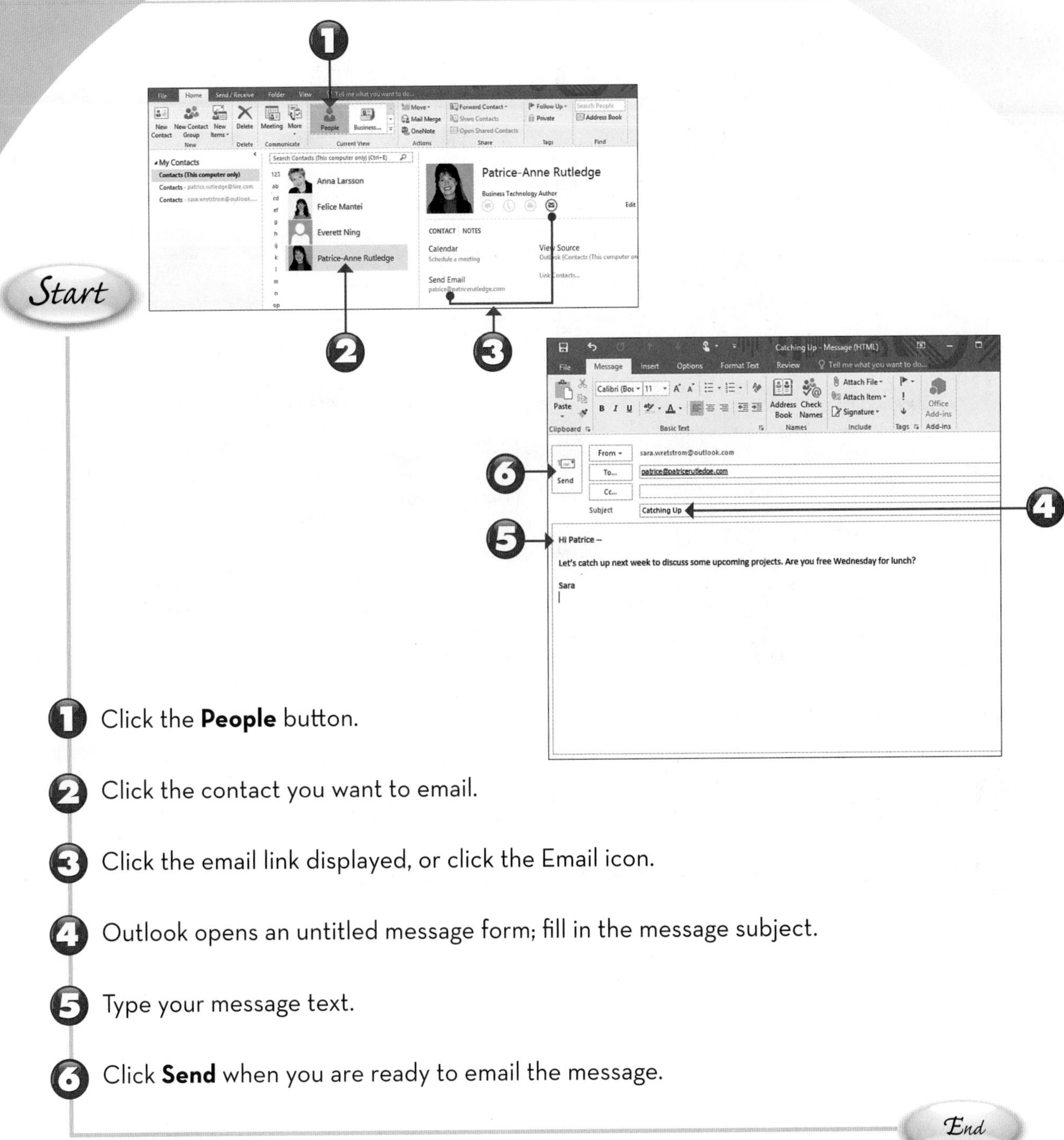


1. Click the **People** button.
2. Click the contact you want to email.
3. Click the email link displayed, or click the Email icon.
4. Outlook opens an untitled message form; fill in the message subject.
5. Type your message text.
6. Click **Send** when you are ready to email the message.

End

### TIP

**Add More Recipients** You can add more email addresses to the To field. Be sure to separate each with a semicolon. If you click the To button, you can display a list of your contacts' email addresses and choose one from the list.

# VIEWING THE CALENDAR

You can use Outlook's Calendar component to keep track of your appointments, dates, and other scheduled events. Depending on how you want to view your information, Calendar offers several view modes you can switch between, such as Day, Week, and Month. You can also view just the work week or scheduled appointments.

Start

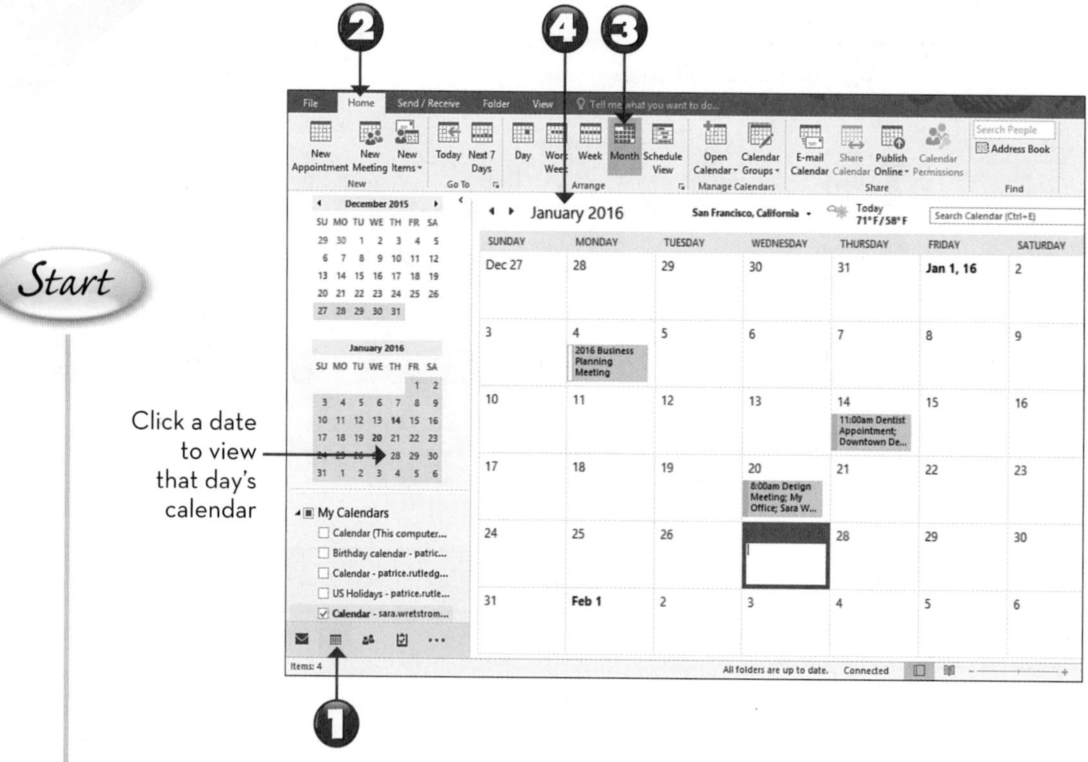


1. Click the **Calendar** icon.
2. Click the **Home** tab.
3. Click a calendar view, such as Month, Week, or Day.
4. Outlook changes the calendar view; in this example, Month view appears.

End

**TIP**

**Current Day** In Month view, you can click a date from the Date Navigator (mini-calendar) to view a specific day in your calendar.

**TIP**

**Weather at a Glance** The weather bar at the top of the calendar enables you to see the current weather at a glance (if you're connected to the Internet, that is). You can change locations or view more details with a click.

# SCHEDULING AN APPOINTMENT

You can schedule an appointment on your calendar using a form to fill out appointment details, such as setting a reminder alarm or specifying start and end times for the appointment.

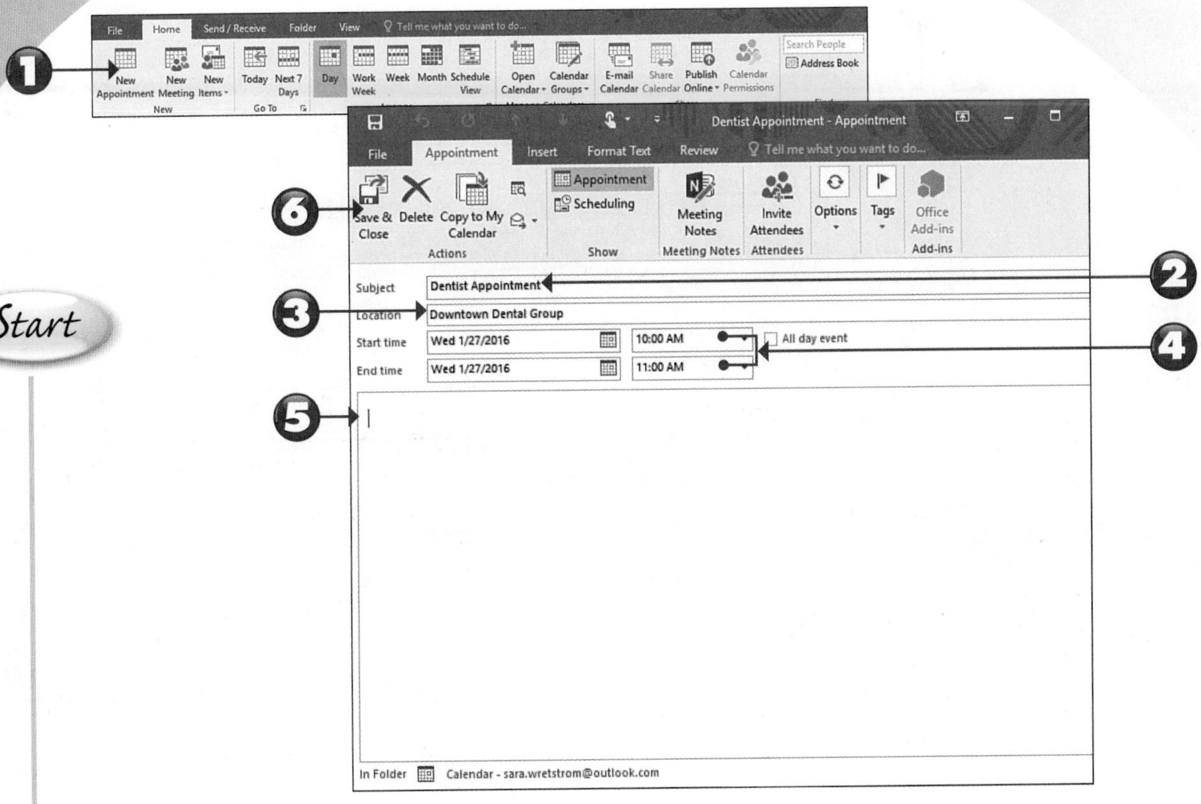

Start

1. Click **New Appointment** on the Home tab.
2. An untitled appointment form opens; type a subject title for the appointment.
3. Optionally, you can specify a location if needed.
4. Set a start and end time using the drop-down menus and choosing specific times.
5. Optionally, type any notes you want to include about the appointment.
6. Click **Save & Close** to save the appointment and add it to the calendar.

End

**TIP**

**Shortcut** In Month view, you can also double-click a date on the calendar to open the appointment form. When you do, be sure to unselect the **All Day Event** check box to create a regular appointment.

**TIP**

**Appointment Options** Click the **Options** drop-down arrow on the Appointment tab in the form to choose from display options for shared calendars, set a recurring appointment, or assign a reminder alarm.

# SCHEDULING A MEETING

You can use Outlook's Calendar to set up meetings and email attendees. You can keep track of who is attending your meeting and check their calendars for availability as well.

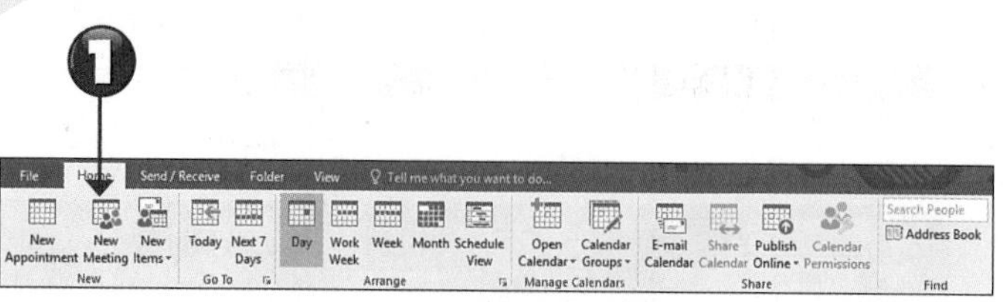

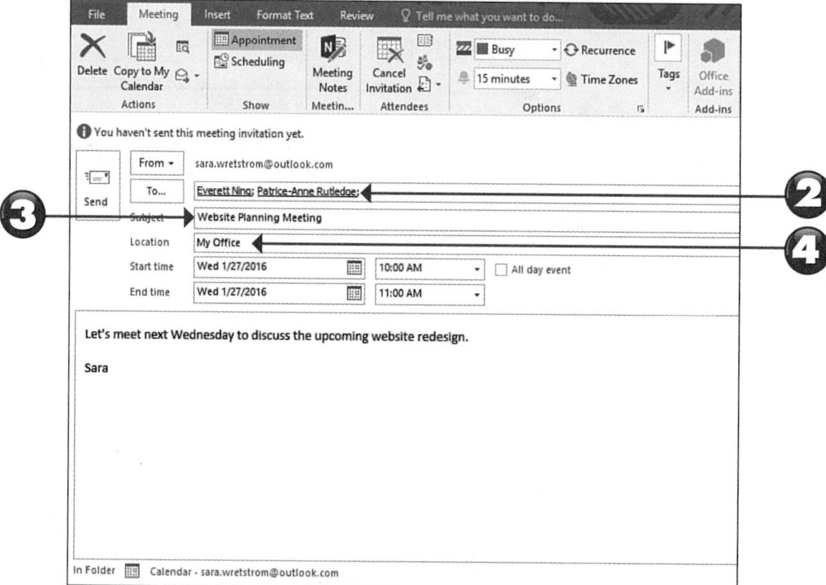


1. From the Calendar's Home tab, click **New Meeting**.
2. An untitled meeting form opens; type the attendees' email addresses.
3. Type a subject.
4. Optionally, enter or select a meeting location.

*Continued*

**TIP**

**Reserve a Conference Room** If your company has enabled you to reserve conference rooms using Outlook, you can search for and select an available room using the Location field. Otherwise, you can manually enter a location in this field.

**TIP**

**Meeting Versus Appointment?** In Outlook, a meeting is an event that you can invite other people to attend and optionally reserve resources, such as a conference room. An appointment is an event that doesn't involve sending invitations or reserving resources, such as a dental appointment.

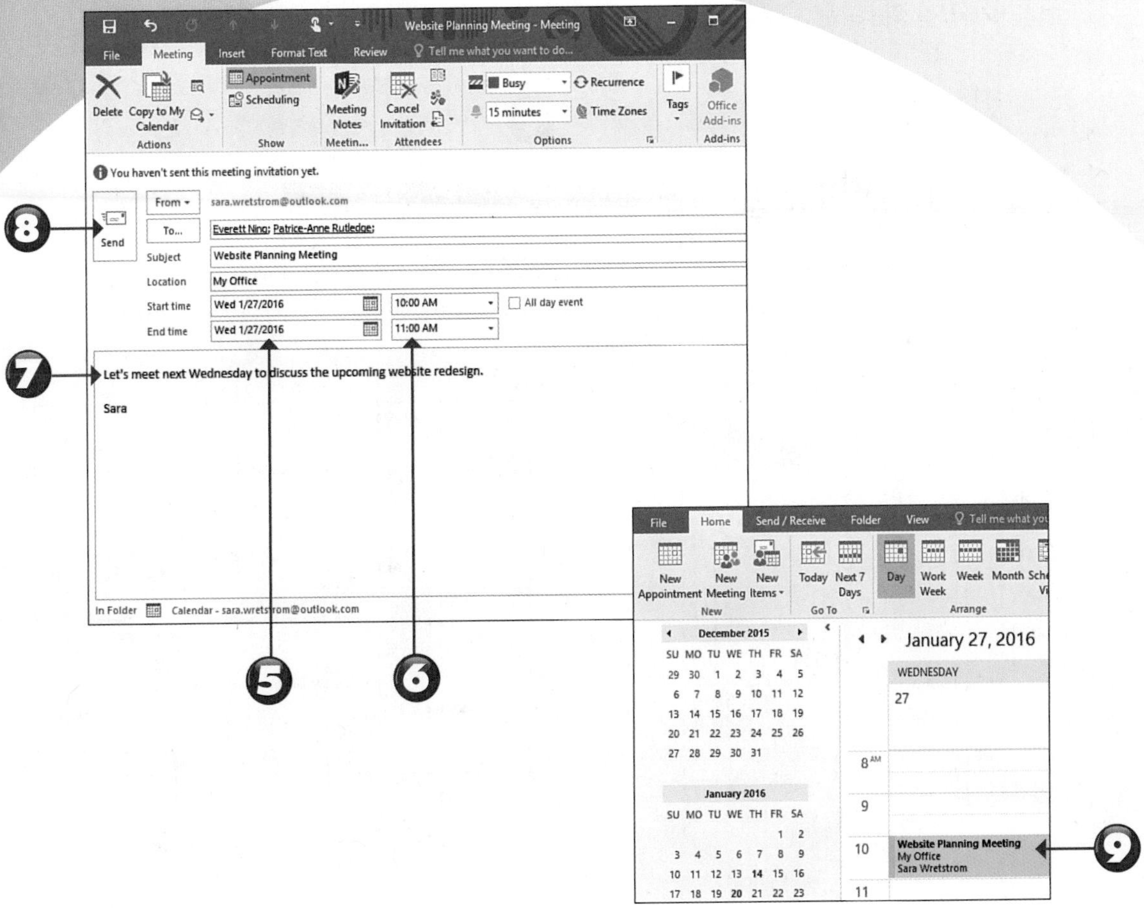

5 Specify a date.

6 Indicate start and end times for the meeting.

7 Type a message or notes about the meeting.

8 Click **Send**.

9 Outlook adds the meeting to your calendar and sends a message to notify others.

End

## TIP

**Check Responses** To see who is attending, double-click the appointment in the calendar to open the appointment form window. Expand the People Pane at the bottom of the form to view who has accepted, declined, or not responded to your invitation.

# SHARING YOUR CALENDAR

You can share your calendar with others or online. One way to share it is to email it, which attaches the file and embeds it into the email message.

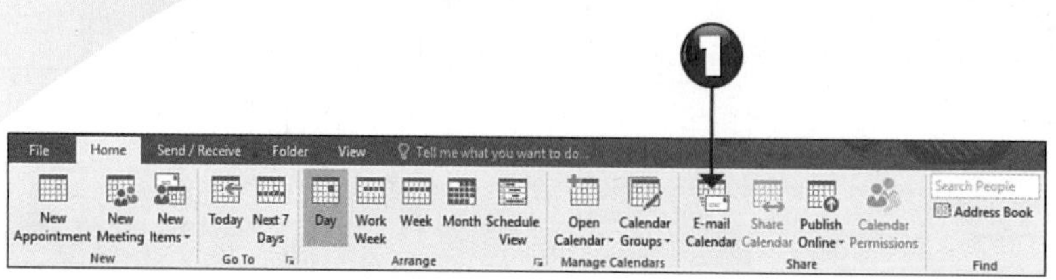

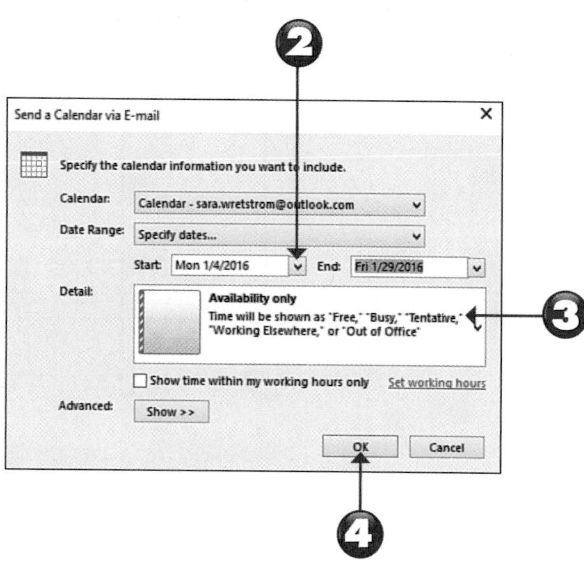


1. From the Home tab, click the **E-mail Calendar** button.
2. The Send a Calendar via E-mail dialog box opens; specify a date range from your calendar, or click the drop-down list and choose an option.
3. Choose any detail information you want to include, or leave the default setting in place.
4. Click **OK**.

Continued

**TIP**

**Share with Exchange** If you use Microsoft Exchange with your email account, you can share your Outlook calendar with other people who have Exchange accounts or even with other email accounts. Click the **Share Calendar** button on the Home tab to send a notification and set any additional options.

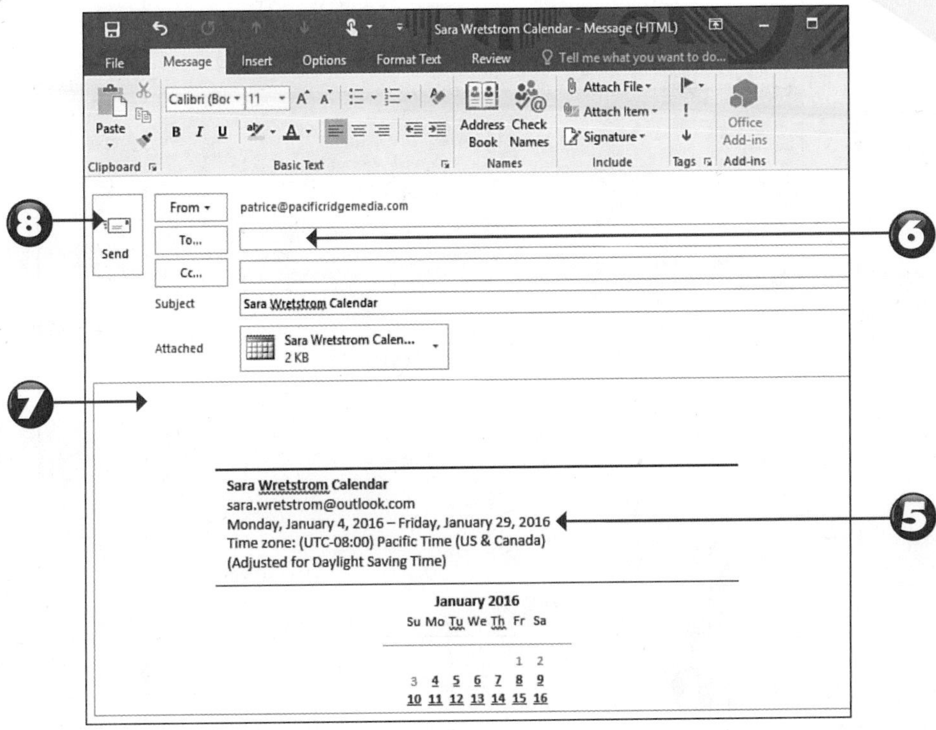


5 Outlook adds the calendar data as an attachment and embeds it in the message text.

6 Type the recipient's email address.

7 Type any additional message text you want to include.

8 Click **Send**.

End

## NOTE

**Publish It** You can also publish your calendar online if you have space on a server using Microsoft's WebDAV feature. Click the **Publish Online** button on the Home tab, and choose **Publish to WebDAV Server** to start the process.

# CREATING A TASK

Use Outlook's tasking feature to create to-do items, projects, and more. Tasks can help you keep track of and manage project steps and other important things you need to accomplish.

Start

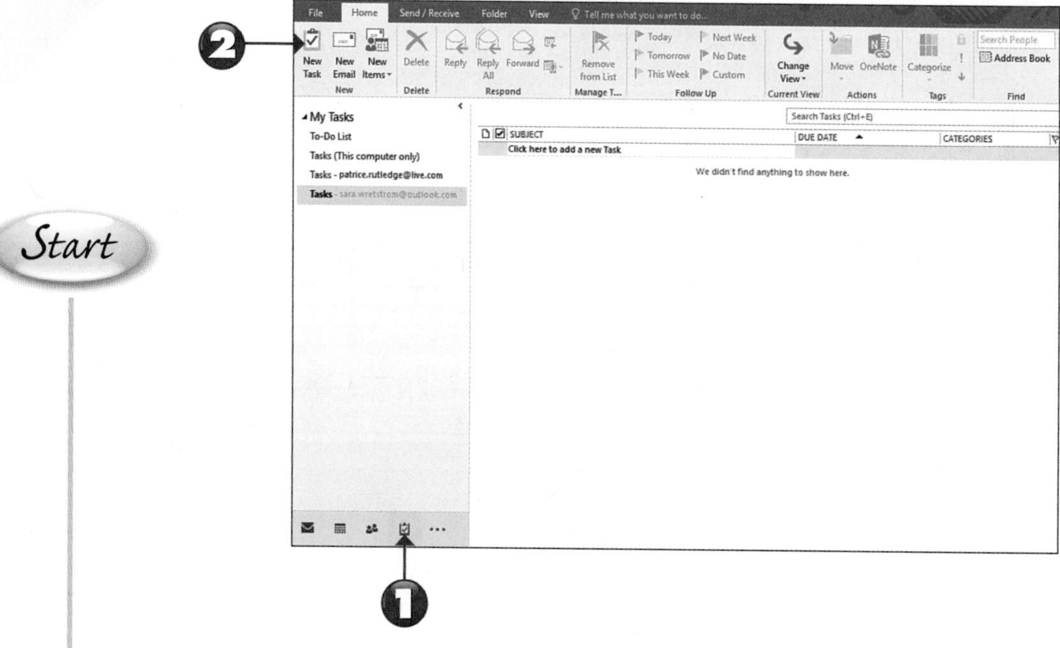


1. Click the **Tasks** icon.
2. On the Home tab, click **New Task**.

Continued

**TIP**

**Change Task Views** You can view your tasks in a variety of ways. The To-Do List view is the default when you first open Tasks. You can choose to view tasks by details, a simple list, priority, completion, and so on. To change views, click the **Change View** button on the Home tab, and choose another view.

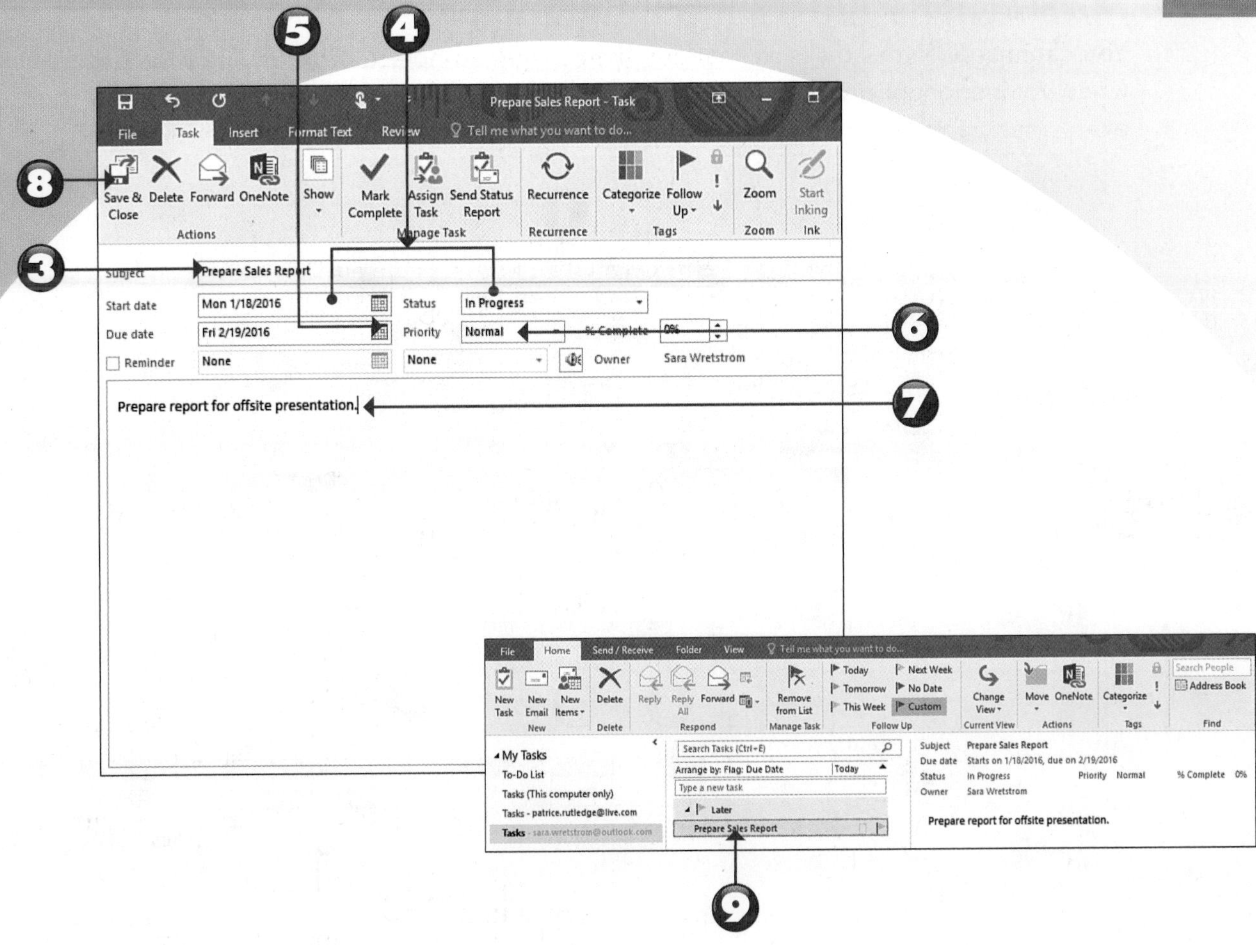


1. An untitled task form opens; type a subject for the task.
2. Specify a start date and status, if needed.
3. Choose a due date for task completion.
4. Set any additional options, such as priority level or a reminder alarm.
5. Type your task information.
6. Click **Save & Close**.
7. Outlook adds the task; this example shows the To-Do List view.

End

# MANAGING TASKS

You can manage your tasks by marking them when complete or removing them from the list when you no longer need to see them. You can edit tasks in any Tasks view. To see the tasks, even when complete, you must use another view besides the To-Do List view.

Start

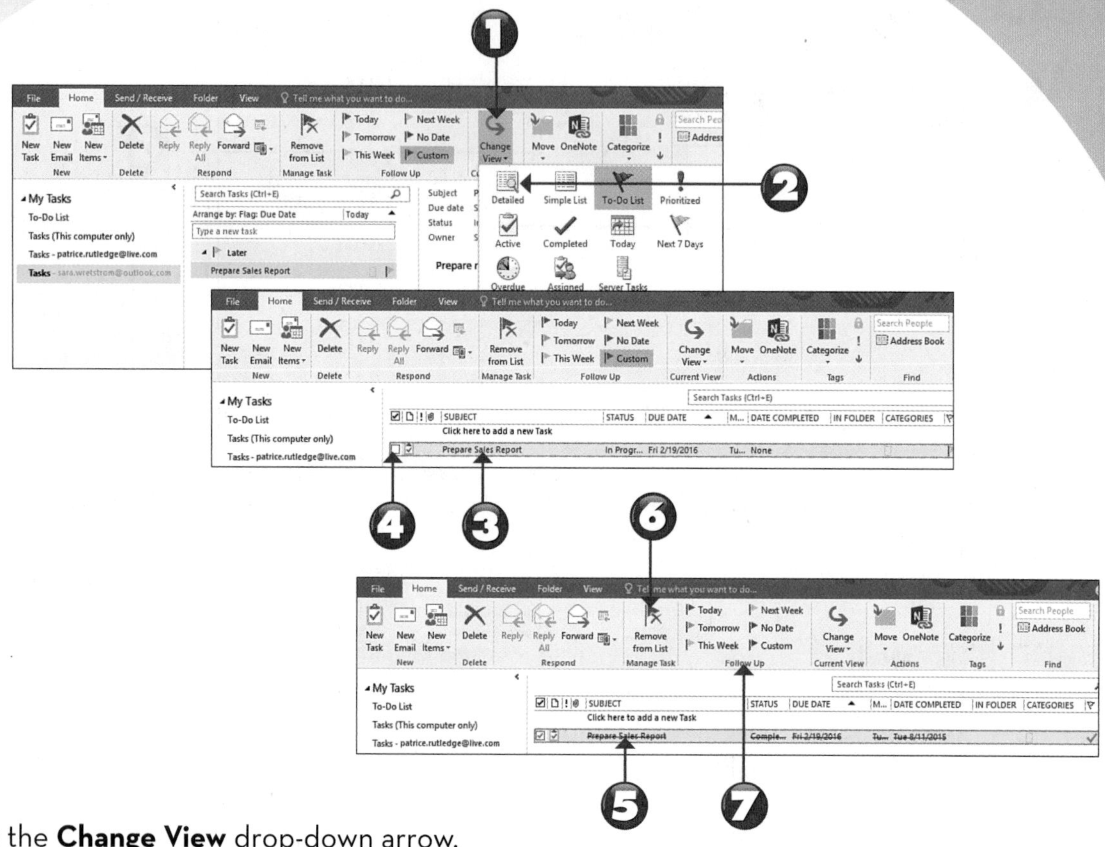


1. Click the **Change View** drop-down arrow.
2. Click **Detailed**.
3. Click the task you want to edit.
4. To mark a task as completed, click the check box in front of the task name.
5. Outlook marks out the task.
6. To remove a task, click **Remove from List**.
7. You can also use the Follow Up tags to flag other date priorities for the task.

End

**TIP**

**Color Coding** You can color code tasks by assigning Categories. For example, you might want all your work-related tasks coded in red and all the home tasks in green. To assign a color, click the **Categorize** drop-down button on the Home tab, and choose a color.

# CREATING NOTES

You can use Outlook's Notes feature to jot down notes for yourself. Notes resemble sticky notes that you can move around, even onto the Microsoft Windows desktop.

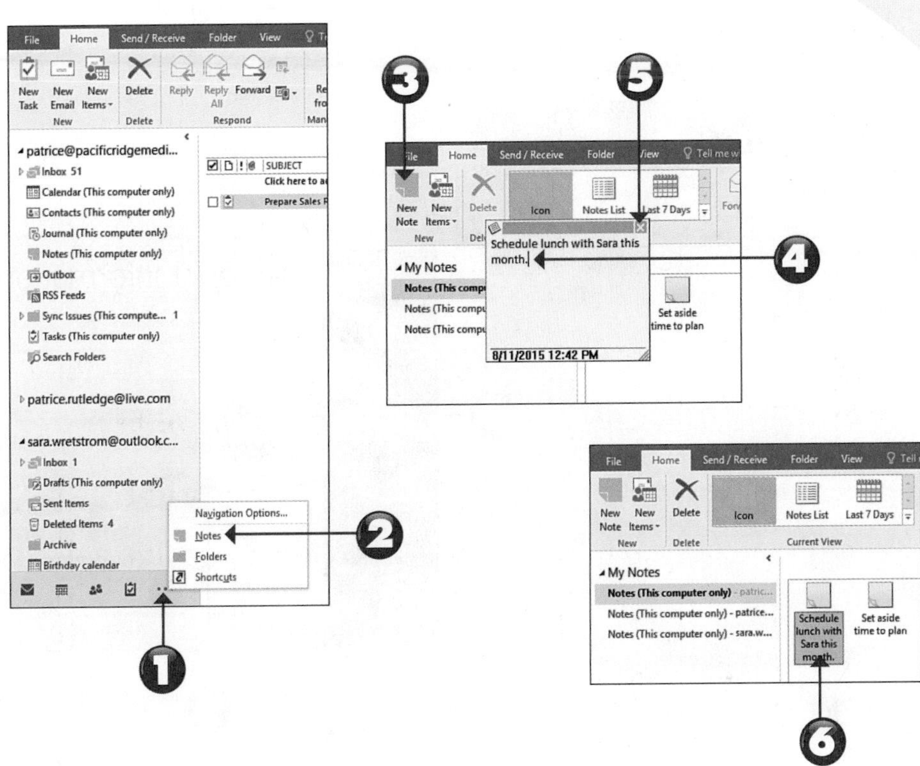


1. Click the **...** icon.
2. Click **Notes**.
3. Outlook opens the Notes component; from the Home tab, click **New Note**.
4. Type your note text.
5. Click **Close**.
6. You can now read the note listed in the list box.

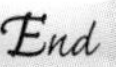

**TIP**

**Notes Views** By default, Outlook starts in Icon view in the Notes component. You can switch to other views, such as a list or current notes using the views available through the Current View gallery.

# SUBSCRIBING TO RSS FEEDS

RSS feeds, or Really Simple Syndication, is a technology that enables web content to be converted into a feed that is viewed as message posts. You can receive RSS feeds for blogs, podcasts, news, and more. You can use Outlook to check the latest updates of your favorite RSS feeds. Feeds you subscribe to appear in the RSS Feeds folder in the Mail component.

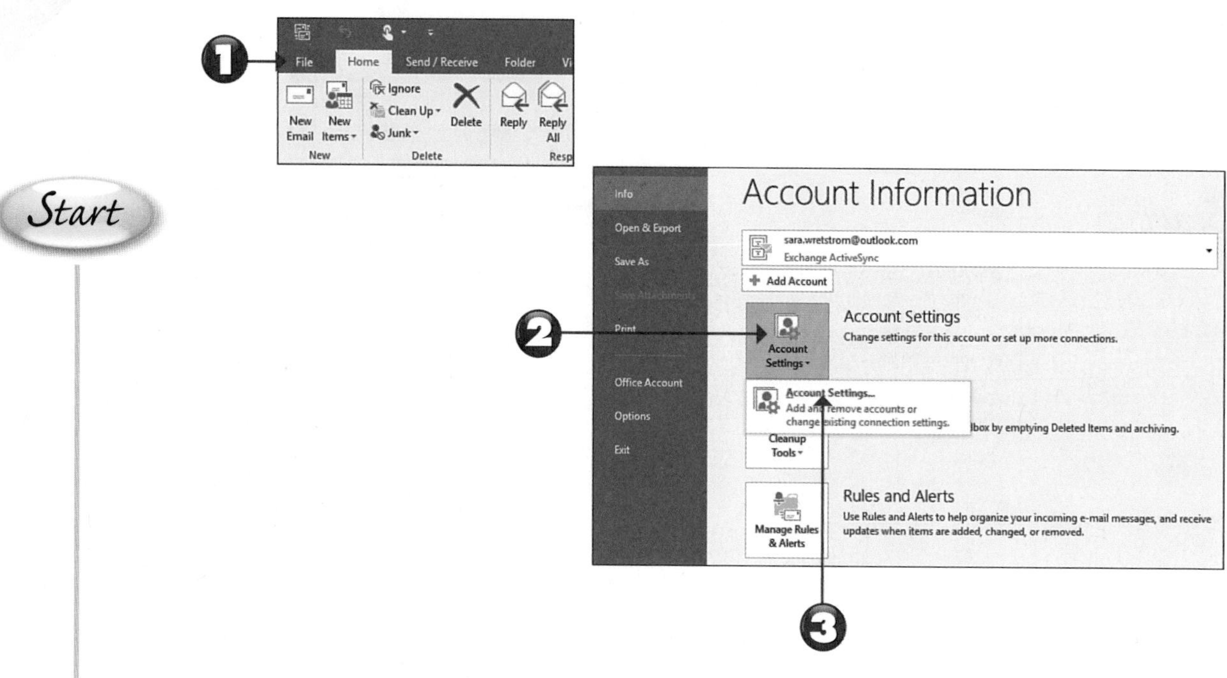


Start

1. Click **File**.
2. From the Info tab, click the **Account Settings** drop-down arrow.
3. Click **Account Settings**.

Continued

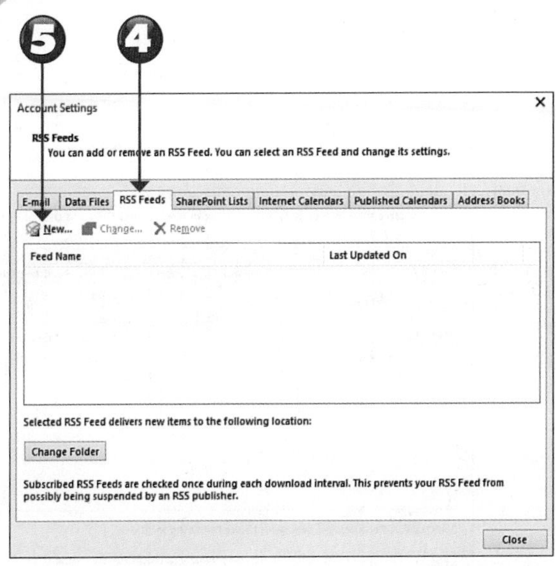


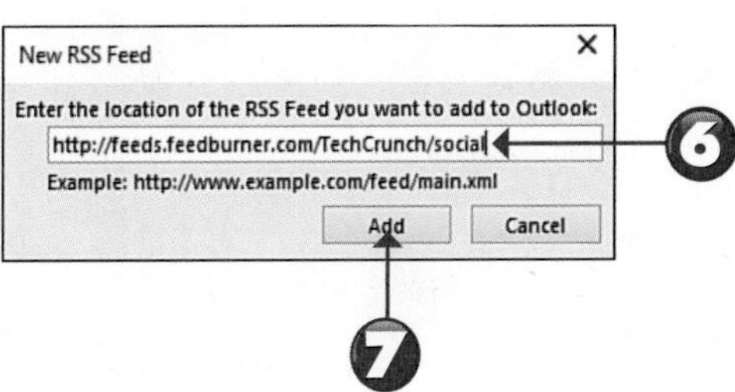


4. The Account Settings dialog box opens; click the **RSS Feeds** tab.

5. Click **New**.

6. Type the RSS Feed address.

7. Click **Add**.

*Continued*

**TIP**

**Find RSS Feeds** Many of your favorite sites might offer RSS feeds. You can find the feed address by clicking the RSS icon on a site (usually an orange square with a small circle and two curved lines).

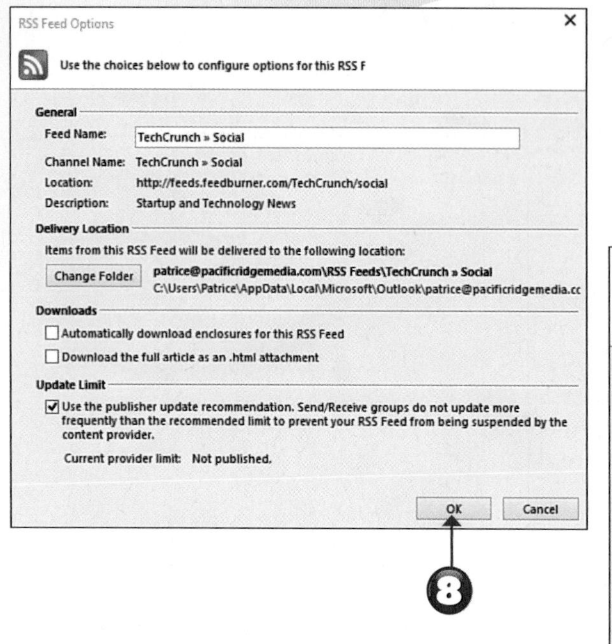


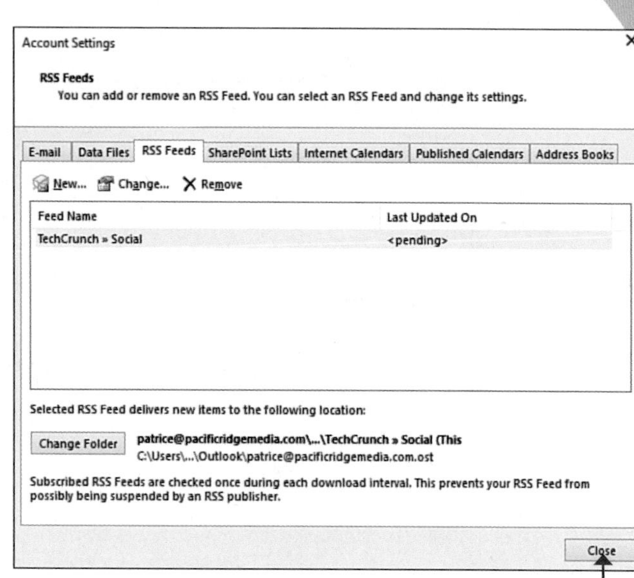


8 The RSS Feed Options dialog box appears with a general name for the feed already assigned. Click **OK** to continue.

9 The RSS Feed is added to the list box; click **Close**.

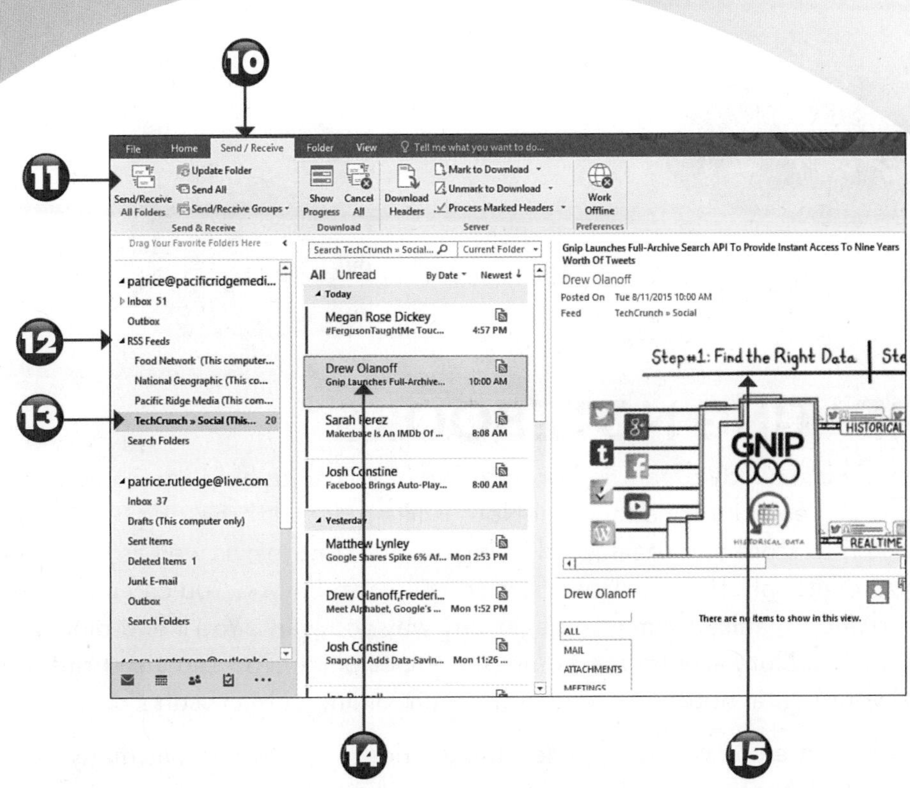


10. Click the **Send/Receive** tab.

11. Click **Send/Receive All Folders** to update the latest posts.

12. Click the **RSS Feeds** folder to view your RSS feed subfolders to which you are subscribed.

13. Click the folder you want to open.

14. Click the message you want to view.

15. You can read the message in the Preview pane.

*End*

**TIP**

**Unsubscribe to a Feed** If you no longer want to subscribe to an RSS Feed, reopen the Account Settings dialog box to the RSS Feeds tab, select the feed name, and then click the **Remove** button.

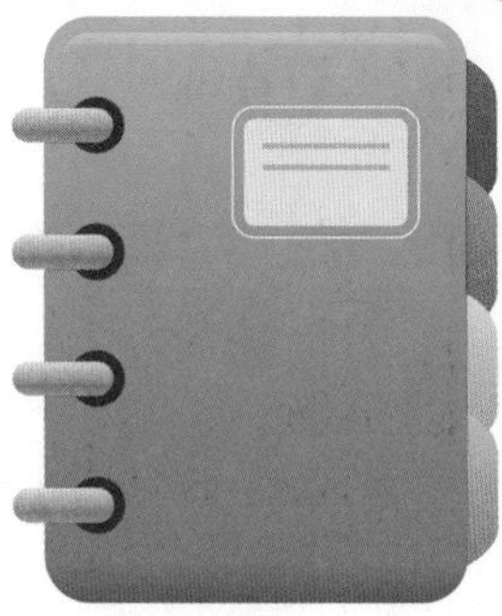

# CREATING NOTEBOOKS

OneNote is a handy organizing program you can use to help keep track of various pieces of information. OneNote is like a digital three-ring binder; you can use it to store and organize clippings and text notes, as well as visual items such as digital photos and artwork, video clips, and more. You can move notes around and organize them into pages any way you want. You'll find plenty of uses for OneNote around the home, school, or office. You can also print and share your digital notebooks and store them online in Microsoft's cloud storage.

Notebooks are composed of pages and sections. You can add as many of each as you need. Sections display as tabs across the top of the page, whereas pages appear as tabs along the right side of the screen. Like all the other Office programs, OneNote displays commands, tools, and features on the Ribbon at the top of the program window. However, to give you plenty of space to work with your notebook pages, the Ribbon may be minimized until you need it. You never need to save your work in OneNote; the program saves things automatically for you as you go along.

# ADDING NOTES IN A NOTEBOOK

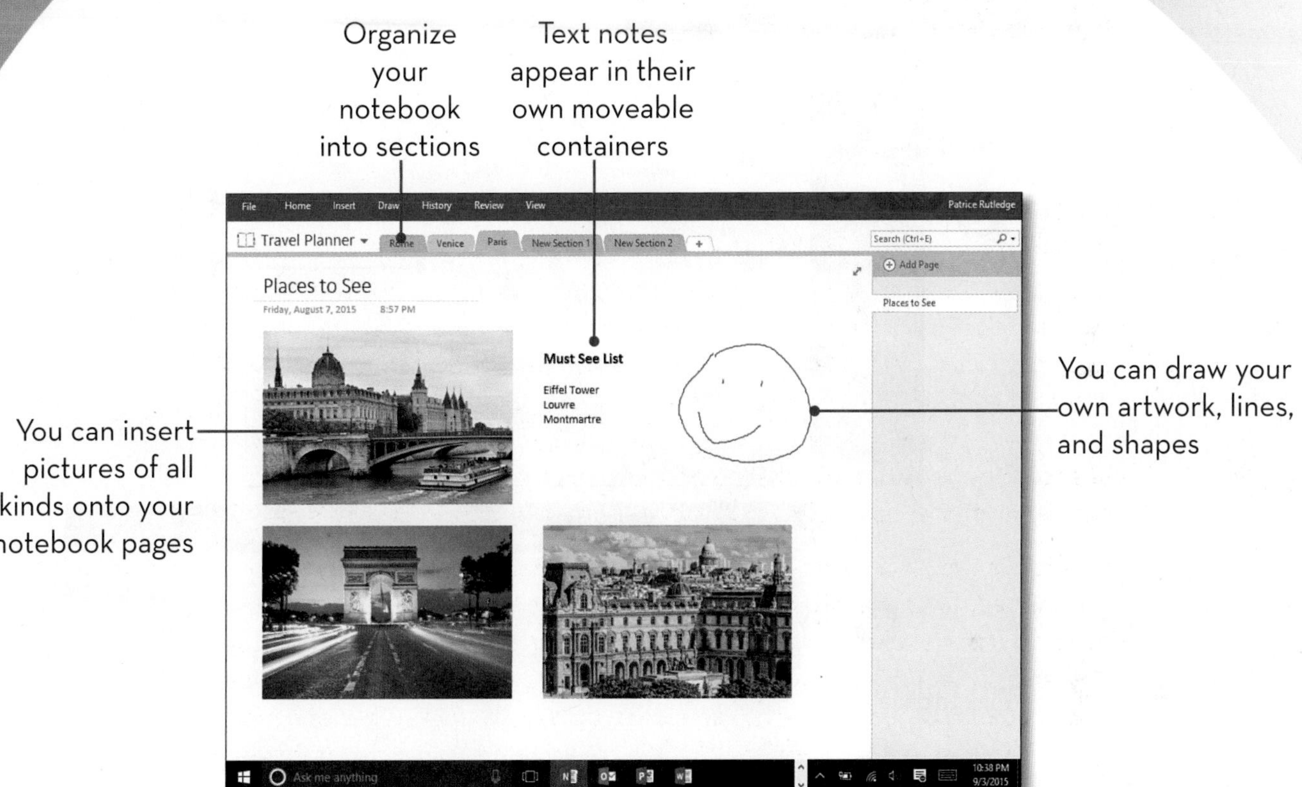

# CREATING A NEW NOTEBOOK

Items you collect and store digitally with OneNote are placed into *notebooks*. Like a regular paper notebook, your digital notebooks are built page by page. When you create a notebook, OneNote starts with a single, blank page. You can start adding notes anywhere on the page.

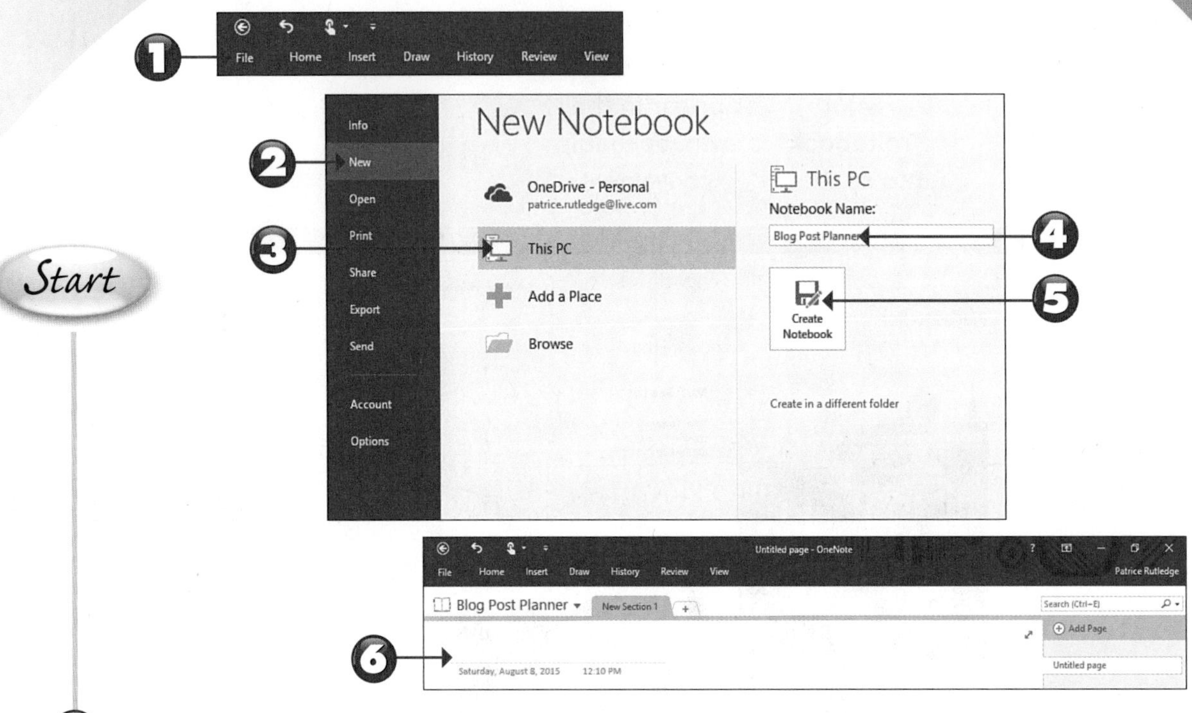


Start

1. Click the **File** tab.
2. Click **New**.
3. Specify a location for the file, such as on your computer or cloud storage.
4. Type a name for the notebook.
5. Click **Create Notebook**.
6. OneNote creates the notebook and displays an untitled page. Click anywhere on the page, and begin typing to start adding notes.

End

## TIP

**No Saving Required** OneNote saves your notebooks and the work you do in them automatically, so there's no need to activate a Save command. Notebooks are saved to the place you designated when you first created the notebook. ■

## TIP

**Switch Between Notebooks** You can click the notebook name's drop-down arrow at the top of the page to display a menu of your notebooks. Click the one you want to work with and OneNote switches to it. ■

# ADDING A PAGE TITLE

You can add titles to your notebook pages to help you keep your information organized and easy to identify. Titles appear at the top of the page and in the page tab area to the right.

1. Click in the title area of the page.
2. Type a title and press **Enter**.
3. OneNote adds the page title to the page tab.

End

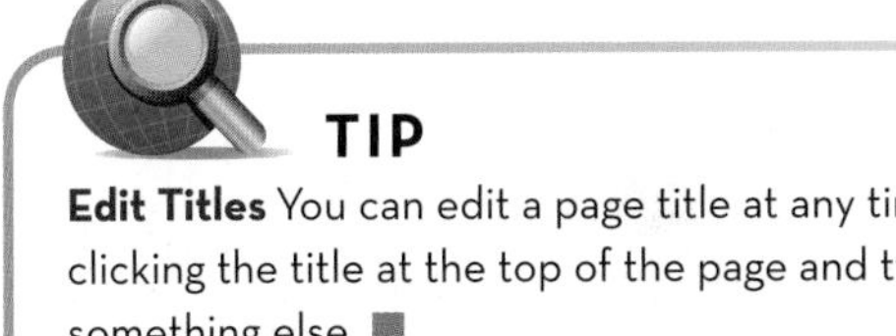

**TIP**

**Edit Titles** You can edit a page title at any time by clicking the title at the top of the page and typing something else.

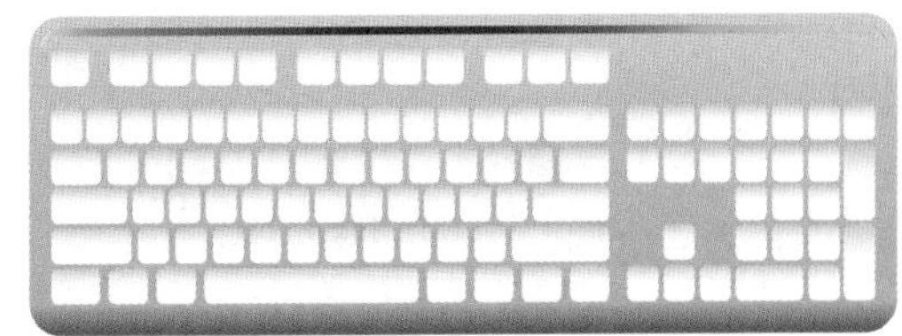

# CREATING A SECTION

You can add sections to a notebook to create logical groups of pages. Sections are much like the color tabs in a binder notebook and appear as tabs at the top of the page. You can add as many sections as you need to your digital notebook. To view a section, click the section tab.

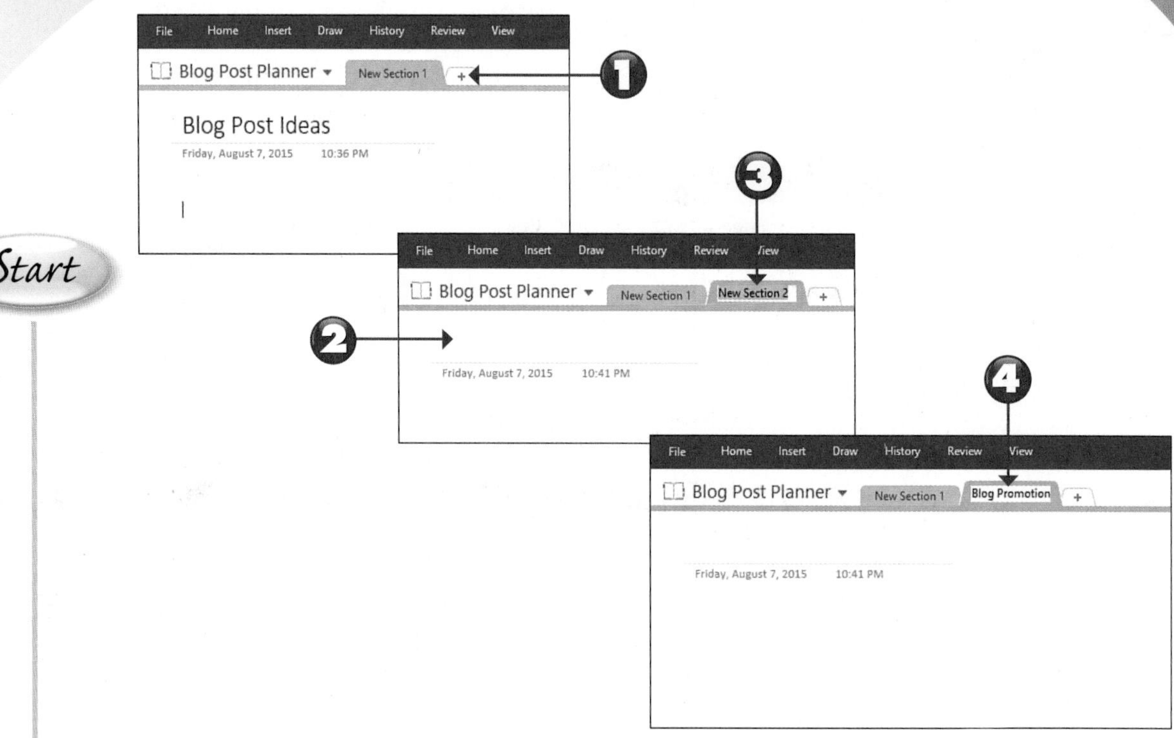


Start

1. Click the **Create a New Section** icon (plus sign).
2. OneNote adds a new section with a blank page.
3. Type a new name and press **Enter**.
4. OneNote applies the new name.

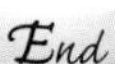

**TIP**

**Color Section Tabs** You can assign different colors to your section tabs by right-clicking the section name tab, choosing **Section Color**, and then choosing a new color to assign. ■

**TIP**

**Delete It!** To remove a section you no longer want, right-click the section tab and choose **Delete**. OneNote prompts you to verify the deletion; click **Yes**. ■

# MOVING A SECTION

You can easily move sections within your notebook. For example, you might want to move a section to the front of the notebook or move another to the back.

Start

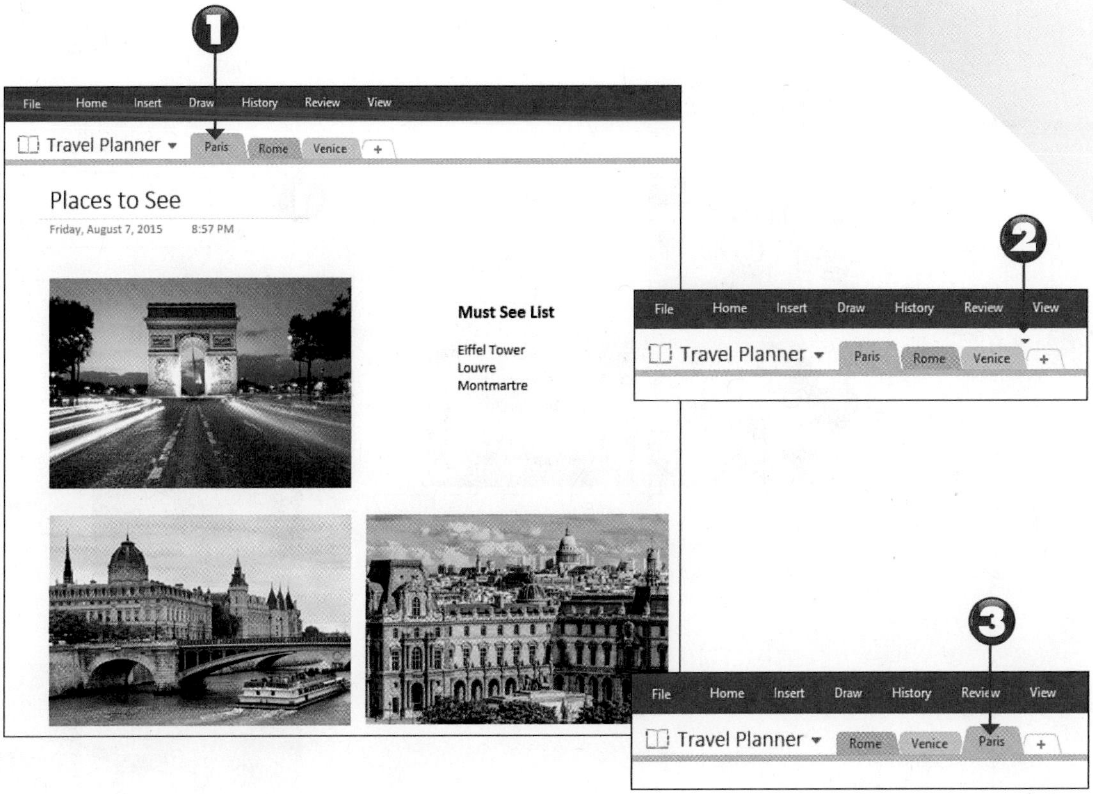

1. Click the section tab you want to move.
2. Drag it to a new location and drop it into place; an indicator marker appears as you drag the section tab.
3. OneNote rearranges the existing tabs to fit the change in order.

End

## TIP

**Merge Sections** You can merge sections, if needed, to create one large section. Right-click the section tab you want to merge and click **Merge into Another Section**. This opens the Merge Section dialog box. Select the section you want to merge into and click **Merge**. ■

# ADDING NOTES

You can add all kinds of notes to a page in a notebook simply by typing on the page. Although typing in notes is similar to typing text in Microsoft Word, notes are contained in their own boxes, which you can move around the page, resize, and format. Although boxed, no actual borders appear around the note text.

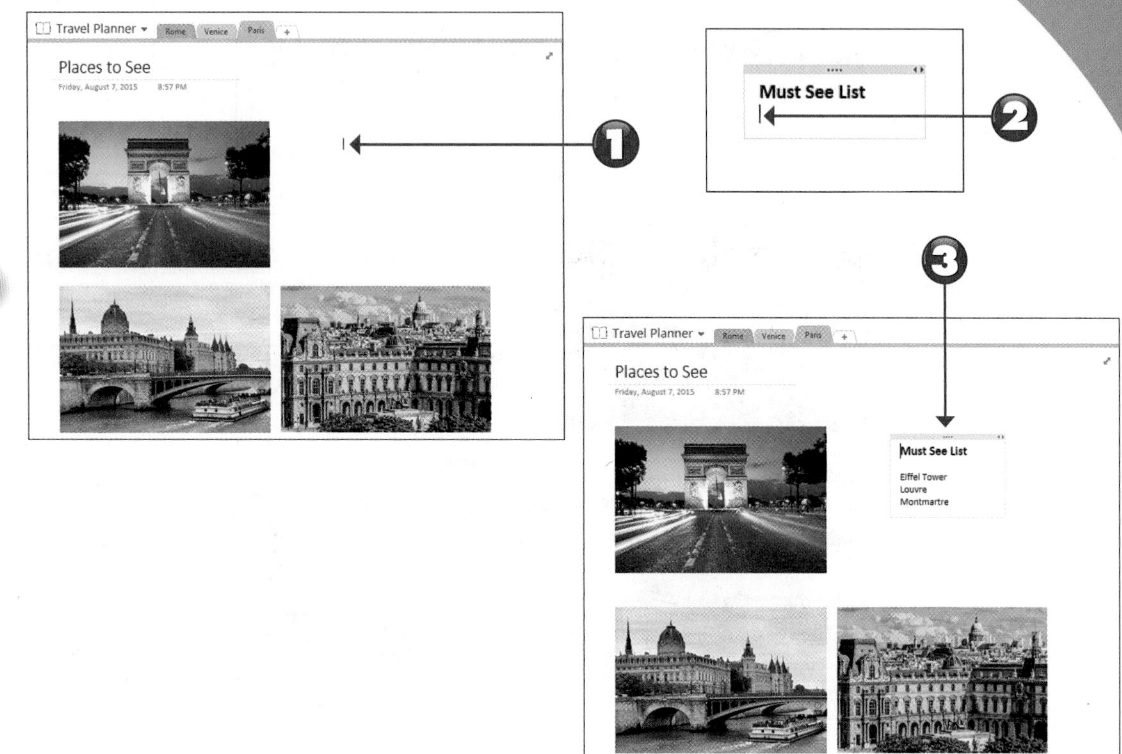


1. Click the page where you want to insert a note.
2. Type your note text. The note box expands as you type.
3. To move a note, click and drag the top of the note, and drop it where you want it to go.

End

## TIP

**Format Text** You can format your note text using the formatting commands on the Ribbon's Home tab or using the mini toolbar that appears when you select text. OneNote's basic formatting tools include fonts, sizes, font colors, and alignment settings, just to name a few. ■

## TIP

**Add Other Elements** You can also add other elements to your notebook, including artwork, video clips, sound files, and more. See Chapter 22, "Enhancing and Managing Notebooks," to learn more about including several of these elements in your notebooks. ■

# ADDING PAGES

You can add pages to your notebook just as easily as you can add sections.

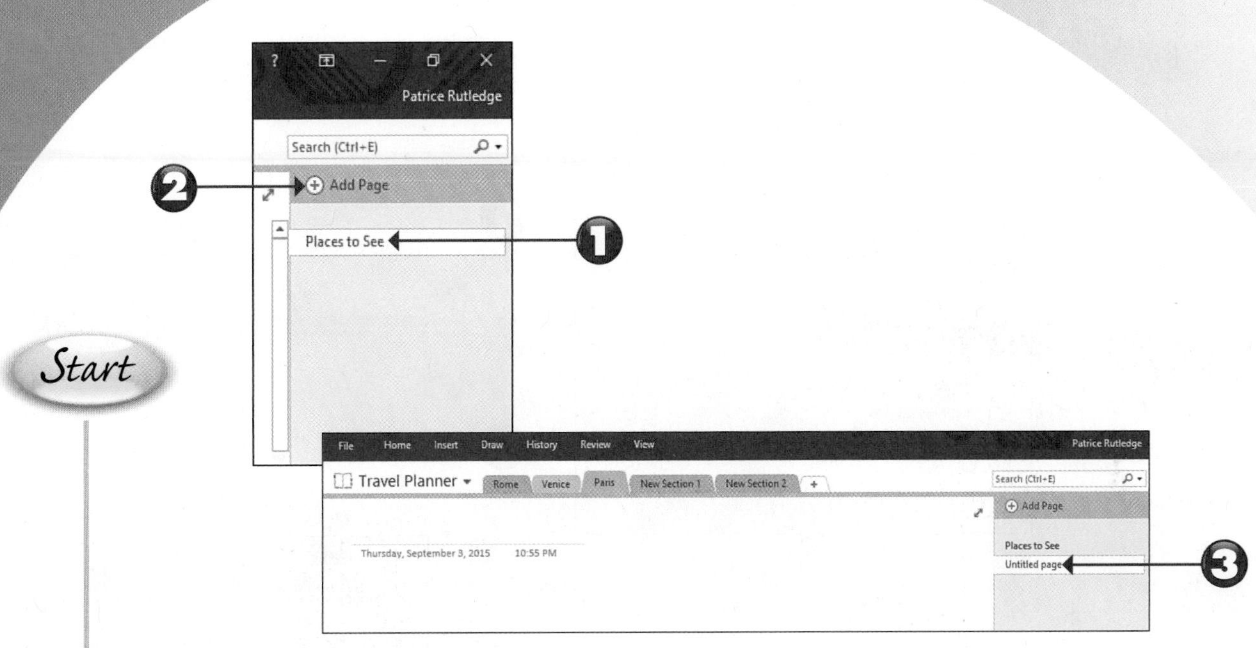


Start

1. Display the page you want to precede the new page.
2. Click the **Add Page** icon.
3. OneNote adds a new page.

End

## TIP

**Delete Pages** To remove a page, right-click the page tab and click **Delete**. ■

## TIP

**Rearrange Pages** You drag and drop page tabs on the right side of the OneNote window to rearrange the order of pages in a section. ■

# CREATING SUBPAGES

You can make a page subordinate to another page, which is handy when you want to group similar subjects together yet keep them on separate pages.

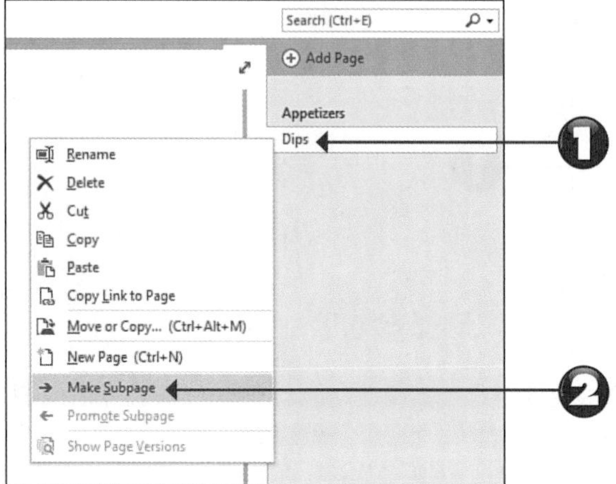


Start

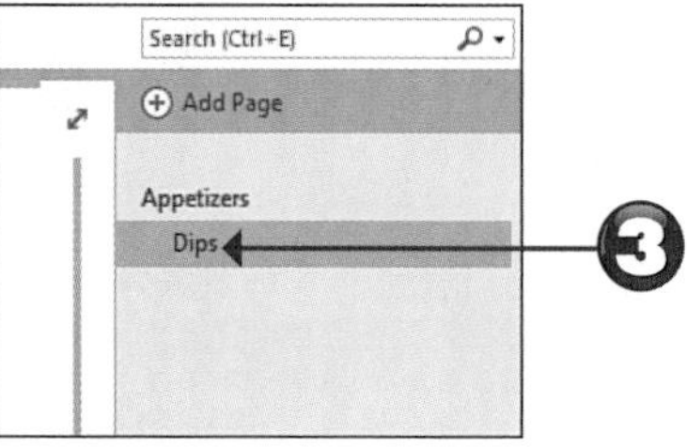


1. Display the page you want to turn into a subpage.
2. Right-click the page tab and click **Make Subpage**.
3. OneNote turns the page into a subpage subordinate to the page above it.

End

## TIP

**Promote a Page** Just as you can make a page subordinate to another, you can also promote a subordinate page. Right-click the page tab and choose **Promote Subpage**. ■

# ADDING A PICTURE

You can add pictures from your computer, the Web, a scanner, or a digital camera. In this task, you see how to add a picture stored on your computer. After you insert a picture, you can move it and resize it.

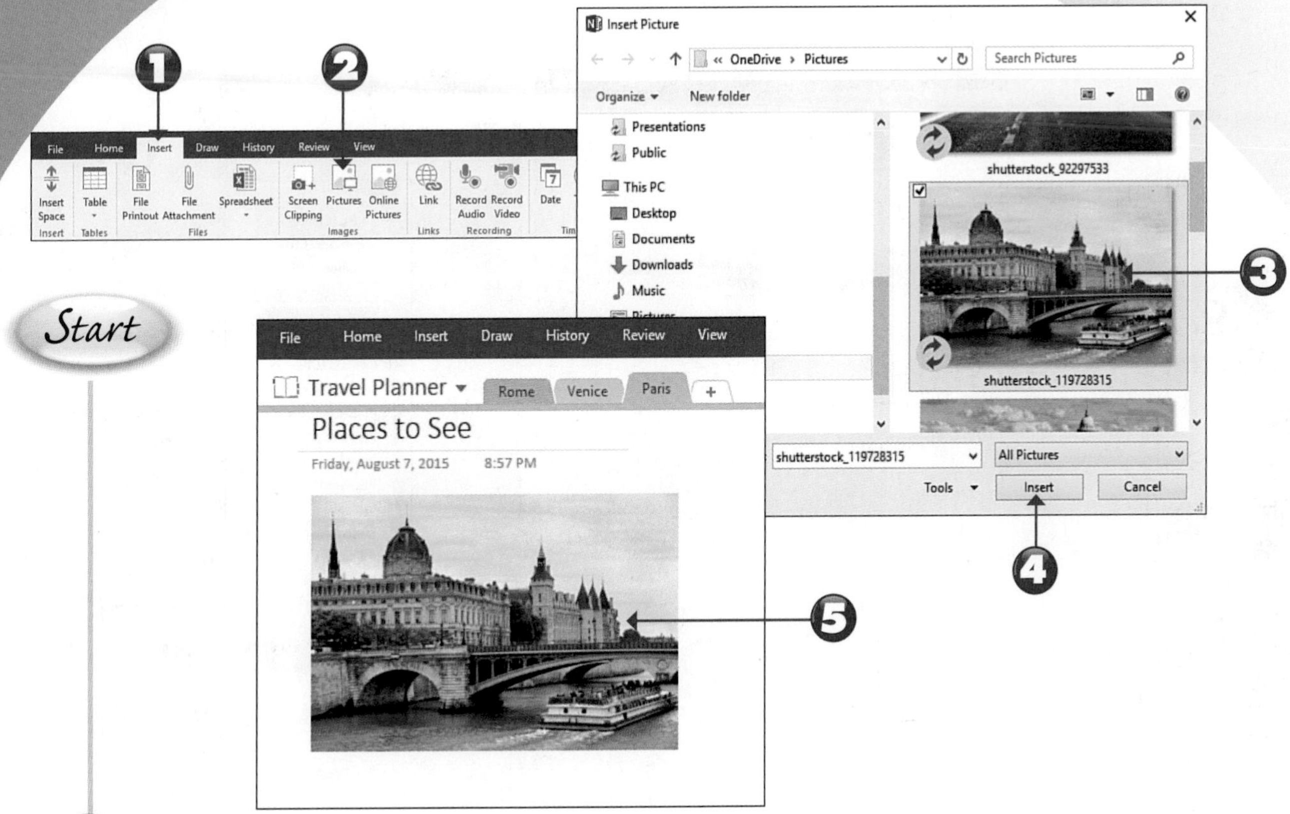

Start

1. Click the **Insert** tab.
2. Click **Pictures**.
3. The Insert Picture dialog box opens; navigate to and select the picture you want to insert.
4. Click **Insert**.
5. The picture is added to the notebook page.

End

**TIP**

**Delete Pictures** To remove a picture, right-click the image and press the **Delete** key.

**TIP**

**Resize Pictures** You can resize a picture by dragging any of its handles—the tiny squares that surround a selected picture.

# APPLYING TAGS

You can use tags to help you remember important things or mark important notes in your notebooks. You can find a list of preset tags on the Ribbon's Home tab.

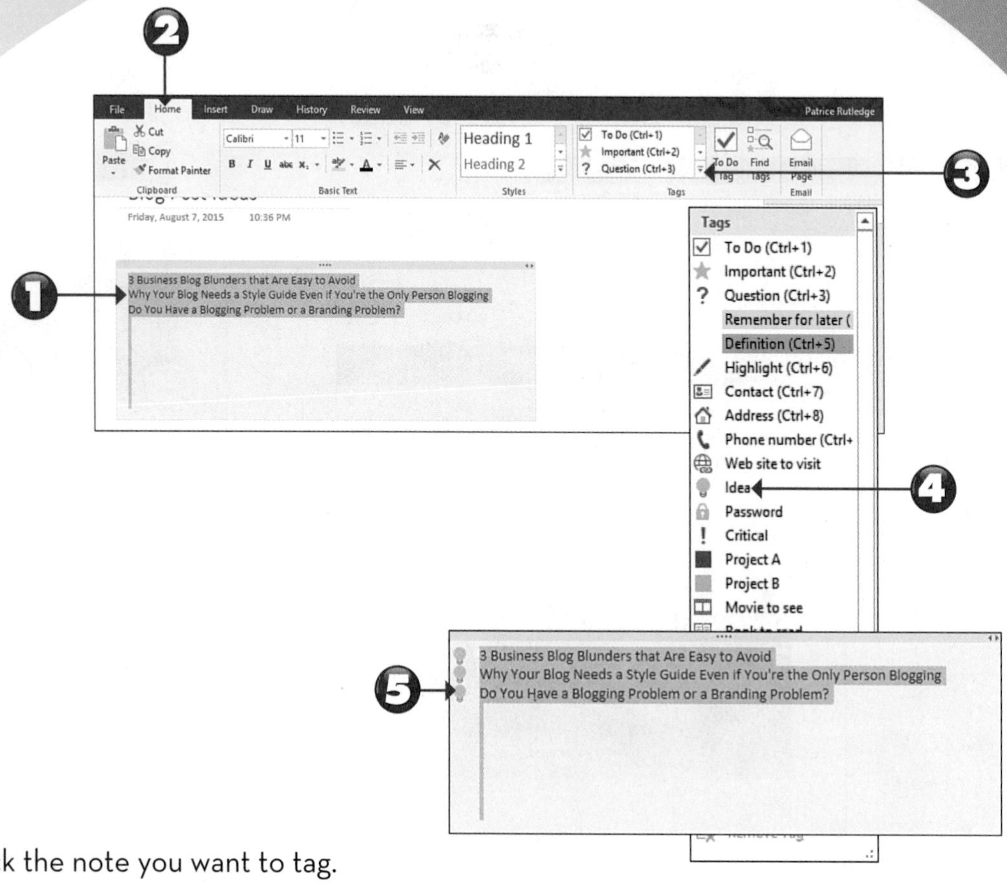

Start

1. Click the note you want to tag.
2. Click the **Home** tab.
3. Click the **More** button on the Tags gallery.
4. Click a tag.
5. OneNote applies the tag to the note.

End

## TIP

**Create Custom Tags** You can create your own custom tags. Display the tags list on the Home tab, and click **Customize Tags**. This opens the Customize Tags dialog box where you can add a new tag or modify an existing tag. ■

# INSERTING LINKS

You can add links in your notes to other notebooks, pages, or websites. If you know a web address, you can type it or use your default browser program to navigate to a page.

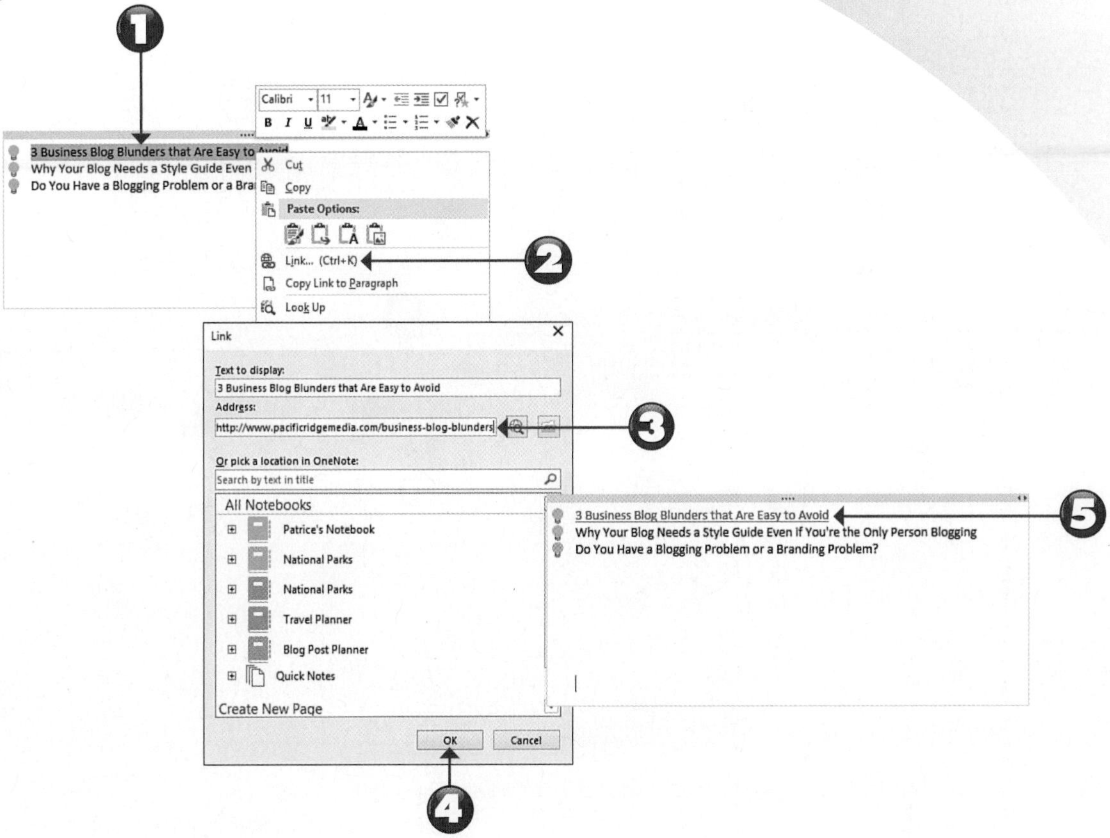

Start

1. Right-click the text or picture you want to turn into a link.

2. Click **Link**.

3. The Link dialog box opens; type the URL for the page you want to link to, or use the **Browse the Web** button to navigate to the page and copy the URL.

4. Click **OK**.

5. OneNote creates the link.

End

## TIP

**Alternative Method** You can also use the Link button on the Ribbon's Insert tab to open the Link dialog box. ■

# APPLYING A TEMPLATE

OneNote includes a variety of templates you can use to create all kinds of notebook pages. For example, you can apply templates for business meeting notes, lecture notes for classroom situations, to-do lists, and more.

Start

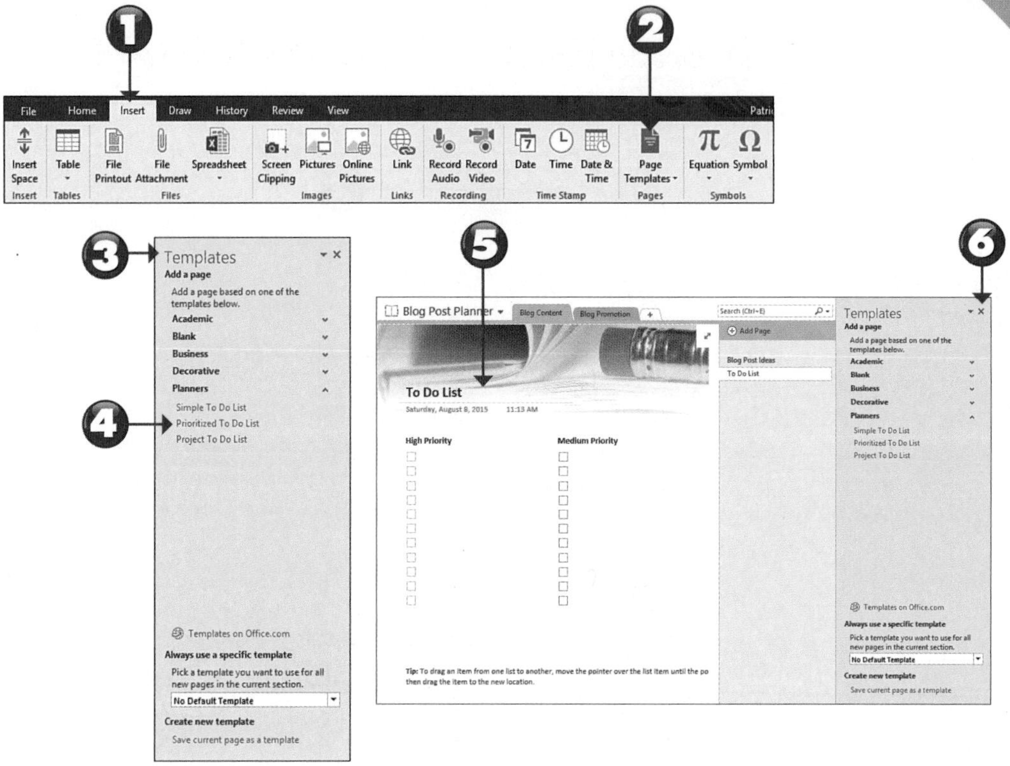

1. Click the **Insert** tab.
2. Click **Page Templates**.
3. The Templates pane appears; click a template category.
4. Click a template.
5. OneNote applies the template to a new page.
6. Click to close the Templates pane.

End

## TIP

**Get Other Templates** You can click the **Templates on Office.com** link in the Templates pane to look for more OneNote templates online. ■

# CHANGE NOTEBOOK VIEWS

You can switch between Normal view (the default) and Full Page view, which enables you to view more of your notebook page onscreen.

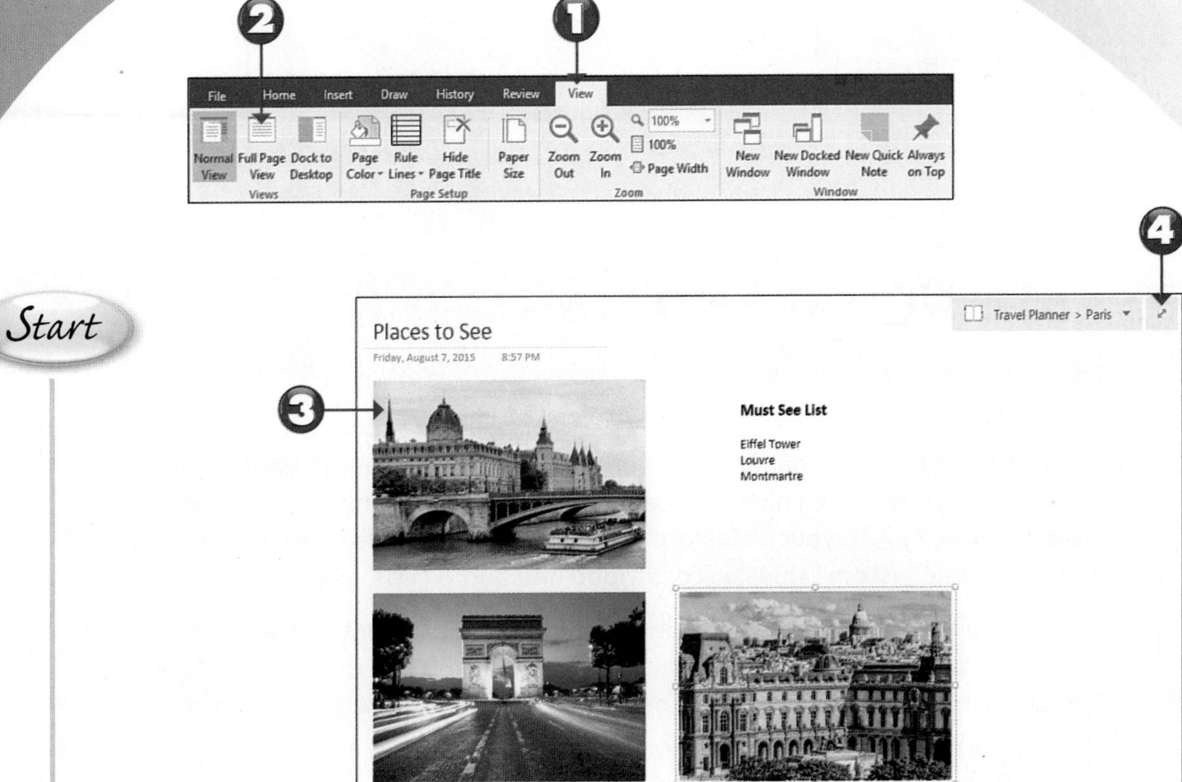


Start

1. Click the **View** tab.

2. Click **Full Page View**.

3. OneNote displays the full page.

4. Click **Normal View** to return to the default view.

End

## TIP

**Dock OneNote** You can use the Dock to Desktop view to dock the notebook on the right side of your Windows desktop screen, which enables you to move items into your notebook or work with the notes while performing other computer tasks. ■

# ENHANCING AND MANAGING NOTEBOOKS

Text notes and artwork aren't the only parts of building notebooks. You might need to collect other types of items for a project, such as video data or an entire folder of research files. You can add more than text notes and images inserted directly into your OneNote notebooks. You can also add the contents of files, create custom tables, record video and audio clips, and more.

OneNote also includes an entire tab of tools on the Ribbon to create drawings, shapes, and other free-form designs. For example, you can use the Highlighter Pen to highlight text in your notes, or you can use the Shapes tools to draw arrows and circles on your pages.

In addition to other types of information you can add, you can tap in to OneNote's other powers to quickly swap tasks with Microsoft Outlook and import files into your notebook pages.

# ADDING VIDEO TO A NOTEBOOK

The playback tools help you work with video and audio clips

You can use the Record Video tool with your computer's built-in camera to record video clips

# ATTACHING FILES

OneNote is a great place to organize information about a particular project or subject, including keeping copies of files. You can add file attachments of all kinds. You can choose to attach files as icons, which can be clicked to open the original file, or you can attach files as printouts to insert a copy of their content as a note on the page.

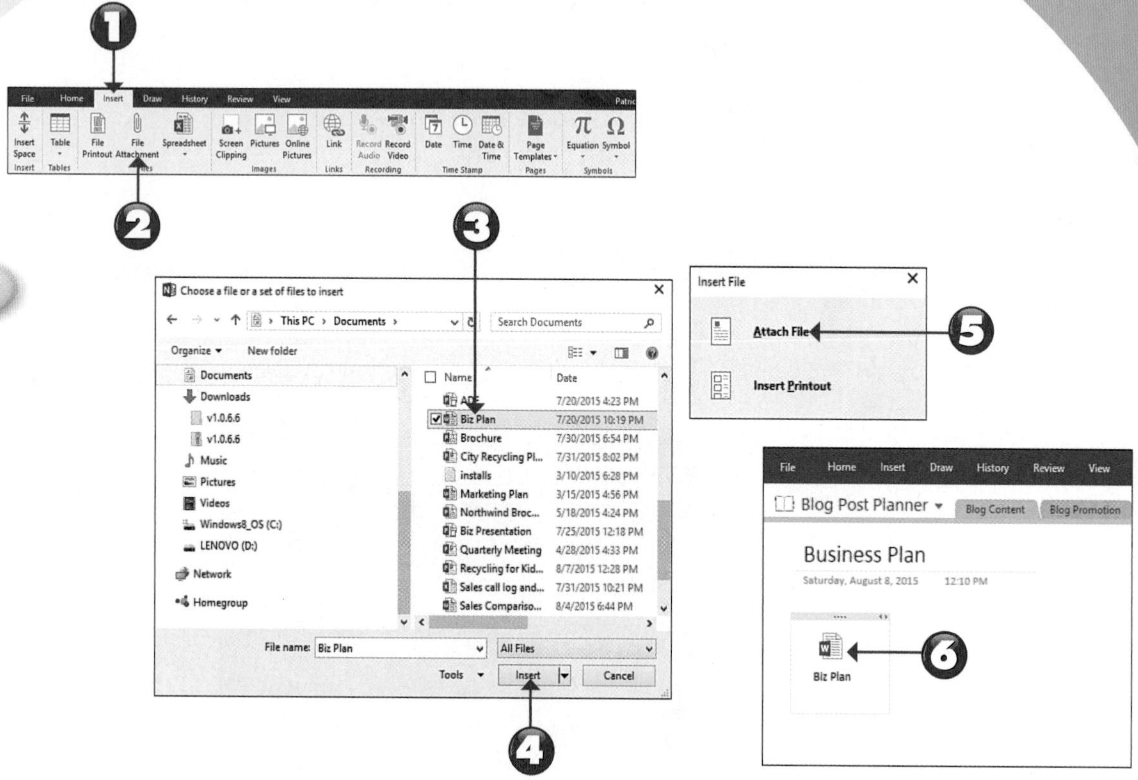

Start

1. Click the **Insert** tab.
2. Click **File Attachment**.
3. Navigate to and select the file or files you want to insert.
4. Click **Insert**.
5. The Insert File dialog box opens; click **Attach File** or **Insert Printout**. (The options might vary based on the type of file you're inserting.)
6. Depending on what you select, the file either appears as an icon or the actual file content appears as a note on the page with an attachment icon.

End

## TIP

**Open Attachments** To open an attachment, double-click the attachment icon. Microsoft might display a warning prompt asking you to make sure you're opening a trusted file. Click **OK** to continue.

# INSERTING TABLES

You can insert basic tables as notes on a page. You can specify how many rows and columns you want and populate the cells with data. When you add a table, a special tab appears on the Ribbon with tools for working with the table.

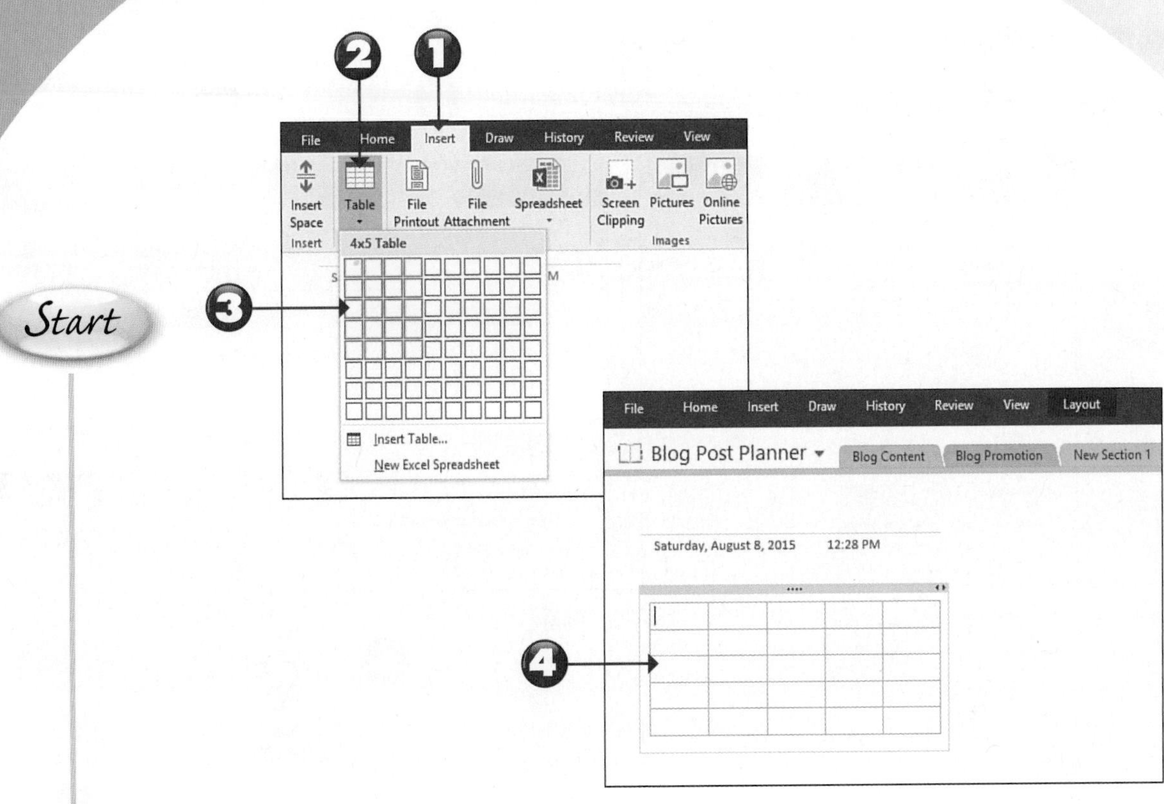


1. Click the **Insert** tab.

2. Click **Table**.

3. Drag across the number of rows and columns you want to create.

4. OneNote inserts the table as a note on the page; click in a cell and type to add text.

End

**TIP**

**Table Formatting** The Table Tools–Layout tab on the Ribbon offers all kinds of table tools for controlling the structure and appearance of the selected table note. You can add rows and columns, change the alignment, control the table gridlines, and more.

# RECORDING AUDIO

If your computer has a built-in microphone, which most computers do, you can record audio to a notebook page. This is handy if you need to record a lecture or presentation.

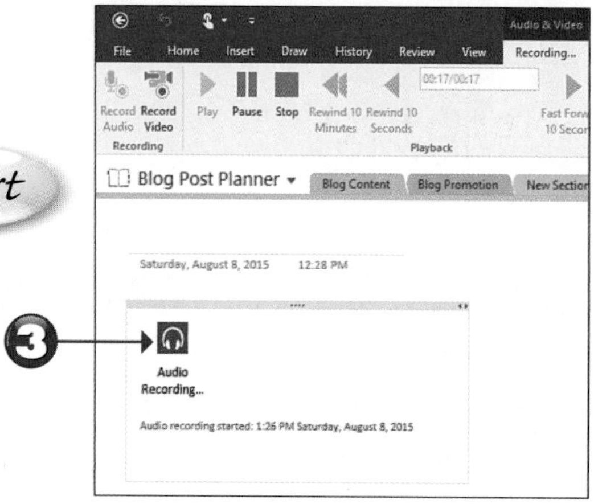

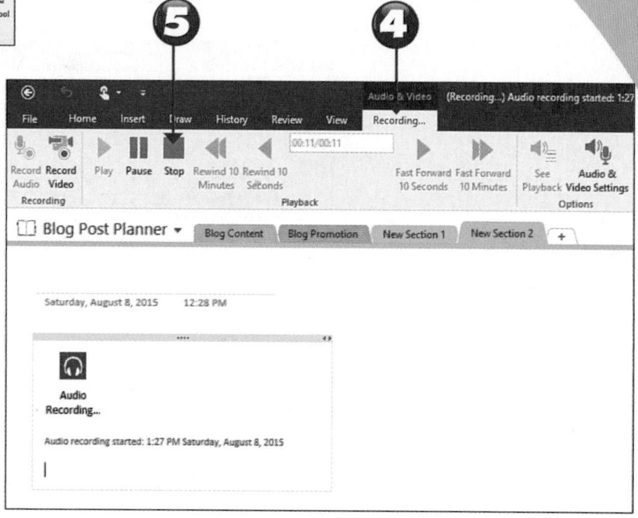

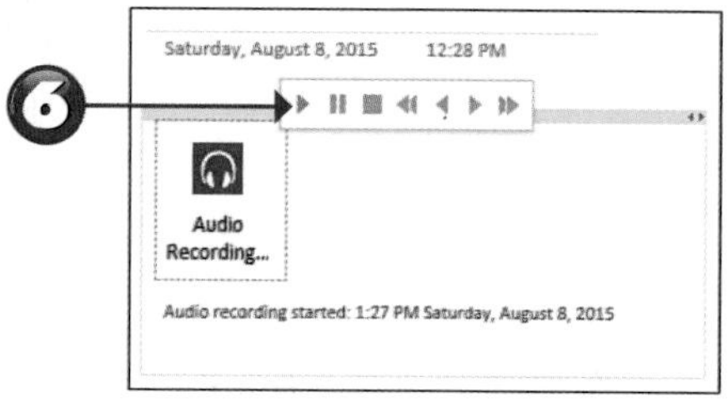

Start

1. Click the **Insert** tab.
2. Click **Record Audio**.
3. OneNote displays an audio icon and immediately starts recording; you can type associated text notes here.
4. To view audio controls while recording, click the **Recording** tab.
5. Click **Stop** to end the recording.
6. To play back the recording at any time, click the audio icon and click **Play**, or click the **Play** button on the Audio & Video-Playback tab.

End

## TIP

**Playback Controls** You can use the audio playback controls to stop, pause, rewind, and fast forward. Playback controls appear as a mini toolbar when you click an audio icon, or you can display the Audio & Video-Playback tab to access the same controls. This tab is available only when you select an audio note on the page.

# RECORDING VIDEO

You can use your computer's built-in video camera to record video clips as notes on your notebook page.

Start

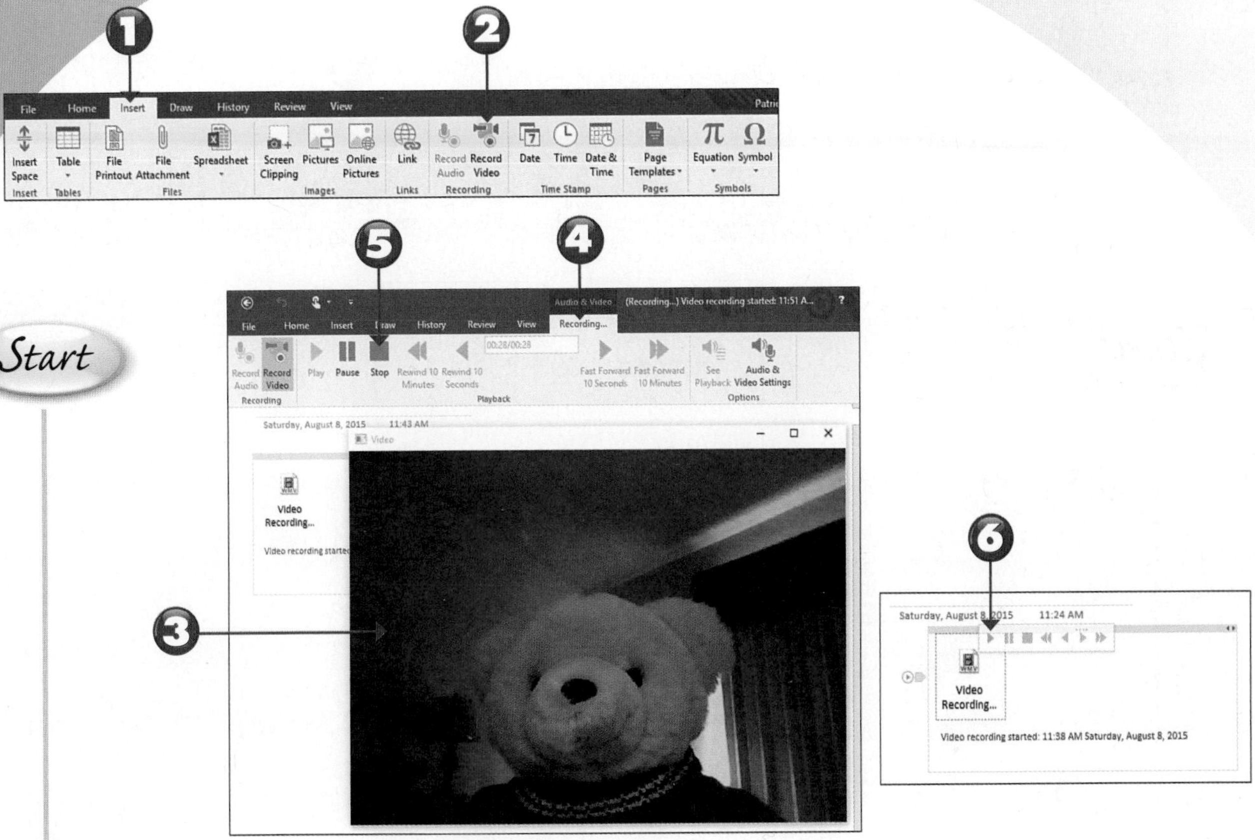

1. Click the **Insert** tab.
2. Click **Record Video**.
3. OneNote displays a video window and immediately starts recording.
4. To view video controls while recording, click the **Recording** tab.
5. Click **Stop** to end the recording.
6. To play back the recording at any time, click the video icon and click **Play**, or click the **Play** button on the Audio & Video-Playback tab.

End

## TIP

**Set Video Options** You can adjust a few settings for audio and video recordings before you begin taping. Select the video clip note, and click the **Audio & Video-Playback** tab on the Ribbon. Click the **Audio & Video Settings** button. This opens the OneNote Options dialog box to the Audio & Video tab, where you can change recording devices and profiles.

# ADDING A TIMESTAMP

Some of the notes and pages you create might need a date or time added so that you can keep track of when you made the note. You can use OneNote's Timestamp tools to instantly add a note containing the date or the time, or both.

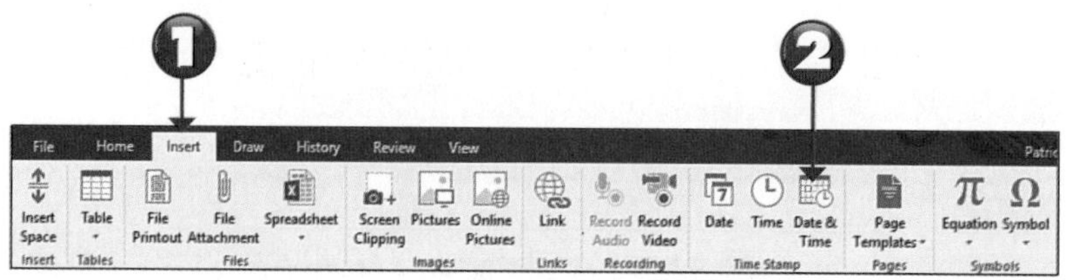


Start

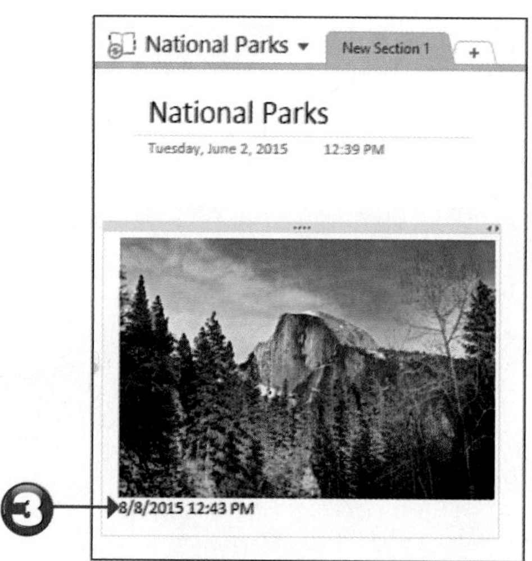


1. Click the **Insert** tab.
2. Click a Time Stamp tool; choose either **Date**, **Time**, or **Date & Time**.
3. OneNote adds a timestamp to the page.

End

## TIP

**Change It** You can edit a timestamp simply by clicking and changing the information. For example, you might need to set a different date for a project.

# EMAILING A PAGE

You can use OneNote with Microsoft Outlook to email a notebook page.

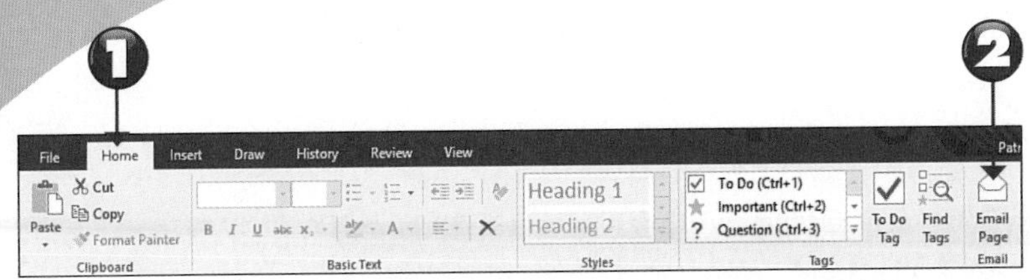


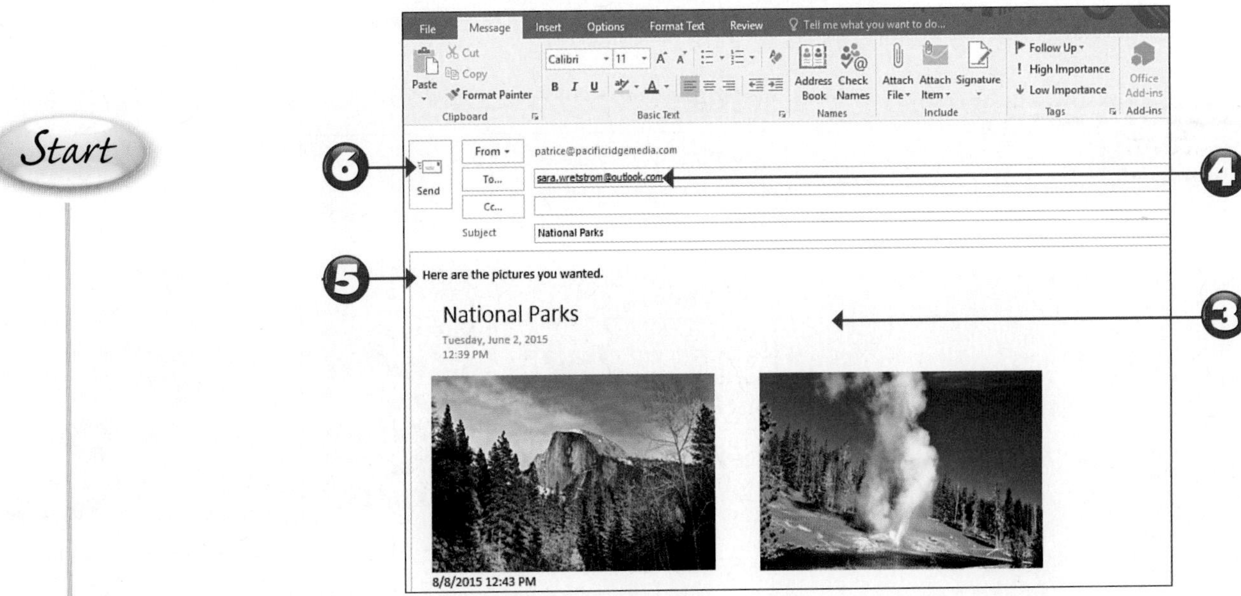


Start

1. Click the **Home** tab.
2. Click **Email Page**.
3. An Outlook message window opens with the notebook page inserted into the message body and the page title as the subject heading.
4. Type the recipient's email address.
5. Type any additional message text, as needed.
6. Click **Send**.

**TIP**

**Other Sending Options** You can also send an entire notebook as an attachment, PDF file, Word file, or blog. Click the **File** tab and choose **Send** to view your options.

# DRAWING IN YOUR NOTEBOOK

The Draw tab on OneNote's Ribbon has an array of drawing tools and controls for adding all kinds of freehand drawings and shapes to your pages. You can use the tools to create charts and graphs, pointer arrows, and more.

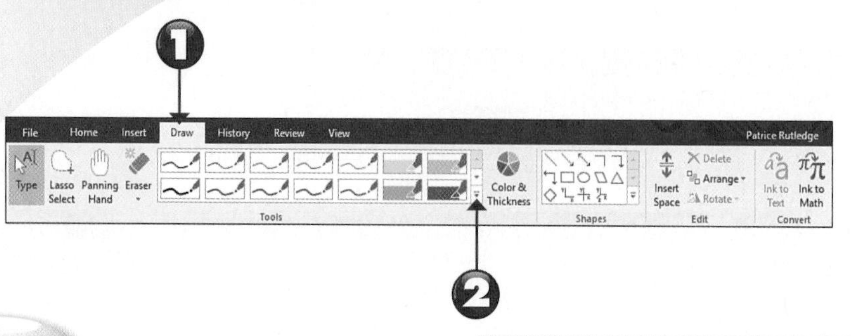


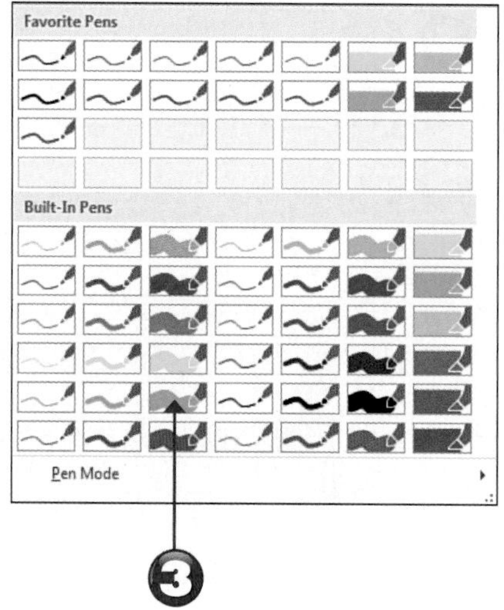


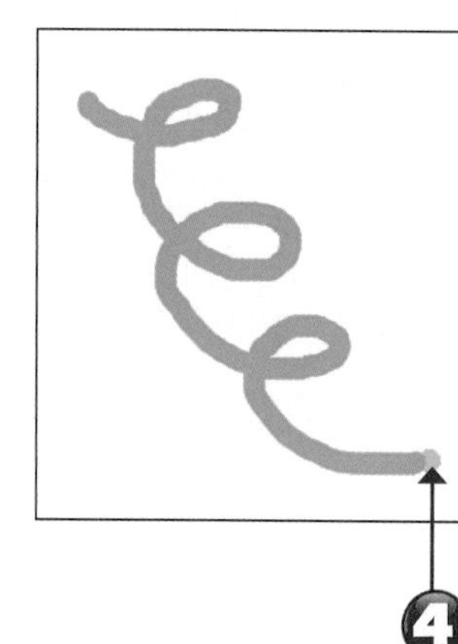

Start

1. Click the **Draw** tab.
2. Click the **More** button.
3. Click a drawing pen.
4. Click and drag on the page to draw freehand style.

Continued

**TIP**

**Draw Onscreen** If your computer supports onscreen drawing or uses a touchscreen monitor, you can draw directly onscreen.

**TIP**

**Change Colors and Thickness** You can change the color and line thickness of your drawing pens. Click the **Color & Thickness** button on the Draw tab, and choose another color or thickness from the Color & Thickness dialog box. Click **OK** to exit and apply the changes.

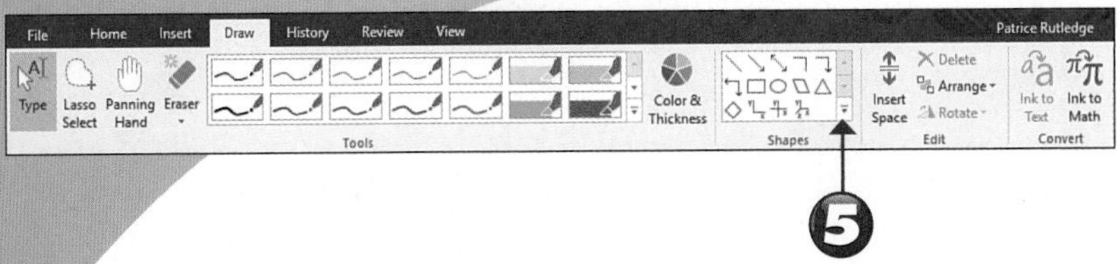

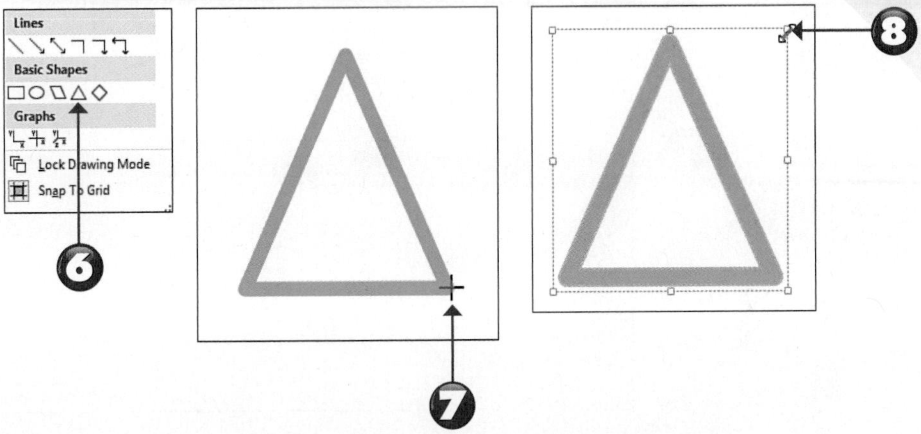

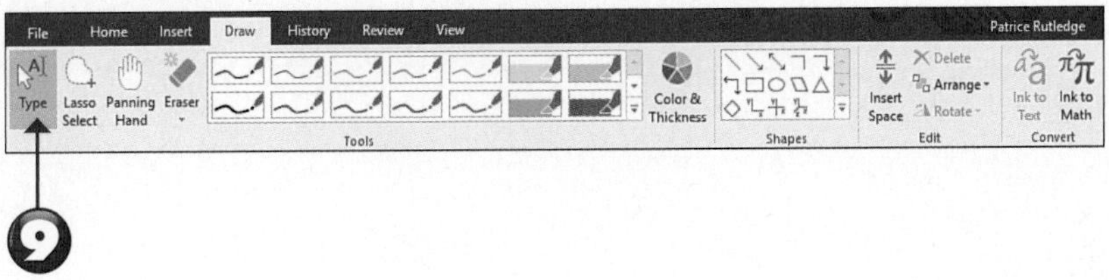

5 To draw a shape with your selected pen, click the Shapes palette's **More** button.

6 Click a shape.

7 Click and drag on the page to draw.

8 To resize a shape, click and drag a handle.

9 To turn off the drawing tool, click the **Type** button on the Draw tab.

End

TIP

**Highlight It** You can use the highlighter pens to highlight in your text notes. You might find this useful when taking notes in class or in meetings, or when reviewing information later.

TIP

**Undo It** You can use the Undo button on the Quick Access toolbar to undo a drawing. You can also erase parts of a drawing using the Eraser tool on the Draw tab.

# SENDING A TASK TO OUTLOOK

You can turn a note into an Outlook task. For example, you might want to take a to-do list in a notebook and use it as a to-do list in Outlook to assign it to a co-worker or coordinate it with calendar dates.

Start

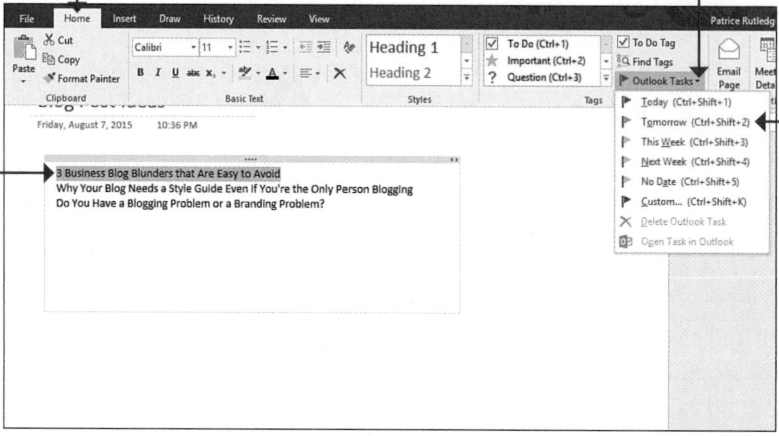

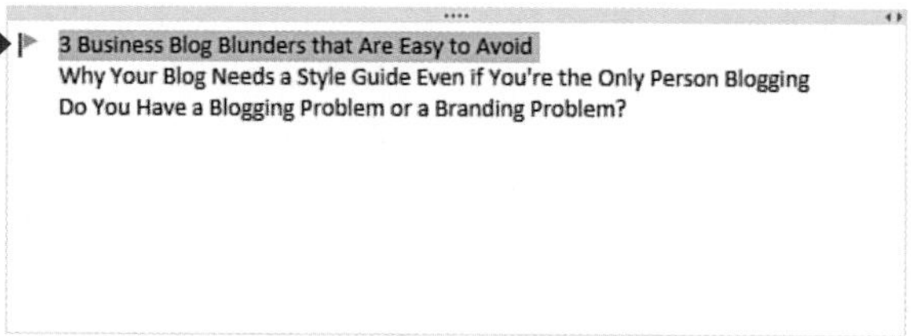

1. Select the words or note you want to turn into a task.
2. Click the **Home** tab.
3. Click **Outlook Tasks**.
4. Click a priority flag setting.
5. OneNote adds flags to the text.

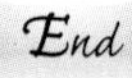

**TIP**

**Delete an Outlook Task** To delete an Outlook task, select it, click the **Home** tab, click **Outlook Tasks**, and click the **Delete Outlook Task** command.

# VIEWING A TASK IN OUTLOOK

You can view a task you sent to Outlook directly from OneNote.

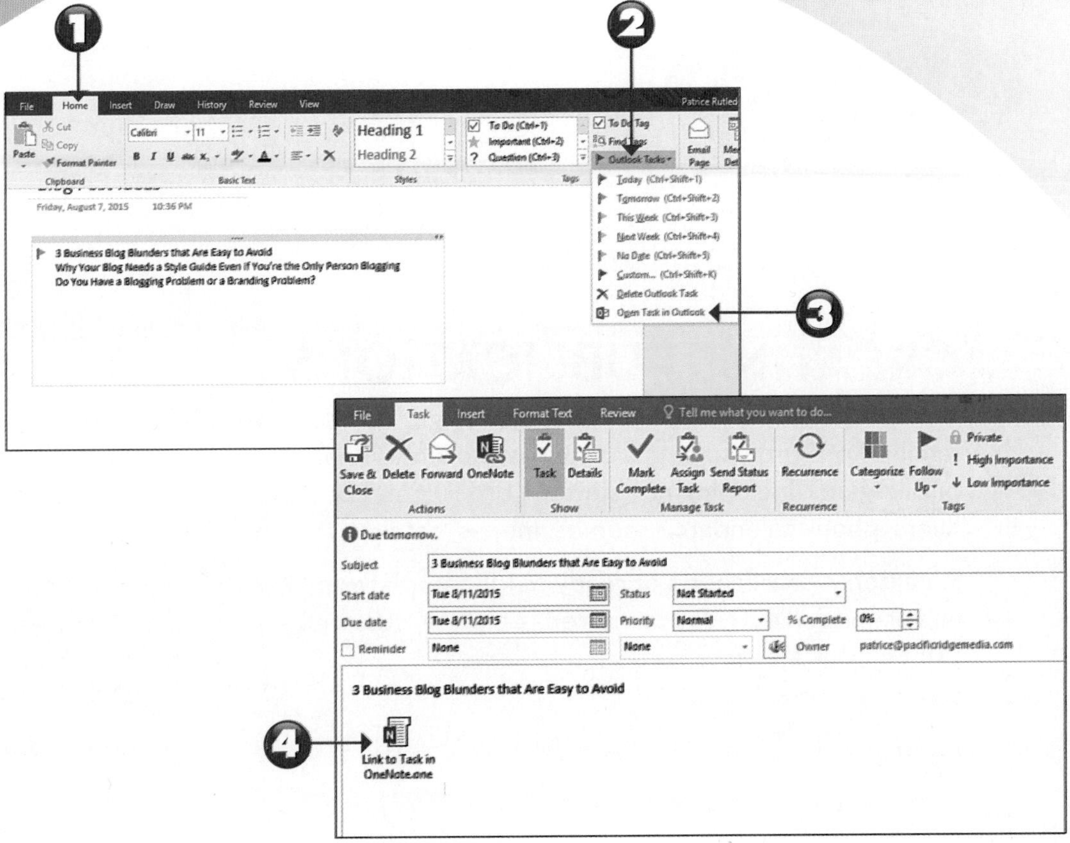

Start

1. Click the **Home** tab.
2. Click **Outlook Tasks**.
3. Click **Open Task in Outlook**.
4. Outlook opens the task.

End

## TIP

**More OneNote Options** If you want to do even more with OneNote, check out the collection of OneNote apps at https://www.onenote.com/apps. Other interesting options include the OneNote Clipper, which lets you send web clips to OneNote (https://www.onenote.com/Clipper), and Office Lens, which functions as a smartphone scanner that sends scanned images to OneNote (https://www.microsoft.com/en-us/store/apps/office-lens/9wzdncrfj3t8).

# CREATING PUBLICATIONS

Publisher 2016 simplifies publication design. Using many tools that are familiar to Word users, you can create professional-quality print and digital publications, including newsletters, brochures, cookbooks, thank-you cards, flyers, photo calendars, resumes, menus, catalogs, and much more.

An extensive collection of ready-made templates makes the process even easier—just select your preferred template, customize its text and pictures, and print or share online.

# GETTING STARTED WITH PUBLISHER

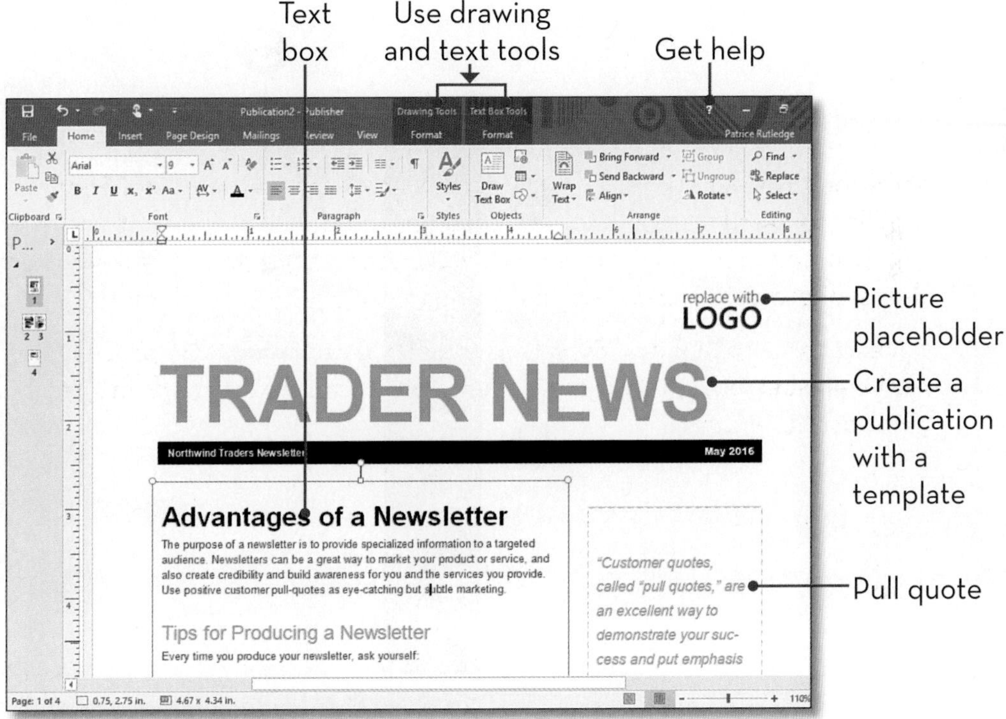

# CREATING A NEW PUBLICATION FROM A TEMPLATE

Publisher offers an extensive collection of templates that can help make the publication process much easier.

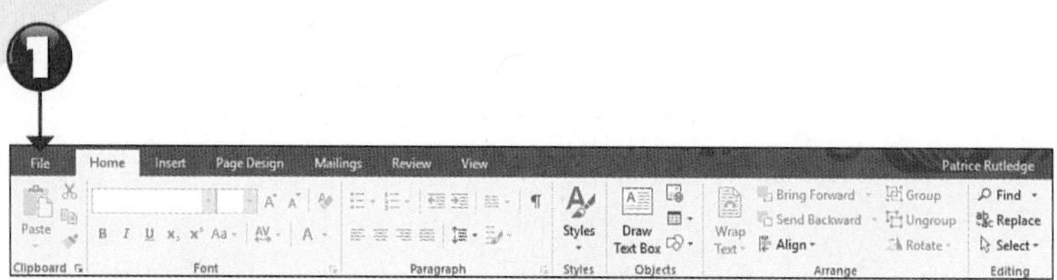

Start

1. Click the **File** tab.
2. Click **New**.
3. Click **Built-In**.
4. Click a template category.

Continued

**TIP**

**Search Online for More Templates** Looking for even more templates? Use the search box at the top of the New page to search Microsoft's online collection with thousands of additional options.

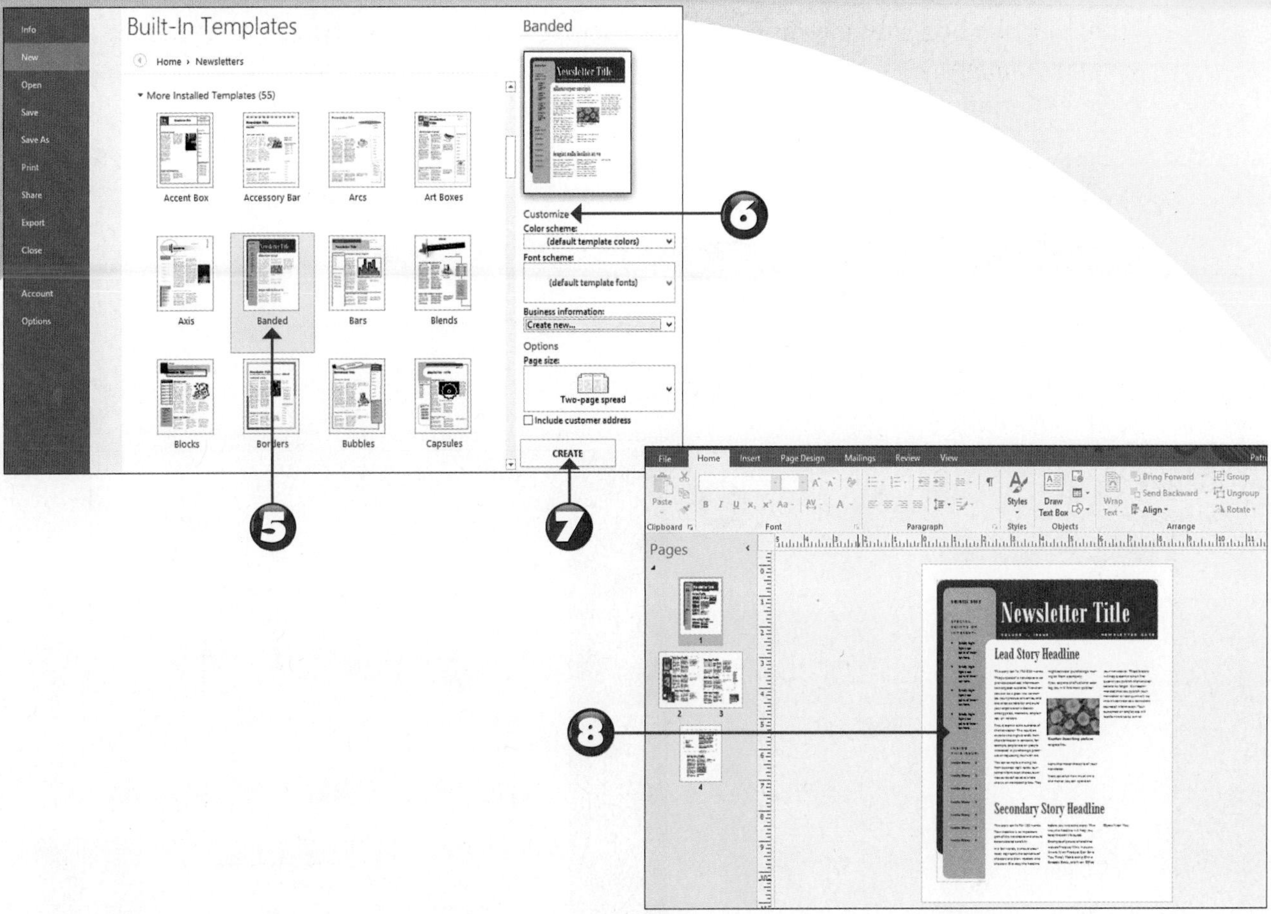

5 Select the template you want to apply.

6 Optionally, customize the template.

7 Click **Create**.

8 Publisher opens a new publication using your selected template.

End

## NOTE

**Template Customization** Publisher enables you to customize a template's color scheme, font scheme, business information, and more. See Chapter 24, "Enhancing and Managing Publications," for more information about color schemes and business information sets.

## TIP

**More Options** Be sure to scroll down the page to view additional options, including those from manufacturers such as Avery and Staples.

# CREATING A NEW BLANK PUBLICATION

Although starting with a template is the easiest way to create a publication, there are times when you might want to start with a blank canvas. This is particularly useful if you already have experience with Publisher and know exactly what you want to create.

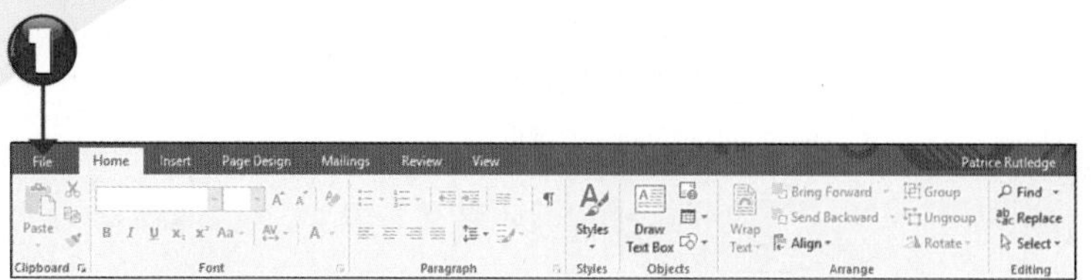

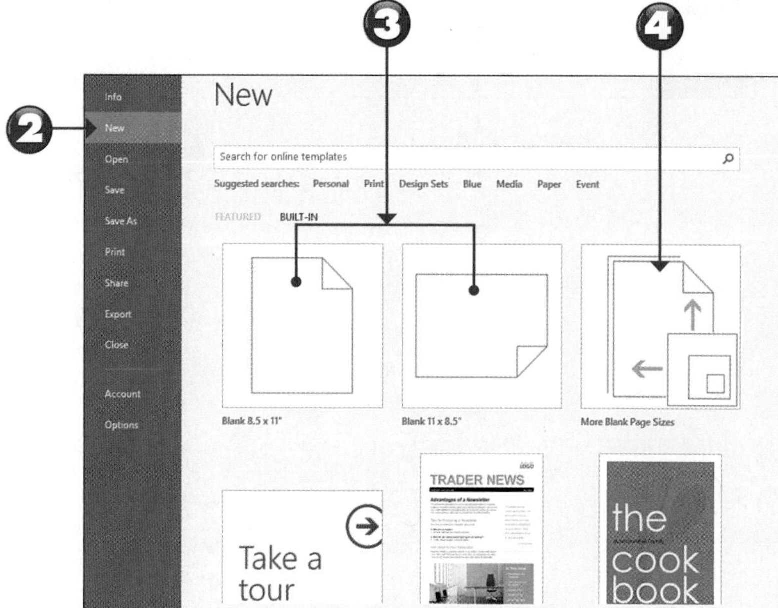

1. Click the **File** tab.
2. Click **New**.
3. Click the blank page template you want to apply.
4. Click **More Blank Page Sizes** if you need a size other than 8.5" x 11".

Continued

## NOTE

**Standard Page Size** The standard page size for a publication is 8.5" x 11" with options for portrait or landscape orientation. If you select a standard size, your blank publication opens automatically after step 3.

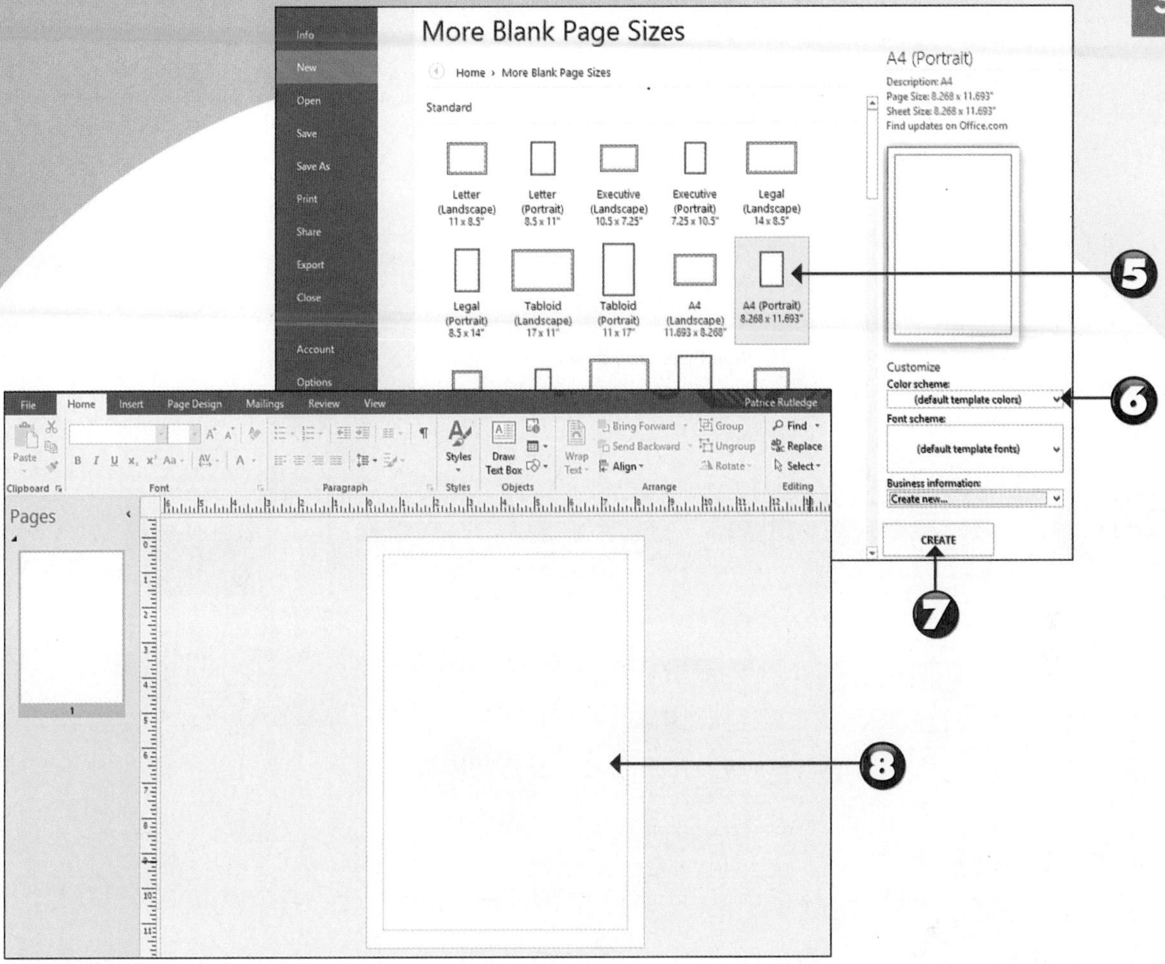

5 Select your preferred page size.

6 Optionally, customize the template.

7 Click **Create**.

8 Publisher opens a new blank publication.

*End*

**TIP**

**Additional Blank Templates** Scroll down the page to view additional blank page templates by publication type (booklets, postcards, and so forth) or by manufacturer (such as 3M labels).

**TIP**

**Customize Colors and Fonts** Optionally, you can customize the colors and fonts you use in your blank template by using the options above the Create button.

# VIEWING A PUBLICATION

Publisher offers several options for viewing your publications, including precise zooming, two-page spreads, and more.

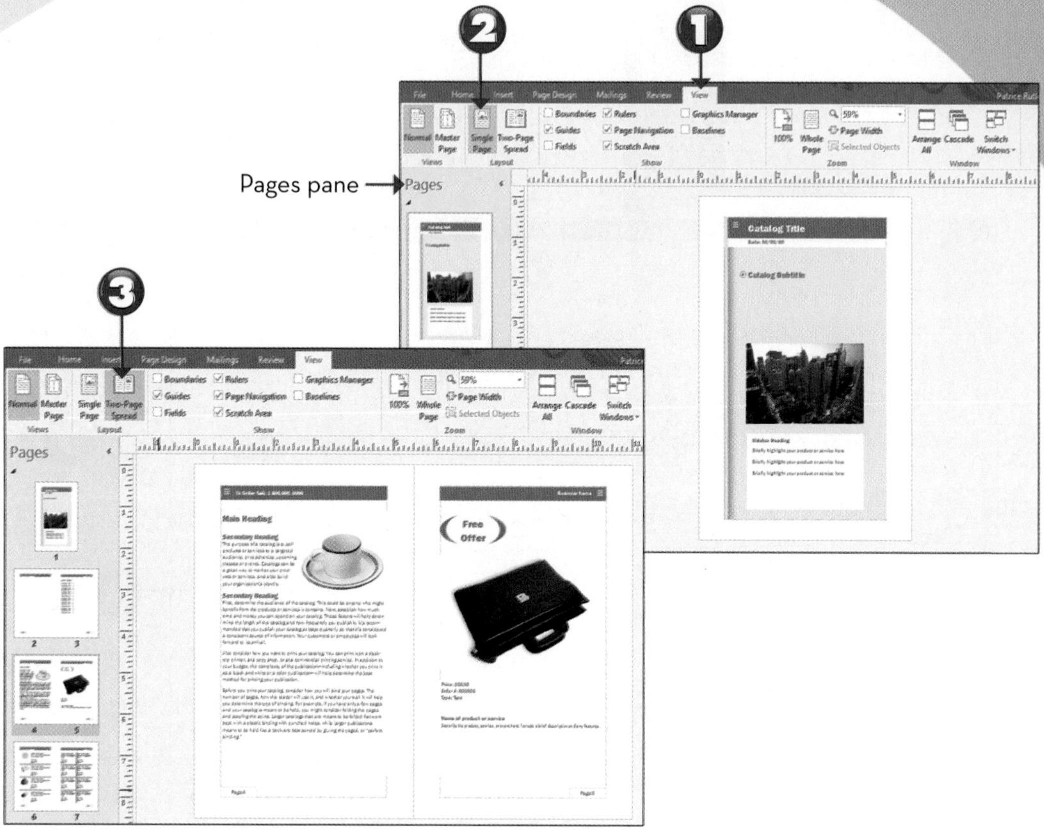

Pages pane

Start

1. Click the **View** tab.

2. Click **Single Page** to view each single page separately.

3. Click **Two-Page Spread** to display two pages at a time on your screen (only for multipage publications).

Continued

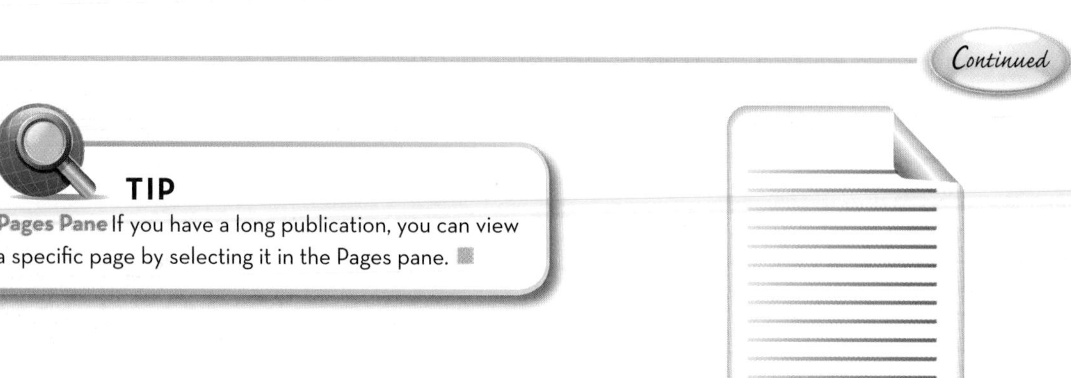

**TIP**

**Pages Pane** If you have a long publication, you can view a specific page by selecting it in the Pages pane.

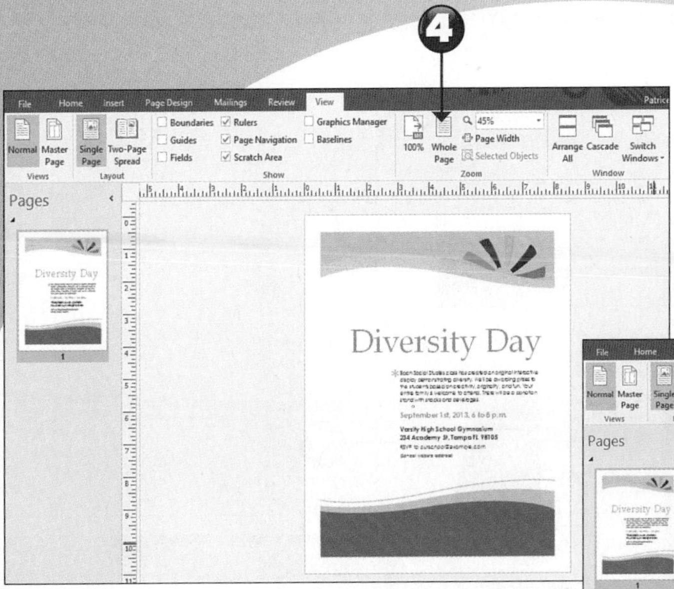

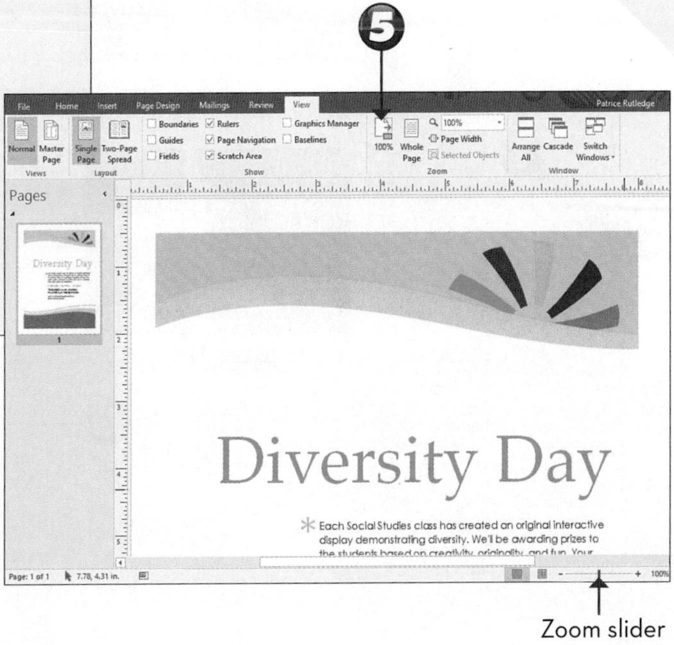

Zoom slider

1. Click **Whole Page** to fit the page on the screen.

2. Click **100%** to zoom into the page at 100 percent of its size.

End

**TIP**

**Zoom Slider** Use the Zoom slider in the lower-right corner of the screen to precisely control the zoom level.

# REPLACING TEXT IN A TEMPLATE

If you create a publication using a template, your next step is to customize it. Publisher includes placeholder content that's easy to replace.

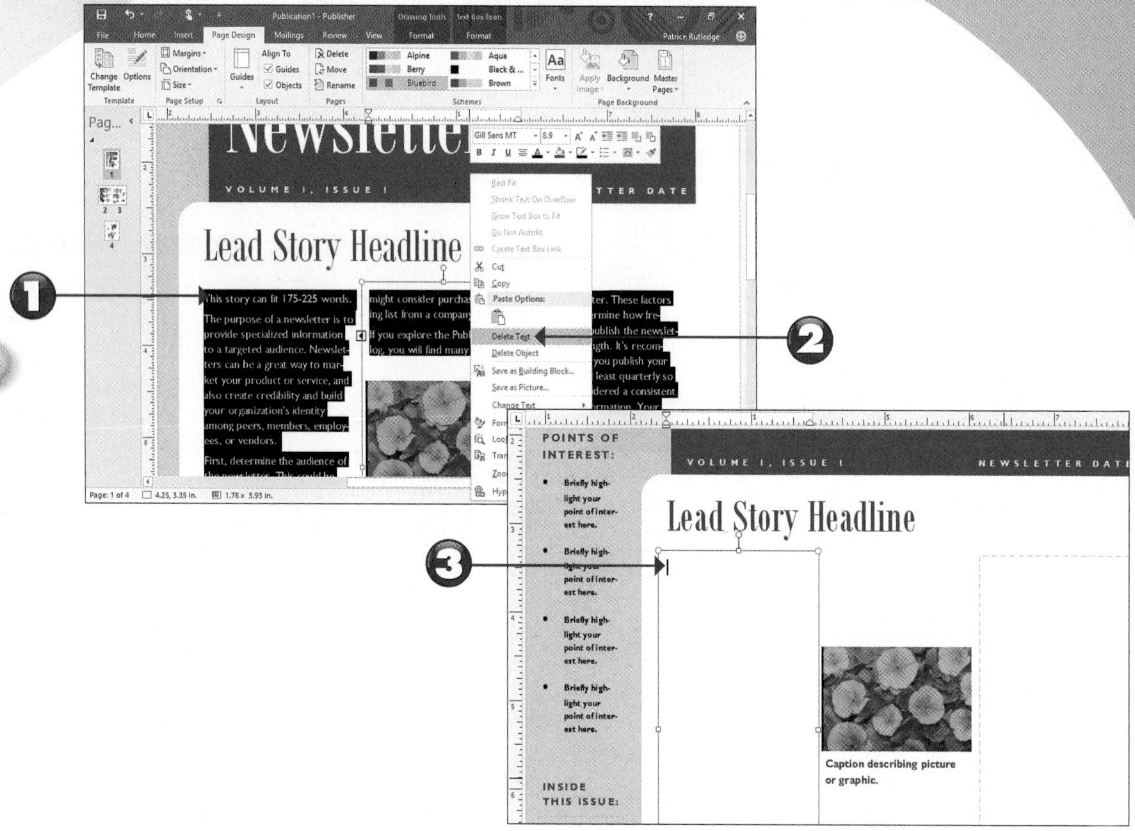

Start

1. View the number of words that can fit in the text box. Note that this information is available only for certain publication types.
2. Right-click the text box and select **Delete Text**.
3. Type your replacement text.

## TIP

**Plan Ahead** When using a template, plan your content to fit into the allotted space. Having a plan makes it much easier to create publications quickly.

## CAUTION

**Copy and Paste** An alternative to typing your replacement text into the text box is to copy and paste the text from another source, such as a text file. Be aware, however, that if you paste in too much text it won't fit in the text box. An ellipsis (...) displays at the end of the box to alert you of this. Although you can make the text flow into a subsequent box, this is often complicated for a beginning user. When you're just getting started with Publisher, it's best to type in your text or ensure a fit before pasting.

# REPLACING A PICTURE IN A TEMPLATE

Replacing pictures in a template is another common Publisher task.

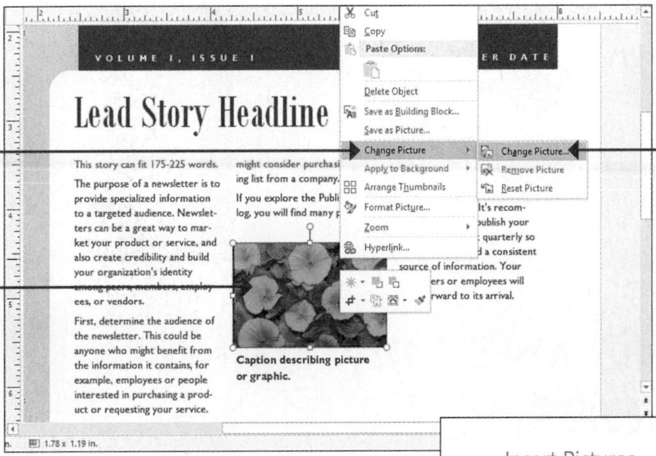

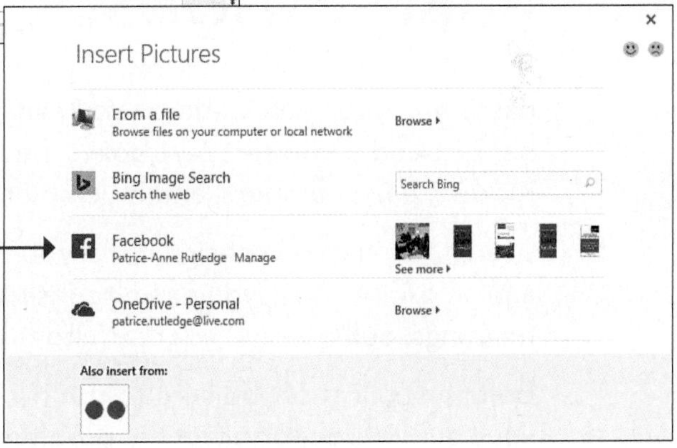

Start

1. Double-click a picture to select it.

2. Right-click the picture and select **Change Picture**.

3. Click **Change Picture**.

4. Select a replacement picture from your computer, Bing Image Search, Facebook, or OneDrive.

End

**TIP**

**How Do I Insert a Picture?** For a reminder of how to insert pictures in Office 2016, see Chapter 4, "Working with Pictures."

**CAUTION**

**Don't Customize Too Much!** Although you can customize a template extensively using Publisher's many tools, it's best to focus on minor text, picture, and color changes if you're a new user. As you become more familiar with Publisher, you can explore more advanced customization techniques.

# ENHANCING AND MANAGING PUBLICATIONS

Publisher 2016 offers an array of powerful features that enable you to customize your publications. You can modify your color scheme and background and insert text boxes, new pages, picture placeholders, headers, footers, page numbers, and much more.

Even if you have no design skills, you can use Publisher's building blocks. For a professional look, you can also insert ready-made design elements such as headings, pull quotes, sidebars, story elements, borders, and accents.

Before publication, be sure to run the built-in Design Checker, which analyzes your publication for potential problems. If you're sending your publication to a commercial printer, the Pack and Go Wizard ensures that your printer has everything needed for optimal printing.

# FORMATTING PUBLICATION TEXT

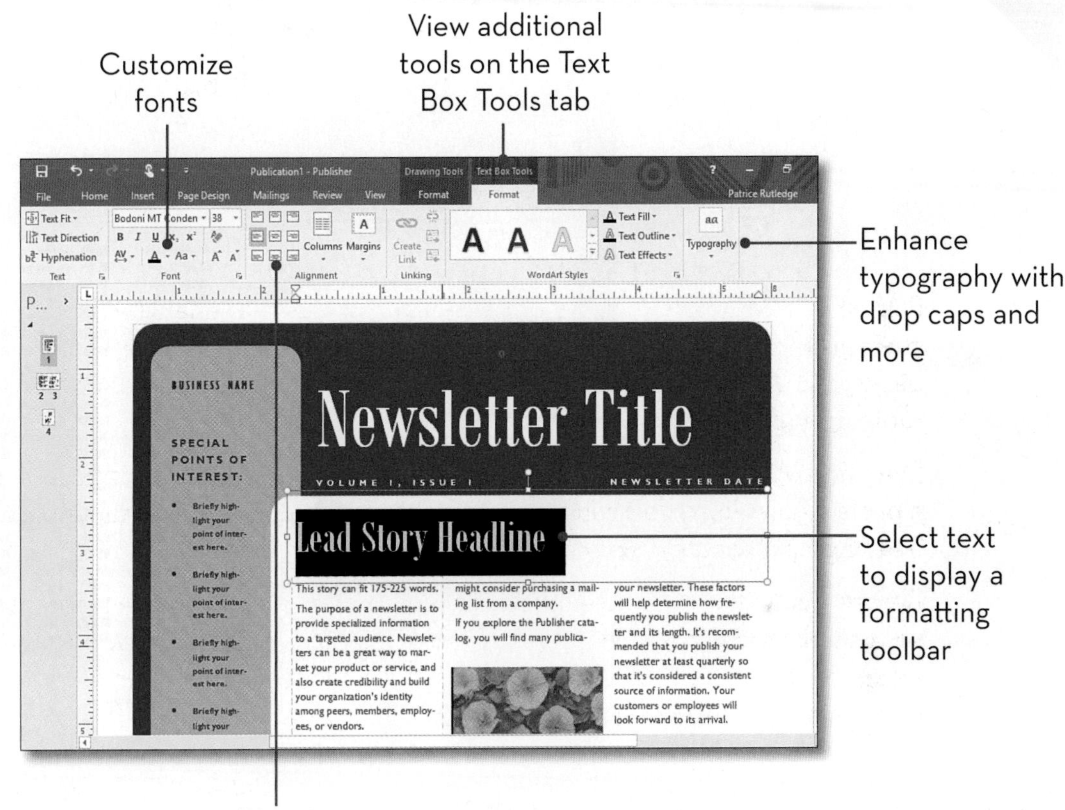

# APPLYING A COLOR SCHEME

When you create a publication, Publisher applies a color scheme, a collection of four coordinated colors identified by name, such as Flow, Moss, and Citrus. If you don't like your current color scheme, you can choose another.

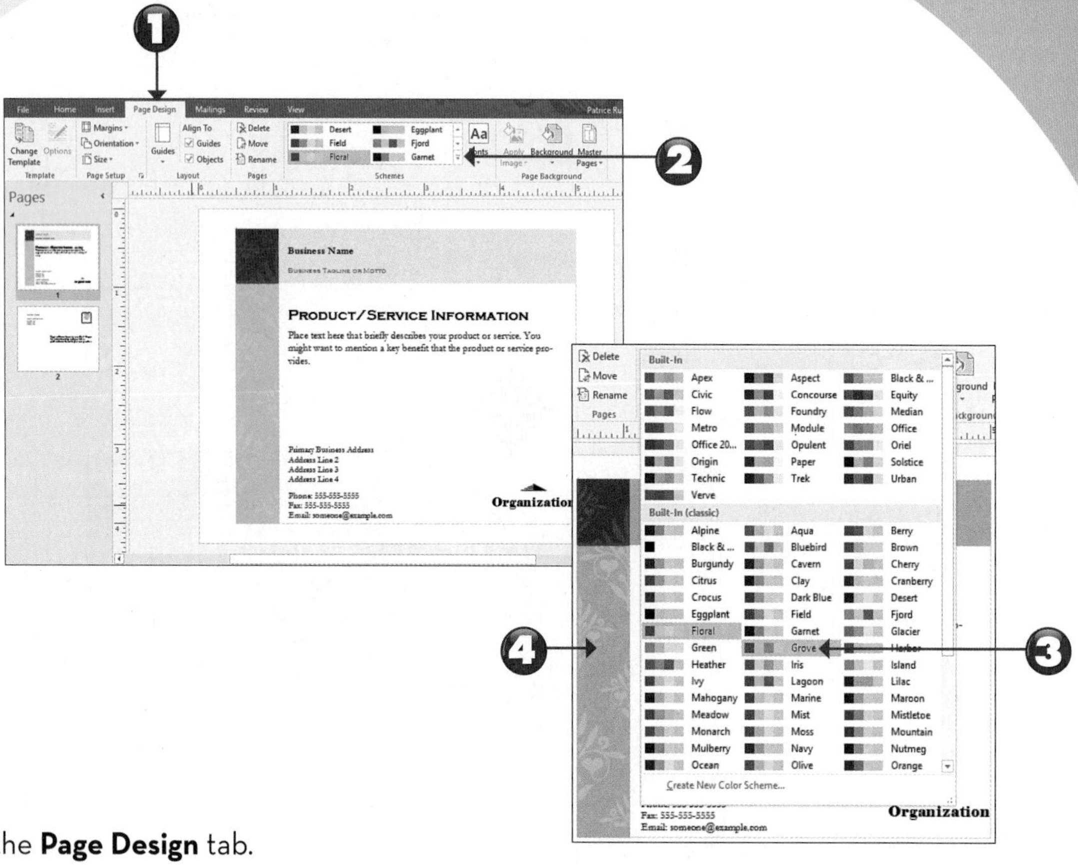

Start

1. Click the **Page Design** tab.
2. Click the **More** button in the Schemes group.
3. Select your preferred color scheme.
4. Publisher applies the scheme to your publication.

End

## TIP

**Color Scheme Shortcut** The number of color schemes Publisher displays in the Schemes group on the Page Design tab is determined by your monitor size. If you see a scheme you want to use and you don't want to view more options in the gallery, you can click the theme to apply it directly to your publication.

## TIP

**Create Your Own Color Scheme** Despite the abundance of existing color schemes, you might want to create your own. For example, you might want to match the colors of an existing publication or logo. Click **Create New Color Scheme** at the bottom of the Color Scheme gallery to select your own combination of colors.

# APPLYING A BACKGROUND

Publisher enables you to apply a solid color or gradient background to one or more pages in your publication. The background colors available in the gallery coordinate with your selected color scheme.

Start

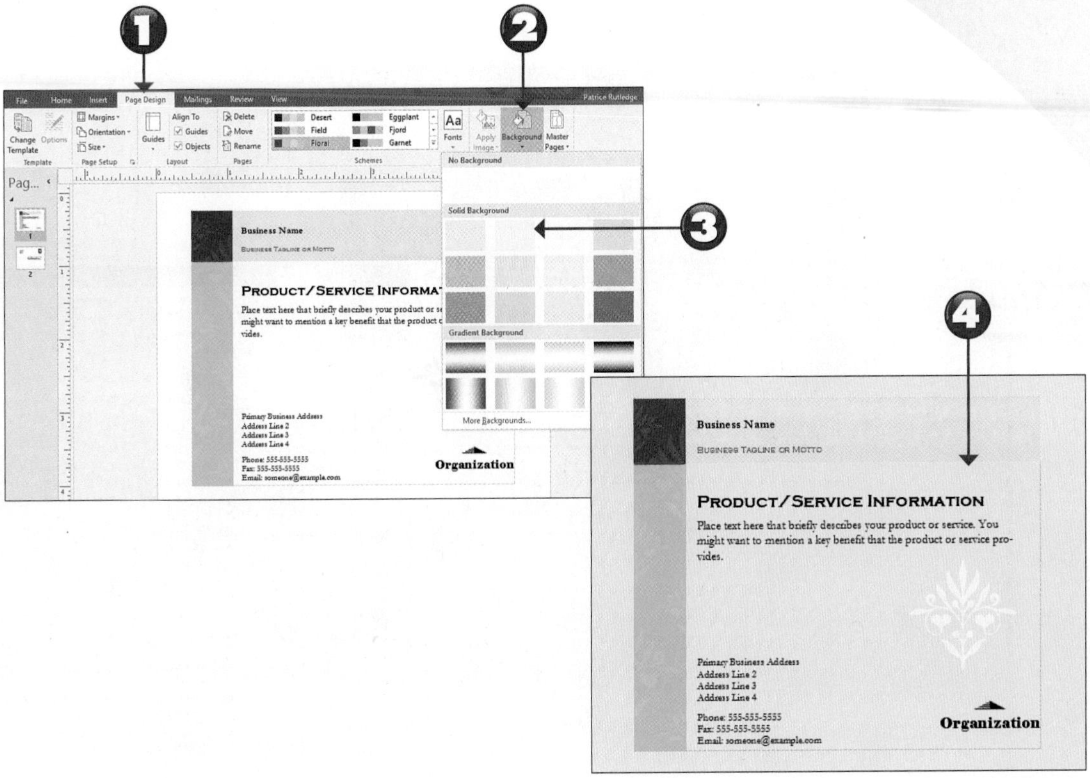

1. Click the **Page Design** tab.
2. Click **Background**.
3. Select your preferred background.
4. Publisher applies the background to your publication.

End

**TIP**

**Customize Your Background** If none of the backgrounds in the gallery suit your needs, click **More Backgrounds** to create a custom background. This option enables you to use any solid or gradient color (not just the ones from your color scheme) or a picture, texture, or pattern as a page background.

**TIP**

**Delete a Background** If you don't like the background you applied, click the **Background** button again and select **No Background** to delete it.

# INSERTING A NEW PAGE

You can insert one or more pages at the beginning, end, or middle of your publication. Inserting duplicate pages is another option.

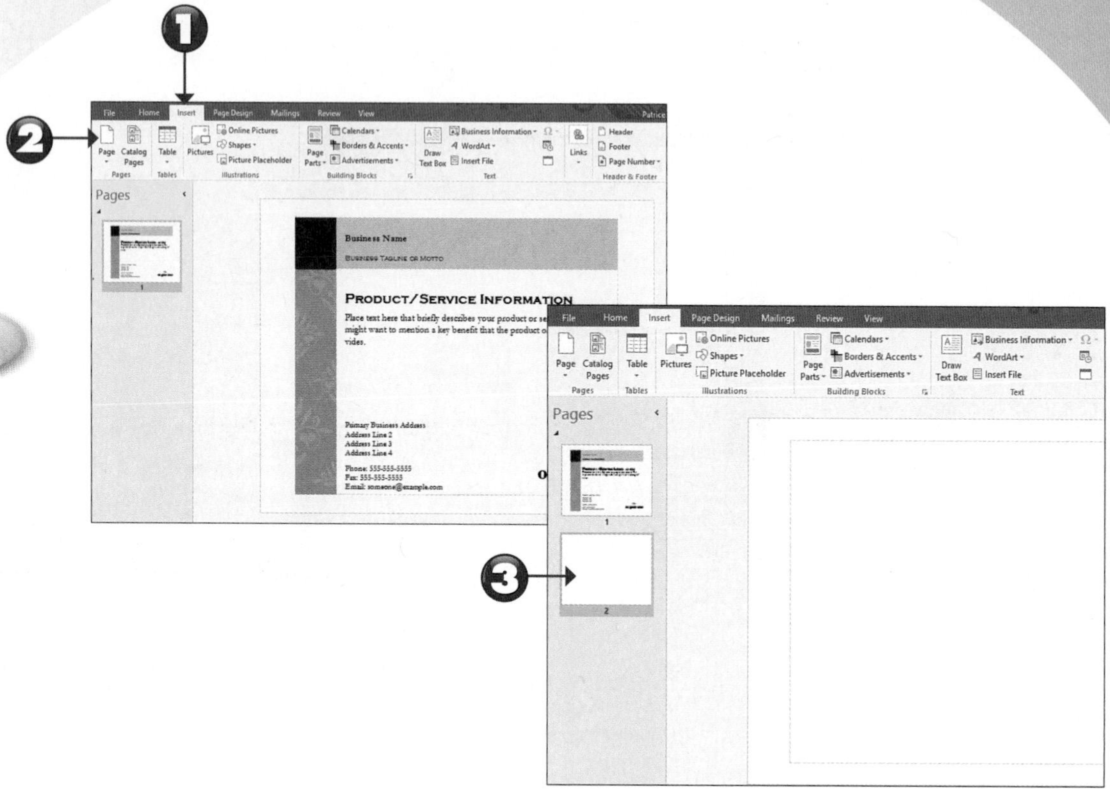

Start

1. Click the **Insert** tab.

2. Click the top portion of the **Page** button.

3. Publisher inserts a blank page after the current page.

End

## TIP

**Insert a Duplicate Page** To insert a duplicate of the current page, click the lower portion of the **Page** button and select **Insert Duplicate Page**.

## TIP

**Other Page Insertion Options** Other options include inserting multiple pages, a page at the beginning of a publication, or new pages with a text box. To view these options, click the lower portion of the Page button and select **Insert Page**.

# DRAWING A TEXT BOX

Add text to a page by drawing a text box. This is particularly useful if you're starting with a blank publication. Text boxes act as moveable containers that you can reposition anywhere on a page.

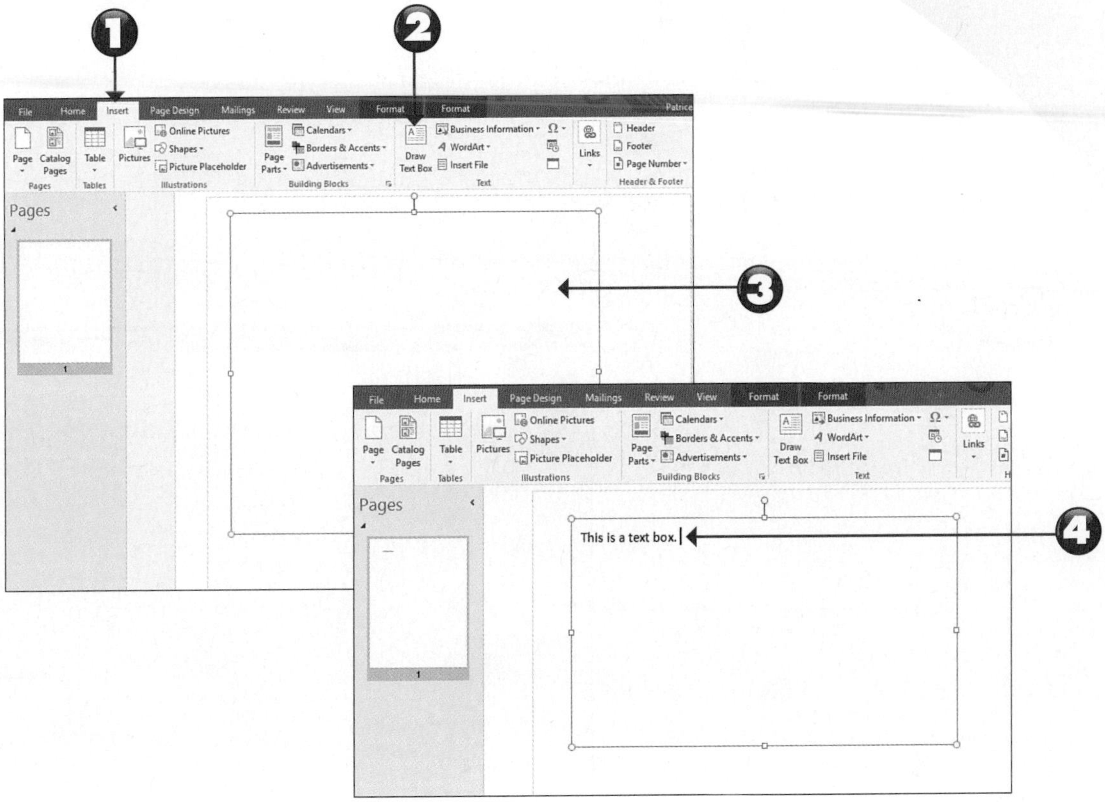

Start

1. Click the **Insert** tab.
2. Click **Draw Text Box**.
3. Click where you want the box to appear, and then drag until the box is the size you want.
4. Enter the desired text in the text box.

End

**TIP**

**Modify a Text Box** To move a text box, position the mouse pointer over an edge of the box, and then drag it to a new location. To resize a box, click and drag a selection handle. To delete a box, select it and press the **Delete** key on your keyboard.

**TIP**

**Text Box Tools** Use the options on the Text Box Tools tab to format your text. Refer to Chapter 3, "Working with Text," for more information about text-formatting options in Office 2016.

# INSERTING A PICTURE PLACEHOLDER

Another piece of content you might want to add to a blank page is a picture. You can do this by inserting a picture placeholder. Like a text box, a picture placeholder is a moveable container that you can reposition anywhere on a page.

Start

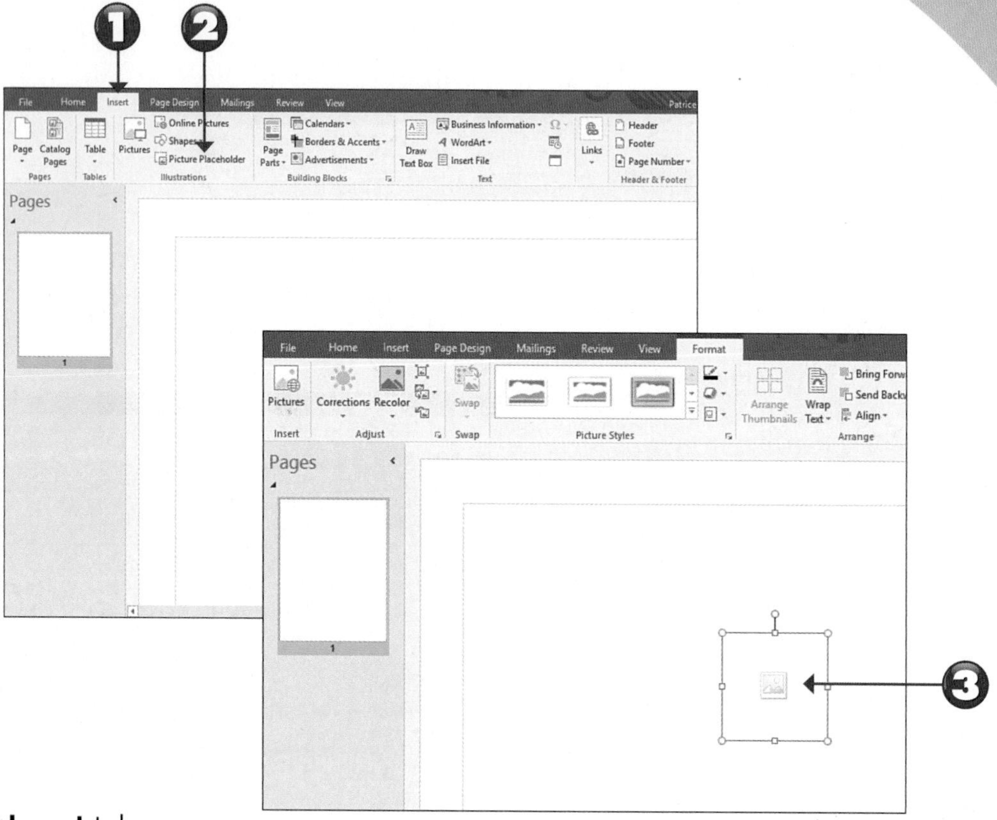

1. Click the **Insert** tab.
2. Click **Picture Placeholder**.
3. Publisher inserts a picture placeholder; click the placeholder to insert a picture.

## TIP

**How Do I Insert a Picture?** For a reminder of how to insert pictures in Office 2016, see Chapter 4, "Working with Pictures."

4 Select a picture from your computer, Bing Image Search, Facebook, or OneDrive.

5 Publisher inserts the picture on the page.

End

**TIP**

**Modify a Picture** To move a picture placeholder, position the mouse pointer over an edge of the box, and then drag it to a new location. To resize a placeholder, click and drag a selection handle. To delete a placeholder, select it and press the Delete key on your keyboard.

**TIP**

**Format a Picture** Use the tools on the Picture Tools—Format tab to format and enhance your picture. For example, you can apply a picture style or recolor a picture. See Chapter 4 for more information about formatting pictures in Office 2016.

# INSERTING HEADERS AND FOOTERS

You can use headers and footers in your documents to add special information to every page, such as a title and date at the top of each page, or a company name and address at the bottom. Header and footer information appears outside the regular text margins at the top (headers) or bottom (footers) of the document.

Start

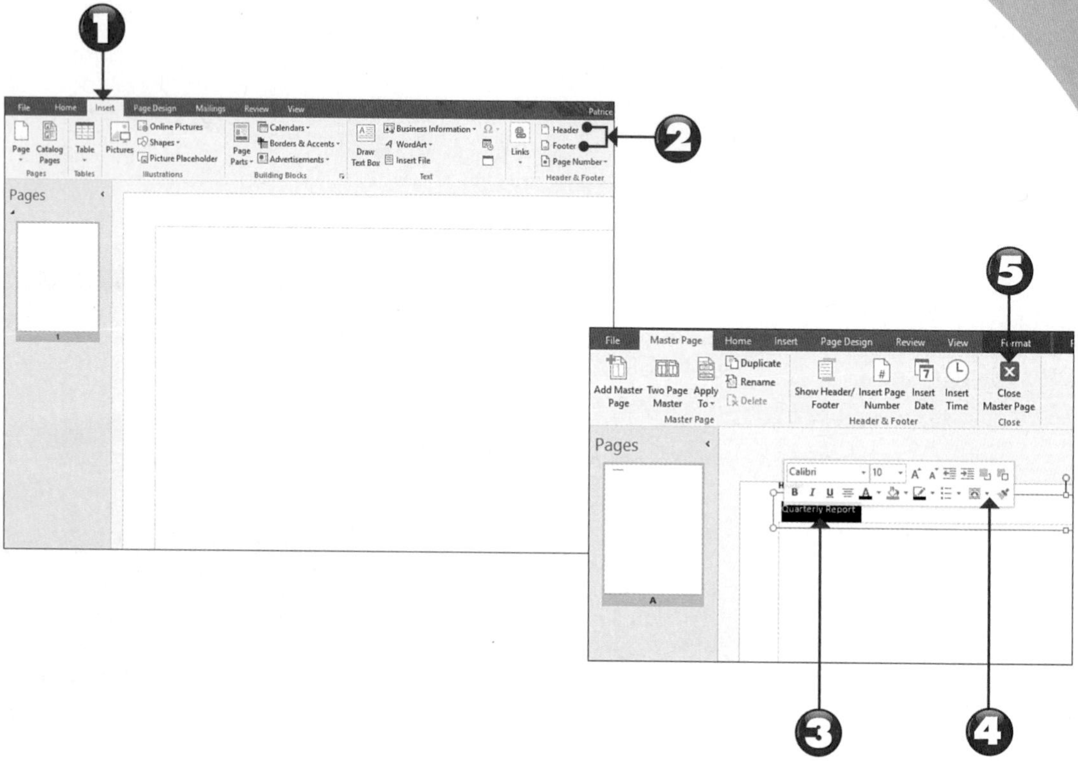

1. Click the **Insert** tab.
2. Click **Header** or **Footer**.
3. Type text into your header or footer.
4. Select your text to display the formatting mini toolbar; format as desired.
5. Click **Close Master Page**.

End

**TIP**

**Insert a Page Number, Date, or Time** Optionally, you can insert a page number, date, or time in a header or footer by using the options on the Master Page tab. You can also insert a page number by clicking the **Page Number** button on the Insert tab. See "Inserting Page Numbers" in the next section for more information.

# INSERTING PAGE NUMBERS

In a longer publication, such as a report or catalog, it's a good idea to include page numbers. Publisher enables you to choose where to place numbers on your page and the numbering format you prefer.

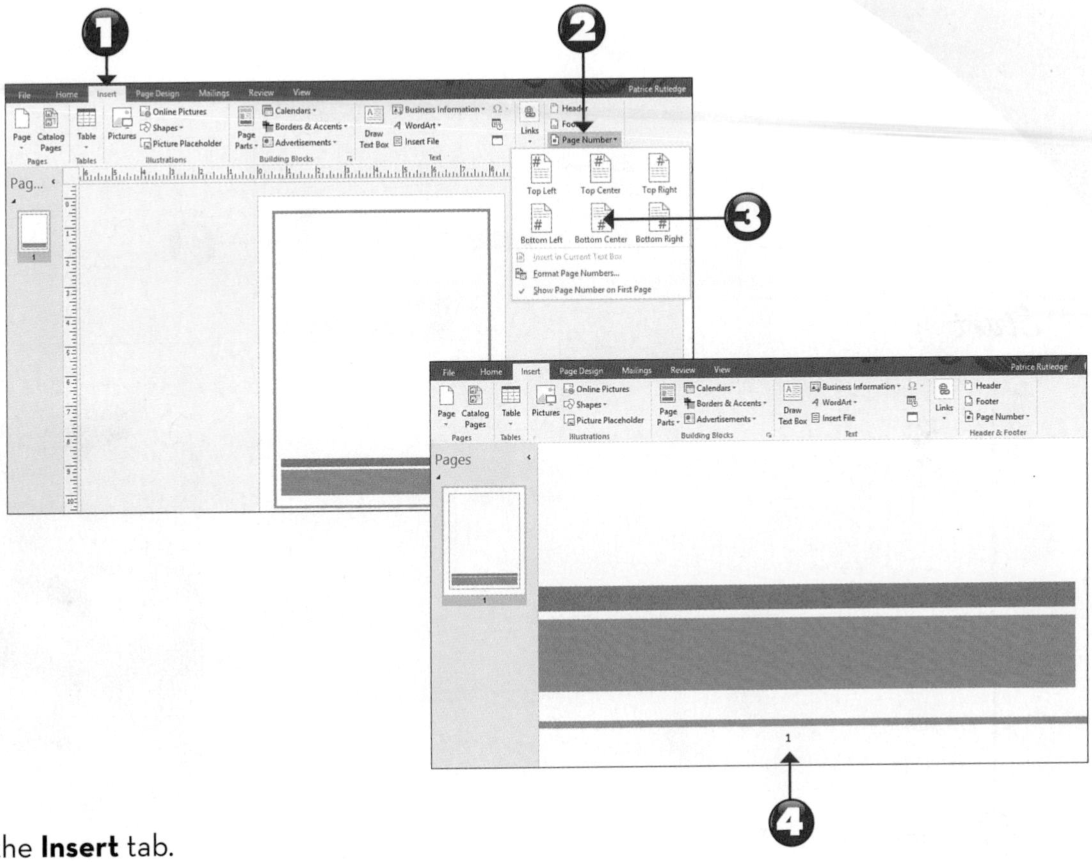

Start

1. Click the **Insert** tab.
2. Click **Page Number**.
3. Specify where you want to place page numbers.
4. Publisher displays the page numbers in your publication.

End

## TIP

**Hide Numbers on the First Page** If you don't want to place a page number on the first page, remove the check mark next to **Show Page Number on First Page** before selecting a location. This is particularly useful if your first page is a cover or title page.

## TIP

**Format Page Numbers** To select another page-numbering format, such as Roman numerals or letters of the alphabet, select **Format Page Numbers** on the Page Numbers menu.

# INSERTING PAGE PARTS

Page parts are part of Publisher's ready-made collection of building blocks, reusable content that you can insert into your publications. Page parts include headings, pull quotes, sidebars, and stories and use the colors of your publication's current color scheme.

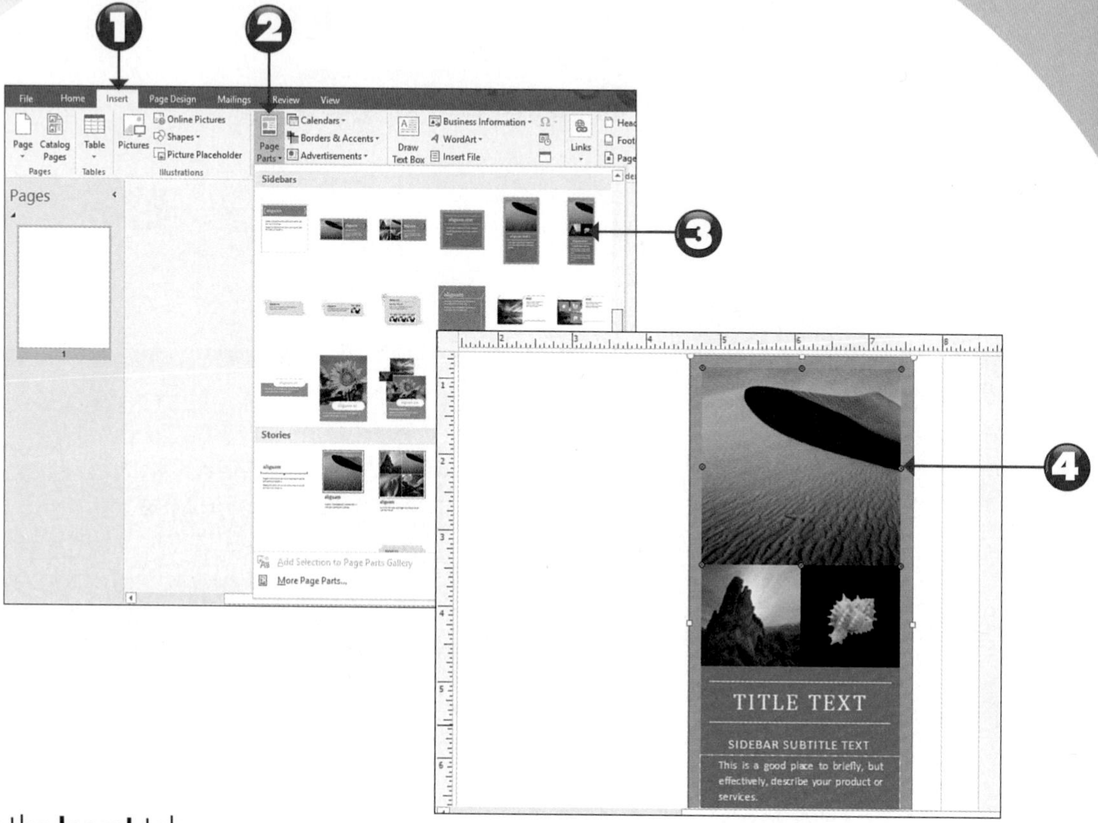

Start

1. Click the **Insert** tab.
2. Click **Page Parts**.
3. Select a part from the gallery.
4. Publisher inserts the part.

End

**TIP**

**More Page Part Options** Click **More Page Parts** at the bottom of the gallery to view even more page parts, including options for reply forms and tables of contents.

**TIP**

**Customize Page Parts** A page part is just like a placeholder in a Publisher template. You replace the text or pictures with your own custom content. You can also select and drag a page part to another location on the page or resize it by dragging a corner.

# INSERTING BORDERS AND ACCENTS

The selected use of borders and accents can add a splash of color and style to your publication. Options include bars, boxes, frames, emphasis, lines, and patterns, which use the colors from your publication's current color scheme.

Start

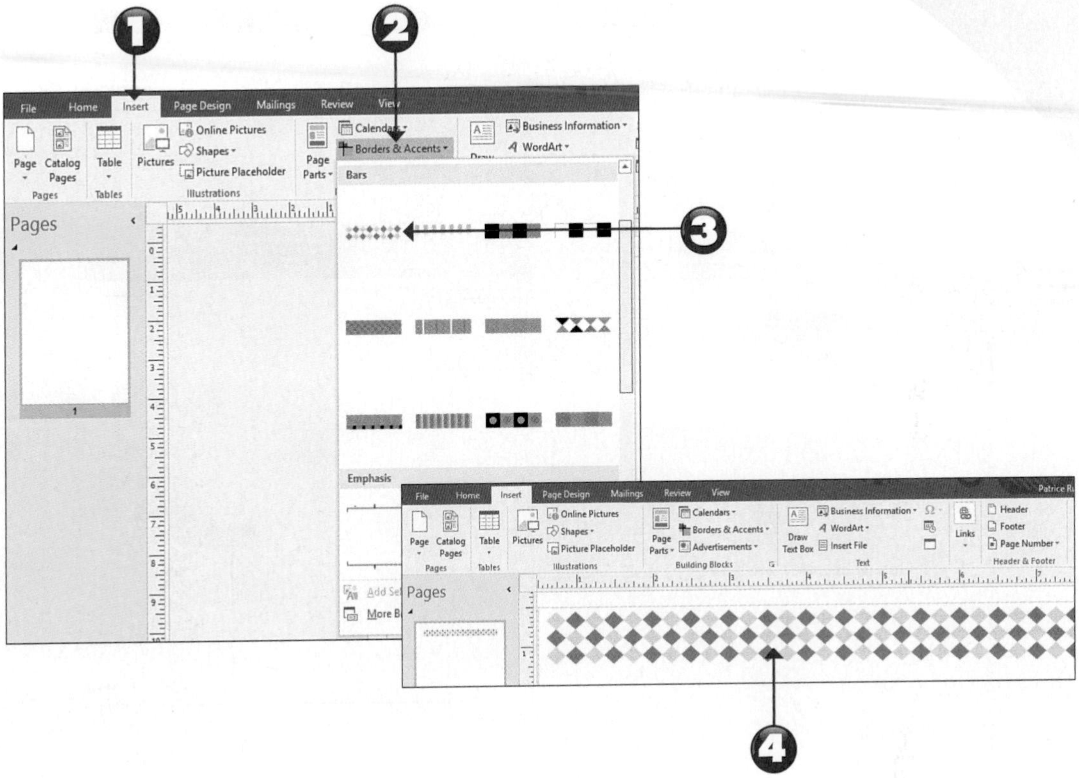

1. Click the **Insert** tab.
2. Click **Borders & Accents**.
3. Select an option from the gallery.
4. Publisher inserts the border or accent; resize or reposition as needed.

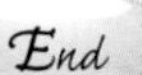

**TIP**

**More Border and Accent Options** Click **More Borders and Accents** at the bottom of the gallery to view even more options.

**TIP**

**Calendars and Advertisements** Other building blocks available on the Insert tab include ready-made calendars and advertisements you can insert into your publications.

# INSERTING A TABLE

A table helps you present information in an organized fashion using rows and columns.

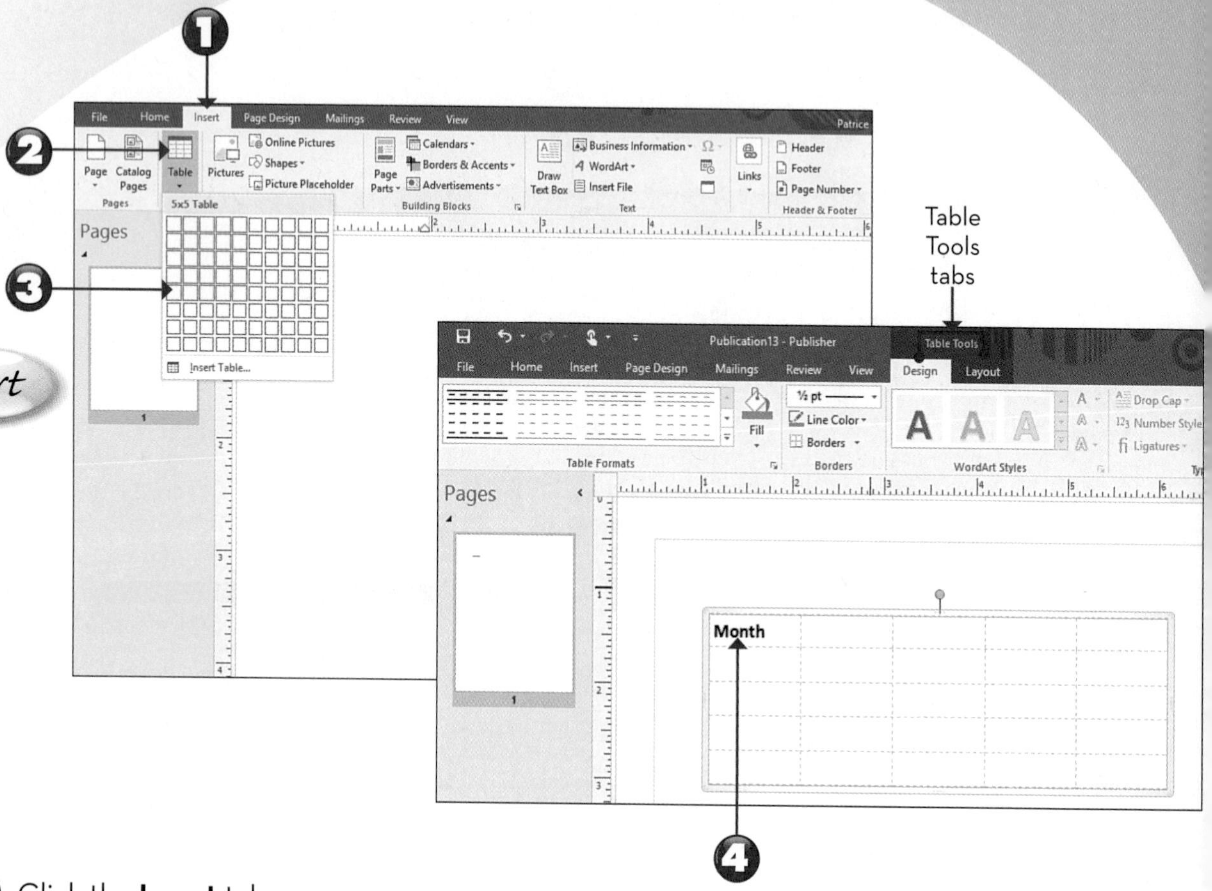

Table Tools tabs

Start

1 Click the **Insert** tab.

2 Click **Table**.

3 Click and drag across the number of rows and columns you want to insert.

4 Publisher inserts your table, and you can start typing in each cell.

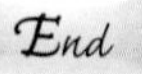

## TIP

**Format a Table** You can use the options on the Table Tools–Design and Table Tools–Layout tabs to format your table. See Chapter 7, "Creating a Document in Microsoft Word," to learn more about Word's table-formatting options, which are similar to Publisher's.

# INSERTING BUSINESS INFORMATION

In Publisher, you can create business information sets that include reusable content about a person or business. For example, you could create a set for your business with your business name, address, phone number, and logo that you can use on business cards, flyers, and so forth.

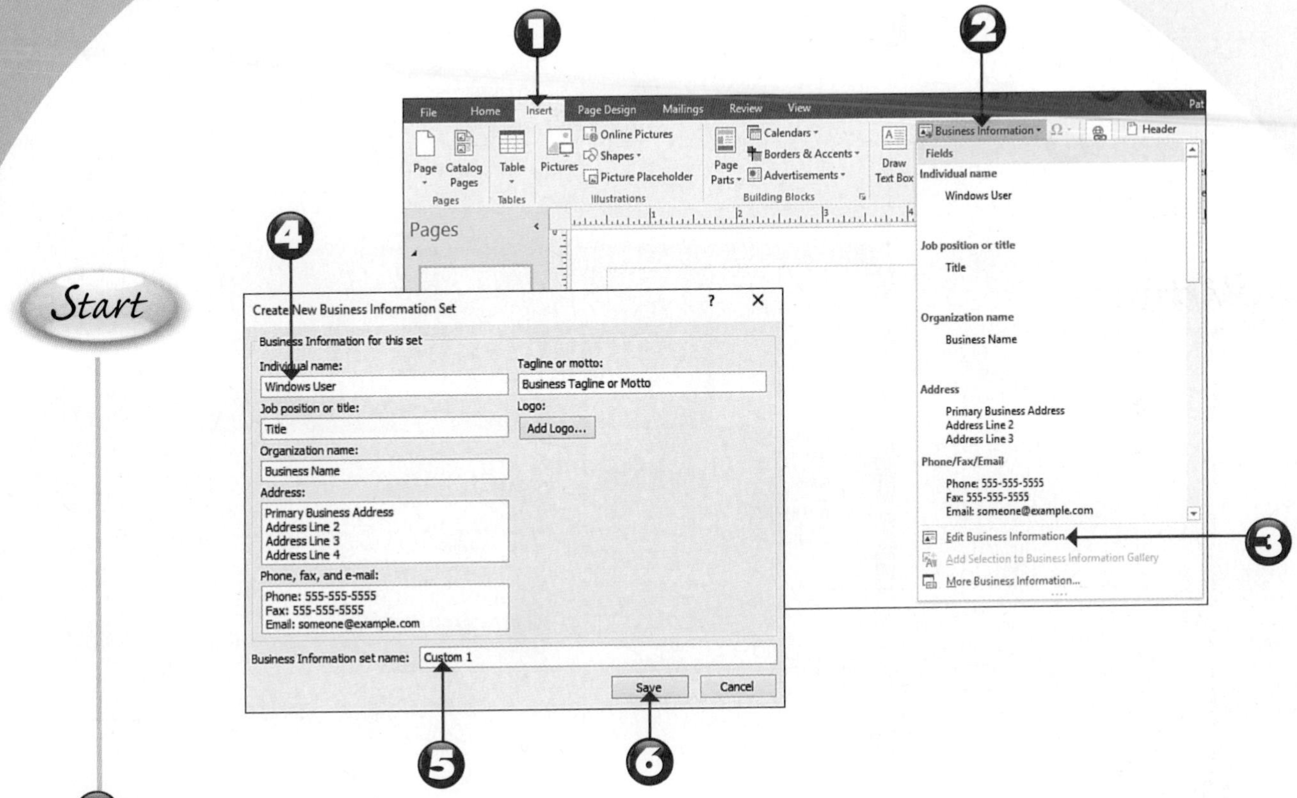

Start

1. Click the **Insert** tab.
2. Click **Business Information**.
3. Click **Edit Business Information**.
4. Enter the information for this business set.
5. Enter a name for this set.
6. Click **Save**.

End

**NOTE**

**How Do I Use Business Information?** You select a business information set when you create a publication that includes this data, such as a newsletter, as described in Chapter 23, "Creating Publications."

# MANAGING PUBLICATION PAGES

The Page Design tab offers numerous options for setting up, laying out, and managing your publication pages.

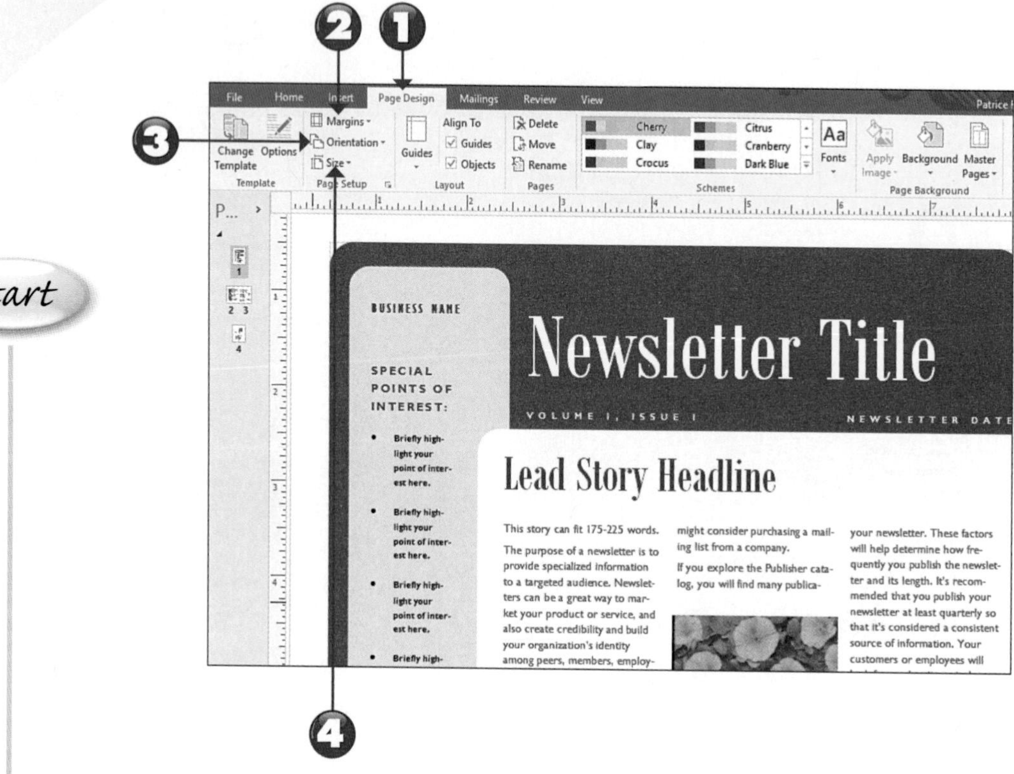


Start

1. Click the **Page Design** tab.
2. Click **Margins** to specify your page margins: wide, moderate (the default), narrow, or custom margins.
3. Click **Orientation** to specify portrait or landscape page orientation.
4. Click **Size** to select a new page size.

Continued

**TIP**

**More Page Setup Options** To open a dialog box with even more page setup options, click the small arrow in the lower-right corner of the Page Setup group on the Page Design tab.

**CAUTION**

**Modification Consequences** Changing the margins, orientation, or size of a publication can cause the existing content to no longer fit on the page. It's best to modify these elements before adding content to a blank publication, and leave them alone if you're using a template.

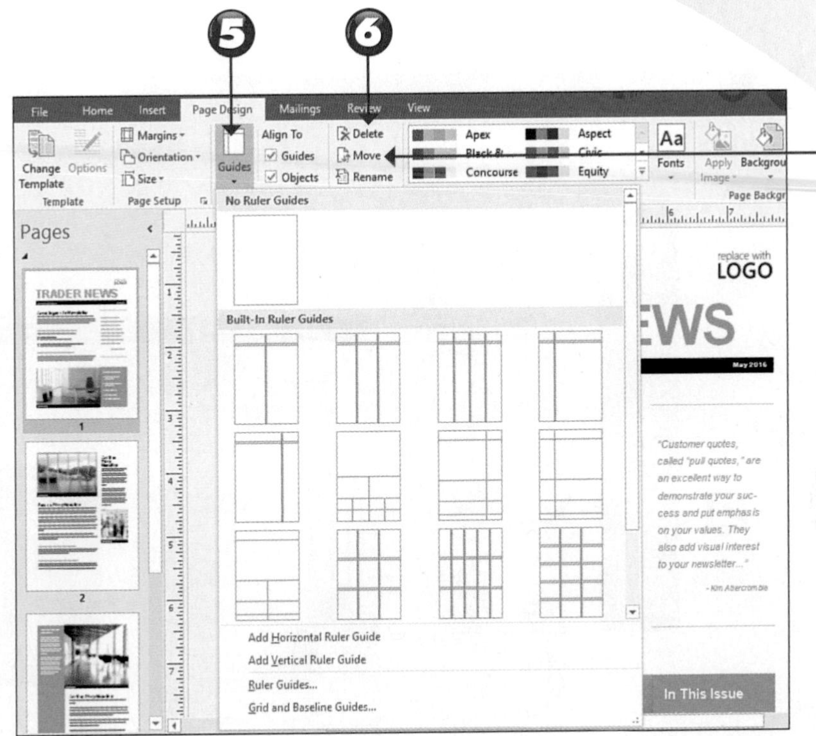


5 Select **Guides** to apply a built-in ruler guide.

6 Click **Delete** to delete the selected page.

7 Click **Move** to move the selected page to a new location in the publication.

End

## NOTE

**Ruler Guides** Applying a ruler guide makes it easier to position pictures, text boxes, tables, and other objects on a page. You can apply one of the built-in ruler guides, such as 2 Columns with Heading or Uneven Columns with Heading, or create your own guide.

## TIP

**Page Options Shortcut** You can also manage your publication pages by right-clicking a page in the Pages pane and selecting an option from the shortcut menu. For example, you can delete or move a page, insert pages or page numbers, and so forth.

# RUNNING THE DESIGN CHECKER

The Design Checker analyzes your publication for potential errors before printing or posting online. Running this tool displays the Design Checker pane, which lists items to fix and enables you to resolve these problems.

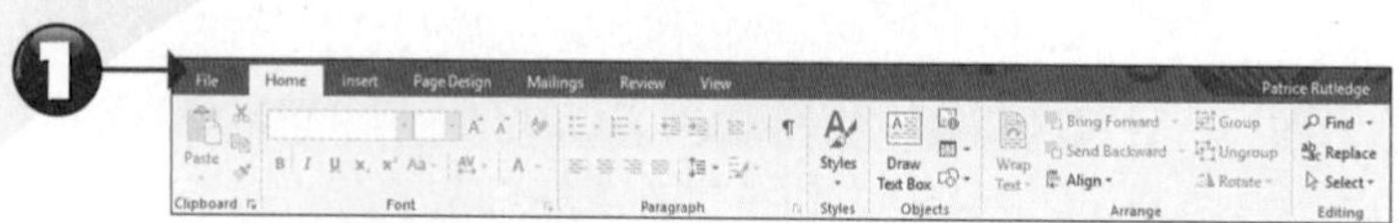

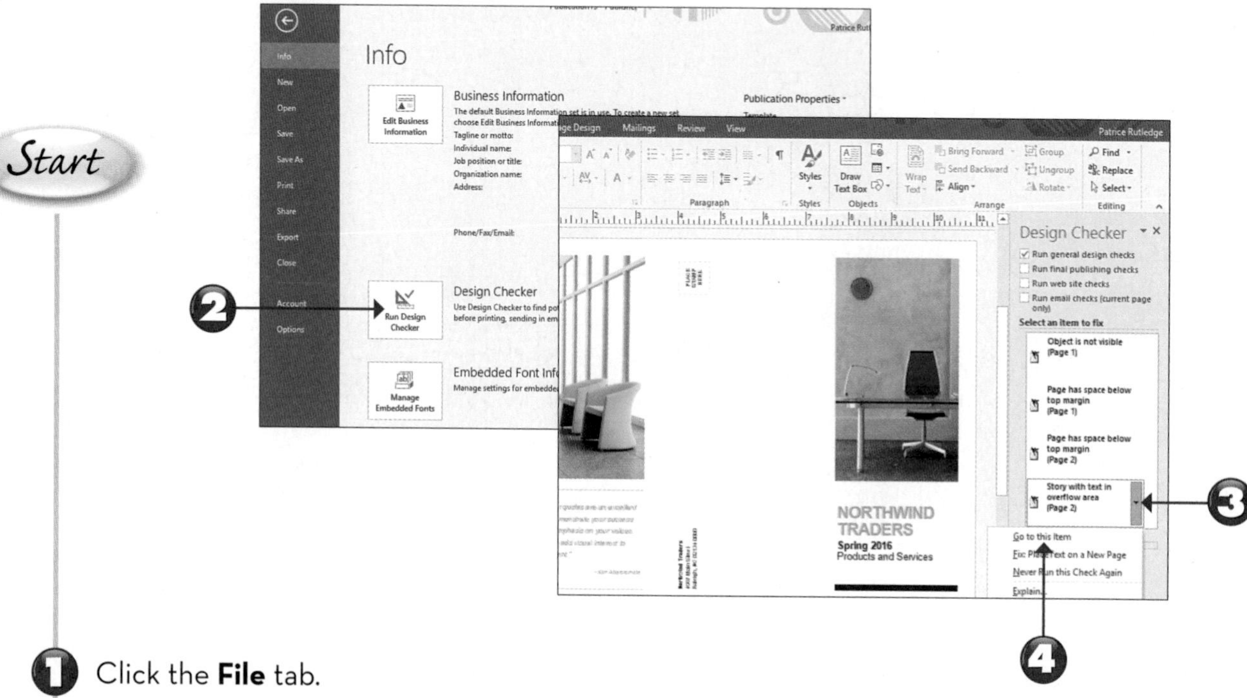


1. Click the **File** tab.
2. Click the **Run Design Checker** button.
3. Click the down arrow next to an item to fix.
4. Click **Go to this item**.

Continued

**TIP**

**Select the Checks You Want** By default, the Design Checker runs general checks, but you can also run final publishing, website, or email checks if needed by selecting those check boxes at the top of the pane.

**TIP**

**Customize the Design Checker** To view and customize the available checks, click **Design Checker Options** at the bottom of the pane. This opens the Design Checker Options dialog box where you can specify the exact checks you want to run from a long list of choices.

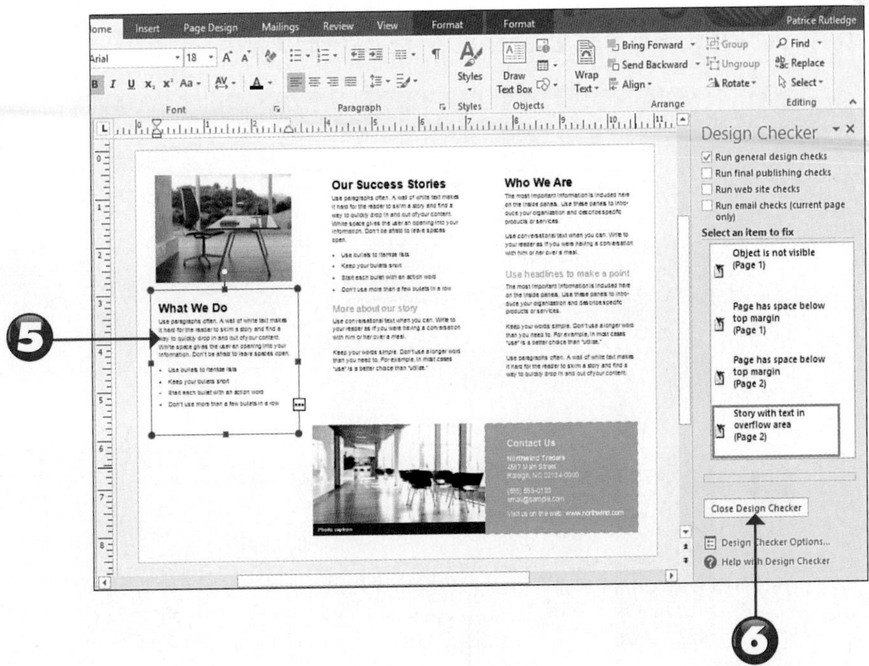


5 Publisher displays the problem area in your publication; fix as needed.

6 Click **Close Design Checker**.

*End*

## NOTE

**Design Checker Limitations** The Design Checker is a great tool for finding potential publication problems, but remember that it is still an automated tool. You're in control of whether you really need to fix each item in the Select an Item to Fix list.

# SAVING A PUBLICATION FOR COMMERCIAL PRINTING

If you plan to send your publication, such as a brochure or newsletter, to a commercial printer for professional printing, Publisher offers a Pack and Go Wizard to help ensure a successful print job.

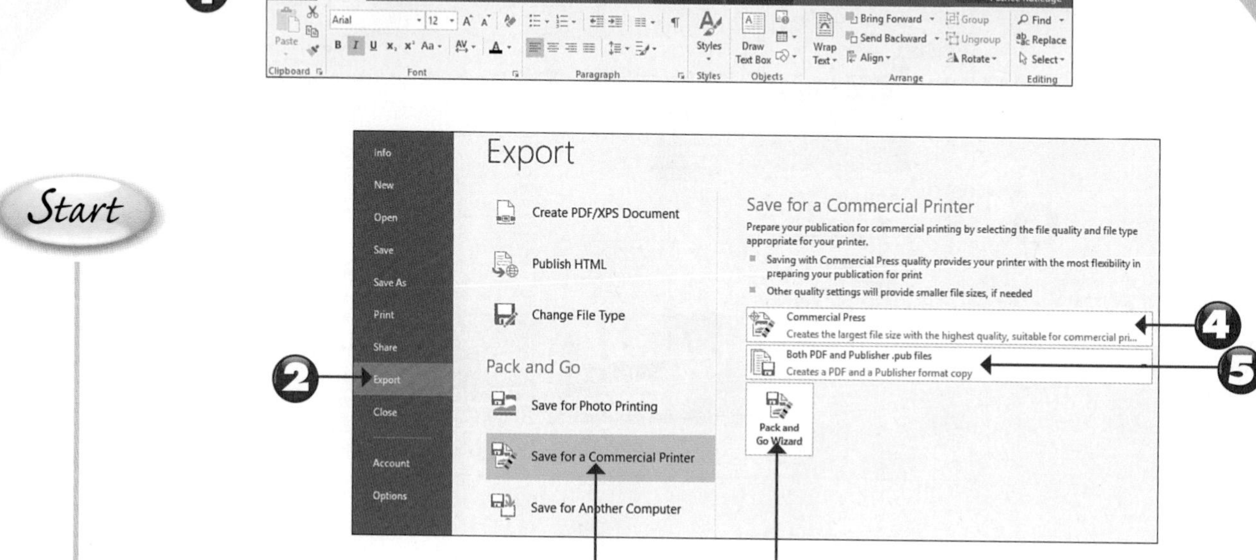

Start

1. Click the **File** tab.
2. Click **Export**.
3. Click **Save for a Commercial Printer**.
4. Select a file quality, such as Commercial Press.
5. Select a file type, such as PDF, Publisher file, or both.
6. Click the **Pack and Go Wizard** button.

Continued

### TIP

**Plan Ahead** Before you create any publication that you plan to send to a commercial printer, ask your printer for advice on the best way to use colors, fonts, pictures, and other objects to ensure optimal printing results. Your printer can also specify the file quality and type required so that you select the appropriate options on this page.

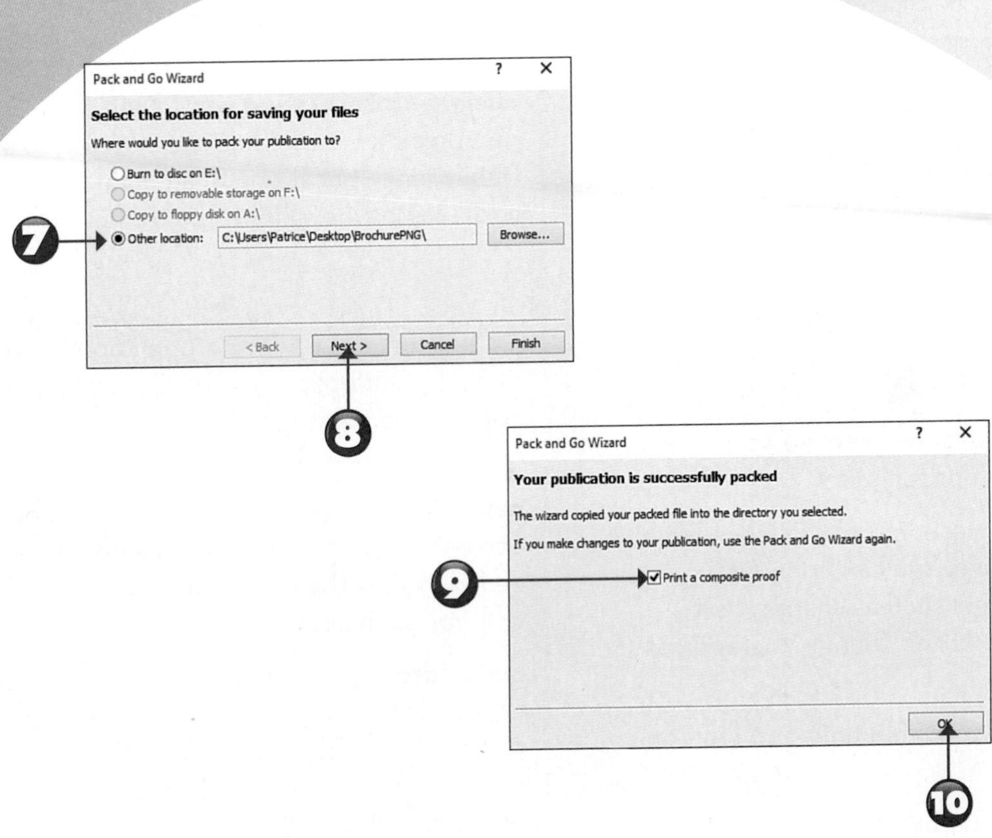


7 Specify where you want to save your file.

8 Click **Next**.

9 Deselect the **Print a composite proof** check box unless your printer asks you to print a proof.

10 Click **OK**.

End

## NOTE

**Composite Proof** A composite proof is a final proof of your publication with color separations, type, and graphics. Your printer will let you know whether you need to do this.

## NOTE

**Photo Printing** You can also save your publication as a series of images that you can send to a photo center for printing. Running this process saves each page as a JPEG or TIFF image (ask your photo center which they prefer) optimized for photo printing. To save as an image set, select **Save for Photo Printing** on the Export page.

## A

**active cell** The selected cell in Excel, highlighted with a border.

**animation** A PowerPoint design tool that makes objects move. You can apply basic animation to objects such as shapes, text placeholders, text boxes, SmartArt graphics, and charts.

**appointment** A specified date and time on an Outlook calendar.

**AutoSum** An Excel button that sums a series of numbers in a row or column automatically.

## B

**Backstage view** Area of Office, accessed by clicking the File tab, in which you can perform common file and account-related tasks in one place.

**Bcc** Abbreviation for *blind courtesy copy* or *blind carbon copy*. In Outlook, using the Bcc box sends a copy of the message to listed recipients without notifying other recipients.

**bitmap** A picture type composed of pixels (tiny dots of color), such as photos from a digital camera. Common bitmap file formats include .bmp, .gif, .jpg, .png, and .tif.

**bookmark** An identification of a section or place in a Word document. You can add bookmarks to lengthy documents that jump you to another location within the document.

**building block** The building block library offers a gallery of ready-made content—including quotes, sidebars, stories, borders, accents, and advertisements—that you can insert in your document or publication.

**business information set** Data about a person or business that you can add to a Publisher publication. It can include a name, address, tagline, phone, and email address.

## C

**Cc** Abbreviation for *carbon copy* or *courtesy copy*. In Outlook, using the Cc box sends a copy of the message to the listed recipients and notifies other recipients of the copy.

**cell** A box in an Excel worksheet where you can enter data and perform calculations. Each cell identifies the intersection of a row and column, such as A1.

**cell address** The intersection of an Excel column letter and row number, such as cell A1 or cell D8. The name box in the upper-left corner of the screen displays the cell address of the selected cell.

**chart** A graphical representation of data displaying numbers as shapes that can be compared to one another. Common chart types include column, pie, line, and bar.

**Clipboard** A pane that stores cut, copied, and pasted objects.

**color scheme** In Publisher, a collection of four coordinated colors identified by name, such as Flow, Moss, and Citrus.

**content palette** A group of six buttons that displays on selected PowerPoint slide layouts, enabling you to add a table, chart, SmartArt graphic, picture, online picture, or video to your slide.

**contextual tab** A tab that displays only when you perform a specific task. For example, the Drawing Tools–Format tab displays only when you select a shape.

**crop** A tool that removes excess content in a picture.

## D

**Design Checker** An automated tool in Publisher that searches for design problems before you print or publish.

**dialog box launcher** A diagonal arrow in the lower-right corner of selected groups on the Ribbon that opens a related dialog box.

## E

**email signature** Text or graphics that display at the bottom of Outlook email messages.

**event** An all-day occurrence in an Outlook calendar, such as a birthday, anniversary, or conference.

## F–G

**footer** Text that repeats at the bottom of every page in a Word, Excel, or PowerPoint document, such as a page number.

**Format Painter** A button on the Home tab that enables you to reuse formatting you applied to an existing object.

**formula** An Excel calculation that adds, subtracts, multiplies, or divides two or more numbers.

**function** A predefined formula in Excel. For example, you could use the AVERAGE function to average a series of numbers.

## H

**header** Text that repeats at the top of every page in a Word, Excel, or PowerPoint document, such as a title or date.

## I–L

**ink** An annotation you create and save during a PowerPoint slide show using the onscreen pen.

**Microsoft account** A free online account sometimes required to access Microsoft applications, such as OneDrive, Skype, Windows 8 and 10, Office 365, or Outlook.

**mini toolbar** A small contextual toolbar that displays only when you perform a specific task. For example, when you select text, a mini toolbar displays with options related to text formatting.

## N

**notebook** A OneNote electronic document for collecting and storing data.

## O

**object** A component you include in an Office document, such as text, shapes, pictures, text boxes, placeholders, SmartArt, charts, WordArt, and so forth.

**Office theme** A theme that controls the appearance of the Office interface rather than the appearance of any documents you create.

**OneDrive** Microsoft's online storage and file-sharing solution, available at https://onedrive.live.com/.

**operator** An indicator of an action to perform in Excel: plus (+), minus (–), multiply (*), or divide (/).

## P

**pane** A window in which you can perform common tasks; it differs from a dialog box because a pane does not cover your screen.

**PDF** Abbreviation for Portable Document Format, a file format that makes your Office documents readable by anyone who has the free Adobe Reader software.

**PivotTable** A table that summarizes and analyzes Excel data.

**placeholder** Container on a PowerPoint slide layout in which you can insert and position content.

**Presenter View** A PowerPoint view that displays a full-screen presentation your audience can see and another view for you (the presenter) that includes slide previews, speaker notes, a timer, and more.

## Q

**Quick Access toolbar** A small toolbar that displays in the upper-left corner of your screen and is available no matter which Ribbon tab you select.

## R

**Ribbon** A navigation tool divided into tabs that displays across the top of all Office applications and provides an easy way to access common commands and buttons.

**RSS feed** Abbreviation for Really Simple Syndication feed, a technology that enables web content to be converted into a feed that you can view as message posts. In Outlook, you can receive RSS feeds for blogs, podcasts, news, and more.

## S

**shape** An object, such as a line, arrow, rectangle, circle, square, or callout.

**slide layout** A PowerPoint tool for adding specific types of content to your slides, such as text, tables, charts, and pictures.

**slide master** A PowerPoint design tool that helps you achieve uniformity by storing data about a presentation's theme and slide layouts, such as colors, fonts, effects, background, placeholders, and positioning—and applying it consistently throughout your presentation. Each presentation contains at least one slide master.

**Slide Sorter view** A PowerPoint view that displays smaller versions of slides in several rows and columns.

**slide transition** A PowerPoint animation effect between two slides, such as a fade, wipe, or reveal.

**SmartArt** A design tool for combining shapes and text to create informative lists, matrixes, pyramids, and more.

**sparkline** An Excel mini chart that graphically represents the data in adjacent cells.

## T–U

**template** The underlying structure for a document; a fill-in-the-blanks skeleton to help you build files.

**theme** A standalone file with coordinated colors, fonts, and effects that you apply to an Office document.

## V

**vector** A picture type composed of points, lines, and curves. Common vector file formats include .eps and .wmf.

**video embed code** A string of HTML code that enables you to share web videos in PowerPoint presentations. For example, YouTube and Vimeo offer video embed codes for embedding their videos.

## W

**Web App** An abbreviated version of a Microsoft Office application that you can access online via OneDrive. Web apps are available for Word, Excel, PowerPoint, and OneNote.

**WordArt** A design tool for creating special text effects such as shadowed, rotated, stretched, and multicolored text.

**workbook** An Excel file, identified with the extension .xls.

**worksheet** An individual "page" in an Excel workbook consisting of a series of rows and columns. Each Excel workbook contains one or more worksheets, identified with a unique tab at the bottom of the screen.

## X–Z

**XPS** Abbreviation for XML Paper Specification, a format that enables you to create documents readable with the XPS Viewer.

# Index

## Symbols



## A



## B

## C

## D

## E

## F

## G



## H

## I



## J-K-L

## P

## R

## S

## T

## U



## V

## W

## X-Y-Z

# More Best-Selling **My** Books!

Learning to use your smartphone, tablet, camera, game, or software has never been easier with the full-color My Series. You'll find simple, step-by-step instructions from our team of experienced authors. The organized, task-based format allows you to quickly and easily find exactly what you want to achieve.

**Visit quepublishing.com/mybooks to learn more.**